Borland® C++ Programmer's Reference

James W. McCord

Borland® C++ Programmer's Reference

For information, address Que Corporation, 11711 N. College Ave., Carmel, IN 46032.

Library of Congress Catalog No.: 91-61722

ISBN: 0-88022-714-1

94 93 92 91 8 7 6 5 4 3 2 1

Interpretation of the printing code: the rightmost double-digit number is the year of the book's printing; the rightmost single-digit number, the number of the book's printing. For example, a printing code of 91-1 shows that the first printing of the book occurred in 1991.

Publisher
Richard K. Swadley

Publishing Manager
Joseph Wikert

Managing Editor
Neweleen Trebnik

Acquisitions Editor
Gregory Croy

Senior Editor
Rebecca Whitney

Production Editor
Katherine Stuart Ewing

Editor
Susan Christophersen

Technical Editor
Derrel Blain

Cover Design
Tim Amrhein

Indexer
Hilary Adams

Book Design
Scott Cook

Production
Claudia Bell
Scott Boucher
Martin Coleman
Sandy Grieshop
Betty Kish
Bob LaRoche
Kim Mays
Howard Peirce
Cindy L. Phipps
Suzanne Tully
Lisa Wilson

Composed in ITC Garamond and OCRB
by Que Corporation

About the Author

James W. McCord

James W. McCord is a captain in the United States Air Force and is stationed at Wright-Patterson Air Force Base, Ohio. He currently works as a computer research scientist at Wright Laboratories, the Avionics Directorate, performing research on software support technologies. James has a bachelor's degree in electrical engineering from Auburn University and a master of science degree in administration from Central Michigan University. He is the author of *C Programmer's Guide to Graphics*, published by SAMS.

Content Overview

TABLE OF CONTENTS

II Borland C++ Reference Guide

Thumb Tab Index

Acknowledgments

I would like to thank Que for the opportunity to write this book. I also thank my wife Jill, son Joshua, and daughter Jamie for supporting me during this project. I also thank T.B.T. for all the great things in my life.

Trademark Acknowledgments

Que Corporation has made every reasonable attempt to supply trademark information about company names, products, and services mentioned in this book. Trademarks indicated below were derived from various sources. Que Corporation cannot attest to the accuracy of this information.

AT&T C++ is a registered trademark of American Telephone and Telegraph Company.

Borland C and Borland C++ are registered trademarks of Borland International.

Microsoft, Microsoft C Compiler, and MS-DOS are registered trademarks of Microsoft Corporation.

PREFACE

Borland C++ is a powerful tool for developing software applications using the C and C++ languages. It provides full ANSI C compatibility and provides the features of AT&T C++ Version 2.0. The product is rich with features including hundreds of functions in the run-time library. Borland C++ adds the power of Turbo Assembler, the Resource Toolkit, Turbo Profiler, and Turbo Debugger to create an unprecedented software development package.

My purpose in writing this book was to weed through the hundreds of pages of Borland C++, Turbo Assembler, Resource Toolkit, Turbo Profiler, and Turbo Debugger documentation and provide you, the programmer, with the straightforward information you need to develop software applications using Borland C++.

This book provides fundamental information on C, object-oriented programming, and C++ that will get you "up and programming" using these languages and techniques. It also provides critical information on using the Turbo Assembler, Turbo Debugger, Turbo Profiler, and Resource Toolkit environments. Most important, it provides full documentation on each of the functions in the Borland C++ run-time library.

This book is useful to both the first-time programmer and the experienced programmer because it provides hundreds of examples, as well as in-depth technical information. No matter what your level of experience, this book will provide the information you need to use Borland C++ effectively.

Introduction

The purpose of this book is to provide reference information on the Borland C++ run-time library and the Borland C++, Turbo Assembler, Turbo Profiler, Turbo Debugger, and Resource Toolkit environments. Part I, Programming with Borland C++, includes chapters 1 through 4 and introduces the Borland C++ environment, providing information on C, C++, and object-oriented programming. Part II, Borland C++ Reference Guide, includes chapters 5 through 18 and provides reference information on the various functions in the run-time library. Part III, Borland C++ Programming Tools, includes Chapters 19 through 22 and introduces programming tools that enhance the capabilities of the C++ compiler.

Each chapter is briefly described in the following paragraphs.

Programming with Borland C++

Chapter 1 introduces the Borland C++ environment and provides information on the menus and command-line options. In Chapter 2 you'll find a description of the C language with its advantages, disadvantages, and code structure. Chapter 3 presents concepts of object-oriented programming. These include encapsulation, inheritance, and polymorphism. Chapter 4 describes the C++ language, documenting enhancements made to C. The basic principles behind classes are introduced in this chapter.

Borland C++ Reference Guide

The reference guide begins with Chapter 5, providing reference information for the character classification macros in the Borland C++ run-time library. Functions used for data conversion are introduced in Chapter 6, and Chapter 7 gives a full description of each of the directory control functions in the Borland C++ run-time library.

An introduction to the principles of graphics programming is presented in Chapter 8, along with reference information for graphics programming functions. Chapter 9 provides full documentation for input/output functions, and in Chapter 10 you'll find descriptions of the functions that interface with DOS, BIOS, or the 8086.

Chapter 11 documents the functions for memory and string manipulation, and reference information for mathematical functions can be found in Chapter 12.

Chapter 13 describes the basic principles behind dynamic memory allocation. This chapter also documents the dynamic memory allocation functions provided in the Borland C++ library. Process control functions are presented in Chapter 14, and Chapter 15 introduces functions that display text and manipulate text windows.

Standard library functions are described in Chapter 16, and Chapter 17 provides reference information on the functions that manipulate the time and date. Finally, miscellaneous functions of the run-time library that don't fall easily into the categories presented in Chapters 5 through 17 are described in Chapter 18.

Borland C++ Programming Tools

The final section of this book begins with Chapter 19, which introduces the capabilities of the Whitewater Resource Toolkit and provides basic user information for the Resource Manager and various editors, including the Accelerator, Bitmap, Cursor, Icon, Dialog Box, Menu, String, and Header editors.

Command-line options, processor instructions, co-processor instructions, directives, operators, and predefined symbols for Turbo Assembler are discussed in Chapter 20. Chapter 21 introduces Turbo Debugger, providing reference information on command-line options and menus for the Turbo Debugger environment.

Chapter 22 offers an introduction to Turbo Profiler, a performance analyzer software tool that helps you optimize your program. Lists of command-line options, along with explanations of environment menus and menu options, are presented in this chapter so that you can easily identify the many features of the Turbo Profiler environment.

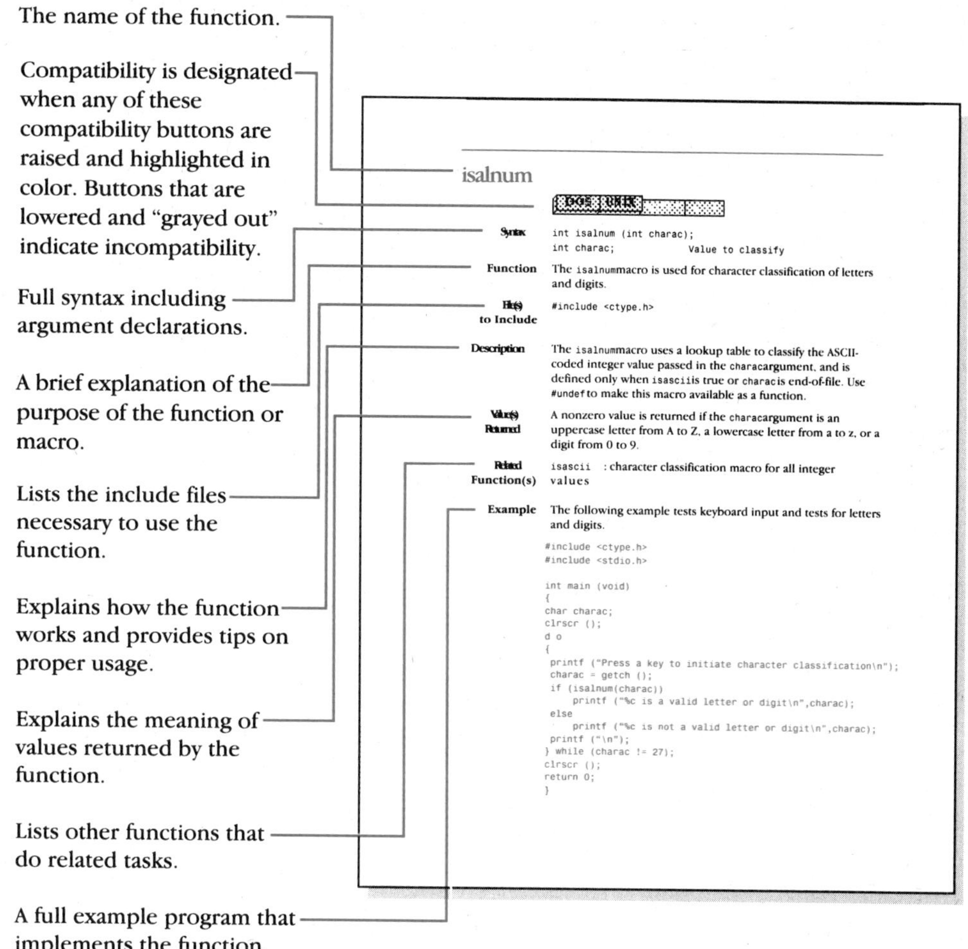
The name of the function.
Compatibility is designated when any of these compatibility buttons are raised and highlighted in color. Buttons that are lowered and "grayed out" indicate incompatibility.
Full syntax including argument declarations.
A brief explanation of the purpose of the function or macro.
Lists the include files necessary to use the function.
Explains how the function works and provides tips on proper usage.
Explains the meaning of values returned by the function.
Lists other functions that do related tasks.
A full example program that implements the function.
isalnum
DOS UNIX
Syntax
int isalnum (int charac);
int charac; Value to classify
Function
The isalnummacro is used for character classification of letters and digits.
File(s) to Include
#include <ctype.h>
Description
The isalnummacro uses a lookup table to classify the ASCII-coded integer value passed in the characargument, and is defined only when isasciiis true or characis end-of-file. Use #undef to make this macro available as a function.
Value(s) Returned
A nonzero value is returned if the characargument is an uppercase letter from A to Z, a lowercase letter from a to z, or a digit from 0 to 9.
Related Function(s)
isascii : character classification macro for all integer values
Example
The following example tests keyboard input and tests for letters and digits.
#include <ctype.h>
#include <stdio.h>
int main (void)
{
char charac;
clrscr ();
d o
{
printf ("Press a key to initiate character classification\n");
charac = getch ();
if (isalnum(charac))
printf ("%c is a valid letter or digit\n",charac);
else
printf ("%c is not a valid letter or digit\n",charac);
printf ("\n");
} while (charac != 27);
clrscr ();
return 0;
}

Part I

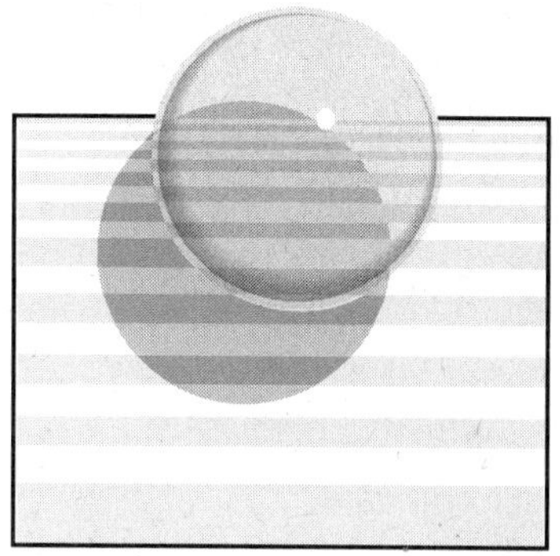

Programming with Borland C++

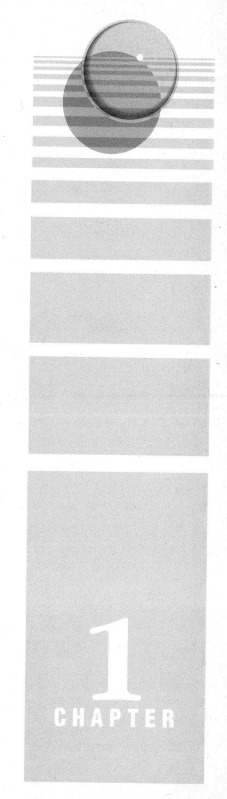

Introduction to Borland C++

Borland C++ provides the ability to program C and C++ programs using the American National Standards Institute (ANSI) C standard, the AT&T C++ version 2.0 definition, and the Kernighan and Ritchie definition. C and C++ programs can be compiled at the command line or inside the Integrated Development Environment (IDE). This chapter introduces the components of the IDE and provides information on command-line compiling and linking.

The Command-Line Compiler

Although Borland provides the IDE for program development, some users prefer the command-line compiler because it provides more direct control over the compilation process. The command-line compiler provided by Borland, BCC, will automatically compile and link the specified files while invoking the Turbo Assembler, TASM, if it is needed to compile .ASM source files.

The command-line compiler is very flexible, and Borland offers many options to control the compilation process. The following format is used to invoke the command-line compiler:

BCC [option [option...]] filename [filename...]
or
BCCX [option [option...]] filename [filename...]

in which

option = optional compiler options; can be none or several
filename = the filename(s) to be compiled and linked

Table 1.1 lists the options for the command-line compiler.

Table 1.1. *Command-line compiler options.*

Option	*Meaning*
@filename	Response files
+filename	Use the alternate configuration file specified in filename
-A	Use only ANSI keywords
-A- or -AT	Use Borland C++ keywords (the default)
-AK	Use only Kernighan and Ritchie keywords
-AU	Use only UNIX keywords
-a	Align word
-a-	Align byte (default)
-B	Compile and call the assembler to process inline assembly code
-b	Make enums word-sized (default)
-b-	Make enums signed or unsigned
-C	Nested comments on
-C-	Nested comments off
-c	Compile to .OBJ, do not link
-D*name*	Define the specified name to the string consisting of the null character
-D*name*=*string*	Define the specified name to the specified string
-d	Merge duplicate strings on
-d-	Merge duplicate strings off (default)
-E*filename*	Use the specified filename as the assembler
-e*filename*	Link and produce the specified filename

Option	*Meaning*
-Fc	Generate COMDEFS
-Ff	Automatically create far variables
-Ff=size	Automatically create far variables and sets the threshold
-Fm	Enable -Fc, -Ff, and -Fs options
-Fs	For all memory models assume DS=SS
-f	Emulate floating-point (the default)
-f-	Don't do floating-point
-ff	Fast floating-point (the default)
-ff-	String ANSI floating-point
-f87	Use 8087 instructions
-f287	Use 80287 instructions
-G	Optimize for speed
-G-	Optimize for size (the default)
-g*n*	Stop warnings after *n* messages
-H	Generate and use precompiled headers
-H-	Do not generate or use precompiled headers (the default)
-Hu	Use but do not generate precompiled headers
-H=*filename*	Set the name of the file for precompiled headers
-h	Use fast huge pointer arithmetic
-I*pathname*	Directories for include files
-in	Set significant identifier length to *n*
-jn	Stop errors after *n* messages
-K	Default character type unsigned
-K-	Default character type signed (the default)
-k	Standard stack frame on (the default)
-L*pathname*	Directories for libraries
-l*x*	Pass option in *x* to the linker
-l-*x*	Suppress the option in *x* for the linker
-M	Instruct the linker to create a map file
-mc	Compile using the compact memory model
-mh	Compile using the huge memory model
-ml	Compile using the large memory model
-mm	Compile using the medium memory model
-mm!	Compile using the medium memory model; assume DS != SS
-ms	Compile using the small memory model

continues

Table 1.1. (continued)

Option	*Meaning*
-ms!	Compile using the small memory model; assume DS != SS
-mt	Compile using the tiny memory model
-mt!	Compile using the tiny memory model; assume DS != SS
-N	Check for stack overflow
-n*pathname*	Output directory
-O	Optimize jumps
-O-	No optimization (the default)
-o*filename*	Compile source file to *filename.obj*
-P	Perform a C++ compile
-P*ext*	Perform a C++ compile and set the default extension to the extension specified in *ext*
-P-	Perform a C++ or C compile depending on the source file extension (the default)
-P-ext	Perform a C++ or C compile depending on the source file extension; set the default extension to the extension specified in *ext*
-p	Use Pascal calling convention
-p-	Use C calling convention (the default)
-Qe	Use all available EMS memory
-Qe-	Use no EMS memory
-Qx	Use all available extended memory
-Qx=*nnnn*	Reserve the number of Kbytes in *nnnn* for other programs
-Qx=*nnnn,yyyy*	Reserve *nnnn* Kybtes of extended memory for other programs and *yyyy* for the compiler
-Qx=*yyyy*	Reserve *yyyy* Kbytes of extended memory for the compiler
-Qx-	Use no extended memory
-r	Use register variables (the default)
-r-	Do not use register variables
-rd	Keep only declared register variables in the registers
-S	Produce .ASM output
-T*string*	Pass the specified string as an option to TASM or the assembler specified with the -E option
-T-	Remove all assembler options
-U*name*	Undefine the specified name
-u	Generate underscores (the default)

Option	*Meaning*
-u-	Do not generate underscores
-V	Smart C++ virtual tables
-Vs	Local C++ virtual tables
-V0,-V1	External and public C++ virtual tables
-Vf	Far C++ virtual tables
-v,-v-	Source debugging on
-vi,-vi-	Controls the expansion of inline functions
-W	Creates an .OBJ for Windows with all functions exportable
-WD	Creates an .OBJ for Windows to be linked as a .DLL with all functions exportable
-WDE	Create an .OBJ for Windows to be linked as a .DLL with explicit export functions
-WE	Create an .OBJ for Windows with explicit export functions
-WS	Create an .OBJ for Windows that uses smart callbacks
-w	Display warnings
-w*xxx*	Allow the warning message in *xxx*
-w-*xxx*	Do not allow the warning message in *xxx*
-X	Disable compiler autodependency output
-Y	Enable overlay code generation
-Yo	Overlay the compiled files
-y	Line numbers on
-Z	Enable register usage optimization
-zA*name*	Code class
-zB*name*	BSS class
-zC*name*	Code segment
-zD*name*	BSS segment
-zE*name*	Far segment
-zF*name*	Far class
-zG*name*	BSS group
-zH*name*	Far group
-zP*name*	Code group
-zR*name*	Data segment
-zS*name*	Data group
-zT*name*	Data class
-zX*	Use default name for X

continues

Table 1.1. (continued)

Option	*Meaning*
-1	Generate 80186 instructions
-1-	Generate 8088/8086 instructions and 80286 real-mode instructions
-2	Generate 80286 protected-mode compatible instructions

An example of a command line for the command-line compiler is as follows:

```
BCC -f87 -G -ml -erunprog File1 File2 File3
```

This command line instructs the compiler to compile File1, File2, and File3 to .OBJ files, then link them to produce an executable file called `runprog.exe` using 8087 hardware instructions, speed optimization, and the large memory mode.

The IDE

The Integrated Development Environment, or IDE, allows you to create, edit, compile, link, execute, and debug your programs. The IDE is very powerful and flexible and can be operated in either protected (BCX) or real (BC) modes. Real mode is supported by all IBM PCs and compatibles. Protected mode is supported only on 80286, 80386, or i486 machines with at least 640K or base RAM and 576K of extended or expanded RAM. The remainder of this chapter provides information on the menus and options of the IDE.

The IDE can be invoked in real mode by typing BC or in protected mode by typing BCX. The format for invoking the IDE is as follows:

BC|BCX [option [option...]][sourcename|projectname[sourcename]]

in which

BC|BCX =	the IDE in real or protected mode, respectively
option =	a command-line compiler option
sourcename|projectname =	the name of the ASCII or project file

As the format for invoking the IDE shows, there are command-line options which allow you to customize the environment. Table 1.2 lists the command-line options for the IDE.

Table 1.2. Command-line options for the IDE.

Option	*Meaning*
/b	Recompiles and links all the files in the project, prints compiler messages to the standard output device, then returns control to the operating system
/d	Forces dual monitor mode if the appropriate hardware is detected
/e	Swaps to expanded memory when allocating memory
/h	Generates a list of all the command-line options available
/l	Used when running on an LCD screen
/m	Does a make rather than a build
/p	Controls palette swapping on EGA video adapters
/r	Used if all the extended or expanded memory has been allocated to a RAM disk
/x	Swaps to extended memory when allocating memory

The IDE is extremely easy to use and is menu-driven. The Menu Bar of the IDE has eleven menus. Each of these menus offers several selections. The following sections provide information on each option in these menus.

The ≡, or System, Menu

The ≡, or System, Menu offers four selections (see Fig. 1.1). These selections are About, Clear Desktop, Repaint Desktop, and Transfer Items. Table 1.3 describes these options.

Table 1.3. Options of the ≡ Menu.

Option	*Purpose*
About	Provides copyright and version information on Borland C++
Clear Desktop	Closes all windows and clears the history lists
Repaint Desktop	Redraws the screen
Transfer Items	All programs that have been installed with the Transfer dialog box are listed under this option

Fig. 1.1. The System Menu.

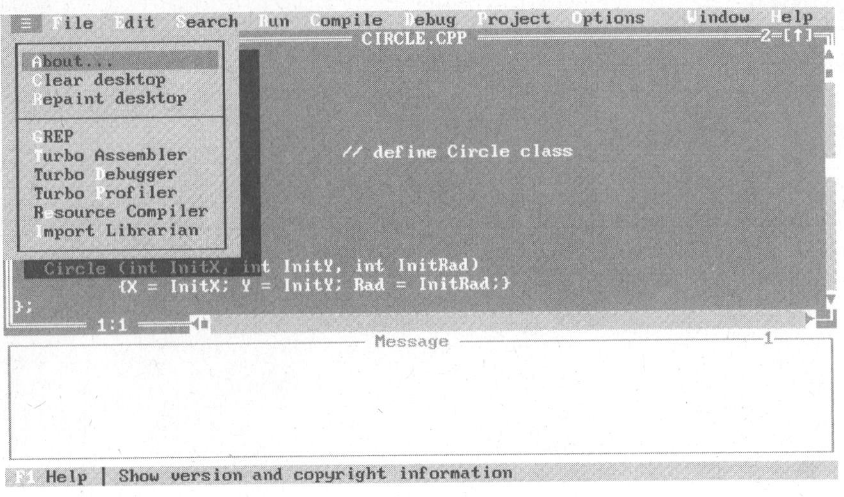

The File Menu

The File Menu provides several options for manipulating files (see Fig. 1.2). In addition, you can quit the IDE and get a DOS prompt from inside this menu. Options under the File Menu include Open, New, Save, Save As, Save All, Change Dir, Print, Get Info, DOS Shell, and Quit. These options are described in table 1.4.

Table 1.4. *Options of the File Menu.*

Option	*Purpose*
Open	Allows you to either open an existing file from the file selection dialog box, or create a new file with the file name typed into the input box
New	Allows you to create a new file with a default name of NONAMExx.C
Save	Saves the file in the active window
Save As	Saves the file in the active window under a different name and, if desired, under a different drive and path

Option	Purpose
Save All	Saves all modified files in the open windows
Change Dir	Permits you to specify the current drive and path
Print	Prints the contents of the active Edit, Output, or Message window
Get Info	Provides information on the current file
DOS Shell	Allows you to get to the DOS prompt; typing EXIT takes you back into the IDE
Quit	Quits the IDE and returns you to the DOS prompt

Fig. 1.2. The File Menu.

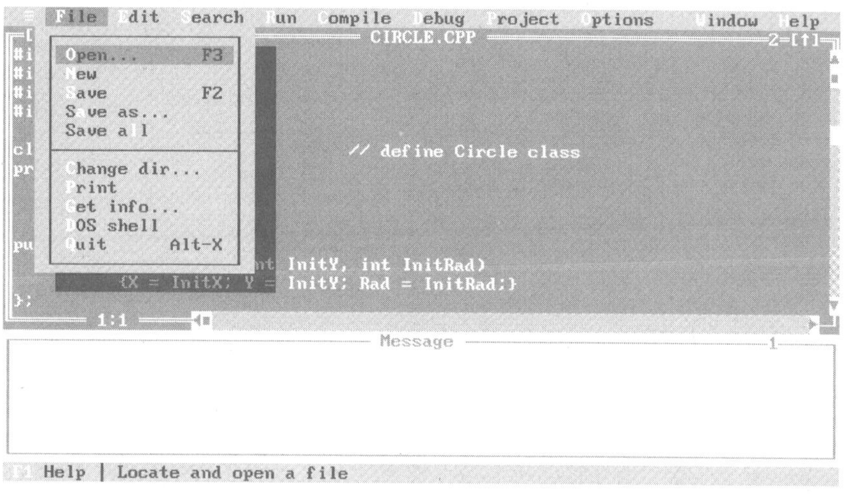

The Edit Menu

The Edit Menu allows you to cut, copy, and paste text between edit windows (see Fig. 1.3). The Edit Menu has eight options, which are Undo, Redo, Cut, Copy, Paste, Copy Example, Show Clipboard, and Clear. These options are described in table 1.5.

Table 1.5. Options of the Edit Menu.

Option	*Purpose*
Undo	Restores the file in the active window to its state before the last edit or cursor movement
Redo	Reverses the last Undo
Cut	Removes highlighted text from an Edit window and places it onto the Clipboard
Copy	Places a copy of highlighted text from an Edit window onto the Clipboard
Paste	Copies the contents of the Clipboard to the location of the cursor
Copy Example	Copies a preselected example from the current Help window to the Clipboard
Show Clipboard	Displays the contents of the Clipboard
Clear	Removes highlighted text from an Edit window; the removed text cannot be recovered with Paste because text is not copied onto the Clipboard

Fig. 1.3. The Edit Menu.

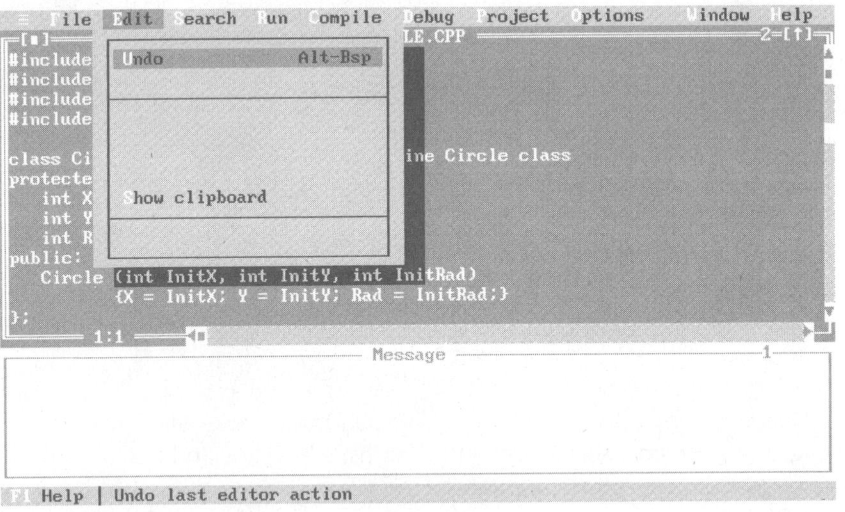

The Search Menu

The Search Menu provides the capability to search for text, function declarations, and error locations (see Fig. 1.4). The options under the Search Menu are Find, Replace, Search Again, Go to Line Number, Previous Error, Next Error, and Locate Function. These options are described in table 1.6.

Table 1.6. *Options of the Search Menu.*

Option	*Purpose*
Find	Allows you to search for a text string; you input the text string in the Find dialog box; the Find dialog box also offers several options to control the search
Replace	Conducts a search for the user-defined text string and replaces it with another user-defined text string; as with Find, the Replace dialog box has several options which control the search and replace
Search Again	Executes the last Find or Replace
Go to Line Number	Takes you to a specified line number; you are prompted by Go to Line Number for the line number
Previous Error	Moves the cursor to the location that caused the previous error or warning message
Next Error	Moves the cursor to the location that caused the next error or warning message
Locate Function	Searches for the specified function; you are prompted for the function name; this option is available only during debugging

The Run Menu

The Run Menu is used to run the programs you create and to start and end debugging sessions (see Fig. 1.5). The options under the Run Menu are Run, Program Reset, Go to Cursor, Trace Into, Step Over, and Arguments. These options are described in table 1.7.

Fig. 1.4. The Search Menu.

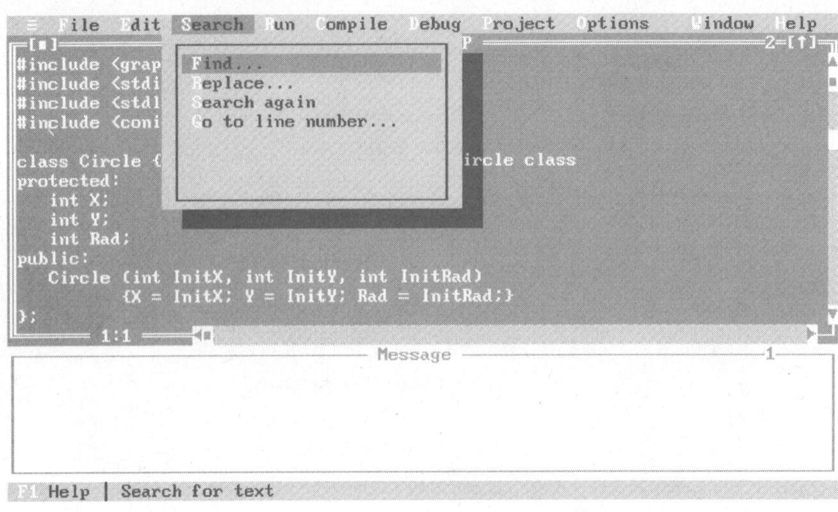

Table 1.7. *Options of the Run Menu.*

Option	*Purpose*
Run	Runs your program; also compiles and links your program if the source code has been modified
Program Reset	Stops the current debugging session, releases all memory allocated by your program, and closes all open files used by your program
Go to Cursor	Runs your program from the run bar to the current position of the cursor
Trace Into	Runs your program step-by-step
Step Over	Allows you to execute the next statement in the current function
Arguments	Permits you to pass command-line arguments to your program

Fig. 1.5. The Run Menu.

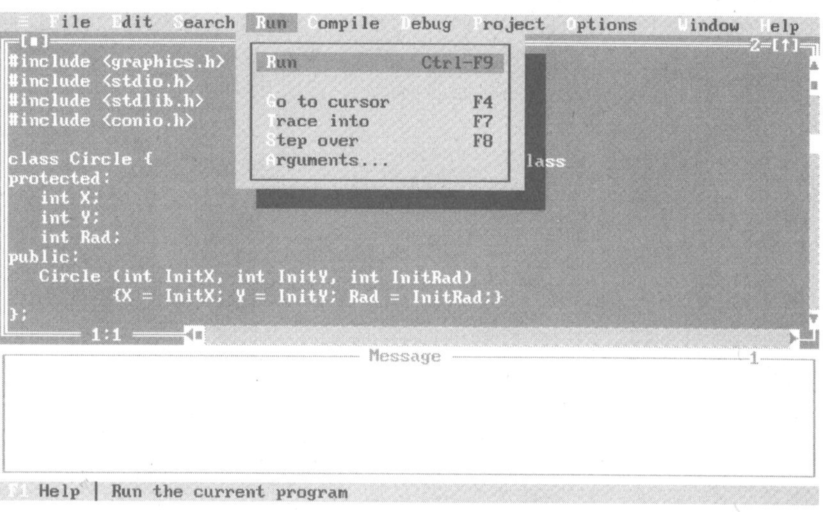

The Compile Menu

The Compile Menu allows you to compile your programs and to make or build a project (see Fig. 1.6). The options under the Compile Menu are Compile to OBJ, Make EXE File, Link EXE File, Build All, and Remove Messages. Table 1.8 describes these options.

Table 1.8. *Options of the Compile Menu.*

Option	*Purpose*
Compile to OBJ	The source code in the active window is compiled to an .OBJ file
Make EXE File	Compiles and links the source code in the active window. The result is an executable file
Link EXE File	Links the current .OBJ and .LIB files and produces an executable file
Build All	Rebuilds all the files in a project even if they have not recently been modified
Remove Messages	Removes all the messages in the Message window

Fig. 1.6. The Compile Menu.

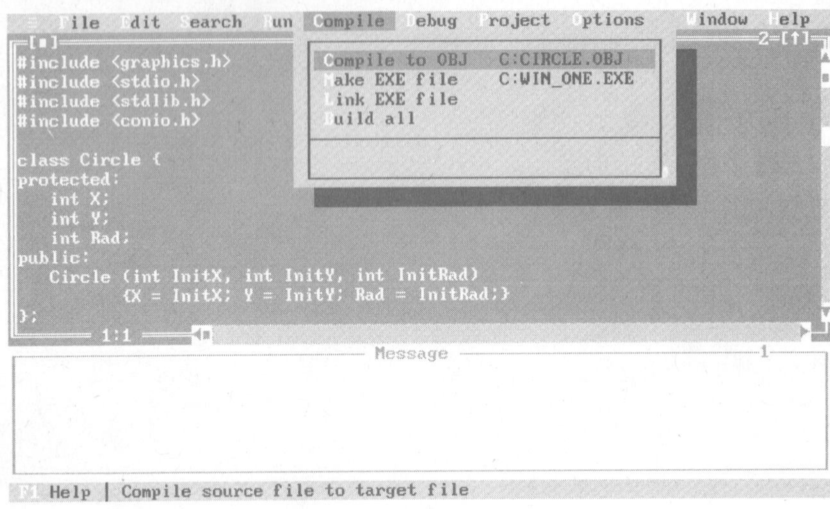

The Debug Menu

The Debug Menu controls the debugger (see Fig. 1.7). The options under the Debug Menu are Inspect, Evaluate/Modify, Call Stack, Watches, Toggle Breakpoint, and Breakpoints. Table 1.9 describes these options.

Table 1.9. *Options of the Debug Menu.*

Option	*Purpose*
Inspect	Opens an Inspector Window that allows you to see and modify data elements
Evaluate/Modify	Evaluates and displays a variable or expression; some variables and expressions can be modified under this option
Call Stack	Displays the call stack
Watch	Provides four additional options, as follows:
Add Watch	Inserts a watch expression into the watch window
Delete Watch	Deletes the current watch expression from the watch window
Edit Watch	Provides the ability to edit the current watch expression in the watch window

Option	Purpose
Remove All Watches	Deletes all watch expressions from the watch window
Toggle Breakpoint	Allows you to toggle unconditional breakpoints on the current cursor line
Breakpoints	Allows you to control both the conditional and unconditional breakpoints in the program

Fig. 1.7. The Debug Menu.

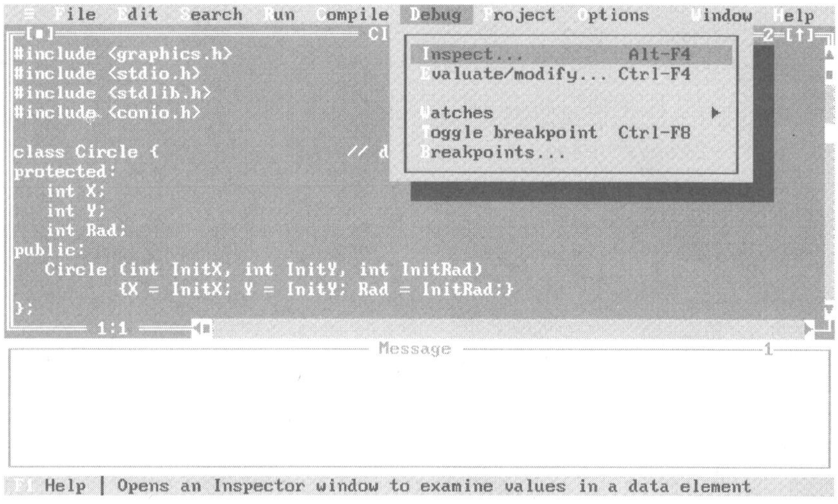

The Project Menu

The Project Menu is provided for project management (see Fig. 1.8). The options of the Project Menu include Open Project, Close Project, Add Item, Delete Item, Local Options, and Include Files. These options are described in table 1.10.

***Table 1.10.** Options of the Project Menu.*

Option	Purpose
Open Project	Allows you to select a previously created project or create a new one

continues

Table 1.10. (continued)

Option	*Purpose*
Close Project	Allows you to close a project and return to the TCDEF.DPR default project
Add Item	Lets you add a file to the project list
Delete Item	Lets you delete a file from the project list
Local Options	Allows you to set command-line options, specify a path and name for the object file, and choose a translator for the project
Include Files	Allows you to view the include files for each file in the project

Fig. 1.8. The Project Menu.

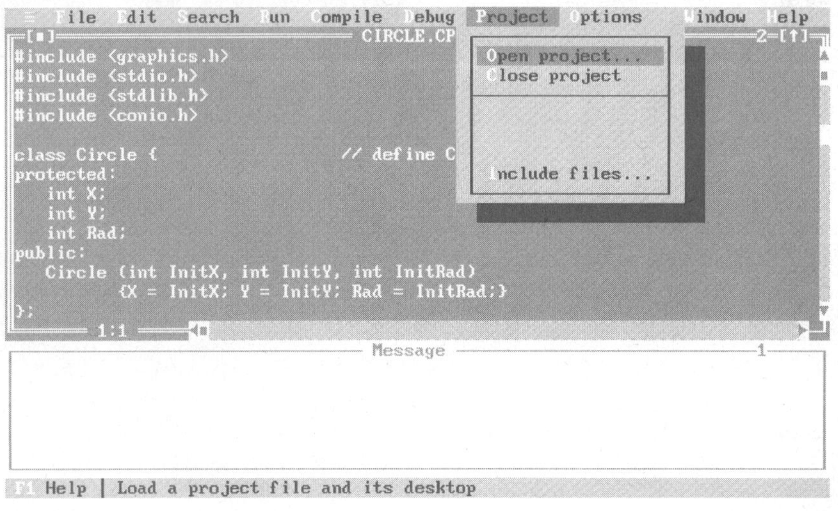

The Options Menu

The Options Menu lets you customize Borland C++ Pro (see Fig. 1.9). The options under the Options Menu are Compiler, Transfer, Make, Linker, Application, Debugger, Directories, Environment, and Save. Table 1.11 describes these options.

Table 1.11. Options of the Options Menu.

Option	*Purpose*
Compiler	Allows you to control the compiler with the following options:
Code Generation	Allows you to specify the memory model, code generation defaults, and macro definitions
Entry/Exit Code	Allows you to specify the kind of prolog or epilog to create for each of a module's functions
C++ Options	Lets you specify the C++ options such as the use of virtual tables
Optimizations	Specifies compiler optimizations such as whether to optimize by speed or size
Source	Specifies source code type
Messages	Controls the display of compiler error and warning messages
Names	Allows you to set the segment, group, and class names for code, data, and BSS sections
Transfer	Allows you to add or delete names in the ≡ (System) Menu
Make	Specifies the conditions for project management
Linker	Specifies the linker settings such as map file and output controls
Application	Allows you to quickly and easily set up the compiler and linker for DOS or Windows executables
Debugger	Sets controls for the debugger
Directories	Allows you to specify the paths for the Include, Library, and Output directories
Environment	Allows you to set up a customized environment using the following options:
Preferences	Allows you to set the screen size, source tracking, and autosave environment settings
Editor	Lets you choose the setting for the editor
Mouse	Allows you to make changes to the mouse features including the behavior of the right mouse key and the speed of the double click
Desktop	Allows you to specify whether you want the History lists, Clipboard contents, watch expressions, and breakpoints saved across sessions
Save	Offers the chance to save the settings modified in Find, Replace, and Options

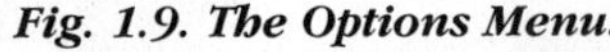

Fig. 1.9. The Options Menu.

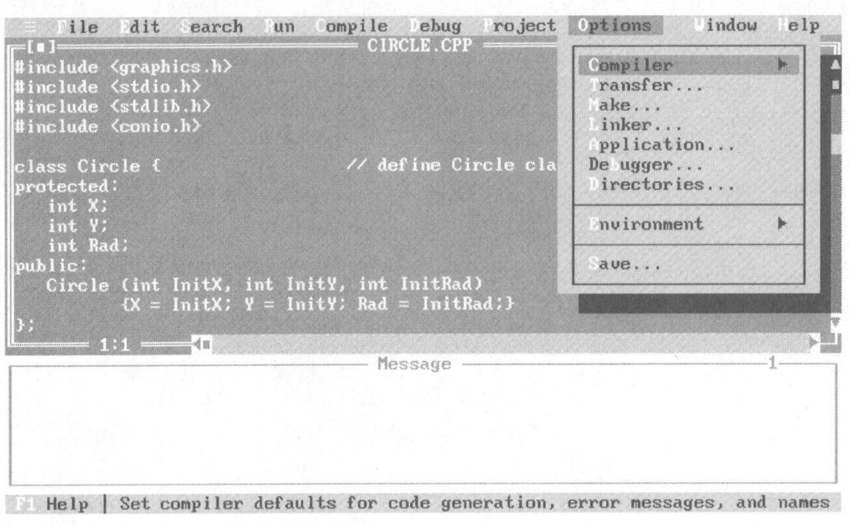

The Windows Menu

The Windows Menu provides window management options (see Fig. 1.10). The window management options include Size/Move, Zoom, Tile, Cascade, Next, Close, Message, Output, Watch, User Screen, Register, Project, Project Notes, and List. These options are described in table 1.12.

***Table 1.12.** Options of the Windows Menu.*

Option	*Purpose*
Size/Move	Changes the size or position of the active window
Zoom	Sets the active window to its maximum size
Tile	Tiles all the open windows
Cascade	Stacks all the open windows
Next	Makes the next window active
Close	Closes the active window

Option	*Purpose*
Message	Makes the Message window active
Output	Makes the Output window active
Watch	Makes the Watch window active
User Screen	Views the full-screen output of a program
Register	Makes the Register window active
Project	Allows you to view the files which create a program
Project Notes	Provides the capability to jot down notes on the project
List	Makes a list of all the windows that have been opened

Fig. 1.10. The Windows Menu.

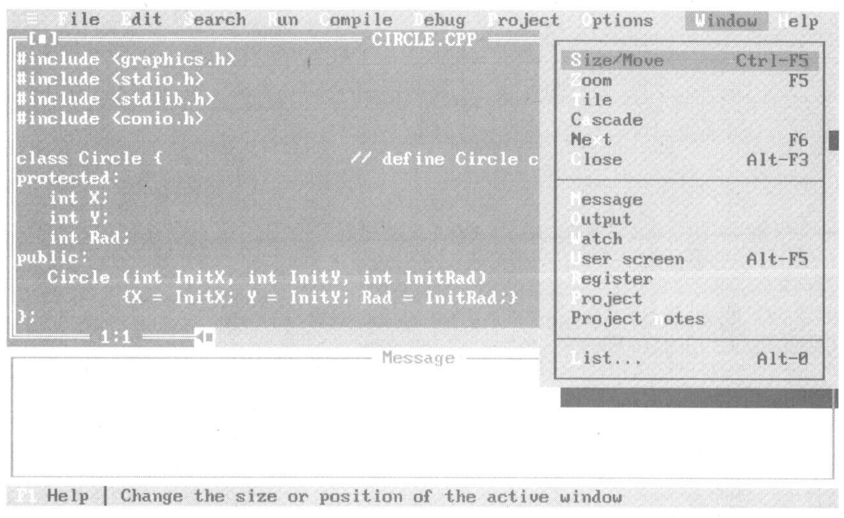

The Help Menu

The Help Menu provides on-line help (see Fig. 1.11). The options for the Help Menu are Contents, Index, Topic Search, Previous Topic, and Help on Help. These options are described in table 1.13.

Table 1.13. Options of the Help Menu.

Option	*Purpose*
Contents	Opens the Help window to the main table of contents
Index	Provides a full list of help keywords which can be selected to bring up help information
Topic Search	Provides help on a selected item from the active edit window
Previous Topic	Displays the last help information viewed
Help on Help	Explains how to use the help system

Fig. 1.11. The Help Menu.

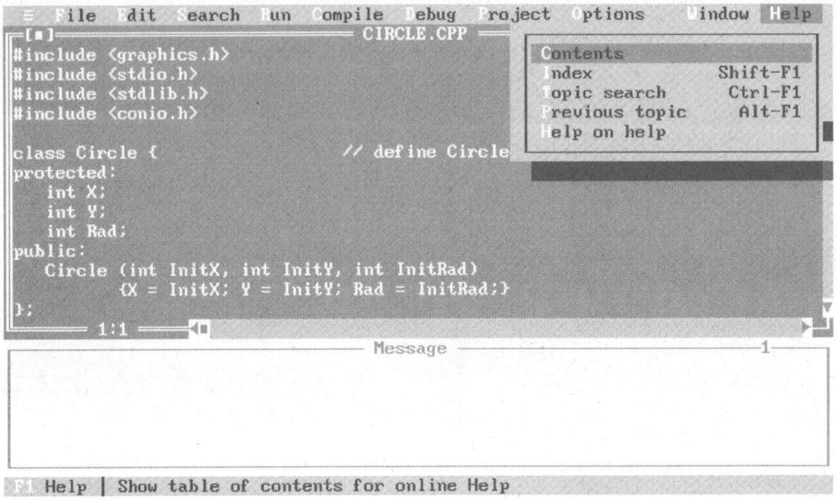

```
 ≡  File  Edit  Search  Run  Compile  Debug  Project  Options    Window  Help
[■]                         CIRCLE.CPP
#include <graphics.h>                       Contents
#include <stdio.h>                          Index            Shift-F1
#include <stdlib.h>                         Topic search      Ctrl-F1
#include <conio.h>                          Previous topic     Alt-F1
                                            Help on help
class Circle {                    // define Circle
protected:
   int X;
   int Y;
   int Rad;
public:
   Circle (int InitX, int InitY, int InitRad)
          {X = InitX; Y = InitY; Rad = InitRad;}
};
      1:1
                           Message                                1
 F1 Help | Show table of contents for online Help
```

The menus, as well as many of the menu options, can be selected using *hot keys*, or keystrokes that automatically invoke a particular menu item without using the mouse or cursor keys. Tables 1.14 through 1.22 provide information on the hot keys available for each menu and menu item. Additionally, information on the use of the function keys is provided.

Table 1.14. The function keys.

Function Key	Menu Option
F1	Help
F2	File | Save
F3	File | Open
F4	Run | Go to Cursor
F5	Window | Zoom
F6	Window | Next
F7	Run | Trace Into
F8	Run | Step Over
F9	Compile | Make Exe file

Table 1.15. Hot keys to get to the menus.

Hot Keys	Menu Selected
Alt-Spacebar	≡ (System) Menu
Alt-C	Compile Menu
Alt-D	Debug Menu
Alt-E	Edit Menu
Alt-F	File Menu
Alt-H	Help Menu
Alt-O	Options Menu
Alt-P	Project Menu
Alt-R	Run Menu
Alt-S	Search Menu
Alt-W	Window Menu

Table 1.16. Hot keys for the File Menu.

Hot Keys	Menu Option
F3	File | Open
F2	File | Save
Alt-X	File | Quit

Table 1.17. Hot keys for the Edit Menu.

Hot Keys	*Menu Option*
Ctrl-Del	Edit | Clear
Ctrl-Ins	Edit | Copy
Shift-Del	Edit | Cut
Shift-Ins	Edit | Paste
Alt-Bkspc	Edit | Undo

Table 1.18. Hot keys for the Search Menu.

Hot Keys	*Menu Option*
Alt-F7	Search | Previous Error
Alt-F8	Search | Next Error

Table 1.19. Hot keys for the Run Menu.

Hot Keys	*Menu Option*
Ctrl-F9	Run | Run
Ctrl-F2	Run | Program Reset
F4	Run | Go to cursor
F7	Run | Trace Into
F8	Run | Step Over

Table 1.20. Hot keys for the Debug Menu.

Hot Keys	*Menu Option*
Alt-F4	Debug | Inspect
Ctrl-F4	Debug | Evaluate/Modify
Ctrl-F3	Debug | Call Stack
Ctrl-F7	Debug | Watches | Add Watch
Ctrl-F8	Debug | Toggle Breakpoint

Table 1.21. Hot keys for the Window Menu.

Hot Keys	*Menu Option*
Ctrl-F5	Window | Size/Move
F5	Window | Zoom
F6	Window | Next
Alt-F3	Window | Close
Alt-F5	Window | User Screen
Alt-O	Window | List

Table 1.22. Hot keys for the Help Menu.

Hot Keys	*Menu Option*
F1	Help | Contents
F1 F1	Help | Help on Help
Shift-F1	Help | Index
Alt-F1	Help | Previous Topic
Ctrl-F1	Help | Topic Search

The C Language

In recent years, the C language has become one of the most popular and powerful development languages. The primary reason for this popularity is that C produces fast, compact code. This chapter introduces the basic concepts and code structure of the C language.

Advantages of the C Language

The C language is considered a high-level language because it offers functions that to some degree resemble English syntax. C can also be considered a mid-level language, however, because the syntax and structure of many standard C functions closely resemble the actual operations of the computer's internal registers. Therefore, the programmer can gain machine-level control over the actual operations of the computer while maintaining a high-level language feel.

The C language produces fast executable code. The flexibility of the C language allows the programmer to optimize the design of the software by using specialized low- and mid-level functions. Because most high-level languages trade efficiency in the executable code for ease in programming and maintenance, the low-level characteristics of the C language allow C code to run more efficiently and quickly.

The C language is very versatile even though the ANSI C standard has only 32 keywords. Because it is a mature language, many functions are provided in the C run-time libraries which offer flexibility in design and implementation. Therefore, the programmer/designer can optimize the design to meet the specific needs of the application. The many methods for memory management provided in the C language, such as the use of pointers, structures, and so forth, offer ways to meet the needs of specific applications, ranging from database management to graphics to statistical applications.

Many high-level languages, such as Ada and PASCAL, are strongly typed. Not C. Because data in the C language is not strongly typed, the data can easily be viewed in several formats, such as character, integer, or ASCII. C also offers the advantages of being a structured language, supporting the concepts of modular programming, and readily interfacing with assembly language routines.

Disadvantages of the C Language

Although C has many advantages, it also has a few disadvantages. Its primary weakness is not being strongly typed. This "typing" feature has both positive and negative side effects. The absence of strongly typed variables gives the programmer more flexibility when manipulating the data in a program. However, this flexibility can result in unexpected—and almost untraceable—errors when a data value is compromised by changes such as roundoff errors, or mistaking an integer for a pointer address.

C Programming Structure

When you use Borland C++ without the recently added object-oriented features, the structure of every program will be generally the same. As with other modular languages such as PASCAL and Ada, there is one main function recognized by the operating system as the controlling function. For the C language, this controlling function is referred to as the `main()` function.

The `main()` function, in normal operations, is the beginning and end of every C program. Other functions, often referred to as subroutines in other languages, are often called from the main program but can be called from any function in the program. Once each function has completed its intended task, control is returned to the calling function. In this way, control is always returned to the `main()` function.

As mentioned earlier, C is designed to be a modular language. This means that sections of code designed to perform a specific task are usually removed from the `main()` function and placed inside their own functions. For example, suppose that you need to display tabular data several times during the execution of the program. Because this is a specific and repetitive task, a separate function which displays the tabular data could easily be developed.

Modular design has several advantages. First, modular design reduces redundant code. It is easier and more efficient to produce a function that can be called to perform a particular task than it is to add the required lines of code every time that task is needed. Second, code which is modular in design is easier to read and understand. By giving functions names which accurately reflect their designed task, the interpretation of the program's operation is a simple matter. Finally, modular code is easy to maintain because it is easier to read and understand. Maintenance is not that important to the casual programmer. It *is* important when designing code for professional applications, however, because this code will probably have to be enhanced and updated in the future.

The examples in this book are developed using traditional C programming methods, with the exception of those in chapters 3 and 4. Because the examples are short, there is no need to use the features of the C++ language. The examples use C programming methods, so it is important to understand the basic structure of C programs. A description of the main features of the C program structure follows.

Preprocessor Directives

A preprocessor directive is a command to the C preprocessor. A common preprocessor directive is `#include`. This directive allows external text files to be incorporated into a C program. The `#include` directive instructs the preprocessor to substitute the contents of the specified file for the `#include` directive.

The `#include` directive is often used to include header files. The header files contain common variable and function declarations for the proper use of certain functions. For example, the header file `graphics.h` must be included to use the graphics functions. Without the header file, the required definitions, declarations, and constants are not available for use.

The format of the `#include` directive determines the search path for the specified file. There are three formats used with the `#include` statement. Each of these formats is presented with an explanation that follows.

```
#include <stdio.h>
```

In this format, the computer searches for the `stdio.h` file in the standard directories. The working directory is not searched.

```
#include "stdio.h"
```

In this format, the search for the `stdio.h` file begins in the current directory, then moves to the standard directories, if necessary.

```
#include "c:\borlandc\include\stdio.h"
```

In this format, the computer searches for the `stdio.h` file in only the specified path.

Declarations

A declaration establishes the names and attributes of variables, functions, and types used in the program. The declaration also specifies the visibility of the variable. When declaring variables and functions, there is a set of standard data types used by the C language. Table 2.1 lists the available data types.

Table 2.1. *Data types.*

Type	*Number of Bits*
unsigned char	8
char	8
enum	16
unsigned int	16
short int	16
int	16
unsigned long	32
long	32
float	32
double	64
long double	80
near pointer	16
far pointer	32

The visibility of a variable is determined by the location of the declaration. Visibility can be defined as the availability of that variable to the various functions in the program. Global variables are declared prior to the `main()` function and are visible to all functions. Local variables are declared inside the function and are therefore visible only inside the function.

A function declaration consists of a return type, the function name, and an argument-type list (if any). A function declaration is used to define the characteristics of the function. The contents of the function are not defined.

Definitions

A definition assigns the contents of a variable or function and allocates storage for the variable or function. A function definition contains a function header and body. The function header contains the type of data returned by the function, the function name, and the list of formal parameters required by the function. The body of the function definition consists of local declarations and a compound statement that describes the operation of the function.

Expressions

An expression can be defined as the combination of operators and operands which yields a single value. The operand is a constant or variable value which is manipulated in an expression. The operator defines the method by which the operands will interact. Table 2.2 lists the operators defined in the C language.

Table 2.2. *Operators for the C language.*

Arithmetic Operators

Operator	*Name*	*Use*	*Meaning*
*	Multiplication	x*y	Multiply x and y
/	Division	x/y	Divide x by y
%	Modulo	x%y	Divide x remainder by y
+	Addition	x+y	Add x and y
–	Subtraction	x–y	Subtract y from x
++	Increment	x++	Increment x
--	Decrement	-- x	Decrement x
–	Negation	–x	Negate x

continues

Table 2.2. (continued)

Relational and Logical Operators

Operator	*Name*	*Use*	*Meaning*
>	Greater than	x>y	1 if x greater than y
>=	Greater than or equal to	x>=y	1 if x greater than or equal to y
<	Less than	x<y	1 if x less than y
<=	Less than or equal to y	x<=y	1 if x less than or equal to y
==	Equal to	x==y	1 if x equals y
!=	Not equal to	x!=y	1 if x not equal to y
!	Logical NOT	!x	1 if x is 0
&&	Logical AND	x&&y	0 if both x and y are 0
||	Logical OR	x||y	0 if either x or y is 0

Note: 1 indicates TRUE, 0 indicates FALSE

Assignment Operators

Operator	*Name*	*Use*	*Meaning*
=	Assignment	x=y	Set x to y value
?=	Compound Assignment	x?=y	Same as x=x?y where ? is one of the following: - * / % << >> & ^ |

Data Access and Size Operators

Operator	*Name*	*Use*	*Meaning*
[]	Array element	x[0]	First element of x
->	Select member	p->x	Member x in structure p points to
*	Indirection	*p	Contents of address p
&	Address of	&x	Address of x
sizeof	Size in bytes	sizeof(x)	Size of x in bytes

Bitwise Operators

Operator	*Name*	*Use*	*Meaning*
~	Bitwise Complement	~x	Switches 1s and 0s
&	Bitwise AND	x&y	Bitwise AND of x and y

Bitwise Operators			
Operator	*Name*	*Use*	*Meaning*
|	Bitwise OR	x|y	Bitwise OR of x and y
^	Bitwise XOR	x^y	Exclusive OR of x and y
<<	Left shift	x<<2	Shift x left 2 bits
>>	Right shift	x>>2	Shift x right 2 bits

Miscellaneous Operators			
Operator	*Name*	*Use*	*Meaning*
()	Function	malloc(x)	Call `malloc` function
(type)	Type cast	(int)x	Set x to type int
?:	Conditional	x1?x2:x3	If x1 is not 0, x2 is evaluated; else x3
,	Sequential	x++,y++	Increment x, then y evaluation

Statements

Statements control the order of execution of a C program. A statement ends in a semicolon and contains keywords, expressions, and other statements. The following paragraphs briefly describe the C statements.

The `assignment` statement (=) assigns the value of the expression on the right to the variable on the left.

```
z = 1000;
```

The `break` statement (`break;`) ends the innermost `do`, `for`, `switch`, or `while` statement.

```
while (x < 1000)
{
        if (x == 123)
                break;
}
```

The `continue` statement (`continue;`) begins the next iteration of the innermost `do`, `for`, or `while` statement in which it appears, skipping the loop body.

```
while (x < 1000)
{
        if (x == 123)
                continue;
}
```

The do-while loop executes a block of statements until the expression in the while statement fails.

```
do
{
        x = x + 1;
} while (x < 1000);
```

The for loop evaluates the first of its three expressions once. The third expression is then evaluated after each pass through the loop until the second expression becomes false.

```
for (x = 1; x < 100; x = x + 10)
{
        y = y + x;
}
```

The goto statement transfers program control to the statement defined by the label.

```
        if (x == 200)
                goto X;
        x == x - 1;
X:      x == x + 1;
```

The if statement executes the following statements (enclosed in brackets) or the next statement (if no brackets) if the expression is true; otherwise, the second expression is executed.

```
if (x == 0)
        y = 10;
else
        y = 0;
```

The null statement is used to indicate that nothing is to happen.

```
if (x == 100)
        ;                       /* do nothing */
```

The return statement stops the execution of the current function and returns control to the calling function. A single value can be returned.

```
if (z == 500)
        return (y);
```

The switch statement evaluates an expression and attempts to match it to a set of case statements. If there is no match, the default statement is executed.

```
switch (x)
{
        case BUY:    buy();
                     break;
        case SELL:   sell();
                     break;
        default:     do_nothing();
                     break;
}
```

The `while` loop executes a statement or block of statements as long as the expression evaluates to a nonzero value.

```
while (x > 1000)
{
        y = y + x;
}
```

Functions

A function is a set of declarations, definitions, expressions, and statements that performs a specific job.

The following code structure illustrates the use of the preprocessor directives, declarations, definitions, expressions, statements, and functions.

```
#include <stdio.h>          /* preprocessor directives */
#include <math.h>           /* include header files    */

#define TRUE 1              /* define a constant */

int calc_diameter (int);   /* function prototype */


int main ()
{                           /* begin main function */

        int radius, dia;    /* declare local variables */

        radius = 10;
        dia = calc_diameter (radius);

        return 0;
}                           /* end main function */


int calc_diameter (rad)   /* function head */
{
```

continues

```
        int diameter;           /* declare local variable */

        diameter = 2 * rad;
        return (diameter);      /* return value */
    }                           /* end calc_diameter */
```

The first lines of any C program are the preprocessor directives. The preprocessor directives are commands to the C preprocessor, which is invoked before compiling the program. In the code structure above, the `#define` and `#include` statements are the preprocessor directives.

The other statements prior to the `main()` function are often declaration statements. A declaration establishes the name and attributes of variables, functions, and types used in the program. Global variables are declared outside the `main()` function and are visible to all functions.

The `main()` function is next. Once inside the `main()` function, local variables are declared. Local variables are declared inside the function and are visible only inside the function. For the most part, the examples in this book do not use functions other than the `main()` function. This is due primarily to the short length of the programs. Although the examples in this book are not always structured as efficiently as possible, they are designed to be simple to understand.

The code structure described in this chapter is followed throughout the book and should provide a simple but effective framework for the interpretation of the enclosed programming examples.

Borland C++ and ANSI C

Many of the run-time library functions provided by Borland C++ are compatible with the ANSI C standard. Therefore, when developing portable C code, only these run-time library functions should be used. Table 2.3 lists functions compatible with ANSI C.

***Table 2.3.** Run-time library functions compatible with ANSI C.*

Function	*Meaning*
`abort`	Abnormally terminates a program
`abs`	Returns the absolute value of an integer
`acos`	Calculates the arc cosine
`asctime`	Converts date and time to ASCII
`asin`	Calculates the arc sine
`assert`	Tests a condition and possibly aborts
`atan`	Calculates the arc tangent

Function	*Meaning*
atan2	Calculates the arc tangent of y/x
atexit	Registers termination function
atof	Converts a string to a floating-point number
atoi	Converts a string to an integer
atol	Converts a string to a long
bsearch	Binary search of an array
calloc	Allocates main memory
ceil	Rounds up
clearerr	Resets error indication
clock	Determines processor time
cos	Calculates the cosine of a value
cosh	Calculates the hyperbolic cosine of a value
ctime	Converts date and time to a string
difftime	Computes the difference between two times
div	Divides two integers
exit	Terminates program
exp	Calculates the exponential e to the x
fabs	Returns the absolute value of a floating-point
fclose	Closes a stream
feof	Detects end-of-file on a stream
ferror	Detects errors on a stream
fflush	Flushes a stream
fgetc	Gets a character from a stream
fgetpos	Gets the current file pointer
fgets	Gets a string from a stream
floor	Rounds down
fmod	Calculates x modulo y
fopen	Opens a stream
fprintf	Writes formatted output to a stream
fputc	Puts a character on a stream
fputs	Outputs a string on a stream
fread	Reads data from a stream
free	Frees an allocated block
freopen	Associates a new file with an open stream
frexp	Splits a double number into mantissa and exponent

continues

Table 2.3. (continued)

Function	*Meaning*
`fscanf`	Scans and formats input from a stream
`fseek`	Repositions a file pointer on a stream
`fsetpos`	Positions the file pointer of a stream
`fstat`	Gets open file information
`ftell`	Returns the current file pointer
`fwrite`	Writes to a stream
`getc`	Gets a character from a stream
`getchar`	Gets a character from `stdin`
`getenv`	Gets a string from the environment
`gets`	Gets a string from `stdin`
`gmtime`	Converts date and time to Greenwich mean time
`isalpha`	Tests for letters
`iscntrl`	Tests for control characters
`isdigit`	Tests for digits
`isgraph`	Tests for printing characters
`islower`	Tests for lowercase letters
`isprint`	Tests for printable characters
`ispunct`	Tests for punctuation characters
`isspace`	Tests for space, tab, newline, formfeed, return
`isupper`	Tests for uppercase letters
`isxdigit`	Tests for hexadecimal digits
`labs`	Gives the absolute value of a long integer
`ldexp`	Calculates $x * 2^{exp}$
`ldiv`	Divides two long integers
`localeconv`	Gets the current locale structure
`localtime`	Converts date and time to a structure
`log`	Calculates the natural logarithm
`log10`	Calculates $\log_{10}(x)$
`longjmp`	Performs a nonlocal goto
`malloc`	Allocates main memory
`memchr`	Searches for a character
`memcmp`	Compares two blocks
`memcpy`	Copies a block
`memmove`	Copies a block

Function	*Meaning*
`memset`	Sets bytes of a block to a specified value
`mktime`	Converts time to calendar format
`perror`	Prints a system error message
`pow`	Calculates x to the power of y
`printf`	Writes formatted output to `stdout`
`putc`	Outputs a character to a stream
`putchar`	Outputs a character to `stdout`
`puts`	Outputs a string to `stdout`
`qsort`	Sorts using the quicksort algorithm
`raise`	Sends a software signal to the program
`rand`	Random number generator
`realloc`	Reallocates main memory
`remove`	Removes a file
`rename`	Renames a file
`rewind`	Repositions a file pointer to beginning of stream
`rmdir`	Removes a directory
`scanf`	Scans and formats input from `stdin`
`setbuf`	Assigns buffering to a stream
`setjmp`	Sets up for nonlocal goto
`setlocale`	Selects a locale
`setvbuf`	Assigns buffering to a stream
`signal`	Specifies signal-handling actions
`sin`	Calculates the sine of a value
`sinh`	Calculates the hyperbolic sine
`sprintf`	Writes formatted output to a string
`sqrt`	Calculates the square root
`srand`	Initializes the random number generator
`sscanf`	Scans and formats input from a string
`stat`	Gets information about a file
`strcat`	Appends one string to another
`strchr`	Scans a string for a character
`strcmp`	Compares two strings
`strcoll`	Compares two strings
`strcpy`	Copies one string into another
`strcspn`	Scans a string for a subset of characters

continues

Table 2.3. (continued)

Function	*Meaning*
`strerror`	Gets an error message string
`strftime`	Formats time for output
`strlen`	Gets the length of a string
`strncat`	Appends a portion of one string to another
`strncmp`	Compares a part of one string with another
`strncpy`	Copies bytes from one string to another
`strpbrk`	Scans a string for a character
`strrchr`	Scans a string for a character
`strspn`	Scans a string for a subset of characters
`strstr`	Scans a string for a substring
`strtod`	Converts a string to a double
`strtok`	Searches a string for tokens
`strtol`	Converts a string to a long
`strtoul`	Converts a string to an unsigned long
`strxfrm`	Transforms a portion of a string
`system`	Issues a system command
`tan`	Calculates the tangent of a value
`tanh`	Calculates the hyperbolic tangent
`time`	Gets the time of day
`tmpfile`	Opens a temporary file in binary mode
`tmpnam`	Creates a unique file name
`tolower`	Converts characters to lowercase
`toupper`	Converts characters to uppercase
`ungetc`	Pushes a character back into the input stream
`vfprintf`	Writes formatted output to a stream
`vprintf`	Writes formatted output to `stdout`
`vsprintf`	Writes formatted output to a string

Object-Oriented Programming

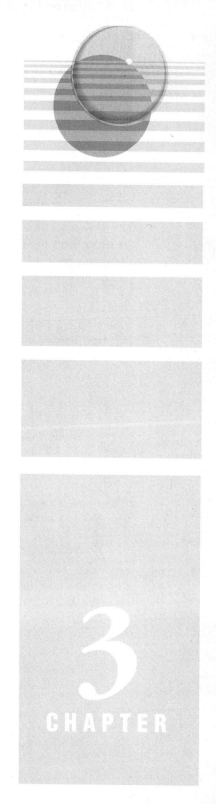

Object-oriented programming is a relatively new programming methodology. A computer environment is modelled as a collection of objects that interact with each other through messages. Object-oriented programming makes a program more modular and maintainable.

Object-oriented programs, of course, contain objects. Objects contain properties and behaviors. Properties are not directly accessible from outside the object. Instead, the properties are manipulated by the behaviors of the object. The behaviors of the object are invoked when a message is received by the object. This is confusing for newcomers to object-oriented programming, so let's take this one step at a time.

First, we will define an object. In the real world, an object has properties and behaviors. For example, a basketball is round and usually orange (its properties) and can be dribbled, passed, or shot (its behaviors). In the programming world, an object also has properties and behaviors. For example, in a graphics application, a circle is described by certain data such as its center, color, radius, and fill pattern (its properties) and can be created, moved, sized, or deleted (its behaviors). Objects in a program can represent the physical entities, such as circles and rectangle, or the more abstract entities, such as stacks and complex data structures.

Object-oriented programming has several characteristics and advantages. First, because objects contain properties and behaviors, objects support modular programming. Modular programming supports ease of development and maintainability of code. The other characteristics and advantages of object-oriented programming involve the properties of encapsulation, inheritance, and polymorphism. These properties are explained in the following paragraphs.

Encapsulation

Encapsulation is described in the Borland C++ tutorial as combining a data structure with the functions (actions or methods) dedicated to manipulating the data. Encapsulation is achieved by means of a new structuring and data-typing mechanism, the class.

To simplify this definition, encapsulation is the practice of using classes to link data and the code used to manipulate the data. In the traditional C programming style, data is usually kept in data structures; functions are then created to manipulate the data. This style is shown as follows:

```
struct data_items
      {
      int a;
      int b;
      int c;
      };

void manipulate_data (int x, int y, int z)
{
data_items.a = data_items.a + x;
data_items.b = data_items.b + y;
data_items.c = data_items.c + z;
}
```

This structure and function would then be put into a source file, compiled separately, and treated as a module. The problem with this method is that even though the structure and function are created to be used together, the data can be accessed without using the described function.

The property of encapsulation solves this problem. Encapsulation is provided in C++ by the `struct`, `union`, and `class` keywords. These keywords allow you to combine data and functions into a class entity. The data items are called data members, whereas the functions are called member functions.

The following is an example of a class:

```
class Circle {
      int x;
      int y;
      int radius;
```

```
        int DrawCircle (int a, int b, int rad);
        int DeleteCircle (int a, int b, int rad);
};
```

The data members of the class are `x`, `y`, and `radius`. The member functions of the class are `DrawCircle` and `DeleteCircle`.

By defining the class `Circle`, the properties of the object cannot be directly accessed from outside the object. Only the behaviors of the object, `DrawCircle` and `DeleteCircle`, can manipulate the data. The behaviors of the object can be invoked only by sending a message to the object. By defining an object in this way, the implementation details of the object are not visible to, or accessible by, the outside. This is encapsulation, which leads to modular programming and maintainable, reusable code.

Inheritance

Inheritance is described in the Borland C++ tutorial as building new, derived classes that inherit the data and functions from one or more previously defined base classes, while possibly redefining or adding new data and actions. This creates a hierarchy of classes.

In other words, inheritance is the ability to create a class which has the properties and behaviors of another class. For example, suppose that you start with a class called DOG. This class has several properties, including four legs, a tail, two eyes, two ears, a mouth, and a nose. Under this class you can add classes which provide more specific information.

For our purposes we'll add the `BigDog` class and the `LittleDog` class. The `BigDog` class has the properties of heavy and tall. The `LittleDog` class has the properties of light and short. More classes could be added which provide even more detail. For example, `LongHairBigDog`, `ShortHairBigDog`, `LongHairLittleDog`, and `ShortHairLittleDog` classes could be added. The `LongHairBigDog` and `LongHairLittleDog` classes add the property of long hair. The `ShortHairBigDog` and `ShortHairLittleDog` classes add the property of short hair.

Additional classes could be added which provide even more specifics. We'll add the `IrishSetter` class and the `Chihuahua` class. The `IrishSetter` class adds the property of red hair. The `Chihuahua` class adds the properties of very small and nervous. This hierarchy is shown in figure 3.1. By developing a hierarchy, it is possible to classify and inherit properties of objects.

Now let's look at applying this hierarchy. An Irish Setter, for example, has the property of red hair as determined from the derived class `IrishSetter`. Derived classes inherit properties from other classes, called base classes. Therefore, the Irish Setter also has the property of the `LongHairBigDog` class, which is long hair. The

`LongHairBigDog` class also inherits properties from the `BigDog` class which, in turn, inherits properties from the DOG class. Therefore, we can determine that the Irish Setter has long red hair, is heavy and tall, and has two ears, two eyes, a tail, a mouth, a nose, and four legs. Similarly, we can determine that the Chihuahua is very small and nervous, has short hair, is light and short, and has two ears, two eyes, a tail, a mouth, a nose, and four legs.

Fig. 3.1. The DOG hierarchy.

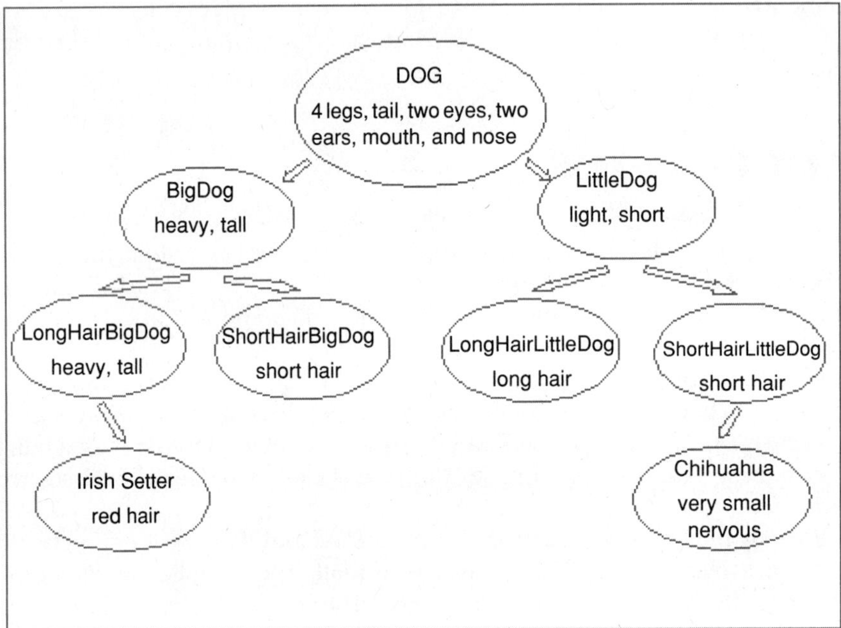

Although this is a simple illustration of inheritance, it provides a basic understanding of the power of inheritance. The ability to inherit properties from other classes allows you to generalize data and properties, thus improving programmer efficiency and reducing redundancy in code.

The following example demonstrates the use of the C++ features of inheritance and encapsulation for the implementation of a graphics program.

```
#include <graphics.h>
#include <stdio.h>
#include <stdlib.h>
#include <conio.h>
```

```
class Circle {
protected:
   int X;
   int Y;
   int Rad;
public:
   Circle (int InitX, int InitY, int InitRad)
      {X = InitX; Y = InitY; Rad = InitRad;}
};

class SolidCircle : public Circle {
protected:
   int Color;
public:
   SolidCircle (int InitX, int InitY, int InitRad,
   int InitColor);
};

class ShadedCircle : public Circle {
protected:
   int Color;
public:
   ShadedCircle (int InitX, int InitY, int InitRad,
   int InitColor);
};

SolidCircle::SolidCircle(int InitX, int InitY, int
InitRad,
   int InitColor) : Circle (InitX, InitY, InitRad) {
   setfillstyle (SOLID_FILL, InitColor);
   fillellipse (InitX, InitY, InitRad, InitRad);
};

ShadedCircle::ShadedCircle(int InitX, int InitY, int
InitRad,
   int InitColor) : Circle (InitX, InitY, InitRad) {
   setfillstyle (HATCH_FILL, InitColor);
   fillellipse (InitX, InitY, InitRad, InitRad);
};


int main()
{
int gdriver = VGA;
int gmode = VGAHI;

int x, y, color, rad, selection;

registerbgidriver(EGAVGA_driver);
registerbgifont(sansserif_font);

initgraph(&gdriver,&gmode,"");
```

```
do
{
x = random (639);
y = random (479);
rad = random (51);
color = random (15);
selection = random (2);

if (selection == 0)
     ShadedCircle (x, y, rad + 5, color + 1);
else
     SolidCircle (x, y, rad + 5, color + 1);

} while (! kbhit());

closegraph();
return 0;
}
```

The program begins by declaring the class `Circle`. The `Circle` class demonstrates the properties of encapsulation through its data `X`, `Y`, and `Rad`. Inheritance is demonstrated by the two derived classes, `ShadedCircle` and `SolidCircle`, of the base class `Circle`.

The program randomly selects the horizontal and vertical coordinates for the center position of a circle. The radius and fill color are then randomly selected. A selection is then made to determine which type of circle will be drawn, either a shaded or solid circle. The shaded or solid circle is then drawn. This continues until a key is pressed.

Polymorphism

Polymorphism is described in the Borland C++ tutorial as giving an action one name or symbol that is shared up and down a class hierarchy, with each class in the hierarchy implementing the action in a way appropriate to itself.

Very simply stated, polymorphism, in C++, is the ability to create several versions of the same function or operator. The Borland C++ Run-Time Library contains several functions which have been "overloaded" to work with various data types. Let's look, for example, at the following function prototypes:

```
int square (int value);
float square (float value);
double square (double square);
```

Each function is designed to accept and return a particular data type: int, float, or double; however, each function is called `square`. In C, you can have only one function with a given name. In C++, on the other hand, function overloading is fully supported as long as the argument lists differ. Therefore, if you call `square` while passing an integer value, the proper function will be called and an integer value will be returned. Similarly, if you call `square` with a float or double value, a float or double value, respectively, will be returned.

The ability to overload functions and operators provides greater flexibility in program design.

The following example demonstrates the overloading of a function.

```
#include <stdio.h>
#include <stdlib.h>
#include <conio.h>
#include <iostream.h>

class squared {
public:
  int squ(int);
  double squ(double);
  long squ(long);
};

int squared::squ(int intval)
{
   int result;

   result = intval * intval;
   return (result);
}

double squared::squ(double dblval)
{
   double result;

   result = dblval * dblval;
   return (result);
}

long squared::squ(long longval)
{
   long result;

   result = longval * longval;
   return (result);
}


int main()
{
squared value;
```

```
clrscr();
cout << "The square of 3 is " << value.squ(3) << endl;
cout << "The square of 3.5 is " << value.squ(3.5) << endl;
cout << "The square of 6L is " << value.squ(6L) << endl;

return 0;
}
```

In this example, the class `squared` has three functions called `squ` associated with it. Each function is designed to work with either int, double, or long values. When the function `squ` is called, the value passed as a parameter determines which version of the `squ` function is executed.

Polymorphism is also known as late, or dynamic, binding and is often accomplished using virtual functions.

The C++ Language

The C++ language is an extension to the C language and adds object-oriented programming features such as encapsulation, inheritance, and polymorphism. Borland's implementation of the C++ language, Borland C++, provides full compatibility with AT&T's C++ version 2.0.

C++ Enhancements to the C Language

The overall structure of a C++ program looks similar to the standard C code structure with a few exceptions. The primary difference is that the C++ language is structured for object-oriented programming methods as described in Chapter 3. In addition, there are several enhancements that make C++ code distinguishable from C code. The following descriptions are provided to briefly explain some of the C++ enhancements to the C language.

Classes, Structures, and Unions

A class is a user-defined data type which allows you to encapsulate data and functions. The class is the most distinguishable enhancement in the C++ language and provides the fundamental object-oriented features of C++. A class can be defined with the `struct`, `union`, or `class` keywords. These keywords create a single class that combines functions, called *member functions*, and data, called *data members*.

A member function is declared inside the class definition and is associated with that class type. Member functions are used to manipulate the *data* members for the class.

The `class` keyword is used to define a class. The following is the general format of the class definition:

```
class classname {
    vartype variable1;    // variables are private by default
    vartype variable2;
    vartype variable3;
    vartype variable4;
              .
              .
              .
public:
    constructor (argument list);
    destructor (argument list);
    member_function1 (argument list);
    member_function2 (argument list);
              .
              .
              .
};
```

The class definition begins with the keyword `class` followed by the class name. In the class definition, data members and member functions are declared inside the brackets. Data members are private by default and can be manipulated only by the member functions. The data members are usually followed by the public declaration, then the member functions. The public declaration allows the member functions to be accessed from outside the class.

As the previous class definition illustrates, there are two functions in the declaration that are not special member functions. These functions are the constructor and the destructor.

The constructor is one of the class's member functions. The constructor initializes the class variables, allocates memory, shares the name of the class, and is automatically invoked. The destructor is another one of the class's member functions. The destructor frees all memory allocated by the constructor and is automatically invoked when needed.

Another way to create a class is with the `struct` keyword. For C++, the `struct` keyword creates a class type with public access by default. The following generalized format is used with the `struct` keyword:

```
struct structname {
   vartype variable1;
   vartype variable2;
   vartype variable3;
          .
          .
          .
   constructor (argument list);
   member_function1 (argument list);
   member_function2 (argument list);
          .
          .
          .
};
```

As with the class keyword, data members and member functions are declared inside the class definition.

The `union` keyword is very similar to the `struct` keyword; however, the union type cannot use the class access specifiers (public, private, protected). The fields of the union type are public. Furthermore, union types cannot be a derived or base class. The following generalized format is used with the `union` keyword:

```
union unionname {
   vartype variable1;
   vartype variable2;
   vartype variable3;
          .
          .
          .
   constructor (argument list);
   member_function1 (argument list);
   member_function2 (argument list);
          .
          .
          .
};
```

The use of the class for object-oriented programming is described and demonstrated in Chapter 3.

Streams

Borland C++ has added a new library, *iostreams*, that provides classes and functions for input/output. The four predefined stream objects offered by this library are as follows:

cin : standard input, similar to stdin in C
cout : standard output, similar to stdout in C
cerr : standard error output, similar to stderr in C
clog : buffered version of cerr

The new library offers several advantages over the use of traditional C input/output libraries. One advantage is that you can direct the standard streams to and from other devices. Another advantage is that the >> and << operators have been overloaded to permit the transfer of various types of data. Furthermore, the formatting of output is more efficient because data type conversion is minimized. Chapter 3 provides an example which uses the iostreams library for input/output using C++.

Operators

The C++ language provides several additional operators and supports operator overloading. Operator overloading is similar to function overloading in that operators can be redefined to work with various types of data. The following paragraphs briefly describe the operators added to the C++ language.

The scope resolution operator (::) is used to resolve name conflicts. One use of this operator is to specify a function from another scope rather than use the function of that name in the current scope. For example, DrawCircle::GetInput() indicates that the GetInput function associated with the DrawCircle class should be called. By using the scope resolution operator, the GetInput function associated with the DrawCircle class will not be confused with any other GetInput function, if there is one.

The delete and new operators are additional operators provided by C++. The delete operator is used with the new operator to provide dynamic storage capabilities. The new operator creates an object of the specified type by allocating space on the heap. The delete operator deallocates the heap storage. The following format is used for the new and delete operators:

```
pointer = new name <name-initializer>
delete pointer;
```

Modifiers, Delimiters, and Specifiers

The C++ language has also added the following modifiers, delimiters, and specifiers.

The // delimiter is used for single-line comments in C++. In C, the /* */ delimiters are used. An example of the // delimiter is as follows:

```
class Circle {                        // begin definition
   int X;
   int Y;
public:
   Circle (int InitX, int InitY);
    };                                // end definition
```

The `const` modifier is used to lock the specified value within its scope. For example,

```
const max_x = 639;
const may_y = 479;
```

The `inline` specifier instructs the compiler to perform inline substitution for the specified function whenever possible. The scope of the function name and its arguments is not affected. An example of the `inline` specifier is as follows:

```
inline float square(const float x) {return x * x}
```

C++ Run-Time Library Functions

Borland C++ provides several functions in the run-time library which are used to implement C++ features. Table 4.1 lists these functions.

Table 4.1. *C++ Run-time library functions.*

Function	*Meaning*
`abs`	Complex version - returns the absolute value
`acos`	Complex version - calculates the arc cosine
`arg`	Gives the angle of a number in the complex plane
`asin`	Complex version - calculates the arc sine

continues

Table 4.1. (continued)

Function	*Meaning*
`atan`	Complex version - calculates the arc tangent
`bcd`	Converts a number to binary coded decimal
`complex`	Creates complex numbers
`conj`	Returns the complex conjugate of a complex number
`cos`	Complex version - calculates the cosine
`cosh`	Complex version - calculates the hyperbolic cosine
`imag`	Returns the imaginary part of a complex number
`log`	Complex version - calculates natural logarithm
`log10`	Complex version - calculates the $\log_{10}$ of x
`norm`	Returns the square of the absolute value
`polar`	Returns the complex number of a given magnitude and angle
`pow`	Complex version - calculates x to the power of y
`real`	Returns the real part of a complex number or converts a BCD number back to float, double, or long double
`sin`	Complex version - calculates the sine
`sinh`	Complex version - calculates the hyperbolic sine
`tan`	Complex version - calculates the tangent
`tanh`	Complex version - calculates the hyperbolic tangent

Part II

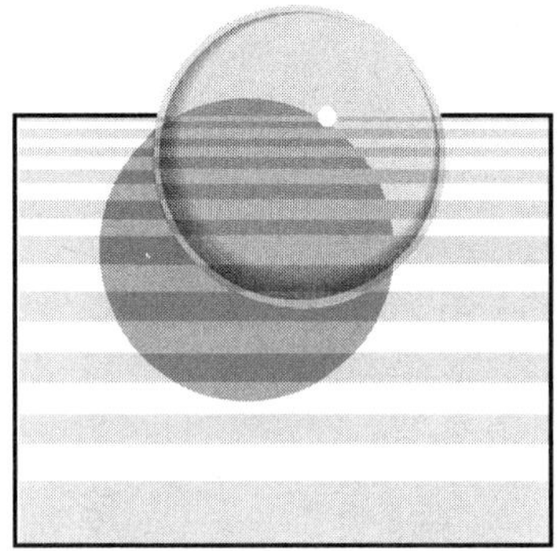

Borland C++ Reference Guide

Character Classification

At some time during your programming adventures, you may find it necessary to classify an ASCII-coded integer value as a digit, uppercase letter, lowercase letter, printable character, control character, punctuation character, or some combination of these. The macros shown in table 5.1, prototyped in the `ctype.h` header file, are provided to classify an ASCII-coded integer value. These macros are often used for testing the validity and range of user input. Only the low-order byte of the integer value is used for classification.

Table 5.1. *Character classification macros.*

Function	*Meaning*
`isalnum`	Tests for letters or digits
`isalpha`	Tests for letters
`isascii`	Tests for valid ASCII characters
`iscntrl`	Tests for control characters
`isdigit`	Tests for digits
`isgraph`	Tests for printable characters (space is excluded)
`islower`	Tests for lowercase letters
`isprint`	Tests for printable characters
`ispunct`	Tests for punctuation characters
`isspace`	Tests for space, tab, carriage return, new line, vertical tab, and formfeed
`isupper`	Tests for uppercase letters
`isxdigit`	Tests for hexadecimal digits

Each of these macros returns a nonzero value for true and a 0 for false.

Table 5.2 shows the 128 characters of the ASCII character set, numbered 0 to 127 decimal. The IBM PC extended ASCII character set, not shown, extends the total number of ASCII characters to 256. The IBM PC extended ASCII characters, numbered 128 to 255 decimal, add several Greek, accented, and graphical characters. Only the first 128 ASCII characters work with the classification macros in this chapter.

Table 5.2. *The ASCII character set.*

Decimal	*Hexadecimal*	*Character or Code*	*Control Character (if applicable)*
0	00	NUL	^@
1	01	SOH	^A
2	02	STX	^B
3	03	ETX	^C
4	04	EOT	^D
5	05	ENQ	^E

Decimal	*Hexadecimal*	*Character or Code*	*Control Character (if applicable)*
6	06	ACK	^F
7	07	BEL	^G
8	08	BS	^H
9	09	HT	^I
10	0A	LF	^J
11	0B	VT	^K
12	0C	FF	^L
13	0D	CR	^M
14	0E	SO	^N
15	0F	SI	^O
16	10	DLE	^P
17	11	DC1	^Q
18	12	DC2	^R
19	13	DC3	^S
20	14	DC4	^T
21	15	NAK	^U
22	16	SYN	^V
23	17	ETB	^W
24	18	CAN	^X
25	19	EM	^Y
26	1A	SUB	^Z
27	1B	ESC	^[
28	1C	FS	^\
29	1D	GS	^]
30	1E	RS	^^
31	1F	US	^_
32	20	SP	
33	21	!	

continues

***Table 5.2.** (continued)*

Decimal	*Hexadecimal*	*Character or Code*	*Control Character (if applicable)*
34	22	"	
35	23	#	
36	24	$	
37	25	%	
38	26	&	
39	27	'	
40	28	(	
41	29	)	
42	2A	*	
43	2B	+	
44	2C	,	
45	2D	—	
46	2E	.	
47	2F	/	
48	30	0	
49	31	1	
50	32	2	
51	33	3	
52	34	4	
53	35	5	
54	36	6	
55	37	7	
56	38	8	
57	39	9	
58	3A	:	
59	3B	;	
60	3C	<	

Decimal	*Hexadecimal*	*Character or Code*	*Control Character (if applicable)*
61	3D	=	
62	3E	>	
63	3F	?	
64	40	@	
65	41	A	
66	42	B	
67	43	C	
68	44	D	
69	45	E	
70	46	F	
71	47	G	
72	48	H	
73	49	I	
74	4A	J	
75	4B	K	
76	4C	L	
77	4D	M	
78	4E	N	
79	4F	O	
80	50	P	
81	51	Q	
82	52	R	
83	53	S	
84	54	T	
85	55	U	
86	56	V	
87	57	W	
88	58	X	

continues

Table 5.2. (continued)

Decimal	*Hexadecimal*	*Character or Code*	*Control Character (if applicable)*
89	59	Y	
90	5A	Z	
91	5B	[	
92	5C	\	
93	5D	]	
94	5E	^	
95	5F	_	
96	60	'	
97	61	a	
98	62	b	
99	63	c	
100	64	d	
101	65	e	
102	66	f	
103	67	g	
104	68	h	
105	69	i	
106	6A	j	
107	6B	k	
108	6C	l	
109	6D	m	
110	6E	n	
111	6F	o	
112	70	p	
113	71	q	
114	72	r	
115	73	s	

Decimal	*Hexadecimal*	*Character or Code*	*Control Character (if applicable)*
116	74	t	
117	75	u	
118	76	v	
119	77	w	
120	78	x	
121	79	y	
122	7A	z	
123	7B	{	
124	7C	|	
125	7D	}	
126	7E	~	
127	7F	DEL	

Borland C++ Character Classification Macros Reference Guide

The remainder of this chapter provides detailed information on the use of each character classification macro.

isalnum

DOS UNIX ANSI C C++

Syntax
```
int isalnum(int charac);

int charac;                    Value to classify
```

Function The `isalnum` macro is used for character classification of letters and digits.

File(s) to Include `#include <ctype.h>`

Description The `isalnum` macro uses a lookup table to classify the ASCII-coded integer value passed in the `charac` argument, and is defined only when `isascii` is true or `charac` is end-of-file. Use `#undef` to make this macro available as a function.

Value(s) Returned A nonzero value is returned if the `charac` argument is an uppercase letter from A to Z, a lowercase letter from a to z, or a digit from 0 to 9.

Related Function(s)

`isascii` : character classification macro for all integer values

Example The following example tests keyboard input and tests for letters and digits.

```
#include <ctype.h>
#include <stdio.h>

int main (void)
{
char charac;
clrscr ();
do
{
 printf ("Press a key to initiate character
     classification\n");
 charac = getch ();
 if (isalnum(charac))
     printf ("%c is a valid letter or
          digit\n",charac);
 else
     printf ("%c is not a valid letter or
          digit\n",charac);
 printf ("\n");
} while (charac != 27);
clrscr ();
return 0;
}
```

isalpha

DOS | UNIX | ANSI C | C++

Syntax `int isalpha(int charac);`

`int charac;` *Value to classify*

Function The `isalpha` macro is used for character classification of letters.

File(s) to Include `#include <ctype.h>`

Description The `isalpha` macro uses a lookup table to classify the ASCII-coded integer value passed in the `charac` argument, and is defined only when `isascii` is true or `charac` is end-of-file. Use `#undef` to make this macro available as a function.

Value(s) Returned A nonzero value is returned if `charac` is an uppercase letter from A to Z or a lowercase letter from a to z.

Related Function(s) `isascii` : character classification macro for all integer values

Example The following example tests keyboard input for uppercase and lowercase letters.

```
#include <ctype.h>
#include <stdio.h>

int main (void)
{
char charac;
clrscr ();
do
{
 printf ("Press a key to initiate character
     classification\n");
 charac = getch ();
 if (isalpha(charac))
     printf ("%c is a valid letter\n",charac);
 else
     printf ("%c is not a valid letter\n",charac);
 printf ("\n");
} while (charac != 27);
clrscr ();
return 0;
}
```

isascii

DOS | UNIX | ANSI C | C++

Syntax

```
int isascii(int charac);

int charac;                    Value to classify
```

Function The `isascii` macro is used for character classification of all integer values.

File(s) to Include `#include <ctype.h>`

Description The `isascii` macro uses a lookup table to classify the ASCII-coded integer value passed in the `charac` argument. The `isascii` macro is defined for all integer values.

Value(s) Returned A nonzero value is returned if the low-order byte of the `charac` argument ranges from 0 to 127 decimal, or 0x00 to 0x7F hexadecimal.

Related Function(s)

- `isalnum` : classification macro for letters and numbers
- `isalpha` : classification macro for letters
- `iscntrl` : classification macro for control characters
- `isdigit` : classification macro for numbers
- `isgraph` : classification macro for print characters
- `islower` : classification macro for lowercase letters
- `isprint` : classification macro for print characters
- `ispunct` : classification macro for punctuation characters
- `isspace` : classification macro for whitespace characters
- `isupper` : classification macro for uppercase letters
- `isxdigit` : classification macro for hexadecimal digits

Example The following example tests the keyboard input for ASCII values.

```
#include <ctype.h>
#include <stdio.h>

int main (void)
{
```

```
char charac;
clrscr ();
do
{
 printf ("Press a key to initiate character
classification\n");
 charac = getch ();
 if (isascii(charac))
     printf ("%c is ASCII\n",charac);
 else
     printf ("%c is not ASCII\n",charac);
 printf ("\n");
} while (charac != 27);
clrscr ();
return 0;
}
```

iscntrl

DOS | UNIX | ANSI C | C++

Syntax `int iscntrl(int charac);`

`int charac;` *Value to classify*

Function The `iscntrl` macro is a character classification macro for the delete and control characters.

File(s) to Include `#include <ctype.h>`

Description The `iscntrl` macro uses a lookup table to classify the ASCII-coded value passed in the `charac` argument, and is defined only when `isascii` is true or `charac` is end-of-file. Use `#undef` to make this macro available as a function.

Value(s) Returned A nonzero value is returned when `charac` is a delete character (0x7F) or ordinary control character ranging from 0x00 to 0x1F.

Related Function(s) `isascii` : character classification macro for all integer values

Example The following example tests the keyboard input for control characters.

```
#include <ctype.h>
#include <stdio.h>

int main (void)
{
char charac;
clrscr ();
do
{
 printf ("Press a key to initiate character
     classification\n");
 charac = getch ();
 if (iscntrl(charac))
     printf ("%c is a valid control character\n",charac);
 else
     printf ("%c is not a valid control
        character\n",charac);
 printf ("\n");
} while (charac != 27);
clrscr ();
return 0;
}
```

isdigit

DOS | UNIX | ANSI C | C++

Syntax `int isdigit(int charac);`

`int charac;` *Value to classify*

Function The `isdigit` macro is a character classification macro for digits.

File(s) to Include `#include <ctype.h>`

Description The `isdigit` macro uses a lookup table to classify the ASCII-coded integer value passed in the `charac` argument, and is defined only when `isascii` is true or `charac` is end-of-file. Use `#undef` to make this macro available as a function.

Value(s) Returned A nonzero value is returned if `charac` is a digit ranging from 0 to 9.

Related Function(s) `isascii` : character classification macro for all integer values

Example The following example tests keyboard input for digits ranging from 0 to 9.

```
#include <ctype.h>
#include <stdio.h>

int main (void)
{
char charac;
clrscr ();
do
{
 printf ("Press a key to initiate character
      classification\n");
 charac = getch ();
 if (isdigit(charac))
      printf ("%c is a valid digit\n",charac);
 else
      printf ("%c is not a valid digit\n",charac);
 printf ("\n");
} while (charac != 27);
clrscr ();
return 0;
}
```

isgraph

DOS | UNIX | ANSI C | C++

Syntax `int isgraph(int charac);`

`int charac;` *Value to classify*

Function The `isgraph` macro is a character classification macro for printable characters.

File(s) to Include `#include <ctype.h>`

Description The `isgraph` macro uses a lookup table to classify the ASCII-coded integer value passed in the `charac` argument, and is defined only when `isascii` is true or `charac` is end-of-file. Use `#undef` to make this macro available as a function.

Value(s) Returned A nonzero value is returned if `charac` is a printable character. 0 is returned if `charac` is the space character or a nonprintable character.

Related Function(s) `isascii` : character classification macro for all integer values

Example The following example tests the keyboard input for printable characters. The space character is excluded.

```
#include <ctype.h>
#include <stdio.h>

int main (void)
{
char charac;
clrscr ();
do
{
 printf ("Press a key to initiate character
      classification\n");
 charac = getch ();
 if (isgraph(charac))
      printf ("%c is a printable character\n",charac);
 else
      printf ("%c is not a printable character\n",charac);
 printf ("\n");
} while (charac != 27);
clrscr ();
return 0;
}
```

islower

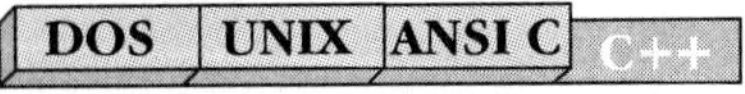

Syntax `int islower(int charac);`

`int charac;` *Value to classify*

Function The `islower` macro is a character classification macro for lowercase letters.

File(s) to Include `#include <ctype.h>`

Description The `islower` macro uses a lookup table to classify the ASCII-coded integer value passed in the `charac` argument, and is defined when isascii is true or charac is end-of-file. Use #undef to make this macro available as a function.

Value(s) Returned A nonzero value is returned when charac is a lowercase letter ranging from a to z.

Related Function(s) isascii : character classification macro for all integer values

Example The following example tests keyboard input for lowercase letters.

```
#include <ctype.h>
#include <stdio.h>

int main (void)
{
char charac;
clrscr ();
do
{
 printf ("Press a key to initiate character
     classification\n");
 charac = getch ();
 if (islower(charac))
     printf ("%c is a lowercase letter\n",charac);
 else
     printf ("%c is not a lowercase
letter\n",charac);
 printf ("\n");
  while (charac != 27);
  clrscr ();
  return 0;
```

isprint

DOS UNIX ANSI C C++

Syntax `int isprint(int charac);`

`int charac;` *Value to classify*

Function The isprint macro is a character classification macro for printable characters.

File(s) to Include `#include <ctype.h>`

Description The `isprint` macro uses a lookup table to classify the ASCII-coded integer value passed in the `charac` argument, and is defined when `isascii` is true or `charac` is end-of-file. Use `#undef` to make this macro available as a function.

Value(s) Returned A nonzero value is returned when `charac` is a printable character ranging from 0x20 to 0x7E.

Related Function(s) `isascii` : character classification macro for all integer values

Example The following example tests the keyboard input for printable characters.

```
#include <ctype.h>
#include <stdio.h>

int main (void)
{
char charac;
clrscr ();
do
{
 printf ("Press a key to initiate character
      classification\n");
 charac = getch ();
 if (isprint(charac))
     printf ("%c is a printable
      character\n",charac);
 else
     printf ("%c is not a printable
      character\n",charac);
 printf ("\n");
} while (charac != 27);
clrscr ();
return 0;
}
```

ispunct

Syntax `int ispunct(int charac);`

`int charac;` *Value to classify*

Function The `ispunct` macro is a character classification routine for punctuation characters.

File(s) to Include `#include <ctype.h>`

Description The `ispunct` macro uses a lookup table to classify the ASCII-coded integer value passed in the `charac` argument, and is defined only when `isascii` is true or `charac` is end-of-file. Use `#undef` to make this macro available as a function.

Value(s) Returned A nonzero value is returned if `charac` is a punctuation character.

Related Function(s) `isascii` : character classification macro for all integer values

Example The following example tests keyboard input for punctuation characters.

```
#include <ctype.h>
#include <stdio.h>

int main (void)
{
char charac;
clrscr ();
do
{
 printf ("Press a key to initiate character
    classification\n");
 charac = getch ();
 if (ispunct(charac))
     printf ("%c is a punctuation
         character\n",charac);
 else
     printf ("%c is not a punctuation
         character\n",charac);
 printf ("\n");
} while (charac != 27);
clrscr ();
return 0;
}
```

isspace

DOS | UNIX | ANSI C | C++

Syntax

```
int isspace(int charac);
```

`int charac;` *Value to classify*

Function The `isspace` macro is a character classification macro for space, tab, carriage return, newline, vertical tab, or formfeed.

File(s) to Include `#include <ctype.h>`

Description The `isspace` macro uses a lookup table to classify the ASCII-coded integer value passed in the `charac` argument, and is defined when `isascii` is true or `charac` is end-of-file. Use `#undef` to make this macro available as a function.

Value(s) Returned A nonzero value is returned when `charac` is a space, tab, carriage return, newline, vertical tab, or formfeed (0x09 through 0x0D, and 0x20).

Related Function(s) `isascii` : character classification macro for all integer values

Example The following example tests keyboard input for the space, tab, carriage return, newline, vertical tab, and formfeed characters.

```
#include <ctype.h>
#include <stdio.h>

int main (void)
{
char charac;
clrscr ();
do
{
 printf ("Press a key to initiate character
      classification\n");
 charac = getch ();
 if (isspace(charac))
      printf ("%c is a whitespace
          character\n",charac);
 else
      printf ("%c is not a whitespace
          character\n",charac);
```

```
 printf ("\n");
} while (charac != 27);
clrscr ();
return 0;
}
```

isupper

DOS | UNIX | ANSI C | C++

Syntax `int isupper(int charac);`

`int charac;` *Value to classify*

Function The `isupper` macro is a character classification macro for uppercase letters.

File(s) to Include `#include <ctype.h>`

Description The `isupper` macro uses a lookup table to classify the ASCII-coded integer value passed in the `charac` argument, and is defined when `isascii` is true or `charac` is end-of-file. Use `#undef` to make this macro available for use as a function.

Value(s) Returned A nonzero value is returned when `charac` is an uppercase letter ranging from A to Z.

Related Function(s) `isascii` : character classification macro for all integer values

Example The following example tests keyboard input for uppercase letters.

```
#include <ctype.h>
#include <stdio.h>

int main (void)
{
char charac;
clrscr ();
do
{
 printf ("Press a key to initiate character
    classification\n");
```

```
        charac = getch ();
        if (isupper(charac))
            printf ("%c is an uppercase character\n",charac);
        else
            printf ("%c is not an uppercase
               character\n",charac);
        printf ("\n");
    } while (charac != 27);
    clrscr ();
    return 0;
}
```

---

isxdigit

DOS | UNIX | ANSI C | C++

Syntax `int isxdigit(int charac);`

`int charac;` *Value to classify*

Function The `isxdigit` macro is a character classification macro for hexadecimal digits.

File(s) to Include `#include <ctype.h>`

Description The `isxdigit` macro uses a lookup table to classify the ASCII-coded value passed in the `charac` argument, and is defined when `isascii` is true or `charac` is end-of-file. Use `#undef` to make this macro available for use as a function.

Value(s) Returned A nonzero value is returned if `charac` is a hexadecimal digit ranging from 0 to 9, A to F, or a to f.

Related Function(s) `isascii` : character classification macro for all integer values

Example The following example tests keyboard input for hexadecimal digits.

```
#include <ctype.h>
#include <stdio.h>

int main (void)
{
```

```
char charac;
clrscr ();
do
{
 printf ("Press a key to initiate character
            classification\n");
 charac = getch ();
 if (isxdigit(charac))
     printf ("%c is a hexadecimal
digit\n",charac);
 else
     printf ("%c is not a hexadecimal
digit\n",charac);
 printf ("\n");
} while (charac != 27);
clrscr ();
return 0;
```

Data Conversion

This chapter introduces the Borland C++ functions and macros used for data conversion. Because data can take any of several forms, the capability to convert the data to meet the specifications for particular applications is often necessary. The data conversion functions and macros introduced in this chapter provide the capability to convert between strings and integers, long values, unsigned long values, and double values. In addition, several functions and macros are described for the conversion of lowercase to uppercase, uppercase to lowercase, and character to ASCII. Table 6.1 lists the functions described in this chapter.

Table 6.1. *Data conversion functions and macros.*

Function	*Meaning*
`atof`	Converts a string to floating-point
`atoi`	Converts a string to integer
`atol`	Converts a string to long integer
`ecvt`	Converts floating-point to a string; the low-order digit is rounded
`fcvt`	Converts floating-point to a string; the digit is rounded for a specified number of digits
`gcvt`	Converts floating-point to a string; uses FORTRAN F or `printf` E format
`itoa`	Converts an integer to a string in the given radix
`ltoa`	Converts a long integer to a string
`strtod`	Converts a string to a double value
`strtol`	Converts a string to a long value
`strtoul`	Converts a string to unsigned long
`toascii`	Converts a character to ASCII (macro)
`_tolower`	Converts uppercase to lowercase (macro)
`tolower`	Converts uppercase to lowercase
`_toupper`	Converts lowercase to uppercase (macro)
`toupper`	Converts lowercase to uppercase
`ultoa`	Converts unsigned long to a string

These functions and macros accomplish one of three tasks. They convert a string to a value, convert a value to a string, or convert a single character. The string values used in the conversion functions and macros are converted to and from types int, double, long, and unsigned long. The limitations for each of the data types supported by Borland C++ are shown in table 6.2

Table 6.2. *Data types.*

Type	*Size in Bits*	*Range*
unsigned char	8	0 to 255
char	8	–128 to 127

Type	*Size in Bits*	*Range*
enum	16	–32,768 to 32,767
unsigned int	16	0 to 65,535
short int	16	–32,768 to 32,767
int	16	–32,768 to 32,767
unsigned long	32	0 to 4,294,967,295
long	32	–2,147,483,648 to 2,147,483,647
float	32	3.4e–38 to 3.4e38
double	64	1.7e–308 to 1.7e308
long double	80	3.4e–4932 to 1.1e4932

Borland C++ Data Conversion Reference Guide

The remainder of this chapter contains detailed information for each of the functions and macros listed in table 6.1.

atof

DOS | UNIX | ANSI C | C++

Syntax

```
double atof(const char *str);

const char *str;            String to convert
```

Function The `atof` function converts a string to a floating-point value.

File(s) to Include `#include <math.h>`
or
`#include <stdlib.h>`

Description The `atof` function converts the string pointed to by the `str` argument to a double value. The character string must be the character representation of a floating-point number and use the format that follows. Conversion ends when an unrecognized character is encountered.

[whitespace] [sign] [ddd] . [ddd] [e|E[sign]ddd]

in which

[whitespace] = an optional string of tabs and spaces
[sign] = the sign of the value
[ddd] = a string of digits on either or both sides of the decimal
[e|E[sign]ddd] = the exponential notation of the value

Note: +INF and –INF, for plus and minus infinity, and +NAN and –NAN, for not-a-number, are recognized by the `atof` function.

Value(s) Returned The double value of the string is returned unless there is an overflow.

Related Function(s)

`atoi` : converts a string to an integer value
`atol` : converts a string to a long value
`strtod` : converts a string to a double value

Example The following example converts the specified string to its floating-point value. Both the string and the value are then displayed.

```
#include <stdio.h>
#include <stdlib.h>

int main (void)
{
float value;
char *string = "532.5596";

clrscr();
value = atof(string);
printf ("Floating-point value = %3.4f\n",value);
printf ("String = %s\n",string);

return 0;
}
```

atoi

DOS | UNIX | ANSI C | C++

Syntax

```
int atoi(const char *str);

const char *str;          String to convert
```

Function The `atoi` function converts a string to an integer value.

File(s) to Include

```
#include <stdlib.h>
```

Description The `atoi` function converts the string pointed to by the `str` argument to an integer value. The string must be the character representation of an integer value and must use the format that follows. Conversion ends when the first unrecognized character is encountered.

[whitespace] [sign] [ddd]

in which

[whitespace] = an optional string of tabs and spaces
[sign] = an optional sign for the value
[ddd] = the string of digits

Value(s) Returned The integer value of the string is returned when `atoi` is successful. If the `atoi` function is unable to convert the string, a 0 is returned.

Related Function(s)

`atof` : converts a string to a floating-point value
`atol` : converts a string to a long value

Example The following example converts the specified string to its equivalent integer value. Both the string and integer value are then displayed.

```
#include <stdlib.h>
#include <stdio.h>

int main (void)
{
int value;
char *string = "8726";
```

continues

```
clrscr();
value = atoi (string);
printf ("Integer value = %d\n",value);
printf ("String = %s\n",string);

return 0;
}
```

atol

DOS | UNIX | ANSI C | C++

Syntax `long atol(const char *str);`

`const char *str;` *String to convert*

Function The `atol` function converts a string to a long value.

File(s) to Include `#include <stdlib.h>`

Description The `atol` function converts the string pointed to by the `str` argument to a long value. The string must be the character representation of an integer value and use the format that follows. Conversion ends when the first unrecognized character is encountered.

[whitespace] [sign] [ddd]

in which

[whitespace] = an optional string of tabs and spaces
[sign] = the optional sign for the following digits
[ddd] = a string of digits

Value(s) Returned The value of the converted string is returned when the `atol` function is successful. If the string cannot be converted, the `atol` function returns a 0.

Related Function(s)
`atof` : converts a string to a floating-point value
`atoi` : converts a string to an integer value

Example The following example converts the specified string to its equivalent long value. Both the value and the string are then displayed.

```
#include <stdlib.h>
#include <stdio.h>

int main (void)
{
long value;
char *string = "45332754";

clrscr();
value = atol(string);
printf ("String = %s\n",string);
printf ("Value = %ld\n",value);

return 0;
}
```

ecvt

DOS | UNIX | ANSI C | C++

Syntax

```
char *ecvt(double value, int ndig, int *dec, int
           *sign);
```

`double value;`	*Value to convert*
`int ndig;`	*Number of digits*
`int *dec;`	*Decimal point position*
`int *sign;`	*Sign of the value*

Function The `ecvt` function converts a floating-point number to a string. The low-order digit is rounded.

File(s) to Include `#include <stdlib.h>`

Description The `ecvt` function converts the floating-point value specified in the `value` argument to a null-terminated string. The length of the string is specified with the `ndig` argument. The `dec` argument is a pointer to the position of the decimal point relative to the beginning of the resulting string (there is no decimal in the string). The `sign` argument points to the value indicating the sign of `value`. A zero indicates positive; a nonzero value indicates negative.

Value(s) Returned The pointer to the converted string is returned by the `ecvt` function.

Related Function(s)
`fcvt` : converts a floating-point value to a string
`gcvt` : converts a floating-point value to a string

Example The following example converts the specified floating-point value to a string value.

```
#include <stdlib.h>
#include <stdio.h>

int main (void)
{
char *string;
double value = 12.756;
int dec, sign, ndig = 8;

clrscr();
string = ecvt (value,ndig,&dec,&sign);
printf ("Value = 12.756\n");
printf ("Significant digits = 8\n");
printf ("String = %s\n", string);
printf ("Decimal point position = %d\n", dec);
printf ("Sign = %d\n", sign);

return 0;
}
```

fcvt

DOS UNIX ANSI C C++

Syntax

```
char *fcvt(double value, int ndig, int *dec, int
          *sign);
```

`double value;`	*Value to convert*
`int ndig;`	*Number of digits in string*
`int *dec;`	*Position of decimal*
`int *sign;`	*Sign of value*

Function The `fcvt` function converts a floating-point value to a string. The digit is rounded for the specified number of digits.

File(s) to Include `#include <stdlib.h>`

Description The `fcvt` function converts the floating-point number described by the `value` argument to a null-terminated string with the length specified in the `ndig` argument. The `dec` argument defines the position of the decimal relative to the beginning of the string. When the `dec` argument is negative, the decimal is placed to the left of the returned digits. The `sign` argument points to the integer representing the sign of the `value` argument. When the `value` argument is negative, the word pointed to by the `sign` argument is a nonzero value. When the `value` argument is positive, the word pointed to by the `sign` argument is 0.

Value(s) Returned The pointer to the resulting string is returned.

Related Function(s)
`ecvt` : converts a floating-point value to a string
`gcvt` : converts a floating-point value to a string

Example The following example converts the floating-point value to a character string using the `fcvt` function.

```
#include <stdlib.h>
#include <stdio.h>

int main (void)
{
char *string;
double value = 54.7259;
int dec, sign, ndig = 7;

clrscr();
string = fcvt(value,ndig,&dec,&sign);
printf ("Value = 54.7259\n");
printf ("Significant digits = 7\n");
printf ("String = %s\n", string);
printf ("Decimal position = %d\n",dec);
printf ("Sign = %d\n",sign);

return 0;
}
```

gcvt

DOS | UNIX | ANSI C | C++

Syntax `char *gcvt(double value, int ndec, char *buf);`

`double value;`	*Value to convert*
`int ndec;`	*Number of significant digits*
`char *buf;`	*Resulting string*

Function The `gcvt` function converts a floating-point value to a string. FORTRAN F or `printf` E format is used.

File(s) to Include `#include <stdlib.h>`

Description The `gcvt` function converts the floating-point value defined in the `value` argument to a null-terminated ASCII string, and stores the string at the location pointed to by the `buf` argument. The resulting string contains the number of significant digits specified in the `ndec` argument and is in FORTRAN F format whenever possible. When `gcvt` is unable to use FORTRAN F format, `printf` E format is used.

Value(s) Returned The `gcvt` function returns the address of the string pointed to by the `buf` argument.

Related Function(s)
`ecvt` : converts a floating-point number to a string
`fcvt` : converts a floating-point number to a string

Example The following example converts the floating-point value to a character string using the `gcvt` function.

```
#include <stdlib.h>
#include <stdio.h>

int main (void)
{
char string[20];
double value = 54.7259;
int ndec = 4;

clrscr();
gcvt(value,ndec,string);
printf ("Value = 54.7259\n");
```

continues

```
printf ("Significant digits = 4\n");
printf ("String = %s\n", string);

return 0;
}
```

itoa

DOS UNIX ANSI C C++

Syntax

```
char *itoa(int value, char *string, int radix);
```

`int value;`	*Value to convert*
`char *string;`	*Resulting string*
`int radix;`	*Base used for conversion*

Function The `itoa` function converts an integer value to a string.

File(s) to Include `#include <stdlib.h>`

Description The `itoa` function converts the integer value defined in the `value` argument to a null-terminated string. The converted string is stored in the location pointed to by the `string` argument. The `radix` argument is an integer value that specifies the base (ranging between 2 and 36) used in converting the `value` argument.

Value(s) Returned The pointer to the resulting string is returned.

Related Function(s)

`ltoa` : converts a long value to a string
`ultoa` : converts an unsigned long value to a string

Example The following example converts the integer value to a character string.

```
#include <stdlib.h>
#include <stdio.h>

int main (void)
{
int value = 8377;
char string[20];
```

continues

```
clrscr();
itoa (value,string,10);
printf ("Value = 8377\n");
printf ("String = %s\n",string);
printf ("Base = 10\n");

return 0;
}
```

ltoa

DOS UNIX ANSI C C++

Syntax

```
char *ltoa(long value, char *string, int radix);
```

`long value;`	*Value to convert*
`char *string;`	*Converted string*
`int radix;`	*Base for conversion*

Function The `ltoa` function converts a long value to a string.

File(s) to Include `#include <stdlib.h>`

Description The `ltoa` function converts the long value defined in the `value` argument to a null-terminated string. The string is stored at the location pointed to by the `string` argument. The `radix` argument specifies the base (ranging from 2 to 36) used to convert the `value` argument.

Value(s) Returned The pointer to the resulting string is returned.

Related Function(s)

`itoa` : converts an integer to a string
`ultoa` : converts an unsigned long value to a string

Example In the following example, `ltoa` converts the long value to a character string.

```
#include <stdlib.h>
#include <stdio.h>

int main (void)
```

```
{
long value = 99288377L;
char string[20];

clrscr();
ltoa (value,string,10);
printf ("Value = 99288377\n");
printf ("String = %s\n",string);
printf ("Base = 10\n");

return 0;
}
```

strtod

DOS | UNIX | ANSI C | C++

Syntax

```
double strod(const char *s, char **endptr);

const char *s;          String to convert
char **endptr;          Useful for error detection
```

Function The `strtod` function converts a string to a double value.

File(s) to Include `#include <stdlib.h>`

Description The `strtod` function converts the character string pointed to by the `s` argument to a double value. The character string to be converted must use the following format:

[whitespace] [sign] [ddd] [.] [ddd] [fmt[sign]ddd]

in which

[whitespace] = optional whitespace
[sign] = optional sign of the value
[ddd] = optional digits
[.] = optional decimal point
[ddd] = optional digits
[fmt] = optional e or E
[sign] = optional sign of exponent
[ddd] = optional digits

The `strtod` function recognizes +INF and –INF for plus and minus infinity. It also recognizes +NAN and –NAN for not-a-number. Conversion stops when the first character that cannot be recognized is encountered.

If `endptr` is not null, the `strtod` function sets `*endptr` to the location of the character that stopped the conversion. Therefore, `endptr` is useful for detecting errors.

Value(s) Returned The double value of the string is returned. `HUGE_VAL` is returned when overflow occurs.

Related Function(s) `atof` : converts a string to a floating-point number

Example The following example converts the character string to its equivalent double value.

```
#include <stdlib.h>
#include <stdio.h>

int main (void)
{
double value;
char string[20] = "254.938";
char *endptr;

clrscr();
value = strtod (string,&endptr);
printf ("Value = %lf\n",value);
printf ("String = %s\n",string);

return 0;
}
```

strtol

DOS | UNIX | ANSI C | C++

Syntax

```
long strtol(const char *s, char **endptr, int
            radix);
```

`const char *s;`	*String to convert*
`char **endptr;`	*Useful for error detection*
`int radix;`	*Base for conversion*

Function The `strtol` function converts a string to a long value.

File(s) to Include `#include <stdlib.h>`

Description The `strtol` function converts the character string pointed to by the `s` argument to a long value. The character string must be in the following format:

[whitespace] [sign] [0] [x] [ddd]

in which

[whitespace] = optional whitespace
[sign] = sign of value
[0] = optional 0
[x] = optional x or X
[ddd] = optional digits

When the `radix` argument ranges from 2 to 36, the returned long value is expressed in the base defined by the `radix` argument. When the `radix` argument is 0, the first few characters of the `s` string determine the base of the returned long value, shown as follows:

First character	*Second character*	*String interpreted as*
0	1 to 7	Octal
0	x or X	Hexadecimal
1 to 9		Decimal

When the `radix` argument is 1, less than 0, or greater than 36, the argument is invalid.

If `endptr` is not null, the `*endptr` argument points to the character that stopped the conversion.

Value(s) Returned The value of the converted string is returned when `strotol` is successful. A 0 is returned when unsuccessful.

Related Function(s)
`atoi` : converts a string to an integer
`atol` : converts a string to a long value
`strtoul` : converts a string to an unsigned long value

Example The following example converts the string to its equivalent long value.

```
#include <stdlib.h>
#include <stdio.h>

int main (void)
{
long value;
char *string = "6568595";
char *endptr;

clrscr();
value = strtol (string,&endptr,10);
printf ("Value = %ld\n",value);
printf ("String = %s\n",string);
printf ("Base = 10\n");

return 0;
}
```

strtoul

Syntax

```
unsigned long strtoul(const char *s, char
                      **endptr, int radix);
```

`const char *s;`	*String to convert*
`char **endptr;`	*Useful for error detection*
`int radix;`	*Base for conversion*

Function The `strtoul` function converts a string to an unsigned long value.

File(s) to Include `#include <stdlib.h>`

Description The `strtoul` function converts the character string pointed to by the `s` argument to an unsigned long value. The character string must be in the following format:

[whitespace] [sign] [0] [x] [ddd]

in which

[whitespace] = optional whitespace
[sign] = sign of value
[0] = optional 0

[x] = optional x or X
[ddd] = optional digits

When the `radix` argument ranges from 2 to 36, the returned long value is expressed in the base defined by the `radix` argument. When the `radix` argument is 0, the first few characters of the `s` string determine the base of the returned long value, shown as follows:

First character	*Second character*	*String interpreted as*
0	1 to 7	Octal
0	x or X	Hexadecimal
1 to 9		Decimal

When the `radix` argument is 1, less than 0, or greater than 36, the argument is invalid.

If `endptr` is not null, the `*endptr` argument points to the character that stopped the conversion.

Value(s) Returned The unsigned long value is returned when `strtoul` is successful. A 0 is returned when unsuccessful.

Related Function(s)

`atol` : converts a string to a long value
`strtol` : converts a string to a long value

Example This example converts the string to its equivalent unsigned long value.

```
#include <stdlib.h>
#include <stdio.h>

int main (void)
{
unsigned long value;
char *string = "6568595";
char *endptr;

clrscr();
value = strtoul (string,&endptr,10);
printf ("Value = %lu\n",value);
printf ("String = %s\n",string);
printf ("Base = 10\n");

return 0;
}
```

toascii

DOS | UNIX | ANSI C | C++

Syntax
```
int toascii(int ch);

int ch;                              Character to convert
```

Function The `toascii` macro converts characters to ASCII format.

File(s) to Include `#include <ctype.h>`

Description The `toascii` function is a macro used to convert the integer defined in the `ch` argument to its ASCII value. This conversion is accomplished by clearing all but the lower 7 bits of the argument.

Value(s) Returned The converted value of the `ch` argument, in the range of 0 to 127, is returned.

Related Function(s)
`tolower` : translates characters to lowercase
`toupper` : translates characters to uppercase

Example The following example converts the integer value 178 to ASCII.

```
#include <stdio.h>
#include <ctype.h>

int main (void)
{
int ch = 178;
int convch;

clrscr();
convch = toascii(ch);
printf ("Converted %d to %d\n",ch,convch);

return 0;
}
```

_tolower

DOS | UNIX | ANSI C | C++

Syntax

```
int _tolower(int ch);

int ch;                    Character to convert
```

Function The `_tolower` macro translates characters to lowercase.

File(s) to Include `#include <ctype.h>`

Description The `_tolower` macro converts known uppercase letters to lowercase. The `ch` argument must specify an uppercase letter from A to Z.

Value(s) Returned The converted lowercase value is returned when `ch` is uppercase. The result is undefined when `ch` is not uppercase.

Related Function(s)

`tolower` : function for converting characters to lowercase
`_toupper` : macro for converting characters to uppercase
`toupper` : function for converting characters to uppercase

Example The following example converts the uppercase character 87 to its lowercase equivalent.

```
#include <stdio.h>
#include <ctype.h>

int main (void)
{
int ch = 87;
int convch;

clrscr();
convch = _tolower(ch);
printf ("Converted %d to %d\n",ch,convch);

return 0;
}
```

tolower

DOS | UNIX | ANSI C | C++

Syntax `int tolower(int ch);`

`int ch;` *Character to convert*

Function The `tolower` function converts characters to lowercase.

File(s) to Include `#include <ctype.h>`

Description The `tolower` function converts the integer defined in the `ch` argument to lowercase. The `ch` argument can range from `EOF` to 255.

Value(s) Returned The lowercase value of `ch` is returned when `ch` is uppercase. All other values are passed unchanged.

Related Function(s)

- `_tolower` : macro for converting characters to lowercase
- `toupper` : function for converting characters to uppercase
- `_toupper` : macro for converting characters to uppercase

Example The following example converts the uppercase character 77 to its lowercase equivalent.

```
#include <stdio.h>
#include <ctype.h>

int main (void)
{
int ch = 77;
int convch;

clrscr();
convch = tolower(ch);
printf ("Converted %d to %d\n",ch,convch);

return 0;
}
```

_toupper

DOS | UNIX | ANSI C | C++

Syntax `int _toupper(int ch);`

`int ch;` *Character to convert*

Function The `_toupper` macro converts characters to uppercase.

File(s) to Include `#include <ctype.h>`

Description The `_toupper` macro converts the character defined in the `ch` argument to uppercase. This macro should be used only when the `ch` argument ranges from a to z.

Value(s) Returned The converted value of the `ch` argument is returned if the `ch` argument ranges from a to z. The result is undefined if the `ch` argument is not lowercase.

Related Function(s)
`toupper` : function to convert a character to uppercase
`tolower` : function to convert a character to lowercase
`tolower` : macro to convert a character to lowercase

Example The following example converts the lowercase character 119 to its uppercase equivalent.

```
#include <stdio.h>
#include <ctype.h>

int main (void)
{
int ch = 119;
int convch;

clrscr();
convch = _toupper(ch);
printf ("Converted %d to %d\n",ch,convch);
return 0;
}
```

toupper

DOS | UNIX | ANSI C | C++

Syntax `int toupper(int ch);`

`int ch;` *Character to convert*

Function The `toupper` function converts characters to uppercase.

File(s) to Include `#include <ctype.h>`

Description The `toupper` function converts the integer value specified in the `ch` argument to its uppercase value. The `ch` argument can range from `EOF` to 255.

Value(s) Returned The converted value of the `ch` argument is returned when the `ch` argument is lowercase. If the `ch` argument is not lowercase, the character is returned unchanged.

Related Function(s)

`_tolower` : macro for converting characters to lowercase
`tolower` : function for converting characters to lowercase
`_toupper` : macro for converting characters to uppercase

Example The following example converts the lowercase letter 109 to its uppercase equivalent.

```
#include <stdio.h>
#include <ctype.h>

int main (void)
{
int ch = 109;
int convch;

clrscr();
convch = toupper(ch);
printf ("Converted %d to %d\n",ch,convch);
return 0;
}
```

ultoa

DOS ~~UNIX~~ ~~ANSI C~~ ~~C++~~

Syntax

```
char *ultoa(unsigned long value, char *string, int
         radix);

unsigned long value;        Value to convert
char *string;               Converted string
int radix;                  Base for conversion
```

Function The `ultoa` function converts an unsigned long value to a string.

File(s) to Include `#include <stdlib.h>`

Description The `ultoa` function converts the unsigned long value defined in the `value` argument to a null-terminated string. The converted string is stored at the location pointed to by the `string` argument. The `radix` argument (ranging from 2 to 36) specifies the base for converting the `value` argument.

Value(s) Returned The converted string is returned.

Related Function(s)

`itoa` : converts an integer to a string
`ltoa` : converts a long value to a string

Example The following example converts the unsigned long value to a character string.

```
#include <stdio.h>
#include <stdlib.h>

int main (void)
{
unsigned long value = 62259374L;
char string [20];

clrscr();
ultoa (value,string,10);
printf ("Value = %lu\n",value);
printf ("String = %s\n",string);
printf ("Base = 10");

return 0;
```

Directory Control

This chapter introduces the functions that control directories and path names. The functions used for directory control are listed in table 7.1.

With directory control functions you can locate files, create, change, or remove directories, and merge or split pathnames. The pathname refers to the descriptor, which explains where a file is located. The elements of a pathname occur in the following order: the drive letter and a colon; the hierarchy of directories leading to the file; the filename, a period, and the file extension. A backslash separates each of the elements. The following example of a directory shows the default location of the `graphics.h` header file:

```
c:\bc\include\graphics.h
```

When you use the functions in table 7.1, you might find that defining a path as a string is necessary. When you create the string, you must use `\\` for the `\` symbol in the pathname. Because `\` is used with other descriptors, such as `\n` for newline, C requires that `\\` be used for the `\` symbol. Therefore the `c:\bc\bc.exe` path would be defined in a string as `c:\\bc\\bc.exe`.

Table 7.1. Directory control functions.

Function	*Description*
`chdir`	Changes the current path
`findfirst`	Finds the first file matching the specifications
`findnext`	Continues the `findfirst` search
`fnmerge`	Creates a path from its component parts
`fnsplit`	Divides a path into its component parts
`getcurdir`	Retrieves the current directory for the specified drive
`getcwd`	Gets the current working directory
`getdisk`	Gets the current drive
`mkdir`	Creates a directory
`mktemp`	Creates a unique file name
`rmdir`	Removes a directory
`searchpath`	Searches the DOS path for a file
`setdisk`	Makes the specified drive the current drive

Borland C++ Directory Control Functions Reference Guide

The remainder of this chapter contains detailed information for each of the directory control functions listed in table 7.1.

chdir

Syntax `int chdir(const char *path);`

`const char *path;` *Path of new directory*

Function The `chdir` function changes the current directory.

File(s) to Include `#include <dir.h>`

Description The `chdir` function changes the current working directory to the path specified in the `path` argument. When a drive is specified in the `path` argument, the current working directory on the specified drive is changed. The current working directory on the active drive is not altered.

Value(s) Returned When the `chdir` function is successful, a 0 is returned. When unsuccessful, a –1 is returned and the global variable `errno` is set to ENOENT, which indicates that the specified path or file name was not found.

Related Function(s)

`getcurdir` : gets the current working directory
`mkdir` : creates a directory
`rmdir` : removes a directory

Example The following example creates a directory called `junk`, changes to that directory, returns from the `junk` directory, then deletes the `junk` directory.

```
#include <dir.h>
#include <stdio.h>

int main (void)
{
int result;
char buffer[MAXPATH];

clrscr();
getcwd (buffer,MAXPATH);
result = mkdir ("junk");
if (!result)
    printf ("junk directory created\n");
result = chdir ("junk");
if (!result)
    printf ("changed directory to junk\n");
result = chdir (buffer);
if (!result)
    printf ("changed back to working
directory\n");
result = rmdir ("junk");
if (!result)
    printf ("removed junk directory\n");

return 0;
}
```

findfirst

DOS | UNIX | ANSI C | C++

Syntax

```
in findfirst(const char *pathname, struct ffblk
                *ffblk, int attrib);
```

`const char *pathname;`	*Path and file name*
`struct ffblk *ffblk;`	*Structure of file information*
`int attrib;`	*Used to select eligible files*

Function The `findfirst` function searches a disk directory for the specific file(s).

File(s) to Include

```
#include <dir.h>
#include <dos.h>DOS
```

Description The `findfirst` function uses the DOS system call 0x4E to search a disk directory for a specified file or files. The `pathname` argument specifies the drive, path, and file name(s) of the file(s) to be located. Wild-card characters can be used in the `pathname` argument.

If the specified file (or files) is found, the `ffblk` structure is filled with the file directory information (see following example).

```
struct ffblk
     {
     char ff_reserved[21];        /* reserved by DOS */
     char ff_attrib;              /* attribute */
     int ff_ftime;                /* file time */
     int ff_fdate;                /* file date */
     long ff_fsize;               /* file size */
     char ff_name[13];            /* file name */
     };
```

The `ff_ftime` and `ff_fdate` members of the `ffblk` structure are 16-bit structures which can be interpreted with the following information:

`ff_ftime`	bits 0 to 4	seconds/2 (15 means 30)
	bits 5 to 10	minutes
	bits 11 to 15	hours

`ff_fdate`	bits 0 to 4	day
	bits 5 to 8	month
	bits 9 to 15	years since 1980

The `attrib` argument selects eligible files for the search. It is selected from the following constants defined in `dos.h`.

`FA_RDONLY`	Read only
`FA_HIDDEN`	Hidden file
`FA_SYSTEM`	System file
`FA_LABEL`	Volume label
`FA_DIREC`	Directory
`FA_ARCH`	Archive

Value(s) Returned If a file matching the specifications is found, a 0 is returned. After the search is exhausted, or if the specified file has an error, a –1 is returned and the global variable `errno` is set to the appropriate value as follows:

ENOENT	Path or file not found
ENMFILE	No more files

Related Function(s) `findnext` : continues the `findfirst` search

Example In the following example, `findfirst` locates the first file in the current directory. The filename is then displayed.

```
#include <stdio.h>
#include <dir.h>

int main (void)
{
struct ffblk ffblk;

clrscr ();
findfirst ("*.*",&ffblk,0);
printf ("First file in current directory :
       %s\n",ffblk.ff_name);

return 0;
}
```

findnext

DOS | UNIX | ANSI C | C++

Syntax

```
int findnext(struct ffblk *ffblk);
```

`struct ffblk *ffblk;` *Structure of file information*

Function The `findnext` function continues the search initiated by the `findfirst` function.

File(s) to Include `#include <dir.h>`

Description The `findnext` function finds subsequent files that match the drive, path, and file name given in the `pathname` argument of the `findfirst` function. Information on only one file is retrieved with each call to the `findnext` function. All information on the found file is stored in the `ffblk` structure. The `ffblk` structure is described with the `findfirst` function.

Value(s) Returned If a matching file is found, a 0 is returned. When the search is exhausted, or if the file name has an error, a –1 is returned and the global variable `errno` is set to the appropriate value as follows:

ENOENT	Path or file not found
ENMFILE	No more files

Related Function(s) `findfirst:` searches a directory of a specified file

Example In the following example, `findfirst` finds the first file in the current directory. The `findnext` function is then used to find the second and third files in the directory. All three file names are displayed.

```
#include <stdio.h>
#include <dir.h>

int main (void)
{
struct ffblk ffblk;

clrscr ();
findfirst ("*.*",&ffblk,0);
```

```
printf ("First file in current directory :
       %s\n",ffblk.ff_name);
findnext (&ffblk);
printf ("Second file in current directory :
       %s\n",ffblk.ff_name);
findnext (&ffblk);
printf ("Third file in current directory :
       %s\n",ffblk.ff_name);

return 0;
}
```

fnmerge

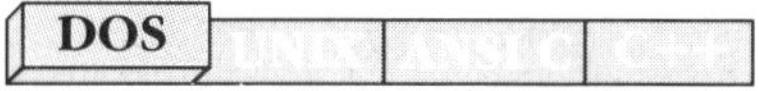

Syntax

```
void fnmerge(char *path, const char *drive, const
             char *dir, const char *name, const
             char *ext);
```

`char *path;`	*Pointer to merged path*
`const char *drive;`	*Drive*
`const char *dir;`	*Directory*
`const char *name;`	*File name*
`const char *ext;`	*File extension*

Function The `fnmerge` function builds a path from its component parts.

File(s) to Include `#include <dir.h>`

Description The `fnmerge` function creates a path name from the components specified in the `drive`, `dir`, `name`, and `ext` arguments. The resulting path is in the following format:

`a:\dir\subdir1\subdir2\filename.ext`

in which `drive` is `a:`, `dir` is `\dir\subdir1\subdir2`, `name` is a filename, and `ext` is a three-letter extension. The `path` argument is a pointer to the location where the constructed path is stored. The MAXPATH variable, defined as 80, determines the maximum length of the constructed path.

Value(s) Returned There is no return value.

Related Function(s) `fnsplit`: divides a path into its component parts

Example In the following example, `fnmerge` creates a path from the `drive`, `dir`, `file`, and `ext` arguments. The merged path is then displayed.

```
#include <dir.h>
#include <stdio.h>

int main (void)
{
char path[MAXPATH];
char drive[MAXDRIVE] = "C:";
char dir[MAXDIR] = "\\TC\\INCLUDE\\";
char file[MAXFILE] = "GRAPHICS";
char ext[MAXEXT] = ".H";

clrscr();
fnmerge (path,drive,dir,file,ext);
printf ("Merged path : %s\n", path);

return 0;
}
```

---

fnsplit

DOS | UNIX | ANSI C | C++

Syntax

```
int fnsplit(const char *path, char *drive, char
*dir,
            char *name, char *ext);
```

`const char *path;`	*Path to split*
`char *drive;`	*Drive*
`char *dir;`	*Directory*
`char *name;`	*Name*
`char *ext;`	*Extension*

Function The `fnsplit` function breaks the specified path into its component parts.

File(s) to Include `#include <dir.h>`

Description The `fnsplit` function divides the path specified in the `path` argument into its component parts. The `drive`, `dir`, `name`, and ext arguments point to the stored locations of the drive name, directory path, file name, and extension strings, respectively. These parameters are defined and limited as follows:

Argument	*Limiting Constant*	*Description*
path	MAXPATH	Maximum of 80 characters
drive	MAXDRIVE	Maximum of 3 characters including the colon
dir	MAXDIR	Maximum of 66 characters including the leading and trailing backslashes
name	MAXFILE	Maximum of 9 characters
ext	MAXEXT	Maximum of 5 characters including the leading dot

Note: All maximum lengths include the space for a NULL terminator.

Value(s) Returned An integer value, which uses five flags to indicate which path components were present in the path argument, is returned. The five flags of the integer value are as follows:

EXTENSION	An extension
FILENAME	A file name
DIRECTORY	A directory and applicable subdirectories
DRIVE	A drive specification
WILDCARDS	Wild cards

Related Function(s) fnmerge: builds a path from its component parts

Example In the following example, fnsplit divides the path argument into its component parts. These parts are then displayed.

```
#include <stdio.h>
#include <stdlib.h>
#include <dir.h>
#include <string.h>
```

continues

```
int main (void)
{
char path[MAXPATH] =
"C:\\TC\\INCLUDE\\GRAPHICS.H";
char drive[MAXDRIVE];
char dir[MAXDIR];
char file[MAXFILE];
char ext[MAXEXT];

clrscr();
fnsplit (path,drive,dir,file,ext);
printf ("The components for the path %s
        are:\n",path);
printf ("Drive : %s\n",drive);
printf ("Directory : %s\n",dir);
printf ("File Name : %s\n",file);
printf ("File Extension : %s\n",ext);

return 0;
}
```

getcurdir

DOS UNIX ANSI C C++

Syntax `int getcurdir(int drive, char *directory);`

`int drive;`	*Drive*
`char *directory;`	*Pointer to retrieved directory*

Function The `getcurdir` function retrieves the current directory for a specified drive.

File(s) to Include `#include <dir.h>`

Description The `getcurdir` function retrieves the name of the current working directory for the drive specified in the `drive` argument. The `drive` argument uses an integer value to specify the drive. A 0 is used for the default drive, a 1 for the A drive, a 2 for the B drive, and so forth. The `directory` argument points to an area of memory where the directory name will be placed. The retrieved directory name does not contain the drive specification and does not begin with a backslash.

Value(s) Returned When the `getcurdir` function is successful, a 0 is returned. A –1 is returned when an error occurs.

Related Function(s)

chdir : changes the current directory
mkdir : makes a directory
rmdir : removes a directory
getcwd : gets the drive and current working directory

Example In the following example, getcurdir gets the current directory of the default drive. The directory is then displayed.

```
#include <stdio.h>
#include <dir.h>

int main (void)
{
char *directory;
int result;

clrscr();
result = getcurdir (0,directory);
if (!result)
    printf ("Directory for default drive is :
            %s\n", directory);
else
    printf ("Directory not retrieved");

return 0;
}
```

getcwd

DOS | UNIX | ANSI C | C++

Syntax

```
char *getcwd(char *buf, int buflen);
```

char *buf;	*Pointer to retrieved directory*
int buflen;	*Length of buffer*

Function The getcwd function retrieves the current working directory.

File(s) to Include #include <dir.h>

Description The getcwd function retrieves the drive and path name of the current working directory and stores it in the location pointed to by the buf argument. The buflen argument specifies the length of the storage buffer.

When the `buf` argument is null, a buffer of length `buflen` is allocated using the `malloc` function. The buffer can be deallocated by passing the return value of the `getcwd` function to the `free` function.

Value(s) Returned If the `buf` argument is null on input, the pointer to the allocated buffer is returned. If the `buf` argument is not null on input, the `buf` argument is returned when successful; null is returned when unsuccessful and the `errno` global variable is set to one of the following:

ENODEV	No such device
ENOMEM	Not enough core
ERANGE	Result out of range

Related Function(s) `getcurdir`: gets the directory of the specified drive

Example In the following example, `getcwd` retrieves the current working directory. The retrieved directory is then displayed.

```
#include <dir.h>
#include <stdio.h>

int main (void)
{
char directory[40];

clrscr ();
getcwd(directory, 40);
printf ("Current directory : %s\n", directory);

return 0;
}
```

getdisk

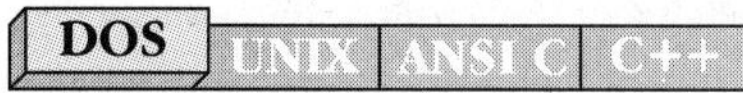

Syntax `int getdisk(void);`

Function The `getdisk` function retrieves the current drive number.

File(s) to Include

```
#include <dir.h>
```

Description The `getdisk` function retrieves the integer value which represents the current drive. For example, 0 represents A, 1 represents B, 2 represents C, and so forth. This function is equivalent to the DOS function 0x19.

Value(s) Returned The current drive number is returned.

Related Function(s) `setdisk`: sets the current drive

Example In the following example, `getdisk` retrieves the current drive. The drive is then displayed.

```
#include <stdio.h>
#include <dir.h>

int main (void)
{
int drive;

clrscr();
drive = getdisk();
printf ("The current drive is %d\n",drive);

return 0;
}
```

mkdir

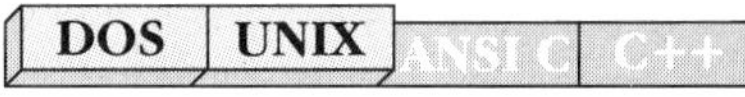

Syntax

```
int mkdir(const char *path);

const char *path;
```

Directory to create

Function The `mkdir` function creates a new directory.

File(s) to Include

```
#include <dir.h>
```

Description The mkdir function creates the directory specified in the path argument.

Value(s) Returned If the directory was successfully created, a 0 is returned. If unsuccessful, a –1 is returned and the global variable errno is set to one of the following:

EACCES	Permission denied
ENOENT	No such file or directory

Related Function(s) chdir: changes the current directory
rmdir: removes the specified directory

Example The following example creates, then removes, a directory called junk.

```
#include <stdio.h>
#include <dir.h>

int main (void)
{
int result;

clrscr ();
result = mkdir ("junk.$$$");
if (!result)
     printf ("Directory JUNK created\n");
else
     printf ("Directory JUNK not created\n");

result = rmdir ("junk.$$$");
if (!result)
     printf ("Directory JUNK removed\n");
else
     printf ("Directory JUNK not removed\n");

return 0;
}
```

mktemp

DOS | UNIX | ANSI C | C++

Syntax `char *mktemp(char *template);`

`char *template;` *Character string for holding file name*

Function The `mktemp` function makes a unique file name.

File(s) to Include `#include <dir.h>`

Description The `mktemp` function replaces the string pointed to by the `template` argument with a unique file name. The `template` argument should be a null-terminated string with six trailing X's that will be replaced by two letters, a period, and three suffix letters. The unique new file name is assigned starting with AA.AAA.

Value(s) Returned The `mktemp` function returns the address of the template string. If an error occurs, null is returned.

Related Function(s) `mkdir`: makes a directory

Example In the following example, `mktemp` creates a unique filename. The filename is then displayed.

```
#include <dir.h>
#include <stdio.h>

int main (void)
{
char *filename = "XXXXXX";
char *ptr;
clrscr ();
ptr = mktemp (filename);
printf ("Unique file name is %s\n",ptr);
return 0;
}
```

rmdir

DOS | UNIX | ANSI C | C++

Syntax `int rmdir(const char *path);`

`const char *path;` *Directory to remove*

Function The `rmdir` function removes the DOS file directory.

File(s) to Include `#include <dir.h>`

Description The `rmdir` function removes the directory specified in the `path` argument. The directory specified in the `path` argument must be empty, and must not be the current working directory or the root directory.

Value(s) Returned The `rmdir` function returns 0 if the `dir` is deleted. When an error occurs, a –1 is returned and the `errno` function is set to one of the following:

EACCES	Permission denied
ENOENT	Path or file function not found

Related Function(s) `chdir:` changes the current directory
`mkdir:` creates a directory

Example The following example creates, then removes, a directory called `junk`.

```
#include <stdio.h>
#include <dir.h>

int main (void)
{
int result;

clrscr ();
result = mkdir ("junk.$$$");
if (!result)
     printf ("Directory JUNK created\n");
else
     printf ("Directory JUNK not created\n");
```

```
result = rmdir ("junk.$$$");
if (!result)
     printf ("Directory JUNK removed\n");
else
     printf ("Directory JUNK not removed\n");

return 0;
}
```

searchpath

DOS | UNIX | ANSI C | C++

Syntax `char *searchpath(const char *file);`

`const char *file;` *File to locate*

Function The `searchpath` function searches the DOS path for a file.

File(s) to Include `#include <dir.h>`

Description The `searchpath` function searches along the DOS path for the file specified in the `file` argument. The DOS path is the path(s) specified in the `path =` statement. The current directory of the current drive is searched first. If the file is not found, each directory specified in the DOS path is searched. When the file is found, the full path name is returned.

Value(s) Returned The pointer to the string containing the file name is returned if the file is located. When unsuccessful, null is returned.

Related Function(s)

`findfirst` : searches for a file in the specified path
`findnext` : continues the `findfirst` search

Example The following example searches for the `bc.exe` file. If the file is found, as in this case, a message showing the path is displayed. If the file is not found, a null follows the message string.

```
#include <stdio.h>
#include <dir.h>

int main (void)
```

continues

```
{
char *path;

/* look for file BC.EXE */

clrscr ();
path = searchpath ("BC.EXE");
if (path != NULL)
        printf ("Found BC.EXE in path %s\n",path);
else
        printf ("File Not Found\n");

return 0;
}
```

setdisk

DOS | UNIX | ANSI C | C++

Syntax `int setdisk(int drive);`

`int drive;` *New drive*

Function The `setdisk` function specifies the current disk drive.

File(s) to Include `#include <dir.h>`

Description The `setdisk` function sets the current drive to the value specified in the `drive` argument. A 0 sets the current drive to A, 1 to B, 2 to C, and so forth.

Value(s) Returned The number of drives available is returned.

Related Function(s) `getdisk`: gets the current disk drive

Example In the following example, `setdisk` sets the disk to the current drive and retrieves the number of drives available on the system.

```
#include <stdio.h>
#include <dir.h>
```

```
int main (void)
{
int numdrives;
int currdrive;

clrscr();
currdrive = getdisk();
numdrives = setdisk (currdrive);
printf ("Current drive is %d\n",currdrive);
printf ("Number of drives is %d\n",numdrives);

return 0;
}
```

Graphics Functions

IBM personal computers and their compatibles operate in two basic modes: text and graphics. In text mode, the screen is divided into rows and columns of character cells. In graphics mode, the screen is divided into pixels, the smallest part of the screen. Figure 8.1 shows the differences between these modes. The resolution of the Video Graphics Array (VGA) adapter in text mode is usually set to 25-character rows by 80-character columns. In graphics mode, the resolution of the VGA is up to 640 pixels wide by 480 pixels high. It should be obvious that the computer can process the 25-by-80 text screen (2000 character cells) much more quickly than the 640-by-480 pixel screen (307,200 pixels). This speed differential is one reason that most applications use the text modes. Applications that use text modes include most word processors and spreadsheets.

Fig. 8.1. Text vs. graphics modes.

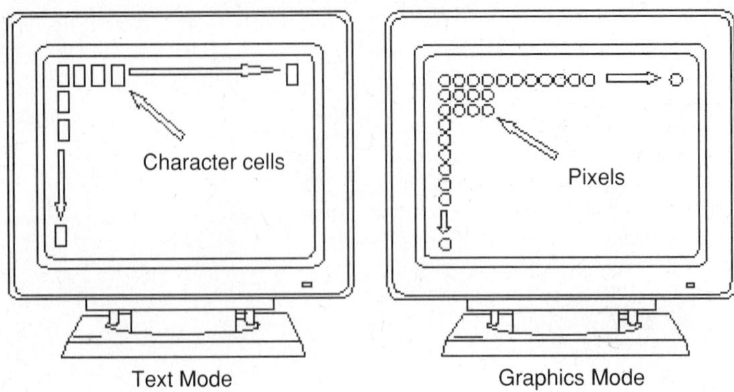

The current trend in computer applications is toward graphics-based programs. The newer, faster computers, usually 32-bit machines operating at 20+ MHz, account for the rise in popularity of Microsoft Windows and "what-you-see-is-what-you-get" (WYSIWYG) applications. With the faster computers, graphics screens can be processed as quickly as text screens with the older 8086/8088 machines. This chapter introduces the basics of graphics programming and the graphics functions provided in the Borland graphics library.

Graphics Modes

IBM personal computers and their compatibles use a video subsystem, which consists of a monitor and video adapter card, to display both text and graphics. The combination of monitor and adapter card defines the range of available colors and screen resolutions. The following table lists the video adapters and graphics drivers supported by the Borland graphics library. Graphics drivers will be explained in more detail in the following paragraphs.

Table 8.1. *Video adapters supported by Borland.*

Adapter	*Driver(s)*
Color Graphics Adapter	CGA
Multi-Color Graphics Array	MCGA
Enhanced Graphics Adapter	EGA, EGAHI, EGAMONO
Video Graphics Array	VGA

Adapter	*Driver(s)*
Hercules Graphics Adapter	HERCMONO
AT&T 400-line Graphics Adapter	ATT400
3270 PC Graphics Adapter	PC3270
IBM 8514 Graphics Adapter	IBM8514

The first task in graphics programming is to put the computer and video subsystem into an appropriate graphics mode. This is accomplished with a call to the `initgraph` function (see `initgraph` in the reference section of this chapter). The `initgraph` function requires that the graphics driver and mode be specified. The graphics driver is adapter-specific and provides all the necessary information for using the adapter. The drivers are listed in table 8.1, shown previously. Each adapter can operate in several modes. Therefore, an operating mode must be specified. The modes are listed in table 8.2 that follows. The specified graphics driver and mode must be valid for the video subsystem. If the graphics driver and mode are valid, a 0 is returned by the `initgraph` function and the system is ready to display graphics information.

***Table 8.2.** Graphics modes supported by Borland.*

Driver	*Mode*	*Value*	*Description*
CGA	CGAC0	0	320x200 - 4 color
	CGAC1	1	320x200 - 4 color
	CGAC2	2	320x200 - 4 color
	CGAC3	3	320x200 - 4 color
	CGAHI	4	640x200 - 2 color
MCGA	MCGAC0	0	320x200 - 4 color
	MCGAC1	1	320x200 - 4 color
	MCGAC2	2	320x200 - 4 color
	MCGAC3	3	320x200 - 4 color
	MCGAMED	4	640x200 - 2 color
	MCGAHI	5	640x480 - 2 color
EGA	EGALO	0	640x200 - 16 color
	EGAHI	1	640x350 - 16 color
EGA64	EGA64LO	0	640x200 - 16 color
	EGA64HI	1	640x350 - 4 color
EGAMONO	EGAMONOHI	3	640x350 - 2 color

continues

Table 8.2. *(continued)*

Driver	*Mode*	*Value*	*Description*
VGA	VGALO	0	640x200 - 16 color
	VGAMED	1	640x350 - 16 color
	VGAHI	2	640x480 - 16 color
ATT400	ATT400C0	0	320x200 - 4 color
	ATT400C1	1	320x200 - 4 color
	ATT400C2	2	320x200 - 4 color
	ATT400C3	3	320x200 - 4 color
	ATT400MED	4	640x200 - 2 color
	ATT400HI	5	640x400 - 2 color
HERC	HERCMONOHI	0	720x348 - 2 color
PC3270	PC3270HI	0	720x350 - 2 color
IBM8514	IBM8514LO	0	640x480 - 256 color
	IBM8514HI	1	1024x768 - 256 color

Coordinate Systems

Once in graphics mode, the computer and video subsystem recognize the screen as a series of pixels. The number of pixels on the screen is determined by the video mode specified when calling the `initgraph` function. For example, when you use the VGA driver with VGAHI mode, the screen is 640 pixels wide by 480 pixels high (see preceding table 8.2). Each pixel is identified by a coordinate pair and can be set to only one color.

There are two coordinate systems recognized by the Borland graphics library. These are the physical and viewport coordinate systems shown in figure 8.2 that follows. The physical coordinate system has its origin in the upper left corner of the screen. The positive horizontal axis extends to the right and has a range from 0 to maximum width minus one. The positive vertical axis extends downward and has a range of maximum height minus one. For the VGA driver with VGAHI mode, the horizontal and vertical axes of the physical coordinate system range from 0 to 639 and 0 to 479, respectively. The physical coordinate system is used only as a reference for the position of the viewport coordinate system.

Fig. 8.2. The physical and viewport coordinate systems.

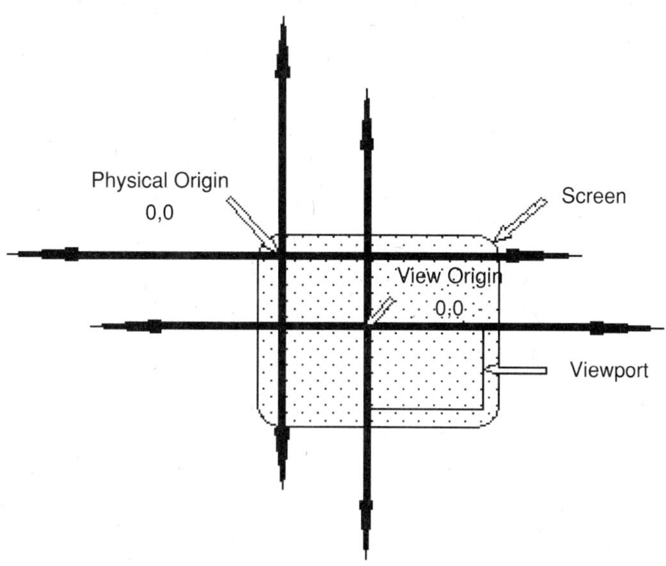

The second coordinate system, the viewport, has its origin in the upper left corner of the current viewport. A viewport, which is set with the `setviewport` function, can be defined as any portion of the physical screen. The positive horizontal axis of the viewport function extends to the right of the origin; the negative axis extends to the left. The positive vertical axis extends downward from the origin; the negative vertical axis extends upward. The default viewport is set to cover the entire physical screen. When the viewport covers the entire screen, the physical and viewport coordinate systems are the same. The viewport coordinate system is used by all the drawing functions and shares the same resolution as the physical coordinate system.

The Graphics Cursor

The graphics library maintains the x and y coordinates of a point called the graphics cursor. The graphics cursor is used as a marker or starting point for many of the graphics functions such as the `lineto` and `linerel` functions. The graphics cursor position is maintained in viewport coordinates and can be manipulated with the `moveto` and `moverel` functions.

Colors and Palettes

Each pixel on the screen can be set to only one color. This color is often referred to as the pixel value. The pixel value, a numeric value, does not actually relate to a color. Instead, the pixel value refers to an index in the current color palette.

The color palette is a table of pixel values which represents colors. The current color palette is limited by the video hardware and mode in use. For example, CGA modes support no more than four colors. EGA modes support up to 16 colors. Table 8.2, shown previously, lists the number of available colors for each video driver and mode.

The following table 8.3 lists the four-color palettes available for the CGA, MCGA, and ATT400 video drivers. For example, CGAC0, MCGAC0, and ATT400C0 video modes have four colors available. The first color, Color 0, is the background color, defined with the `setbkcolor` function. The remaining colors, shown in table 8.3, are Color 1, `CGA_LIGHTGREEN`; Color 2, `CGA_LIGHTRED`; and Color 3, `CGA_YELLOW`.

Table 8.3. *The four-color palettes.*

Palette Number	*Color 1*	*Color 2*	*Color 3*
0	CGA_LIGHTGREEN	CGA_LIGHTRED	CGA_YELLOW
1	CGA_LIGHTCYAN	CGA_LIGHTMAGENTA	CGA_WHITE
2	CGA_GREEN	CGA_RED	CGA_BROWN
3	CGA_CYAN	CGA_MAGENTA	CGA_LIGHTGRAY

Note: Color 0 is defined with the `setbkcolor` function.

As mentioned previously, Color 0 of the four-color palette is defined with the `setbkcolor` function. The available background colors for the four color palettes are listed in table 8.4.

Table 8.4. *Background colors for the four-color palettes.*

Color Constant	*Value*
BLACK	0
BLUE	1
GREEN	2
CYAN	3
RED	4
MAGENTA	5
BROWN	6

Color Constant	*Value*
LIGHTGRAY	7
DARKGRAY	8
LIGHTBLUE	9
LIGHTGREEN	10
LIGHTCYAN	11
LIGHTRED	12
LIGHTMAGENTA	13
YELLOW	14
WHITE	15

For the CGA, MCGA, and ATT400 adapters in two-color modes, the user has the option of selecting a foreground color. The background color is black and the foreground color is selected with the `setbkcolor` function with options from table 8.4. The selection of the foreground color with the `setbkcolor` function seems odd, but the design of the CGA adapter makes this necessary. The two color-modes which operate in this way are the CGAHI, MCGAMED, MCGAHI, ATT400MED, and ATT400HI.

The EGA and VGA adapters support two, four, and sixteen color modes. In two- and four-color modes, the palettes are used in the same manner described in the previous paragraphs. For 16-color modes, the EGA and VGA adapters use the predefined palette shown in table 8.5.

Table 8.5. *The EGA and VGA 16-color palette.*

Color Constant	*Value*	*Palette Index*
EGA_BLACK	0	0
EGA_BLUE	1	1
EGA_GREEN	2	2
EGA_CYAN	3	3
EGA_RED	4	4
EGA_MAGENTA	5	5
EGA_LIGHTGRAY	7	6
EGA_BROWN	20	7
EGA_DARKGRAY	56	8
EGA_LIGHTBLUE	57	9
EGA_LIGHTGREEN	58	10
EGA_LIGHTCYAN	59	11
EGA_LIGHTRED	60	12
EGA_LIGHTMAGENTA	61	13
EGA_YELLOW	62	14
EGA_WHITE	63	15

Fill Patterns

Many of the drawing functions, such as `fillpoly`, `floodfill`, and `bar`, are provided in the graphics library to create filled figures. The functions used to create filled figures use the current fill pattern and fill color. The fill pattern and fill color are specified by either the `setfillpattern` or `setfillstyle` functions.

The `setfillstyle` function selects a fill pattern, predefined by Borland, and a fill color. The fill pattern is an 8-by-8 bit pattern used to fill the figure. The predefined fill patterns are listed in table 8.6. The fill color is selected from the current palette.

***Table 8.6.** Predefined fill patterns.*

Constant	*Value*	*Meaning*
EMPTY_FILL	0	No fill
SOLID_FILL	1	Fill with current color
LINE_FILL	2	Fill with horizontal lines
LTSLASH_FILL	3	Fill with thin slashes
SLASH_FILL	4	Fill with heavy slashes
BKSLASH_FILL	5	Fill with heavy backslashes
LTBKSLASH_FILL	6	Fill with light backslashes
HATCH_FILL	7	Fill with light hatch marks
XHATCH_FILL	8	Fill with heavy hatch marks
INTERLEAVE_FILL	9	Fill with interleaving pattern
WIDE_DOT_FILL	10	Fill with wide, dotted pattern
CLOSE_DOT_FILL	11	Fill with close, dotted pattern
USER_FILL	12	Fill with user-defined pattern

The `setfillpattern` function specifies a user-defined fill pattern and the current fill color. Again, the fill pattern is an 8-by-8 bit pattern. Each bit in the pattern corresponds to a pixel on the screen. If the bit is 1, the corresponding screen pixel is set to the current fill color. If the bit is 0, the corresponding screen pixel remains unchanged. Therefore, a solid fill pattern would correspond to an 8-by-8 fill pattern of 1's. The fill pattern would then be defined by eight rows of 11111111 binary, or 0xFF, 0xFF, 0xFF, 0xFF, 0xFF, 0xFF, 0xFF, 0xFF hexadecimal.

Line Styles

Many of the drawing functions use the current line style. The current line style consists of the current line pattern and line thickness. The line pattern is a 16-bit pattern which describes the appearance of the line. Each bit of the line pattern corresponds to a pixel on the screen. A 1 bit sets the corresponding pixel to the current color. A 0 bit leaves the corresponding pixel unchanged. The line pattern can be defined by the user, or it can be selected from the predefined line patterns listed in table 8.7 that follows. An example of a user-defined pattern is 1111111111111111 binary, or 0xFFFF hexadecimal, for a solid line. The line thickness is set to either 1 or 3 (see table 8.8).

Table 8.7. *Predefined line patterns.*

Constant	*Value*	*Meaning*
`SOLID_LINE`	0	Solid line
`DOTTED_LINE`	1	Dotted line
`CENTER_LINE`	2	Centered line
`DASHED_LINE`	3	Dashed line
`USERBIT_LINE`	4	User-defined line style

Table 8.8. *Line thickness parameters.*

Constant	*Value*	*Meaning*
`NORM_WIDTH`	1	Line 1 pixel wide
`THICK_WIDTH`	3	Line 3 pixels wide

Combining Text with Graphics

The standard text output functions, such as `printf`, cannot be used with graphics modes. Borland provides an 8-by-8 bit-mapped font and several stroked fonts for the display of text while in graphics modes. There are four basic steps to using these fonts.

1. Register the fonts: All desired fonts must be registered before they are used. The font files (.CHR) should be converted into .OBJ files and linked to the executable file. (This procedure is described in UTIL.DOC, which is included on the Borland C++ distribution disks.) The fonts can then be registered with the `registerbgifont` function. The font files and public names for each stroked font are listed in table 8.9.

Table 8.9. Public names used to register the BGI stroked fonts.

Font File	*Description*	*Public Name*
SANS.CHR	Stroked sans-serif font	`sansserif_font`
TRIP.CHR	Stroked triplex font	`triplex_font`
LITT.CHR	Stroked small font	`small_font`
GOTH.CHR	Stroked gothic font	`gothic_font`

Fig. 8.3. Borland fonts.

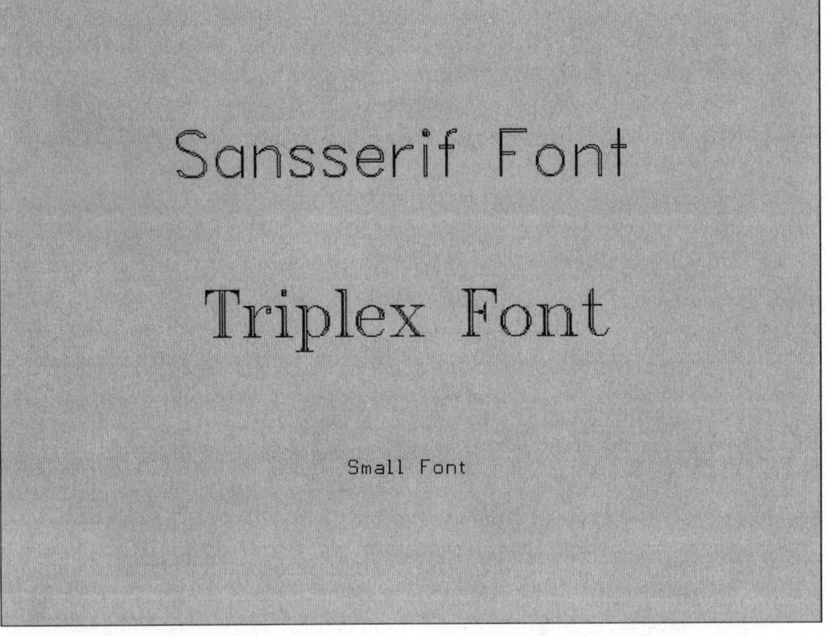

2. Set the text style: Setting the text style consists of selecting a registered font, specifying a text direction, and choosing a character size. The `settextstyle` function is used for these purposes. The font constants are listed in table 8.10 that follows. The text direction constants are listed in table 8.11. The `charsize` argument of the `settextstyle` argument specifies the size of the text output.

Fig. 8.4. Borland fonts.

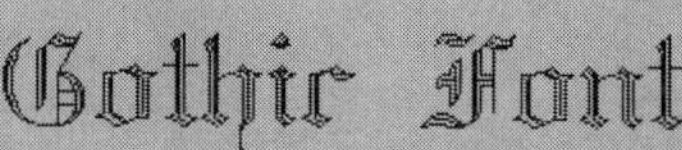

Table 8.10. *Text font constants.*

Constant	*Value*	*Meaning*
DEFAULT_FONT	0	8-by-8 bit-mapped font
TRIPLEX_FONT	1	Stroked triplex font
SMALL_FONT	2	Stroked small font
SANS_SERIF_FONT	3	Stroked sans-serif font
GOTHIC_FONT	4	Stroked gothic font

Table 8.11. *Text directions.*

Constant	*Value*	*Meaning*
HORIZ_DIR	0	Normal, horizontal text
VERT_DIR	1	Text rotated 90 degrees counterclockwise

3. Set the text justification: The `settextjustify` function defines how the text will be placed on the screen relative to the current position of the graphics cursor. Table 8.12 lists the constants used to define the vertical and horizontal justifications.

***Table 8.12.** Text justifications.*

Horizontal Justification

Constant	*Value*	*Meaning*
`LEFT_TEXT`	0	Left justify
`CENTER_TEXT`	1	Center text
`RIGHT_TEXT`	2	Right justify

Vertical Justification

Constant	*Value*	*Meaning*
`BOTTOM_TEXT`	0	Bottom justify
`CENTER_TEXT`	1	Center text
`TOP_TEXT`	2	Top justify

4. Display the text: The actual displaying of the text is accomplished by the `outtext` and `outtextxy` functions using the settings and fonts identified in steps 1 through 3.

Graphics Functions by Category

The graphics functions provided in the Borland C++ graphics library can be divided into six general categories. The functions in each of these categories are briefly described in tables 8.13 through 8.19 that follow. Because some functions fall into more than one category, they are described with each appropriate category.

***Table 8.13.** Graphic system control functions.*

Function	*Meaning*
`closegraph`	Closes the graphics system
`detectgraph`	Determines which driver and mode to use
`graphdefaults`	Resets graphics variables to their defaults

Function	*Meaning*
`_graphfreemem`	Frees graphics memory
`_graphgetmem`	Allocates graphics memory
`getgraphmode`	Retrieves the current mode
`getmoderange`	Retrieves the range of valid modes for the current driver
`initgraph`	Initializes the graphics mode
`installuserdriver`	Installs a third-party device driver
`installuserfont`	Installs a third-party font
`registerbgidriver`	Registers a driver
`restorecrtmode`	Resets the graphics system to its default mode
`setgraphbufsize`	Defines the size of the internal graphics buffer
`setgraphmode`	Puts the graphics system into the specified graphics mode

Table 8.14. *Drawing functions.*

Function	*Meaning*
`arc`	Creates a circular arc
`bar`	Creates a filled bar
`bar3d`	Creates a filled 3-D bar
`circle`	Creates a circle
`drawpoly`	Creates a polygon
`ellipse`	Creates an ellipse
`fillellipse`	Creates a filled ellipse
`fillpoly`	Creates a filled polygon
`floodfill`	Fills a defined area
`getarccoords`	Gets the parameters of the last call to the `arc` or `ellipse` functions
`getaspectratio`	Gets the aspect ratio for the current graphics mode
`getfillpattern`	Gets the current user-defined fillpattern
`getfillsettings`	Gets the current fill pattern and color
`getlinesettings`	Gets the current line style, line pattern, and line thickness
`line`	Creates a line between two specified points
`linerel`	Creates a line with an endpoint some relative distance from the graphics cursor
`lineto`	Creates a line from the graphics cursor to a specified point
`moveto`	Moves the graphics cursor to a specified point
`moverel`	Moves the graphics cursor some relative distance
`pieslice`	Creates a filled circular pie slice
`rectangle`	Creates a rectangle
`sector`	Draws a filled elliptical pie slice

continues

Table 8.14. *(continued)*

Function	*Meaning*
`setaspectratio`	Modifies the default aspect ratio
`setfillpattern`	Sets a user-defined fill pattern
`setfillstyle`	Sets the fill pattern and color
`setlinestyle`	Sets the line style and width
`setwritemode`	Sets the write mode for straight lines

Table 8.15. *Screen and viewport manipulation functions.*

Function	*Meaning*
`cleardevice`	Clears the graphics screen
`clearviewport`	Clears the current viewport
`getimage`	Stores a rectangular part of the screen
`getpixel`	Gets the pixel value of a specified pixel
`getviewsettings`	Gets information on the current viewport
`imagesize`	Determines the required buffer size of an image when using `getpixel`
`putimage`	Places a stored image on the screen
`putpixel`	Sets a specified pixel to the current color
`setactivepage`	Sets the active page
`setviewport`	Defines the current viewport
`setvisualpage`	Sets the visual page

Table 8.16. *Text output functions.*

Function	*Meaning*
`gettextsettings`	Gets the current font, text direction, character size, and text justification
`outtext`	Displays a character string relative to the current position of the graphics cursor
`outtextxy`	Displays a character string relative to a specified point
`registerbgifont`	Registers a font
`settextjustify`	Sets the text justification
`settextstyle`	Sets the font, text style, and character size
`setusercharsize`	Defines the width and height parameters for the stroked fonts
`textheight`	Determines the height, in pixels, of a character string
`textwidth`	Determines the width, in pixels, of a character string

Table 8.17. Colors and palette control functions.

Function	*Meaning*
`getbkcolor`	Gets the current background color
`getcolor`	Gets the current color
`getdefaultpalette`	Gets the default palette
`getmaxcolor`	Gets the maximum color value for the current graphics mode
`getpalette`	Gets the current palette and palette size
`getpalettesize`	Gets the size of the current palette
`setallpalette`	Redefines the entire palette
`setbkcolor`	Defines the background color
`setcolor`	Defines the current color
`setallpalette`	Redefines the entire palette
`setpalette`	Redefines one entry in the current palette
`setrgbpalette`	Defines colors for IBM 8514

Table 8.18. Error handling and state query functions.

Function	*Meaning*
`getarccoords`	Gets the coordinates from the last call to the `arc` or `ellipse` functions
`getapectratio`	Gets the aspect ratio for the current mode
`getbkcolor`	Gets the current background color
`getcolor`	Gets the current color
`getdefaultpalette`	Gets the default palette
`getdrivername`	Gets the name of the current driver
`getfillpattern`	Gets the current user-defined fill pattern
`getfillsettings`	Gets the current fill pattern and color
`getgraphmode`	Gets the current graphics mode
`getlinesettings`	Gets the line style, line pattern, and line thickness
`getmaxcolor`	Gets the highest color value in the current palette
`getmaxmode`	Gets the highest mode number for the current driver
`getmaxx`	Gets the maximum x coordinate of the current mode
`getmaxy`	Gets the maximum y coordinate of the current mode
`getmodename`	Gets the name of the specified mode
`getmoderange`	Gets the range of modes available for the current driver
`getpalette`	Gets the current palette and palette size
`getpalettesize`	Gets the size of the current palette
`getpixel`	Gets the color of the specified pixel
`gettextsettings`	Gets the current font, text direction, character size, and text justification
`getviewsettings`	Gets the settings of the current viewport
`getx`	Gets the x coordinate of the graphics cursor

continues

Table 8.18. *(continued)*

Function	*Meaning*
`gety`	Gets the y coordinate of the graphics cursor
`grapherrormsg`	Gets an error message string for a specified error code
`graphresult`	Gets an error code for the last unsuccessful graphics call

Borland C++ Graphics Functions Reference Guide

The remainder of this chapter provides detailed information on the use of each of the functions provided in the Borland C++ graphics library.

arc

DOS | UNIX | ANSI C | C++

Syntax

```
void far arc(int x, int y, int startangle, int
                  endangle,int radius);
```

`int x, y;`	*Center of arc*
`int startangle;`	*Starting angle*
`int endangle;`	*Ending angle*
`int radius;`	*Radius of arc*

Function The `arc` function creates a circular arc on the screen.

File(s) to Include `#include <graphics.h>`

Description The `arc` function creates a circular arc. The arc is centered at the point specified by the `x` and `y` arguments and is drawn with the specified radius. The arc is not filled but is drawn using the current color. The arc begins at the angle specified by the `startangle` argument and is drawn in a counterclockwise direction until it reaches the angle specified by the `endangle` argument. The `arc` function uses east (extending to the right of the arc's center in the horizontal direction) as its 0 degree point.

The `setlinestyle` function can be used to set the width of the arc. The pattern argument of the `setlinestyle` function, however, will be ignored by the `arc` function. Figure 8.5 illustrates the use of the `arc` function.

Fig. 8.5. The `arc` *function.*

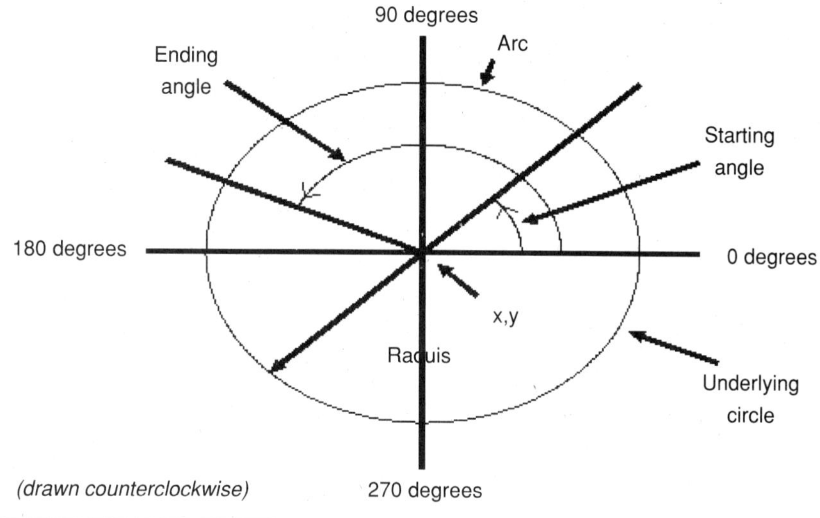

Value(s) Returned There is no return value.

Related Function(s)

`getarccoords` : gets coordinates of last call to `arc`
`setcolor` : sets the current color

Example The following example demonstrates the `arc` function by creating a series of circular arcs. Each arc is centered in the display screen; each subsequent arc has a decreasing radius.

```
#include <graphics.h>
#include <stdio.h>
#include <stdlib.h>
#include <conio.h>

int main ()
{
int gdriver = EGA;
int gmode = EGAHI;
int radius;
```

```
    /* register EGAVGA_driver and sansserif_font
       */
    /* ... these have been added to graphics.lib
       */
    /* as described in UTIL.DOC
       */

registerbgidriver (EGAVGA_driver);
registerbgifont (sansserif_font);

    /* set EGA video mode  */

initgraph (&gdriver,&gmode,"");
rectangle (0,0,639,349);

    /* Draw a series of arcs */

for(radius = 25; radius < 175; radius = radius+25)
{
   arc (320,175,0,270,radius);
}

    /* Delay and Exit */

settextjustify(CENTER_TEXT,BOTTOM_TEXT);
outtextxy (320,320,"Press Any Key To Exit");
getch ();
closegraph();
return 0;
}
```

bar

DOS | UNIX | ANSI C | C++

Syntax

```
void far bar(int left, int top, int right, int
             bottom);

int left, top;          Upper left corner of bar
int right, bottom;      Lower right corner of bar
```

Function The `bar` function creates a filled, rectangular, two-dimensional bar.

File(s) to Include `#include <graphics.h>`

Description The `bar` function draws a filled, rectangular, two-dimensional bar. The upper left corner of the rectangular bar is defined by the `left` and `top` arguments. These arguments correspond to the x and y values of the upper left corner. Similarly, the `right` and `bottom` arguments define the lower right corner of the bar. The bar is not outlined but is filled with the current fill pattern and fill color as set by the `setfillstyle` function. Figure 8.6 illustrates the use of the bar function.

Fig. 8.6. The `bar` *function.*

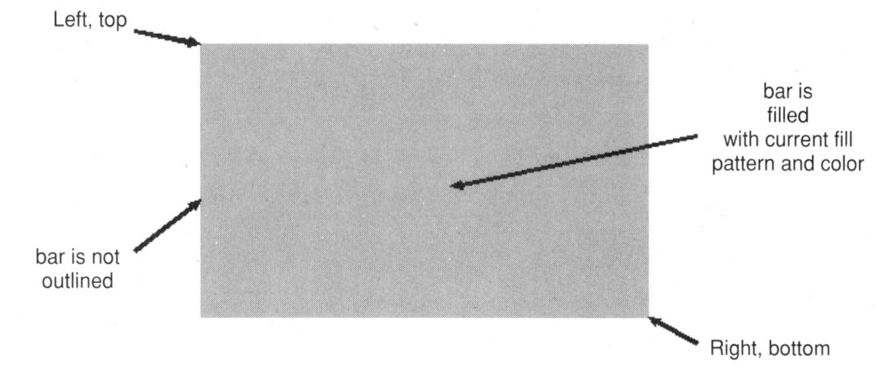

Value(s) Returned There is no return value.

Related Function(s)

`setcolor`	:	sets the current color
`rectangle`	:	generates a rectangle
`setfillstyle`	:	sets the current fill pattern

Example In the following example, the `bar` function displays a series of bars extending from the left to the right side of the screen. Each bar is drawn using a different fill pattern, color, and height.

```
#include <graphics.h>
#include <stdio.h>
#include <stdlib.h>
#include <conio.h>

int main ()
{
```

continues

```
int gdriver = EGA;
int gmode = EGAHI;
int x, y, color,fill;

     /* register EGAVGA_driver and sansserif_font
        */
     /* ... these have been added to graphics.lib
        */
     /* as described in UTIL.DOC */

registerbgidriver(EGAVGA_driver);
registerbgifont(sansserif_font);

     /* set EGA high-resolution 16-color mode */

initgraph (&gdriver,&gmode,"");
rectangle (0,0,639,349);

x = 20;
y = 20;
color = 1;
fill=1;

do
{
     setfillstyle (fill,color);
     bar (x,y,x+40,320);
     x = x+40;
     y = y+10;
     color = color+1;
     if (color > 15)
          color = 1;
     fill = fill+1;
     if (fill > 11)
          fill = 1;
} while (x < 620);

     /* Delay and Exit */

settextjustify(CENTER_TEXT,BOTTOM_TEXT);
outtextxy (330,345,"Press Any Key To Exit");

getch ();
closegraph();
return 0;
}
```

bar3d

DOS | UNIX | ANSI C | C++

Syntax

```
void far bar3d(int left, int top, int right, int
               bottom, int depth, int topflag);
```

`int left, top;`	*Upper left corner of bar*
`int right, bottom;`	*Lower right corner of bar*
`int depth;`	*Depth of 3D bar*
`int topflag;`	*0 - bar is topped, 1 - not topped*

Function The `bar3d` function creates a three-dimensional rectangular bar.

File(s) to Include `#include <graphics.h>`

Description The `bar3d` function creates a three-dimensional rectangular bar. The `left` and `top` arguments define the upper left corner of the front-most rectangle. Similarly, the `right` and `bottom` arguments define the lower right corner of the front-most rectangle. The depth argument defines the three-dimensional depth, in pixels, of the bar. The bar is outlined, in all three dimensions, in the current color and line style. The front-most rectangle is filled using the current fill pattern and fill color. The `topflag` argument specifies whether stacking several bars on top of each other is possible. If `topflag` is set to a nonzero value, a top is placed on the figure. If `topflag` is set to 0, no top is placed on the figure so that other bars can be stacked on top of the figure. Figure 8.7 illustrates the use of the `bar3d` function.

Value(s) Returned There is no return value.

Related Function(s)

`bar`	: creates a two-dimensional bar
`setcolor`	: sets the current color
`setfillstyle`	: sets the current fill pattern

Fig. 8.7. The `bar3d` *function.*

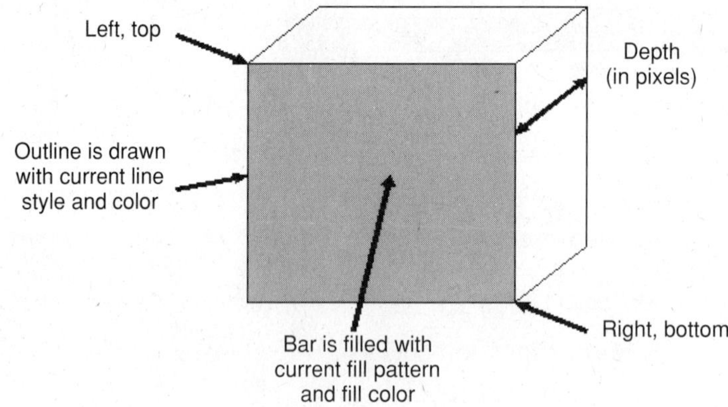

Example The following example demonstrates how `bar3d` creates a filled, three-dimensional bar. The depth of the bar is 50 pixels.

```
#include <graphics.h>
#include <stdio.h>
#include <stdlib.h>
#include <conio.h>

int main ()
{
int gdriver = EGA;
int gmode = EGAHI;
int pattern, color;

     /* register EGAVGA_driver and sansserif_font
        */
     /* ... these have been added to graphics.lib
        */
     /* as described in UTIL.DOC
        */

registerbgidriver(EGAVGA_driver);
registerbgifont(sansserif_font);

     /* set EGA high-resolution 16-color mode */

initgraph (&gdriver,&gmode,"");
rectangle (0,0,639,349);
```

```
        /* Draw 3d bar using white borders and fill
           */
        /* pattern 11 - has depth of 50
           */

pattern = 11;
color = 15;

setfillstyle (pattern,color);
bar3d (220,50,420,300,50,1);

        /* Delay and Exit */

settextjustify(CENTER_TEXT,BOTTOM_TEXT);
outtextxy (320,320,"Press Any Key To Exit");
getch ();
closegraph();
return 0;
}
```

circle

DOS | UNIX | ANSI C | C++

Syntax

```
void far circle(int x, int y, int radius);

int x, y;                    Center of circle
int radius;                  Radius of circle
```

Function The `circle` function generates a circle centered at x,y.

File(s) to Include `#include <graphics.h>`

Description The `circle` function draws a circle. The `x` and `y` arguments define the center of the circle, whereas the `radius` argument defines the horizontal radius of the circle. The circle is not filled but is drawn using the current color. The thickness of the circle's outline can be set by the `setlinestyle` function; however, the linestyle is ignored by the `circle` function. The aspect ratio for the current mode is taken into account when calculating the circle; therefore, the altering of the default x and y aspect factors will affect the circle (it will no longer be round). Figure 8.8 illustrates the use of the `circle` function.

Fig. 8.8. The `circle` ***function.***

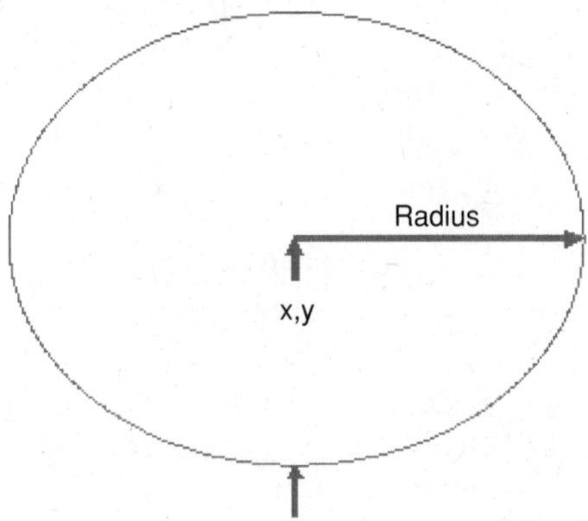

Value(s) Returned There is no return value.

Related Function(s)
`setcolor` : sets the current color
`ellipse` : draws an ellipse

Example In the following example, `circle` creates five series of concentric circles. One series is centered on the screen, whereas the others are displayed in the corners of the screen.

```
#include <graphics.h>
#include <stdio.h>
#include <stdlib.h>
#include <conio.h>

int main ()
{
int gdriver = EGA;
int gmode = EGAHI;
int width, radius;
int style, pattern;
     /* register EGAVGA_driver and sansserif_font
        */
     /* ... these have been added to graphics.lib
        */
     /* as described in UTIL.DOC
        */
registerbgidriver(EGAVGA_driver);
registerbgifont(sansserif_font);
     /* set EGA high-resolution 16-color mode   */
```

```
initgraph (&gdriver,&gmode,"");
rectangle (0,0,639,349);
     /* Draw a series of concentric circles  */
     /* with wide line thickness             */
style = SOLID_LINE;
pattern = 1;
width = THICK_WIDTH;
for (radius = 150; radius != 0; radius = radius-
  25)
     {
     setlinestyle (style,pattern,width);
     circle (320,175,radius);
     }

     /* Draw circles in the four corners using */
     /* normal width line thickness            */

width = NORM_WIDTH;
for (radius = 30; radius != 0; radius = radius -
  5)
     {
     setlinestyle (style,pattern,width);
     circle (50,50,radius);
     circle (50,299,radius);
     circle (589,50,radius);
     circle (589,299,radius);
     }
     /* Delay and Exit */

settextjustify(CENTER_TEXT,BOTTOM_TEXT);
outtextxy (320,320,"Press Any Key To Exit");
getch ();
closegraph();
return 0;
}
```

cleardevice

DOS UNIX ANSI C C++

Syntax `void far cleardevice(void);`

Function The `cleardevice` function clears the graphics screen.

File(s) to Include `#include <graphics.h>`

Description The `cleardevice` function clears a graphics screen. This function uses the current background color, as set by the `setbkcolor` function, to fill the screen. The position of the graphics cursor is placed in the upper left corner of the screen, position (0,0), after the screen has been cleared.

Value(s) Returned There is no return value.

Related Function(s)
`clearviewport` : clears the current viewport
`setbkcolor` : sets the current background color

Example In the following example, `cleardevice` clears the screen with a different color each time a key is pressed. This continues until the Esc key is pressed.

```
#include <graphics.h>
#include <stdio.h>
#include <stdlib.h>
#include <conio.h>

int main ()
{
int gdriver = EGA;
int gmode = EGAHI;
int color;
int ch;

     /* register EGAVGA_driver and sansserif_font
        */
     /* ... these have been added to graphics.lib
        */
     /* as described in UTIL.DOC
        */
registerbgidriver(EGAVGA_driver);
registerbgifont(sansserif_font);

     /* set EGA high-resolution 16-color mode  */

initgraph (&gdriver,&gmode,"");
rectangle (0,0,639,349);
color = 1;

     /* each time a key a pressed, the background
        */
     /* color is incremented and the screen is
        */
     /* cleared - press ESC to exit          */

do
```

```
{
     setbkcolor (color);
     cleardevice();
     rectangle (0,0,639,349);

          /* Delay  */

     settextstyle (SANS_SERIF_FONT,HORIZ_DIR,2);
     settextjustify(CENTER_TEXT,BOTTOM_TEXT);
     outtextxy (320,320,"Press Any Key To Clear
      Screen -
                            ESC to Exit");
     ch = getch ();
     color = color + 1;
     if (color > 15)
          color = 0;
} while (ch != 27);

closegraph();
return 0;
}
```

clearviewport

Syntax `void far clearviewport(void);`

Function The `clearviewport` function clears the current viewport.

File(s) to Include `#include <graphics.h>`

Description The `clearviewport` function fills the current viewport with the current background color. The background color can be set with the `setbkcolor` function. The current position of the graphics cursor is then set to the upper left corner of the current viewport. This position is (0,0) in viewport coordinates.

Value(s) Returned There is no return value.

Related Function(s) `cleardevice` : clears the screen

Example In the following example, `clearviewport` clears the current viewport by filling the viewport with a new color each time a key is pressed. This continues until the Esc key is pressed.

```
#include <graphics.h>
#include <stdio.h>
#include <stdlib.h>
#include <conio.h>

int main ()
{
int gdriver = EGA;
int gmode = EGAHI;
int color;
int ch;

      /* register EGAVGA_driver and sansserif_font
         */
      /* ... these have been added to graphics.lib
         */
      /* as described in UTIL.DOC
         */
registerbgidriver(EGAVGA_driver);
registerbgifont(sansserif_font);

      /* set EGA high-resolution 16-color mode */

initgraph (&gdriver,&gmode,"");
rectangle (0,0,639,349);
rectangle (50,50,590,300);
color = 1;

      /* each time a key a pressed, the background
         */
      /* color is incremented and the viewport is
         */
      /* cleared - press ESC to exit
         */

settextstyle (SANS_SERIF_FONT,HORIZ_DIR,2);
settextjustify(CENTER_TEXT,BOTTOM_TEXT);
outtextxy (320,330,"Press Any Key to Clear
      Viewport - ESC to Exit");

setviewport (50,50,590,300,0);

do
{
      setbkcolor (color);
      clearviewport();
      rectangle (0,0,540,250);
```

```
            /* Delay  */

        ch = getch ();
        color = color + 1;
        if (color > 15)
            color = 0;
    } while (ch != 27);


    closegraph();
    return 0;
    }
```

closegraph

Syntax `void far closegraph(void);`

Function The `closegraph` function closes the graphics system.

File(s) to Include `#include <graphics.h>`

Description The `closegraph` function closes the graphics system as initiated by the `initgraph` function. The `closegraph` function frees all the memory used by the graphics system, then restores the video mode to the screen mode that was in use before the call to the `initgraph` function.

Value(s) Returned There is no return value.

Related Function(s) `initgraph` : initializes the graphics system

Example The following example demonstrates using `closegraph` to shut down the graphics system and restore the screen mode.

```
#include <graphics.h>
#include <stdio.h>
#include <stdlib.h>
#include <conio.h>

int main ()
{
```

continues

```
int gdriver = EGA;
int gmode = EGAHI;

     /* register EGAVGA_driver and sansserif_font
        */
     /* ... these have been added to graphics.lib
        */
     /* as described in UTIL.DOC
        */

registerbgidriver(EGAVGA_driver);
registerbgifont(sansserif_font);

     /* set EGA high-resolution 16-color mode */

initgraph (&gdriver,&gmode,"");
setbkcolor (1);
rectangle (0,0,639,349);

setcolor (4);
circle (320,175,100);
setcolor (2);
rectangle(220,75,420,275);

     /* Delay and Exit */

settextstyle (SANS_SERIF_FONT,HORIZ_DIR,2);
settextjustify(CENTER_TEXT,BOTTOM_TEXT);
outtextxy (320,330,"Press Any Key To Exit and
  Close Graphics System");

getch ();
closegraph();

return 0;
}
```

detectgraph

DOS UNIX ANSI C C++

Syntax

```
void far detectgraph(int far *driver, int far
                     *mode);
```

`int far *driver;`	*Graphics driver*
`int far *mode;`	*Graphics mode*

Function The `detectgraph` function determines the graphics driver and mode to use with the current graphics hardware.

File(s) to Include `#include <graphics.h>`

Description The `detectgraph` function detects the graphics adapter and optimal mode to use for the computer system in use. If the `detectgraph` function detects no graphics hardware, the `*driver` argument is set to `grNotDetected` (–2). A call to `graphresult` will result in a return value of –2, or `grNotDetected`.

Table 8.1, at the beginning of this chapter, lists the graphics drivers that can be used for the `*driver` argument. A value of 0, or DETECT, initiates the `autodetection` feature which determines the optimal driver for use.

Table 8.2, also shown earlier, lists the constants and values for the `*mode` argument. However, if the `*driver` argument is set to 0, or DETECT, the `*mode` argument is automatically set to the highest resolution mode for the driver.

Value(s) Returned There is no return value.

Related Function(s) `initgraph` : initializes the graphics system

Example In the following example, `detectgraph` determines the current graphics driver and mode. The retrieved information is then displayed on the screen.

```
#include <graphics.h>
#include <stdio.h>
#include <stdlib.h>
#include <conio.h>

int main ()
{
char buffer [40];
int gdriver;
int gmode;

    /* register EGAVGA_driver and sansserif_font
       */
    /* ... these have been added to graphics.lib
       */
    /* as described in UTIL.DOC
       */
```

continues

```
registerbgidriver(EGAVGA_driver);
registerbgifont(sansserif_font);

    /* set EGA high-resolution 16-color mode */

detectgraph (&gdriver,&gmode);
initgraph(&gdriver,&gmode,"");
rectangle (0,0,639,349);

    /* get and display graphics driver and mode */

settextjustify (CENTER_TEXT,BOTTOM_TEXT);
sprintf (buffer,"Graphics Driver Value :
%d",gdriver);
outtextxy(320,100,buffer);

sprintf (buffer,"Graphics Mode Value : %d",gmode);
outtextxy(320,200,buffer);

    /* Delay and Exit */

settextjustify(CENTER_TEXT,BOTTOM_TEXT);
outtextxy (320,320,"Press Any Key To Exit");

getch ();

closegraph();
return 0;
}
```

drawpoly

DOS | UNIX | ANSI C | C++

Syntax

```
void far drawpoly(int numpoints, int far
*polypoints);
```

`int numpoints;`	*Number of points*
`int far *polypoints;`	*Points in polygon*

Function The `drawpoly` function draws an unfilled polygon.

File(s) to Include `#include <graphics.h>`

Description The `drawpoly` function creates a polygon with a specified number of points. The `numpoints` argument defines the number of points in the polygon. For the drawpoly function, the number of points must be the actual number of points plus one in order to create a closed polygon. In other words, the first point must equal the last point. For example, numpoints would be equal to 4 for a triangle and 9 for an octagon. The *polypoints argument points to an array of numbers of length numpoints times 2. The first two members of the array identify the x and y coordinates of the first point, respectively, whereas the next two specify the next point, and so forth. Therefore, the *polypoints array would be of length 8 for a triangle and of length 18 for an octagon. The drawpoly function draws the outline of the polygon with the current line style and color but does not fill the polygon. Figure 8.9 illustrates the use of the drawpoly function.

Fig. 8.9. The drawpoly *function.*

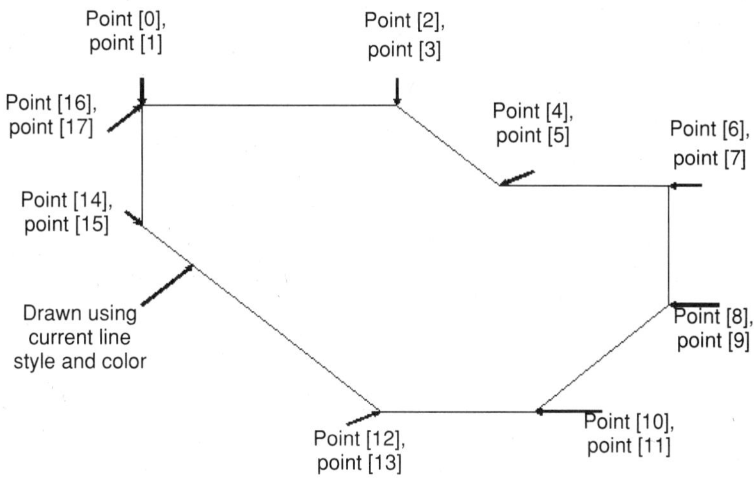

Value(s) Returned There is no return value.

Related Function(s)
fillpoly : draws a filled polygon
setcolor : sets the current color

Example The drawpoly function in the following example creates a nine-point polygon. Note that the last point is the same as the first. The drawpoly function does not automatically close the polygon; therefore, if the polygon is to be closed, the first point must be the same as the last point.

```
#include <graphics.h>
#include <stdio.h>
#include <stdlib.h>
#include <conio.h>

int main ()
{
int gdriver = EGA;
int gmode = EGAHI;
int point[18];

    /* register EGAVGA_driver and sansserif_font
        */
    /* ... these have been added to graphics.lib
        */
    /* as described in UTIL.DOC
        */

registerbgidriver(EGAVGA_driver);
registerbgifont(sansserif_font);

    /* set EGA high-resolution 16-color mode
        */

initgraph (&gdriver,&gmode,"");
rectangle (0,0,639,349);


    /* define 9 point polygon - note that the last
        point */
    /* is equal to the first - the polygon is not
        */
    /* automatically closed by the drawpoly
        function */

point[0] = 50;
point[1] = 50;

point[2] = 320;
point[3] = 100;

point[4] = 590;
point[5] = 50;

point[6] = 370;
point[7] = 175;

point[8] = 590;
point[9] = 300;

point[10] = 320;
point[11] = 250;
```

```
point[12] = 50;
point[13] = 300;

point[14] = 270;
point[15] = 175;

point[16] = 50;
point[17] = 50;

drawpoly(9,point);

    /* Delay and Exit */

settextjustify(CENTER_TEXT,BOTTOM_TEXT);
outtextxy (320,320,"Press Any Key To Exit");

getch ();

closegraph();
return 0;
}
```

ellipse

DOS UNIX ANSI C C++

Syntax

```
void far ellipse(int x, int y, int startangle,
                 int endangle, int xradius, int
                 yradius);
```

`int x, y;`	*Center of ellipse*
`int startangle;`	*Starting angle*
`int endangle;`	*Ending angle*
`int xradius;`	*Radius in horizontal (x) direction*
`int yradius;`	*Radius in vertical (y) direction*

Function The `ellipse` function generates an elliptical arc.

File(s) to Include `#include <graphics.h>`

Description The `ellipse` function draws an elliptical arc in the current color. The elliptical arc is centered at the point specified by the `x` and `y` arguments. Because the arc is elliptical, the `xradius` argument specifies the horizontal radius and the `yradius` argument specifies the vertical radius. The elliptical arc begins at the angle specified by the `startangle` argument and extends in a counterclockwise direction to the angle specified by the `endangle` argument. The `ellipse` function considers east, or the horizontal axis to the right of the ellipse center, to be 0 degrees. The elliptical arc is drawn with the current line thickness as set by the `setlinestyle` function. However, the linestyle is ignored by the `ellipse` function. Figure 8.10 illustrates the use of `ellipse`.

Fig. 8.10. The `ellipse` *function.*

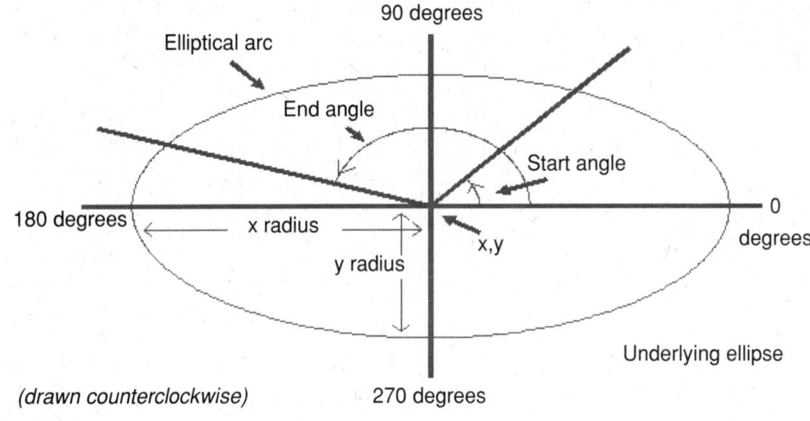

Value(s) Returned There is no return value.

Related Function(s)

`circle` : generates a circle
`arc` : generates a circular arc
`setcolor` : sets the current color

Example The `ellipse` function is used in the following example to display a set of partial ellipses, each with a varying x and y radius. The starting point of each ellipse is 180 degrees from the endpoint of the previous one.

```
#include <graphics.h>
#include <stdio.h>
#include <stdlib.h>
#include <conio.h>

int main ()
{
int gdriver = EGA;
int gmode = EGAHI;
```

```
int xradius = 250;
int yradius = 150;
int angle = 0;
    /* register EGAVGA_driver and sansserif_font
       */
    /* ... these have been added to graphics.lib
       */
    /* as described in UTIL.DOC
       */
registerbgidriver(EGAVGA_driver);
registerbgifont(sansserif_font);
    /* set EGA high-resolution 16-color mode */
initgraph (&gdriver,&gmode,"");
rectangle (0,0,639,349);

    /* draw concentric ellipses - each with a
       starting */
    /* and ending angle 90 degrees from the
       previous */

do
{

ellipse (320,175,angle,angle + 270, xradius,
yradius);
angle = angle + 90;
xradius = xradius - 25;
yradius = yradius - 25;

} while (yradius != 0);

     /* Delay and Exit */

settextjustify(CENTER_TEXT,BOTTOM_TEXT);
outtextxy (320,320,"Press Any Key To Exit");
getch ();
closegraph();
return 0;
}
```

fillellipse

DOS UNIX ANSI C C++

Syntax

```
void far fillellipse(int x, int y, int xradius,
                         int yradius);
```

```
int x, y;          Center of ellipse
int xradius;       Radius in horizontal (x) direction
int yradius;       Radius in vertical (y) direction
```

Function The `fillellipse` function draws a filled ellipse.

File(s) to Include `#include <graphics.h>`

Description The `fillellipse` function draws and fills an ellipse. The center of the ellipse is specified by the `x` and `y` arguments. The `xradius` argument identifies the radius of the ellipse in the horizontal direction, whereas the `yradius` argument identifies the radius of the ellipse in the vertical direction. The ellipse is outlined in the current color and filled with the current fill color and fill pattern. Figure 8.11 illustrates the use of the `fillellipse` function.

Fig. 8.11. The `fillellipse` ***function.***

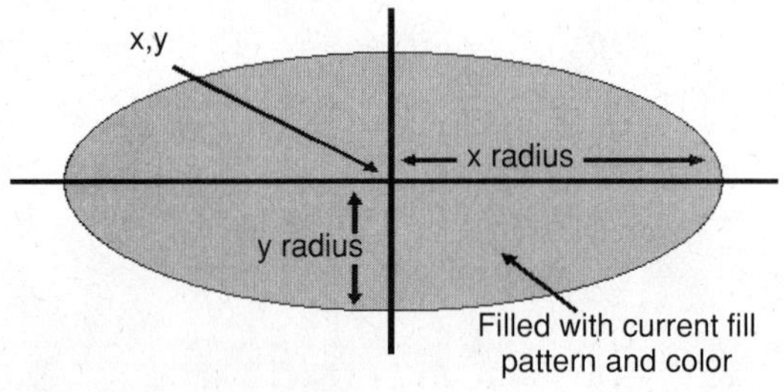

Value(s) Returned There is no return value.

Related Function(s)
`ellipse` : draws an elliptical arc
`circle` : draws a circle
`arc` : draws a circular arc

Example In the following example, `fillellipse` creates two ellipses. The first is filled with a solid fill pattern; the second uses an interleaving fill pattern.

```
#include <graphics.h>
#include <stdio.h>
#include <stdlib.h>
#include <conio.h>
```

```
int main ()
{
int gdriver = EGA;
int gmode = EGAHI;
int pattern, color;

    /* register EGAVGA_driver and sansserif_font
       */
    /* ... these have been added to graphics.lib
       */
    /* as described in UTIL.DOC
       */

registerbgidriver(EGAVGA_driver);
registerbgifont(sansserif_font);

     /* set EGA high-resolution 16-color mode */

initgraph (&gdriver,&gmode,"");
rectangle (0,0,639,349);

     /* draw two ellipses - solid, pattern */

pattern = SOLID_FILL;
color = 14;
setfillstyle (pattern,color);
fillellipse(180,175,100,150);

pattern = INTERLEAVE_FILL;
color = 1;
setfillstyle (pattern,color);
fillellipse(450,175,100,150);

     /* Delay and Exit */

settextjustify(CENTER_TEXT,BOTTOM_TEXT);
outtextxy (320,320,"Press Any Key To Exit");
getch ();
closegraph();
return 0;
}
```

fillpoly

DOS UNIX ANSI C C++

Syntax

```
void far fillpoly(int numpoints, int far
                  *polypoints);
```

```
int numpoints;              Number of points
int far *polypoints;        Points describing the polygon
```

Function The `fillpoly` function generates a filled polygon.

File(s) to Include `#include <graphics.h>`

Description The `fillpoly` function creates a filled polygon. The `numpoints` argument defines the number of points in the polygon. Unlike the `drawpoly` function, the polygon is closed automatically. Therefore, `numpoints` would be set to 3 for a triangle and 8 for an octagon. The `*polypoints` argument is a pointer to an array of length `numpoints` times 2. This array contains the x and y values of each point. The first two members of the array specify the location of the first point, the next two members of the array specify the location of the next point, and so forth. The outline of the polygon is drawn first using the current color and linestyle. The polygon is then filled with the current fill pattern and fill color. Figure 8.12 illustrates the use of the `fillpoly` function.

Value(s) Returned There is no return value.

Related Function(s)

`drawpoly` : draws an unfilled polygon
`setfillstyle` : sets the current fill style

Example In the following example, `fillpoly` displays an eight-point, filled polygon. `fillpoly` automatically closes the border of the polygon. Therefore, there is no need to make the first point equal to the last as with the `drawpoly` function. The polygon is filled with a red slash fill.

```
#include <graphics.h>
#include <stdio.h>
#include <stdlib.h>
#include <conio.h>

int main ()
{
int gdriver = EGA;
int gmode = EGAHI;
int point[16];
int pattern, color;

     /* register EGAVGA_driver and sansserif_font
        */
```

```
    /* ... these have been added to graphics.lib
       */
    /* as described in UTIL.DOC
       */

registerbgidriver(EGAVGA_driver);
registerbgifont(sansserif_font);

    /* set EGA high-resolution 16-color mode */

initgraph (&gdriver,&gmode,"");
rectangle (0,0,639,349);

pattern = SLASH_FILL;
color = 4;

point[0] = 320;
point[1] = 50;

point[2] = 590;
point[3] = 100;

point[4] = 370;
point[5] = 175;

point[6] = 590;
point[7] = 250;

point[8] = 320;
point[9] = 300;

point[10] = 50;
point[11] = 250;

point[12] = 270;
point[13] = 175;

point[14] = 50;
point[15] = 100;
setfillstyle (pattern,color);
fillpoly (8,point);

     /* Delay and Exit */

settextjustify(CENTER_TEXT,BOTTOM_TEXT);
outtextxy (320,320,"Press Any Key To Exit");

getch ();

closegraph();
return 0;
}
```

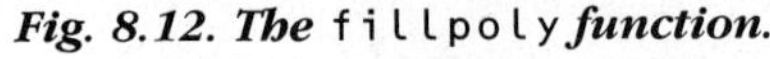

Fig. 8.12. The fillpoly *function.*

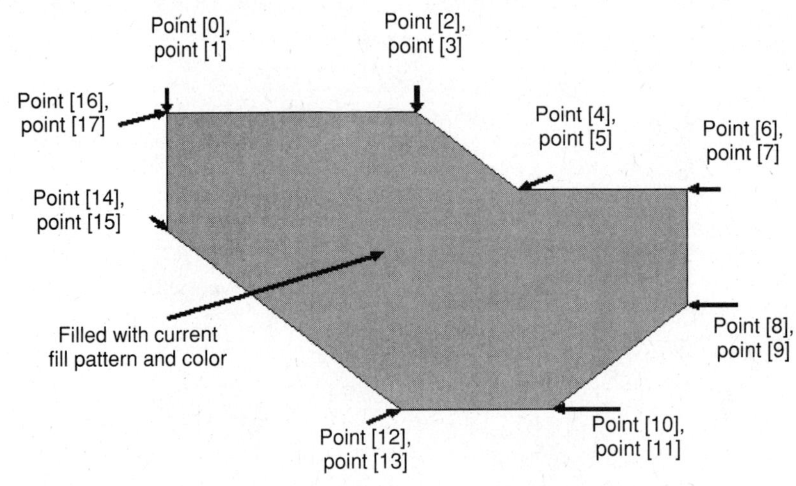

floodfill

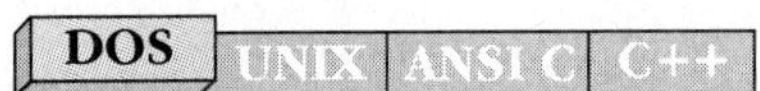

Syntax

```
void far floodfill(int x, int y, int border);
```

`int x, y;`	*Starting point for fill*
`int border;`	*Border color*

Function The `floodfill` function fills a bound area with the current color.

File(s) to Include

```
#include <graphics.h>
```

Description The `floodfill` function fills a bound area with the current fill color and fill pattern. The `x` and `y` arguments specify the starting point for the filling algorithm. The `border` argument specifies the color value of the area's border. For the `floodfill` function to work as expected, the area to be filled must be surrounded by the color specified in the `border` argument. When the point specified by the `x` and `y` arguments lies within the area to be filled, the inside will be filled. If it lies outside the area, the outside will be filled.

Value(s) Returned A –7 is returned via the `graphresult` function if an error occurs while filling a region.

Related Function(s)
`setcolor` : sets the current color
`setfillstyle` : sets the current fill style

Example In the following example, `floodfill` fills a polygon with a blue dotted fill pattern.

```
#include <graphics.h>
#include <stdio.h>
#include <stdlib.h>
#include <conio.h>

int main ()
{
int gdriver = EGA;
int gmode = EGAHI;
int point[18];
int pattern, color;

    /* register EGAVGA_driver and sansserif_font
*/
    /* ... these have been added to graphics.lib
*/
    /* as described in UTIL.DOC
*/

registerbgidriver(EGAVGA_driver);
registerbgifont(sansserif_font);

    /* set EGA high-resolution 16-color mode */

initgraph (&gdriver,&gmode,"");
rectangle (0,0,639,349);

    /* define 9 point polygon - note that the last
       point */
    /* is equal to the first - the polygon is not
*/
    /* automatically closed by the drawpoly
function - */
    /* then fill the polygon
*/

point[0] = 50;
point[1] = 50;

point[2] = 320;
point[3] = 100;
```

continues

```
point[4] = 590;
point[5] = 50;

point[6] = 370;
point[7] = 175;

point[8] = 590;
point[9] = 300;

point[10] = 320;
point[11] = 250;

point[12] = 50;
point[13] = 300;

point[14] = 270;
point[15] = 175;

point[16] = 50;
point[17] = 50;

drawpoly(9,point);
pattern = 10;
color = 1;
setfillstyle (pattern, color);
floodfill (320,175,15);

     /* Delay and Exit */

settextjustify(CENTER_TEXT,BOTTOM_TEXT);
outtextxy (320,320,"Press Any Key To Exit");

getch ();
closegraph();
return 0;
}
```

getarccoords

Syntax

```
void far getarccoords(struct arccoordstype far
                                 *arccoords);
```

`struct arccoordstype far *arccoords;` *Holds returned values*

Function The `getarccoords` function retrieves the parameters used in the last call to the `arc` function.

File(s) to Include `#include <graphics.h>`

Description The `getarccoords` function retrieves the coordinates of the center, starting, and ending points of the last successful call to the `arc` function. The `*arccoords` argument points to the structure of type `arccoordstype`, which holds the retrieved information. The syntax for the `arccoordstype` structure follows.

```
struct arccoordstype
     {
     int x, y;
     int xstart, ystart;
     int xend, yend;
     };
```

The `x` and `y` members define the center of the arc. The `xstart` and `ystart` members define the x and y coordinates of the starting point for the arc. Similarly, the `xend` and `yend` members define the x and y coordinates of the ending point of the arc.

Value(s) Returned There is no return value.

Related Function(s) `arc` : draws a circular arc

Example In the following example, `getarccoords` retrieves information on each arc drawn. This information is then used to draw a line from the starting point to the ending point for each arc.

```
#include <graphics.h>
#include <stdio.h>
#include <stdlib.h>
#include <conio.h>

int main ()
{
struct arccoordstype arcinfo;
int gdriver = EGA;
int gmode = EGAHI;
int radius;

    /* register EGAVGA_driver and sansserif_font
       */
    /* ... these have been added to graphics.lib
       */
```

continues

```
    /* as described in UTIL.DOC
       */

registerbgidriver(EGAVGA_driver);
registerbgifont(sansserif_font);

    /* set EGA high-resolution 16-color mode */

initgraph (&gdriver,&gmode,"");
rectangle (0,0,639,349);

    /* Draw a series of arcs      */
    /* and connect the endpoints */

for (radius = 25; radius < 175; radius = radius +
  25)
{
   arc (320,175,0,270,radius);
   getarccoords(&arcinfo);
   moveto(arcinfo.xstart,arcinfo.ystart);
   lineto(arcinfo.xend,arcinfo.yend);
}
    /* Delay and Exit */

settextjustify(CENTER_TEXT,BOTTOM_TEXT);
outtextxy (320,320,"Press Any Key To Exit");
getch ();
closegraph();
return 0;
}
```

getaspectratio

DOS | UNIX | ANSI C | C++

Syntax

```
void far getaspectratio(int far *xaspect, int far
                        *yaspect);
```

`int far *xaspect;` *Aspect ratio of x axis*

`int far *yaspect;` *Aspect ratio of y axis*

Function The `getaspectratio` function retrieves the aspect ratio of the current graphics mode.

File(s) to Include `#include <graphics.h>`

Description The `getaspectratio` function retrieves the aspect ratio of the current graphics mode. The aspect ratio can be defined as the ratio of the width of the graphics mode's pixel as compared to the height of the pixel. This ratio, using existing graphics modes, is always less than or equal to 1. The value for determining the aspect ratio with respect to the horizontal axis is returned in the `*xaspect` argument. Similarly, the value for the vertical axis is returned in the `*yaspect` argument. The `*yaspect` argument is set to 10,000, which is returned upon calling the `getaspectratio` function. The `*xaspect` argument is almost always less than the `*yaspect` value, because most graphics modes have pixels that are taller than they are wide. The only exception is in VGA modes, which produce square pixels (that is, `xaspect = yaspect`).

Value(s) Returned There is no return value.

Related Function(s) `setaspectratio` : changes the default aspect ratio

Example In the following example, `getaspectratio` retrieves the current screen aspect ratio. The x and y aspect ratios are then displayed.

```
#include <graphics.h>
#include <stdio.h>
#include <stdlib.h>
#include <conio.h>

int main ()
{
int gdriver = EGA;
int gmode = EGAHI;
int xaspect, yaspect;
char buffer[40];

    /* register EGAVGA_driver and sansserif_font
       */
    /* ... these have been added to graphics.lib
       */
    /* as described in UTIL.DOC
       */

registerbgidriver(EGAVGA_driver);
registerbgifont(sansserif_font);

    /* set EGA high-resolution 16-color mode */
```

continues

```
initgraph (&gdriver,&gmode,"");
rectangle (0,0,639,349);

    /* get aspect ratios and display them */

getaspectratio (&xaspect,&yaspect);

settextjustify (CENTER_TEXT,CENTER_TEXT);
sprintf (buffer,"The x aspect ratio is :
     %d",xaspect);
outtextxy (320,100,buffer);

sprintf (buffer,"The y aspect ratio is :
     %d",yaspect);
outtextxy (320,200,buffer);

    /* Delay and Exit */

settextjustify(CENTER_TEXT,BOTTOM_TEXT);
outtextxy (320,320,"Press Any Key To Exit");
getch ();
closegraph();
return 0;
}
```

getbkcolor

DOS UNIX ANSI C C++

Syntax `int far getbkcolor(void);`

Function The `getbkcolor` function retrieves the current background color.

File(s) to Include `#include <graphics.h>`

Description The `getbkcolor` function retrieves the color value of the current background color. The background color, by default, is color value 0. However, this value can be changed by a call to the `setbkcolor` function. Table 8.4 at the start of this chapter lists the background colors.

Value(s) Returned The value of the current background color is returned.

Related Function(s) `setbkcolor` : sets the background color

Example In the following example, `getbkcolor` retrieves the value of the current background color. This value is then displayed on the screen.

```
#include <graphics.h>
#include <stdio.h>
#include <stdlib.h>
#include <conio.h>

int main ()
{
int gdriver = EGA;
int gmode = EGAHI;
int background;
char buffer [40];

    /* register EGAVGA_driver and sansserif_font
       */
    /* ... these have been added to graphics.lib
       */
    /* as described in UTIL.DOC
       */

registerbgidriver(EGAVGA_driver);
registerbgifont(sansserif_font);
    /* set EGA high-resolution 16-color mode */

initgraph (&gdriver,&gmode,"");
rectangle (0,0,639,349);

    /* set, get, and display the background color
       */

setbkcolor (1);
background = getbkcolor();

sprintf (buffer,"The background color is :
%d",background);
settextjustify (CENTER_TEXT,CENTER_TEXT);
outtextxy (320,175,buffer);

    /* Delay and Exit */

settextjustify(CENTER_TEXT,BOTTOM_TEXT);
outtextxy (320,320,"Press Any Key To Exit");

getch ();
```

continues

```
closegraph();
return 0;
}
```

getcolor

DOS UNIX ANSI C C++

Syntax `int far getcolor(void);`

Function The `getcolor` function retrieves the value of the current color.

File(s) to Include `#include <graphics.h>`

Description The `getcolor` function retrieves the value of the current color. The current color, which is not the same as the fill color, is the color used for drawing lines, arcs, and so forth. The retrieved color value is interpreted according to which mode is in use. For example, Color 1 varies in CGA modes depending on which palette is in use. Tables 8.3 and 8.5 at the start of this chapter help interpret the returned value according to the mode and palette in use.

Value(s) Returned The value of the current color is returned.

Related Function(s) `setcolor` : sets the current color

Example In the following example, `getcolor` retrieves the value of the current color. Three lines are drawn using three colors. The color value is retrieved after each line has been completed and the color value is displayed.

```
#include <graphics.h>
#include <stdio.h>
#include <stdlib.h>
#include <conio.h>

int main ()
{
int gdriver = EGA;
int gmode = EGAHI;
int color;
char buffer [40];
int y, colnum;
```

```
    /* register EGAVGA_driver and sansserif_font
       */
    /* ... these have been added to graphics.lib
       */
    /* as described in UTIL.DOC
       */

registerbgidriver(EGAVGA_driver);
registerbgifont(sansserif_font);

    /* set EGA high-resolution 16-color mode */

initgraph (&gdriver,&gmode,"");
rectangle (0,0,639,349);

    /* set, get, and display several colors */

colnum = 15;

settextjustify(LEFT_TEXT,CENTER_TEXT);

for (y = 75; y < 230; y = y + 75)
     {
     setcolor (colnum);
     line (20,y,400,y);
     color = getcolor();
     sprintf (buffer,"Color : %d",color);
     outtextxy (450,y,buffer);
     colnum = colnum   5;
     }
     /* Delay and Exit */

settextjustify(CENTER_TEXT,BOTTOM_TEXT);
outtextxy (320,320,"Press Any Key To Exit");

getch ();

closegraph();
return 0;
}
```

getdefaultpalette

DOS UNIX ANSI C C++

Syntax `struct palettetype *far getdefaultpalette(void);`

Function The `getdefaultpalette` function retrieves the structure which defines the palette.

File(s) to Include `#include <graphics.h>`

Description The `getdefaultpalette` function returns the pointer to the palette which was defined by the driver upon initialization. The pointer identifies a structure of type `palettetype`. The `palettetype` structure is defined as follows:

```
#define MAXCOLORS 15

struct palettetype
   {
   unsigned char size;
   signed char colors[MAXCOLORS + 1];
   };
```

Value(s) Returned The `getdefaultpalette` function returns a pointer to the palette which was initialized by the `initgraph` function.

Related Function(s) `initgraph` : initializes the graphics environment

Example In the following example, `getdefaultpalette` returns the color values of the current palette in a structure of type `palettetype`. These color values are then displayed on the screen.

```
#include <graphics.h>
#include <stdio.h>
#include <stdlib.h>
#include <conio.h>

int main ()
{
struct palettetype far *palette = NULL;
int gdriver = EGA;
int gmode = EGAHI;
int x, a, b;
char buffer[40];

    /* register EGAVGA_driver and sansserif_font
       */
    /* ... these have been added to graphics.lib
       */
    /* as described in UTIL.DOC
       */
```

```
registerbgidriver(EGAVGA_driver);
registerbgifont(sansserif_font);

    /* set EGA high-resolution 16-color mode */

initgraph (&gdriver,&gmode,"");
rectangle (0,0,639,349);

    /* get palette and print colors */

a = 5;
b = 5;
palette = getdefaultpalette();

for (x=0; x<palette->size; x = x + 1)
{
     gotoxy (a,b);
     printf("Color %d : %d", x, palette-
       >colors[x]);
     b = b + 1;
}
   /* Delay and Exit */

settextjustify(CENTER_TEXT,BOTTOM_TEXT);
outtextxy (320,320,"Press Any Key To Exit");
getch ();
closegraph();
return 0;
}
```

getdrivername

DOS UNIX ANSI C C++

Syntax `char *far getdrivername(void);`

Function The `getdrivername` function returns a pointer to the string that contains the name of the current graphics driver.

File(s) to Include `#include <graphics.h>`

Description The `getdrivername` function returns the pointer to a string which contains the name of the current graphics driver. This function should be called only after a driver has been defined and initialized (after the `initgraph` function).

Value(s) Returned The pointer to the string which contains the current graphics driver is returned by the `getdrivername` function.

Related Function(s) `initgraph` : initializes the graphics environment

Example In the following example, `getdrivername` returns the pointer to the current driver name. The driver name is then displayed.

```
#include <graphics.h>
#include <stdio.h>
#include <stdlib.h>
#include <conio.h>

int main ()
{
char *driver;
int gdriver = EGA;
int gmode = EGAHI;

    /* register EGAVGA_driver and sansserif_font
       */
    /* ... these have been added to graphics.lib
       */
    /* as described in UTIL.DOC
       */

registerbgidriver(EGAVGA_driver);
registerbgifont(sansserif_font);

    /* set EGA high-resolution 16-color mode */

initgraph (&gdriver,&gmode,"");
rectangle (0,0,639,349);

    /* get the driver name and display */

driver = getdrivername();

settextstyle (SANS_SERIF_FONT,HORIZ_DIR,2);
settextjustify (CENTER_TEXT,CENTER_TEXT);
outtextxy(320,145,"The driver name is :");
outtextxy(320,175,driver);

    /* Delay and Exit */

settextjustify(CENTER_TEXT,BOTTOM_TEXT);
outtextxy (320,320,"Press Any Key To Exit");
```

```
getch ();
closegraph();
return 0;
}
```

getfillpattern

DOS | UNIX | ANSI C | C++

Syntax

```
void far getfillpattern(char far *pattern);
```

`char far *pattern;` *Fill pattern*

Function The `getfillpattern` function copies a specified fill pattern to memory.

File(s) to Include `#include <graphics.h>`

Description The `getfillpattern` function retrieves a user-defined fill pattern, as defined by the `setfillpattern` function, and stores it in memory. The `*pattern` argument is a pointer to an 8-byte series that represents an 8-by-8 bit fill pattern. Each byte represents an 8-bit row in which each bit is either on or off (0 or 1). A 1 bit indicates that the corresponding pixel should be set to the current fill color. A 0 bit indicates that the corresponding pixel will not be changed.

Value(s) Returned There is no return value.

Related Function(s) `setfillpattern` : sets the current fill pattern

Example In the following example, `getfillpattern` stores the default fill pattern. Once stored, the fill pattern is changed twice and rectangles are drawn with the new fill patterns. The fill pattern is then reset to the default and a rectangle is filled with the default pattern.

```
#include <graphics.h>
#include <stdio.h>
#include <stdlib.h>
#include <conio.h>
```

continues

```
int main ()
{
int gdriver = EGA;
int gmode = EGAHI;

    /* set 50% and 25% fill patterns          */
    /* also set a holder for the old pattern */

char pattern1[8] =
{0x55,0xAA,0x55,0xAA,0x55,0xAA,0x55,0xAA};
char pattern2[8] =
{0x44,0x11,0x44,0x11,0x44,0x11,0x44,0x11};
char patternhold[8] =
{0x00,0x00,0x00,0x00,0x00,0x00,0x00,0x00};

    /* register EGAVGA_driver and sansserif_font
       */
    /* ... these have been added to graphics.lib
       */
    /* as described in UTIL.DOC
       */

registerbgidriver(EGAVGA_driver);
registerbgifont(sansserif_font);

    /* set EGA high-resolution 16-color mode */

initgraph (&gdriver,&gmode,"");
rectangle (0,0,639,349);

    /* first get the current fill pattern and save
       in    */
    /* in patternhold - next set the pattern to
       pattern1 */
    /* and fill the upper half of the screen -
       next      */
    /* fill the lower half of screen with pattern
       2  -    */
    /* lastly get the old pattern and fill center
       square */

getfillpattern (patternhold);

setcolor (15);
rectangle (0,0,639,175);
setfillpattern(pattern1,1);
floodfill (1,1,15);

rectangle (0,175,639,349);
setfillpattern(pattern2,1);
floodfill (1,176,15);
```

```
rectangle (200,175,440,225);
setfillpattern(patternhold,0);
floodfill (201,176,15);

     /* Delay and Exit */

settextjustify(CENTER_TEXT,CENTER_TEXT);
outtextxy (320,200,"Press Any Key To Exit");
getch ();
closegraph();
return 0;
}
```

getfillsetting

Syntax

```
void far getfillsettings(struct fillsettingstype
                                    far *info);
```

`struct fillsettingstype far *info;` *Fill information*

Function The `getfillsettings` function retrieves information concerning the current fill pattern and current fill color.

File(s) to Include `#include <graphics.h>`

Description The `getfillsettings` function retrieves the current fill settings. The `*info` argument points to the structure of type `fillsettingstype`, which is updated when the `getfillsettings` function is called. This structure is as follows:

```
struct fillsettingstype
     {
     int pattern;
     int color;
     };
```

Table 8.6, appearing early in this chapter, can assist with interpreting the returned pattern value. If the returned value is 12, a user-defined fill pattern is in use.

Value(s) Returned There is no return value.

Related Function(s)

`setfillpattern` : sets a user-defined fill pattern
`setfillstyle` : sets the current fill pattern and color

Example In the following example, `getfillsettings` retrieves the current fill settings. These fill settings are then displayed on the screen.

```
#include <graphics.h>
#include <stdio.h>
#include <stdlib.h>
#include <conio.h>

int main ()
{
struct fillsettingstype fillsettings;
int gdriver = EGA;
int gmode = EGAHI;
char buffer [40];

    /* register EGAVGA_driver and sansserif_font
       */
    /* ... these have been added to graphics.lib
       */
    /* as described in UTIL.DOC
       */

registerbgidriver(EGAVGA_driver);
registerbgifont(sansserif_font);

    /* set EGA high-resolution 16-color mode */

initgraph (&gdriver,&gmode,"");
rectangle (0,0,639,349);

    /* get fill settings and display information
       */

rectangle (200,150,440,250);
setfillstyle (SLASH_FILL,15);
floodfill (1,1,15);

getfillsettings (&fillsettings);

sprintf (buffer, "Fill Style : %d",
  fillsettings.pattern);
settextjustify (CENTER_TEXT,CENTER_TEXT);
outtextxy (320,175,buffer);
sprintf (buffer,"Fill Color : %d",
  fillsettings.color);
outtextxy (320,200,buffer);
```

```
     /* Delay and Exit */

outtextxy (320,225,"Press Any Key To Exit");

getch ();
closegraph();
return 0;
}
```

getgraphmode

Syntax `int far getgraphmode(void);`

Function The `getgraphmode` function returns the current graphics mode.

File(s) to Include `#include <graphics.h>`

Description The `getgraphmode` function retrieves the value of the current graphics mode. The current driver must be considered when interpreting the return value. This function should be called only after the graphics system has been initialized with the `initgraph` function. Table 8.2, at the start of this chapter, can assist with interpreting the returned value.

Value(s) Returned The graphics mode as set by the `initgraph` or `setgraphmode` functions is returned when the `getgraphmode` function is called.

Related Function(s)
`setgraphmode` : sets the graphics mode
`initgraph` : initializes the graphics system

Example In the following example, `getgraphmode` retrieves the current graphics mode. The mode is then displayed on the screen.

```
#include <graphics.h>
#include <stdio.h>
#include <stdlib.h>
#include <conio.h>
int main ()
{
int gdriver = EGA;
int gmode = EGAHI;
```

continues

```
char buffer [40];
int mode;

     /* register EGAVGA_driver and sansserif_font
        */
     /* ... these have been added to graphics.lib
       */
     /* as described in UTIL.DOC
       */

registerbgidriver(EGAVGA_driver);
registerbgifont(sansserif_font);

     /* set EGA high-resolution 16-color mode */

initgraph (&gdriver,&gmode,"");
rectangle (0,0,639,349);

     /* get mode and display */

mode = getgraphmode ();
sprintf (buffer,"The Mode Number is : %d",mode);
settextstyle (SANS_SERIF_FONT,HORIZ_DIR,2);
settextjustify (CENTER_TEXT,CENTER_TEXT);
outtextxy (320,175,buffer);

     /* Delay and Exit */

outtextxy (320,320,"Press Any Key To Exit");
getch ();
closegraph();
return 0;
}
```

getimage

DOS | UNIX | ANSI C | C++

Syntax

```
void far getimage(int left, int top, int right,
                  int bottom, void far *image);
```

`int left, top;`	*Upper left corner of image*
`int right, bottom;`	*Lower right corner of image*
`void far *image;`	*Image buffer*

Function The `getimage` function stores a rectangular image in memory.

File(s) to Include `#include <graphics.h>`

Description The `getimage` function stores a rectangular portion of the screen for later use. The upper left corner of the rectangular area to be stored is defined by the `left` and `top` arguments. These arguments represent the x and y coordinates of the upper left corner, respectively. The `right` and `bottom` arguments define the lower right corner of the rectangular image. These arguments define the x and y values of the lower right corner. The `*image` argument points to the memory buffer in which the image is stored. The `getimage` function is often used with the `putimage` function to create partial page animation.

Value(s) Returned There is no return value.

Related Function(s)

`imagesize` : determines the required size of the image buffer
`putimage` : places a stored image on the screen

Example In the following example, `getimage` stores the rectangular image displayed in the center of the screen. This image is then placed in the four corners of the screen with the `putimage` function.

```
#include <graphics.h>
#include <stdio.h>
#include <stdlib.h>
#include <conio.h>
int main ()
{
int gdriver = EGA;
int gmode = EGAHI;
void *image;
unsigned int imsize;

     /* register EGAVGA_driver and sansserif_font
        */
     /* ... these have been added to graphics.lib
        */
     /* as described in UTIL.DOC
        */

registerbgidriver(EGAVGA_driver);
registerbgifont(sansserif_font);

     /* set EGA high-resolution 16-color mode */
```

continues

```
initgraph (&gdriver,&gmode,"");
rectangle (0,0,639,349);

    /* draw and store an image - then place it */
    /* in the four corners of the screen       */

setfillstyle(SOLID_FILL,2);
bar (280,135,360,215);
setfillstyle(SOLID_FILL,4);
fillellipse(320,175,40,40);

imsize = imagesize(280,135,360,215);
image = malloc(imsize);
getimage(280,135,360,215,image);
putimage (20,20,image,COPY_PUT);
putimage (540,20,image,COPY_PUT);
putimage (20,240,image,COPY_PUT);
putimage (540,240,image,COPY_PUT);

    /* Delay and Exit */

settextjustify(CENTER_TEXT,BOTTOM_TEXT);
outtextxy (320,320,"Press Any Key To Exit");

getch ();

closegraph();
return 0;
}
```

getlinesettings

DOS | UNIX | ANSI C | C++

Syntax

```
void far getlinesettings(struct linesettingstype
                                   far *info);

struct linesettingstype far *info;
```
Line information

Function The `getlinesettings` function retrieves the current line style, line pattern, and line thickness.

File(s) to Include `#include <graphics.h>`

Description The `getlinesettings` function retrieves the current line settings. These settings are placed in a structure of type `linesettingstype`, which is pointed to by the `*info` argument. The current line style, pattern, and thickness are placed in this structure. The syntax for the `linesettingstype` structure is as follows:

```
struct linesettingstype
    {
    int linestyle;
    unsigned upattern;
    int thickness;
    };
```

The `linestyle` member of this structure specifies the style of the lines to be drawn. Table 8.7, at the start of this chapter, lists the predefined linestyle constants and values. Table 8.8, also appearing earlier in this chapter, lists the predefined line thickness constants and values.

The `upattern` member of the structure contains the user-defined line pattern only when the linestyle member is equal to USERBIT_LINE, or 4. When the `linestyle` member is equal to USERBIT_LINE, the `upattern` member contains a 16-bit user defined line pattern. A 1 bit in this line pattern indicates that the corresponding pixel will be set to the current color. A 0 bit indicates that the corresponding pixel will remain unchanged. For example, a user-defined line pattern of 0001000100010001 binary, or 0x1111 hex, indicates that every fourth pixel on the line will be set to the current color.

Value(s) Returned There is no return value.

Related Function(s) `setlinestyle` : sets the current line style

Example In the following example, `getlinesettings` retrieves the current line settings, including the current line style, user pattern, and line thickness. These settings are then displayed.

```
#include <graphics.h>
#include <stdio.h>
#include <stdlib.h>
#include <conio.h>

int main ()
{
struct linesettingstype lineset;
int gdriver = EGA;
int gmode = EGAHI;
```

continues

```
char buffer[40];

     /* register EGAVGA_driver and sansserif_font
        */
     /* ... these have been added to graphics.lib
        */
     /* as described in UTIL.DOC
        */

registerbgidriver(EGAVGA_driver);
registerbgifont(sansserif_font);

     /* set EGA high-resolution 16-color mode */

initgraph (&gdriver,&gmode,"");
rectangle (0,0,639,349);

     /* define, use, and retrieve line settings */

setlinestyle (DOTTED_LINE,0xFFFF,THICK_WIDTH);
getlinesettings (&lineset);
rectangle (50,50,590,300);
settextjustify(CENTER_TEXT,CENTER_TEXT);
sprintf (buffer,"The Line Style is :
  %d",lineset.linestyle);
outtextxy (320,75,buffer);
sprintf (buffer,"The User Pattern is :
  0x%x",lineset.upattern);
outtextxy (320,150,buffer);

sprintf (buffer,"The Line Thickness is :
  %d",lineset.thickness);
outtextxy (320,225,buffer);
     /* Delay and Exit */

outtextxy (320,320,"Press Any Key To Exit");
getch ();
closegraph();
return 0;
}
```

getmaxcolor

DOS | UNIX | ANSI C | C++

Syntax `int far getmaxcolor(void);`

Function The `getmaxcolor` function retrieves the value of the maximum color in the current palette.

File(s) to Include

```
#include <graphics.h>
```

Description

The `getmaxcolor` function gets the highest color value in the current palette. The palette in use depends upon the driver and mode initialized. For 16-color modes, the return value is 15. Similarly, for two-color modes, the return value is 1.

Value(s) Returned

The highest color value in the current palette is returned when the `getmaxcolor` function is called.

Related Function(s)

`getcolor` : gets the current color
`setcolor` : sets the current color

Example

In the following example, `getmaxcolor` retrieves the maximum color number in the current palette. The color number is then displayed.

```
#include <graphics.h>
#include <stdio.h>
#include <stdlib.h>
#include <conio.h>

int main ()
{
int gdriver = EGA;
int gmode = EGAHI;
int maxcolor;
char buffer[40];

     /* register EGAVGA_driver and sansserif_font
        */
     /* ... these have been added to graphics.lib
        */
     /* as described in UTIL.DOC
          */

registerbgidriver(EGAVGA_driver);
registerbgifont(sansserif_font);

     /* set EGA high-resolution 16-color mode */

initgraph (&gdriver,&gmode,"");
rectangle (0,0,639,349);

     /* get and display the maximum color number
          */

maxcolor = getmaxcolor();
```

continues

```
settextstyle(SANS_SERIF_FONT,HORIZ_DIR,2);
settextjustify (CENTER_TEXT,CENTER_TEXT);
sprintf (buffer,"The Maximum Color Number is :
  %d",maxcolor);
outtextxy (320,175,buffer);

     /* Delay and Exit */

settextjustify(CENTER_TEXT,BOTTOM_TEXT);
outtextxy (320,320,"Press Any Key To Exit");

getch ();

closegraph();
return 0;
}
```

getmaxmode

DOS | UNIX | ANSI C | C++

Syntax `int far getmaxmode(void);`

Function The `getmaxmode` function returns the maximum mode number for the current driver.

File(s) to Include `#include <graphics.h>`

Description The `getmaxmode` function determines the highest mode value for the current driver. The highest mode value generally represents the mode with the highest resolution. This function works with all drivers, including installed vendor-added drivers.

Value(s) Returned The maximum mode number for the current driver is returned when the `getmaxmode` function is called.

Related Function(s)
`getmoderange` : retrieves the range of modes for the driver
`getmodename` : returns the name of the graphics mode

Example In the following example, `getmaxmode` retrieves the maximum mode number for the current driver. The maximum mode number is then displayed.

```
#include <graphics.h>
#include <stdio.h>
#include <stdlib.h>
#include <conio.h>
```

```
int main ()
{
int gdriver = EGA;
int gmode = EGAHI;
int maxmode;
char buffer[40];

     /* register EGAVGA_driver and sansserif_font
        */
     /* ... these have been added to graphics.lib
        */
     /* as described in UTIL.DOC
        */

registerbgidriver(EGAVGA_driver);
registerbgifont(sansserif_font);

     /* set EGA high-resolution 16-color mode */

initgraph (&gdriver,&gmode,"");
rectangle (0,0,639,349);

     /* get and display the maximum mode */

maxmode = getmaxmode();

settextstyle (SANS_SERIF_FONT,HORIZ_DIR,2);
settextjustify (CENTER_TEXT,CENTER_TEXT);
sprintf (buffer,"The Maximum Mode Number is: %d",
maxmode);
outtextxy(320,175,buffer);

     /* Delay and Exit */

outtextxy (320,320,"Press Any Key To Exit");
getch ();
closegraph();
return 0;
}
```

getmaxx

Syntax `int far getmaxx(void);`

Function The `getmaxx` function returns the maximum horizontal (x) screen coordinate.

File(s) to Include `#include <graphics.h>`

Description The `getmaxx` function gets the maximum screen coordinate in the horizontal direction. This value is usually the maximum horizontal resolution minus 1. For example, in EGA modes with 640-by-350 resolution, the returned value is 640 – 1, or 639. This value occurs because of the way the coordinates are numbered. The x axis begins at 0 and extends 640 pixels to 639. The y axis is numbered in a similar manner.

Value(s) Returned The maximum horizontal (x) screen coordinate is returned when the `getmaxx` function is called.

Related Function(s) `getmaxy` : retrieves the maximum y coordinate

Example In the following example, `getmaxx` retrieves the maximum horizontal, or x, coordinate for the current screen mode. This x coordinate is then displayed on the screen.

```
#include <graphics.h>
#include <stdio.h>
#include <stdlib.h>
#include <conio.h>

int main ()
{
int gdriver = EGA;
int gmode = EGAHI;
int maxx;
char buffer[40];

     /* register EGAVGA_driver and sansserif_font
        */
     /* ... these have been added to graphics.lib
        */
     /* as described in UTIL.DOC
        */

registerbgidriver(EGAVGA_driver);
registerbgifont(sansserif_font);

     /* set EGA high-resolution 16-color mode */

initgraph (&gdriver,&gmode,"");
rectangle (0,0,639,349);

     /* get and display the maximum x value for
        the mode */
```

```
maxx = getmaxx();

settextstyle (SANS_SERIF_FONT,HORIZ_DIR,2);
settextjustify(CENTER_TEXT,CENTER_TEXT);
sprintf (buffer,"The Maximum 'x' value is:
%d",maxx);
outtextxy(320,175,buffer);

     /* Delay and Exit */

outtextxy (320,320,"Press Any Key To Exit");

getch ();

closegraph();
return 0;
}
```

getmaxy

DOS UNIX ANSI C C++

Syntax `int far getmaxy(void);`

Function The `getmaxy` function returns the maximum vertical (y) screen coordinate.

File(s) to Include `#include <graphics.h>`

Description The `getmaxy` function gets the maximum screen coordinate in the vertical direction. This value is usually the maximum vertical resolution minus 1. For example, in EGA modes with 640-by-350 resolution, the returned value is 350 – 1, or 349. This value occurs because of the way the coordinates are numbered. The y axis begins at 0 and extends 350 pixels to 349. The x axis is numbered in a similar manner.

Value(s) Returned The maximum vertical (y) screen coordinate is returned when the `getmaxy` function is called.

Related Function(s) `getmaxx` : retrieves the maximum vertical (y) coordinate

Example In the following example, `getmaxy` retrieves the maximum vertical, or y, coordinate for the current screen mode. This y coordinate is then displayed on the screen.

```
#include <graphics.h>
#include <stdio.h>
#include <stdlib.h>
#include <conio.h>

int main ()
{
int gdriver = EGA;
int gmode = EGAHI;
int maxy;
char buffer[40];

     /* register EGAVGA_driver and sansserif_font
        */
     /* ... these have been added to graphics.lib
        */
     /* as described in UTIL.DOC
        */

registerbgidriver(EGAVGA_driver);
registerbgifont(sansserif_font);

     /* set EGA high-resolution 16-color mode */

initgraph (&gdriver,&gmode,"");
rectangle (0,0,639,349);

     /* get and display the maximum y value for
        the mode */

maxy = getmaxy();

settextstyle (SANS_SERIF_FONT,HORIZ_DIR,2);
settextjustify(CENTER_TEXT,CENTER_TEXT);
sprintf (buffer,"The Maximum 'y' value is :
%d",maxy);
outtextxy(320,175,buffer);

     /* Delay and Exit */

outtextxy (320,320,"Press Any Key To Exit");

getch ();

closegraph();
return 0;
}
```

getmodename

DOS ~~UNIX~~ ~~ANSI C~~ ~~C++~~

Syntax

```
char *far getmodename(int modenumber);
```

`int modenumber;` *Graphics mode number*

Function The `getmodename` function returns the pointer to the string that contains the name of the graphics mode.

File(s) to Include `#include <graphics.h>`

Description The `getmodename` function retrieves the name of the graphics mode specified in the `modenumber` argument. The returned pointer indicates the string containing the mode name, embedded in each driver.

Value(s) Returned The pointer to the string that contains the name of the specified graphics mode is returned when the `getmodename` function is called.

Related Function(s)

`getmaxmode` : returns the maximum mode number
`getmoderange` : returns the range of modes

Example In the following example, `getmodename` displays the name of the retrieved mode. The mode and associated mode name are then displayed.

```
#include <graphics.h>
#include <stdio.h>
#include <stdlib.h>
#include <conio.h>

int main ()
{
int gdriver = EGA;
int gmode = EGAHI;
int mode;
char buffer[40];
     /* register EGAVGA_driver and sansserif_font
        */
     /* ... these have been added to graphics.lib
        */
```

continues

```
    /* as described in UTIL.DOC
       */

registerbgidriver(EGAVGA_driver);
registerbgifont(sansserif_font);

    /* set EGA high-resolution 16-color mode */

initgraph (&gdriver,&gmode,"");
rectangle (0,0,639,349);

    /* get mode number and name - display them */

mode = getgraphmode();
settextstyle(SANS_SERIF_FONT,HORIZ_DIR,2);
settextjustify(CENTER_TEXT,CENTER_TEXT);

sprintf(buffer,"Current Mode Number : %d =>
                %s",mode,getmodename(mode));
outtextxy(320,175,buffer);

    /* Delay and Exit */

outtextxy (320,320,"Press Any Key To Exit");

getch ();

closegraph();
return 0;
}
```

getmoderange

DOS UNIX ANSI C C++

Syntax

```
void far getmoderange(int driver, int far *lowmode,
                      int far *highmode);
```

`int driver;`	*Graphics driver*
`int far *lowmode;`	*Lowest mode*
`int far *highmode;`	*Highest mode*

Function The `getmoderange` function retrieves the range of modes for the specified graphics driver.

File(s) to Include

```
#include <graphics.h>
```

Description

The `getmoderange` function retrieves the high and low mode values for the driver specified in the `driver` argument. The lowest mode value is returned in `*lowmode` and the highest mode value is returned in `*highmode`. If the specified driver is invalid, a –1 is returned in both `*lowmode` and `*highmode`. However, if `driver` is set to –1, the high and low modes for the current driver are retrieved.

Value(s) Returned

There is no return value.

Related Function(s)

`getmodename` : retrieves the name of the current mode

Example

In the following example, `getmoderange` retrieves the minimum and maximum modes (the mode range) for the current screen mode. The mode range is then displayed.

```
#include <graphics.h>
#include <stdio.h>
#include <stdlib.h>
#include <conio.h>

int main ()
{
int gdriver = EGA;
int gmode = EGAHI;
int lowmode, highmode;
char buffer[40];

    /* register EGAVGA_driver and sansserif_font
       */
    /* ... these have been added to graphics.lib
       */
    /* as described in UTIL.DOC
       */

registerbgidriver(EGAVGA_driver);
registerbgifont(sansserif_font);

    /* set EGA high-resolution 16-color mode */
    /* assumes driver is in current directory */

initgraph (&gdriver,&gmode,"");
rectangle (0,0,639,349);
```

continues

```
    /* get and display mode range */

getmoderange(gdriver,&lowmode,&highmode);

settextjustify (CENTER_TEXT,CENTER_TEXT);
sprintf (buffer,"The mode range is : %d to
  %d",lowmode,highmode);
outtextxy (320,175,buffer);

    /* Delay and Exit */

outtextxy (320,320,"Press Any Key To Exit");
getch ();
closegraph();
return 0;
}
```

getpalette

DOS | UNIX | ANSI C | C++

Syntax

```
void far getpalette(struct palettetype far
                        *palette)
```

`struct palettetype far *palette;` *Palette information*

Function The `getpalette` function retrieves information on the current palette.

File(s) to Include `#include <graphics.h>`

Description The `getpalette` function gets the current palette settings. The `*palette` argument points to the structure of type `palettetype` in which the palette information is stored. The syntax for the `palettetype` structure is as follows:

```
#define MAXCOLORS 15

struct palettetype
    {
    unsigned char size;
    signed char colors[MAXCOLORS + 1];
    };
```

The `size` member of the structure indicates the number of color entries in the current palette. The `colors` array contains the color numbers for the palette entry.

Value(s) Returned There is no return value.

Related Function(s)
`setpalette` : modifies one color in the current palette
`setallpalette` : modifies all colors in the palette

Example In the following example, `getpalette` retrieves the values of the current palette. These values are then displayed.

```
#include <graphics.h>
#include <stdio.h>
#include <stdlib.h>
#include <conio.h>

int main ()
{
struct palettetype palette;
int gdriver = EGA;
int gmode = EGAHI;
int x, y;
char buffer[40];

    /* register EGAVGA_driver and sansserif_font
       */
    /* ... these have been added to graphics.lib
       */
    /* as described in UTIL.DOC
       */

registerbgidriver(EGAVGA_driver);
registerbgifont(sansserif_font);

    /* set EGA high-resolution 16-color mode */

initgraph (&gdriver,&gmode,"");
rectangle (0,0,639,349);

    /* get and display palette information */

getpalette (&palette);
y = 50;

settextjustify (CENTER_TEXT,CENTER_TEXT);

sprintf (buffer,"Palette Size : %d",palette.size);
outtextxy (320,25,buffer);
```

continues

```
for (x = 0; x < palette.size; x = x + 1)
     {
     sprintf (buffer,"Color [%02d] : 0x%02X",
                      x,palette.colors[x]);
     outtextxy (320,y,buffer);
     y = y + 15;
     }

     /* Delay and Exit */

settextjustify(CENTER_TEXT,CENTER_TEXT);
outtextxy (320,320,"Press Any Key To Exit");

getch ();

closegraph();
return 0;
}
```

getpalettesize

DOS UNIX ANSI C C++

Syntax `int far getpalettesize(void);`

Function The `getpalettesize` function returns the size of the current palette.

File(s) to Include `#include <graphics.h>`

Description The `getpalettesize` function determines the number of valid palette entries for the current palette considering the graphics mode in use. For 16-color modes, the `getpalettesize` function returns a 16.

Value(s) Returned The number of colors in the current palette is returned when `getpalettesize` is called.

Related Function(s)
`setpalette` : modifies one color in the current palette
`setallpalette` : modifies all colors in the palette

Example In the following example, `getpalettesize` retrieves the size of the current palette. The size is then displayed on the screen.

```
#include <graphics.h>
#include <stdio.h>
#include <stdlib.h>
#include <conio.h>

int main ()
{
int gdriver = EGA;
int gmode = EGAHI;
int palsize;
char buffer[40];

     /* register EGAVGA_driver and sansserif_font
        */
     /* ... these have been added to graphics.lib
        */
     /* as described in UTIL.DOC
        */

registerbgidriver(EGAVGA_driver);
registerbgifont(sansserif_font);

     /* set EGA high-resolution 16-color mode */

initgraph (&gdriver,&gmode,"");
rectangle (0,0,639,349);

     /* get and display palette size */

palsize = getpalettesize ();

settextstyle (SANS_SERIF_FONT,HORIZ_DIR,2);
settextjustify (CENTER_TEXT,CENTER_TEXT);
sprintf (buffer,"The palette size is :
%d",palsize);
outtextxy (320,175,buffer);

     /* Delay and Exit */

outtextxy (320,320,"Press Any Key To Exit");

getch ();

closegraph();
return 0;
}
```

getpixel

DOS UNIX ANSI C C++

Syntax `unsigned far getpixel(int x, int y);`

`int x, y;` *Coordinates of pixel*

Function The `getpixel` function returns the color of the specified pixel.

File(s) to Include `#include <graphics.h>`

Description The `getpixel` function retrieves the color value of the pixel specified by the `x` and `y` arguments. The `x` and `y` arguments specify the screen coordinates of the pixel to evaluate. When evaluating the returned color value, the graphics mode in use must be considered. Tables 8.3 and 8.5, at the start of this chapter, are provided for the evaluation of the returned color value.

Value(s) Returned The color value of the specified pixel is returned when the `getpixel` function is called.

Related Function(s) `putpixel` : sets the specified pixel to the specified color

Example In the following example, `getpixel` evaluates every pixel on the screen. If the pixel has a color value of 15 (white), that pixel is then set to color value 14 (yellow).

```
#include <graphics.h>
#include <stdio.h>
#include <stdlib.h>
#include <conio.h>

int main ()
{
int gdriver = EGA;
int gmode = EGAHI;
int x,y;
int color;
     /* register EGAVGA_driver and sansserif_font
        */
     /* ... these have been added to graphics.lib
        */
```

```
     /* as described in UTIL.DOC
        */

registerbgidriver(EGAVGA_driver);
registerbgifont(sansserif_font);

     /* set EGA high-resolution 16-color mode */

initgraph (&gdriver,&gmode,"");
rectangle (0,0,639,349);
bar3d (50,50,590,300,25,1);

     /* evaluate each pixel on the screen */
     /* if the pixel is 15, set to 14     */

for (x = 0; x <640; x = x+1)
{
     for (y = 0; y < 350; y = y + 1)
          {
          color = getpixel (x,y);
          if (color == 15)
               putpixel (x,y,14);
          }
}
     /* Delay and Exit */

settextjustify(CENTER_TEXT,BOTTOM_TEXT);
outtextxy (320,320,"Press Any Key To Exit");
getch ();
closegraph();
return 0;
}
```

gettextsettings

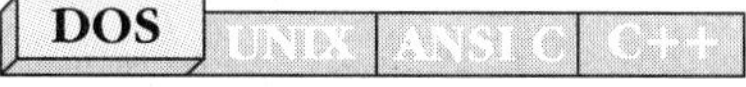

Syntax

```
void far gettextsettings(struct textsettingstype
                                 far *info);
```

`struct textsettingstype far *info;` *Text settings*

Function The `gettextsettings` function retrieves information on the current graphics font.

File(s) to Include `#include <graphics.h>`

Description The `gettextsettings` function gets information about the current graphics font. This information is placed in a structure of type `textsettingstype`, which is pointed to by the `*info` argument. This structure contains information on the current font in use, the text direction, the character size, and horizontal and vertical text justification. The syntax for the `textsettingstype` structure is as follows:

```
struct textsettingstype
     {
     int font;
     int direction;
     int charsize;
     int horiz;
     int vert;
     };
```

Tables 8.10, 8.11, and 8.12 earlier in this chapter list the predefined constants, values, and meanings for the available fonts, text direction, and vertical and horizontal justifications. The `charsize` member contains the integer value representing the magnification factor for the current font.

Value(s) Returned There is no return value.

Related Function(s) `settextstyle` : sets the current font characteristics

Example In the following example, `gettextsettings` retrieves the current text settings including the current font, text direction, character size, and vertical/horizontal justification. These text settings are then displayed on the screen.

```
#include <graphics.h>
#include <stdio.h>
#include <stdlib.h>
#include <conio.h>

int main ()
{
struct textsettingstype textset;
int gdriver = EGA;
int gmode = EGAHI;
char buffer [40];

    /* register EGAVGA_driver and sansserif_font
       */
    /* ... these have been added to graphics.lib
       */
```

```
     /* as described in UTIL.DOC
        */

registerbgidriver (EGAVGA_driver);
registerbgifont (sansserif_font);

     /* set EGA 16-color high resolution video
        mode  */

initgraph (&gdriver,&gmode,"");
rectangle (0,0,639,349);

     /* set, get, and display text settings */

settextstyle(SANS_SERIF_FONT,HORIZ_DIR,2);
settextjustify(CENTER_TEXT,CENTER_TEXT);
gettextsettings(&textset);
sprintf (buffer,"Font Value : %d",textset.font);
outtextxy (320,75,buffer);
sprintf (buffer,"Text Direction :
  %d",textset.direction);
outtextxy (320,125,buffer);
sprintf (buffer,"Character Size :
  %d",textset.charsize);
outtextxy (320,175,buffer);
sprintf (buffer,"Horizontal Justification :
  %d",textset.horiz);
outtextxy (320,225,buffer);
sprintf (buffer,"Vertical Justification :
  %d",textset.vert);
outtextxy (320,275,buffer);

     /* Delay and Exit */
settextjustify(CENTER_TEXT,BOTTOM_TEXT);
outtextxy (320,320,"Press Any Key To Exit");
getch ();
closegraph();
return 0;
}
```

getviewsettings

Syntax `void far getviewsettings(struct viewporttype far *viewport);`

`struct viewporttype far *viewport;` *Viewport information*

Function The `getviewsettings` function retrieves information regarding the current viewport.

File(s) to Include `#include <graphics.h>`

Description The `getviewsettings` function gets information about the current viewport. This information is placed in a structure of type `viewporttype`, which is pointed to by the `*viewport` argument. This structure contains information about the upper left and lower right corners, as well as the setting of the viewport's clipping flag. The syntax for the `viewporttype` structure is as follows:

```
struct viewportype
      {
      int left, top;
      int right, bottom;
      int clip;
      };
```

The `left` and `top` members of the structure define the x and y coordinates, respectively, of the upper left corner of the viewport. In the same manner, the `right` and `bottom` members define the lower-right corner of the viewport. The `clip` member indicates whether graphics output extending beyond the border of the viewport will be clipped. If the `clip` member is a nonzero value, graphics output is clipped at the borders of the viewport. If the `clip` member is 0, output can extend beyond the borders of the viewport.

Value(s) Returned There is no return value.

Related Function(s) `setviewport` : sets the current viewport

Example In the following example, `getviewsettings` retrieves the parameters for the current viewport. These parameters are then displayed on the screen.

```
#include <graphics.h>
#include <stdio.h>
#include <stdlib.h>
#include <conio.h>
```

```
int main ()
{
struct viewporttype viewset;
int gdriver = EGA;
int gmode = EGAHI;
char buffer[40];

     /* register EGAVGA_driver and sansserif_font
        */
     /* ... these have been added to graphics.lib
        */
     /* as described in UTIL.DOC
        */

registerbgidriver (EGAVGA_driver);
registerbgifont (sansserif_font);

     /* set EGA 16-color high resolution video
        mode  */

initgraph (&gdriver,&gmode,"");
rectangle (0,0,639,349);

     /* get and display current viewport settings
         */

getviewsettings (&viewset);
settextjustify (CENTER_TEXT,CENTER_TEXT);
sprintf (buffer,"Upper left corner : %d,
  %d",viewset.left,viewset.top);
outtextxy (320,100,buffer);
sprintf (buffer,"Lower right corner : %d,
  %d",viewset.right,viewset.bottom);
outtextxy (320,150,buffer);
sprintf (buffer,"Clipping Value :
%d",viewset.clip);
outtextxy (320,200,buffer);

     /* Delay and Exit */

settextjustify(CENTER_TEXT,BOTTOM_TEXT);
outtextxy (320,320,"Press Any Key To Exit");
getch ();
closegraph();
return 0;
}
```

getx

DOS | UNIX | ANSI C | C++

Syntax `int far getx(void);`

Function The `getx` function returns the horizontal (x) position of the graphics cursor.

File(s) to Include `#include <graphics.h>`

Description The `getx` function retrieves the position, in the horizontal direction, of the graphics cursor. The returned value specifies the horizontal pixel location (the x coordinate), relative to the current viewport, of the graphics cursor.

Value(s) Returned The horizontal (x) coordinate of the current graphics cursor position is returned when the `getx` function is called.

Related Function(s) `gety` : returns the y position of the graphics cursor

Example In the following example, `getx` retrieves the current horizontal, or x, coordinate of the cursor position. This x coordinate is displayed along with the y coordinate.

```
#include <graphics.h>
#include <stdio.h>
#include <stdlib.h>
#include <conio.h>

int main ()
{
int gdriver = EGA;
int gmode = EGAHI;
char buffer [40];

      /* register EGAVGA_driver and sansserif_font
         */
      /* ... these have been added to graphics.lib
         */
      /* as described in UTIL.DOC
         */

registerbgidriver (EGAVGA_driver);
registerbgifont (sansserif_font);
```

```
 /* set EGA 16-color high resolution video mode*/
initgraph (&gdriver,&gmode,"");
rectangle (0,0,639,349);

     /* set and display position of cursor */

moveto (320,175);
settextjustify (CENTER_TEXT,CENTER_TEXT);

sprintf (buffer,"The 'x' position of cursor is
  %d",getx());
outtextxy (320,175,buffer);

sprintf (buffer,"The 'y' position of cursor is
  %d",gety());
outtextxy (320,225,buffer);

     /* Delay and Exit */

settextjustify(CENTER_TEXT,BOTTOM_TEXT);
outtextxy (320,320,"Press Any Key To Exit");

getch ();
closegraph();
return 0;
}
```

gety

DOS UNIX ANSI C C++

Syntax `int far gety(void);`

Function The `gety` function returns the vertical (y) coordinate of the current graphics cursor position.

File(s) to Include #include <graphics.h>

Description The `gety` function retrieves the vertical position of the graphics cursor. The value returned by this function specifies the vertical pixel location (the y coordinate), relative to the current viewport, of the graphics cursor.

Value(s) Returned The vertical (y) coordinate of the current graphics cursor position is returned when the `gety` function is called.

Related Function(s)

`getx` : gets the x coordinate of the graphics cursor

Example

In the following example, `gety` retrieves the vertical, or y, coordinate of the current cursor position. The y coordinate is then displayed along with the x coordinate.

```
#include <graphics.h>
#include <stdio.h>
#include <stdlib.h>
#include <conio.h>

int main ()
{
int gdriver = EGA;
int gmode = EGAHI;
char buffer [40];

     /* register EGAVGA_driver and sansserif_font
        */
     /* ... these have been added to graphics.lib
        */
     /* as described in UTIL.DOC
        */

registerbgidriver (EGAVGA_driver);
registerbgifont (sansserif_font);

     /* set EGA 16-color high resolution video
        mode  */

initgraph (&gdriver,&gmode,"");
rectangle (0,0,639,349);

     /* set and display position of cursor */

moveto (320,175);
settextjustify (CENTER_TEXT,CENTER_TEXT);

sprintf (buffer,"The 'x' position of cursor is
 %d",getx());
outtextxy (320,175,buffer);

sprintf (buffer,"The 'y' position of cursor is
 %d",gety());
outtextxy (320,225,buffer);

     /* Delay and Exit */

settextjustify(CENTER_TEXT,BOTTOM_TEXT);
outtextxy (320,320,"Press Any Key To Exit");
```

```
getch ();
closegraph();
return 0;
}
```

graphdefaults

DOS UNIX ANSI C C++

Syntax `void far graphdefaults(void);`

Function The `graphdefaults` function resets all settings in the graphics environment to their default values.

File(s) to Include `#include <graphics.h>`

Description The `graphdefaults` function resets all graphics settings to their original, or default, values. This function resets the viewport to cover the entire screen, moves the graphics cursor to position (0,0), resets the current palette to its default colors, resets the background color and current color to their default values, resets the fill style and pattern to their defaults, and resets the text font and justification.

Value(s) Returned There is no return value.

Related Function(s) `initgraph` : initializes the graphics environment

Example In the following example, `graphdefaults` resets all altered values to their default settings.

```
#include <graphics.h>
#include <stdio.h>
#include <stdlib.h>
#include <conio.h>

int main ()
{
int gdriver = EGA;
int gmode = EGAHI;
```

```
    /* register EGAVGA_driver and sansserif_font
       */
    /* ... these have been added to graphics.lib
       */
    /* as described in UTIL.DOC
       */

registerbgidriver (EGAVGA_driver);
registerbgifont (sansserif_font);

    /* set EGA 16-color high resolution video mode
       */

initgraph (&gdriver,&gmode,"");
rectangle (0,0,639,349);

    /* modify settings - call graphdefaults to
       reset */
    /* these to the defaults - use the defaults
       */

setcolor (4);
setviewport (20,20,100,100,1);
settextstyle (SANS_SERIF_FONT,HORIZ_DIR,2);
settextjustify (CENTER_TEXT,CENTER_TEXT);

graphdefaults ();

line (0,0,639,349);
outtextxy(320,175,"EXAMPLE OF graphdefaults();");

     /* Delay and Exit */

settextjustify(CENTER_TEXT,BOTTOM_TEXT);
outtextxy (320,320,"Press Any Key To Exit");

getch ();
closegraph();
return 0;
}
```

grapherrormsg

DOS | UNIX | ANSI C | C++

Syntax `char *far grapherrormsg(int errorcode);`

`int errorcode;` *Error code*

Function The `grapherrormsg` function returns the pointer to the error message string.

File(s) to Include `#include <graphics.h>`

Description The `grapherrormsg` function gets the pointer to the error message string for a specified error code. The `errorcode` argument specifies the value of the error code. The `graphresult` function must be used to retrieve the error code used for the `errorcode` argument.

Value(s) Returned The pointer to the error message string is returned when the `grapherrormsg` function is called.

Related Function(s) `graphresult` : returns an error code

Example In the following example, `grapherrormsg` returns the pointer to an error message string. This pointer is then used to display the error string.

```
#include <graphics.h>
#include <stdio.h>
#include <stdlib.h>
#include <conio.h>

int main ()
{
int gdriver = EGA;
int gmode = EGAHI;
int errorcode;
char buffer [40];

     /* register EGAVGA_driver and sansserif_font
        */
     /* ... these have been added to graphics.lib
        */
     /* as described in UTIL.DOC
        */

registerbgidriver (EGAVGA_driver);
registerbgifont (sansserif_font);

     /* set EGA 16-color high resolution video
        mode  */

initgraph (&gdriver,&gmode,"");
rectangle (0,0,639,349);
```

```
     /* draw rectangle-get error message-display
        code */

rectangle (50,50,590,200);
errorcode = graphresult ();

sprintf (buffer,"Error Message :
  %s",grapherrormsg(errorcode));
settextjustify (CENTER_TEXT,CENTER_TEXT);
outtextxy (320,175,buffer);

     /* Delay and Exit */

settextjustify(CENTER_TEXT,BOTTOM_TEXT);
outtextxy (320,320,"Press Any Key To Exit");

getch ();

closegraph();
return 0;
}
```

_graphfreemem

DOS | UNIX | ANSI C | C++

Syntax

```
void far _graphfreemem(void far*ptr, unsigned
                       size);

void far *ptr;          Pointer
unsigned size;          Size of buffer
```

Function The `_graphfreemem` function frees graphics memory.

File(s) to Include `#include <graphics.h>`

Description The `_graphfreemem` function is used by the graphics library to deallocate memory previously reserved by a call to the `_graphgetmem` function. Because this function is provided for use by the graphics library, no example is provided for this function. However, it is possible to control the graphics library memory management by declaring a function similar to the `_graphfreemem` function.

Value(s) Returned There is no return value.

Related Function(s) `_graphgetmem` : allocates graphics memory

_graphgetmem

DOS UNIX ANSI C C++

Syntax

```
void far * far _graphgetmem(unsigned size);
unsigned size;            Size of buffer
```

Function The `_graphgetmem` function allocates graphics memory.

File(s) to Include `#include <graphics.h>`

Description The `_graphgetmem` function allocates graphics memory for internal buffers, graphics drivers, and fonts. This function is for use by the graphics library; therefore, no example is provided. However, it is still possible to manage the graphics memory by creating a similar version of this function.

Value(s) Returned There is no return value.

Related Function(s) `_graphfreemem` : frees graphics memory

graphresult

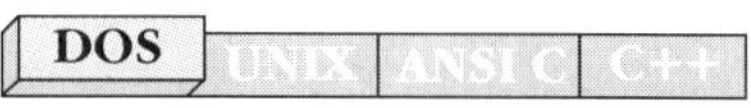

Syntax

```
int far graphresult(void);
```

Function The `graphresult` function returns the error code for the latest unsuccessful graphics call.

File(s) to Include `#include <graphics.h>`

Description The `graphresult` function retrieves and returns the error code for the last unsuccessful graphics call. In addition, it resets the error level to 0, or `grOk`. Table 8.13 lists the possible return values and constants for the `graphresult` function.

Table 8.13. Error codes.

Code	*Constant*	*Meaning*
0	`grOK`	No error
–1	`grNoInitGraph`	Graphics not initiated
–2	`grNotDetected`	No graphics hardware detected
–3	`grFileNotFound`	Driver file not found
–4	`grInvalidDriver`	Invalid driver file
–5	`grNoLoadMem`	No memory to load driver
–6	`grNoScanMem`	No memory in scan fill
–7	`grNoFloodMem`	No memory in `floodfill`
–8	`grFontNotFound`	Font file not found
–9	`grNoFontMem`	No memory to load font
–10	`grInvalidMode`	Invalid graphics mode
–11	`grError`	Graphics error
–12	`grIOerror`	Graphics IO error
–13	`grInvalidFont`	Invalid font file
–14	`grInvalidFontNum`	Invalid font number
–15	`grInvalidDeviceNum`	Invalid device number
–18	`grInvalidVersion`	Invalid version number

Value(s) Returned The current graphics error code is returned when the `graphresult` function is called.

Related Function(s) `grapherrormsg` : returns the pointer to the error string

Example In the following example, `graphresult` retrieves the status of the last graphics function. If an error occurs, an appropriate message is displayed. Similarly, a message is displayed if no error occurs.

```
#include <graphics.h>
#include <stdio.h>
#include <stdlib.h>
#include <conio.h>

int main ()
{
int gdriver = EGA;
int gmode = EGAHI;
int errorcode;
char buffer [40];
```

```
     /* register EGAVGA_driver and sansserif_font
        */
     /* ... these have been added to graphics.lib
        */
     /* as described in UTIL.DOC
        */

registerbgidriver (EGAVGA_driver);
registerbgifont (sansserif_font);

     /* set EGA 16-color high resolution video
        mode */

initgraph (&gdriver,&gmode,"");
rectangle (0,0,639,349);

     /* draw figure - get error message - display
        code */

rectangle (50,50,590,200);
ellipse (320,125,0,360,270,75);
errorcode = graphresult ();
if (errorcode == 0)
     sprintf (buffer,"No Error - Error Code :
  %d",errorcode);
if (errorcode != 0)
     sprintf (buffer,"Error - Error Code :
  %d",errorcode);
settextjustify (CENTER_TEXT,CENTER_TEXT);
outtextxy (320,175,buffer);

     /* Delay and Exit */

settextjustify(CENTER_TEXT,BOTTOM_TEXT);
outtextxy (320,320,"Press Any Key To Exit");
getch ();
closegraph();
return 0;
}
```

imagesize

Syntax

```
unsigned far imagesize(int left, int top, int
                          right, int bottom);
```

```
int left, top;          Upper left corner of image
int right, bottom;      Lower right corner of image
```

Function The `imagesize` function returns the required number of bytes to store the specified image.

File(s) to Include `#include <graphics.h>`

Description The `imagesize` function determines the buffer size needed to store an image with the `getimage` function. The `left` and `top` arguments define the x and y coordinates of the upper left corner of the rectangular image. Similarly, the `right` and `bottom` arguments define the lower right corner of the image. The `imagesize` function returns the actual number of bytes needed if the required size is less than 64K –1 bytes. If this is not the case, the returned value is 0xFFFF, or –1.

Value(s) Returned The number of bytes required to store the specified image is returned when the `imagesize` function is called.

Related Function(s)
`getimage` : stores as image to memory
`putimage` : places an image on the screen

Example In the following example, `imagesize` sizes the buffer used to store the rectangular image. This image is then placed on the screen several times in a diagonal fashion.

```
#include <graphics.h>
#include <stdio.h>
#include <stdlib.h>
#include <conio.h>

int main ()
{
int gdriver = EGA;
int gmode = EGAHI;
void *image;
unsigned int imsize;
int x, y;

    /* register EGAVGA_driver and sansserif_font
       */
    /* ... these have been added to graphics.lib
       */
    /* as described in UTIL.DOC
       */

registerbgidriver(EGAVGA_driver);
```

```
registerbgifont(sansserif_font);

     /* set EGA high-resolution 16-color mode */

initgraph (&gdriver,&gmode,"");
rectangle (0,0,639,349);

     /* draw and store an image - then place it */
     /* in a diagonal fashion over the screen   */

setfillstyle(SOLID_FILL,14);
bar (280,135,360,215);
setfillstyle(SOLID_FILL,1);
fillellipse(320,175,40,40);

imsize = imagesize(280,135,360,215);
image = malloc(imsize);
getimage(280,135,360,215,image);

cleardevice ();
rectangle (0,0,639,349);
y = 20;

for (x=20; x<550; x=x+60)
{
     putimage (x,y,image,COPY_PUT);
     y = y + 25;
}

     /* Delay and Exit */

settextjustify(CENTER_TEXT,BOTTOM_TEXT);
outtextxy (320,320,"Press Any Key To Exit");

getch ();

closegraph();
return 0;
}
```

initgraph

Syntax

```
void far initgraph(int far *driver, int far *mode,
                   char far *path);
```

continues

```
int far *driver;        Graphics driver
int far *mode;          Graphics mode
int far *path;          Path to the driver
```

Function The `initgraph` function initializes the graphics system.

File(s) to Include `#include <graphics.h>`

Description The `initgraph` function loads or validates a graphics driver and places the video system into graphics mode. This function must be called before any graphics functions that produce output are used. Table 8.1 at the start of this chapter lists the graphics drivers provided in the Borland environment. These constants and values are used for the `*driver` argument. If `*driver` is set to DETECT, or 0, the `detectgraph` function is called and an appropriate driver and graphics mode are selected. Setting `*driver` to any other predefined value initiates the loading of the corresponding graphics driver.

Table 8.2 at the start of this chapter lists the graphics modes associated with the drivers listed in Table 8.1. These values and constants are used for the `*mode` argument. These values and constants, should, of course, correspond to the driver specified in the `*driver` argument.

The `*path` argument specifies the directory path where the graphics drivers are located. The `initgraph` function will search this path for the driver first. Then, if the driver is not found, the current directory will be searched. When the `*path` argument is null, only the current directory is searched.

One way to avoid having to load the driver from the disk each time the program is run is to "link" the appropriate driver to the executable program. The examples in this book use this format. However, the drivers must first be made into a .OBJ file, added to the `graphics.lib` file, and then registered in the current program. The UTIL.DOC file, included in the distribution disks, explains in detail how to create the driver object files and add them to the `graphics.lib` file.

Value(s) Returned When the `initgraph` function is called, the internal error code is set. If the `initgraph` function is successful, the code is set to 0. If not, the code is set as follows:

```
-2   grNotDetected      Graphics card not found
-3   grFileNotFound     Driver file not found
```

```
-4    grInvalidDriver       Driver file invalid
-5    grNoLoadMem           Not enough memory to load
                            driver
```

Related Function(s) closegraph : closes the graphics system

Example In the following examples, initgraph initializes the graphics environment. The current mode and mode name are then displayed.

```
#include <graphics.h>
#include <stdio.h>
#include <stdlib.h>
#include <conio.h>

int main ()
{
int gdriver = EGA;
int gmode = EGAHI;
int mode;
char buffer [40];

     /* register EGAVGA_driver and sansserif_font
        */
     /* ... these have been added to graphics.lib
        */
     /* as described in UTIL.DOC
        */

registerbgidriver(EGAVGA_driver);
registerbgifont(sansserif_font);

     /* set EGA high-resolution 16-color mode */

initgraph (&gdriver,&gmode,"");
setbkcolor (1);
rectangle (0,0,639,349);

     /* get and display the graphics mode */

settextjustify (CENTER_TEXT,CENTER_TEXT);
outtextxy (320,150,"Graphics System Intialized");
mode = getgraphmode();
sprintf (buffer,"Mode : %d",mode);
outtextxy (320,200,buffer);
sprintf (buffer,"Mode Name :
%s",getmodename(mode));
outtextxy (320,250,buffer);
```

continues

```
        /* Delay and Exit */

settextjustify(CENTER_TEXT,BOTTOM_TEXT);
outtextxy (320,330,"Press Any Key To Exit and
Close Graphics
System");

getch ();
closegraph();
return 0;
}
```

installuserdriver

DOS UNIX ANSI C C++

Syntax

```
int far installuserdriver(char far *name, int huge
                                (*detect)(void));
```

`char far *name;` *New device driver file*

`int huge (*detect)(void));` *Pointer to optional autodetect*

Function The `installuserdriver` function installs a vendor-added device driver to the BGI device driver table.

File(s) to Include `#include <graphics.h>`

Description The `installuserdriver` function allows the user to add additional, third-party device drivers to the internal BGI device driver table. The `*name` argument defines the name of the new .BGI driver file. The `*detect` parameter is a pointer to an optional `autodetect` function that might be provided with the new driver. The `autodetect` function is expected to receive no parameters and return an integer value. Because this function requires a third-party device driver, no example is provided.

Value(s) Returned The driver number parameter, which would be passed to the `initgraph` function to select the new driver, is returned when the `installuserdriver` function is called.

Related Function(s) `registerbgidriver` : registers a driver file

installuserfont

DOS UNIX ANSI C C++

Syntax

```
int far installuserfont(char far *name);

char far *name;              Path to font file
```

Function The `installuserfont` function loads a font file that is not built into the BGI system.

File(s) to Include

```
#include <graphics.h>
```

Description The `installuserfont` function loads a stroked font file that is not provided with the BGI system. The `*name` parameter specifies the name of the font file to load. The graphics system can have up to twenty fonts installed at any time. No example is provided for this function because no user font file is available for loading.

Value(s) Returned The font identification number, used to select the new font through the `settextstyle` function, is returned when the `installuserfont` function is called. If the internal font table is full, –11 is returned, indicating an error.

Related Function(s) `settextstyle` : sets the font characteristics

line

Syntax

```
void far line(int x1, int y1, int x2, int y2);

int x1, y1;                  Starting point
int x2, y2;                  Ending point
```

Function The `line` function draws a line between the two specified points.

File(s) to Include

```
#include <graphics.h>
```

continues

Description The `line` function connects two points with a line. The first point is specified by the `x1` and `y1` arguments. The second point is specified by the `x2` and `y2` arguments. The connecting line is drawn using the current line style, thickness, and color. The position of the graphics cursor is not affected by the `line` function.

Value(s) Returned There is no return value.

Related Function(s)

`lineto` : draws a line from the graphics cursor to a specified point

`linerel` : draws a line a specified distance relative to the graphics cursor

Example In the following example, `line` draws a line between two points which bounce around the screen. The color of the line changes every 500 iterations.

```
#include <graphics.h>
#include <stdio.h>
#include <stdlib.h>
#include <conio.h>

int main ()
{
int gdriver = EGA;
int gmode = EGAHI;
int x1, y1;
int x2, y2;
int x1dir, y1dir;
int x2dir, y2dir;
int color;
int counter;

     /* register EGAVGA_driver and sansserif_font
        */
     /* ... these have been added to graphics.lib
        */
     /* as described in UTIL.DOC
        */

registerbgidriver (EGAVGA_driver);
registerbgifont (sansserif_font);

     /* set EGA 16-color high resolution video
        mode  */

initgraph (&gdriver,&gmode,"");
rectangle (0,0,639,349);
```

```
          /* draw line which bounces around on screen
             */

     x1 = 300;
     y1 = 175;
     x2 = 300;
     y2 = 200;

     x1dir = 1;
     y1dir = 1;
     x2dir = 1;
     y2dir = 1;

     color = 1;
     counter = 0;

     do
     {
          setcolor (color);
          line (x1,y1,x2,y2);
          if (x1 == 638)
               x1dir = -1;
          if (x1 == 1)
               x1dir = 1;
          if (x2 == 638)
               x2dir = -1;
          if (x2 == 1)
               x2dir = 1;
          if (y1 == 348)
               y1dir = -1;
          if (y1 == 1)
               y1dir = 1;
          if (y2 == 348)
               y2dir = -1;
          if (y2 == 1)
               y2dir = 1;

          x1 = x1 + x1dir;
          x2 = x1 + x2dir;
          y1 = y1 + y1dir;
          y2 = y2 + y2dir;

          counter = counter + 1;

          if (counter == 500)
               {
               counter = 0;
               color = color + 1;
               }

          if (color > 15)
               color = 1;
```

continues

```
} while (!kbhit());

     /* Delay and Exit */

closegraph();
return 0;
}
```

linerel

DOS UNIX ANSI C C++

Syntax

```
void far linerel(int dx, int dy);

int dx, dy;
```

Relative distance to draw line

Function The `linerel` function draws a line a relative distance from the current graphics cursor position.

File(s) to Include

```
#include <graphics.h>
```

Description The `linerel` function draws a line a predetermined distance and direction from the current position of the graphics cursor. The `dx` argument specifies the relative number of pixels to travel in the horizontal direction. The `dy` argument specifies the relative number of pixels to travel in the vertical direction. These arguments can be either positive or negative values. The line is drawn in the current color, line style, and line thickness from the current graphics cursor position through the specified relative distance. When the line is finished, the cursor position is updated to the endpoint of the line.

Value(s) Returned There is no return value.

Related Function(s)

`line` : draws a line between two specified points

`lineto` : draws a line from the cursor position to the specified point

Example In the following example, `linerel` draws several lines (in the shape of an asterisk) relative to a point which bounces around the screen. The current color changes each time the asterisk is drawn.

```
#include <graphics.h>
#include <stdio.h>
#include <stdlib.h>
#include <conio.h>

int main ()
{
int gdriver = EGA;
int gmode = EGAHI;
int x, y;
int xdir, ydir;
int color;

    /* register EGAVGA_driver and sansserif_font
       */
    /* ... these have been added to graphics.lib
       */
    /* as described in UTIL.DOC
       */

registerbgidriver (EGAVGA_driver);
registerbgifont (sansserif_font);

    /* set EGA 16-color high resolution video mode
       */

initgraph (&gdriver,&gmode,"");
rectangle (0,0,639,349);

   /* draw asterisk which bounces around on screen
      */

x = 320;
y = 175;

xdir = 1;
ydir = 1;
color = 1;
do
{
     setcolor (color);
     moveto (x,y);
     linerel (0,5);
     linerel (5,5);
     linerel (5,0);
     linerel (0,-5);
     linerel (-5,-5);
     linerel (-5,0);
     linerel (-5,5);
     linerel (5,-5);
     linerel (5,-5);
```

continues

```
        if (x == 638)
            xdir = -1;
        if (x == 1)
            xdir = 1;
        if (y == 348)
            ydir = -1;
        if (y == 1)
            ydir = 1;

        x = x + xdir;
        y = y + ydir;

        color = color + 1;

        if (color > 15)
            color = 1;

    } while (!kbhit());

        /* Delay and Exit */

    closegraph();
    return 0;
    }
```

lineto

DOS | UNIX | ANSI C | C++

Syntax `void far lineto(int x, int y);`

`int x, y;` *Endpoint of line*

Function The `lineto` function draws a line from the current position of the graphics cursor to the point specified by `x, y`.

File(s) to Include `#include <graphics.h>`

Description The `lineto` function draws a line from the current position of the graphics cursor to the point specified by the `x` and `y` arguments. The line is drawn using the current color, line style, and line thickness. After the line has been drawn, the graphics cursor position is set to the position specified by the `x` and `y` arguments (the endpoint of the line).

Value(s) Returned There is no return value.

Related Function(s)

`line` : draws a line between two specified points
`linerel` : draws a line a relative distance from the graphics cursor

Example In the following example, `moveto` and `lineto` draw a line between two points which bounce around the screen. The current color changes every 100 iterations.

```
#include <graphics.h>
#include <stdio.h>
#include <stdlib.h>
#include <conio.h>

int main ()
{
int gdriver = EGA;
int gmode = EGAHI;
int x1, y1;
int x2, y2;
int x1dir, y1dir;
int x2dir, y2dir;
int color;
int counter;

      /* register EGAVGA_driver and sansserif_font
         */
      /* ... these have been added to graphics.lib
         */
      /* as described in UTIL.DOC
         */

registerbgidriver (EGAVGA_driver);
registerbgifont (sansserif_font);

      /* set EGA 16-color high resolution video
         mode   */

initgraph (&gdriver,&gmode,"");
rectangle (0,0,639,349);

      /* draw line which bounces around on screen
         */

x1 = 100;
y1 = 1;
x2 = 1;
y2 = 130;

x1dir = 1;
y1dir = 1;
```

continues

```
x2dir = 1;
y2dir = 1;
color = 1;
counter = 0;
do
{
     setcolor (color);
     moveto (x1,y1);
     lineto (x2,y2);
     if (x1 == 638)
          x1dir = -1;
     if (x1 == 1)
          x1dir = 1;
     if (x2 == 638)
          x2dir = -1;
     if (x2 == 1)
          x2dir = 1;
     if (y1 == 348)
          y1dir = -1;
     if (y1 == 1)
          y1dir = 1;
     if (y2 == 348)
          y2dir = -1;
     if (y2 == 1)
          y2dir = 1;
     x1 = x1 + x1dir;
     x2 = x1 + x2dir;
     y1 = y1 + y1dir;
     y2 = y2 + y2dir;

     counter = counter + 1;

     if (counter == 100)
          {
          color = color + 1;
          counter = 0;
          }

     if (color > 15)
          color = 1;

} while (!kbhit());

     /* Delay and Exit */

closegraph();
return 0;
}
```

moverel

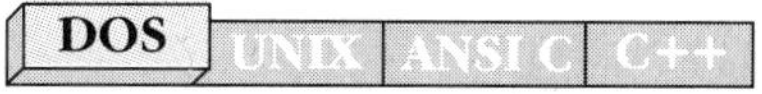

Syntax `void far moverel(int dx, int dy);`

`int dx, dy;` *Distance to move cursor*

Function The `moverel` function moves the graphics cursor a relative distance from the present location.

File(s) to Include `#include <graphics.h>`

Description The `moverel` function moves the position of the graphics cursor a relative distance as specified by the `dx` and `dy` arguments. The `dx` argument defines the relative distance to move in the horizontal direction, whereas the `dy` argument defines the relative distance to move in the vertical direction. These values can be either positive or negative. No drawing takes place as the cursor is moved.

Value(s) Returned There is no return value.

Related Function(s) `moveto` : moves the cursor to the specified point

Example In the following example, `moverel` moves the cursor a relative distance each iteration. `lineto` draws a line from the new cursor position to the center of the screen. The current color changes every 50 iterations.

```
#include <graphics.h>
#include <stdio.h>
#include <stdlib.h>
#include <conio.h>

int main ()
{
int gdriver = EGA;
int gmode = EGAHI;
int x, y;
int xdir, ydir;
int color;
int counter;
```

continues

```
     /* register EGAVGA_driver and sansserif_font
        */
     /* ... these have been added to graphics.lib
        */
     /* as described in UTIL.DOC
        */

registerbgidriver (EGAVGA_driver);
registerbgifont (sansserif_font);

     /* set EGA 16-color high resolution video
        mode  */

initgraph (&gdriver,&gmode,"");
rectangle (0,0,639,349);

     /* move cursor around screen - draw line to
        center */
moveto (1,175);
xdir = 1;
ydir = 1;
color = 1;
do
{
     setcolor (color);
     moverel (xdir,ydir);
     x = getx();
     y = gety();
     lineto (320,175);
     moveto (x,y);
     if (x == 638)
          xdir = -1;
     if (x == 1)
          xdir = 1;
     if (y == 348)
          ydir = -1;
     if (y == 1)
          ydir = 1;
     counter = counter + 1;
     if (counter > 50)
          {
          counter = 0;
          color = color + 1;
          }
     if (color > 15)
          color = 1;
} while (!kbhit());
     /* Delay and Exit */
closegraph();
return 0;
}
```

moveto

DOS UNIX ANSI C C++

Syntax `void far moveto(int x, int y);`

`int x, y;` *Point to move cursor*

Function The `moveto` function moves the graphics cursor to the specified point.

File(s) to Include `#include <graphics.h>`

Description The `moveto` function places the graphics cursor at the point specified by the `x` and `y` arguments. As the cursor is moved from its previous position to the point specified by the `x` and `y` arguments, no drawing takes place.

Value(s) Returned There is no return value.

Related Function(s) `moverel` : moves the cursor a relative distance

Example In the following example, `moveto` moves the cursor to a predetermined point which bounces around the screen. A line is then drawn to the center of the screen with `lineto`. The line color changes every 25 iterations.

```
#include <graphics.h>
#include <stdio.h>
#include <stdlib.h>
#include <conio.h>

int main ()
{
int gdriver = EGA;
int gmode = EGAHI;
int x, y;
int xdir, ydir;
int color;
int counter;
     /* register EGAVGA_driver and sansserif_font
        */
     /* ... these have been added to graphics.lib
        */
```

continues

```
     /* as described in UTIL.DOC
        */

registerbgidriver (EGAVGA_driver);
registerbgifont (sansserif_font);

     /* set EGA 16-color high resolution video
        mode  */

initgraph (&gdriver,&gmode,"");
rectangle (0,0,639,349);

     /* move cursor around screen - draw line to
        center */

x = 1;
y = 175;
xdir = 1;
ydir = 1;
color = 1;

do
{
     setcolor (color);
     moveto (x,y);
     lineto (320,175);

     if (x == 638)
          xdir = -1;
     if (x == 1)
          xdir = 1;
     if (y == 348)
          ydir = -1;
     if (y == 1)
          ydir = 1;
     x = x + xdir;
     y = y + ydir;
     counter = counter + 1;
     if (counter > 25)
          {
          counter = 0;
          color = color + 1;
          }
     if (color > 15)
          color = 1;
} while (!kbhit());
     /* Delay and Exit */
closegraph();
return 0;
}
```

outtext

DOS UNIX ANSI C C++

Syntax

```
void far outtext(char far *textstring);
```

`char far *textstring;` *String to display*

Function The `outtext` function displays a text string at the current graphics cursor position.

File(s) to Include `#include <graphics.h>`

Description The `outtext` function displays a text string. The `*textstring` argument defines the text string to display. The text string is displayed at the current graphics cursor position using the current color and text font, direction, settings, and justifications. The cursor position remains unchanged unless the current horizontal justification is `LEFT_TEXT` and the text direction is `HORIZ_DIR`. When this is the case, the cursor position is placed in the x direction the pixel width of the text string. In addition, when you use the default font, any text which extends outside the current viewport is truncated.

Although the `outtext` function is designed for unformatted text, formatted text can be displayed by using a character buffer and the `sprintf` function. This method of displaying formatted text with the `outtext` and `outtextxy` functions is demonstrated in many examples in this chapter.

Value(s) Returned There is no return value.

Related Function(s) `outtextxy` : displays a string at the specified location

Example In the following example, `outtext` displays both vertical and horizontal text using the sans serif font.

```
#include <graphics.h>
#include <stdio.h>
#include <stdlib.h>
#include <conio.h>

int main ()
{
```

continues

```
int gdriver = EGA;
int gmode = EGAHI;

     /* register EGAVGA_driver and sansserif_font
        */
     /* ... these have been added to graphics.lib
        */
     /* as described in UTIL.DOC
        */

registerbgidriver (EGAVGA_driver);
registerbgifont (sansserif_font);

     /* set EGA 16-color high resolution video
        mode  */

initgraph (&gdriver,&gmode,"");
rectangle (0,0,639,349);

     /* display text using outtext function */

settextstyle (SANS_SERIF_FONT,HORIZ_DIR,2);
settextjustify (CENTER_TEXT,CENTER_TEXT);

moveto (320,175);
outtext ("Horizontal Text");

settextstyle (SANS_SERIF_FONT,VERT_DIR,2);
moveto (20,175);
outtext ("Vertical Text");
moveto (619,175);
outtext ("Vertical Text");

     /* Delay and Exit */

settextstyle (SANS_SERIF_FONT,HORIZ_DIR,2);
settextjustify(CENTER_TEXT,BOTTOM_TEXT);
outtextxy (320,320,"Press Any Key To Exit");

getch ();
closegraph();
return 0;
}
```

outtextxy

DOS | UNIX | ANSI C | C++

Syntax
```
void far outtextxy(int x, int y, char far
                   *textstring);
```

```
int x, y;                    Location to place text
char far *textstring;        String to display
```

Function The `outtextxy` function displays a text string at the specified location.

File(s) to Include `#include <graphics.h>`

Description The `outtextxy` function displays a text string. The `*textstring` argument defines the text string to display. The text string is displayed at the position specified in the `x` and `y` arguments using the current color and text font, direction, settings, and justifications. When you use the default font, any text that extends outside the current viewport is truncated.

Although the `outtextxy` function is designed for unformatted text, formatted text can be displayed by using a character buffer and the `sprintf` function. This method of displaying formatted text with the `outtext` and `outtextxy` functions is demonstrated in many of the examples in this chapter.

Value(s) Returned There is no return value.

Related Function(s) `outtext` : displays text at the graphics cursor position

Example In the following example, `outtextxy` displays both vertical and horizontal text using the sans serif font.

```
#include <graphics.h>
#include <stdio.h>
#include <stdlib.h>
#include <conio.h>

int main ()
{
int gdriver = EGA;
int gmode = EGAHI;

     /* register EGAVGA_driver and sansserif_font
        */
     /* ... these have been added to graphics.lib
        */
     /* as described in UTIL.DOC
        */

registerbgidriver (EGAVGA_driver);
registerbgifont (sansserif_font);
```

continues

```
     /* set EGA 16-color high resolution video
        mode  */

initgraph (&gdriver,&gmode,"");
rectangle (0,0,639,349);

     /* display text using outtextxy function */

settextstyle (SANS_SERIF_FONT,HORIZ_DIR,2);
settextjustify (CENTER_TEXT,CENTER_TEXT);
outtextxy (320,175,"Horizontal Text");

settextstyle (SANS_SERIF_FONT,VERT_DIR,2);
outtextxy (20,175,"Vertical Text");
outtextxy (619,175,"Vertical Text");

     /* Delay and Exit */

settextstyle (SANS_SERIF_FONT,HORIZ_DIR,2);
settextjustify(CENTER_TEXT,BOTTOM_TEXT);
outtextxy (320,320,"Press Any Key To Exit");
getch ();
closegraph();
return 0;
}
```

pieslice

DOS UNIX ANSI C C++

Syntax

```
void far pieslice(int x, int y, int startangle,
                  int endangle, int radius);
```

`int x, y;`	*Center of pie*
`int startangle;`	*Starting angle*
`int endangle;`	*Ending angle*
`int radius;`	*Radius of pie*

Function The `pieslice` function draws a filled circular pie slice.

File(s) to Include `#include <graphics.h>`

Description The `pieslice` function draws and fills a circular pie slice. The pie slice is centered at the point specified by the x and y arguments. The circular portion of the pie begins at the angle specified by the `startangle` argument and is drawn in a counterclockwise direction until it reaches the angle specified by the `endangle` argument. The pie slice is outlined in the current color and filled with the current fill pattern and fill color. The `pieslice` function uses east (extending to the right of center in the horizontal direction) as its 0 degree reference point. Figure 8.13 illustrates the use of `pieslice`.

*Fig. 8.13. **The*** `pieslice` ***function.***

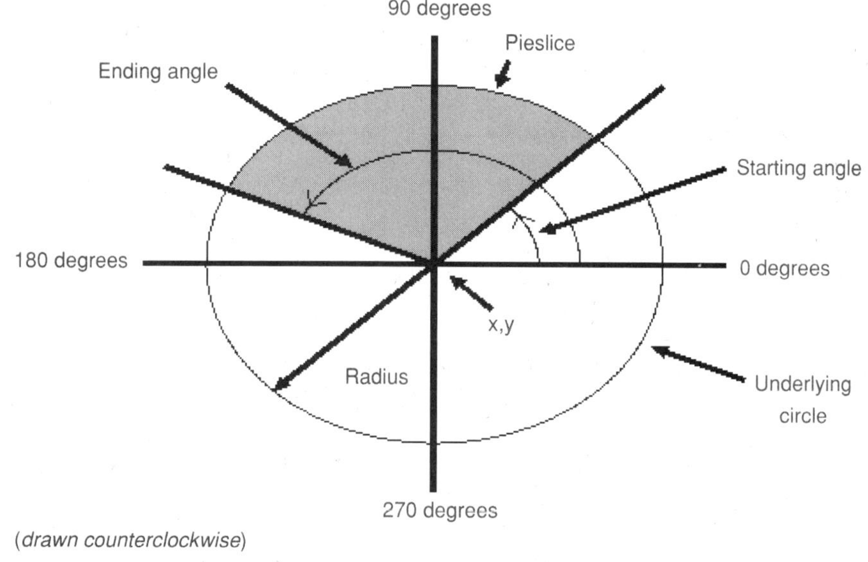

(*drawn counterclockwise*)

Value(s) Returned There is no return value.

Related Function(s)

`arc` : draws a circular arc
`sector` : draws a filled elliptical pie slice

Example In the following example, `pieslice` creates a 5-slice pie chart. Each wedge is filled with a different fill pattern.

```
#include <graphics.h>
#include <stdio.h>
#include <stdlib.h>
```

continues

```
#include <conio.h>

int main ()
{
int gdriver = EGA;
int gmode = EGAHI;

     /* register EGAVGA_driver and sansserif_font
        */
     /* ... these have been added to graphics.lib
        */
     /* as described in UTIL.DOC
        */

registerbgidriver (EGAVGA_driver);
registerbgifont (sansserif_font);

     /* set EGA 16-color high resolution video
        mode  */

initgraph (&gdriver,&gmode,"");
rectangle (0,0,639,349);

     /* draw a pie chart using various fill
        patterns */

setfillstyle (SOLID_FILL, 15);
pieslice (320,175,0,45,150);

setfillstyle (WIDE_DOT_FILL, 15);
pieslice (320,175,45,135,150);

setfillstyle (SLASH_FILL, 15);
pieslice (320,175,135,195,150);

setfillstyle (HATCH_FILL, 15);
pieslice (320,175,195,275,150);

setfillstyle (EMPTY_FILL, 15);
pieslice (320,175,275,360,150);

     /* Delay and Exit */

settextjustify(CENTER_TEXT,BOTTOM_TEXT);
outtextxy (320,320,"Press Any Key To Exit");

getch ();
closegraph();
return 0;
}
```

putimage

DOS | UNIX | ANSI C | C++

Syntax

```
void far putimage(int left, int top, void far
                        *image, int action);

int left, top;              Upper left corner of image
void far *image;            Image buffer
int action;                 Method used to place image
```

Function The `putimage` function places a stored image on the screen.

File(s) to Include `#include <graphics.h>`

Description The `putimage` function places an image previously stored by the `getimage` function onto the screen. The `left` and `top` arguments define the position at which to place the upper left corner of the image. The `*image` argument points to the memory location where the image is stored. The image is placed on the screen with the action defined in the `action` argument. Table 8.20 describes the values and constants used for the `action` argument. The `putimage` function is often used with the `getimage` function to create partial page animation.

Table 8.20. *Operators for the* `putimage` *function.*

Constant	*Value*	*Meaning*
COPY_PUT	0	Overwrite existing pixels
XOR_PUT	1	Exclusive OR pixels
OR_PUT	2	Inclusive OR pixels
AND_PUT	3	AND Pixels
NOT_PUT	4	Invert image

Value(s) Returned There is no return value.

Related Function(s)

`getimage` : stores a rectangular image in memory

`imagesize` : determines the number of bytes required to store an image

Example In the following example, `putimage` places a stored rectangular image on the screen in three rows.

```
#include <graphics.h>
#include <stdio.h>
#include <stdlib.h>
#include <conio.h>

int main ()
{
int gdriver = EGA;
int gmode = EGAHI;
void *image;
unsigned int imsize;
int x;

    /* register EGAVGA_driver and sansserif_font
       */
    /* ... these have been added to graphics.lib
       */
    /* as described in UTIL.DOC
       */

registerbgidriver(EGAVGA_driver);
registerbgifont(sansserif_font);

     /* set EGA high-resolution 16-color mode */

initgraph (&gdriver,&gmode,"");
rectangle (0,0,639,349);

     /* draw and store an image - then place it */
     /* on the screen                            */

setfillstyle(SOLID_FILL,14);
bar (280,135,360,215);
setfillstyle(SOLID_FILL,1);
fillellipse(320,175,40,40);

imsize = imagesize(280,135,360,215);
image = malloc(imsize);
getimage(280,135,360,215,image);

cleardevice ();
rectangle (0,0,639,349);

for (x=30; x<550; x=x+60)
{
     putimage (x,20,image,COPY_PUT);
     putimage (x,120,image,COPY_PUT);
     putimage (x,220,image,COPY_PUT);
}
```

```
      /* Delay and Exit */

settextjustify(CENTER_TEXT,BOTTOM_TEXT);
outtextxy (320,320,"Press Any Key To Exit");
getch ();
closegraph();
return 0;
}
```

putpixel

DOS | UNIX | ANSI C | C++

Syntax `void far putpixel(int x, int y, int color);`

`int x, y;` *Coordinates of pixel*
`int color;` *Desired color*

Function The `putpixel` function sets the specified pixel to the specified color.

File(s) to Include `#include <graphics.h>`

Description The `putpixel` function sets a particular pixel to a certain color. The position of the target pixel is specified by the `x` and `y` arguments. The `color` argument specifies the color value for the pixel.

Value(s) Returned There is no return value.

Related Function(s) `getpixel` : gets the color of the specified pixel

Example In the following example, `getpixel` evaluates each pixel on the screen. If the pixel color is blue, `putpixel` changes it to red. Similarly, `putpixel` changes red pixels to blue.

```
#include <graphics.h>
#include <stdio.h>
#include <stdlib.h>
#include <conio.h>

int main ()
```

continues

```
{
int gdriver = EGA;
int gmode = EGAHI;
int x,y;
int color;

    /* register EGAVGA_driver and sansserif_font
       */
    /* ... these have been added to graphics.lib
       */
    /* as described in UTIL.DOC
       */

registerbgidriver(EGAVGA_driver);
registerbgifont(sansserif_font);

    /* set EGA high-resolution 16-color mode */

initgraph (&gdriver,&gmode,"");
rectangle (0,0,639,349);

setfillstyle (SOLID_FILL,1);
bar (1,1,638,348);
setfillstyle (SOLID_FILL,4);
fillellipse (320,175,200,75);

     /* evaluate each pixel on the screen */
     /* switch pixel colors blue and red   */

for (x = 0; x <640; x = x+1)
     {
     for (y = 0; y < 350; y = y + 1)
          {
          color = getpixel (x,y);
          if (color == 1)
               putpixel (x,y,4);
          if (color == 4)
               putpixel (x,y,1);
          }
     }

     /* Delay and Exit */

settextjustify(CENTER_TEXT,BOTTOM_TEXT);
outtextxy (320,320,"Press Any Key To Exit");

getch ();
closegraph();
return 0;
}
```

rectangle

DOS ~~UNIX~~ ~~ANSI C~~ ~~C++~~

Syntax

```
void far rectangle(int left, int top, int right,
                   int bottom);

int left, top;          Upper left corner of rectangle
int right, bottom;      Lower right corner of rectangle
```

Function The `rectangle` function draws a rectangle with the specified opposing corners.

File(s) to Include `#include <graphics.h>`

Description The `rectangle` function creates an unfilled rectangle using the current color. The upper left corner of the rectangle is specified by the `left` and `top` arguments. These arguments represent the x and y coordinates of the upper left corner. Similarly, the `right` and `bottom` arguments are used to specify the lower right corner of the rectangle. The borders of the rectangle are drawn using the current line style and thickness. Figure 8.14 illustrates the use of the `rectangle` function.

Fig. 8.14. The `rectangle` ***function.***

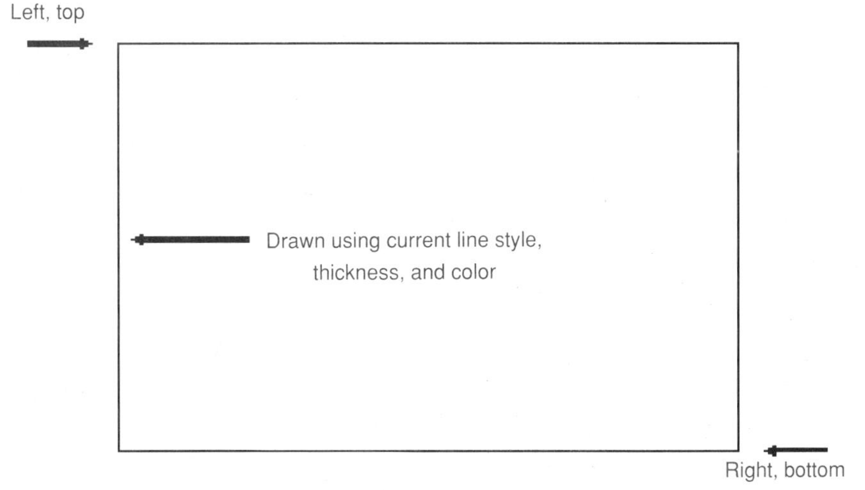

Value(s) Returned There is no return value.

Related Function(s)
ba : draws a two-dimensional bar
bar3d : draws a three-dimensional bar

Example In the following example, `rectangle` creates a series of rectangles with varying corner points.

```
#include <graphics.h>
#include <stdio.h>
#include <stdlib.h>
#include <conio.h>
int main ()
{
int gdriver = EGA;
int gmode = EGAHI;
int x1,y1;
int x2,y2;
int color = 1;

    /* register EGAVGA_driver and sansserif_font
       */
    /* ... these have been added to graphics.lib
       */
    /* as described in UTIL.DOC
       */

registerbgidriver (EGAVGA_driver);
registerbgifont (sansserif_font);

   /* set EGA 16-color high resolution video mode
       */

initgraph (&gdriver,&gmode,"");
rectangle (0,0,639,349);

   /* draw a series of multi-colored rectangles */

x1 = 0;
y1 = 0;
x2 = 639;
y2 = 349;

for (x1 = 0; x1 < x2; x1 = x1 + 1)
     {
     setcolor (color);
     rectangle (x1,y1,x2,y2);
     color = color + 1;
```

```
        if (color > 15)
            color = 1;
        x2 = x2 - 1;
        y1 = y1 + 1;
        y2 = y2 - 1;
        }
        /* Delay and Exit */

    setcolor (0);
    settextjustify(CENTER_TEXT,CENTER_TEXT);
    outtextxy (320,320,"Press Any Key To Exit");
    getch ();
    closegraph();
    return 0;
    }
```

registerbgidriver

DOS UNIX ANSI C C++

Syntax `int registerbgidriver(void (*driver)(void));`

`void (*driver)(void);` *Driver included during link*

Function The `registerbgidriver` function registers a user-loaded or linked graphics driver code.

File(s) to Include `#include <graphics.h>`

Description The `registerbgidriver` function loads and registers a graphics driver. The `*driver` argument points to the driver. A registered driver file can either be loaded from the disk or converted to .OBJ form and linked-in to the program. The examples in this chapter use the `registerbgidriver` function to register the `EGAVGA_driver`. However, before this could be done, the EGAVGA.BGI file had to be converted to .OBJ form and added to the `graphics.lib` file. This process is described in the UTIL.DOC file included with the Borland C++ distribution disks. By registering the driver in this way, the .EXE file is not dependent on an external driver file to run.

Value(s) Returned The `registerbgidriver` function returns the driver number when successful. An error code is returned if the specified driver is invalid.

Related Function(s) `installuserdriver` : installs a vendor-added device driver

Example In the following example, `registerbgidriver` registers the EGAVGA_driver. The driver name is then retrieved and displayed.

```
#include <graphics.h>
#include <stdio.h>
#include <stdlib.h>
#include <conio.h>

int main ()
{
int gdriver = EGA;
int gmode = EGAHI;
char *drivername;

      /* register EGAVGA_driver and sansserif_font
         */
      /* ... these have been added to graphics.lib
         */
      /* as described in UTIL.DOC
         */

registerbgidriver (EGAVGA_driver);
registerbgifont (sansserif_font);

      /* set EGA 16-color high resolution video
         mode */

initgraph (&gdriver,&gmode,"");
rectangle (0,0,639,349);

      /* get and display the current driver */
drivername = getdrivername();

settextjustify (CENTER_TEXT,CENTER_TEXT);
outtextxy (320,125,"Driver Name Is :");
outtextxy (320,150,drivername);

      /* Delay and Exit */

settextjustify(CENTER_TEXT,BOTTOM_TEXT);
outtextxy (320,320,"Press Any Key To Exit");

getch ();

closegraph();
return 0;
}
```

registerbgifont

DOS | UNIX | ANSI C | C++

Syntax `int registerbgifont(void (*font)(void));`

`void (*font)(void);` *Font included during link*

Function The `registerbgifont` function registers a linked font code.

File(s) to Include `#include <graphics.h>`

Description The `registerbgifont` function informs the system that the font pointed to by the `*font` argument was included during linking. The examples in this chapter use the `registerbgifont` function to register the `sansserif_font`. To do this, the SANS.BGI file first had to be converted to .OBJ form and added to the `graphics.lib` file. This process is described in UTIL.DOC, which is included in the Borland C++ distribution disks. By registering the font file this way, the .EXE file is not dependent on any outside files for proper execution.

Value(s) Returned If successful, the font number of the registered font is returned. If unsuccessful, an error code is returned.

Related Function(s) `installuserfont` : loads a non-BGI font

Example In the following example, `registerbgifont` registers the `sansserif_font`. This font is then selected and used to display the various text settings.

```
#include <graphics.h>
#include <stdio.h>
#include <stdlib.h>
#include <conio.h>

int main ()
{
struct textsettingstype textset;
int gdriver = EGA;
int gmode = EGAHI;
char buffer [40];
```

continues

```
      /* register EGAVGA_driver and sansserif_font
         */
      /* ... these have been added to graphics.lib
         */
      /* as described in UTIL.DOC
         */

registerbgidriver (EGAVGA_driver);
registerbgifont (sansserif_font);

     /* set EGA 16-color high resolution video mode
        */

initgraph (&gdriver,&gmode,"");
rectangle (0,0,639,349);

     /* set, get, and display text settings */

settextstyle(SANS_SERIF_FONT,HORIZ_DIR,2);
settextjustify(CENTER_TEXT,CENTER_TEXT);

gettextsettings(&textset);

sprintf (buffer,"Font Value : %d",textset.font);
outtextxy (320,75,buffer);

sprintf (buffer,"Text Direction :
  %d",textset.direction);
outtextxy (320,125,buffer);

sprintf (buffer,"Character Size :
  %d",textset.charsize);
outtextxy (320,175,buffer);

sprintf (buffer,"Horizontal Justification :
  %d",textset.horiz);
outtextxy (320,225,buffer);

sprintf (buffer,"Vertical Justification :
  %d",textset.vert);
outtextxy (320,275,buffer);

      /* Delay and Exit */

settextjustify(CENTER_TEXT,BOTTOM_TEXT);
outtextxy (320,320,"Press Any Key To Exit");

getch ();

closegraph();
return 0;
}
```

restorecrtmode

DOS | UNIX | ANSI C | C++

Syntax `void far restorecrtmode(void);`

Function The `restorecrtmode` function restores the video system to the original mode set before the call to the `initgraph` function.

File(s) to Include `#include <graphics.h>`

Description The `restorecrtmode` function resets the video graphics mode to the mode in use before the initialization of the graphics system. This function is often used with the `setgraphmode` function to switch between graphics and text modes, as shown in the example that follows.

Value(s) Returned There is no return value.

Related Function(s) `initgraph` : initializes the graphics environment

Example In the following example, `restorecrtmode` sets the video mode to the default text mode. The `setgraphmode` function is then used to restore the system to graphics mode.

```
#include <graphics.h>
#include <stdio.h>
#include <stdlib.h>
#include <conio.h>

int main ()
{
int gdriver = EGA;
int gmode = EGAHI;

     /* register EGAVGA_driver and sansserif_font
        */
     /* ... these have been added to graphics.lib
        */
     /* as described in UTIL.DOC
        */

registerbgidriver (EGAVGA_driver);
registerbgifont (sansserif_font);
```

continues

```
      /* set EGA 16-color high resolution video
         mode  */

initgraph (&gdriver,&gmode,"");
rectangle (0,0,639,349);

      /* press a key to go to text mode */

settextjustify (CENTER_TEXT,CENTER_TEXT);
outtextxy (320,175,"Press a key to go to text
mode");
getch ();
restorecrtmode ();

      /* press another key to go back to graphics
         mode */

printf ("Press a key to go back to graphics
mode");
getch ();
setgraphmode (gmode);
rectangle (0,0,639,349);

      /* Delay and Exit */

settextjustify(CENTER_TEXT,BOTTOM_TEXT);
outtextxy (320,320,"Press Any Key To Exit");

getch ();
closegraph();
return 0;
}
```

sector

Syntax

```
void far sector(int x, int y, int startangle, int
                endangle, int xradius, int
                yradius);
```

`int x, y;`	*Center of pie*
`int startangle;`	*Starting angle*
`int endangle;`	*Ending angle*
`int xradius;`	*Radius about x axis*
`int yradius;`	*Radius about y axis*

Function The `sector` function draws a filled elliptical pie slice.

File(s) to Include `#include <graphics.h>`

Description The `sector` function creates an elliptical pie slice. The resulting pie slice is centered at the point specified by the `x` and `y` arguments. The elliptical arc of the pie slice begins at the angle specified by the `startangle` argument and is drawn in a counterclockwise direction until the angle specified by the `endangle` argument is reached. The radius of the elliptical arc is specified by the `xradius` argument for the horizontal radius and the `yradius` argument for the vertical radius. The pie slice is outlined using the current color and filled with the current fill pattern and fill color. Figure 8.15 illustrates the use of `sector`.

Fig. 8.15. The `sector` ***function.***

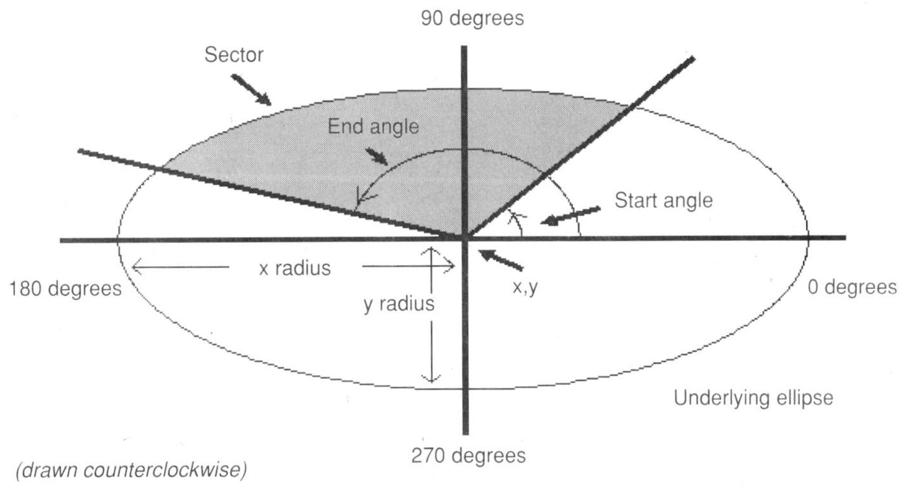

Value(s) Returned There is no return value.

Related Function(s)
`ellipse` : draws an elliptical arc
`pieslice`: draws a filled circular pie slice

Example In the following example, `sector` creates a five-wedge elliptical pie chart. Each wedge is filled with a different fill pattern.

```
#include <graphics.h>
#include <stdio.h>
```

continues

```
#include <stdlib.h>
#include <conio.h>

int main ()
{
int gdriver = EGA;
int gmode = EGAHI;

     /* register EGAVGA_driver and sansserif_font
        */
     /* ... these have been added to graphics.lib
        */
     /* as described in UTIL.DOC
       */

registerbgidriver (EGAVGA_driver);
registerbgifont (sansserif_font);

     /* set EGA 16-color high resolution video
        mode */

initgraph (&gdriver,&gmode,"");
rectangle (0,0,639,349);

     /* draw an elliptical pie chart   */
     /* using various fill patterns    */

setfillstyle (SOLID_FILL, 15);
sector (320,175,0,45,250,125);

setfillstyle (WIDE_DOT_FILL, 15);
sector (320,175,45,135,250,125);

setfillstyle (SLASH_FILL, 15);
sector (320,175,135,195,250,125);

setfillstyle (HATCH_FILL, 15);
sector (320,175,195,275,250,125);

setfillstyle (EMPTY_FILL, 15);
sector (320,175,275,360,250,125);

     /* Delay and Exit */

settextjustify(CENTER_TEXT,BOTTOM_TEXT);
outtextxy (320,320,"Press Any Key To Exit");

getch ();

closegraph();
return 0;
}
```

setactivepage

Syntax

```
void far setactivepage(int page);

int page;
```

Page number

Function The `setactivepage` function sets the active page, or section of memory, to which all subsequent graphics output is sent.

File(s) to Include `#include <graphics.h>`

Description Video memory may include several pages. The `setactivepage` function specifies the page number which represents the section of video memory to which all graphics output is sent. This section of memory is called the active page. The `page` argument specifies the active page number. To use this function effectively, you must have an EGA or VGA video adapter that has sufficient memory to support multiple pages of graphics. This function is used with the `setvisualpage` function to draw on nonvisual pages and to create full screen animation.

Value(s) Returned There is no return value.

Related Function(s) `setvisualpage` : sets the visual page

Example In the following example, `setactivepage` sends all graphics output to a nonvisual page. `setvisualpage` is then used to display the page.

```
#include <graphics.h>
#include <stdio.h>
#include <stdlib.h>
#include <conio.h>

int main ()
{
int gdriver = EGA;
int gmode = EGAHI;
int activepage;
int visualpage;
int holder;
int ch;
```

continues

```
     /* register EGAVGA_driver and sansserif_font
        */
     /* ... these have been added to graphics.lib
        */
     /* as described in UTIL.DOC
        */

registerbgidriver (EGAVGA_driver);
registerbgifont (sansserif_font);

     /* set EGA 16-color high resolution video
        mode  */
initgraph (&gdriver,&gmode,"");
rectangle (0,0,639,349);

     /* draw figure and message on two pages of
        EGA   */
     /* video memory - pressing a key will switch
        */
     /* visual and active pages until ESC is
        pressed */

activepage = 1;
visualpage = 0;
setactivepage (activepage);
setvisualpage (visualpage);
setbkcolor (1);
cleardevice();
setfillstyle (SOLID_FILL,4);
bar (100,50,540,250);
settextjustify (CENTER_TEXT,CENTER_TEXT);
outtextxy (320,310,"PAGE ONE - PRESS ANY KEY TO
CHANGE PAGE");
outtextxy (320,330,"PRESS ESC TO EXIT");
holder = activepage;
activepage = visualpage;
visualpage = holder;
setactivepage (activepage);
setvisualpage (visualpage);
cleardevice ();
fillellipse (320,150,220,100);
outtextxy (320,310,"PAGE ZERO - PRESS ANY KEY TO
CHANGE PAGE");
outtextxy (320,330,"PRESS ESC TO EXIT");
do
{
     holder = activepage;
     activepage = visualpage;
     visualpage = holder;
     setactivepage (activepage);
     setvisualpage (visualpage);
```

```
        ch = getch ();
    } while (ch != 27);
        /* Exit */
    closegraph();
    return 0;
    }
```

setallpalette

DOS UNIX ANSI C C++

Syntax

```
void far setallpalette(struct palettetype far
                        *palette);
```

`struct palettetype far *palette;` *New palette colors*

Function The `setallpalette` function resets all the current palette colors to those specified.

File(s) to Include `#include <graphics.h>`

Description The `setallpalette` function sets the current palette to the palette defined in the structure of `palettetype`, which is pointed to by the `*palette` argument. All the colors of the current palette are set to those defined in the `palettetype` structure. The syntax for the `palettetype` structure is as follows:

```
#define MAXCOLORS 15

struct palettetype
     {
     unsigned char size;
    signed char color[MAXCOLORS + 1];
     };
```

The `size` member of the structure defines the number of colors in the current palette. The `colors` member is an array of color values for the palette. If the entry for any element of the array is set to –1, the color value of that element will not change. It should be noted that all changes to the palette are immediately visible and that the `setallpalette` function should not be used with the IBM-8514 driver. Table 8.5 at the start of this chapter lists the predefined palettes for the EGA and VGA drivers.

Value(s) Returned If the passed values are invalid, a –11 is returned and the palette is unchanged.

Related Function(s) `setpalette` : resets one color in the palette

Example In the following example, `setallpalette` inverts the current palette. For example, colors 0 and 15 are switched.

```
#include <graphics.h>
#include <stdio.h>
#include <stdlib.h>
#include <conio.h>

int main ()
{
struct palettetype palette;
int gdriver = EGA;
int gmode = EGAHI;
int y, color;
char buffer[40];

     /* register EGAVGA_driver and sansserif_font
        */
     /* ... these have been added to graphics.lib
        */
     /* as described in UTIL.DOC
        */

registerbgidriver(EGAVGA_driver);
registerbgifont(sansserif_font);

     /* set EGA high-resolution 16-color mode */

initgraph (&gdriver,&gmode,"");
rectangle (0,0,639,349);

     /* get and change palette information */

getpalette (&palette);
y = 20;

for (color = 1; color < 16; color = color + 1)
{
     setcolor (palette.colors[color]);
     line (20,y,620,y);
     y = y + 20;
}
```

```
settextjustify (CENTER_TEXT,CENTER_TEXT);
outtextxy (320,300,"PRESS ANY KEY TO MODIFY
PALETTE");
getch ();

palette.colors[0] = EGA_WHITE;
palette.colors[1] = EGA_YELLOW;
palette.colors[2] = EGA_LIGHTMAGENTA;
palette.colors[3] = EGA_LIGHTRED;
palette.colors[4] = EGA_LIGHTCYAN;
palette.colors[5] = EGA_LIGHTGREEN;
palette.colors[6] = EGA_LIGHTBLUE;
palette.colors[7] = EGA_DARKGRAY;
palette.colors[8] = EGA_BROWN;
palette.colors[9] = EGA_LIGHTGRAY;
palette.colors[10] = EGA_MAGENTA;
palette.colors[11] = EGA_RED;
palette.colors[12] = EGA_CYAN;
palette.colors[13] = EGA_GREEN;
palette.colors[14] = EGA_BLUE;
palette.colors[15] = EGA_BLACK;

setallpalette(&palette);

     /* Delay and Exit */

settextjustify(CENTER_TEXT,CENTER_TEXT);
outtextxy (320,320,"Press Any Key To Exit");

getch ();

closegraph();
return 0;
}
```

setaspectratio

Syntax `void far setaspectratio(int xaspect, int yaspect);`

`int xaspect;`	*Horizontal (x) aspect ratio*
`int yaspect;`	*Vertical (y) aspect ratio*

Function The `setaspectratio` function modifies the default aspect ratio for the current mode.

File(s) to Include `#include <graphics.h>`

Description The `setaspectratio` function modifies the aspect ratio for the current screen mode. The aspect ratio is used by the graphics system to calculate circles and arcs. Therefore, altering the aspect ratio will affect the output of these functions. The `getaspectratio` function can be used to retrieve the default settings of the current mode before modifying them.

Value(s) Returned There is no return value.

Related Function(s) `getaspectratio` : gets the current aspect ratio

Example In the following example, `setaspectratio` modifies the x and y aspect ratios of the screen. Therefore, the circles that are drawn are not circular.

```
#include <graphics.h>
#include <stdio.h>
#include <stdlib.h>
#include <conio.h>

int main ()
{
int gdriver = EGA;
int gmode = EGAHI;
int width, radius;
int style, pattern;
int xaspect, yaspect;

  /* register EGAVGA_driver and sansserif_font */
  /* ... these have been added to graphics.lib */
  /* as described in UTIL.DOC                  */

registerbgidriver(EGAVGA_driver);
registerbgifont(sansserif_font);

  /* set EGA high-resolution 16-color mode  */

initgraph (&gdriver,&gmode,"");
rectangle (0,0,639,349);

     /* get old and set new aspect ratios */
     /* circles will not be round         */

getaspectratio (&xaspect,&yaspect);
```

```
setaspectratio ((xaspect * 2), yaspect);

     /* Draw a series of concentric circles  */
     /* with wide line thickness              */

style = SOLID_LINE;
pattern = 1;
width = THICK_WIDTH;
for (radius = 150; radius != 0; radius = radius -
  25)
     {
     setlinestyle (style,pattern,width);
     circle (320,175,radius);
     }

     /* Draw circles in the four corners using */
     /* normal width line thickness            */

width = NORM_WIDTH;
for (radius = 30; radius != 0; radius =
  radius - 5)
     {
     setlinestyle (style,pattern,width);
     circle (50,50,radius);
     circle (50,299,radius);
     circle (589,50,radius);
     circle (589,299,radius);
     }

     /* Delay and Exit */

settextjustify(CENTER_TEXT,BOTTOM_TEXT);
outtextxy (320,320,"Press Any Key To Exit");
getch ();
closegraph();
return 0;
}
```

setbkcolor

DOS | UNIX | ANSI C | C++

Syntax `void far setbkcolor(int color);`

`int color;` *Desired color*

Function The `setbkcolor` function sets the background color to the specified color.

File(s) to Include `#include <graphics.h>`

Description The `setbkcolor` function sets the background color to the color value specified in the `color` argument. Table 8.4 at the start of this chapter lists the predefined constants and values available for the color argument.

For the CGA, MCGA, and ATT400 adapters in two-color modes, the user has the option of selecting a foreground color. The background color is black and the foreground color is selected with the `setbkcolor` function with options from table 8.4. The selection of the foreground color with the `setbkcolor` function seems odd, but the design of the CGA adapter makes this necessary. The two-color modes which operate in this way are the CGAHI, MCGAMED, MCGAHI, ATT400MED, and ATT400HI.

Value(s) Returned There is no return value.

Related Function(s) `getbkcolor` : gets the current background color

Example In the following example, `setbkcolor` sets the background color to blue. This background color is then retrieved and displayed on the screen.

```
#include <graphics.h>
#include <stdio.h>
#include <stdlib.h>
#include <conio.h>

int main ()
{
int gdriver = EGA;
int gmode = EGAHI;
int background;
char buffer [40];

     /* register EGAVGA_driver and sansserif_font
        */
     /* ... these have been added to graphics.lib
        */
     /* as described in UTIL.DOC
        */

registerbgidriver(EGAVGA_driver);
registerbgifont(sansserif_font);
```

```
     /* set EGA high-resolution 16-color mode */

initgraph (&gdriver,&gmode,"");
rectangle (0,0,639,349);

     /* set, get, and display the background color
        */

setbkcolor (1);
background = getbkcolor();

sprintf (buffer,"The background color is :
%d",background);
settextjustify (CENTER_TEXT,CENTER_TEXT);
outtextxy (320,175,buffer);

     /* Delay and Exit */

settextjustify(CENTER_TEXT,BOTTOM_TEXT);
outtextxy (320,320,"Press Any Key To Exit");

getch ();

closegraph();
return 0;
}
```

setcolor

DOS UNIX ANSI C C++

Syntax `void far setcolor(int color);`

`int color;` *Desired color*

Function The `setcolor` function sets the current color to the specified color.

File(s) to Include `#include <graphics.h>`

Description The `setcolor` function sets the current color to the color value specified in the `color` argument. The current color is used for drawing lines, arc, circles, text, and so forth. The predefined constants and values for 16-color modes and the CGA are listed in tables 8.3 and 8.5 at the start of this chapter.

Value(s) Returned There is no return value.

Related Function(s) `getcolor` : retrieves the current color

Example In the following example, `setcolor` sets the color of the line drawn between a point which bounces around the screen and the center of the screen.

```
#include <graphics.h>
#include <stdio.h>
#include <stdlib.h>
#include <conio.h>

int main ()
{
int gdriver = EGA;
int gmode = EGAHI;
int x, y;
int xdir, ydir;
int color;
int counter;

     /* register EGAVGA_driver and sansserif_font
        */
     /* ... these have been added to graphics.lib
        */
     /* as described in UTIL.DOC
        */

registerbgidriver (EGAVGA_driver);
registerbgifont (sansserif_font);

     /* set EGA 16-color high resolution video
        mode */

initgraph (&gdriver,&gmode,"");
rectangle (0,0,639,349);

     /* move cursor around screen - draw line to
        center */

x = 1;
y = 175;
xdir = 1;
ydir = 1;
color = 1;
```

```
do
{
     setcolor (color);
     moveto (x,y);
     lineto (320,175);

     if (x == 638)
          xdir = -1;
     if (x == 1)
          xdir = 1;
     if (y == 348)
          ydir = -1;
     if (y == 1)
          ydir = 1;

     x = x + xdir;
     y = y + ydir;
     counter = counter + 1;
     if (counter > 25)
          {
          counter = 0;
          color = color + 1;
          }
     if (color > 15)
          color = 1;
} while (!kbhit());
     /* Delay and Exit */
closegraph();
return 0;
}
```

setfillpattern

DOS UNIX ANSI C C++

Syntax

```
void far setfillpattern(char far *pattern, int
                                    color);

char far *pattern;          Fill pattern
int color;                  Desired color
```

Function The `setfillpattern` function specifies the fill pattern.

File(s) to Include `#include <graphics.h>`

Description The `setfillpattern` function selects a user-defined fill pattern. The `*pattern` argument points to an 8-byte, 8-by-8 bit pattern that represents the fill pattern. Each byte represents an 8-bit row in which each bit describes how the fill pattern will behave. A 1 bit in the fill pattern indicates that the corresponding pixel will be set to the current fill color. A 0 bit indicates that the corresponding pixel will remain unchanged. For example, a fill pattern of

```
char pattern [8] =
{0xFF,0xFF,0xFF,0xFF,0xFF,0xFF,0xFF,0xFF};
```

will generate a solid fill pattern in which every pixel is set to the current fill color. The fill color is specified by the color argument.

Value(s) Returned There is no return value.

Related Function(s) `getfillpattern` : copies a fill pattern into memory

Example In the following example, `setfillpattern` sets the fill pattern to two user-defined fill patterns, then fills two rectangles using these fill patterns.

```
#include <graphics.h>
#include <stdio.h>
#include <stdlib.h>
#include <conio.h>
int main ()
{
int gdriver = EGA;
int gmode = EGAHI;

     /* set 50% and 25% fill patterns          */
     /* also set a holder for the old pattern */

char pattern1[8] =
  {0x55,0xAA,0x55,0xAA,0x55,0xAA,0x55,0xAA};
char pattern2[8] =
  {0x44,0x11,0x44,0x11,0x44,0x11,0x44,0x11};
char patternhold[8] =
  {0x00,0x00,0x00,0x00,0x00,0x00,0x00,0x00};

     /* register EGAVGA_driver and sansserif_font
        */
```

```
      /* ... these have been added to graphics.lib
         */
      /* as described in UTIL.DOC
         */

registerbgidriver(EGAVGA_driver);
registerbgifont(sansserif_font);

      /* set EGA high-resolution 16-color mode */

initgraph (&gdriver,&gmode,"");
rectangle (0,0,639,349);

      /* first get the current fill pattern and
         save it    */
      /* in patternhold - next set the pattern to
         pattern1   */
      /* and fill the upper half of the screen -
         next       */
      /* fill the lower half of screen with
         pattern2    -   */
      /* lastly get the old pattern and fill
center         square */

getfillpattern (patternhold);

setcolor (15);
rectangle (0,0,639,175);
setfillpattern(pattern1,1);
floodfill (1,1,15);

rectangle (0,175,639,349);
setfillpattern(pattern2,1);
floodfill (1,176,15);
rectangle (200,175,440,225);
setfillpattern(patternhold,0);
floodfill (201,176,15);

      /* Delay and Exit */

settextjustify(CENTER_TEXT,CENTER_TEXT);
outtextxy (320,200,"Press Any Key To Exit");
getch ();
closegraph();
return 0;
}
```

setfillstyle

DOS UNIX ANSI C C++

Syntax

```
void far setfillstyle(int pattern, int color);
```

`int pattern;`	*Predefined pattern*
`int color;`	*Desired color*

Function The `setfillstyle` function selects a predefined fill pattern and a fill color.

File(s) to Include `#include <graphics.h>`

Description The `setfillstyle` function selects a predefined fill pattern and a fill color. The `pattern` argument specifies the predefined pattern, whereas the `color` argument specifies the fill color. Table 8.6 at the start of this chapter lists the predefined fill patterns. However, the `USER_FILL`, value 12 pattern should not be used to set a user-defined fill pattern. The `setfillpattern` function should be used instead.

Value(s) Returned There is no return value.

Related Function(s) `getfillsettings` : gets the current fill pattern and color

Example In the following example, `setfillstyle` selects various fill patterns for displaying a five-wedge pie chart.

```
#include <graphics.h>
#include <stdio.h>
#include <stdlib.h>
#include <conio.h>

int main ()
{
int gdriver = EGA;
int gmode = EGAHI;

    /* register EGAVGA_driver and
       sansserif_font */
    /* ... these have been added to
       graphics.lib */
    /* as described in UTIL.DOC
       */
```

```
registerbgidriver (EGAVGA_driver);
registerbgifont (sansserif_font);

     /* set EGA 16-color high resolution video
        mode  */

initgraph (&gdriver,&gmode,"");
rectangle (0,0,639,349);

     /* draw a pie chart using various fill
        styles     */
     /* and colors as set by the setfillstyle
        function */

setfillstyle (SOLID_FILL, 1);
pieslice (320,175,0,45,150);

setfillstyle (WIDE_DOT_FILL, 15);
pieslice (320,175,45,135,150);

setfillstyle (SLASH_FILL, 4);
pieslice (320,175,135,195,150);

setfillstyle (HATCH_FILL, 14);
pieslice (320,175,195,275,150);

setfillstyle (EMPTY_FILL, 15);
pieslice (320,175,275,360,150);

     /* Delay and Exit */

settextjustify(CENTER_TEXT,BOTTOM_TEXT);
outtextxy (320,320,"Press Any Key To Exit");
getch ();
closegraph();
return 0;
}
```

setgraphbufsize

DOS | UNIX | ANSI C | C++

Syntax

```
unsigned far setgraphbufsize(unsigned
buffersize);
unsigned buffersize;      Buffer size
```

Function The setgraphbufsize function modifies the default size of the internal graphics buffer.

File(s) to Include `#include <graphics.h>`

Description The setgraphbufsize function changes the size of the internal graphics buffer as set by the initgraph function when the graphics system is initialized.

The graphics buffer is used by several of the graphics functions; therefore, extreme care should be taken when altering this buffer of default size 4,096.

It should be noted that the setgraphbufsize function should be called before calling the initgraph function.

Value(s) Returned The previous size of the internal graphics buffer is returned when the setgraphbufsize function is called.

Related Function(s)

_graphfreemem : deallocates graphics memory
_graphgetmem : allocates graphics memory

Example In the following example, setgraphbufsize sets a new graphics buffer size. The old and the new buffer sizes are then displayed.

```
#include <graphics.h>
#include <stdio.h>
#include <stdlib.h>
#include <conio.h>

int main ()
{
int gdriver = EGA;
int gmode = EGAHI;
int originalsize, newsize;
char buffer [40];

     /* register EGAVGA_driver and sansserif_font
        */
     /* ... these have been added to graphics.lib
        */
     /* as described in UTIL.DOC
        */

registerbgidriver (EGAVGA_driver);
registerbgifont (sansserif_font);
```

```
        /* set EGA 16-color high resolution video
           mode  */

initgraph (&gdriver,&gmode,"");
rectangle (0,0,639,349);

        /* get old buffer size, set new size, display
           both */

newsize = 10000;

originalsize = setgraphbufsize(newsize);

sprintf (buffer,"The original buffer size was
  %d",originalsize);
settextjustify (CENTER_TEXT,CENTER_TEXT);
outtextxy (320,100,buffer);

sprintf (buffer,"The current buffer size is
  %d",newsize);
outtextxy (320,150,buffer);

setgraphbufsize(originalsize);

        /* Delay and Exit */

settextjustify(CENTER_TEXT,BOTTOM_TEXT);
outtextxy (320,320,"Press Any Key To Exit");
getch ();
closegraph();
return 0;
}
```

setgraphmode

Syntax `void far setgraphmode(int mode);`

`int mode;` *Graphics mode*

Function The `setgraphmode` function sets the graphics system to the specified video mode.

File(s) to Include `#include <graphics.h>`

Description The `setgraphmode` function selects a graphics mode only after the graphics system has been initialized by the `initgraph` function. The `mode` argument defines the desired mode and must be a valid mode for the current driver. In addition to setting a new mode, `setgraphmode` clears the screen and resets all graphics settings to their default values. This function is often used with the `restorecrtmode` function to switch between text and graphics modes, as in the example that follows.

Value(s) Returned A –10, for `grInvalidMode`, is returned when the specified video mode is invalid for the current device driver.

Related Function(s) `initgraph` : initializes the graphics environment

Example In the following example, `setgraphmode` sets the video mode to graphics mode after being placed in text mode with the `restoremode` function.

```
#include <graphics.h>
#include <stdio.h>
#include <stdlib.h>
#include <conio.h>

int main ()
{
int gdriver = EGA;
int gmode = EGAHI;

     /* register EGAVGA_driver and sansserif_font
        */
     /* ... these have been added to graphics.lib
        */
     /* as described in UTIL.DOC
        */

registerbgidriver (EGAVGA_driver);
registerbgifont (sansserif_font);

     /* set EGA 16-color high resolution video
        mode  */

initgraph (&gdriver,&gmode,"");
rectangle (0,0,639,349);

     /* press a key to go to text mode */

settextjustify (CENTER_TEXT,CENTER_TEXT);
outtextxy (320,175,"Press a key to go to text
```

```
   mode");
getch ();
restorecrtmode ();

     /* press another key to go back to graphics
        mode */

printf ("Press a key to go back to graphics
  mode");
getch ();
setgraphmode (gmode);
rectangle (0,0,639,349);

     /* Delay and Exit */

settextjustify(CENTER_TEXT,BOTTOM_TEXT);
outtextxy (320,320,"Press Any Key To Exit");

getch ();
closegraph();
return 0;
}
```

setlinestyle

DOS UNIX ANSI C C++

Syntax

```
void far setlinestyle(int linestyle, unsigned
                      pattern, int thickness);
```

`int linestyle;`	*Line style*
`unsigned pattern;`	*User-defined line pattern*
`int thickness;`	*Thickness of line*

Function The `setlinestyle` function sets the characteristics for straight lines including the style and width.

File(s) to Include `#include <graphics.h>`

Description The `setlinestyle` function defines the line characteristics for straight lines. The `linestyle` parameter specifies the predefined line pattern to use. The predefined line styles are shown in table 8.7 at the start of this chapter. The `thickness` parameter defines the width of the line. The constants for the `thickness` argument are shown in table 8.8, also at the start of this chapter.

The `pattern` argument is a 16-bit pattern that describes the line style when the `linestyle` argument is `USERBIT_LINE`, or 4. This 16-bit pattern describes the line. A 1 bit in the pattern indicates that the corresponding pixel on the line will be set to the current color. A 0 bit indicates that the corresponding pixel will remain unchanged. For example, a pattern of 1111111111111111 binary, or 0xFFFF hex, indicates that all pixels on the line will be set to the current color; therefore, 0xFFFF represents a solid line.

Value(s) Returned If an invalid parameter is passed to the `setlinestyle` function, a –11 is returned via the `graphresult` function.

Related Function(s)

`getlinesettings` : gets the current line style, pattern, and thickness

Example In the following example, `setlinestyle` sets the current line style. These line settings are then retrieved and displayed.

```
#include <graphics.h>
#include <stdio.h>
#include <stdlib.h>
#include <conio.h>

int main ()
{
struct linesettingstype lineset;
int gdriver = EGA;
int gmode = EGAHI;
char buffer[40];

     /* register EGAVGA_driver and sansserif_font
        */
     /* ... these have been added to graphics.lib
        */
     /* as described in UTIL.DOC
        */

registerbgidriver(EGAVGA_driver);
registerbgifont(sansserif_font);

     /* set EGA high-resolution 16-color mode */

initgraph (&gdriver,&gmode,"");
rectangle (0,0,639,349);

     /* define, use, and retrieve line settings */
```

```
setlinestyle (DOTTED_LINE,0xFFFF,THICK_WIDTH);

getlinesettings (&lineset);

rectangle (50,50,590,300);
settextjustify(CENTER_TEXT,CENTER_TEXT);

sprintf (buffer,"The Line Style is :
  %d",lineset.linestyle);
outtextxy (320,75,buffer);

sprintf (buffer,"The User Pattern is :
  0x%x",lineset.upattern);
outtextxy (320,150,buffer);

sprintf (buffer,"The Line Thickness is :
  %d",lineset.thickness);
outtextxy (320,225,buffer);

     /* Delay and Exit */

outtextxy (320,320,"Press Any Key To Exit");
getch ();
closegraph();
return 0;
}
```

setpalette

DOS | UNIX | ANSI C | C++

Syntax `void far setpalette(int palettenumber, int color);`

`int palettenumber;`	*Palette number to change*
`int color;`	*New color*

Function The `setpalette` function modifies one entry in the current palette.

File(s) to Include `#include <graphics.h>`

Description The `setpalette` function modifies a single entry in the current palette. The `palettenumber` argument specifies the palette member to change. The `color` argument specifies the new color value for the palette member. Note that all changes made to the palette are immediately visible and that the `setpalette` function cannot be used with the IBM 8514 driver. Table 8.5 at the start of this chapter shows the predefined color values and constants for the EGA and VGA.

Value(s) Returned If an invalid parameter is passed to the `setpalette` function, a –11 is returned via the `graphresult` function.

Related Function(s) `setallpalette` : resets the entire palette

Example In the following example, `setpalette` inverts two colors, one pair at a time, each time a key is pressed. The Esc key can be pressed to exit the program.

```
#include <graphics.h>
#include <stdio.h>
#include <stdlib.h>
#include <conio.h>

int col[16] =
{EGA_WHITE,EGA_YELLOW,EGA_LIGHTMAGENTA,EGA_LIGHTRED,
  EGA_LIGHTCYAN,EGA_LIGHTGREEN,EGA_LIGHTBLUE,
  EGA_DARKGRAY,EGA_BROWN,EGA_LIGHTGRAY,EGA_MAGENTA,
  EGA_RED,EGA_CYAN,EGA_GREEN,EGA_BLUE,EGA_BLACK};

int main ()
{
struct palettetype palette;
int gdriver = EGA;
int gmode = EGAHI;
int y, color;
char buffer[40];
int ch;

     /* register EGAVGA_driver and sansserif_font
        */
     /* ... these have been added to graphics.lib
        */
     /* as described in UTIL.DOC
        */

registerbgidriver(EGAVGA_driver);
registerbgifont(sansserif_font);

     /* set EGA high-resolution 16-color mode */

initgraph (&gdriver,&gmode,"");
rectangle (0,0,639,349);

     /* change one palette color with each key
        stroke */
```

```
getpalette (&palette);
color = 1;

for (y = 10; y < 160; y = y + 10)
{
      setcolor (color);
      line (20,y,620,y);
      color = color + 1;
}
color = 0;
settextjustify (CENTER_TEXT,CENTER_TEXT);
outtextxy (320,320,"Press ESC to Exit");

do
{
      ch =  getch ();
      setpalette (color,col[color]);
      color = color + 1;
} while (ch != 27);


      /* Exit */
closegraph();
return 0;
}
```

setrgbpalette

DOS UNIX ANSI C C++

Syntax

```
void far setrgbpalette(int palettenum, int red,
                       int green, int blue);
```

`int palettenum;`	*Palette entry to modify*
`int red;`	*Red component*
`int green;`	*Green component*
`int blue;`	*Blue component*

Function The `setrgbpalette` function defines colors for the IBM 8514.

File(s) to Include `#include <graphics.h>`

Description The `setrgbpalette` function is used with the IBM 8514 and VGA drivers. The `palettenum` argument specifies the palette entry to be modified. For the IBM 8514, the palette range is 0 to 255. For VGA modes, the palette range is 0 to 15. The `red`, `green`, and `blue` arguments define the color intensity of the palette entry.

Value(s) Returned There is no return value.

Related Function(s)

`setpalette` : modifies one color in the current palette
`setallpalette` : modifies all colors in the current palette

Example The following example modifies one member of the VGA palette.

```
#include <graphics.h>
#include <stdio.h>
#include <stdlib.h>
#include <conio.h>

int main ()
{
struct palettetype palette;
int gdriver = VGA;
int gmode = VGAHI;

     /* register EGAVGA_driver and sansserif_font
        */
     /* ... these have been added to graphics.lib
        */
     /* as described in UTIL.DOC
        */

registerbgidriver (EGAVGA_driver);
registerbgifont (sansserif_font);

     /* set VGA high resolution video mode   */

initgraph (&gdriver,&gmode,"");
rectangle (0,0,639,349);

     /* get palette and modify a palette entry */

getpalette (&palette);

setrgbpalette (palette.colors[3],6,4,1);

     /* Delay and Exit */

settextjustify(CENTER_TEXT,BOTTOM_TEXT);
outtextxy (320,320,"Press Any Key To Exit");
```

```
getch ();

closegraph();
return 0;
}
```

settextjustify

DOS UNIX ANSI C C++

Syntax

```
void far settextjustify(int horizontal, int
                        vertical);
```

`int horizontal;` *Horizontal justification*
`int vertical;` *Vertical justification*

Function The `settextjustify` function sets the text justification for the graphics functions.

File(s) to Include `#include <graphics.h>`

Description The `settextjustify` function specifies the method in which the text is placed on the screen relative to the cursor position. The `horizontal` argument specifies the horizontal justification, whereas the `vertical` argument specifies the vertical justification. The predefined constants and values for the horizontal and vertical justifications are shown in table 8.12 at the start of this chapter. The default settings for the text justifications are `LEFT_TEXT` for horizontal and `TOP_TEXT` for vertical.

Value(s) Returned If an invalid parameter is passed to the `settextjustify` function, a –11 is returned via the `graphresult` function.

Related Function(s) `outtext` : used to display text in graphics mode

Example In the following example, `settextjustify` displays text using different vertical and horizontal justifications.

```
#include <graphics.h>
#include <stdio.h>
#include <stdlib.h>
#include <conio.h>
```

continues

```
int main ()
{
struct textsettingstype textset;
int gdriver = EGA;
int gmode = EGAHI;
char buffer [40];

     /* register EGAVGA_driver and sansserif_font
        */
     /* ... these have been added to graphics.lib
        */
     /* as described in UTIL.DOC
        */

registerbgidriver (EGAVGA_driver);
registerbgifont (sansserif_font);

     /* set EGA 16-color high resolution video
        mode  */

initgraph (&gdriver,&gmode,"");
rectangle (0,0,639,349);

     /* display text with different justifications
        */

settextjustify (LEFT_TEXT,BOTTOM_TEXT);
outtextxy (320,175,"LEFT_TEXT - BOTTOM_TEXT");

settextjustify (RIGHT_TEXT,TOP_TEXT);
outtextxy (320,175,"RIGHT_TEXT - TOP_TEXT");

     /* Delay and Exit */

settextjustify(CENTER_TEXT,BOTTOM_TEXT);
outtextxy (320,320,"Press Any Key To Exit");
getch ();
closegraph();
return 0;
}
```

settextstyle

DOS | UNIX | ANSI C | C++

Syntax

```
void far settextstyle(int font, int direction,
                      int charsize);
```

```
int font;                  Font to use
int direction;             Direction to display text
int charsize;              Character size
```

Function The `settextstyle` function sets the graphics font output characteristics.

File(s) to Include `#include <graphics.h>`

Description The `settextstyle` function specifies the characteristics for font text output. The `font` argument specifies the registered font to use. To achieve predictable results, the font should be registered (see `registerbgifont` in the reference section of this chapter). The `direction` argument specifies the direction in which text will be displayed. Tables 8.10 and 8.11 at the start of this chapter list the available fonts and directions. The default direction is `HORIZ_DIR`. The `charsize` argument defines the factor by which the current font will be multiplied. A nonzero `charsize` argument can be used with bit-mapped or stroked fonts. However, a `charsize` of 0, which selects the user-defined character size as defined in the `setusercharsize` function, works only with stroked fonts. The `charsize` argument can magnify the size of the font up to 10 times its normal size.

Value(s) Returned There is no return value.

Related Function(s) `gettextsettings` : gets information on the current text characteristics

Example In the following example, `settextstyle` selects the sans serif font in the horizontal direction with character size of 2. The text settings are then retrieved and displayed.

```
#include <graphics.h>
#include <stdio.h>
#include <stdlib.h>
#include <conio.h>

int main ()
{
struct textsettingstype textset;
int gdriver = EGA;
int gmode = EGAHI;
char buffer [40];

    /* register EGAVGA_driver and sansserif_font
       */
```

continues

```
     /* ... these have been added to graphics.lib
        */
     /* as described in UTIL.DOC
        */

registerbgidriver (EGAVGA_driver);
registerbgifont (sansserif_font);

     /* set EGA 16-color high resolution video
        mode  */

initgraph (&gdriver,&gmode,"");
rectangle (0,0,639,349);

     /* set, get, and display text settings */

settextstyle(SANS_SERIF_FONT,HORIZ_DIR,2);
settextjustify(CENTER_TEXT,CENTER_TEXT);
gettextsettings(&textset);
sprintf (buffer,"Font Value : %d",textset.font);
outtextxy (320,75,buffer);
sprintf (buffer,"Text Direction :
  %d",textset.direction);
outtextxy (320,125,buffer);
sprintf (buffer,"Character Size :
  %d",textset.charsize);
outtextxy (320,175,buffer);
sprintf (buffer,"Horizontal Justification :
  %d",textset.horiz);
outtextxy (320,225,buffer);
sprintf (buffer,"Vertical Justification :
  %d",textset.vert);
outtextxy (320,275,buffer);

     /* Delay and Exit */

settextjustify(CENTER_TEXT,BOTTOM_TEXT);
outtextxy (320,320,"Press Any Key To Exit");

getch ();

closegraph();
return 0;
}
```

setusercharsize

DOS UNIX ANSI C C++

Syntax

```
void far setusercharsize(int multx, int divx, int
                         multy, int divy);

int multx, divx;          Set ratio for character width
int multy, divy;          Set ratio for character height
```

Function The `setusercharsize` function sets the character width and height for stroked fonts.

File(s) to Include `#include <graphics.h>`

Description The `setusercharsize` function sets the size characteristics for stroked fonts. For this function to affect the character size, the `charsize` argument of the `settextstyle` function must be set to 0. The width of the character is set by the `multx` and `divx` arguments. For example, to double the size of the character, `multx` could be set to 2 whereas `divx` could be set to 1. The resulting width is 2/1 or 2 times the default width. Similarly, the `multy` and `divy` arguments specify the height of the character.

Value(s) Returned There is no return value.

Related Function(s) `gettextsettings` : gets the characteristics of the current font

Example In the following example, `setusercharsize` sets the character size to 50% height and 33% width. The height and width ratios are then displayed.

```
#include <graphics.h>
#include <stdio.h>
#include <stdlib.h>
#include <conio.h>
```

continues

```
int main ()
{
int gdriver = EGA;
int gmode = EGAHI;
int multx, divx;
int multy, divy;
char buffer[40];

     /* register EGAVGA_driver and sansserif_font
        */
     /* ... these have been added to graphics.lib
        */
     /* as described in UTIL.DOC
        */

registerbgidriver (EGAVGA_driver);
registerbgifont (sansserif_font);

     /* set EGA 16-color high resolution video
        mode  */

initgraph (&gdriver,&gmode,"");
rectangle (0,0,639,349);

     /* set font and character size */

multx = 1;
divx = 2;
multy = 1;
divy = 3;

settextstyle (SANS_SERIF_FONT,HORIZ_DIR,0);

setusercharsize (multx,divx,multy,divy);

settextjustify (CENTER_TEXT,CENTER_TEXT);
sprintf (buffer,"The Width Ratio is %d to
  %d",multx,divx);
outtextxy (320,150,buffer);

sprintf (buffer,"The Height Ratio is %d to
  %d",multy,divy);
outtextxy (320,200,buffer);

     /* Delay and Exit */

settextjustify(CENTER_TEXT,BOTTOM_TEXT);
outtextxy (320,320,"Press Any Key To Exit");

getch ();
```

```
closegraph();
return 0;
}
```

setviewport

DOS UNIX ANSI C C++

Syntax

```
void far setviewport(int left, int top, int right,
                     int bottom, int clip);
```

`int left, top;`	*Upper left corner of viewport*
`int right, bottom;`	*Lower right corner of viewport*
`int clip;`	*Clip flag*

Function The `setviewport` function specifies the current viewport and its characteristics.

File(s) to Include `#include <graphics.h>`

Description The `setviewport` function defines the current viewport. The `left` and `top` arguments define the upper left corner of the viewport. The `left` and `top` arguments correspond to the x and y coordinates of this corner, respectively. Similarly, the `right` and `bottom` arguments define the lower right corner of the viewport. The `clip` argument defines whether subsequent graphics output will be clipped at the viewport's border. A clip value of 0 indicates that the output will not be clipped, whereas a nonzero value indicates that output will be clipped. When the viewport is initialized, the cursor position is moved to the position (0,0), the upper left corner. All output after the viewport is initialized is relative to this point. The default viewport covers the entire screen.

Value(s) Returned A –11 is returned via the `graphresult` function when an invalid parameter is passed to the `setviewport` function.

Related Function(s)

`getviewsettings` : gets the settings of the current viewport
`clearviewport` : clears the current viewport

Example In the following example, `setviewport` creates a viewport, which clips output at its border. The attempt is then made to draw a line outside the border of the viewport.

```
#include <graphics.h>
#include <stdio.h>
#include <stdlib.h>
#include <conio.h>

int main ()
{
int gdriver = EGA;
int gmode = EGAHI;

     /* register EGAVGA_driver and sansserif_font
        */
     /* ... these have been added to graphics.lib
        */
     /* as described in UTIL.DOC
        */

registerbgidriver(EGAVGA_driver);
registerbgifont(sansserif_font);

     /* set EGA high-resolution 16-color mode */

initgraph (&gdriver,&gmode,"");
rectangle (0,0,639,349);

     /* highlight and create viewport --      */
     /* attempt to draw outside of viewport */
     /* reset viewport to entire screen      */

rectangle (50,50,590,300);
setviewport (50,50,590,300,1);
line (0,0,639,349);

setviewport (0,0,639,349,1);

     /* Delay and Exit */

settextjustify (CENTER_TEXT,CENTER_TEXT);
outtextxy (320,330,"Press Any Key to Exit");
getch ();

closegraph();
return 0;
}
```

setvisualpage

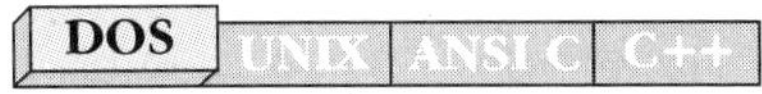

Syntax `void far setvisualpage(int page);`

`int page;` *Page number*

Function The `setvisualpage` function sets the visual, or display, page to the specified page number.

File(s) to Include `#include <graphics.h>`

Description The `setvisualpage` function sets the visual page as specified in the `page` argument. A page is a section of memory in which video information is stored. When used with a system (EGA or VGA) with sufficient video memory to support multiple pages of graphics, `setvisualpage` (in conjunction with `setactivepage`) allows the programmer to create graphics on hidden pages and flip among multiple pages of graphics information. Using careful planning of the video pages, simple full-screen animation can easily be created by flipping between the pages of video memory.

Value(s) Returned There is no return value.

Related Function(s) `setactivepage` : sets the active page

Example In the following example, `setvisualpage` sets the current active page to the visual page after all output to that page is finished.

```
#include <graphics.h>
#include <stdio.h>
#include <stdlib.h>
#include <conio.h>

int main ()
{
int gdriver = EGA;
int gmode = EGAHI;
int activepage;
int visualpage;
```

```
int holder;
int ch;

     /* register EGAVGA_driver and sansserif_font
        */
     /* ... these have been added to graphics.lib
        */
     /* as described in UTIL.DOC
        */
registerbgidriver (EGAVGA_driver);
registerbgifont (sansserif_font);

     /* set EGA 16-color high resolution video
        mode  */
initgraph (&gdriver,&gmode,"");
rectangle (0,0,639,349);

     /* draw figure and message on two pages of
        EGA     */
     /* video memory - pressing a key will switch
               */
     /* visual and active pages until ESC is
        pressed */

activepage = 1;
visualpage = 0;
setactivepage (activepage);
setvisualpage (visualpage);
setbkcolor (1);
cleardevice();
setfillstyle (SOLID_FILL,4);
bar (100,50,540,250);
rectangle (100,50,540,250);
settextjustify (CENTER_TEXT,CENTER_TEXT);
outtextxy (320,310,"PAGE ONE - PRESS ANY KEY TO
CHANGE PAGE");
outtextxy (320,330,"PRESS ESC TO EXIT");
holder = activepage;
activepage = visualpage;
visualpage = holder;
setactivepage (activepage);
setvisualpage (visualpage);
cleardevice ();
fillellipse (320,150,220,100);
outtextxy (320,310,"PAGE ZERO - PRESS ANY KEY TO
CHANGE PAGE");
outtextxy (320,330,"PRESS ESC TO EXIT");
do
{
     holder = activepage;
     activepage = visualpage;
     visualpage = holder;
```

```
        setactivepage (activepage);
        setvisualpage (visualpage);
        ch = getch ();
    } while (ch != 27);
        /* Exit */
    closegraph();
    return 0;
    }
```

setwritemode

Syntax

```
void far setwritemode(int mode);
int mode;                    Write mode
```

Function The `setwritemode` function sets the writing mode for drawing straight lines in graphics mode.

File(s) to Include `#include <graphics.h>`

Description The `setwritemode` function sets the logical writing mode for straight lines. The `mode` argument specifies the writing mode. The writing mode determines the interaction between existing pixel values and the pixel values on the line. Table 8.21 lists the values and constants for the mode argument.

Table 8.21. *Write modes.*

Constant	*Value*	*Meaning*
COPY_PUT	0	Line pixels overwrite existing pixels
XOR_PUT	1	Screen pixels are the exclusive OR of line and existing pixels

Value(s) Returned There is no return value.

Related Function(s)

`drawpoly` : uses the write mode to draw the polygon
`line` : uses the write mode to draw lines
`linerel` : uses the write mode to draw lines
`lineto` : uses the write mode to draw lines
`rectangle` : uses the write mode to draw the rectangle

Example In the following example, `setwritemode` sets the logical line writing mode. A line is then drawn using the two write modes.

```
#include <graphics.h>
#include <stdio.h>
#include <stdlib.h>
#include <conio.h>

int main ()
{
int gdriver = EGA;
int gmode = EGAHI;

     /* register EGAVGA_driver and sansserif_font
        */
     /* ... these have been added to graphics.lib
        */
     /* as described in UTIL.DOC
        */

registerbgidriver (EGAVGA_driver);
registerbgifont (sansserif_font);

     /* set EGA 16-color high resolution video
        mode */

initgraph (&gdriver,&gmode,"");
rectangle (0,0,639,349);
setfillstyle (SOLID_FILL,1);
bar (1,1,638,348);

     /* draw lines using the write modes */

setcolor (14);
setwritemode (COPY_PUT);
line (20,40,620,40);
settextjustify (CENTER_TEXT,CENTER_TEXT);
outtextxy (320,80,"COPY_PUT Line");

setwritemode (XOR_PUT);
line (20,150,620,150);
outtextxy (320,190,"XOR_PUT Line");

     /* Delay and Exit */

settextjustify(CENTER_TEXT,BOTTOM_TEXT);
outtextxy (320,320,"Press Any Key To Exit");

getch ();
closegraph();
return 0;
}
```

textheight

DOS UNIX ANSI C C++

Syntax `int far textheight(char far *textstring);`

`char far *textstring;` *Text string to evaluate*

Function The `textheight` function determines and returns the height, in pixels, of the specified text string.

File(s) to Include `#include <graphics.h>`

Description The `textheight` function determines the height, in pixels, of the text string specified by the `*textstring` argument. The text height is determined by using the current font and character size.

Value(s) Returned The height, in pixels, of the specified text string is returned when `textheight` is called.

Related Function(s) `textwidth` : returns the width of a text string

Example In the following example, `textheight` determines the height, in pixels, of the current font. The width and height of the specified string are then displayed.

```
#include <graphics.h>
#include <stdio.h>
#include <stdlib.h>
#include <conio.h>

int main ()
{
int gdriver = EGA;
int gmode = EGAHI;
int multx, divx;
int multy, divy;
char buffer[40];
int textht;
int textwid;

      /* register EGAVGA_driver and sansserif_font
         */
      /* ... these have been added to graphics.lib
```

continues

```
                */
           /* as described in UTIL.DOC
                */

        registerbgidriver (EGAVGA_driver);
        registerbgifont (sansserif_font);

           /* set EGA 16-color high resolution video
                mode  */

        initgraph (&gdriver,&gmode,"");
        rectangle (0,0,639,349);

           /* set font and get character size */

        multx = 1;
        divx = 2;
        multy = 1;
        divy = 3;

        settextstyle (SANS_SERIF_FONT,HORIZ_DIR,2);
        setusercharsize (multx,divx,multy,divy);

        textht = textheight ("X");

        textwid = textwidth ("Width : xxx - Height : xx");

        settextjustify (CENTER_TEXT,CENTER_TEXT);
        sprintf (buffer,"Width Ratio : %d - Height:
          %d",textwid,textht);
        outtextxy (320,150,buffer);

           /* Delay and Exit */

        settextjustify(CENTER_TEXT,BOTTOM_TEXT);
        outtextxy (320,320,"Press Any Key To Exit");

        getch ();
        closegraph();
        return 0;
        }
```

textwidth

DOS UNIX ANSI C C++

Syntax `int far textwidth(char far *textstring);`

`char far *textstring;` *Text string to evaluate*

Function The textwidth function determines and returns the width, in pixels, of the specified text string.

File(s) to Include `#include <graphics.h>`

Description The textwidth function determines the width of the text string specified by the *textstring argument. The current font and character size are used for determining the width of the string.

Value(s) Returned The width, in pixels, of the specified text string is returned when textwidth is called.

Related Function(s) textheight : determines the height of a text string

Example In the following example, the width of the specified text string is determined by the textwidth function. The height and width of this string are then displayed.

```
#include <graphics.h>
#include <stdio.h>
#include <stdlib.h>
#include <conio.h>

int main ()
{
int gdriver = EGA;
int gmode = EGAHI;
int multx, divx;
int multy, divy;
char buffer[40];
int textht;
int textwid;

     /* register EGAVGA_driver and sansserif_font
        */
     /* ... these have been added to graphics.lib
        */
     /* as described in UTIL.DOC
        */

registerbgidriver (EGAVGA_driver);
registerbgifont (sansserif_font);

     /* set EGA 16-color high resolution video
        mode */

initgraph (&gdriver,&gmode,"");
```

continues

```
rectangle (0,0,639,349);

     /* set font and get character size */

multx = 1;
divx = 2;
multy = 1;
divy = 3;

settextstyle (SANS_SERIF_FONT,HORIZ_DIR,2);
setusercharsize (multx,divx,multy,divy);

textht = textheight ("X");
textwid = textwidth ("Width : xxx - Height : xx");

settextjustify (CENTER_TEXT,CENTER_TEXT);
sprintf (buffer,"Width Ratio : %d - Height:
%d",textwid,textht);
outtextxy (320,150,buffer);

     /* Delay and Exit */

settextjustify(CENTER_TEXT,BOTTOM_TEXT);
outtextxy (320,320,"Press Any Key To Exit");

getch ();
closegraph();
return 0;
}
```

Input/Output

This chapter introduces the functions and macros used for text screen, keyboard, file, stream, and device input/output. There are three fundamental types of I/O functions. These types are stream I/O functions, low-level I/O functions, and console I/O functions.

Stream I/O functions treat data items or files as a stream of characters. These functions perform both formatted, buffered I/O and unformatted, buffered I/O.

Low-level I/O functions use the operating system for I/O and do not provide buffering or formatting.

Console I/O functions provide access to the console. These functions allow you to read from, and write to, the screen and the keyboard buffer.

These basic terms used for defining the I/O functions and macros are described more in the following sections.

Stream I/O

The stream I/O functions and macros use a buffer to store the data traveling to and from a file. Stream I/O is more efficient than low-level I/O for most applications because the buffering of data reduces the number of times the disk has to be accessed. The term *flush* describes writing this buffer to the disk file. Stream I/O can be formatted, which provides greater flexibility in processing and displaying data.

Low-Level I/O

The low-level I/O functions and macros do not use a buffer to store data traveling to and from a file. In addition, low-level I/O has no formatting capability. Low-level I/O functions use the capabilities of the operating system to perform I/O.

Console I/O

Several of the functions and macros in table 9.1 that follows provide the capability to directly access the keyboard and screen. It is not necessary to open these devices for access and there is no buffering involved. The term *console* is used when discussing the keyboard and screen collectively.

Table 9.1 lists I/O functions and macros.

Table 9.1. *Input/output functions and macros.*

Function	*Meaning*
`access`	Checks the accessibility of a file
`cgets`	Reads a string from the console
`_chmod`	Reads or sets the DOS file attributes
`chmod`	Changes the file access mode
`chsize`	Changes the size of a file
`clearerr`	Resets the error indication
`_close`	Closes a file; used with `_open`
`close`	Closes a file; used with `open`
`cprintf`	Displays formatted output on the screen

Function	*Meaning*
`cputs`	Writes a string to the screen
`_creat`	Creates a new file; the file is opened in binary mode
`creat`	Creates a new file; the file can be opened in either binary or textmode
`creatnew`	Creates a new file; will not overwrite an existing file
`creattemp`	Creates a unique file
`cscanf`	Scans and formats input from the console
`dup`	Duplicates a file handle
`dup2`	Duplicates a file handle onto an existing one
`eof`	Checks for end-of-file
`fclose`	Closes a stream
`fcloseall`	Closes all open streams
`fdopen`	Associates a stream with a file handle
`feof`	Checks a stream for end-of-file
`ferror`	Tests a stream for errors
`fflush`	Flushes a stream
`fgetc`	Gets a character from a stream
`fgetchar`	Gets a character from `stdin`
`fgetpos`	Gets the current file pointer
`fgets`	Gets a string from a stream
`filelength`	Determines the size of a file
`fileno`	Gets the file handle for a stream
`flushall`	Flushes all streams
`fopen`	Opens a stream
`fprintf`	Writes formatted output to a stream
`fputc`	Puts a character on a stream
`fputchar`	Puts a character on `stdout`
`fputs`	Puts a string on a stream
`fread`	Reads data from a stream

continues

Table 9.1. (continued)

Function	*Meaning*
`freopen`	Associates a new file with an open stream
`fscanf`	Formats input from a stream
`fseek`	Repositions the file pointer on a stream
`fsetpos`	Sets the file pointer position for a stream
`fstat`	Retrieves information on an open file
`ftell`	Gets the file pointer for a stream
`fwrite`	Adds data to a stream
`getc`	Gets a character from a stream
`getch`	Gets a character from the keyboard
`getchar`	Gets a character from `stdin`
`getche`	Gets and echoes a character from the keyboard
`getftime`	Gets file date and time information
`getpass`	Reads a password
`gets`	Gets a stream from `stdin`
`getw`	Gets an integer from a stream
`ioctl`	Controls an I/O device
`isatty`	Checks for a device type
`kbhit`	Checks for available keystrokes
`lock`	Sets the file-sharing locks
`lseek`	Moves the position of the file pointer
`_open`	Opens a file in binary mode
`open`	Opens a file in either binary or text mode
`perror`	Prints a system error message
`printf`	Writes formatted output to `stdout`
`putc`	Outputs a character to a stream
`putch`	Outputs a character to the screen
`putchar`	Outputs a character to `stdout`
`puts`	Outputs a string to `stdout`

Function	*Meaning*
`putw`	Outputs an integer value to a stream
`_read`	Reads from a file; does not remove carriage returns
`read`	Reads from a file; removes carriage returns and reports end-of-file
`remove`	Removes a file
`rename`	Changes the name of a file
`rewind`	Moves file pointer to beginning of a stream
`scanf`	Scans and formats input from `stdin`
`setbuf`	Sets I/O buffering for a stream
`_setcursortype`	Defines the appearance of the cursor
`setftime`	Sets the date and time for a file
`setmode`	Sets the mode for an open file
`setvbuf`	Sets I/O buffering for a stream
`sopen`	Opens a shared file
`sprintf`	Writes formatted output to a string
`sscanf`	Scans and formats input from a string
`stat`	Gets information about a file
`_strerror`	Generates a custom error message
`strerror`	Gets the error message for an error number
`tell`	Gets the file pointer position
`tmpfile`	Opens a temporary file in binary mode
`tmpnam`	Creates a unique file name
`ungetc`	Pushes a character into the input stream
`ungetch`	Pushes a character into the keyboard buffer
`unlock`	Releases file sharing locks
`va_arg`	Provides access to a variable argument list; used with `va_end` and `va_start`
`va_end`	Provides access to a variable argument list; used with `va_arg` and `va_start`

continues

Table 9.1. (continued)

Function	*Meaning*
`va_start`	Provides access to a variable argument list; used with `va_arg` and `va_end`
`vfprintf`	Writes formatted output to a stream
`vfscanf`	Scans and formats input from a stream
`vprintf`	Writes formatted output to `stdout`
`vscanf`	Scans and formats input from `stdin`
`vsprintf`	Writes formatted output to a string
`vsscanf`	Scans and formats input from a stream
`_write`	Writes to a file; does not translate linefeed characters to carriage return/linefeed pairs
`write`	Writes to a file; translates linefeed characters to carriage return/linefeed pairs

Borland C++ Input/Output Reference Guide

The remainder of this chapter provides detailed information on the use of each of the input/output functions and macros listed in table 9.1

access

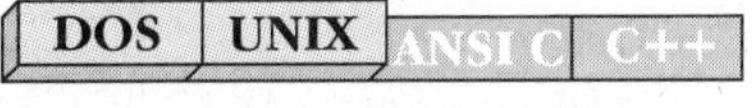

Syntax

```
int access(const char *filename, int amode);

const char *filename;     File name
int amode;                Access mode
```

Function The `access` function checks the accessibility of a file.

File(s) to Include `#include <io.h>`

Description The `access` function checks the accessibility of the file specified in the `filename` argument. The file in the `filename` argument is checked for the access mode specified in the `amode` argument. The possible values for the `amode` argument are as follows:

06	Check for read and write permission
04	Check for read permission
02	Check for write permission
01	Execute
00	Check for existence of file

Value(s) Returned When the specified access is allowed, 0 is returned. If an error occurs, –1 is returned and the global variable `errno` is set to ENOENT, for path or file name not found, or to EACCES, for permission denied.

Related Function(s) `chmod:` changes the accessibility of a file

Example The following example tests the accessibility of the newly created file `test.tst`.

```
#include <stdio.h>
#include <stdlib.h>
#include <conio.h>
#include <io.h>

int main (void)
{
int result;

clrscr ();
creatnew ("test.tst",0);
result = access("test.tst",4);
if (result == 0)
     printf ("TEST.TST has read access\n");
else
     printf ("TEST.TST doesn't have read
access\n");

return 0;
}
```

cgets

DOS | UNIX | ANSI C | C++

Syntax

```
char *cgets(char *str);

char *str;                    Retrieved string
```

Function The `cgets` function reads a string from the console.

File(s) to Include `#include <conio.h>`

Description The `cgets` function gets a string of characters from the console. The string is stored in the location pointed to by the `str` argument. Characters are read until a carriage return/linefeed combination is found, or the maximum number of characters has been read. The `str[0]` element holds the maximum length of the string to read. The `str[1]` element is set, upon return, to the actual number of characters read. Therefore, the length of the `str` argument should be the length of the `str[0]` element plus two.

Value(s Returned The pointer to the `str[2]` element is returned when successful.

Related Function(s)

`getch` : gets a character from the keyboard
`getche` : gets and echoes a character from the keyboard
`gets` : gets a string from `stdin`

Example In the following example, `cgets` reads a name from the console.

```
#include <stdio.h>
#include <stdlib.h>
#include <conio.h>
#include <io.h>

int main (void)
{
char buffer[83];
char *name;
```

```
clrscr ();
printf ("Input your name\n");
name = cgets (buffer);
printf ("\nPointer to name is %p\n",name);

return 0;
}
```

_chmod

DOS UNIX ANSI C C++

Syntax

```
int _chmod(const char *path, int func[,int
           attrib]);
```

`const char *path;`	*File to modify*
`int func[,int attrib];`	*Specifies set or retrieve*

Function The `_chmod` function reads or sets the DOS file attributes.

File(s) to Include

```
#include <io.h>
#include <dos.h>
```

Description The `_chmod` function either reads or sets the DOS file attributes for the file specified in the `path` argument. The `func` argument specifies whether the file attributes will be read or changed. If the `func` argument is 0, the current DOS attributes are returned. If the `func` argument is 1, the DOS attribute is set to the value in the `attrib` argument. The `attrib` argument is selected from one of the following:

FA_RDONLY	Read-only
FA_HIDDEN	Hidden file
FA_SYSTEM	System file
FA_LABEL	Volume label
FA_DIREC	Directory
FA_ARCH	Archive

Value(s) Returned When successful, the file attribute word is returned. When unsuccessful, the global variable `errno` is set to ENOENT, for path or file name not found, or to EACCES, for permission denied.

Related Function(s)
`access` : determines the accessibility of a file
`chmod` : changes the file access mode

Example The following example creates the file `testcase.tst` as a hidden file, then changes its access mode to read-only using the `_chmod` function.

```
#include <stdio.h>
#include <stdlib.h>
#include <conio.h>
#include <io.h>
#include <dos.h>

int main (void)
{
int result;

clrscr ();
creatnew ("testcase.tst",FA_HIDDEN);
_chmod ("testcase.tst",1,FA_RDONLY);
result = access ("testcase.tst",4);
if (result == 0)
     printf ("Access changed to read only\n");
else
     printf ("Access not changed\n");

return 0;
}
```

---

chmod

DOS | UNIX | ANSI C | C++

Syntax `int chmod(const char *path, int amode);`

`const char *path;`	*Path of file*
`int amode;`	*Access mode*

Function The `chmod` function changes the file access mode.

File(s) to Include
`#include <io.h>`
`#include <sys\stat.h>`

Description The `chmod` function sets the file access mode of the file specified in the `path` argument to the access mode specified in the `amode` argument. The `amode` argument can be set to one of the following:

`S_IWRITE`	Allowed to write
`S_IREAD`	Allowed to read
`S_IREAD|S_IWRITE`	Allowed to read and write

Value(s) Returned When successful, zero is returned. When unsuccessful, –1 is returned and the global variable `errno` is set to ENOENT, for path or file name not found, or to EACCES, for permission denied.

Related Function(s)
`access` : determines the accessibility of a file
`_chmod` : retrieves or sets the file access mode

Example The following example creates `testone.tst` and then sets its access mode for permission to read using the `chmod` function.

```
#include <stdio.h>
#include <stdlib.h>
#include <conio.h>
#include <io.h>
#include <sys\stat.h>

int main (void)
{
int result;

clrscr ();
creatnew ("testone.tst",0);
result = chmod ("testone.tst",S_IREAD);
if (result == 0)
     printf ("chmod on testone.tst successful\n");
else
     printf ("chmod on testone.tst
unsuccessful\n");

return 0;
}
```

chsize

DOS | UNIX | ANSI C | C++

Syntax
```
int chsize(int handle, long size);

int handle;                 File
long size;                  New size
```

Function The `chsize` function changes the size of a file.

File(s) to Include `#include <io.h>`

Description The `chsize` function changes the size of the file specified in the `handle` argument. If the size specified in the `size` argument is greater than the current size, the file is expanded and null characters are added. If the new size is smaller than the current size, the file is truncated and data extending beyond the new end-of-file is lost.

Value(s) Returned Zero is returned when successful. When unsuccessful, –1 is returned and the global variable `errno` is to set EACCES, for permission denied, EBADF, for bad file number, or ENOSPC, for UNIX not DOS.

Related Function(s)
`_creat` : creates a new file or overwrites existing one
`creat` : creates a new file or overwrites existing one

Example The following example changes the size of `size.tst` using the `chsize` function.

```
#include <stdio.h>
#include <stdlib.h>
#include <conio.h>
#include <io.h>
#include <fcntl.h>
#include <sys\stat.h>

int main (void)
{
int filehandle;
int result;
char buffer[10] = "**********";
```

```
clrscr ();
filehandle = creat("size.tst",S_IREAD|S_IWRITE);
write (filehandle,buffer,strlen(buffer));
result = chsize (filehandle,6L);
if (result == 0)
     printf ("size.tst modified\n");
else
     printf ("size.tst not modified\n");

return 0;
}
```

clearerr

DOS | UNIX | ANSI C | C++

Syntax

```
void clearerr(FILE *stream);

FILE *stream;
```

Stream

Function The `clearerr` function resets the error indication for the stream.

File(s) to Include `#include <stdio.h>`

Description The `clearerr` function resets the error indicator and end-of-file indicator to zero for the stream in the `stream` argument.

Value(s) Returned There is no return value.

Related Function(s)

`ferror` : detects stream errors
`perror` : prints a system error message

Example In the following example, `clearerr` clears the error that occurs when attempting to read from `clearerr.tst`.

```
#include <stdio.h>
#include <stdlib.h>
#include <conio.h>
#include <io.h>

int main (void)
```

continues

```
{
FILE *filepointer;
char grabchar;

clrscr ();
filepointer = fopen ("clearerr.tst","w");
grabchar = getc(filepointer);
if ferror(filepointer)
     {
     printf ("Error - Resetting error
indicator\n");
     clearerr (filepointer);
     }
else
     printf ("Character Retrieved\n");

fclose (filepointer);

return 0;
}
```

_close

DOS UNIX ANSI C C++

Syntax `int _close(int handle);`

`int handle;` *File handle*

Function The `_close` function closes a file. This function is used with `_open`.

File(s) to Include `#include <io.h>`

Description The `_close` function closes the file with the handle specified in the `handle` argument. The file handle to specify in the `handle` argument can be obtained from the `_creat`, `creat`, `creatnew`, `creattemp`, `dup`, `dup2`, `_open`, or `open` functions.

Value(s) Returned A zero is returned when successful. A –1 is returned when the handle in the `handle` argument does not identify a valid, open file. The global variable `errno` is also set to EBADF, for bad file number, when unsuccessful.

Related Function(s)
`close` : closes a file
`open` : opens a file

Example The following example uses the `_close` function to close the `-close.tst` file.

```
#include <stdio.h>
#include <stdlib.h>
#include <conio.h>
#include <io.h>
#include <fcntl.h>

int main (void)
{
int filehandle;
int result;

clrscr ();
filehandle = open ("-close.tst",O_CREAT);

result = _close (filehandle);
if (result == 0)
      printf ("-close.tst has been closed\n");
else
      printf ("Unable to close -close.tst\n");

return 0;
}
```

close

Syntax `int close(int handle);`

`int handle;` *File handle*

Function The `close` function closes a file. This function is used with `open`.

File(s) to Include `#include <io.h>`

Description The `close` function closes the file specified by the file handle in the `handle` argument. The file handle can be obtained from the `_creat`, `creat`, `creatnew`, `creattemp`, `dup`, `dup2`, `_open`, or `open` functions.

Value(s) Returned A zero is returned when successful. If the file handle in the `handle` argument does not identify a valid, open file, a –1 is returned and the global variable `errno` is set to EBADF, for bad file number.

Related Function(s)
`_close` : closes a file
`open` : opens a file

Example The following example uses the `close` function to close the file `close.tst`.

```
#include <stdio.h>
#include <stdlib.h>
#include <conio.h>
#include <io.h>
#include <fcntl.h>

int main (void)
{
int filehandle;
int result;

clrscr ();
filehandle = open ("close.tst",O_CREAT);

result = close (filehandle);
if (result == 0)
     printf ("close.tst has been closed\n");
else
     printf ("Unable to close close.tst\n");

return 0;
}
```

cprintf

DOS UNIX ANSI C C++

Syntax `int cprintf(const char *format[, argument, ...]);`

`const char *format[, argument, ...];` *Characters and formats*

Function The `cprintf` function displays formatted output on the screen.

File(s) to Include `#include <conio.h>`

Description The `cprintf` function displays the formatted string described by the series of arguments and the format specifiers in the format string pointed to by the `format` argument. The format specifiers are the same as those described in this chapter under the `printf` function.

Value(s) Returned The number of characters sent to the screen is returned.

Related Function(s)
`fprintf` : writes formatted output to a stream
`printf` : writes formatted output to `stdout`
`vprintf` : writes formatted output to a stream

Example In the following example, `cprintf` displays two text strings.

```
#include <stdio.h>
#include <stdlib.h>
#include <conio.h>

int main (void)
{
clrscr ();
cprintf ("The cprintf function displays\r\n");
cprintf ("formatted output\r\n");

return 0;
}
```

cputs

Syntax `int cputs(const char *str);`

`const char *str;` *String to write*

Function The `cputs` function writes a string to the screen.

File(s) to Include `#include <conio.h>`

Description The `cputs` function writes the string in the `str` argument to the screen. This function does not add a newline character and does not translate linefeed characters (`\n`) into carriage return/linefeed characters (`\r\n`).

Value(s) Returned The last character printed is returned.

Related Function(s)
`fputs` : outputs a string on a stream
`puts` : outputs a string to `stdout`

Example In the following example, `cputs` displays two text strings.

```
#include <stdio.h>
#include <stdlib.h>
#include <conio.h>

int main (void)
{
clrscr ();
cputs ("The cputs function writes a\r\n");
cputs ("string to the screen\r\n");

return 0;
}
```

_creat

DOS | UNIX | ANSI C | C++

Syntax `int _creat(const char *path, int attrib);`

`const char *path;`	*File*
`int attrib;`	*DOS attribute*

Function The `_creat` function creates a new file. The file is opened in binary mode.

File(s) to Include
`#include <io.h>`
`#include <dos.h>`

Description The `_creat` function creates a new file with the file name specified in the `path` argument. The new file has the DOS attribute specified in the `attrib` argument. The valid arguments for the `attrib` argument are as follows:

FA_RDONLY	Read-only
FA_HIDDEN	Hidden file
FA_SYSTEM	System file

When the file specified in the `path` argument exists, it is deleted and a new file with that name is created.

Value(s) Returned The file handle for the new file is returned when successful. When the function is unsuccessful, a –1 is returned and the global variable `errno` is set to ENOENT, for path or file name not found, EMFILE, for too many open files, or EACCES, for permission denied.

Related Function(s)

`creat` : creates a new file
`creatnew` : creates a new file
`creattemp` : creates a unique file

Example The following example uses the `_creat` function to create the file `_creat.tst`.

```
#include <stdio.h>
#include <stdlib.h>
#include <conio.h>
#include <dos.h>
#include <io.h>

int main (void)
{
int filehandle;

clrscr ();
filehandle = _creat ("  creat.tst", 0);
if (filehandle < 0)
     printf ("Error in creating  creat.tst\n");
else
     printf ("File handle for  creat.tst is %d\n",
            filehandle);
close (filehandle);

return 0;
}
```

creat

DOS | UNIX | ANSI C | C++

Syntax
```
int creat(const char *path, int amode);
```

`const char *path;`	*File name*
`int amode;`	*Access mode*

Function The `creat` function creates a new file. The file can be opened in either binary or text mode.

File(s) to Include
```
#include <io.h>
#include <sys\stat.h>
```

Description The `creat` function creates a new file with the file name specified in the `path` argument. If a file with the specified file name does not exist, a new file is created with the access mode specified in the `amode` argument. If a file with the specified file name exists, the associated file is truncated but the file attributes are not changed. If the associated file has a read-only attribute, the file is not modified at all. The valid values for the `amode` argument are as follows:

`S_IWRITE`	Allowed to write
`S_IREAD`	Allowed to read
`S_IREAD|S_IWRITE`	Allowed to read and write

Value(s) Returned The new file handle for the file is returned when successful. When unsuccessful, a –1 is returned and the global variable `errno` is set to ENOENT, for path or file not found, EMFILE, for too many open files, or EACCES, for permission denied.

Related Function(s)
`_creat` : creates a new file
`creanew` : creates a new file
`creattemp` : creates a unique file

Example The following example uses the `creat` function to create the `creat.tst` file.

```
#include <stdio.h>
#include <stdlib.h>
```

```
#include <conio.h>
#include <sys/stat.h>
#include <io.h>

int main (void)
{
int filehandle;

clrscr ();
filehandle = creat ("creat.tst",S_IREAD|S_IWRITE);
if (filehandle < 0)
     printf ("Error in creating creat.tst\n");
else
     printf ("File handle for creat.tst is %d\n",
          filehandle);
close (filehandle);

return 0;
}
```

creatnew

DOS UNIX ANSI C C++

Syntax

```
int creatnew(const char *path, int mode);
```

`const char *path;`	*File name*
`int mode;`	*Access mode*

Function The `creatnew` function creates a new file. This function will not overwrite an existing file.

File(s) to Include

```
#include <io.h>
#include <dos.h>
```

Description The `creatnew` function creates a new file with the file name and access mode specified in the `path` and `mode` arguments, respectively. If a file with the specified file name exists, the file is not modified and an error is returned. The valid values for the `mode` argument are as follows:

`FA_RDONLY`	Read-only
`FA_HIDDEN`	Hidden file
`FA_SYSTEM`	System file

Value(s) Returned The file handle of the new file is returned when successful. When unsuccessful, a –1 is returned and the global variable `errno` is set to one of the following values:

EEXIST	File exists
ENOENT	Path or file name not found
EMFILE	Too many open files
EACCES	Permission denied

Related Function(s)

`_creat` : creates a new file in binary mode
`creat` : creates a new file in either binary or text mode
`creattemp` : creates a unique file

Example In the following example, `creatnew` creates the file `creatnew.tst`.

```
#include <stdio.h>
#include <stdlib.h>
#include <conio.h>
#include <dos.h>
#include <io.h>

int main (void)
{
int filehandle;

clrscr ();
filehandle = creatnew ("creatnew.tst",FA_RDONLY);
if (filehandle < 0)
     printf ("Error in creating creatnew.tst\n");
else
     printf ("File handle for creatnew.tst is
%d\n",
             filehandle);
close (filehandle);

return 0;
}
```

creattemp

DOS UNIX ANSI C C++

Syntax

```
int creattemp(char *path, int attrib);
```

`char *path;`	*Path*
`int attrib;`	*DOS attribute*

Function The `creattemp` function creates a unique file.

File(s) to Include

```
#include <io.h>
#include <dos.h>
```

Description The `creattemp` function creates a unique file in the path, which should end with \, specified in the `path` argument. The file is created with the DOS attribute specified in the `attrib` argument. The valid values for the `creattemp` argument are as follows:

`FA_RDONLY`	Read only
`FA_HIDDEN`	Hidden file
`FA_SYSTEM`	System file

Value(s) Returned If successful, the file handle of the new file is returned. If unsuccessful, a –1 is returned and the global variable `errno` is set to ENOENT, for path or file name not found, EMFILE, for too many open files, or EACCES, for permission denied.

Related Function(s)

`_creat`	: creates a new file in binary mode
`creat`	: creates a new file in binary or text mode
`creatnew`	: creates a new file; will not overwrite an existing file

Example In the following example, `creattemp` creates a unique file.

```
#include <stdio.h>
#include <stdlib.h>
#include <conio.h>
#include <string.h>
#include <dos.h>

int main (void)
{
int filehandle;
char name[40];

clrscr ();
strcpy (name,"\\");
filehandle = creattemp (name,0);
if (filehandle ==  1)
     printf ("Error in creating temporary
file\n");
else
     printf ("File name : %s\n", name);
close (filehandle);

return 0;
}
```

cscanf

DOS | UNIX | ANSI C | C++

Syntax `int cscanf(char *format[, address, ...]);`

`char *format[, address, ...];` *String to scan*

Function The `cscanf` function scans and formats input from the console.

File(s) to Include `#include <conio.h>`

Description The `cscanf` function reads and formats a string that is read from the console. The string can contain a series of fields, with each field separated by whitespace and having a corresponding format specifier. The `format` argument points to the formatted string. The format specifiers used with this function are described in this chapter with the `scanf` function.

Value(s) Returned The number of input fields scanned, converted, and stored is returned.

Related Function(s)

`fscanf` : scans and formats input from a stream
`scanf` : scans and formats input from the `stdin` stream
`sscanf` : scans and formats input from a string

Example

In the following example, `cscanf` scans the name entered from the console.

```
#include <stdio.h>
#include <stdlib.h>
#include <conio.h>

int main (void)
{
char instring[80];

clrscr ();
cprintf ("Enter your name\r\n");
cscanf ("%s",instring);
cprintf ("\r\nHello %s\r\n",instring);

return 0;
}
```

dup

DOS | UNIX | ANSI C | C++

Syntax

```
int dup(int handle);

int handle;
```

File handle

Function

The `dup` function duplicates a file handle.

File(s) to Include

```
#include <io.h>
```

Description

The `dup` function duplicates the file handle in the `handle` argument. The value for the `handle` argument can be obtained from calling the `_creat`, `creat`, `_open`, `open`, or `dup2` functions. The new file handle has the same open file or device, the same file pointer, and the same access mode as the previous handle.

Value(s) Returned The new file handle is returned when successful. When unsuccessful, –1 is returned and the global variable `errno` is set to EMFILE, for too many open files, or EBADF, for bad file number.

Related Function(s) `dup2` : duplicates a file handle onto an existing one

Example In the following example, `dup` duplicates the file handle.

```
#include <stdio.h>
#include <stdlib.h>
#include <conio.h>
#include <io.h>

int main (void)
{
int oldhandle;
int newhandle;
int result;

clrscr ();
oldhandle = creat ("duptest.tst",0);
newhandle = dup (oldhandle);
printf ("Old handle : %d\n", oldhandle);
printf ("New handle : %d\n", newhandle);

return 0;
}
```

---

dup2

DOS | UNIX | ANSI C | C++

Syntax `int dup2(int oldhandle, int newhandle);`

`int oldhandle;`	*Old file handle*
`int newhandle;`	*New file handle*

Function The `dup2` function duplicates a file handle onto an existing one.

File(s) to Include `#include <io.h>`

Description The `dup2` function copies the file handle in the `oldhandle` argument over the file handle in the `newhandle` argument. Both the `oldhandle` and `newhandle` arguments are obtained by calling the `_creat`, `creat`, `_open`, `open`, or `dup` functions. The new file handle has the same open file or device, the same file pointer, and the same access mode as the original file handle.

Value(s) Returned When successful, 0 is returned. When unsuccessful, –1 is returned and the global variable `errno` is set to EMFILE, for too many open files, or to EBADF, for bad file number.

Related Function(s) `dup` : duplicates a file handle

Example In the following example, `dup2` copies `firsthandle` onto `secondhandle`.

```
#include <stdio.h>
#include <stdlib.h>
#include <conio.h>
#include <io.h>

int main (void)
{
int firsthandle;
int secondhandle;
int result;

clrscr ();
firsthandle = creat ("dup1.tst",0);
secondhandle = creat ("dup2.tst",0);
result = dup2 (firsthandle,secondhandle);
if (result == 0)
     printf ("Duplication successful\n");
else
     printf ("Duplication unsuccessful\n");

return 0;
}
```

eof

DOS | UNIX | ANSI C | C++

Syntax

```
int eof(int handle);

int handle;
```

File handle of file to check

Function The `eof` function checks a file for end-of-file.

File(s) to Include `#include <io.h>`

Description The `eof` function checks whether the file specified by the file handle in the `handle` argument has reached the end-of-file marker.

Value(s) Returned A 1 is returned if the end-of-file is reached. A 0 is returned if the end-of-file has not been reached. On error, a –1 is returned and the global variable `errno` is set to EBADF, for bad file number.

Related Function(s) `feof` : detects end-of-file on a stream

Example In the following example, `eof` checks `eof.tst` for end-of-file.

```
#include <stdio.h>
#include <stdlib.h>
#include <conio.h>
#include <io.h>

int main (void)
{
int handle;
int result;

clrscr ();
handle = creat ("eof.tst",0);
result = eof (handle);
if (result == 1)
     printf ("End of file reached\n");
else
     printf ("Not at end of file\n");

return 0;
}
```

fclose

DOS | UNIX | ANSI C | C++

Syntax `int fclose(FILE *stream);`

`FILE *stream;` *Stream to close*

Function The `fclose` function closes a stream.

File(s) to Include `#include <stdio.h>`

Description The `fclose` function closes the stream specified in the `stream` argument. All stream buffers are flushed and the system-allocated buffers are freed before closing.

Value(s) Returned A 0 is returned when successful. `EOF` is returned upon error.

Related Function(s)

`close` : closes a file
`fcloseall` : closes open streams
`fopen` : opens a stream

Example: In the following example, `fclose` closes the stream.

```
#include <stdio.h>
#include <stdlib.h>
#include <conio.h>
#include <io.h>

int main (void)
{
FILE *filepointer;
int result;

clrscr ();
filepointer = fopen ("fclose.tst","w");
result = fclose (filepointer);
if (result == 0)
     printf ("File closed\n");
else
     printf ("Can't close file\n");

return 0;
}
```

fcloseall

DOS | UNIX | ANSI C | C++

Syntax `int fcloseall(void);`

Function The `fcloseall` function closes all open streams.

File(s) to Include `#include <stdio.h>`

Description The `fcloseall` function closes all the open streams with the exception of the `stdin`, `strprn`, `stderr`, and `stdaux` streams.

Value(s) Returned The number of streams closed is returned. If an error occurs, `EOF` is returned.

Related Function(s)
`fclose` : closes a stream
`fopen` : opens a stream

Example In the following example, `fcloseall` closes all the open streams.

```
#include <stdio.h>
#include <stdlib.h>
#include <conio.h>
#include <io.h>

int main (void)
{
FILE *filepointer1;
FILE *filepointer2;
int result;

clrscr ();
filepointer1 = fopen ("fclose1.tst","w");
filepointer2 = fopen ("fclose2.tst","w");
result = fcloseall ();
if (result != EOF)
     printf ("%d files closed\n",result);
else
     printf ("Can't close files\n");

return 0;
}
```

fdopen

DOS | UNIX | ANSI C | C++

Syntax

```
FILE *fdopen(int handle, char *type);

int handle;                 File handle
char *type;                 Stream type
```

Function The `fdopen` function associates a stream with a file handle.

File(s) to Include `#include <stdio.h>`

Description The `fdopen` function associates a stream with the file handle specified in the `handle` argument. The `type` argument specifies the type of stream. The type of stream must correspond to the mode in the file handle and is selected from one of the following:

r	Read only
w	Write only
a	Append
r+	Read and write existing file
w+	Write to new file
a+	Append

The character `t` can be added to the end of the `type` string to specify that the file is opened or created in text mode. Similarly, the character `b` can be used to open or create a file in binary mode. When the `t` or `b` character is not used, the value of the global variable `_fmode` (`O_BINARY` or `_OTEXT`) determines the file mode.

Value(s) Returned The pointer to the opened stream is returned when successful. If unsuccessful, null is returned.

Related Function(s)
`fclose` : closes a stream
`fopen` : opens a stream
`freopen` : associates a new file with an open stream

Example In the following example, `fdopen` associates `filehandle` with `filepointer`.

```
#include <stdio.h>
#include <stdlib.h>
#include <conio.h>
#include <io.h>
#include <fcntl.h>
#include <sys\stat.h>

int main (void)
{
FILE *filepointer;
int filehandle;

clrscr ();
filehandle = open ("fdopen.tst",S_IREAD|S_IWRITE);
filepointer = fdopen (filehandle,"w");
if (filepointer != NULL)
      {
      printf ("fdopen was successful\n");
      fclose (filepointer);
      }
else
      printf ("fdopen wasn't successful\n");

return 0;
}
```

feof

DOS | UNIX | ANSI C | C++

Syntax `int feof(FILE *stream);`

`FILE *stream;` *Stream to check*

Function The `feof` macro checks a stream for end-of-file.

File(s) to Include `#include <stdio.h>`

Description The `feof` macro checks the stream specified in the `stream` argument for the end-of-file indicator. When the end-of-file is found, read operations on the file return the value of the indicator until the `rewind` function is called. Each input operation results in a reset of the end-of-file indicator.

Value(s) Returned A nonzero value is returned if the end-of-file indicator was detected on the last input operation to the stream. If the end-of-file indicator was not detected, a 0 is returned.

Related Function(s) eof : checks for end-of-file

Example The following example checks for end-of-file on the open stream using the feof macro.

```
#include <stdio.h>
#include <stdlib.h>
#include <conio.h>
#include <io.h>

int main (void)
{
FILE *filepointer;
int result;
int inchar;

clrscr ();
filepointer = fopen ("feof.tst","w");
inchar = fgetc (filepointer);
result = feof (filepointer);
if (result == 0)
     printf ("EOF not reached\n");
else
     printf ("EOF reached\n");
fclose (filepointer);

return 0;
}
```

ferror

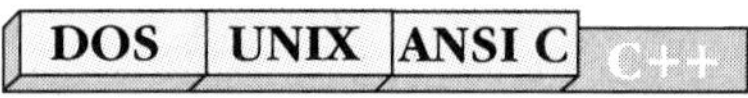

Syntax `int ferror(FILE *stream);`

`FILE *stream;` *Stream to test*

Function The ferror macro tests the specified stream for errors.

File(s) to Include `#include <stdio.h>`

Description The ferror macro tests the stream specified in the stream argument for read and write errors. Once the stream's error indicator has been set, it remains set until the `clearerr` or `rewind` function is called.

Value(s) Returned A nonzero value is returned if an error is detected.

Related Function(s)
`clearerr` : resets the error indicator
`perror` : prints a system error message

Example In the following example, the `ferror` macro tests the open stream for errors.

```
#include <stdio.h>
#include <stdlib.h>
#include <conio.h>
#include <io.h>

int main (void)
{
FILE *filepointer;
char grabchar;

clrscr ();
filepointer = fopen ("clearerr.tst","w");
grabchar = getc(filepointer);
if ferror(filepointer)
     {
     printf ("Error - Resetting error
indicator\n");
     clearerr (filepointer);
     }
else
     printf ("Character Retrieved\n");
fclose (filepointer);

return 0;
}
```

fflush

DOS	UNIX	ANSI C	C++

Syntax `int fflush(FILE *stream);`

`FILE *stream;` *Stream to flush*

Function The `fflush` function flushes the specified stream.

File(s) to Include `#include <stdio.h>`

Description The `fflush` function writes the output of the stream specified by the `stream` argument to the associated file when the stream has buffered output. When the stream has no buffered output, the `fflush` function does nothing. The stream remains open after the function has completed.

Value(s) Returned A 0 is returned when successful. If an error is detected, `EOF` is returned.

Related Function(s)
`fclose` : closes a stream
`flushall` : flushes all streams

Example In the following example, the `fflush` function flushes the buffered output of the stream.

```
#include <stdio.h>
#include <stdlib.h>
#include <conio.h>
#include <io.h>

int main (void)
{
FILE *filepointer;
char buffer[] = "Put into file fflush.tst";
int result;

clrscr ();
filepointer = fopen ("fflush.tst","w");
fwrite (buffer,strlen(buffer),1,filepointer);
result = fflush (filepointer);
if (result == 0)
     printf ("Stream flushed\n");
else
     printf ("Unable to flush stream\n");
fclose (filepointer);

return 0;
}
```

fgetc

DOS | UNIX | ANSI C | C++

Syntax `int fgetc(FILE *stream);`

`FILE *stream;` *Input stream*

Function The `fgetc` function gets a character from a stream.

File(s) to Include `#include <stdio.h>`

Description The `fgetc` function gets the next character from the stream specified in the `stream` argument.

Value(s) Returned The retrieved character, converted to type `int` without sign extension, is returned. If an error occurs, or the end-of-file is reached, `EOF` is returned.

Related Function(s)

`fgetchar` : gets a character from `stdin`
`fputc` : puts a character on a stream
`getc` : gets a character from a stream

Example In the following example, `fgetc` attempts to get a character from the open stream.

```
#include <stdio.h>
#include <stdlib.h>
#include <conio.h>
#include <io.h>

int main (void)
{
FILE *filepointer;
int result;
int inchar;

clrscr ();
filepointer = fopen ("feof.tst","w");
inchar = fgetc (filepointer);
result = feof (filepointer);
if (result == 0)
     {
```

```
     printf ("EOF not reached\n");
     printf ("Got character %d \n",inchar);
     }
else
     printf ("EOF reached\n");
fclose (filepointer);

return 0;
}
```

fgetchar

DOS | UNIX | ANSI C | C++

Syntax `int fgetchar(void);`

Function The `fgetchar` function gets a character from `stdin`.

File(s) to Include `#include <stdio.h>`

Description The `fgetchar` function retrieves a character from `stdin`.

Value(s) Returned The retrieved character, converted to type `int` without sign extension, is returned. If an error or end-of-file is encountered, `EOF` is returned.

Related Function(s)
`fgetc` : gets a character from a stream
`fputchar` : puts a character on `stdout`
`getchar` : gets a character from `stdin`

Example In the following example, `fgetchar` retrieves a character.

```
#include <stdio.h>
#include <stdlib.h>
#include <conio.h>
#include <io.h>

int main (void)
{
int inchar;

clrscr ();
printf ("Enter a character - then press
<ENTER>\n");
```

continues

```
inchar = fgetchar ();
printf ("Input Character : %c\n",inchar);

return 0;
}
```

fgetpos

DOS UNIX ANSI C C++

Syntax
```
int fgetpos(FILE *stream, fpos_t *pos);
```

`FILE *stream;`	*Stream*
`fpos_t *pos;`	*File pointer*

Function The `fgetpos` function gets the current file pointer.

File(s) to Include `#include <stdio.h>`

Description The `fgetpos` function stores the position of the file pointer that corresponds to the stream specified in the `stream` argument in the location pointed to by the `pos` argument.

Value(s) Returned A 0 is returned when successful. When unsuccessful, a nonzero value is returned and the global variable `errno` is set to EBADF, for bad file number, or EINVAL, for invalid argument.

Related Function(s) `fsetpos` : sets the current file pointer

Example In the following example, `fgetpos` gets the position of the file pointer.

```
#include <stdio.h>
#include <stdlib.h>
#include <conio.h>
#include <io.h>

int main (void)
{
FILE *filepointer;
fpos_t position;
char buffer[] = "Put this string into
fgetpos.tst";
```

```
clrscr ();
filepointer = fopen("fgetpos.tst","w+");
fwrite (buffer,strlen(buffer),1,filepointer);
fgetpos (filepointer,&position);
printf ("File Pointer : %ld\n",position);
fclose (filepointer);

return 0;
}
```

fgets

DOS | UNIX | ANSI C | C++

Syntax `char *fgets(char s, int n, FILE *stream);`

`char s;`	*String*
`int n;`	*Number of characters to read*
`FILE *stream;`	*Stream to read*

Function The `fgets` function gets a string from a stream.

File(s) to Include `#include <stdio.h>`

Description The `fgets` function reads a number of characters from the stream specified in the `stream` argument and places these characters in the `string` argument. Reading stops when a newline character is read or the number of characters specified in the `n` argument, minus one, is read. A null byte is added to the string to mark the end.

Value(s) Returned The string pointed to by the `s` argument is returned when successful. If an error or end-of-line is encountered, null is returned.

Related Function(s)
`cgets` : gets a string from the console
`fputs` : outputs a string on a stream
`gets` : gets a string from `stdin`

Example In the following example, `fgets` reads the `fgets.tst` file.

```
#include <stdio.h>
#include <stdlib.h>
#include <conio.h>
#include <io.h>

int main (void)
{
FILE *filepointer;
char buffer[] = "Put this string into fgets.tst";
char instring[40];

clrscr ();
filepointer = fopen("fgets.tst","w+");
fwrite (buffer,strlen(buffer),1,filepointer);
fseek (filepointer,0,SEEK_SET);
fgets (instring,strlen(buffer)+1,filepointer);
printf ("String : %s\n",instring);
fclose (filepointer);

return 0;
}
```

filelength

DOS | UNIX | ANSI C | C++

Syntax `long filelength(int handle);`

`int handle;` *File handle*

Function The `filelength` function determines the file size of a specified file.

File(s) to Include `#include <io.h>`

Description The `filelength` function retrieves the file size, in bytes, of the file specified by the `handle` argument.

Value(s) Returned The file length, in bytes, is returned when successful. When unsuccessful, a –1 is returned and the global variable `errno` is set to EBADF, for bad file number.

Related Function(s)
`fopen` : opens a stream
`open` : opens a file

Example In the following example, `filelength` determines the length of `fileleng.tst`.

```
#include <stdio.h>
#include <stdlib.h>
#include <conio.h>
#include <io.h>
#include <fcntl.h>
#include <sys/stat.h>

int main (void)
{
int filehandle;
long result;

clrscr ();
filehandle = open
("fileleng.tst",S_IREAD|S_IWRITE);
result = filelength (filehandle);
if (result ==  1)
     printf ("Error\n");
else
     printf ("File length (bytes) :
%ld\n",result);
close (filehandle);

return 0;
}
```

fileno

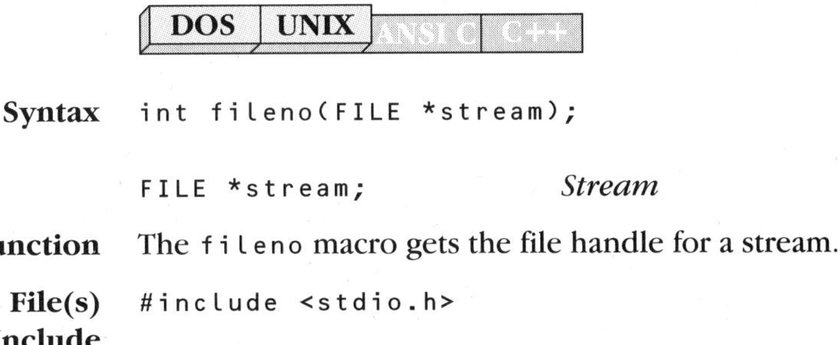

Syntax `int fileno(FILE *stream);`

`FILE *stream;` *Stream*

Function The `fileno` macro gets the file handle for a stream.

File(s) to Include `#include <stdio.h>`

Description The `fileno` macro retrieves the file handle for the stream specified in the `stream` argument. When the specified stream has more than one handle, the handle assigned when the stream was first opened is returned.

Value(s) Returned The file handle is returned.

Related Function(s)
`fdopen` : associates a stream with a file handle
`fopen` : opens a stream

Example In the following example, the `fileno` macro gets the file handle for the stream.

```
#include <stdio.h>
#include <stdlib.h>
#include <conio.h>
#include <io.h>
#include <fcntl.h>
#include <sys/stat.h>

int main (void)
{
FILE *filepointer;
int filehandle;

clrscr ();
filepointer = fopen ("fileno.tst","w");
filehandle = fileno (filepointer);
printf ("File Handle : %d\n",filehandle);
fclose (filepointer);

return 0;
}
```

flushall

DOS | UNIX | ANSI C | C++

Syntax `int flushall(void);`

Function The `flushall` function flushes all streams.

File(s) to Include `#include <stdio.h>`

Description The `flushall` function clears all buffers that correspond to open input streams and writes all buffers that correspond to open output streams. All streams stay open.

Value(s) Returned The number of open input and output streams is returned.

Related Function(s)

fclose : closes a stream
fcloseall : closes open streams
fflush : flushes a stream

Example In the following example, flushall flushes the open streams.

```
#include <stdio.h>
#include <stdlib.h>
#include <conio.h>
#include <io.h>

int main (void)
{
FILE *filepointer1;
FILE *filepointer2;
int result;

clrscr ();
filepointer1 = fopen ("flush1.tst","w");
filepointer2 = fopen ("flush2.tst","w");
result = flushall ();
printf ("%d streams flushed\n",result);
fclose (filepointer1);
fclose (filepointer2);

return 0;
}
```

fopen

DOS | UNIX | ANSI C | C++

Syntax

```
FILE *fopen(const char *filename, const char
            *mode);
```

const char *filename; *File name*
const char *mode; *Associated mode*

Function The fopen function opens a stream.

File(s) to Include #include <stdio.h>

Description The `fopen` function opens the file specified in the `filename` argument and its associated stream. The `mode` argument is one of the following and specifies the mode of the stream.

r	Read only
w	Write only
a	Append
r+	Read or write an existing file
w+	Read or write a new file
a+	Append

The character `b` can be added to the `mode` string to open or create a file in binary mode. The character `t` can be added to the `mode` string to open or create a file in text mode. If neither `b` nor `t` is used, the file mode is determined by the value of the `_fmode` global variable (`O_BINARY` or `O_TEXT`).

Value(s) Returned The pointer to the opened stream is returned when successful. Null is returned when unsuccessful.

Related Function(s) `fclose` : closes a stream
`fdopen` : associates a stream with a file handle

Example In the following example, `fopen` opens the stream.

```
#include <stdio.h>
#include <stdlib.h>
#include <conio.h>
#include <io.h>

int main (void)
{
FILE *filepointer;

clrscr ();
filepointer = fopen ("fopen.tst","w");
if (filepointer == NULL)
     printf ("Can't open file\n");
else
     printf ("fopen.tst opened\n");
fclose (filepointer);

return 0;
}
```

fprintf

DOS | UNIX | ANSI C | C++

Syntax

```
int fprintf(FILE *stream, const char
            *format[,argument,...]);

FILE *stream;                          Stream
const char *format[, argument, ...];   Format string
```

Function The `fprintf` function writes formatted output to a stream.

File(s) to Include `#include <stdio.h>`

Description The `fprintf` function writes formatted data. This data is created from a series of arguments and the format specifier string pointed to by the `format` argument. The data is written to the stream specified in the `stream` argument. The format specifier and argument pairs determine the format of the output. The format specifiers used with the `fprintf` function are the same as those explained in this chapter under the `printf` function.

Value(s) Returned The number of bytes output is returned when successful. When unsuccessful, `EOF` is returned.

Related Function(s)
`cprintf` : writes formatted output to the screen
`printf` : writes formatted output to `stdout`
`sprintf` : writes formatted output to a string

Example In the following example, `fprintf` sends a formatted string to the stream.

```
#include <stdio.h>
#include <stdlib.h>
#include <conio.h>
#include <io.h>

int main (void)
{
FILE *filepointer;
int value = 5;
int result;
```

```
clrscr ();
filepointer = fopen ("fprintf.tst","w");
result = fprintf (filepointer,"send to file
%d",value);
if (result == EOF)
     printf ("Error\n");
else
     printf ("Number of bytes output :
%d\n",result);
fclose (filepointer);

return 0;
}
```

fputc

DOS | UNIX | ANSI C | C++

Syntax `int fputc(int c, FILE *stream);`

`int c;` *Character to output*
`FILE *stream;` *Stream for output*

Function The `fputc` function puts a character on a stream.

File(s) to Include `#include <stdio.h>`

Description The `fputc` function places the character specified in the `c` argument on the stream specified in the `stream` argument.

Value(s) Returned The character `c` is returned when successful. `EOF` is returned when unsuccessful.

Related Function(s)
`fgetc` : gets a character from a stream
`putc` : outputs a character to a stream

Example In the following example, `fputc` outputs `A` on the stream.

```
#include <stdio.h>
#include <stdlib.h>
#include <conio.h>
#include <io.h>

int main (void)
{
```

```
#include <io.h>

int main (void)
{
FILE *filepointer;
int result;

clrscr ();
filepointer = fopen ("fputs.tst","w");
result = fputs ("Output to stream",filepointer);
if (result == EOF)
     printf ("\nError\n");
else
     printf ("\n%c : last character
sent\n",result);
fclose (filepointer);

return 0;
}
```

fread

DOS | UNIX | ANSI C | C++

Syntax

```
size_t fread(void *ptr, size_t size, size_t n,
             FILE *stream);
```

`void *ptr;`	*Pointer to block*
`size_t size;`	*Length of data items*
`size_t n;`	*Number of data items*
`FILE *stream;`	*Stream to read from*

Function The `fread` function reads data from a stream.

File(s) to Include `#include <stdio.h>`

Description The `fread` function reads a number of data items from the stream specified in the `stream` argument. The number of items read is defined in the `n` argument. The size, in bytes, of each data item is defined in the `size` argument. The `ptr` argument points to the block of data items read from the stream.

Value(s) Returned The number of items read is returned when successful. A short count is returned if an error or end-of-file is encountered.

Related Function(s)

`fopen` : opens a stream
`fwrite` : writes to a stream
`read` : reads from a file

Example In the following example, `fread` reads data from the stream.

```
#include <stdio.h>
#include <stdlib.h>
#include <conio.h>
#include <io.h>

int main (void)
{
FILE *filepointer;
char buffer[] = "Put this in fread.tst";
char buffer1[40];
int result;

clrscr ();
filepointer = fopen ("fread.tst","w+");
fwrite (buffer, strlen(buffer)+1,1,filepointer);
fseek (filepointer,SEEK_SET,0);
result = fread
(buffer1,strlen(buffer)+1,1,filepointer);
printf ("\n%d item(s) read\n",result);
printf ("String : %s\n",buffer1);
fclose (filepointer);

return 0;
}
```

freopen

DOS | UNIX | ANSI C | C++

Syntax

```
FILE *freopen(const char *filename, const char
                *mode, FILE *stream);

const char *filename;     File name
const char *mode;         File mode
FILE *stream;             Stream
```

Function The `freopen` function associates a new file with an open stream.

File(s) to Include `#include <stdio.h>`

Description The `freopen` function substitutes the file specified in the `filename` argument for the stream in the `stream` argument. The `mode` argument specifies the file mode and is chosen from one of the following:

r	Read only
w	Write only
a	Append
r+	Open existing file for read or write
w+	Create a new file for read or write
a+	Append

The character `t` can be added to the `mode` string to open or create the file in text mode. The character `b` can be added to the `mode` string to open or create the file binary mode. If the `t` or `b` character is not added, the file is opened or created in the mode specified by the value in the `_fmode` global variable (`O_TEXT` or `O_BINARY`).

Value(s) Returned The `stream` argument is returned when successful. When unsuccessful, null is returned.

Related Function(s)
`fclose` : closes a stream
`fdopen` : associates a stream with a file handle
`fopen` : opens a stream

Example In the following example, `freopen` associates `freopen.tst` with `stdout`.

```
#include <stdio.h>
#include <stdlib.h>
#include <conio.h>
#include <io.h>

int main (void)
{
char buffer[] = "Send this to the file";
char buffer1[40];

clrscr ();
freopen ("freopen.tst","w",stdout);
printf ("%s",buffer);
fclose (stdout);

return 0;
}
```

fscanf

DOS | UNIX | ANSI C | C++

Syntax

```
int fscanf(FILE *stream, const char
            *format[,address,...]);
```

```
FILE *stream;                          Stream
const char *format[,address,...]); Format string
```

Function The `fscanf` function formats input from a stream.

File(s) to Include `#include <stdio.h>`

Description The `fscanf` function reads a series of input fields from the stream specified in the `stream` argument, formats each field according to a format specifier, and stores the formatted input. The format specifiers are pointed to by the `format` argument. The format specifiers are explained in this chapter under the `scanf` function.

Value(s) Returned The number of input fields scanned, converted, and stored is returned when successful. `EOF` is returned if an attempt is made to read at the end-of-file. Zero is returned when no fields are stored.

Related Function(s)
`cscanf` : scans and formats input from the console
`scanf` : scans and formats input from `stdin`

Example In the following example, `fscanf` retrieves input from the stream.

```
#include <stdio.h>
#include <stdlib.h>
#include <conio.h>
#include <io.h>

int main (void)
{
char x;

clrscr ();
printf ("Enter a character - then press
<Enter>\n");
fscanf (stdin,"%c",&x);
```

```
printf ("Value entered : %c\n",x);

return 0;
}
```

fseek

DOS | UNIX | ANSI C | C++

Syntax `int fseek(FILE *stream, long offset, int whence);`

```
FILE *stream;          Stream
long offset;           Number of offset bytes
int whence;            File location
```

Function The `fseek` function repositions the file pointer on a stream.

File(s) to Include `#include <stdio.h>`

Description The `fseek` function sets the file pointer associated with the stream in the `stream` argument. The file pointer is set to a position that is offset from its position in the `whence` argument by the number of bytes specified in the `offset` argument. The `whence` argument is selected from one of the following:

Constant	*Value*	*Meaning*
SEEK_SET	0	File beginning
SEEK_CUR	1	Current file pointer position
SEEK_END	2	End-of-file

Value(s) Returned A 0 is returned when successful. A nonzero value is returned when unsuccessful.

Related Function(s)
`fgetpos` : gets the position of the file pointer
`fopen` : opens a stream
`fsetpos` : positions the file pointer of a stream

Example In the following example, `fseek` moves the file pointer to the beginning of the stream.

```
#include <stdio.h>
#include <stdlib.h>
#include <conio.h>
#include <io.h>

int main (void)
{
FILE *filepointer;
char buffer[] = "Put this in fseek.tst";
char buffer1[40];
int result;

clrscr ();
filepointer = fopen ("fseek.tst","w+");
fwrite (buffer, strlen(buffer)+1,1,filepointer);
fseek (filepointer,SEEK_SET,0);
result = fread
(buffer1,strlen(buffer)+1,1,filepointer);
printf ("\n%d item(s) read\n",result);
printf ("String : %s\n",buffer1);
fclose (filepointer);

return 0;
}
```

fsetpos

DOS | UNIX | ANSI C | C++

Syntax `int fsetpos(FILE *stream, const fpos_t *pos);`

`FILE *stream;`	*Stream*
`const fpos_t *pos;`	*New position*

Function The `fsetpos` function sets a new position for the file pointer of a stream.

File(s) to Include `#include <stdio.h>`

Description The `fsetpos` function sets the file pointer that corresponds to the stream specified in the `stream` argument to the position specified in the `pos` argument. The value of the `pos` argument is the value returned by calling the `fgetpos` function.

Value(s) Returned Zero is returned when successful. When unsuccessful, a nonzero value is returned and the global variable `errno` is set to a nonzero value.

Related Function(s) `fgetpos` : gets the position of the file pointer

Example In the following example, `fsetpos` sets the position of the file pointer.

```
#include <stdio.h>
#include <stdlib.h>
#include <conio.h>
#include <io.h>

int main (void)
{
FILE *filepointer;
fpos_t position;
int result;

clrscr ();
filepointer = fopen ("fsetpos.tst","w+");
fgetpos (filepointer,&position);
result = fsetpos (filepointer,&position);
if (result == 0)
     printf ("File position : %ld\n",position);
else
     printf ("Unable to set file position\n");
fclose (filepointer);

return 0;
}
```

---

fstat

DOS | UNIX | ANSI C | C++

Syntax `int fstat(int handle, struct stat *statbuf);`

`int handle;`	*File handle*
`struct stat *statbuf;`	*File information*

Function The `fstat` function retrieves information on an open file or directory.

File(s) to Include `#include <sys\stat.h>`

Description The `fstat` function retrieves information on the open file or directory that corresponds to the file handle specified in the `handle` argument. The information is stored in a structure of type `stat`, which is pointed to by the `statbuf` argument. The `stat` structure is as follows:

```
struct stat
     {
     short st_dev;           Drive number
     short st_ino;           No meaning under DOS
     short st_mode;          File mode information
     short st_nlink;         Set to integer constant 1
     int st_uid;             No meaning under DOS
     int st_gid;             No meaning under DOS
     short st_rdev;          Same as st_dev
     long st_size;           File size in bytes
     long st_atime;          Time file was modified
     long st_mtime;          Same as st_atime
     long st_ctime;          Same as st_atime
     };
```

Value(s) Returned Zero is returned when successful. When unsuccessful, a –1 is returned and the global variable `errno` is set to EBADF, for bad file handle.

Related Function(s) `stat` : retrieves information about a file

Example In the following example, `fstat` gets information on `fstat.tst`.

```
#include <stdio.h>
#include <stdlib.h>
#include <conio.h>
#include <io.h>
#include <sys\stat.h>

int main (void)
{
FILE *filepointer;
struct stat bufstats;
int filehandle;
```

```
clrscr ();
filepointer = fopen ("fstat.tst","w+");
filehandle = fileno (filepointer);
fstat (filehandle,&bufstats);
printf ("File on drive : %c\n",
'A'+bufstats.st_dev);
printf ("Size of file : %ld\n",bufstats.st_size);
fclose (filepointer);

return 0;
}
```

ftell

DOS | UNIX | ANSI C | C++

Syntax `long int ftell(FILE *stream);`

`FILE *stream;` *Stream*

Function The `ftell` function retrieves the current file pointer for a stream.

File(s) to Include `#include <stdio.h>`

Description The `ftell` function retrieves the current file pointer for the stream specified in the `stream` argument.

Value(s) Returned The position of the file pointer is returned when successful. When unsuccessful, a –1L is returned and the global variable `errno` is set to a positive value.

Related Function(s)
`fgetpos` : retrieves the current file pointer
`fseek` : repositions the file pointer
`fsetpos` : positions the file pointer

Example In the following example, `ftell` determines the position of the current file pointer.

```
#include <stdio.h>
#include <stdlib.h>
#include <conio.h>
#include <io.h>
```

```
int main (void)
{
FILE *filepointer;
long position;

clrscr ();
filepointer = fopen ("ftell.tst","w+");
position = ftell (filepointer);
printf ("File pointer at byte : %ld\n",position);
fclose (filepointer);

return 0;
}
```

fwrite

DOS | UNIX | ANSI C | C++

Syntax

```
size_t fwrite(const void *ptr, size_t size, size_t n,
              FILE *stream);
```

`const void *ptr;`	*Pointer*
`size_t size;`	*Length (bytes) of data items*
`size_t n;`	*Number of data items*
`FILE *stream;`	*Stream*

Function The `fwrite` function adds data to a stream.

File(s) to Include `#include <stdio.h>`

Description The `fwrite` function adds data items to the end of the stream specified in the `stream` argument. The number of data items to add is specified in the `n` argument. The size, in bytes, of each data item is specified in the `size` argument. The data written begins at the position pointed to by the `ptr` argument.

Value(s) Returned The number of items written is returned when successful. When unsuccessful, a short count is returned.

Related Function(s)
`fopen` : opens a stream
`fread` : reads data from a stream

Example In the following example, `fwrite` writes the buffer to the file `fwrite.tst`.

```
#include <stdio.h>
#include <stdlib.h>
#include <conio.h>
#include <io.h>

int main (void)
{
FILE *filepointer;
char buffer[] = "Put this in fwrite.tst";
char buffer1[40];
int result;

clrscr ();
filepointer = fopen ("fwrite.tst","w+");
fwrite (buffer, strlen(buffer)+1,1,filepointer);
fseek (filepointer,SEEK_SET,0);
result = fread
(buffer1,strlen(buffer)+1,1,filepointer);
printf ("\n%d item(s) read\n",result);
printf ("String : %s\n",buffer1);
fclose (filepointer);

return 0;
}
```

getc

DOS | UNIX | ANSI C | C++

Syntax `int getc(FILE *stream);`

`FILE *stream;` *Stream*

Function The `getc` macro retrieves a character from a stream.

File(s) to Include `#include <stdio.h>`

Description The `getc` macro retrieves a character from the input stream specified in the `stream` argument. The file pointer for the stream is then moved to point to the next character in the stream.

Value(s) Returned The character read from the stream, converted to type `int` without sign extension, is returned when successful. `EOF` is returned if the end-of-file is read or an error occurs.

Related Function(s)
`fgetc` : gets a character from a stream
`getch` : gets a character from the keyboard
`putc` : outputs a character to a stream

Example In the following example, the `getc` macro gets a character from `stdin`.

```
#include <stdio.h>
#include <stdlib.h>
#include <conio.h>
#include <io.h>

int main (void)
{
char inchar;

clrscr ();
printf ("Enter a character - then press
<ENTER>\n");
inchar = getc (stdin);
printf ("Character : %c\n",inchar);

return 0;
}
```

---

getch

DOS | UNIX | ANSI C | C++

Syntax `int getch(void);`

Function The `getch` function gets a character from the keyboard but does not display the character on the screen.

File(s) to Include `#include <conio.h>`

Description The `getch` function retrieves a character from the keyboard. The retrieved character is not displayed on the screen.

Value(s) Returned The character read from the keyboard is returned.

Related Function(s)

getc : gets a character from a stream
getchar : gets a character from stdin
getche : gets a character from the keyboard and echoes

Example In the following example, getch gets a character from the keyboard.

```
#include <stdio.h>
#include <stdlib.h>
#include <conio.h>
#include <io.h>

int main (void)
{
int inchar;

clrscr ();
printf ("Press a key\n");
inchar = getch ();
printf ("ASCII value : %d\n",inchar);

return 0;
}
```

---

getchar

DOS | UNIX | ANSI C | C++

Syntax `int getchar(void);`

Function The getchar macro gets a character from the stdin stream.

File(s) to Include `#include <stdio.h>`

Description The getchar macro retrieves a character from the stdin stream.

Value(s) Returned The retrieved character, converted to type int without sign extension, is returned when successful. When the end-of-file is reached, or an error occurs, EOF is returned.

Related Function(s)

getc : gets a character from a stream
getch : gets a character from the keyboard
getche : gets a character from the keyboard and echoes

Example In the following example, the `getchar` macro gets a character from the `stdin` stream.

```
#include <stdio.h>
#include <stdlib.h>
#include <conio.h>
#include <io.h>

int main (void)
{
int inchar;

clrscr ();
printf ("Press a key - then press <ENTER>\n");
inchar = getchar ();
printf ("ASCII value : %d\n",inchar);

return 0;
}
```

getche

DOS | UNIX | ANSI C | C++

Syntax `int getche(void);`

Function The `getche` function gets a character from the keyboard and displays the character on the screen.

File(s) to Include `#include <conio.h>`

Description The `getche` function retrieves a character from the keyboard. The character is then displayed on the screen.

Value(s) Returned The character read from the keyboard is returned.

Related Function(s)
`getc` : gets a character from a stream
`getch` : gets a character from the keyboard
`getchar` : gets a character from the `stdin` stream

Example In the following example, `getche` gets a character from the keyboard and displays it on the screen.

```
#include <stdio.h>
#include <stdlib.h>
#include <conio.h>
#include <io.h>

int main (void)
{
int inchar;

clrscr ();
printf ("Press a key\n");
inchar = getche ();
printf ("\nASCII value : %d\n",inchar);

return 0;
}
```

getftime

DOS UNIX ANSI C C++

Syntax

```
int getftime(int handle, struct ftime *ftimep);
```

`int handle;`	*File handle*
`struct ftime *ftimep;`	*File information*

Function The `getftime` function gets information on the file date and time.

File(s) to Include `#include <io.h>`

Description The `getftime` function retrieves date and time information on the file specified by the file handle in the `handle` argument. The information is stored in the structure of type `ftime`, which is pointed to by the `ftimep` argument.

Value(s) Returned Zero is returned when successful. When unsuccessful, a –1 is returned and the global variable `errno` is set to EINVFNC, for invalid function number, or EBADF, for bad file number.

Related Function(s) `setftime` : sets file date and time

Example In the following example, `getftime` gets the date and time information for `getftime.tst`.

```
#include <stdio.h>
#include <stdlib.h>
#include <conio.h>
#include <io.h>

int main (void)
{
FILE *filepointer;
int filehandle;
struct ftime datetime;

clrscr ();
filepointer = fopen ("getftime.tst","w");
filehandle = fileno (filepointer);
getftime (filehandle,&datetime);
printf ("Date : %02u : %02u : %02u\n",
datetime.ft_month,
     datetime.ft_day, datetime.ft_year + 1980);
printf ("Time : %02u : %02u : %02u\n",
datetime.ft_hour,
     datetime.ft_min, datetime.ft_tsec/2);
fclose (filepointer);

return 0;
}
```

---

getpass

DOS | UNIX | ANSI C | C++

Syntax `char *getpass(const char *prompt);`

`const char *prompt;` *Prompt string*

Function The `getpass` function reads a password from the console.

File(s) to Include `#include <conio.h>`

Description The `getpass` function reads a system password from the system console. The function prompts password entry by displaying the prompt string specified in the `prompt` argument. The characters read from the console are not displayed on the screen.

Value(s) Returned The pointer to a static string (up to eight characters, not counting the null terminator) that contains the password is returned.

Related Function(s)
`getch` : gets a character from the keyboard
`getche` : gets a character from the keyboard and echoes

Example In the following example, `getpass` accepts and verifies a password.

```
#include <stdlib.h>
#include <stdio.h>
#include <conio.h>
#include <io.h>

int main (void)
{
char *psword;

clrscr ();
psword = getpass ("Enter the password\n");
cprintf ("Password %s\r\n",psword);

getch();
return 0;
}
```

gets

DOS | UNIX | ANSI C | C++

Syntax

```
char *gets(char *s);
```

`char *s;` *String*

Function The `gets` function gets a string from the `stdin` stream.

File(s) to Include `#include <stdio.h>`

Description The `gets` function retrieves a string of characters from the `stdin` stream. The string is placed in the position pointed to by the `s` argument. The `gets` function reads everything until a newline character is encountered. At that point reading stops and the newline character in the copied string is replaced with a null character.

Value(s) Returned The pointer to the string is returned when successful. When the end-of-file is read, or an error occurs, null is returned.

Related Function(s)
`cgets` : reads a string from the console
`fgets` : gets a string from a stream
`puts` : outputs a string to the `stdout` stream

Example In the following example, `gets` retrieves a string from `stdin`.

```
#include <stdio.h>
#include <stdlib.h>
#include <conio.h>
#include <io.h>

int main (void)
{
char instring[80];

clrscr ();
printf ("Type a string - press <ENTER>\n");
gets (instring);
printf ("String : %s\n",instring);

return 0;
}
```

---

getw

DOS | UNIX | ANSI C | C++

Syntax `int getw(FILE *stream);`

`FILE *stream;` *Stream*

Function The `getw` function gets an integer from a stream.

File(s) to Include `#include <stdio.h>`

Description The `getw` function retrieves the next integer in the stream specified in the `stream` argument. This function should not be used when the specified stream has been opened in text mode.

Value(s) Returned The retrieved integer is returned when successful. If the end-of-file is read, or an error occurs, `EOF` is returned.

Related Function(s) `putw` : puts an integer on a stream

Example In the following example, `getw` gets an integer value from the stream.

```
#include <stdio.h>
#include <stdlib.h>
#include <conio.h>
#include <io.h>

int main (void)
{
FILE *filepointer;
int result;

clrscr ();
filepointer = fopen ("getw.tst","w");
result = getw (filepointer);
if (result == EOF)
     printf ("End of file\n");
else
     printf ("Value read : %d\n", result);
fclose (filepointer);

return 0;
}
```

ioctl

DOS UNIX ANSI C C++

Syntax

```
int ioctl(int handle, int func[, void *argdx, int
          argcx]);
```

`int handle;`	*Handle*
`int func[, void *argdx, int argcx];`	*Function to perform*

Function The `ioctl` function controls an I/O device.

File(s) to Include `#include <io.h>`

Description The `ioctl` function provides direct control over DOS device drivers for special functions through the DOS call 0x44. The `func` argument specifies the action taken by this function. The following values are used for the `func` argument:

Value	*Meaning*
0	Gets device information
1	Sets device information using the `argdx` argument
2	Reads the number of bytes specified in the `argcx` argument into the address pointed to by the `argdx` argument
3	Writes the number of bytes specified in the `argcx` argument from the address pointed to by the `argdx` argument
4	Performs the same as 2 except that the `handle` argument specifies the drive number (0=default, 1=A, etc.)
5	Performs the same as 3 except that the `handle` argument specifies the drive number (0=default, 1=A, etc.)
6	Gets input status
7	Gets output status
8	Tests removability
11	Sets retry count for sharing conflict

The results of this function vary because it is dependent on the vendor's hardware and device configuration. The vendor's BIOS documentation should be consulted when using this function.

Value(s) Returned The device information is returned for a `func` value of 0 or 1. For `func` values of 2 through 5, the number of bytes transferred is returned. For `func` values of 6 or 7, the device status is returned. For errors, a –1 is returned and the global variable `errno` is set to EINVAL, for invalid argument, EBADF, for bad file number, or EINVDAT, for invalid data.

Related Function(s) `bdos` : provides access to DOS system calls

Example In the following example, `ioctl` determines whether the default drive is removable.

```
#include <stdio.h>
#include <stdlib.h>
#include <conio.h>
#include <io.h>
#include <dir.h>

int main (void)
{
int result;

clrscr ();
result = ioctl (0,8,0,0);
if (! result)
     printf ("The Default Drive is Removable\n");
else
     printf ("The Default Drive is not
             Removable\n");

return 0;
}
```

isatty

DOS UNIX ANSI C C++

Syntax `int isatty(int handle);`

`int handle;` *Handle*

Function The `isatty` function checks for a device type.

File(s) to Include `#include <io.h>`

Description The `isatty` function determines whether the device specified in the `handle` argument is a character device. The character devices are a terminal, a console, a printer, or a serial port.

Value(s) Returned A nonzero value is returned if the device is a character device. A zero is returned if the device is not a character device.

Related Function(s) `ioctl` : controls an I/O device

Example In the following example, `isatty` determines whether `stdout` is associated with a character device.

```
#include <stdio.h>
#include <stdlib.h>
#include <conio.h>
#include <io.h>

int main (void)
{
int result;
int filehandle;

clrscr ();
filehandle = fileno (stdout);
result = isatty (filehandle);
if (result == 0)
     printf ("stdout isn't a character device\n");
else
     printf ("stdout is a character device\n");

return 0;
}
```

kbhit

DOS | UNIX | ANSI C | C++

Syntax `int kbhit(void);`

Function The `kbhit` function checks to see whether there are any available keystrokes.

File(s) to Include `#include <conio.h>`

Description The `kbhit` function checks for available keystrokes. If there are any keystrokes available, they can be retrieved with the `getch` or `getche` functions.

Value(s) Returned A nonzero value is returned if a keystroke is available. If no keystroke is available, zero is returned.

Related Function(s)
`getch` : gets a character from the keyboard
`getche` : gets a character from the keyboard and echoes

Example The following example uses `kbhit` as a conditional for a loop. When a key is pressed, you can exit from the loop.

```
#include <stdio.h>
#include <stdlib.h>
#include <conio.h>
#include <io.h>

int main (void)
{
clrscr ();
do
{
     printf ("Press a key to stop looping\n");
} while (!kbhit());

return 0;
}
```

lock

DOS | UNIX | ANSI C | C++

Syntax `int lock(int handle, long offset, long length);`

`int handle;`	*File handle*
`long offset;`	*Offset*
`long length;`	*File length*

Function The `lock` function sets the file-sharing locks.

File(s) to Include `#include <io.h>`

Description The `lock` function interfaces the DOS file-sharing mechanism. SHARE.EXE must be loaded before using this function. This function is unique to DOS 3.*X*.

Value(s) Returned Zero is returned when successful. When unsuccessful, –1 is returned.

Related Function(s) `unlock` : releases file-sharing locks

Example In the following example, the `lock` function locks the file `lock.tst`. SHARE.EXE, included with DOS versions after 3.0, must be loaded for the example to work properly.

```
#include <stdio.h>
#include <stdlib.h>
#include <conio.h>
#include <io.h>
#include <fcntl.h>
#include <sys\stat.h>
#include <share.h>

int main (void)
{
int handle;
int result;
int length;

clrscr ();
handle =
sopen("lock.tst",O_RDWR,SH_DENYNO,S_IREAD);
length = filelength (handle);
result = lock (handle,0L,length);
if (result == 0)
     printf ("File locked\n");
else
     printf ("Unable to lock file\n");
result = unlock (handle,0L,length);
if (result == 0)
     printf ("File unlocked\n");
else
     printf ("Unable to unlock file\n");

return 0;
}
```

lseek

DOS | UNIX | ANSI C | C++

Syntax

```
long lseek(int handle, long offset, int
           fromwhere);
```

`int handle;`	*File handle*
`long offset;`	*Offset*
`int fromwhere;`	*File location*

Function The `lseek` function moves the position of the file pointer.

File(s) to Include `#include <io.h>`

Description The `lseek` function moves the file pointer that corresponds to the file handle in the `handle` argument to a position offset from the file location specified in the `fromwhere` argument. The `offset` argument specifies the number of bytes of offset. The `fromwhere` argument should be set to one of the following constants:

Constant	*Value*	*Meaning*
`SEEK_SET`	0	File beginning
`SEEK_CUR`	1	Current position of file pointer
`SEEK_END`	2	End-of-file

Value(s) Returned The offset, in bytes, of the new position is returned when successful. When unsuccessful, –1L is returned and the global variable `errno` is set to EBADF, for bad file number, or EINVAL, for invalid argument.

Related Function(s) `fseek` : moves a file pointer on a stream

Example In the following example, the `lseek` argument sets the file pointer of `lseek.tst` to the end of the file.

```
#include <stdio.h>
#include <stdlib.h>
#include <conio.h>
#include <io.h>
#include <fcntl.h>
#include <sys\stat.h>
#include <share.h>

int main (void)
{
char buffer[] = "Sent to file";
int filehandle;
long result;

clrscr ();
filehandle =
open("lseek.tst",O_CREAT,S_IREAD|S_IREAD);
write (filehandle,buffer,strlen(buffer));
result = lseek (filehandle,0L,SEEK_END);
if (result !=  1L)
     printf ("Pointer position %ld\n",result);
else
     printf ("Error\n");
close (filehandle);

return 0;
}
```

_open

DOS UNIX ANSI C C++

Syntax

```
int _open(const char *filename, int oflags);
```

`const char *filename;`	*File to open*
`int oflags;`	*Open flags*

Function The `_open` function opens a file in binary mode.

File(s) to Include

```
#include <io.h>
#include <fnctl.h>
```

Description The `_open` function opens the file specified in the `filename` argument. The file is opened in binary mode and has the access mode defined by the `oflags` argument. The constants (as defined in `fnctl.h`) for the `_open` function are as follows:

`O_RDONLY`	Read only
`O_WRONLY`	Write only
`O_RDWR`	Read and write
`O_NOINHERIT`	File not passed to child programs
`O_DENYALL`	Only current handle has access
`O_DENYWRITE`	Allows read only from any open file
`O_DENYREAD`	Allows writes only from another open file
`O_DENYNONE`	Gives access to other open files

Value(s) Returned The file handle is returned when successful. When unsuccessful, –1 is returned and the global variable is set to ENOENT, for path or file not found, EMFILE, for too many open files, EACCES, for permission denied, or EINVACC, for invalid access code.

Related Function(s)
`OPEN` : opens a file in either text or binary mode
`SOPEN` : opens a shared file

Example In the following example, the `_open` function opens `_open.tst`.

```
#include <stdio.h>
#include <stdlib.h>
#include <conio.h>
#include <io.h>
#include <fcntl.h>
#include <sys\stat.h>

int main (void)
{
char buffer[] = "Sent to file";
int filehandle;

clrscr ();

if ((filehandle = _open("_open.tst",O_RDWR)) ==
1)
      {
      perror ("Error in _open\n");
      return 1;
      }
printf ("File opened\n");
_write (filehandle,buffer,strlen(buffer));
_close (filehandle);

return 0;
}
```

open

DOS | UNIX | ANSI C | C++

Syntax

```
int open(const char *path, int access[,unsigned
        mode]);
```

`const char *path;`	*File*
`int access[,unsigned mode];`	*Access mode*

Function The `open` function opens a file in either binary or text mode.

File(s) to Include

```
#include <sys\stat.h>
#include <fcntl.h>
#include <io.h>
```

Description The `open` function opens the file specified in the `path` argument. The access mode of the file is specified in the `access` argument. The `access` argument consists of bitwise ORing flags selected from the following lists. One flag is selected from the first list. The flags of the second list can be used with the flag selected from the first list.

Read/write flags	
`O_RDONLY`	Read only
`O_WRONLY`	Write only
`O_RDWR`	Read and write

Access flags	
`O_NDELAY`	Not used
`O_APPEND`	Sets the file pointer to the end of file
`O_CREAT`	File is created and bits in the mode argument are used to set the file attributes
`O_TRUNC`	Truncate file to 0
`O_EXCL`	Used with `O_CREAT`
`O_BINARY`	Open the file in binary mode
`O_TEXT`	Open the file in text mode

The `mode` argument, used when the `access` argument contains `O_CREAT`, is selected from the following constants:

`S_IWRITE`	Write
`S_IREAD`	Read
`S_IREAD|S_IWRITE`	Read and write

Value(s) Returned The file handle is returned when successful. When unsuccessful, –1 is returned and the global variable `errno` is set to ENOENT, for path or file not found, EMFILE, for too many open files, EACCES, for permission denied, or EINVACC, for invalid access code.

Related Function(s)
`open` : opens a file in binary mode
`sopen` : opens a shared file

Example In the following example, the `open` function opens the file `open.tst`.

```
#include <stdio.h>
#include <stdlib.h>
#include <conio.h>
#include <io.h>
#include <fcntl.h>
#include <sys\stat.h>

int main (void)
{
char buffer[] = "Sent to file";
int filehandle;

clrscr ();

if ((filehandle = open("open.tst",O_CREAT)) ==  1)
     {
     perror ("Error in open\n");
     return 1;
     }
printf ("File opened\n");
write (filehandle,buffer,strlen(buffer));
close (filehandle);

return 0;
}
```

perror

DOS | UNIX | ANSI C | C++

Syntax `void perror(const char *s);`

`const char *s;` *Error message*

Function The `perror` function prints a system error message.

File(s) to Include `#include <stdio.h>`

Description The `perror` function prints the message specified in the `s` argument, followed by a colon and the system error from the last function which produced an error.

Value(s) Returned There is no return value.

Related Function(s)
`clearerr` : resets a stream's error indicator
`strerror` : returns a pointer to an error message string

Example The following example attempts to open the file `junk.jnk`. If unable to open the file, a message is displayed using the `perror` function.

```
#include <stdio.h>

int main (void)
{
FILE *ret;

ret = fopen ("junk.jnk","r");
if (!ret)
     perror ("Can't open file");

return 0;
}
```

printf

DOS | UNIX | ANSI C | C++

Syntax

```
int printf(const char *format[,argument,...]);
```

`const char *format[,argument,...];` *Format specifiers and arguments*

Function The `printf` function writes formatted output to the `stdout` stream.

File(s) to Include `#include <stdio.h>`

Description The `printf` function outputs formatted data to the `stdout` stream. The format string which contains a series of format specifiers and is specified by the `format` argument is matched with arguments to create the formatted data.

The format string contains plain characters and conversion specifications. Plain characters are copied "as is." Conversion characters are in the following form:

```
%[flags][width][.prec][F|N|h|l|L]type
```

in which

flags = sequence of flag characters to include: the output justification, numeric signs, decimal signs, trailing zeros, octal and hex prefixes
width = width specifier : the minimum number of characters to print
prec = precision specifier : the maximum number of characters to print
F|N|h|l|L = input-size modifier : override default size of argument
N = near pointer
F = far pointer
h = short int
l = long
L = long double
type = conversion-type character

Table 9.2 provides further information on conversion-type characters.

Table 9.2. Conversion-type characters.

Numeric values

Character	*Input*	*Formatted output*
d	integer	signed decimal integer
i	integer	signed decimal integer
o	integer	unsigned octal integer
u	integer	unsigned decimal integer
x	integer	unsigned hex integer (a,b,c,d,e,f)
X	integer	unsigned hex integer (A,B,C,D,E,F)
f	floating point	signed value of form [–]dddd.dddd
e	floating point	signed value of form [–]d.dddd or e[+/–]ddd
g	floating point	signed value in e or f form using given value and precision
E	floating point	same as e with E for exponent
G	floating point	same as g with E for exponent

Characters

Character	*Input*	*Formatted output*
c	character	single character
s	string pointer	prints until null-terminator or precision is reached
%	none	the % character is printed

Pointers

Character	*Input*	*Formatted output*
n	pointer to int	stores the number of characters written up to that point

Character	*Input*	*Formatted output*
p	pointer	prints the input argument as a pointer in format XXXX:YYYY or YYYY (depends on memory model)

Table 9.3 provides conventions that are used with some of the specifications in table 9.2.

Table 9.3. *Conventions.*

Character	*Convention*
e or E	The argument is made to match the format [–]d.dddd ...e[+/–]ddd in which one digit precedes the decimal, the number of digits after the decimal is equal to the precision, and exponent contains at least two digits.
f	The argument is made to match the format [–]ddd.ddd..., in which the number of digits after the decimal is equal to the precision.
g or G	The argument is printed in e, E, or f format with the number of significant digits matching the precision. Trailing zeros are removed and the decimal is displayed only when necessary. e or f format is used with g. E format is used with G.
x or X	The letters a,b,c,d,e,f are used for output with x. The letters A,B,C,D,E,F are used with X.

Note: +INF and –INF represent plus and minus infinity. IEEE not-a-number is printed as +NAN or –NAN.

Table 9.4 lists the flag characters that can be used in any combination and in any order.

Table 9.4. Flag characters.	
Flag	***Meaning***
–	Left-justifies the result. The right is filled with blanks.
+	Signed conversion.
blank	A non-negative value indicates output will begin with a blank, not a +. A negative value will still begin with a –.
#	Indicates that the argument is to be converted using one of the alternate forms described in table 9.5.

Table 9.5 lists the alternate forms used with the # flag.

Table 9.5. Alternate forms.	
Character	***Meaning***
c,s,d,i,u	Has no effect
0	0 is prepended to a nonzero argument
x or X	0x or 0X is prepended to the argument
e,E,or f	The result will contain a decimal point even if no digit follows it
g or G	Same as e or E, except all trailing zeros are removed

Table 9.6 lists the width specifiers which set the minimum field width for an output value.

Table 9.6. Width specifiers.

Specifier	*Meaning*
n	A minimum of n characters is printed. Blanks are used to pad the right or left (depends on flags) if the output value has less than n characters.
0n	A minimum of n characters is printed. 0s are used to pad the left side when the output value has less than n characters.
*	The argument list contains the width specifier.

Precision specifiers begin with a period and can be defined directly through a decimal digit string or through the * specifier. When the * is used, the next argument in the call is used as the precision. Table 9.7 lists the precision specifiers.

Table 9.7. Precision specifiers.

Specifier	*Meaning*
(none given)	Uses default precisions d,i,o,u,x,X types = 1 e,E,f types = 6 g,G types = all significant digits s types = prints to the first null character
.0	For e,E,f types, no decimal is used. For d,i,o,u,x types, precision is set to defaults.
.n	n characters or decimal places are used. When the output value exceeds n digits, the value is rounded or truncated as follows: For d,i,o,u,x,X: If the input value has less than n digits, the value is left padded with 0s. If the input value has more than n digits, the value is not truncated. For e,E,f: n specifies the number of characters printed after the decimal. The last character is rounded when exceeding the n limitation.

continues

Table 9.7. (continued)	
Specifier	*Meaning*
	For g,G: n specifies the maximum number of significant digits to print.
	For c: n does not affect the output.
	For s: n specifies the maximum number of characters to print.
*	The argument list defines the precision specifier.

The input-size modifier specifies the size of the input argument and affects the way that the data type of the input argument is interpreted. Table 9.8 provides additional information on the input-size modifiers.

Table 9.8. Input-size modifiers.	
Modifier	*Meaning*
F	The argument is read as a far pointer.
N	The argument is read as a near pointer. The N modifier cannot be used with any conversion in the huge model.
h	The argument is interpreted as a short integer with d,i,o,u,x,X.
l	The argument is interpreted as a long integer for d,i,o,u,x,X and as a double for e,E,f,g,G.
L	The argument is interpreted as a long double for e,E,f,g,G.

Value(s) Returned The number of bytes output is returned when `printf` is successful. When unsuccessful, `EOF` is returned.

Related Function(s)
`cprintf` : writes formatted output to the screen
`fprintf` : writes formatted output to a stream
`sprintf` : writes formatted output to a string

Example In the following example, `printf` displays a string.

```
#include <stdio.h>
#include <stdlib.h>
#include <conio.h>
#include <io.h>

int main (void)
{
char buffer[] = "formatted output";

clrscr ();
printf ("The printf function can display
%s\n",buffer);

return 0;
}
```

putc

DOS | UNIX | ANSI C | C++

Syntax `int putc(int c, FILE *stream);`

`int c;`	*Character to output*
`FILE *stream;`	*Stream*

Function The `putc` macro outputs a character to a stream.

File(s) to Include `#include <stdio.h>`

Description The `putc` macro outputs the character specified in the `c` argument to the stream specified in the `stream` argument.

Value(s) Returned The character output to the stream is returned when successful. When unsuccessful, `EOF` is returned.

Related Function(s)
`fputc` : outputs a character to a stream
`putch` : outputs a character to the screen
`putchar` : outputs a character to `stdout`

Example In the following example, the `putc` macro puts `inchar` to `stdout`.

```
#include <stdio.h>
#include <stdlib.h>
#include <conio.h>
#include <io.h>

int main (void)
{
char inchar;

clrscr ();
printf ("Enter a character - then press
<ENTER>\n");
inchar = getc (stdin);
putc(inchar,stdout);
return 0;
}
```

putch

DOS | UNIX | ANSI C | C++

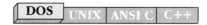

Syntax `int putch(int c);`

`int c;` *Character to display*

Function The `putch` function outputs a character to the screen.

File(s) to Include `#include <conio.h>`

Description The `putch` function outputs the character specified in the `c` argument to the text screen. Linefeed characters (`\n`) are not translated to carriage return/linefeed pairs (`\r\n`).

Value(s) Returned The character in the `c` argument is returned when successful. When unsuccessful, `EOF` is returned.

Related Function(s)
`getch` : gets a character from the keyboard
`getche` : gets a character from the keyboard and echoes
`putc` : outputs a character to a stream
`putchar` : outputs a character to `stdout`

Example In the following example, `putch` displays the retrieved character.

```
#include <stdio.h>
#include <stdlib.h>
#include <conio.h>
#include <io.h>

int main (void)
{
int inchar;

clrscr ();
printf ("Press a key\n");
inchar = getch ();
printf ("Character : ");
putch (inchar);

return 0;
}
```

putchar

DOS | UNIX | ANSI C | C++

Syntax `int putchar(int c);`

`int c;` *Character to output*

Function The `putchar` macro outputs a character to the `stdout` stream.

File(s) to Include `#include <stdio.h>`

Description The `putchar` macro outputs the character in the `c` argument to the `stdout` stream.

Value(s) Returned The character in the `c` argument is returned when successful. When unsuccessful, `EOF` is returned.

Related Function(s)
`fputchar` : outputs a character to `stdout`
`putc` : outputs a character to a stream
`putch` : outputs a character to the screen

Example In the following example, the `putchar` macro puts a character on `stdout`.

```
#include <stdio.h>
#include <stdlib.h>
#include <conio.h>
#include <io.h>

int main (void)
{
int inchar;

clrscr ();
printf ("Press a key - then press <ENTER>\n");
inchar = getchar ();
printf ("Character : ");
putchar (inchar);
return 0;
}
```

puts

DOS | UNIX | ANSI C | C++

Syntax `int puts(const char *s);`

`const char *s;` *String to output*

Function The `puts` function outputs a string to the `stdout` stream.

File(s) to Include `#include <stdio.h>`

Description The `puts` function outputs the string in the `s` argument to the `stdout` output stream. A newline character is appended to the string.

Value(s) Returned A nonnegative value is returned when successful. When unsuccessful, `EOF` is returned.

Related Function(s)
`cputs` : writes a string to the screen
`fputs` : outputs a string on a stream

Example The following example puts the retrieved string on `stdout` using the `puts` function.

```
#include <stdio.h>
#include <stdlib.h>
#include <conio.h>
#include <io.h>

int main (void)
{
char instring[80];

clrscr ();
printf ("Type a string - press <ENTER>\n");
gets (instring);
printf ("String : ");
puts (instring);

return 0;
}
```

putw

DOS | UNIX | ANSI C | C++

Syntax

```
int putw(int w, FILE *stream);
```

`int w;`	*Integer to output*
`FILE *stream;`	*Stream*

Function The `putw` function outputs an integer value to a stream.

File(s) to Include `#include <stdio.h>`

Description The `putw` function outputs the integer value in the `w` argument to the stream specified in the `stream` argument.

Value(s) Returned The integer value in the `w` argument is returned when successful. When unsuccessful, `EOF` is returned.

Related Function(s) `getw` : gets an integer from a stream

Example In the following example, `putw` puts 3 on the open stream.

```
#include <stdio.h>
#include <stdlib.h>
#include <conio.h>
#include <io.h>

int main (void)
{
FILE *filepointer;
int result;

clrscr ();
filepointer = fopen ("putw.tst","w");
result = putw (3,filepointer);
if (result == EOF)
     printf ("Error\n");
else
     printf ("Value put on stream : %d\n",
result);
fclose (filepointer);

return 0;
}
```

_read

DOS | UNIX | ANSI C | C++

Syntax `int _read(int handle, void *buf, unsigned len);`

`int handle;`	*File handle*
`void *buf;`	*Buffer*
`unsigned len;`	*Number of bytes to read*

Function The `_read` function reads from a file. This function does not remove carriage returns.

File(s) to Include `#include <io.h>`

Description The `_read` function reads from the file that corresponds to the file handle specified in the `handle` argument. The number of bytes specified in the `len` argument is read from the file and placed in the buffer pointed to by the `buf` argument. Carriage returns are not removed. When reading from disk files, reading begins at the position of the file pointer. For devices, the bytes are read directly from the device. The maximum number of bytes that can be read is 65,534.

Value(s) Returned The number of bytes read is returned when successful. When unsuccessful, –1 is returned and the global variable `errno` is set to EACCES, for permission denied, or EBADF, for bad file number.

Related Function(s)

`_open` : opens a file in binary mode
`open` : opens a file in either binary or text mode
`read` : reads from a file
`_write` : writes to a file

Example In the following example, the `_read` function reads from `read.tst`.

```
#include <stdio.h>
#include <stdlib.h>
#include <conio.h>
#include <io.h>
#include <fcntl.h>
#include <sys\stat.h>

int main (void)
{
void *buffer;
int filehandle;
int result;
buffer = malloc (1);

clrscr ();
filehandle = open (" read.tst",O_CREAT);
result = _read (filehandle,buffer,1);
if (result == 0)
     printf ("Reached end of file\n");
else
     if (result ==  1)
          printf ("Error\n");
     else
          printf ("%d bytes placed in
buffer\n",result);
close (filehandle);

return 0;
}
```

read

DOS | UNIX | ANSI C | C++

Syntax

```
int read(int handle, void *buf, unsigned len);
```

`int handle;`	*File handle*
`void *buf;`	*Buffer*
`unsigned len;`	*Number of bytes to read*

Function The `read` function reads from a file. This function removes carriage returns and reports end-of-file.

File(s) to Include `#include <io.h>`

Description The `read` function reads from the file that corresponds to the file handle specified in the `handle` argument. The number of bytes specified in the `len` argument are read from the file and placed in the buffer pointed to by the `buf` argument. Carriage returns are removed. When reading from disk files, reading begins at the position of the file pointer. For devices, the bytes are read directly from the device. The maximum number of bytes that can be read is 65,534.

Value(s) Returned The number of bytes read is returned when successful. When unsuccessful, –1 is returned and the global variable `errno` is set to EACCES, for permission denied, or EBADF, for bad file number.

Related Function(s)

`open` : opens a file
`_read` : read from a file
`write` : writes to a file

Example In the following example, the `read` function reads from `read.tst`.

```
#include <stdio.h>
#include <stdlib.h>
#include <conio.h>
#include <io.h>
#include <fcntl.h>
#include <sys\stat.h>

int main (void)
```

```
{
void *buffer;
int filehandle;
int result;
buffer = malloc (1);

clrscr ();
filehandle = open ("read.tst",O_CREAT);
result = read (filehandle,buffer,1);
if (result == 0)
     printf ("Reached end of file\n");
else
     if (result ==  1)
          printf ("Error\n");
     else
          printf ("%d bytes placed in
buffer\n",result);
close (filehandle);

return 0;
}
```

remove

DOS | UNIX | ANSI C | C++

Syntax `int remove(const char *filename);`

`const char *filename;` *File name*

Function The `remove` macro removes a file.

File(s) to Include `#include <stdio.h>`

Description The `remove` macro removes the file specified in the `filename` argument. The file being removed should be closed.

Value(s) Returned Zero is returned when successful. When unsuccessful, –1 is returned and the global variable `errno` is set to ENOENT, for no such file or directory, or EACCES, for permission denied.

Related Function(s) `unlink` : deletes a file

Example The following example removes the `remove.rem` file using the `remove` macro.

```
#include <stdio.h>
#include <stdlib.h>
#include <conio.h>
#include <io.h>
#include <fcntl.h>
#include <sys\stat.h>

int main (void)
{
int filehandle;
int result;

clrscr ();
filehandle = open
("remove.rem",O_CREAT,S_IREAD|S_IWRITE);
close (filehandle);
result = remove ("remove.rem");
if (result == 0)
     printf ("File removed\n");
else
     printf ("Unable to remove file\n");

return 0;
}
```

rename

Syntax

```
int rename(const char *oldname, const char
                *newname);
```

`const char *oldname;`	*Old file name*
`const char *newname;`	*New file name*

Function The `rename` function changes the name of a file.

File(s) to Include `#include <stdio.h>`

Description The `rename` function changes the name of the file specified by the `oldname` argument to the name specified in the `newname` argument. The drive specifiers, if used in the arguments, must be the same. The directories, if used, can differ.

Value(s) Returned Zero is returned when successful. When unsuccessful, –1 is returned and the global variable `errno` is set to ENOENT, for no such file or directory, EACCES, for permission denied, or ENOTSAM, for not same device.

Related Function(s) `creat` : creates new file

Example In the following example, the `rename` function renames `rename.tst` to `rename1.tst`.

```
#include <stdio.h>
#include <stdlib.h>
#include <conio.h>
#include <io.h>
#include <fcntl.h>
#include <sys\stat.h>

int main (void)
{
int filehandle;
int result;

clrscr ();
filehandle = open
("rename.tst",O_CREAT,S_IREAD|S_IWRITE);
close (filehandle);
result = rename ("rename.tst","rename1.tst");
if (result == 0)
     printf ("File renamed\n");
else
     printf ("Unable to rename file\n");

return 0;
}
```

rewind

Syntax `void rewind(FILE *stream);`

`FILE *stream;` *Stream*

Function The `rewind` function moves the file pointer to the beginning of a stream.

File(s) to Include `#include <stdio.h>`

Description The `rewind` function moves the file pointer to the beginning of the stream specified in the `stream` argument. End-of-file and error indicators are cleared.

Value(s) Returned There is no return value.

Related Function(s)
`fopen` : opens a stream
`fseek` : moves a file pointer on a stream
`ftell` : gets the position of the file pointer

Example In the following example, `rewind` moves the file pointer to the beginning of the stream.

```
#include <stdio.h>
#include <stdlib.h>
#include <conio.h>
#include <io.h>

int main (void)
{
FILE *filepointer;
char firstch;
int result;

clrscr ();
filepointer = fopen ("rewind.tst","w+");
fprintf (filepointer, "Send this to file");
rewind (filepointer);
fscanf (filepointer,"%c",&firstch);
printf ("%c is first character of
file\n",firstch);
fclose (filepointer);

return 0;
}
```

scanf

DOS | UNIX | ANSI C | C++

Syntax `int scanf(const char *format[,address,...]);`

`const char *format[,address,...];` *Format string*

Function The `scanf` function scans and formats input from the `stdin` stream.

File(s) to Include `#include <stdio.h>`

Description The `scanf` function reads data from the `stdin` stream. Input fields are scanned from the `stdin` stream and formatted according to the format string in the `format` argument. The formatted input is stored at the address passed in the `address` argument, which follows the format string.

The format string contains whitespace characters, nonwhitespace characters, and format specifiers. Whitespace characters are blanks, tabs, and newlines and are read but not stored by the `scanf` function. Nonwhitespace characters include all other ASCII characters with the exception of %. Nonwhitespace characters are read but not stored. The format specifiers tell the `scanf` function how to read, convert, and store the input field.

Format specifiers are as follows:

`%[*][width][F|N][h|l|L]type`

in which

* = an assignment suppression character : suppresses assignment of the next input field

width = width specifier : maximum number of characters to read

F|N = pointer size modifier : overrides the default size of the address argument

F = far pointer

N = near pointer

h|l|L = argument type modifier :
overrides default type of address argument
h = short int
l = long int for integer conversion
or double for floating-point conversion
L = long double
type = type character

The `scanf` type characters are shown in table 9.9.

Table 9.9. The scanf type characters.

Numerics

Character	*Input*	*Type of argument*
d	Decimal integer	Pointer to int
D	Decimal integer	Pointer to long
o	Octal integer	Pointer to int
O	Octal integer	Pointer to long
i	Decimal, octal, or	Pointer to int hexadecimal integer
I	Decimal, octal, or	Pointer to long hexadecima integer
u	Unsigned decimal	Pointer to unsigned int integer
U	Unsigned decimal	Pointer to unsigned long integer
x	Hexadecimal integer	Pointer to int
X	Hexadecimal integer	Pointer to long
e,E	Floating point	Pointer to float
f	Floating point	Pointer to float
g,G	Floating point	Pointer to float

Characters		
Character	*Input*	*Type of argument*
s	Character string	Pointer to array of characters
c	Character string	Pointer to character if a field width is also given
		Pointer to array of characters
%	% character	The % character is stored

Pointers		
Character	*Input*	*Type of argument*
n		Pointer to int
p	Hexadecimal form	Pointer to an object (the YYYY:ZZZZ or ZZZZ pointer size depends on the memory model being used)

Table 9.10 lists and explains some of the conventions used with the format specifiers.

Table 9.10. *Conventions.*

Convention	*Meaning*
%c	Reads the next character. To skip a whitespace character and read the next nonwhitespace character, use %1s.
%Wc	The address argument is a pointer to an array of characters with W elements.
%s	The address argument is a pointer to an array of characters. The array must contain n+1 elements in which n is the length of the string because a null terminator is appended to the string.

continues

Table 9.10. (continued)

Convention	*Meaning*
%[...]	The address argument is a pointer to an array of characters. The characters between the [] are searched for. The ^ character can be used as the first character in the bracket to search for all characters except those in the []. In addition, a – can be used to specify a range (for example [0-9] checks for 0,1,2,3,4,5,6,7,8,9).
%e,%E,%f, %g,%G	The floating-point numbers in the input field must follow the format: `[+/-]ddddddddd[.]dddd[E|e] [+/-]ddd`
%d,%i,%o,%x, %D,%I,%O,%X, %c,%n	A pointer to unsigned character, unsigned integer, or unsigned long can be used in the conversion in which a pointer to a character, integer, or long is allowed.

The assignment suppression character (*) can follow the percent sign to indicate that the next input field should be scanned but should not be assigned to the next address argument. The input data should be of the type specified in the type character that follows the suppression character (*).

The width specifier (n) defines the maximum number of characters that will be read from the current input field. When the input field has fewer characters than the value of the width specifier, all characters in the field are read. When a whitespace or a nonconvertible character is encountered, all characters read up to that point are converted and stored.

The input size modifiers (F,N) and the argument-type modifiers (h,l,L) are used by the `scanf` function to interpret the corresponding address argument. Table 9.11 explains the use of these modifiers.

Table 9.11. *The input size and argument-type modifiers.*

Modifier	*Meaning*
F	Overrides the default or declared size.
N	Overrides the default or declared size. Cannot be used with the huge model.
h	Converts input to short int and stores in short object for d,i,o,u,x.
l	d,i,o,u,x: Converts input to long int and stores in long object.
	e,f,g: Converts input to double and stores in double object.
	D,I,O,U,X: Has no effect.
	c,s,n,p: Has no effect.
L	e,f,g: Converts input to long double and stores in long double object.
	All other formats: Has no effect.

The `scanf` function will stop scanning the current input field for any of the following reasons:

- An assignment-suppression character (*) is encountered.
- The number of characters in the width specifier have been read.
- The character read from the field cannot be converted under the current format.
- The next character in the input field does not appear in the search set.

When scanning stops, the next character read is considered to be the first character of the next field.

The `scanf` function will terminate when the next character in the input field conflicts with the nonwhitespace character in the format string, the next character in the input field is `EOF`, or the format string is exhausted.

Value(s) Returned The number of input fields scanned, converted, and stored is returned. EOF is returned when the end-of-file is read.

Related Function(s)
cscanf : scans and formats input from the console
fscanf : scans and formats input from a stream
sscanf : scans and formats input from a string
vfscanf : scans and formats input from a stream
vscanf : scans and formats input from the stdin stream
vsscanf : scans and formats input from a stream

Example In the following example, the scanf function scans the input from stdin.

```
#include <stdio.h>
#include <stdlib.h>
#include <conio.h>
#include <io.h>

int main (void)
{
char name[40];

clrscr ();
printf ("Enter your name\n");
scanf ("%s",&name);
printf ("Hello %s\n",name);

return 0;
}
```

setbuf

DOS | UNIX | ANSI C | C++

Syntax `void setbuf(FILE *stream, char *buf);`

`FILE *stream;`	*Stream*
`char *buf;`	*Buffer*

Function The setbuf function sets I/O buffering for a stream.

File(s) to Include `#include <stdio.h>`

Description The `setbuf` argument sends buffered I/O from the stream specified in the `stream` argument to the buffer in the `buf` argument. Buffered I/O indicates that characters are written as a block. The `setbuf` function should be called immediately after opening the stream specified in the `stream` argument.

Value(s) Returned There is no return value.

Related Function(s) `setvbuf` : sets I/O buffering for a stream

Example In the following example, `setbuf` sends the `stdout` traffic to a buffer.

```
#include <stdio.h>
#include <stdlib.h>
#include <conio.h>
#include <io.h>

int main (void)
{
char buffer[80];

clrscr ();
setbuf (stdout,buffer);
printf ("This is sent to the buffer\n");
printf ("until the buffer is flushed\n");
fflush (stdout);

return 0;
}
```

_setcursortype

Syntax `void _setcursortype(int cur_t);`

`int cur_t;` *Cursor type*

Function The `_setcursortype` function defines the appearance of the cursor.

File(s) to Include `#include <conio.h>`

Description The `_setcursortype` function sets the text cursor to the type specified in the `cur_t` argument. The constants which can be used for the `cur_t` argument are as follows:

`_NOCURSOR`	No cursor is shown
`_SOLIDCURSOR`	Solid block cursor is used
`_NORMALCURSOR`	Uses the normal underscore cursor

Value(s) Returned There is no return value.

Related Function(s)
`wherex` : gets the horizontal position of the text cursor
`wherey` : gets the vertical position of the text cursor

Example The following example displays the three cursor types.

```
#include <conio.h>
#include <stdio.h>

int main (void)
{
clrscr();
printf ("Normal Cursor");
printf ("\nPress Enter to continue");
_setcursortype(_NORMALCURSOR);
getch();
printf ("\nSolid Cursor");
printf ("\nPress Enter to continue");
_setcursortype(_SOLIDCURSOR);
getch();
printf ("\nNo Cursor");
printf ("\nPress Enter to continue");
_setcursortype(_NOCURSOR);
getch();
_setcursortype(_NORMALCURSOR);

return 0;
}
```

setftime

DOS UNIX ANSI C C++

Syntax

```
int setftime(int handle, struct ftime *ftimep);
```

`int handle;`	*File handle*
`struct ftime *ftimep;`	*Date and time information*

Function The `setftime` function sets the date and time for a file.

File(s) to Include

```
#include <io.h>
```

Description The `setftime` function sets the date and time of the file that corresponds to the file handle specified in the `handle` argument. The `ftimep` argument, a structure of type `ftime`, stores the date and time information. The `ftime` structure follows.

```
struct ftime
      {
      unsigned ft_tsec: 5;      /* seconds */
      unsigned ft_min: 6;       /* minutes */
      unsigned ft_hour: 5;      /* hours */
      unsigned ft_day: 5;       /* days */
      unsigned ft_month: 4;     /* months */
      unsigned ft_year: 7;      /* year   1980 */
      };
```

Value(s) Returned Zero is returned when successful. When unsuccessful, –1 is returned and the global variable `errno` is set to EINVFNC, for invalid function number, or EBADF, for bad file number.

Related Function(s) `getftime` : gets date and time information for a file

Example In the following example, `setftime` assigns new date and time values to `setftime.tst`.

```
#include <stdio.h>
#include <stdlib.h>
#include <conio.h>
#include <io.h>
```

```
int main (void)
{
FILE *filepointer;
struct ftime fltm;
int filehandle;
int result;

clrscr ();
filepointer = fopen ("setftime.tst","w");
fltm.ft_tsec = 5;
fltm.ft_min = 5;
fltm.ft_hour = 5;
fltm.ft_day = 5;
fltm.ft_month = 5;
fltm.ft_year = 5;
filehandle = fileno(filepointer);
result = setftime (filehandle,&fltm);
if (result == 0)
     printf ("setftime successful\n");
else
     printf ("setftime unsuccessful\n");
fclose (filepointer);

return 0;
}
```

setmode

DOS | UNIX | ANSI C | C++

Syntax `int setmode(int handle, int amode);`

`int handle;`	*File handle*
`int amode;`	*Mode for file*

Function The `setmode` function sets the mode for an open file.

File(s) to Include `#include <fcntl.h>`
`#include <io.h>`

Description The `setmode` function sets the mode for the open file which corresponds to the file handle specified in the `handle` argument. The `amode` argument specifies the mode for the file and is selected from one of the following values:

`O_BINARY`	Binary mode
`O_TEXT`	Text mode

Value(s) Returned Zero is returned when successful. When unsuccessful, –1 is returned and the global variable `errno` is set to EINVAL, for invalid argument.

Related Function(s)

`_creat` : creates a new file; the file is opened in binary mode
`creat` : creates a new file; the file is opened in either text or binary mode
`_open` : opens a file in binary mode
`open` : opens a file in either binary or text mode

Example In the following example, `setmode` sets `stdout` to binary.

```
#include <stdio.h>
#include <stdlib.h>
#include <conio.h>
#include <io.h>
#include <fcntl.h>

int main (void)
{
int result;

clrscr ();
result = setmode (fileno(stdout),O_BINARY);
if (result == 0)
     printf ("stdout is in binary mode\n");
else
     printf ("stdout unchanged\n");

return 0;
}
```

setvbuf

DOS | UNIX | ANSI C | C++

Syntax

```
int setvbuf(FILE *stream, char *buf, int type,
               size_t size);
```

```
FILE *stream;          Stream
char *buf;             Buffer
int type;              Type of buffering
size_t size;           Size of buffer
```

Function The `setvbuf` function sets I/O buffering for a stream.

File(s) to Include `#include <stdio.h>`

Description The `setvbuf` function is used for I/O buffering from the stream specified in the `stream` argument to the buffer specified in the `buf` argument. The `size` argument defines the size of the buffer and must be greater than 0 and less than 32,768. The `type` argument specifies the type of buffering and is selected from one of the following:

`_IOFBF`	File is fully buffered. The buffer is filled prior to writing to a file.
`_IOLBF`	File is line buffered. The entire buffer is filled before writing. However, the buffer is flushed after a newline character is written.
`_IONBF`	File is unbuffered. Each input is read directly and each output is written immediately. The `size` and `buf` arguments are ignored.

Value(s) Returned Zero is returned when successful. When unsuccessful, a nonzero value is returned.

Related Function(s)
`fflush` : flushes a stream
`fopen` : opens a stream
`setbuf` : sets I/O buffering for a stream

Example In the following example, `setvbuf` assigns buffering to the open stream.

```
#include <stdio.h>
#include <stdlib.h>
#include <conio.h>
#include <io.h>

int main (void)
{
FILE *filepointer;
char buffer[512];
int result;
```

```
clrscr ();
filepointer = fopen("setvbuf.tst","w");
result = setvbuf (filepointer,buffer,_IOFBF,512);
if (result == 0)
     printf ("Buffer has been set up\n");
else
     printf ("Unable to set up buffer\n");
fclose (filepointer);

return 0;
}
```

sopen

DOS | UNIX | ANSI C | C++

Syntax

```
int sopen(char *path, int access, int shflag, int
          mode);
```

`char *path;`	*File name*
`int access;`	*Access flags*
`int shflag;`	*Type of file sharing*
`int mode;`	*Used with `O_CREAT` flag*

Function The `sopen` macro opens a shared file.

File(s) to Include

```
#include <fcntl.h>
#include <sys\stat.h>
#include <share.h>
#include <io.h>
```

Description The `sopen` macro opens the shared file specified in the `path` argument. The `access` argument specifies the access mode and consists of ORing flags from the following lists. One flag is selected from the first list while the flags from the second list can be used in any combination.

Read/write flags	
O_RDONLY	Read only
O_WRONLY	Write only
O_RDWR	Read and write
Access flags	
O_NDELAY	Not used
O_APPEND	Sets the file pointer to the end of file
O_CREAT	File is created and bits in the mode argument are used to set the file attributes
O_TRUNC	Truncate file to 0
O_EXCL	Used with O_CREAT. Error if file exists
O_BINARY	Open the file in binary mode
O_TEXT	Open the file in text mode

The mode argument, used when the access argument contains O_CREAT, is selected from the following constants:

S_IWRITE	Write
S_IREAD	Read
S_IREAD|S_IWRITE	Read and write

The shflag argument defines the type of file-sharing for the specified file. The value of the shflag argument is selected from one of the following:

SH_COMPAT	Compatibility mode
SH_DENYRW	Denies read and write
SH_DENYWR	Denies write
SH_DENYRD	Denies read
SH_DENYNONE	Allows read and write
SH_DENYNO	Allows read and write

Value(s) Returned When successful, the file handle is returned and the file pointer is set to the beginning of the file. When unsuccessful, –1 is returned and the global variable errno is set to ENOENT, for path or file not found, EMFILE, for too many open files, EACCES, for permission denied, or EINVACC, for invalid access code.

Related Function(s)
`creat` : creates a file
`open` : opens a file

Example In the following example, the `sopen` macro opens `lock.tst`.

```
#include <stdio.h>
#include <stdlib.h>
#include <conio.h>
#include <io.h>
#include <fcntl.h>
#include <sys\stat.h>
#include <share.h>

int main (void)
{
int handle;
int result;
int length;

clrscr ();
handle =
sopen("lock.tst",O_RDWR,SH_DENYNO,S_IREAD);
length = filelength (handle);
result = lock (handle,0L,length);
if (result == 0)
     printf ("File locked\n");
else
     printf ("Unable to lock file\n");
result = unlock (handle,0L,length);
if (result == 0)
     printf ("File unlocked\n");
else
     printf ("Unable to unlock file\n");

return 0;
}
```

sprintf

DOS | UNIX | ANSI C | C++

Syntax

```
int sprintf(char *buffer,const char
            *format[,argument,...]);
```

`char *buffer;` *Output*
`char *format[,argument,...];` *Format string, arguments*

Function The `sprintf` function writes formatted output to a string.

File(s) to Include `#include <stdio.h>`

Description The `sprintf` function writes formatted output to the string pointed to by the `buffer` argument. The output data is formatted according to the series of arguments following the format specifiers in the format string pointed to by the `format` argument. The `sprintf` function uses the same format specifiers as those described in this chapter under the `printf` function.

Value(s) Returned The number of bytes output to the buffer is returned when successful. The returned count does not include the null byte. `EOF` is returned when unsuccessful.

Related Function(s)
`fprintf` : writes formatted output to a stream
`printf` : writes formatted output to `stdout`

Example In the following example, `sprintf` writes a string to the buffer.

```
#include <stdio.h>
#include <stdlib.h>
#include <conio.h>
#include <io.h>

int main (void)
{
char buffer[40];
char buffer1[] = "the buffer";

clrscr ();
sprintf (buffer, "Send this to %s\n", buffer1);
printf ("%s",buffer);

return 0;
}
```

sscanf

DOS | UNIX | ANSI C | C++

Syntax

```
int sscanf(const char *buffer, const char

     *format[,address,...]);
```

`const char *buffer;`	*Input*
`const char *format[,address,...];`	*Format specifiers, fields*

Function The `sscanf` function scans and formats input from a string.

File(s) to Include `#include <stdio.h>`

Description The `sscanf` function scans and formats the input string pointed to by the `buffer` argument. The input is formatted according to the format specifiers in the format field pointed to by the `format` argument. The formatted input is stored at the addresses specified in the arguments following the format string. The `sscanf` function is very similar to the `scanf` function. The format specifiers and further information for the `sscanf` function can be found in this chapter under the `scanf` function.

Value(s) Returned The number of input fields scanned, converted, and stored is returned. `EOF` is returned when the end-of-string is read.

Related Function(s)

`fscanf` : scans and formats input from a stream
`scanf` : scans and formats input from `stdin`

Example In the following example, `sscanf` scans the buffer for strings.

```
#include <stdio.h>
#include <stdlib.h>
#include <conio.h>
#include <io.h>
```

```
int main (void)
{
char buffer[] = "one two three four";
char one[10];
char two[10];
char three[10];
char four[10];

clrscr ();
sscanf (buffer, "%s %s %s %s",one,two,three,four);
printf ("%s : %s : %s : %s\n",one,two,three,four);

return 0;
}
```

stat

DOS | UNIX | ANSI C | C++

Syntax `int stat(char *path, struct stat *statbuf);`

`char *path;`	*File*
`struct stat *statbuf;`	*File information*

Function The `stat` function retrieves information about a file.

File(s) to Include `#include <sys\stat.h>`

Description The `stat` function retrieves information about the file specified in the `path` argument. The information is stored in a structure of type `stat`, pointed to by the `statbuf` argument. The `stat` structure is as follows:

```
struct stat
    {
    short st_dev;          Drive number
    short st_ino;          No meaning under DOS
    short st_mode;         File mode information
    short st_nlink;        Set to integer constant 1
    int st_uid;            No meaning under DOS
    int st_gid;            No meaning under DOS
    short st_rdev;         Same as st_dev
    long st_size;          File size in bytes
```

```
long st_atime;          Time file was modified
long st_mtime;          Same as st_atime
long st_ctime;          Same as st_atime
};
```

The st_mode field, the bit mask for the file's mode, contains the following bits:

	S_IFREG	Set if ordinary file is specified in path
or	S_IFDIR	Set if path is specified in path argument
	S_IWRITE	Permission to write
and/or	S_IREAD	Permission to read

The bit mask also includes the read/write bits, which are set according to the access mode.

Value(s) Returned Zero is returned if the information is retrieved successfully. When unsuccessful, –1 is returned and the global variable errno is set to ENOENT, for path or file not found.

Related Function(s) fstat : gets information on an open file

Example In the following example, stat retrieves information about stat.tst.

```
#include <stdio.h>
#include <stdlib.h>
#include <conio.h>
#include <io.h>
#include <sys/stat.h>

int main (void)
{
FILE *filepointer;
struct stat sbuf;

clrscr ();
filepointer = fopen ("stat.tst","w+");
stat ("stat.tst",&sbuf);
printf ("Drive : %c\n",sbuf.st_dev + 'A');
printf ("File size in bytes :
%ld\n",sbuf.st_size);
fclose (filepointer);

return 0;
}
```

_strerror

DOS | UNIX | ANSI C | C++

Syntax

```
char *_strerror(const char *s);

const char *s;                Error message
```

Function The _strerror function generates a custom error message.

File(s) to Include

```
#include <string.h>
```

or

```
#include <stdio.h>
```

Description The _strerror function generates the custom error message specified by the s argument. When s is null, the value returned by the _strerror function points to the most recent error message. When s is not null, the return value is the custom error message followed by a colon, a space, and the most recent system error message.

Value(s) Returned The pointer to the complete error string is returned.

Related Function(s)

perror : prints a system error message
strerror : returns a pointer to an error message

Example The following example generates an error message using the _strerror function.

```
#include <stdio.h>
#include <string.h>

int main (void)
{
int file_handle = 100;
char *message;

clrscr();
if (dup(file_handle) ==  1)
     printf ("%s", _strerror ("Cannot duplicate
handle"));

return 0;
}
```

strerror

Syntax

```
char *strerror(int errnum);

int errnum;                    Error number
```

Function The `strerror` function returns the pointer to an error message string for a specified error number.

File(s) to Include `#include <string.h>` or `#include <stdio.h>`

Description The `strerror` function retrieves the pointer to the error message that corresponds to the error number specified in the `errnum` argument.

Value(s) Returned The pointer to the error string is returned.

Related Function(s)

`perror` : prints a system error message
`_strerror` : generates a custom error message

Example In the following example, `strerror` retrieves the error message string for error number 10.

```
#include <stdio.h>
#include <string.h>

int main (void)
{
char *message;

clrscr();
message = strerror(10);
printf ("Error: %s\n",message);

return 0;
}
```

tell

DOS UNIX ANSI C C++

Syntax

```
long tell(int handle);

int handle;                    File handle
```

Function The `tell` function retrieves the position of the file pointer.

File(s) to Include `#include <io.h>`

Description The `tell` function retrieves the position of the file pointer for the file that corresponds to the file handle specified in the `handle` argument. The position is expressed as the number of bytes from the beginning of the file.

Value(s) Returned The current file pointer position is returned when successful. When unsuccessful, –1L is returned and the global variable `errno` is set to EBADF, for bad file number.

Related Function(s)

`fseek` : repositions a file pointer on a stream
`ftell` : returns the position of the file pointer
`lseek` : moves the file pointer

Example In the following example, `tell` gets the position of the file pointer.

```
#include <stdio.h>
#include <stdlib.h>
#include <conio.h>
#include <io.h>
#include <sys/stat.h>

int main (void)
{
FILE *filepointer;
long position;
int filehandle;

clrscr ();
filepointer = fopen ("tell.tst","w+");
filehandle = fileno (filepointer);
position = tell (filehandle);
```

```
printf ("Pointer position : %ld\n",position);
fclose (filepointer);

return 0;
}
```

tmpfile

DOS | UNIX | ANSI C | C++

Syntax `FILE *tmpfile(void);`

Function The `tmpfile` function opens a temporary file in binary mode.

File(s) to Include `#include <stdio.h>`

Description The `tmpfile` function opens a temporary binary file. When the file is closed, or the program ends, the file is removed.

Value(s) Returned The pointer to the stream is returned when the file is successfully created. When the file can't be created, null is returned.

Related Function(s) `tmpnam` : creates a unique file name

Example In the following example, `tmpfile` creates a temporary file.

```
#include <stdio.h>
#include <stdlib.h>
#include <conio.h>
#include <io.h>

int main (void)
{
FILE *filepointer;

clrscr ();
filepointer = tmpfile ();
if (filepointer == NULL)
     printf ("Temporary file not created\n");
else
     printf ("Temporary file created\n");
return 0;
}
```

tmpnam

DOS | UNIX | ANSI C | C++

Syntax

```
char *tmpnam(char *s);

char *s;                    Array for name
```

Function The `tmpnam` function creates a unique file name.

File(s) to Include `#include <stdio.h>`

Description The `tmpnam` function creates a unique file name which is useful for creating temporary files. The `s` argument should be either null or a pointer to an array.

Value(s) Returned When `s` is null, the pointer to an internal static object is returned. Otherwise, `s` is returned.

Related Function(s) `tmpfile` : creates a temporary file

Example In the following example, `tmpnam` creates a unique file name.

```
#include <stdio.h>
#include <stdlib.h>
#include <conio.h>
#include <io.h>

int main (void)
{
char tempname[13];

clrscr ();
tmpnam (tempname);
printf ("Temporary name  %s\n",tempname);

return 0;
}
```

ungetc

DOS | UNIX | ANSI C | C++

Syntax

```
int ungetc(int c, FILE *stream);

int c;                  Character
FILE *stream;           Stream
```

Function The `ungetc` function pushes a character back into the input stream.

File(s) to Include `#include <stdio.h>`

Description The `ungetc` function places the character specified in the `c` argument back into the stream specified in the `stream` argument. The stream must be opened. Only the most recently retrieved character, using the `getc` function, is available to be pushed back into the stream.

Value(s) Returned The character placed into the stream is returned when successful. `EOF` is returned when unsuccessful.

Related Function(s)

`etc` : gets a character from a stream
`ungetch` : pushes a character back into the keyboard buffer

Example In the following example, `ungetc` pushes the retrieved character back into `stdin`.

```
#include <stdio.h>
#include <stdlib.h>
#include <conio.h>
#include <io.h>

int main (void)
{
char ch;

clrscr ();
printf ("Press a key\n");
ch = getch();
printf ("Character entered %c\n",ch);
ungetc (ch,stdin);
ch = getc(stdin);
```

continues

```
printf ("%c still there\n",ch);

return 0;
}
```

ungetch

Syntax `int ungetch(int ch);`

`int ch;` *Character*

Function The `ungetch` function places a character back into the keyboard buffer.

File(s) to Include `#include <conio.h>`

Description The `ungetch` function places the character in the `ch` argument back into the keyboard buffer. Only the last character, retrieved by the `getch` or `getche` functions, is available to be placed back into the keyboard buffer.

Value(s) Returned The character placed into the keyboard buffer is returned when successful. When unsuccessful, `EOF` is returned.

Related Function(s)
`getch` : gets a character from the keyboard
`getche` : gets a character from the keyboard and echoes
`ungetc` : pushes a character back into the input stream

Example In the following example, `ungetch` pushes the retrieved character back into the keyboard buffer.

```
#include <stdio.h>
#include <stdlib.h>
#include <conio.h>
#include <io.h>

int main (void)
{
char ch;

clrscr ();
```

```
printf ("Press a key\n");
ch = getch();
printf ("Character entered %c\n",ch);
ungetch (ch);
ch = getch();
printf ("%c still there\n",ch);

return 0;
}
```

unlock

Syntax `int unlock(int handle, long offset, long length);`

`int handle;`	*File handle*
`int offset;`	*Offset*
`long length;`	*File length*

Function The `unlock` function releases the file sharing locks for a file.

File(s) to Include `#include <io.h>`

Description The `unlock` function releases the file sharing locks for the file that corresponds to the file handle specified in the `handle` argument. To avoid errors, all file-sharing locks for a file, as set by the `lock` function, should be removed before closing the file.

Value(s) Returned Zero is returned when successful. When unsuccessful, –1 is returned.

Related Function(s) `lock` : places file-sharing locks on a file

Example In the following example, `unlock` unlocks the file-sharing locks on `lock.tst`.

```
#include <stdio.h>
#include <stdlib.h>
#include <conio.h>
#include <io.h>
#include <fcntl.h>
```

continues

```
#include <sys\stat.h>
#include <share.h>

int main (void)
{
int handle;
int result;
int length;

clrscr ();
handle = sopen("lock.tst",O_RDWR,SH_DENYNO,
S_IREAD);
length = filelength (handle);
result = lock (handle,0L,length);
if (result == 0)
     printf ("File locked\n");
else
     printf ("Unable to lock file\n");
result = unlock (handle,0L,length);
if (result == 0)
     printf ("File unlocked\n");
else
     printf ("Unable to unlock file\n");

return 0;
}
```

va_arg

Syntax `type va_arg(va_list ap, type);`

`va_list ap;`	*Points to list*
`type;`	*Type*

Function The `va_arg` macro provides access to a variable argument list.

File(s) to Include `#include <stdarg.h>`

Description The `va_arg` macro is used with the `va_start` and `va_end` macros to access variable argument lists. The `ap` argument, type `va_list`, is an array of information needed by the `va_arg` and `va_end` macros. When the `va_start` macro is called, the `ap` argument points to the first argument in the variable argument list. The arguments in the variable list should be of the type specified in the `type` argument. Each successive call to the `va_arg` macro returns the `next` argument in the list. The `va_end` macro allows a normal return.

Value(s) Returned The argument pointed to by the `ap` argument is returned.

Related Function(s)

`va_start` : provides access to a variable argument list
`va_end` : provides a normal return from accessing a variable argument list

Example In the following example, the `va_arg` macro implements a factorial.

```
#include <stdio.h>
#include <stdlib.h>
#include <conio.h>
#include <io.h>
#include <stdarg.h>

void factor(char *msg,...)
{
int result = 1;
va_list aptr;
int arg;

va_start (aptr,msg);
while ((arg = va_arg(aptr,int)) != 0)
      {
      result = result * arg;
      }
printf (msg,result);
va_end(aptr);
}

int main (void)
{
clrscr ();
factor ("Result: %d\n",3,2,1,0);

return 0;
}
```

va_end

DOS | UNIX | ANSI C | C++

Syntax `void va_end(va_list ap);`

`va_list ap;` *Points to list*

Function The `va_end` macro provides access to a variable argument list.

File(s) to Include `#include <stdarg.h>`

Description The `va_end` macro is used with the `va_start` and `va_arg` macros to access variable argument lists. The `ap` argument, type `va_list`, is an array of information needed by the `va_arg` and `va_end` macros. When the `va_start` macro is called, the `ap` argument points to the first argument in the variable argument list. The arguments in the variable list should be of the type specified in the type argument of the `va_arg` macro. Each successive call to the `va_arg` macro returns the next argument in the list. The `va_end` macro allows a normal return from accessing the variable argument list.

Value(s) Returned There is no return value.

Related Function(s)
`va_start` : provides access to a variable argument list
`va_arg` : provides access to a variable argument list

Example In the following example, the `va_end` macro implements the `sendmessage` function.

```
#include <stdio.h>
#include <stdlib.h>
#include <conio.h>
#include <io.h>
#include <stdarg.h>

void sendmessage(char *format,...)
{
va_list aptr;
va_start (aptr,format);
vprintf (format,aptr);
va_end(aptr);
```

```
}

int main (void)
{
char buffer[] = "Hello";

clrscr ();
sendmessage ("%s there!\n",buffer);
sendmessage ("Having fun yet?\n");

getch();
return 0;
}
```

va_start

Syntax

```
void va_start(va_list ap, lastfix);

va_list ap;                 Points to list
lastfix;                    Last fixed parameter
```

Function The `va_start` macro provides access to a variable argument list.

File(s) to Include

```
#include <stdarg.h>
#include <stdio.h>
```

Description The `va_start` macro is used with the `va_arg` and `va_end` macros to access variable argument lists. The `ap` argument, type `va_list`, is an array of information needed by the `va_arg` and `va_end` macros. When the `va_start` macro is called, the `ap` argument points to the first argument in the variable argument list. The arguments in the variable list should be of the type specified in the `type` argument of the `va_arg` macro. Each successive call to the `va_arg` macro returns the next argument in the list. The `lastfix` argument specifies the last fixed parameter to be passed to the calling function. The `va_end` macro allows a normal return from accessing variable argument lists.

Value(s) Returned There is no return value.

Related Function(s)
`va_arg` : provides access to a variable argument list
`va_end` : provides access to a variable argument list

Example In the following example, the `va_start` macro implements the `sendmessage` function.

```
#include <stdio.h>
#include <stdlib.h>
#include <conio.h>
#include <io.h>
#include <stdarg.h>

void sendmessage(char *format,...)
{
va_list aptr;
va_start (aptr,format);
vprintf (format,aptr);
va_end(aptr);
}

int main (void)
{
char buffer[] = "Hello";

clrscr ();
sendmessage ("%s there!\n",buffer);
sendmessage ("Having fun yet?\n");

return 0;
}
```

---

vfprintf

DOS | UNIX | ANSI C | C++

Syntax

```
int vfprintf(FILE *stream, const char *format,
             va_list arglist);
```

`FILE *stream;`	*Stream*
`const char *format;`	*Format string*
`va_list arglist;`	*Argument list*

Function The `vfprintf` function writes formatted output to a stream.

File(s) to Include

`#include <stdio.h>`

Description

The `vfprintf` function sends formatted output to the stream specified in the `stream` argument. The `arglist` argument is a pointer to a list of arguments. Each argument in the list is formatted according to the format specifiers in the format string. The format specifiers in the format string are the same format specifiers used by the `printf` function. More information on the format specifiers can be found in this chapter under the `printf` function. The format string is pointed to by the `format` argument.

Value(s) Returned

The number of bytes output is returned when successful. When unsuccessful, `EOF` is returned.

Related Function(s)

`printf` : writes formatted output to the `stdout` stream
`vprintf` : writes formatted output to the `stdout` stream

Example

In the following example, `vfprintf` writes output to the stream.

```
#include <stdio.h>
#include <stdlib.h>
#include <conio.h>
#include <io.h>
#include <stdarg.h>

FILE *filepointer;

void sendmessage(char *format,...)
{
va_list aptr;
va_start (aptr,format);
vfprintf (filepointer,format,aptr);
va_end(aptr);
}

void getmessage(char *format,...)
{
va_list aptr;
va_start (aptr,format);
vfscanf (filepointer,format,aptr);
va_end(aptr);
}
```

continues

```
int main (void)
{
char buffer[] = "Hello";
char one[10];
char two[10];
char three[10];
char four[10];
char five[10];

clrscr ();
filepointer = fopen ("vf.tst","w+");
sendmessage ("%s there!\n",buffer);
sendmessage ("Having fun yet?\n");
rewind (filepointer);
getmessage ("%s ",one);
printf ("%s",one);
getmessage ("%s ",two);
printf ("%s\n",two);
getmessage ("%s",three);
printf ("%s ",three);
getmessage ("%s",four);
printf ("%s ",four);
getmessage ("%s",five);
printf ("%s\n",five);
fclose(filepointer);

return 0;
}
```

vfscanf

DOS | UNIX | ANSI C | C++

Syntax

```
int vfscanf(FILE *stream, const char *format,
            va_list arglist);
```

`FILE *stream;`	*Stream*
`const char *format;`	*Format string*
`va_list arglist;`	*Argument list*

Function The `vscanf` function scans and formats input from a stream.

File(s) to Include

```
#include <stdio.h>
#include <stdarg.h>
```

Description The `vfscanf` function scans and formats the input from the stream specified in the `stream` argument. The `arglist` argument is a pointer to a list of arguments. The arguments in this list provide addresses for storing the formatted input fields. The input fields are read from the stream and formatted according to the format specifiers in the format string specified in the `format` argument. The format specifiers used with the `vfscanf` function are the same format specifiers described in this chapter under the `scanf` function.

Value(s) Returned The number of input fields scanned, converted, and stored is returned. `EOF` is returned when end-of-file is read.

Related Function(s)

`fscanf` : scans and formats input from a stream
`scanf` : scans and formats input from the `stdin` stream
`vscanf` : scans and formats input from the `stdin` stream

Example In the following example, `vfscanf` scans input from the stream.

```
#include <stdio.h>
#include <stdlib.h>
#include <conio.h>
#include <io.h>
#include <stdarg.h>

FILE *filepointer;

void sendmessage(char *format,...)
{
va_list aptr;
va_start (aptr,format);
vfprintf (filepointer,format,aptr);
va_end(aptr);
}

void getmessage(char *format,...)
{
va_list aptr;
va_start (aptr,format);
vfscanf (filepointer,format,aptr);
va_end(aptr);
}

int main (void)
{
char buffer[] = "Hello";
char one[10];
char two[10];
```

continues

```
char three[10];
char four[10];
char five[10];

clrscr ();
filepointer = fopen ("vf.tst","w+");
sendmessage ("%s there!\n",buffer);
sendmessage ("Having fun yet?\n");
rewind (filepointer);
getmessage ("%s ",one);
printf ("%s",one);
getmessage ("%s ",two);
printf ("%s\n",two);
getmessage ("%s",three);
printf ("%s ",three);
getmessage ("%s",four);
printf ("%s ",four);
getmessage ("%s",five);
printf ("%s\n",five);
fclose(filepointer);

return 0;
}
```

vprintf

DOS | UNIX | ANSI C | C++

Syntax `int vprintf(const char *format, va_list arglist);`

`const char *format;`	*Format string*
`va_list arglist;`	*Argument list*

Function The `vprintf` function writes formatted output to the `stdout` stream.

File(s) to Include `#include <stdarg.h>`

Description The `vprintf` function sends formatted output to the `stdout` stream. The `arglist` argument is a pointer to a list of arguments. Each argument in the list is formatted according to the format specifiers in the format string. The format specifiers in the format string are the same format specifiers used by the `printf` function. More information on the format specifiers can be found in this chapter under the `printf` function. The format string is pointed to by the `format` argument.

Value(s) Returned The number of bytes output is returned when successful. When unsuccessful, `EOF` is returned.

Related Function(s)

`printf` : writes formatted output to `stdout`
`vfprintf` : writes formatted output to a stream

Example In the following example, `vprintf` sends the message to `stdout`.

```
#include <stdio.h>
#include <stdlib.h>
#include <conio.h>
#include <io.h>
#include <stdarg.h>

void sendmessage(char *format,...)
{
va_list aptr;
va_start (aptr,format);
vprintf (format,aptr);
va_end(aptr);
}

int main (void)
{
int num1 = 20;
float num2 = 3.0;

clrscr ();
sendmessage ("Print an int and a float\n");
sendmessage ("Int : %d Float: %f\n",num1,num2);

return 0;
}
```

vscanf

DOS | UNIX | ANSI C | C++

Syntax `int vscanf(const char *format, va_list arglist);`

`const char *format;` *Format string*
`va_list arglist;` *Argument list*

Function The `vscanf` function scans and formats input from the `stdin` stream.

File(s) to Include `#include <stdio.h>`

Description The `vscanf` function scans and formats the input from the stream specified in the `stream` argument. The `arglist` argument is a pointer to a list of arguments. The arguments in this list provide addresses for storing the formatted input fields. The input fields are read from the stream and formatted according to the format specifiers in the format string specified in the `format` argument. The format specifiers used with the `vscanf` function are the same format specifiers described in this chapter under the `scanf` function.

Value(s) Returned The number of input fields scanned, converted, and stored is returned.

Related Function(s)
`scanf` : scans and formats input from the `stdin` stream
`vfscanf` : scans and formats input from a stream

Example In the following example, `vscanf` gets a name from `stdin`.

```
#include <stdio.h>
#include <stdlib.h>
#include <conio.h>
#include <io.h>
#include <stdarg.h>

void getname(char *format,...)
{
va_list aptr;
va_start (aptr,format);
vscanf (format,aptr);
va_end(aptr);
}

int main (void)
{
char first[20];
char middle[20];
char last[20];

clrscr ();
printf ("Enter your first middle and last
name\n");
getname("%s %s %s",first,middle,last);
```

```
printf ("Hello %s %s %s\n",first,middle,last);

return 0;
}
```

vsprintf

DOS | UNIX | ANSI C | C++

Syntax

```
int vsprintf(char *buffer, const char *format,
             va_list arglist);
```

`char *buffer;`	*String buffer*
`const char *format;`	*Format string*
`va_list arglist;`	*Argument list*

Function The `vsprintf` function writes formatted output to a string.

File(s) to Include

```
#include <stdarg.h>
#include <stdio.h>
```

Description The `vsprintf` function sends formatted output to the string specified in the `buffer` argument. The `arglist` argument is a pointer to a list of arguments. Each argument in the list is formatted according to the format specifiers in the format string. The format specifiers in the format string are the same format specifiers used by the `printf` function. More information on the format specifiers can be found in this chapter under the `printf` function. The format string is pointed to by the `format` argument.

Value(s) Returned The number of bytes output is returned when successful. When unsuccessful, `EOF` is returned.

Related Function(s)

`printf` : writes formatted output to the `stdout` stream
`vprintf` : writes formatted output to the `stdout` stream

Example In the following example, `vsprintf` builds and displays a name.

```
#include <stdio.h>
#include <stdlib.h>
#include <conio.h>
#include <io.h>
#include <stdarg.h>
```

continues

```
char name[80];

void buildname(char *format,...)
{
va_list aptr;
va_start (aptr,format);
vsprintf (name,format,aptr);
va_end(aptr);
}

int main (void)
{
char first[20] = "JAMES";
char middle[20] = "WARREN";
char last[20] = "MCCORD";

clrscr ();
buildname("%s %s %s",first,middle,last);
printf ("%s\n",name);

return 0;
}
```

vsscanf

DOS | **UNIX** | ANSI C | C++

Syntax

```
int vsscanf(const char *buffer, const char
            *format, va_list arglist);
```

`const char *buffer;`	*Buffer*
`const char *format;`	*Format string*
`va_list arglist;`	*Argument list*

Function The `vsscanf` function scans and formats input from a stream.

File(s) to Include

```
#include <stdarg.h>
#include <stdio.h>
```

Description The `vsscanf` function scans and formats the input from the stream specified in the `buffer` argument. The `arglist` argument is a pointer to a list of arguments. The arguments in this list provide addresses for storing the formatted input fields. The input fields are read from the stream and formatted according to the format specifiers in the format string specified in the `format` argument. The format specifiers used with the `vsscanf` function are the same format specifiers described in this chapter under the `scanf` function.

Value(s) Returned The number of input fields scanned, converted, and stored is returned.

Related Function(s)

`scanf` : scans and formats input from the `stdin` stream
`vfscanf` : scans and formats input from a stream
`vscanf` : scans and formats input from the `stdin` stream

Example In the following example, `vsscanf` scans the name buffer.

```
#include <stdio.h>
#include <stdlib.h>
#include <conio.h>
#include <io.h>
#include <stdarg.h>

char name[40] = "JAMES WARREN MCCORD";

void getname(char *format,...)
{
va_list aptr;
va_start (aptr,format);
vsscanf (name,format,aptr);
va_end(aptr);
}

int main (void)
{
char first[20];
char middle[20];
char last[20];

clrscr ();
getname("%s %s %s",first,middle,last);
printf ("%s %s %s\n",first,middle,last);

return 0;
}
```

_write

DOS | UNIX | ANSI C | C++

Syntax

```
int _write(int handle, void *buf, unsigned len);
```

`int handle;`	*File handle*
`void *buf;`	*Buffer*
`unsigned len;`	*Number of bytes to write*

Function The `_write` function writes to a file. This function does not translate linefeed characters to carriage return/linefeed pairs.

File(s) to Include `#include <io.h>`

Description The `_write` function writes a number of bytes from the buffer pointed to by the `buf` argument to the file which corresponds to the file handle specified in the `file` argument. The number of bytes to copy from the buffer is specified in the `len` argument. The `_write` function does not convert linefeed characters to carriage return/linefeed pairs. The maximum number of bytes that can be written is 65,534.

Value(s) Returned The number of bytes written is returned when successful. When unsuccessful, –1 is returned and the global variable `errno` is set to EACCES, for permission denied, or EBADF, for bad file number.

Related Function(s) `write` : writes to a file; translates linefeed characters to carriage return/linefeed pairs

Example In the following example, the `_write` function writes the buffer to the open file.

```
#include <stdio.h>
#include <stdlib.h>
#include <conio.h>
#include <io.h>
#include <fcntl.h>
#include <sys\stat.h>

int main (void)
{
```

```
char buffer[] = "Send to file";
int filehandle;
int result;

clrscr ();

if ((filehandle = open("_write.tst",O_CREAT,
                S_IREAD|S_IWRITE)) ==  1)
     {
     perror ("Error in _open\n");
     return 1;
     }
printf ("File opened\n");
result = _write
(filehandle,buffer,strlen(buffer));
if (result ==  1)
     printf ("Error writing to file\n");
else
     printf ("%d bytes written\n",result);
_close (filehandle);

return 0;
}
```

write

DOS | UNIX | ANSI C | C++

Syntax `int write(int handle, void *buf, unsigned len);`

`int handle;`	*File handle*
`void *buf;`	*Buffer*
`unsigned len;`	*Number of bytes to write*

Function The `write` function writes to a file. This function translates linefeed characters to carriage return/linefeed pairs.

File(s) to Include `#include <io.h>`

Description The `write` function writes a number of bytes from the buffer pointed to by the `buf` argument to the file which corresponds to the file handle specified in the `file` argument. The number of bytes to copy from the buffer is specified in the `len` argument.

The `write` function converts linefeed characters to carriage return/linefeed pairs. The maximum number of bytes that can be written is 65,543.

Value(s) Returned The number of bytes written is returned when successful. When unsuccessful, –1 is returned and the global variable `errno` is set to EACCES, for permission denied, or EBADF, for bad file number.

Related Function(s) `_write` : writes to a file

Example In the following example, the `write` function writes the buffer to the open file.

```
#include <stdio.h>
#include <stdlib.h>
#include <conio.h>
#include <io.h>
#include <fcntl.h>
#include <sys\stat.h>

int main (void)
{
char buffer[] = "Sent to file";
int filehandle;
int result;

clrscr ();

if ((filehandle = open("write.tst",O_CREAT,
                S_IREAD|S_IWRITE)) ==  1)
     {
     perror ("Error in _open\n");
     return 1;
     }
printf ("File opened\n");
result = write (filehandle,buffer,strlen(buffer));
if (result ==  1)
     printf ("Error writing to file\n");
else
     printf ("%d bytes written\n",result);
close (filehandle);

return 0;
}
```

Interfaces for DOS, BIOS, and the 8086

This chapter provides information on the macros and functions used to directly interface with the Disk Operating System (DOS), the Basic Input/Output System (BIOS), and 8086 software interrupts. BIOS is a set of input/output routines which provides access to the system's peripherals, including the keyboard, display adapter, disk drives, and ports. BIOS is built into read-only memory (ROM) on IBM-compatible MS-DOS machines. DOS contains a series of utility functions for the manipulation of disks and files. Table 10.1 lists the functions and macros used to interface with DOS, BIOS, and the 8086.

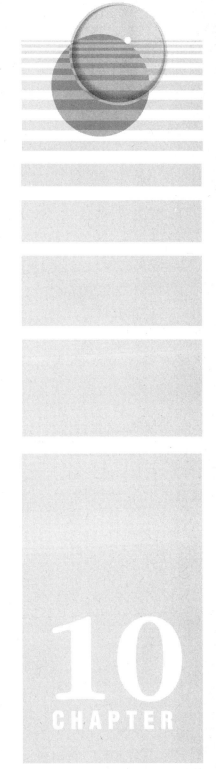

Table 10.1. DOS, BIOS, and 8086 interface functions and macros.

Function	*Meaning*
`absread`	Reads the specified disk sectors
`abswrite`	Writes specific disk sectors
`bdos`	Provides access to DOS system calls
`bdosptr`	Provides access to DOS system calls
`bioscom`	Performs serial I/O
`biosdisk`	Provides BIOS disk drive services
`biosequip`	Checks equipment connected to the system
`bioskey`	Provides a BIOS keyboard interface
`biosmemory`	Returns the size of RAM
`biosprint`	Provides BIOS services for printer I/O
`biostime`	Reads or sets the BIOS timer
`country`	Returns country-specific information
`ctrlbrk`	Specifies the new control-break handler
`disable`	Disables hardware interrupts
`dosexterr`	Retrieves extended DOS error information
`__emit__`	Inserts literal values directly into code
`enable`	Enables hardware interrupts
`FP_OFF`	Gets the far address offset of a far pointer
`FP_SEG`	Gets the far address segment of a far pointer
`freemem`	Frees an allocated DOS memory block
`geninterrupt`	Generates a software interrupt
`getcbrk`	Gets the setting for control-break checking
`getdfree`	Gets information about free space on a disk
`getdta`	Retrieves the disk transfer address
`getfat`	Retrieves file allocation table information for a drive
`getfatd`	Retrieves file allocation table information for the default drive
`getpsp`	Retrieves the program segment prefix
`getvect`	Retrieves the interrupt vector

Function	*Meaning*
`getverify`	Retrieves the status of the DOS verify flag
`harderr`	Defines the hardware error handler function
`hardresume`	Used with the `harderr` function to return to DOS
`hardretn`	Used with the `harderr` function to return control to the program
`inport`	Reads a word from the specified port
`inportb`	Reads a byte from the specified port
`int86`	Generates an 8086 software interrupt
`int86x`	Generates an 8086 software interrupt
`intdos`	Generates a DOS interrupt
`intdosx`	Generates a DOS interrupt
`intr`	Generates an 8086 software interrupt
`keep`	Used to create Terminate Stay Resident programs
`MK_FP`	Creates a far pointer
`outport`	Sends a word to the specified port
`outportb`	Sends a byte to the specified port
`_OvrInitEms`	Initializes expanded memory for swapping
`_OvrInitExt`	Initializes extended memory for swapping
`parsfnm`	Parses a file name
`peek`	Retrieves the word at the specified location
`peekb`	Retrieves the byte at the specified location
`poke`	Stores an integer value at the specified location
`pokeb`	Stores a byte at the specified location
`randbrd`	Reads a random block from a file
`randbwr`	Writes a random block to disk
`segread`	Reads the segment registers
`setcbrk`	Selects the control-break setting
`setdta`	Sets the disk transfer address
`setvect`	Sets an interrupt vector entry

continues

Table 10.1. *(continued)*

Function	*Meaning*
`setverify`	Sets the DOS verify flag
`sleep`	Suspends program execution for a specified number of seconds
`unlink`	Deletes a file

The interrupt numbers for the BIOS functions are shown in table 10.2 that follows. The interrupt numbers for selected DOS functions are shown in table 10.3. All these functions can be accessed through the Borland C++ general purpose interrupt routines `int86` and `int86x`. The *DOS Programmer's Reference*, 2nd Ed., written by Dettman and Kyle and published by Que Corporation, 1989, provides specific user information for each of these functions.

Table 10.2. *BIOS functions.*

Interrupt	*Function*	*Meaning*
00h		Divide-by-zero interrupt
01h		Single step interrupt
02h		Non-maskable interrupt
03h		Breakpoint interrupt
04h		Arithmetic overflow interrupt
05h		Print screen
08h		System timer
09h		Keyboard interrupt
0Bh		Communications
0Ch		Communications
0Dh		Hard disk controller
0Eh		Floppy disk management
0Fh		Printer management
10h		Video Functions
	00h	Set video mode
	01h	Set cursor type
	02h	Set cursor position

Interrupt	*Function*	*Meaning*
	03h	Read cursor position and configuration
	04h	Read light pen position
	05h	Select active display page
	06h	Scroll window up
	07h	Scroll window down
	08h	Read character and attribute
	09h	Write character and attribute
	0Ah	Write character at cursor
	0Bh	Set color palette
	0Ch	Write graphics pixel
	0Dh	Read graphics pixel
	0Eh	Write text in TTY mode
	0Fh	Get current display mode
	10h	Set palette registers
	11h	Character generator
	12h	Alternate select
	13h	Write string
	1Ah	Read/Write display codes
	1Bh	Get display state
	1Ch	Save/Restore display state
11h		Get status of equipment
12h		Get memory size
13h		Diskette functions
	00h	Reset disk system
	01h	Get status of disk system
	02h	Read disk sectors
	03h	Write disk sectors
	04h	Verify disk sectors
	05h	Format disk track

continues

Table 10.2. (continued)

Interrupt	*Function*	*Meaning*
	06h	Format cylinder/Set bad sector flags
	07h	Format drive
	08h	Get disk drive parameters
	09h	Initialize fixed disk table
	0Ah	Read long sector
	0Bh	Write long sector
	0Ch	Seek cylinder
	0Dh	Alternate disk reset
	0Eh	Read sector buffer
	0Fh	Write sector buffer
	10h	Test fixed disk system status
	11h	Recalibrate fixed disk drive
	12h	Controller RAM diagnostic
	13h	Drive diagnostic
	14h	Controller diagnostic
	15h	Return DASD type
	16h	Read disk change line status
	17h	Set DASD type for disk format
	18h	Set media type for format
	19h	Park heads
	1Ah	Format ESDI unit
14h		Asynchronous communication functions
	00h	Initialize communications port
	01h	Write character
	02h	Read character
	03h	Get port status
	04h	Extended initialization
	05h	Extended port control

Interrupt	*Function*	*Meaning*
15h		System services functions
	00h	Turn on cassette motor
	01h	Turn off cassette motor
	02h	Read data blocks from cassette
	03h	Write data blocks to cassette
	0Fh	ESDI unit format periodic interrupt
	21h	Power-on self test error log
	4Fh	Keyboard intercept
	80h	Device open
	81h	Device close
	82h	Program termination
	83h	Event wait
	84h	Joystick support
	85h	System request key pressed
	86h	Delay
	87h	Move block
	88h	Determine size of extended memory
	89h	Switch to protected mode
	90h	Device wait
	91h	Interrupt complete
	C0h	Get system configuration parameters
	C1h	Get extended BIOS data area segment address
	C2h	Pointing device interface
	C3h	Enable/disable watchdog timeout
	C4h	Programmable option select
16h		Keyboard functions
	00h	Read keyboard character
	01h	Read keyboard status
	02h	Get keyboard flags

continues

Table 10.2. (continued)

Interrupt	*Function*	*Meaning*
	03h	Adjust keyboard repeat rate
	04h	Key-click on/off
	05h	Write to keyboard buffer
	10h	Get keystroke
	11h	Check keyboard
	12h	Get keyboard status flags
17h		Printer functions
	00h	Write character to printer
	01h	Initialize printer port
	02h	Get printer port status
18h		Execute ROM BASIC
19h		System warm boot
1Ah		System timer/real-time clock services
	00h	Get clock counter
	01h	Set clock counter
	02h	Read real-time clock
	03h	Set real-time clock
	04h	Read date from real-time clock
	05h	Set date on real-time clock
	06h	Set system alarm
	07h	Disable real-time clock alarm
	09h	Read real-time clock alarm
	0Ah	Get day count
	0Bh	Set day count
	80h	Set sound source
1Bh		Control-break address
1Ch		Timer tick interrupt
1Dh		Video initialization parameter table

Interrupt	*Function*	*Meaning*
1Eh		Disk initialization parameter table
1Fh		Graphics character bitmap table
70h		Real-time clock interrupt

Table 10.3. *DOS functions using interrupt 21h.*

Function	*Subfunction*	*Meaning*
00h		Terminate program
01h		Keyboard input with echo
02h		Display output
03h		Auxiliary input
04h		Auxiliary output
05h		Printer output
06h		Direct console I/O
07h		Direct `stdin` input
08h		`stdin` input
09h		Display string
0Ah		Buffered `stdin` input
0Bh		Check `stdin` status
0Ch		Clear buffer and input
0Dh		Reset disk
0Eh		Select disk
0Fh		Open file
10h		Close file
11h		Search for first entry
12h		Search for next entry
13h		Delete file
14h		Read sequential file
15h		Write sequential file

continues

Table 10.3. *(continued)*

Function	*Subfunction*	*Meaning*
16h		Create file
17h		Rename file
18h		Reserved
19h		Get default drive
1Ah		Set DTA address
1Bh		Get allocation table information
1Ch		Get allocation table information for the specified drive
1Dh		Reserved
1Eh		Reserved
1Fh		Get default disk parameter block
20h		Reserved
21h		Random file read
22h		Random file write
23h		Get file size
24h		Set random record field
25h		Set interrupt vector
26h		Create PSP
27h		Read random block
28h		Write random block
29h		Parse file name
2Ah		Get system date
2Bh		Set system date
2Ch		Get system time
2Dh		Set system time
2Eh		Set verify flag
2Fh		Get DTA address
30h		Get DOS version number

Function	*Subfunction*	*Meaning*
31h		Terminate and stay resident
32h		Get drive parameter block
33h	00h	Get control-break flag
	01h	Set control-break flag
	05h	Get boot drive code
34h		Return address of InDOS flag
35h		Get interrupt vector
36h		Get free disk space
37h	00h	Get `switchchar`
	01h	Set `switchchar`
	02h	Read device availability
	03h	Set device availability
38h		Get/set country information
39h		Create subdirectory
3Ah		Remove subdirectory
3Bh		Set directory
3Ch		Create/truncate file
3Dh		Open file
3Eh		Close file
3Fh		Read file or device
40h		Write to file or device
41h		Delete file
42h		Move file pointer
43h	00h	Get file attributes
	01h	Set file attributes
44h		Device driver control (IOCTL)
	00h	Get device information
	01h	Set device information
	02h	Read device IOCTL

continues

Table 10.3. (continued)

Function	*Subfunction*	*Meaning*
	03h	Write device IOCTL
	04h	Read block driver IOCTL
	05h	Write block drive IOCTL
	06h	Get input status
	07h	Get output status
	08h	Determine whether block drive is removable
	09h	Determine whether block drive is local or remote
	0Ah	Determine whether handle is local or remote
	0Bh	Set sharing retry count
	0Ch	Generic I/O control for handles
	0Dh	Generic I/O control for block devices
	0Eh	Get logical drive map
	0Fh	Set logical drive map
45h		Duplicate handle
46h		Force duplicate handle
47h		Get current directory
48h		Allocate memory
49h		Release memory
4Ah		Modify memory allocation
4Bh	00h	Execute program
	03h	Load overlay
4Ch		Terminate with return code
4Dh		Get return code
4Eh		Search for first match
4Fh		Search for next match
50h		Set PSP segment
51h		Get PSP segment
52h		Get disk list

Function	*Subfunction*	*Meaning*
53h		Translate BPB to DPB
54h		Get verify flag
55h		Create PSP
56h		Rename file
57h	00h	Get file date and time
	01h	Set file date and time
58h	00h	Get allocation strategy
	01h	Set allocation strategy
59h		Get extended error information
5Ah		Create uniquely named file
5Bh		Create new file
5Ch	00h	Set file access locks
	01h	Clear file access locks
5Dh	00h	Copy data to DOS save area
	06h	Get critical-error flag address
	0Ah	Set error data values
5Eh	00h	Get machine name
	01h	Set machine name
	02h	Set network printer setup
	03h	Get network printer setup
5Fh	02h	Get redirection list entry
	03h	Set redirection list entry
	04h	Cancel redirection list entry
60h		Expand path name string
61h		Reserved
62h		Get PSP address
63h	00h	Get system lead byte table
	01h	Set/clear interim console flag
	02h	Get value of interim console flag

continues

Table 10.3. (continued)

Function	Subfunction	Meaning
64h		Set current country byte
65h		Get extended country information
66h	01h	Get global code page
	02h	Set global code page
67h		Set handle count
68h		Flush buffer
69h		Reserved
6Ah		Allocate memory
6Bh		Reserved
6Ch		Extended open/create

Borland C++ DOS, BIOS, and 8086 Interface Reference Guide

The remainder of this chapter provides detailed information on the use of each of the functions and macros listed in table 10.1.

absread

Syntax

```
int absread(int drive, int nsects, int lsect,
            void *buffer);
```

`int drive;`	*Drive to read*
`int nsects;`	*Number of sectors to read*
`int lsect;`	*Logical sector number*
`void *buffer;`	*Memory address*

Function The `absread` function reads the specified disk sectors.

File(s) to Include `#include <dos.h>`

Description The `absread` function reads specific disk sectors from the drive specified in the `drive` argument. The number of sectors to read is defined in the `nsects` argument and is limited to the smaller of 64K or the size of the buffer. The `lsect` argument defines the beginning logical sector number. The `buffer` argument specifies the beginning address in memory where the data is to be placed.

Value(s) Returned If successful, a zero is returned. When unsuccessful, a –1 is returned and the global variable `errno` is set to the value returned by the system call in the AX register.

Related Function(s) `abswrite` : writes specific disk sectors

Example In the following example, `absread` reads the first sector of drive A.

```
#include <stdio.h>
#include <conio.h>
#include <dos.h>
#include <stdlib.h>

int main (void)
{
unsigned char buffer[512];

clrscr ();
printf ("Insert a disk in Drive A, then press a
  key\n");
getch();
if (absread (0,1,1,&buffer) != 0)
     printf ("Cannot read from Drive A\n");
else
     printf ("Drive A, Sector 1 read\n");

return 0;
}
```

abswrite

DOS UNIX ANSI C C++

Syntax

```
int abswrite(int drive, int nsects, int lsect,
             void *buffer);
```

`int drive;`	*Drive to write to*
`int nsects;`	*Number of sectors to write*
`int lsect;`	*Logical sector number*
`void *buffer;`	*Memory address*

Function The `abswrite` function writes specific disk sectors.

File(s) to Include `#include <dos.h>`

Description The `abswrite` function writes to the drive specified in the `drive` argument. The `nsects` argument defines the number of sectors to write to and is limited to the smaller of either 64K or the size of the buffer. The `lsect` argument defines the beginning logical sector number. The `buffer` argument specifies the address in memory where the data will be written.

Value(s) Returned Zero is returned when successful. When unsuccessful, –1 is returned and the global variable `errno` is set to the return value of the system call in the AX register.

Related Function(s) `absread` : reads specific disk sectors

Example In the following example, `abswrite` writes to drive A.

```
#include <stdio.h>
#include <conio.h>
#include <dos.h>
#include <stdlib.h>

int main (void)
{
unsigned char buffer[512];

clrscr ();
printf ("Insert a blank disk in Drive A, then
  press a key\n");
```

Related Function(s)
`bdos` : provides access to DOS system calls
`intdos` : DOS interrupt interface

Example In the following example, `bdosptr` sets the current directory.

```
#include <stdio.h>
#include <conio.h>
#include <dos.h>
#include <dir.h>
#include <stdlib.h>

int main (void)
{
char buffer [80];

clrscr ();
     /* get the current directory */
getcwd (buffer,80);
bdosptr (0x3B,buffer,0);
printf ("Directory set to %s\n",buffer);

return 0;
}
```

bioscom

DOS UNIX ANSI C C++

Syntax

```
int bioscom(int cmd, char abyte, int port);
```

`int cmd;`	*Command*
`char abyte;`	*Settings for communication*
`int port;`	*Port for communication*

Function The `bioscom` function performs serial I/O.

File(s) to Include `#include <bios.h>`

Description The `bioscom` function performs serial I/O via the port specified in the `port` argument. When the `port` argument is 1, the COM1 port is used; when the `port` argument is 2, the COM2 port is used, and so forth.

The `cmd` argument specifies the way that the `abyte` argument will be interpreted. The possible values for the `cmd` argument are as follows:

0	Sets the communications parameters to those set in the `abyte` argument
1	Sends the character defined in `abyte`
2	Receives a character
3	Returns the current status of the port

The `abyte` argument consists of the combination of one value from each of the following groups:

Baud rate

Value	*Meaning*
0x00	110 Baud
0x20	150 Baud
0x40	300 Baud
0x60	600 Baud
0x80	1200 Baud
0xA0	2400 Baud
0xC0	4800 Baud
0xE0	9600 Baud

Parity

Value	*Meaning*
0x00	No parity
0x08	Odd parity
0x18	Even parity

Stop Bits

Value	*Meaning*
0x00	1 stop bit
0x04	2 stop bits

Data Bits

Value	*Meaning*
0x02	7 data bits
0x03	8 data bits

Therefore, for 9600 baud, odd parity, 1 stop bit, and 8 data bits, `abyte` would be 0xEB for 0xE0|0x08|0x00|0x03.

Value(s) Returned A 16-bit integer is returned. The return value is interpreted as follows:

Bit	*Meaning*
15	Time out
14	Transmit shift register empty
13	Transmit holding register empty
12	Break detect
11	Framing error
10	Parity error
9	Overrun error
8	Data ready
7	Received line signal detect
6	Ring indicator
5	Data set ready
4	Clear to send
3	Change in receive line signal detector
2	Trailing edge ring detector
1	Change in data set ready
0	Change in clear to send

Related Function(s) `biosprint` : provides printer I/O

Example In the following example, `bioscom` gets the status of the COM1 port.

```
#include <stdio.h>
#include <conio.h>
```

continues

```
#include <bios.h>
#include <stdlib.h>

int main (void)
{
int status;
int cmd = 3;
char abyte = (0xE0|0x00|0x00|0x03);
int port = 0;

clrscr();
status = bioscom (cmd,abyte,port);
printf ("Status of Comm 1 Port %d\n", status);
status = 0x100 & status;
     /* check data ready */
if (status == 0x100)
     printf ("Comm1 has Data Ready\n");
else
     printf ("Comm1 is not ready\n");

return 0;
}
```

biosdisk

DOS UNIX ANSI C C++

Syntax

```
int biosdisk(int cmd, int drive, int head, int
             track, int sector, int nsects, void
             *buffer);
```

`int cmd;`	*Command*
`int drive;`	*Drive to use*
`int head;`	*Head specifier*
`int track;`	*Track specifier*
`int sector;`	*Sector specifier*
`int nsects;`	*Number of sectors*
`void *buffer;`	*Information*

Function The `biosdisk` function provides BIOS disk drive services.

Filc(s) to Include `#include <bios.h>`

Description The `biosdisk` function accesses interrupt 0x13 for BIOS disk operations on the drive specified in the `drive` argument. For floppy drives, 0 is used to identify the first drive, 1 is for the second drive, and so forth. For hard drives, 0x80 is used to identify the first hard drive, 0x81 for the second drive, 0x82 for the third drive, and so forth.

The `cmd` argument specifies the disk operation to perform. The `head`, `track`, `sector`, `nsects`, and `buffer` arguments are used to support the requirements for the command specified in the `cmd` argument. The following commands are available for use:

Command	*Meaning*
0	Resets disk system by a hard reset; all other parameters are ignored.
1	Returns the status of the last disk operation; all other parameters are ignored.
2	Reads the specified disk sectors. The `head`, `track`, and `sector` arguments specify the starting sector. The `nsects` argument specifies the number of sectors to read. The read data is stored in buffer.
3	Writes disk sectors from memory. The `head`, `track`, and `sector` arguments specify the starting sector. The `nsects` argument specifies the number of sectors to write. The data is read from buffer.
4	Verifies sectors. The `head`, `track`, and `sector` arguments specify the starting sector. The `nsects` argument specifies the number of sectors to verify.
5	Formats a track. The `head` and `track` arguments specify the track to format. Buffer stores the sector headers.
6	Formats a track and sets bad sector flags.
7	Formats the drive beginning as a specific track.
8	Retrieves the current drive parameters and stores them in buffer.
9	Initializes drive-pair characteristics.
10	Does a long read.

Command	*Meaning*
11	Does a long write.
12	Does a disk seek.
13	Alternates disk reset.
14	Reads sector buffer.
15	Writes sector buffer.
16	Tests the specified drive to see whether it is ready.
17	Recalibrates the drive.
18	Performs diagnostics on controller RAM.
19	Performs drive diagnostics.
20	Performs controller internal diagnostics.

Value(s) Returned A status byte is returned that consists of the following bits:

Value	*Meaning*
0x00	Operation successful
0x01	Bad command
0x02	Address mark not found
0x03	Attempt to write to write-protected disk
0x04	Sector not found
0x05	Reset failed (hard disk)
0x06	Disk changed since last operation
0x07	Drive parameter activity failed
0x08	Direct memory access (DMA) overrun
0x09	Attempt to perform DMA across 64K
0x0A	Bad sector detected
0x0B	Bad track detected
0x0C	Unsupported track
0x10	Bad CRC/ECC on disk read

Value	*Meaning*
0x11	CRC/ECC corrected data error
0x20	Controller failure
0x40	Seek operation failed
0x80	Attachment failed to respond
0xAA	Drive not ready (hard disk)
0xBB	Undefined error occurred (hard disk)
0xCC	Write fault occurred
0xE0	Status error
0xFF	Sense operation failed

Related Function(s)

`absread` : reads disk sectors
`abswrite` : writes disk sectors

Example In the following example, `biosdisk` resets the disk system.

```
#include <stdio.h>
#include <conio.h>
#include <bios.h>
#include <stdlib.h>

int main (void)
{
int status;
int cmd = 0;
int drive = 0;
int head = 0;
int track = 1;
int sector = 1;
int nsectors = 1;
char buffer[512];

clrscr();
status = biosdisk
(cmd,drive,head,track,sector,nsectors,buffer);
if (status == 0)
     printf ("Disk System Reset\n");
else
     printf ("Unable to Reset Disk System\n");

return 0;
}
```

biosequip

DOS | UNIX | ANSI C | C++

Syntax `int biosequip(void);`

Function The `biosequip` function checks the equipment connected to the system.

File(s) to Include `#include <bios.h>`

Description The `biosequip` function checks the equipment connected to the system using BIOS interrupt 0x11.

Value(s) Returned The returned 16-bit value is interpreted as follows:

Bits 14-15	Number of parallel printers installed 00 = 0 printers 01 = 1 printer 10 = 2 printers 11 = 3 printers
Bit 13	Serial printer attached
Bit 12	Game I/O attached
Bits 9-11	Number of COM ports 000 = 0 ports 001 = 1 port 010 = 2 ports 011 = 3 ports 100 = 4 ports 101 = 5 ports 110 = 6 ports 111 = 7 ports
Bit 8	Direct Memory Access (DMA) 0 = Machine has DMA 1 = Machine does not have DMA

Bits 6-7	Number of disk drives 00 = 1 drive 01 = 2 drives 10 = 3 drives 11 = 4 drives
Bits 4-5	Initial video mode 00 = Unused 01 = 40x25 BW with color card 10 = 80x25 BW with color card 11 = 80x25 BW with mono card
Bits 2-3	Motherboard RAM size 00 = 16K 01 = 32K 10 = 48K 11 = 64K
Bit 1	Floating-point co-processor
Bit 0	Boot from disk

Related Function(s)

`bioscom` : performs serial I/O
`biosdisk` : performs BIOS disk drive services

Example

In the following example, `biosequip` tests for a math co-processor.

```
#include <stdio.h>
#include <conio.h>
#include <bios.h>
#include <stdlib.h>

int main (void)
{
int result;

clrscr();
result = biosequip();
if (result &0x0002)
     printf ("Math co-processor installed\n");
else
```

```
        printf ("Math co-processor not installed\n");

    return 0;
    }
```

bioskey

Syntax

```
int bioskey(int cmd);

int cmd;                        Command
```

Function The `bioskey` function provides a BIOS keyboard interface.

File(s) to Include `#include <bios.h>`

Description The `bioskey` function interfaces the keyboard through the direct use of BIOS services. The BIOS interrupt 0x16 is used by the function. The `cmd` argument, as described in the following Value(s) Returned, specifies the BIOS operation.

Value(s) Returned The value returned is dependent on the `cmd` statement. One of the following is returned.

Command	*Return value*
0	When the lower 8 bits are nonzero, the ASCII character for the next keystroke is returned. When the lower 8 bits are zero, the upper 8 bits reflect the extended keyboard codes.
1	This command tests to see if a keystroke is ready to be read from the keyboard buffer. A zero return value means that no keystroke is ready. When a keystroke is ready, the value of the keystroke is returned.

Command	*Return value*		
2	This command checks the current Shift key status.		
	Bit 7	0x80	Insert on
	Bit 6	0x40	Caps Lock on
	Bit 5	0x20	Num Lock o
	Bit 4	0x10	Scroll Lock on
	Bit 3	0x08	Alt pressed
	Bit 2	0x04	Ctrl pressed
	Bit 1	0x02	<- Shift pressed
	Bit 0	0x01	-> Shift pressed

Related Function(s) `biosprint` : provides BIOS printer services

Example In the following example, `bioskey` tests the status of the Caps Lock, Num Lock, and Scroll Lock keys.

```
#include <stdio.h>
#include <conio.h>
#include <bios.h>

int main (void)
{
int result;

clrscr();
result = bioskey(2);
if (result & 0x40)
     printf ("Caps Lock key is on\n");
else
     printf ("Caps Lock key is off\n");
if (result & 0x20)
     printf ("Num Lock key is on\n");
else
     printf ("Num Lock key is off\n");
if (result & 0x10)
     printf ("Scroll Lock key is on\n");
else
     printf ("Scroll Lock key is off\n");

return 0;
}
```

biosmemory

DOS | UNIX | ANSI C | C++

Syntax `int biosmemory(void);`

Function The `biosmemory` function returns the size of RAM.

File(s) to Include `#include <bios.h>`

Description The `biosmemory` function retrieves the size of RAM. The `biosmemory` function uses the BIOS interrupt 0x12 and does not count display adapter memory, extended memory, or expanded memory.

Value(s) Returned The size of RAM, in 1K blocks, is returned.

Related Function(s) `biosequip` : checks the equipment attached to the system

Example In the following example, `bioskey` tests the size of RAM.

```
#include <stdio.h>
#include <conio.h>
#include <bios.h>
#include <stdlib.h>

int main (void)
{
int status;

clrscr();
status = biosmemory ();
printf ("Available memory excluding video,\n");
printf ("extended, or expanded memory is
  %dK\n",status);

return 0;
}
```

biosprint

Syntax

```
int biosprint(int cmd, int abyte, int port);

int cmd;                    Command
int abyte;                  Character to print
int port;                   Port to print from
```

Function The `biosprint` function provides BIOS services for printer I/O.

File(s) to Include `#include <bios.h>`

Description The `biosprint` function performs printer functions using BIOS interrupt 0x17. The `port` argument specifies the port to which the printer is connected. A `port` argument of 0 indicates LPT1. A `port` argument of 1 indicates LPT2, and so forth.

The `cmd` argument is selected from one of the following values. The `abyte` argument specifies the character to send.

Command	*Meaning*
0	Prints the character in the abyte argument
1	Initializes the printer port
2	Reads the printer status

Value(s) Returned The current printer status is returned and is interpreted as follows:

Bit	*Value*	*Meaning*
Bit 0	0x01	Device time out
Bit 3	0x08	I/O error
Bit 4	0x10	Selected
Bit 5	0x20	Out of paper
Bit 6	0x40	Acknowledge
Bit 7	0x80	Not busy

Related Function(s)

`bioscom` : performs serial I/O

Example

In the following example, `biosprint` checks the status of the printer on LPT1.

```
#include <stdio.h>
#include <conio.h>
#include <bios.h>
#include <stdlib.h>

int main (void)
{
int status;
int cmd = 0;
int abyte = 0;
int port = 0;

clrscr();
printf ("This program assumes a printer is
  connected\n");
printf ("to LPT1:\n");
status = biosprint (cmd,abyte,port);
if (status & 0x80)
     printf ("Printer is not busy\n");
else
     printf ("Printer is busy\n");

return 0;
}
```

biostime

DOS UNIX ANSI C C++

Syntax

```
long biostime(int cmd, long newtime);
```

`int cmd;`	*Command*
`long newtime;`	*New time when* `cmd` *is 1*

Function

The `biostime` function reads or sets the BIOS timer.

File(s) to Include

```
#include <bios.h>
```

Description The `biostime` function either reads or sets the BIOS timer using BIOS interrupt 0x1A. The BIOS timer counts ticks since midnight at a rate of approximately 18.2 ticks per second. The `cmd` argument specifies whether to read or set the BIOS timer. When the `cmd` argument is 0, the current value of the timer is returned. When the `cmd` argument is 1, the timer is set to the value specified in the `newtime` argument.

Value(s) Returned When the `cmd` argument is 0, the current value of the BIOS timer is returned.

Related Function(s) `time` : returns the time of day

Example In the following example, `biostime` retrieves the current value of the BIOS timer.

```
#include <stdio.h>
#include <conio.h>
#include <bios.h>
#include <stdlib.h>
#include <time.h>

int main (void)
{
long time_status;
int cmd = 0;
long newtime = 0L;

clrscr();
time_status = biostime (cmd,newtime);
printf ("Number of clock ticks since midnight =
       %lu\n", time_status);

return 0;
}
```

---

country

Syntax

```
struct COUNTRY *country(int xcode, struct country
                        *cp);
```

```
int xcode;                Country
struct country *cp;       Country information
```

Function The `country` function returns country-specific information.

File(s) to Include `#include <dos.h>`

Description The `country` function specifies the format for country-specific data such as date, time, and currency. When the `cp` argument is set to –1, the `xcode` argument selects the current country. For any other value of the `cp` argument, information on the country specified in the `xcode` argument is returned in the structure pointed to by the `cp` argument. The COUNTRY structure is as follows:

```
struct COUNTRY
     {
     int co_date;                 /* date format */
     char co_curr[5];             /* currency symbol
                                   */
     char co_thsep[2];            /* thousands
                                   separator */
     char co_desep[2];            /* decimal separator
                                   */
     char co_dtsep[2];            /* date separator */
     char co_tmsep[2];            /* time separator */
     char co_currstyle;           /* currency style */
     char co_digits;              /* significant
                                   digits */
     char co_time;                /* time format */
     char co_case;                /* case map */
     char co_dasep[2];            /* data separator */
     char co_fill[10];            /* filler */
     };
```

The `co_date` member of the structure is interpreted in the following manner:

0	US style of month, day, year
1	European style of day, month, year
2	Japanese style of year, month, day

The `co_currstyle` member of the structure is interpreted in the following manner:

0	Currency symbol precedes the value with no spaces between the symbol and the number

1	Currency symbol follows the value with no spaces between the number and the symbol
2	Currency symbol precedes the value with a space after the symbol
3	Currency symbol follows the number with a space before the symbol

Value(s) Returned The pointer to the structure is returned in the `cp` argument when `country` is successful. When unsuccessful, null is returned.

Example The following example displays information on USA country-specific information.

```
#include <stdio.h>
#include <conio.h>
#include <dos.h>
#include <stdlib.h>

int main (void)
{
struct COUNTRY country_info;

clrscr();
country (0, &country_info);
printf ("USA Date Format :
%d\n",country_info.co_date);
printf ("USA Currency Symbol :
%s\n",country_info.co_curr);
printf ("USA Time Format :
%s\n",country_info.co_time);

return 0;
}
```

ctrlbrk

DOS | UNIX | ANSI C | C++

Syntax `void ctrlbrk(int (*handler)(void));`

`int (*handler)(void);` *Control-break handler function*

Function The `ctrlbrk` function specifies the new control-break handler.

File(s) to Include `#include <dos.h>`

Description The `ctrlbrk` function specifies a new handler function for the control-break. The new function is specified in the `handler` argument. The `handler` function should return 0 to abort the current program, or any other value to continue program execution.

Value(s) Returned There is no return value.

Related Function(s) `getcbrk` : gets the control-break setting

Example In the following example, `ctrlbrk` sets the `ctrl_brk` function (defined in the example) as the control-break handler.

```
#include <stdio.h>
#include <conio.h>
#include <dos.h>

int ctrl_brk (void)
{
printf ("Breaking out of loop\n");
return 0;
}

int main (void)
{
clrscr();
ctrlbrk (ctrl_brk);
printf ("Entering an infinite loop\n");
for (;;)
     {
```

```
        printf ("Press Ctrl-Brk to exit\n");
        }

return 0;
}
```

disable

DOS | UNIX | ANSI C | C++

Syntax `void disable(void);`

Function The `disable` macro disables hardware interrupts.

File(s) to Include `#include <dos.h>`

Description The `disable` macro provides interrupt control through the ability to disable hardware interrupts. The non-maskable interrupt from an external device is still allowed.

Value(s) Returned There is no return value.

Related Function(s) `enable` : enables hardware interrupts

Example In the following example, the `disable` function disables interrupts while in the interrupt service routine.

```
#include <stdio.h>
#include <conio.h>
#include <dos.h>
#include <stdlib.h>

void interrupt (*old)(void);

int counter = 0;

void interrupt new (void)
{
disable();
counter = counter + 1;
```

continues

```
enable();
}

int main (void)
{
int x;

clrscr ();

     /* get the timer interrupt vector */
old = getvect (0x1C);
     /* set new vector */
setvect (0x1C, new);
for (counter = 0; counter < 15; counter = counter
  + 1)
     printf ("Counter Value : %d\n",counter);
     /* reset vector */
setvect (0x1C, old);

return 0;
}
```

dosexterr

DOS | UNIX | ANSI C | C++

Syntax `int dosexterr(struct DOSERROR *eblkp);`

`struct DOSERROR *eblkp;` *Pointer to error information*

Function The `dosexterr` function retrieves extended DOS error information.

File(s) to Include `#include <dos.h>`

Description The `dosexterr` function retrieves extended DOS error information on a failed DOS call. The error information is placed in the DOSERROR structure, which is pointed to by the `eblkp` argument. The DOSERROR structure follows.

```
struct DOSERROR
     {
     int de_exterror;          /* extended error */
     char de_class;            /* error class */
```

```
    char de_action;             /* action */
    char de_locus;              /* error locus */
    };
```

Value(s) Returned The value of the `de_exterror` member of the DOSERROR structure is returned.

Related Function(s)
`bdos` : provides access to DOS calls
`bdosptr` : provides access to DOS calls

Example The following example displays error information when `dosexterr` is unable to open the file `xyz.xyz`.

```
#include <stdio.h>
#include <conio.h>
#include <dos.h>
#include <stdlib.h>

int main (void)
{
struct DOSERROR errinfo;

clrscr();

    /* attempt to open a nonexistent file */
fopen ("xyz.xyz","r");
dosexterr (&errinfo);
printf ("Error : %d\n",errinfo.de_exterror);
printf ("Class : %x\n",errinfo.de_class);
printf ("Action : %x\n",errinfo.de_action);
printf ("Locus : %x\n",errinfo.de_locus);

return 0;
}
```

__emit__

DOS | UNIX | ANSI C | C++

Syntax `void __emit__(argument,...);`

`argument,...;` *Single-byte machine instructions*

Function The `__emit__` function inserts literal values directly into code.

File(s) to Include `#include <dos.h>`

Description The `__emit__` function generates machine language instructions without using inline assembly language by allowing the programmer to insert literal values directly into object code as it compiles. The arguments for the `__emit__` function are usually single-byte machine instructions, but can be more complex with references to C variables. Any number of arguments can be passed to the `__emit__` function, providing that at least one argument is used.

The following restrictions are placed on the arguments to the `__emit__` function: All arguments must be in the form of expressions which can be used to initialize a static object. Therefore, integer values, floating-point values, and the addresses of static objects are valid arguments.

> Extreme caution should be used with this function because Borland C++ makes no attempts to check the correctness of the arguments passed in the `__emit__` function.

Value(s) Returned There is no return value.

Example In the following example, `__emit__` prints the screen.

```
#include <stdio.h>
#include <conio.h>
#include <dos.h>
#include <stdlib.h>

int main (void)
{
int x;

clrscr();
for (x=1; x<20; x=x+1)
printf ("Counting : %d\n",x);
      /* do a print screen */
__emit__ (0xcd,0x05);

return 0;
}
```

enable

DOS | UNIX | ANSI C | C++

Syntax `void enable(void);`

Function The `enable` macro enables hardware interrupts.

File(s) to Include `#include <dos.h>`

Description The `enable` macro provides interrupt control through the capability to enable hardware interrupts.

Value(s) Returned There is no return value.

Related Function(s)
`disable` : disables hardware interrupts
`getvect` : gets the interrupt vector

Example In the following example, the `enable` macro enables interrupts before leaving the interrupt service routine.

```
#include <stdio.h>
#include <conio.h>
#include <dos.h>
#include <stdlib.h>

void interrupt (*old)(void);

int counter = 0;

void interrupt new (void)
{
disable();
counter = counter + 1;
enable();
}

int main (void)
{
int x;

clrscr ();

     /* get the timer interrupt vector */
```

continues

```
old = getvect (0x1C);
     /* set new vector */
setvect (0x1C, new);
for (counter = 0; counter < 15; counter = counter
  + 1)
     printf ("Counter Value : %d\n",counter);
     /* reset vector */
setvect (0x1C, old);

return 0;
}
```

FP_OFF

DOS UNIX ANSI C C++

Syntax `unsigned FP_OFF(void far *p);`

`void far *p;` *Pointer to evaluate*

Function The `FP_OFF` macro gets the far address offset of a far pointer.

File(s) to Include `#include <dos.h>`

Description The `FP_OFF` macro either sets or retrieves the far address offset of the far pointer specified in the `p` argument.

Value(s) Returned The value of the offset is returned.

Related Function(s) `FP_SEG` : gets the far address segment of a far pointer

Example In the following example, the `FP_OFF` macro retrieves the offset of the string.

```
#include <stdio.h>
#include <conio.h>
#include <dos.h>
#include <stdlib.h>

int main (void)
```

```
{
char far *string = "Find the offset and segment";

clrscr();
printf ("%s\n",string);
printf ("Offset : %X\n",FP_OFF(string));
printf ("Segment : %X\n",FP_SEG(string));

return 0;
}
```

FP_SEG

Syntax `unsigned FP_SEG(void far *p);`

`void far *p;` *Pointer to evaluate*

Function The `FP_SEG` macro gets the far address segment of a pointer.

File(s) to Include `#include <dos.h>`

Description The `FP_SEG` macro either retrieves or sets the far address segment of the far pointer specified in the `p` argument.

Value(s) Returned The value representing the address segment is returned.

Related Function(s) `FP_OFF` : gets the far address offset of a far pointer

Example In the following example, the `FP_SEG` macro retrieves the segment of the string.

```
#include <stdio.h>
#include <conio.h>
#include <dos.h>
#include <stdlib.h>

int main (void)
{
```

continues

```
char far *string = "Find the offset and segment";

clrscr();
printf ("%s\n",string);
printf ("Offset : %X\n",FP_OFF(string));
printf ("Segment : %X\n",FP_SEG(string));

return 0;
}
```

freemem

DOS UNIX ANSI C C++

Syntax `int freemem(unsigned segx);`

`unsigned segx;` *Segment address of block*

Function The `freemem` function frees an allocated DOS memory block.

File(s) to Include `#include <dos.h>`

Description The `freemem` function frees the DOS memory block described by the segment address in the `segx` argument and allocated by a previous call to the `allocmem` function.

Value(s) Returned When successful, a zero is returned. When unsuccessful, –1 is returned and the global variable `errno` is set to ENOMEM, for insufficient memory.

Related Function(s)
`allocmem` : allocates a DOS memory segment
`free` : frees a memory block

Example In the following example, `freemem` frees the memory allocated by the `allocmem` function.

```
#include <stdio.h>
#include <conio.h>
#include <dos.h>
#include <alloc.h>
#include <stdlib.h>
```

```
int main (void)
{
int result;
unsigned int seg;

clrscr();
result = allocmem (2,&seg);
if (result ==  1)
     printf ("Memory allocated\n");
else
     printf ("Memory not allocated\n");
result = freemem (seg);
if (result == 0)
     printf ("Memory freed\n");
else
     printf ("Memory not freed\n");

return 0;
}
```

geninterrupt

DOS UNIX ANSI C C++

Syntax `void geninterrupt(int intr_num);`

`int intr_num;` *Interrupt number*

Function The `geninterrupt` macro generates a software interrupt.

File(s) to Include `#include <dos.h>`

Description The `geninterrupt` macro generates the software interrupt specified in the `intr_num` argument.

Value(s) Returned There is no return value.

Related Function(s)
`disable` : disables hardware interrupts
`enable` : enables hardware interrupts
`getvect` : gets the interrupt vector

Example In the following example, `geninterrupt` displays the character `A`.

```
#include <stdio.h>
#include <conio.h>
#include <dos.h>
#include <stdlib.h>

int main (void)
{
struct text_info textinfo;

clrscr ();
gotoxy (1,1);
gettextinfo (&textinfo);
_AH = 9;
_AL = 'A';
_BH = 0;
_BL = textinfo.attribute;
_CX = 1;
geninterrupt (0x10);
gotoxy (1,3);
printf ("Program Completed\n");

return 0;
}
```

getcbrk

DOS | UNIX | ANSI C | C++

Syntax `int getcbrk(void);`

Function The `getcbrk` function gets the current setting for control-break monitoring.

File(s) to Include `#include <dos.h>`

Description The `getcbrk` function generates the DOS system call 0x33 which retrieves the setting for control-break checking.

Value(s) Returned The value of the control-break setting is returned (0 for off, 1 for on).

Related Function(s)

`crtlbrk` : sets the control-break handler function
`setcbrk` : sets the control-break setting

Example

In the following example, `getcbrk` retrieves the status of the control-break flag.

```
#include <stdio.h>
#include <conio.h>
#include <dos.h>
#include <stdlib.h>

int main (void)
{
int result;

clrscr ();
result = getcbrk ();
if (result == 0)
     printf ("Control-break flag is off\n");
else
     printf ("Control-break flag is on\n");
return 0;
}
```

getdfree

DOS | UNIX | ANSI C | C++

Syntax

```
void getdfree(unsigned char drive, struct dfree
              *dtable);
```

`unsigned char drive;`	*Drive*
`struct dfree *dtable;`	*Pointer to disk information*

Function

The `getdfree` function retrieves information on free space available on a disk.

File(s) to Include

`#include <dos.h>`

Description

The `getdfree` function retrieves the disk characteristics of the disk drive specified in the `drive` argument. The disk characteristics are then placed in the structure of type `dfree` pointed to by the `dtable` argument. The `dfree` structure follows.

```
struct dfree
     {
     unsigned df_avail;         /* available
                                   clusters */
     unsigned df_total;         /* total clusters */
     unsigned df_bsec;          /* bytes per sector
                                   */
     unsigned df_sclus;         /* sectors per
                                   cluster */
     };
```

Value(s) Returned There is no return value.

Related Function(s)

`getfat` : gets file allocation information for a drive
`getfatd` : gets file allocation information for the default drive

Example The following example gets disk information from drive A.

```
#include <stdio.h>
#include <conio.h>
#include <dos.h>
#include <stdlib.h>

int main (void)
{
struct dfree dtab;

clrscr ();
printf ("Insert a disk into Drive A\n");
printf ("Press a key when ready\n");
getch();
getdfree (1,&dtab);
if (dtab.df_sclus == 0xFFFF)
     {
     printf ("Error - aborting\n");
     exit (1);
     }
printf ("Available Clusters :
  %u\n",dtab.df_avail);
printf ("Total Clusters : %u\n",dtab.df_total);
printf ("Bytes per sector : %u\n",dtab.df_bsec);
printf ("Sectors per cluster :
  %u\n",dtab.df_sclus);

return 0;
}
```

getdta

DOS UNIX ANSI C C++

Syntax `char far *getdta(void);`

Function The `getdta` function retrieves the disk transfer address.

File(s) to Include `#include <dos.h>`

Description The `getdta` function retrieves the current setting of the disk transfer address.

Value(s) Returned The far pointer to the disk transfer address is returned.

Related Function(s) `setdta` : sets the disk transfer address

Example In the following example, `getdta` retrieves the disk transfer address.

```
#include <stdio.h>
#include <conio.h>
#include <dos.h>
#include <stdlib.h>

int main (void)
{
char far *dtaddress;

clrscr ();
dtaddress = getdta();
printf ("Current Disk Transfer Address :
  %Fp\n",dtaddress);

return 0;
}
```

getfat

DOS UNIX ANSI C C++

Syntax

```
void getfat(unsigned char drive, struct fatinfo
            *dtable);
```

```
unsigned char drive;        Drive
struct fatinfo *dtable;     Retrieved information
```

Function The `getfat` function retrieves the file allocation table information for a specified drive.

File(s) to Include `#include <dos.h>`

Description The `getfat` function retrieves the file allocation table information for the drive specified in the `drive` argument. When the `drive` argument is set to 0, the default drive is used. When the `drive` argument is set to 1, the A drive is used. When the `drive` argument is set to 2, the B drive is used, and so forth. The retrieved information is stored in a structure of type `fatinfo`, pointed to by the `dtable` argument. The `fatinfo` structure follows.

```
struct fatinfo
    {
    char fi_sclus;          /* sectors per cluster */
    char fi_fatid;          /* the FAT id number */
    int fi_nclus;           /* number of clusters */
    int fi_bysec;           /* bytes per sector */
    };
```

Value(s) Returned There is no return value.

Related Function(s) `getfatd` : gets file allocation table information for the default drive

Example In the following example, `getfat` retrieves information on the default drive.

```
#include <stdio.h>
#include <conio.h>
#include <dos.h>
#include <stdlib.h>
```

```
int main (void)
{
struct fatinfo info;

clrscr ();
getfat (0, &info);
printf ("Information on the default drive\n");
printf ("Sectors per cluster :
  %d\n",info.fi_sclus);
printf ("FAT ID byte : %d\n",info.fi_fatid);
printf ("Number of clusters :
  %d\n",info.fi_nclus);
printf ("Bytes per sector : %d\n",info.fi_bysec);

return 0;
}
```

getfatd

DOS UNIX ANSI C C++

Syntax `void getfatd(struct fatinfo *dtable);`

`struct fatinfo *dtable;` *Retrieved information*

Function The `getfatd` function retrieves file allocation table information from the default drive.

File(s) to Include `#include <dos.h>`

Description The `getfatd` function retrieves the file allocation table information for the default drive. The retrieved information is stored in a structure of type `fatinfo`, pointed to by the `dtable` argument. The `fatinfo` structure follows.

```
struct fatinfo
     {
     char fi_sclus;       /* sectors per cluster */
```

continues

```
char fi_fatid;       /* the FAT id number */
int fi_nclus;        /* number of clusters */
int fi_bysec;        /* bytes per sector */
};
```

Value(s) Returned There is no return value.

Related Function(s)

`getdfree` : gets the disk characteristics
`getfat` : gets the file allocation table information for the specified drive

Example In the following example, `getfatd` retrieves information on the default drive.

```
#include <stdio.h>
#include <conio.h>
#include <dos.h>
#include <stdlib.h>

int main (void)
{
struct fatinfo info;

clrscr ();
getfatd (&info);
printf ("Information on the default drive\n");
printf ("Sectors per cluster :
  %d\n",info.fi_sclus);
printf ("FAT ID byte : %d\n",info.fi_fatid);
printf ("Number of clusters :
  %d\n",info.fi_nclus);
printf ("Bytes per sector : %d\n",info.fi_bysec);

return 0;
}
```

getpsp

DOS UNIX ANSI C C++

Syntax `unsigned getpsp(void);`

Function The `getpsp` function retrieves the program segment prefix.

File(s) to Include `#include <dos.h>`

Description The `getpsp` function retrieves the segment address of the program segment prefix. The `getpsp` function uses the DOS call 0x62.

Value(s) Returned The program segment prefix is returned.

Related Function(s) `getenv` : retrieves a string from the environment

Example In the following example, `getpsp` retrieves the program segment prefix.

```
#include <stdio.h>
#include <conio.h>
#include <dos.h>
#include <stdlib.h>

int main (void)
{
unsigned psprefix;

clrscr ();
psprefix = getpsp ();
printf ("Program Segment Prefix : %x\n",psprefix);

return 0;
}
```

getvect

DOS UNIX ANSI C C++

Syntax

```
void interrupt(*getvect(int interruptno))();

int interruptno;          Interrupt vector
```

Function The `getvect` function retrieves the interrupt vector.

File(s) to Include `#include <dos.h>`

Description The `getvect` function retrieves the interrupt vector specified in the `interruptno` argument (ranging from 0 to 255).

Value(s) Returned The 4-byte value, stored in the specified interrupt vector, is returned.

Related Function(s)
`geninterrupt` : generates an interrupt
`setvect` : sets the value of an interrupt vector

Example In the following example, `getvect` retrieves the timer interrupt vector.

```
#include <stdio.h>
#include <conio.h>
#include <dos.h>
#include <stdlib.h>

void interrupt (*old)(void);

int counter = 0;

void interrupt new (void)
{
disable();
counter = counter + 1;
enable();
}

int main (void)
{
int x;

clrscr ();
```

```
     /* get the timer interrupt vector */
old = getvect (0x1C);
     /* set new vector */
setvect (0x1C, new);
for (counter = 0; counter < 15; counter = counter
+ 1)
     printf ("Counter Value : %d\n",counter);
     /* reset vector */
setvect (0x1C, old);

return 0;
}
```

getverify

DOS UNIX ANSI C C++

Syntax `int getverify(void);`

Function The `getverify` function retrieves the status of the DOS verify flag.

File(s) to Include `#include <dos.h>`

Description The `getverify` function retrieves the current status of the DOS verify flag. A verify flag of 0 indicates that verify is off; therefore, writing is not verified. A verify flag of 1 indicates that verify is on; therefore, writing is verified.

Value(s) Returned A 1 or 0 is returned to indicate the status of the verify flag.

Related Function(s) `setverify` : sets the status of the verify flag

Example In the following example, `getverify` retrieves the status of the verify flag.

```
#include <stdio.h>
#include <conio.h>
#include <dos.h>
#include <stdlib.h>
```

continues

```
int main (void)
{
int status;

clrscr ();
status = getverify ();
if (status == 0)
     printf ("Verify Flag is OFF\n");
else
     printf ("Verify Flag is ON\n");
return 0;
}
```

harderr

DOS | UNIX | ANSI C | C++

Syntax `void harderror(int (*handler)());`

`int (*handler)();` *Hardware error handler*

Function The `harderror` function defines the hardware error handler function.

File(s) to Include `#include <dos.h>`

Description The `harderror` function specifies a function that handles the hardware error generated by interrupt 0x24. The hardware error handler function, as pointed to by the `handler` argument, is called with the following arguments each time the interrupt 0x24 occurs:

`handler (int errval, int ax, int bp, int si);`

`int errval;` *Error code set in the DI register.*

`int ax;` *Value for AX register. Indicates whether a disk or device error occurred. If* `ax` *is a nonnegative number, a disk error occurred. Otherwise, a device error occurred. ANDing* `ax` *with 0x00FF gives the drive number with the error when* `ax` *indicates a disk error (0 for drive A, 1 for drive B, etc).*

`int bp;` *Segment address of device driver header for the bad driver.*

`int si;` *Offset address of device driver header for the bad driver.*

Value(s) Returned There is no return value.

Related Function(s)

`hardresume` : hardware error handler
`hardretn` : hardware error handler

Example In the following example, `harderr` defines a new hardware error handler.

```
#include <stdio.h>
#include <conio.h>
#include <dos.h>
#include <stdlib.h>

int handler (int errval, int ax, int bp, int si)
{
int response;

if (ax < 0)
     printf ("Device Error\n");
else
     printf ("Disk Error\n");
printf ("Error Code : %d\n",errval);
printf ("Pointer to device driver header :
  %d:%d\n",bp,si);
printf ("Do you want to return to the program or
  DOS?\n");
printf ("Press 'p' for program or 'd' for DOS\n");
response = getch();
if (response == 'd')
     hardresume (2);
else
     hardretn (2);
return 2;
}


int main (void)
{
clrscr ();

harderr (handler);
printf ("If there is a disk in drive A - remove
  it\n");
```

continues

```
printf ("Press any key to continue\n");
getch();
fopen ("a:test.tmp","w");

return 0;
}
```

hardresume

DOS UNIX ANSI C C++

Syntax `void hardresume(int axret);`

`int axret;` *Return code*

Function The `hardresume` function can be used with the `harderr` function to return to DOS.

File(s) to Include `#include <dos.h>`

Description The `hardresume` function is used with the `harderr` function to return control to DOS. The value defined in the `axret` argument is one of the following: 2 (abort), 1 (retry), or 0 (ignore). When 2 (abort) is defined, the control-break interrupt, DOS interrupt 0x23, is generated.

Value(s) Returned There is no return value.

Related Function(s)
`harderr` : defines a hardware error handler
`hardretn` : hardware error handler

Example In the following example, `hardresume` returns to DOS from inside the error handler.

```
#include <stdio.h>
#include <conio.h>
#include <dos.h>
#include <stdlib.h>

int handler (int errval, int ax, int bp, int si)
{
int response;

if (ax < 0)
     printf ("Device Error\n");
else
     printf ("Disk Error\n");
printf ("Error Code : %d\n",errval);
printf ("Pointer to device driver header :
  %d:%d\n",bp,si);
printf ("Do you want to return to the program or
  DOS?\n");
printf ("Press 'p' for program or 'd' for DOS\n");
response = getch();
if (response == 'd')
     hardresume (2);
else
     hardretn (2);
return 2;
}


int main (void)
{
clrscr ();

harderr (handler);
printf ("If there is a disk in drive A - remove
  it\n");
printf ("Press any key to continue\n");
getch();
fopen ("a:test.tmp","w");

return 0;
}
```

hardretn

DOS UNIX ANSI C C++

Syntax

```
void hardretn(int retn);

int retn;                    Return code
```

Function The `hardretn` function can be used with the `harderr` function to return control to the program.

File(s) to Include `#include <dos.h>`

Description The `hardretn` function is used with the `harderr` function to return control to the application program. The `retn` argument must be set to one of the following: 2 (abort), 1 (retry), or 0 (ignore).

Value(s) Returned There is no return value.

Related Function(s)

`harderr` : defines a hardware error handler
`hardresume` : hardware error handler

Example In the following example, `hardretn` returns control to the application from within the error handler.

```
#include <stdio.h>
#include <conio.h>
#include <dos.h>
#include <stdlib.h>

int handler (int errval, int ax, int bp, int si)
{
int response;

if (ax < 0)
     printf ("Device Error\n");
else
     printf ("Disk Error\n");
printf ("Error Code : %d\n",errval);
printf ("Pointer to device driver header :
  %d:%d\n",bp,si);
printf ("Do you want to return to the program or
  DOS?\n");
```

```
printf ("Press 'p' for program or 'd' for DOS\n");
response = getch();
if (response == 'd')
     hardresume (2);
else
     hardretn (2);
return 2;
}


int main (void)
{
clrscr ();

harderr (handler);
printf ("If there is a disk in drive A - remove
  it\n");
printf ("Press any key to continue\n");
getch();
fopen ("a:test.tmp","w");

return 0;
}
```

inport

DOS UNIX ANSI C C++

Syntax `int inport(int portid);`

`int portid;` *Port to read*

Function The `inport` function reads a word from the specified port.

File(s) to Include `#include <dos.h>`

Description The `inport` function reads the low byte of the word from the port specified in the `portid` argument. The high byte of the word can be read by setting the `portid` argument to `portid + 1`.

Value(s) Returned The read value is returned.

Related Function(s)

`inportb` : reads a byte from the specified port
`outport` : outputs a word to the specified port
`outportb` : outputs a byte to the specified port

Example The following example reads a word from the port using the `inport` function.

```
#include <stdio.h>
#include <conio.h>
#include <dos.h>
#include <stdlib.h>

int main (void)
{
unsigned char wordread;

clrscr ();
wordread = inport (0);
printf ("The byte read from the port is :
  0x%X\n",wordread);

return 0;
}
```

inportb

DOS UNIX ANSI C C++

Syntax `unsigned char inportb(int portid);`

`int portid;` *Port to read*

Function The `inportb` macro reads a byte from the specified port.

File(s) to Include `#include <dos.h>`

Description The `inportb` macro reads a byte from the port specified in the `portid` argument.

Value(s) Returned The read value is returned.

Related Function(s)

`inport` : reads a word from the specified port
`outport` : writes a word to the specified port
`outportb` : writes a byte to the specified port

Example The following example reads a byte from serial port 1 using `inportb`.

```
#include <stdio.h>
#include <conio.h>
#include <dos.h>
#include <stdlib.h>

int main (void)
{
unsigned char byteread;

clrscr ();
byteread = inportb (0);
printf ("The byte read from serial port 1 is :
  0x%X\n",byteread);

return 0;
}
```

int86

DOS | UNIX | ANSI C | C++

Syntax

```
int int86(int intno, union REGS *inregs,
          union REGS *outregs);
```

`int intno;`	*Software interrupt*
`union REGS *inregs;`	*Values to load before interrupt*
`union REGS *outregs;`	*Register values after interrupt*

Function The `int86` function generates an 8086 software interrupt.

File(s) to Include `#include <dos.h>`

Description The `int86` function executes the 8086 software interrupt defined in the `intno` argument. The register values are set to those values specified in the `inregs` argument before generating the interrupt. After the interrupt, the current register values are copied to the location specified in the `outregs` argument.

```
union REGS
     {
     struct WORDREGS x;
     struct BYTEREGS h;
     };

struct WORDREGS
     {
     unsigned int ax, bx, cx, dx, si, di, cflag,
  flags;
     };

struct BYTEREGS
     {
     unsigned char al, ah, bl, bh, cl, ch, dl, dh;
     };
```

Value(s) Returned The value of the AX register is returned upon completion of the software interrupt. If the carry flag of the `outregs` argument is not 0, an error has occurred and the global variable `_doserrno` is set to the error code.

Related Function(s) `int86x` : general 8086 software interrupt

Example The following example determines the date using the `int86` function.

```
#include <stdio.h>
#include <conio.h>
#include <dos.h>
#include <stdlib.h>

int main (void)
{
union REGS xr, yr;

clrscr ();
xr.h.ah = 0x2A;
int86 (0x21, &xr, &yr);
printf ("Today is %.2d - %.2d -
  %.4d\n",yr.h.dh,yr.h.dl,yr.x.cx);

return 0;
}
```

int86x

DOS UNIX ANSI C C++

Syntax

```
int int86x(int intno, union REGS *inregs, union
          REGS *outregs, struct SREGS *segregs);
```

`int intno;`	*Interrupt*
`union REGS *inregs;`	*Values to load before call*
`union REGS *outregs;`	*Register values after call*
`struct SREGS *segregs`	*Values to load before call*

Function The `int86x` function generates an 8086 software interrupt.

File(s) to Include `#include <dos.h>`

Description The `int86x` function generates the 8086 interrupt specified in the `intno` argument. The values in the `inregs` and `segregs` arguments are loaded into the appropriate registers before generating the interrupt. After the interrupt, the new register values are placed in the `outregs` argument.

```
union REGS
     {
     struct WORDREGS x;
     struct BYTEREGS h;
     };

struct WORDREGS
     {
     unsigned int ax, bx, cx, dx, si, di, cflag,
  flags; };

struct BYTEREGS
     {
     unsigned char al, ah, bl, bh, cl, ch, dl, dh;
     };

struct SREGS
     {
     unsigned int es;
     unsigned int cs;
     unsigned int ss;
     unsigned int ds;
     };
```

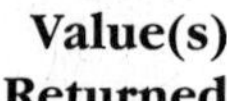

Value(s) Returned The value of the AX register is returned. When the carry flag of the `outregs` argument is not 0, an error has occurred and the global variable `_doserrno` is set to the error code.

Related Function(s) `int86` : generates an 8086 software interrupt

Example The following example determines the date using the `int86x` function.

```
#include <stdio.h>
#include <conio.h>
#include <dos.h>
#include <stdlib.h>

int main (void)
{
union REGS xr, yr;
struct SREGS segregs;

clrscr ();
xr.h.ah = 0x2A;
int86x (0x21, &xr, &yr, &segregs);
printf ("Today is %.2d - %.2d -
  %.4d\n",yr.h.dh,yr.h.dl,yr.x.cx);

return 0;
}
```

intdos

DOS UNIX ANSI C C++

Syntax

```
int intdos(union REGS *inregs, union REGS
           *outregs);
```

`union REGS *inregs;`	*Specifies the DOS function*
`union REGS *outregs;`	*Register values after interrupt*

Function The `intdos` function generates a DOS interrupt.

File(s) to Include `#include <dos.h>`

Description The `intdos` function generates the DOS interrupt 0x21 for the purpose of executing a DOS function. The `ah` member of the `inregs` argument (`inregs -> h.ah`) contains the DOS function to be executed. After completion of the interrupt, the current register values are loaded into the `outregs` argument.

```
union REGS
     {
     struct WORDREGS x;
     struct BYTEREGS h;
     };

struct WORDREGS
     {
     unsigned int ax, bx, cx, dx, si, di, cflag,
   flags;
     };

struct BYTEREGS
     {
     unsigned char al, ah, bl, bh, cl, ch, dl, dh;
     };
```

Value(s) Returned The value of the AX register is returned. If the carry flag of the `outregs` argument is not zero, an error has occurred and the global variable `_doserrno` is set to the error code.

Related Function(s) `intdosx` : generates a DOS interrupt

Example In the following example, `intdos` retrieves the current drive.

```
#include <stdio.h>
#include <conio.h>
#include <dos.h>
#include <stdlib.h>

int main (void)
{
union REGS xr;

clrscr ();
xr.h.ah = 0x19;
intdos (&xr, &xr);
printf ("The current drive is : %c\n",xr.h.al +
  65);

return 0;
}
```

intdosx

DOS UNIX ANSI C C++

Syntax

```
int intdosx(union REGS *inregs, union REGS
            *outregs, struct SREGS *segregs);
```

`union REGS *inregs;`	*DOS interrupt to generate*
`union REGS *outregs;`	*Register values after interrupt*
`struct SREGS *segregs;`	*Values to load before interrupt*

Function The `intdosx` function generates a DOS interrupt.

File(s) to Include `#include <dos.h>`

Description The `intdosx` function generates DOS interrupt 0x21 for the purpose of executing the DOS function specified in the `ah` member of the `inregs` argument (`inregs -> h.ah`). The values in the `segregs` argument are loaded in the appropriate registers before generating the interrupt. Upon completion of the interrupt, the current register values are loaded into the `outregs` argument.

```
union REGS
     {
     struct WORDREGS x;
     struct BYTEREGS h;
     };

struct WORDREGS
     {
     unsigned int ax, bx, cx, dx, si, di, cflag,
  flags;
     };

struct BYTEREGS
     {
     unsigned char al, ah, bl, bh, cl, ch, dl, dh;
     };

struct SREGS
     {
     unsigned int es;
```

```
unsigned int cs;
unsigned int ss;
unsigned int ds;
};
```

Value(s) Returned The value of the AX register is returned. If the carry flag of the `outregs` argument is not 0, an error has occurred and the global variable `_doserrno` is set to the error code.

Related Function(s) `intdos` : generates a DOS interrupt

Example In the following example, `intdosx` retrieves the current drive.

```
#include <stdio.h>
#include <conio.h>
#include <dos.h>
#include <stdlib.h>

int main (void)
{
union REGS xr;
struct SREGS segregs;

clrscr ();
xr.h.ah = 0x19;
intdosx (&xr, &xr, &segregs);
printf ("The current drive is : %c\n",xr.h.al +
  65);

return 0;
}
```

intr

DOS UNIX ANSI C C++

Syntax `void intr(int intno, struct REGPACK *preg);`

`int intno;`	*Interrupt*
`struct REGPACK *preg;`	*Values to load before interrupt*

Function The `intr` function generates an 8086 software interrupt.

File(s) to Include

```
#include <dos.h>
```

Description

The `intr` function generates the 8086 software interrupt specified in the `intno` argument. Before generating the interrupt, the values in the `preg` argument are loaded into the appropriate registers. Upon completion of the interrupt, the current register values are loaded into the `preg` argument. The `preg` argument is a structure of type REGPACK, as follows:

```
struct REGPACK
     {
     unsigned r_ax, r_bx, r_cx, r_dx;
     unsigned r_bp, r_si, r_di, r_ds, r_es,
       r_flags;
     };
```

Value(s) Returned

There is no return value.

Related Function(s)

`int86` : generates an 8086 software interrupt
`int86x` : generates an 8086 software interrupt

Example

The following example displays the current year.

```
#include <stdio.h>
#include <conio.h>
#include <dos.h>
#include <stdlib.h>

int main (void)
{
struct REGPACK reg;

clrscr ();
reg.r_ax = 0x2a << 8;
intr (0x21,&reg);
printf ("The year is : %.4d\n",reg.r_cx);

return 0;
}
```

keep

DOS UNIX ANSI C C++

Syntax

```
void keep(unsigned char status, unsigned size);

unsigned char status;      Exit status
unsigned size;             Size in paragraphs
```

Function The `keep` function exits a program but keeps the program resident in memory.

File(s) to Include `#include <dos.h>`

Description The `keep` function exits the current program while keeping the program resident in memory. The `exit` argument specifies the exit status of the program. The `size` argument specifies the length, in paragraphs, of the program. The `keep` function uses DOS function 0x31.

Value(s) Returned There is no return value.

Related Function(s)

`abort` : abnormally terminates a program
`exit` : terminates a program

Example Terminate Stay Resident (TSR) programs should be created with extreme caution and a full understanding of system design. The MS-DOS technical manuals provide the information required for the development of TSR programs. Due to the complexity of TSR programs and their dependence on system configuration, no example is provided.

MK_FP

DOS UNIX ANSI C C++

Syntax

```
void far *MK_FP(unsigned seg, unsigned ofs);
```

`unsigned seg;` *Segment*
`unsigned ofs;` *Offset*

Function The `MK_FP` macro creates a far pointer from the specified segment and offset.

File(s) to Include `#include <dos.h>`

Description The MK_FP macro creates the far pointer defined by the segment specified in the `seg` argument and the offset specified in the `ofs` argument.

Value(s) Returned The far pointer is returned.

Related Function(s)
`FP_OFF` : retrieves the far address offset
`FP_SEG` : retrieves the far address segment

Example The following example creates a far pointer with the `MK_FP` macro.

```
#include <stlib.h>
#include <stdio.h>
#include <conio.h>
#include <dos.h>

int main (void)
{
unsigned int far *screen;
int ch, x;

clrscr ();
printf ("Press y for yes or n for no\n");
ch = getch();
if (ch == 'y')
        screen = MK_FP (0xB000,0);
if (ch == 'n')
        screen = MK_FP (0xB800,0);
```

```
for (x=0; x<10; x++)
        screen[x]=0x0700 + ('0' + x);

getch()
return 0;
}
```

outport

DOS UNIX ANSI C C++

Syntax

```
void outport(int portid, int value);

int portid;               Port for output
int value;                Word to send
```

Function The `outport` function sends a word to the specified port.

File(s) to Include `#include <dos.h>`

Description The `outport` function sends the low byte of the word defined by the `value` argument to the port specified in the `portid` argument. Setting the `portid` argument to `portid + 1` sends the high byte of the word in the `value` argument.

Value(s) Returned There is no return value.

Related Function(s)

`inport` : reads a word from the specified port
`inportb` : reads a byte from the specified port
`outportb` : sends a byte to the specified port

Example The following example sends 23 out of port 0.

```
#include <stdio.h>
#include <conio.h>
#include <dos.h>
#include <stdlib.h>

int main (void)
{
clrscr ();
```

continues

```
outport (23,0);
printf ("23 sent out port 0\n");

return 0;
}
```

outportb

DOS UNIX ANSI C C++

Syntax

```
void outportb(int portid, unsigned char value);

int portid;                 Port for output
unsigned char value;        Byte to send
```

Function The `outportb` macro sends a byte to the specified port.

File(s) to Include `#include <dos.h>`

Description The `outportb` macro sends the byte specified in the `value` argument to the port specified in the `portid` argument.

Value(s) Returned There is no return value.

Related Function(s)

`inport` : reads a word from the specified port
`inportb` : reads a byte from the specified port
`outport` : sends a word to the specified port

Example The following example sends `A` out port 0 using the `outportb` macro.

```
#include <stdio.h>
#include <conio.h>
#include <dos.h>
#include <stdlib.h>

int main (void)
{
clrscr ();
outportb ('A',0);
printf ("'A' sent out port 0\n");

return 0;
}
```

_OvrInitEms

DOS UNIX ANSI C C++

Syntax

```
int cdecl far _OvrInitEms(unsigned emsHandle,
                          unsigned firstPage,
                          unsigned pages);
```

`unsigned emsHandle;`	*EMS handle*
`unsigned firstPage;`	*First page for swapping*
`unsigned pages;`	*Number of pages*

Function The `_OvrInitEms` function initializes expanded memory swapping for the overlay manager.

File(s) to Include `#include <dos.h>`

Description The `_OvrInitEms` function checks for expanded memory by searching for an EMS driver. When the `emsHandle` argument is 0, the overlay manager allocates EMS pages, which are used for swapping. When the `emsHandle` argument is a nonzero value, the argument should represent a valid EMS handle. The `firstPage` argument specifies the starting location for swapping. The `pages` argument specifies the maximum number of pages to be used by the overlay manager.

Value(s) Returned Zero is returned if expanded memory is available for swapping.

Related Function(s) `_OvrInitExt` : initializes extended memory swapping

Example In the following example, the `_OvrInitEms` function checks expanded memory and tries to use 16 pages for swapping. The result of the function call is then displayed.

```
#include <stdio.h>
#include <conio.h>
#include <dos.h>
#include <stdlib.h>

int main (void)
{
int result;
```

continues

```
clrscr ();
result = _OvrInitEms (0,0,16);
if (result == 0)
     printf ("Able to use Expanded Memory for
  swapping\n");
else
     printf ("Unable to use Expanded Memory\n");

return 0;
}
```

_OvrInitExt

Syntax

```
int cdecl far _OvrInitExt(unsigned long
                          startAddress, unsigned
                          long length);
```

`unsigned long startAddress;`	*Starting address*
`unsigned long length;`	*Amount of extended memory to use for overlay manager*

Function The `_OvrInitExt` function initializes extended memory swapping for the overlay manager.

File(s) to Include `#include <dos.h>`

Description The `_OvrInitExt` function checks for extended memory and allocates memory from it. When the `startAddress` argument is zero, the starting address is determined by the overlay manager and the memory allocated is limited by the smaller of either the `length` argument or the size of the overlays. When the `startAddress` argument is a nonzero value, the overlay manager uses extended memory above the stated address. The `length` argument specifies the maximum amount of extended memory to be used by the overlay manager.

Value(s) Returned If extended memory is available for use by the overlay manager, a zero is returned.

Related Function(s) `_OvrInitEms` : initializes expanded memory swapping

Example The following example attempts to use extended memory above the stated address. The result of the function call is then displayed.

```
#include <stdio.h>
#include <conio.h>
#include <dos.h>
#include <stdlib.h>

int main (void)
{
int result;

clrscr ();
result = _OvrInitExt (0x200000L,0);
if (result == 0)
     printf ("Able to use Extended Memory for
  swapping\n");
else
     printf ("Unable to use Extended Memory\n");

return 0;
}
```

parsfnm

DOS UNIX ANSI C C++

Syntax

```
char *parsfnm(const char *cmdline, struct fcb
              *fcb,int opt);
```

`const char *cmdline;`	*Command line*
`struct fcb *fcb;`	*File control block*
`int opt;`	*DOS parse system call*

Function The `parsfnm` function parses a file name.

File(s) to Include

```
#include <dos.h>
```

Description

The `parsfnm` function parses the command line pointed to by the `cmdline` argument for a file name. The `fcb` argument, a structure of type `fcb`, stores the file control block, which consists of drive, file name, and extension. The `opt` argument is the value documented for AL in the DOS parse system call.

```
struct fcb
     {
     char fcb_drive;        /* 0=default,1=A,etc */
     char fcb_name[8];      /* File name */
     char fcb_ext[3];       /* File extension */
     short fcb_curblk;      /* Current block number*/
     short fcb_recsize;     /* Logical record size */
     long fcb_filsize;      /* File size in bytes  */
     short fcb_date;        /* Date file was last
                               written */
     char fcb_resv[10];     /* Reserved for DOS */
     char fcb_currec;       /* Current record in
                               block */
     long fcb_random;       /* Random record number*/
     };
```

Value(s) Returned

The pointer to the next byte after the end of the file name is returned when `parsfnm` is successful. Null is returned when unsuccessful.

Example

The following example finds and displays the drive and file name of BC.EXE. Note that BC.EXE should be in the current directory or in a path specified in the DOS PATH.

```
#include <stdio.h>
#include <conio.h>
#include <dos.h>
#include <stdlib.h>

int main (void)
{
struct fcb fcblock;

clrscr ();
parsfnm ("BC.EXE",&fcblock,1);
printf ("Drive : %d\n",fcblock.fcb_drive);
printf ("Name  : %s\n",fcblock.fcb_name);

return 0;
}
```

peek

DOS | UNIX | ANSI C | C++

Syntax

```
int peek(unsigned segment, unsigned offset);

unsigned segment;         Segment
unsigned offset;          Offset
```

Function The `peek` macro retrieves the word at the specified memory location.

File(s) to Include `#include <dos.h>`

Description The `peek` macro retrieves the word at the memory location specified by the `segment` and `offset` arguments.

Value(s) Returned The retrieved word is returned.

Related Function(s)
`peekb` : retrieves the byte at the specified location
`poke` : stores a value at the specified location
`pokeb` : stores a byte at the specified location

Example In the following example, the `peek` macro checks the status of the Caps Lock key.

```
#include <stdio.h>
#include <conio.h>
#include <dos.h>
#include <stdlib.h>

int main (void)
{
int result;

clrscr ();
printf ("Checking the status of the Caps Lock
  key\n");
result = peek (0x0040,0x0017);
if (result & 64)
     printf ("Caps Lock is on\n");
else
     printf ("Caps Lock is off\n");

return 0;
}
```

peekb

DOS | UNIX | ANSI C | C++

Syntax

```
char peekb(unsigned segment, unsigned offset);

unsigned segment;        Segment
unsigned offset;         Offset
```

Function The `peekb` macro retrieves the byte at the specified memory location.

File(s) to Include `#include <dos.h>`

Description The `peekb` macro retrieves the byte at the memory location specified by the `segment` and `offset` arguments.

Value(s) Returned The retrieved byte is returned.

Related Function(s)

`peek` : retrieves the word at the specified location
`poke` : stores a value at the specified location
`pokeb` : stores a byte at the specified location

Example In the following example, the `peekb` macro checks the status of the Num Lock key.

```
#include <stdio.h>
#include <conio.h>
#include <dos.h>
#include <stdlib.h>

int main (void)
{
int result;

clrscr ();
printf ("Checking the status of the Num Lock
  key\n");
result = peekb (0x0040,0x0017);
if (result & 32)
     printf ("Num Lock is on\n");
else
     printf ("Num Lock is off\n");

return 0;
}
```

poke

DOS | UNIX | ANSI C | C++

Syntax

```
void poke(unsigned segment, unsigned offset, int
         value);
```

```
unsigned segment;        Segment
unsigned offset;         Offset
int value;               Value to store
```

Function The `poke` macro stores an integer value at the specified memory location.

File(s) to Include `#include <dos.h>`

Description The `poke` macro stores the integer value specified in the `value` argument at the memory location specified by the `segment` and `offset` arguments.

Value(s) Returned There is no return value.

Related Function(s)

`peek` : retrieves the word at the specified location
`peekb` : retrieves the byte at the specified location
`pokeb` : stores a byte at the specified location

Example In the following example, the `poke` macro turns the Caps Lock key on.

```
#include <stdio.h>
#include <conio.h>
#include <dos.h>
#include <stdlib.h>

int main (void)
{
int result;

clrscr ();
printf ("Turning the Caps Lock key on\n");
poke (0x0040,0x0017,64);
result = peek (0x0040,0x0017);
if (result & 64)
     printf ("Caps Lock is on\n");
```

continues

```
else
     printf ("Caps Lock is off\n");

return 0;
}
```

pokeb

DOS UNIX ANSI C C++

Syntax

```
void pokeb(unsigned segment, unsigned offset, char
           value);
```

`unsigned segment;`	*Segment*
`unsigned offset;`	*Offset*
`char value;`	*Byte to store*

Function The `pokeb` macro stores a byte at a specified memory location.

File(s) to Include `#include <dos.h>`

Description The `pokeb` macro stores the byte specified in the `value` argument at the memory location specified in the `segment` and `offset` arguments.

Value(s) Returned There is no return value.

Related Function(s)

`peek` : retrieves the word at the specified location
`peekb` : retrieves the byte at the specified location
`poke` : stores an integer value at the specified location

Example In the following example, the `pokeb` macro turns the Caps Lock key on.

```
#include <stdio.h>
#include <conio.h>
#include <dos.h>
#include <stdlib.h>

int main (void)
{
int result;
```

```
clrscr ();
printf ("Turning the Caps Lock key on\n");
pokeb (0x0040,0x0017,64);
result = peek (0x0040,0x0017);
if (result & 64)
     printf ("Caps Lock is on\n");
else
     printf ("Caps Lock is off\n");

return 0;
}
```

randbrd

DOS | UNIX | ANSI C | C++

Syntax

```
int randbrd(struct fcb *fcb, int rcnt);

struct fcb *fcb;          File control block
int rcnt;                 Number of records to read
```

Function The randbrd function reads a random block from a file.

File(s) to Include `#include <dos.h>`

Description The randbrd function reads records from the open file control block pointed to by the fcb argument. The number of records to read is specified in the rcnt argument. The records are placed in memory at the current disk transfer address.

```
struct fcb
     {
     char fcb_drive;        /* 0=default,1=A,etc */
     char fcb_name[8];      /* File name */
     char fcb_ext[3];       /* File extension */
     short fcb_curblk;      /* Current block number*/
     short fcb_recsize;     /* Logical record size */
     long fcb_filsize;      /* File size in bytes */
     short fcb_date;        /* Date file was last
                               written */
     char fcb_resv[10];     /* Reserved for DOS */
     char fcb_currec;       /* Current record in
                               block */
```

continues

```
long fcb_random;     /* Random record number*/
};
```

Value(s) Returned One of the following is returned:

0	All records are read
1	End-of-file is reached and last record read is complete
2	Reading records would have wrapped around address 0xFFFF; as many records as possible were read
3	End-of-file is reached and last record read is incomplete

Related Function(s) `randbwr` : writes a random block

Example The following example attempts to read a block from `junk.jnk`.

```
#include <stdio.h>
#include <conio.h>
#include <dos.h>
#include <stdlib.h>

int main (void)
{
int result;
struct fcb fcbblk;

clrscr ();
creatnew ("junk.jnk",0);
result = randbrd (&fcbblk,1);
if (result == 0)
     printf ("All records read\n");
if (result == 1)
     printf ("EOF reached - last record
       complete\n");
if (result == 2)
     printf ("Read as many records as
       possible\n");
if (result == 3)
     printf ("EOF reached - last record
       incomplete\n");

return 0;
}
```

randbwr

DOS UNIX ANSI C C++

Syntax

```
int randbwr(struct fcb *fcb, int rcnt);

struct fcb *fcb;          File control block
int rcnt;                 Number of records to write
```

Function The randbwr function writes a random block to disk.

File(s) to Include `#include <dos.h>`

Description The randbwr function writes a number of records to disk using the open file control block specified in the fcb argument. The rcnt argument specifies the number of records to write. When the rcnt argument is set to 0, the file is truncated to the length indicated by the random record field.

```
struct fcb
     {
     char fcb_drive;       /* 0=default,1=A,etc */
     char fcb_name[8];     /* File name */
     char fcb_ext[3];      /* File extension */
     short fcb_curblk;     /* Current block number
                              */
     short fcb_recsize;    /* Logical record size */
     long fcb_filsize;     /* File size in bytes */
     short fcb_date;       /* Date file was last
                              written */
     char fcb_resv[10];    /* Reserved for DOS */
     char fcb_currec;      /* Current record in
                              block */
     long fcb_random;      /* Random record number
                              */
     };
```

Value(s) Returned One of the following is returned.

0	All records are written
1	Insufficient disk space to write records; no records were written
2	Writing records would have wrapped around address 0xFFFF; as many records as possible were written

Related Function(s) `randbrd` : reads a random block

Example The following example attempts to write a block to `junk.jun`.

```
#include <stdio.h>
#include <conio.h>
#include <dos.h>
#include <stdlib.h>

int main (void)
{
int result;
char far *old_dta;
struct fcb fcbblk;
char buffer [256] = "Testing randbwr function";

clrscr ();
creatnew ("junk.jun",0);
old_dta = getdta();
setdta(buffer);
fcbblk.fcb_recsize = 256;
fcbblk.fcb_random = 0L;
result = randbwr (&fcbblk,1);
if (result == 0)
     printf ("All records written\n");
if (result == 1)
     printf ("Not enough disk space\n");
if (result == 2)
     printf ("Wrote as many records as
  possible\n");
setdta (old_dta);

return 0;
}
```

segread

DOS | UNIX | ANSI C | C++

Syntax `void segread(struct SREGS *segp);`

`struct SREGS *segp;` *Segment registers*

Function The `segread` function reads the segment registers.

File(s) to Include `#include <dos.h>`

Description The `segread` function retrieves the values of the segment registers. These values are then placed in the structure of type SREGS, pointed to by the `segp` argument.

```
struct SREGS
      {
      unsigned int es;
      unsigned int cs;
      unsigned int ss;
      unsigned int ds;
      };
```

Value(s) Returned There is no return value.

Related Function(s)

`intdosx` : generates a DOS interrupt
`int86x` : generates an 8086 interrupt

Example In the following example, `segread` reads the segment registers. The segment registers are then displayed.

```
#include <stdio.h>
#include <conio.h>
#include <dos.h>
#include <stdlib.h>

int main (void)
{
struct SREGS values;

clrscr ();
segread (&values);
printf ("CS : %X\n",values.cs);
printf ("DS : %X\n",values.ds);
printf ("ES : %X\n",values.es);
printf ("SS : %X\n",values.ss);

return 0;
}
```

setcbrk

DOS UNIX ANSI C C++

Syntax

```
int setcbrk(int cbrkvalue);

int cbrkvalue;                    Break value
```

Function The `setcbrk` function selects the control-break setting.

File(s) to Include `#include <dos.h>`

Description The `setcbrk` function sets the control-break setting to the value specified in the `cbrkvalue` argument. A `cbrkvalue` of 0 limits checking to console I/O, printer I/O, and other device communications. A `cbrkvalue` of 1 checks at every system call. The `setcbrk` function uses the DOS system call 0x33.

Value(s) Returned The value of the `cbrkvalue` argument is returned.

Related Function(s) `getcbrk` : retrieves the control-break setting

Example In the following example, `setcbrk` sets the control-break flag to limited checking.

```
#include <stdio.h>
#include <conio.h>
#include <dos.h>
#include <stdlib.h>

int main (void)
{
int result;

clrscr ();
setcbrk (0);
result = getcbrk ();
if (result == 0)
     printf ("Control-break flag is off\n");
else
     printf ("Control-break flag is on\n");

return 0;
}
```

setdta

DOS | UNIX | ANSI C | C++

Syntax `void setdta(char far *dta);`

`char far *dta;` *Disk transfer address*

Function The `setdta` function sets the disk transfer address.

File(s) to Include `#include <dos.h>`

Description The `setdta` function sets the disk transfer address to the value specified in the `dta` argument.

Value(s) Returned There is no return value.

Related Function(s) `getdta` : retrieves the disk transfer address

Example In the following example, `setdta` modifies the disk transfer address.

```
#include <stdio.h>
#include <conio.h>
#include <dos.h>
#include <stdlib.h>

int main (void)
{
char far *dtaddress;
char buffer[256] = "TEST";

clrscr();
dtaddress = getdta();
printf ("Current Disk Transfer Address :
  %Fp\n",dtaddress);
setdta (buffer);
printf ("New Disk Transfer Address : %Fp\n",
  getdta ());
setdta (dtaddress);
printf ("DTA returned to : %Fp\n",dtaddress);

return 0;
}
```

setvect

DOS | UNIX | ANSI C | C++

Syntax

```
void setvect(int interruptno, void interrupt
            (*isr)());
```

`int interruptno;` *Interrupt*
`void interrupt (*isr)();` *Pointer to new interrupt*

Function The `setvect` function sets an interrupt vector entry.

File(s) to Include `#include <dos.h>`

Description The `setvect` function sets the interrupt vector specified in the `interruptno` argument to the value specified by the far pointer in the `isr` argument. The far pointer in the `isr` argument contains the address of the new interrupt function. The interrupt vector is a 4-byte value which contains the address of an interrupt function.

Value(s) Returned There is no return value.

Related Function(s) `getvect` : gets the interrupt vector

Example In the following example, `setvect` sets an interrupt vector entry.

```
#include <stdio.h>
#include <conio.h>
#include <dos.h>
#include <stdlib.h>

void interrupt (*old)(void);

int counter = 0;

void interrupt new (void)
{
disable();
counter = counter + 1;
enable();
}
```

```
int main (void)
{
int x;

clrscr ();

     /* get the timer interrupt vector */
old = getvect (0x1C);
     /* set new vector */
setvect (0x1C, new);
for (counter = 0; counter < 15; counter = counter
  + 1)
     printf ("Counter Value : %d\n",counter);
     /* reset vector */
setvect (0x1C, old);

return 0;
}
```

setverify

DOS | UNIX | ANSI C | C++

Syntax `void setverify(int value);`

`int value;` *New value for verify flag*

Function The `setverify` function sets the verify flag in DOS.

File(s) to Include `#include <dos.h>`

Description The `setverify` function sets the verify flag to the value specified in the `value` argument. When the `value` argument is 0, the verify flag is turned off and writes to disk are not verified. When the `value` argument is 1, the verify flag is turned on and all writes to disk are verified.

Value(s) Returned There is no return value.

Related Function(s) `getverify` : retrieves the setting of the verify flag

Example In the following example, `setverify` turns the verify flag off.

```
#include <stdio.h>
#include <conio.h>
#include <dos.h>
#include <stdlib.h>

int main (void)
{
int status;

clrscr ();
status = getverify ();
setverify (0);
if (status == 0)
     printf ("Verify Flag is OFF\n");
else
     printf ("Verify Flag is ON\n");

return 0;
}
```

sleep

DOS | UNIX | ANSI C | C++

Syntax `void sleep(unsigned seconds);`

`unsigned seconds;` *Number of seconds to sleep*

Function The `sleep` function suspends program execution for the specified number of seconds.

File(s) to Include `#include <dos.h>`

Description The `sleep` function suspends the execution of the current program for the number of seconds specified in the `seconds` argument.

Value(s) Returned There is no return value.

Related Function(s)

`delay` : delays execution for the specified number of milliseconds

Example

The following example suspends program execution for 10 seconds using the `sleep` function.

```
#include <stdio.h>
#include <conio.h>
#include <dos.h>
#include <stdlib.h>

int main (void)
{

clrscr ();
printf ("Sleeping for 10 seconds\n");
sleep (10);
printf ("Slept for 10 seconds\n");

return 0;
}
```

unlink

Syntax

```
int unlink(const char *filename);

const char *filename;
```
Path to delete

Function

The `unlink` function deletes a file.

File(s) to Include

`#include <dos.h>`
or
`#include <io.h>`
or
`#include <stdio.h>`

Description

The `unlink` function deletes the file specified in the `filename` argument. The `filename` argument can contain the drive, path, and file name, but no wild cards. Read-only files cannot be deleted with this function.

Value(s) Returned Zero is returned when unlink is successful. When unsuccessful, –1 is returned and the global variable errno is set to ENOENT, for path or file name not found, or EACCESS, for permission denied.

Related Function(s) remove : removes a file

Example The following example creates a file called junkfile.jnk, then deletes it using the unlink function.

```
#include <stdio.h>
#include <conio.h>
#include <sys\stat.h>
#include <io.h>
#include <stdlib.h>

int main (void)
{
int result;

clrscr ();
creat ("junkfile.jnk",S_IWRITE);
result = unlink ("junkfile.jnk");
if (result == 0)
     printf ("unlink was successful\n");
else
     printf ("unlink was not successful\n");

return 0;
}
```

Memory and String Manipulation

This chapter introduces the Borland C++ functions for string and memory manipulation. These functions are mainly used to manipulate strings and blocks of memory that represent text. The C and C++ languages do not have standard operators for manipulating strings and blocks of memory. Fortunately, the Borland C++ compiler provides numerous functions for this purpose.

Memory Manipulation

The memory manipulation functions described in this chapter are used to copy, initialize, search, and compare blocks of memory. A block of memory, often referred to as a buffer, contains either ASCII characters or binary numerical values, and is accessed by the pointer to the first byte. The pointer to the block of memory is a two-part address consisting of a segment and offset.

Strings

Because the C and C++ languages do not have a formal type for strings, strings are treated as arrays of characters in which each character is one byte. In the C and C++ languages, strings end with a null character; therefore, strings in C are referred to as null-terminated strings.

Strings can be declared in several ways, such as the following:

```
char string_one = "George Washington";or   char
string_two[20];
orchar *string_ptr;
```

The length of the string is determined by the number of bytes it contains, excluding the NULL terminator. For example, in the previous declaration of `string_two`, the string length is 20 bytes. Twenty-one bytes are required, however, to store the string and its NULL terminator.

Many of the string manipulation functions discussed in this chapter are used for comparing strings. These functions perform string comparison on a character-by-character basis. Each character pair is compared by its ASCII values.

Table 11.1 lists the functions discussed in this chapter.

Table 11.1. *String and memory manipulation functions.*

Function	*Meaning*
`memccpy`	Copies a block with a specified size
`memchr`	Searches a block for a specified character
`memcmp`	Compares two blocks
`memcpy`	Copies from one block to another
`memicmp`	Compares two arrays; is not case sensitive
`memmove`	Copies a block
`memset`	Sets a number of bytes in a block to the specified character
`movedata`	Moves a block from one address to another
`movmem`	Moves a block
`setmem`	Sets a number of bytes in a block to the specified value
`stpcpy`	Copies a string
`strcat`	Adds one string to another
`strchr`	Searches a string for a given character
`strcmp`	Compares two strings
`strcmpi`	Compares two strings; is not case sensitive
`strcoll`	Compares two strings
`strcpy`	Copies a string
`strcspn`	Searches a string for segments not containing a subset of a second string

Function	*Meaning*
`strdup`	Copies a string to a new location
`_strerror`	Generates a user-defined error message
`strerror`	Gets the error message associated with a specified error value
`stricmp`	Compares two strings; is not case sensitive
`strlen`	Determines the length of a string
`strlwr`	Converts uppercase in a string to lowercase
`strncat`	Adds the contents of one string to another
`strncmp`	Compares a part of one string with a part of another
`strncmpi`	Compares a part of one string with a part of another; is not case sensitive
`strncpy`	Copies a specified number of characters from one string to another
`strnicmp`	Compares parts of two strings; is not case sensitive
`strnset`	Sets a number of characters in a string to specified character
`strpbrk`	Searches one string for the first occurrence of any character from a second string
`strrchr`	Searches a string for the last occurrence of a specified character
`strrev`	Reverses the order of a string
`strset`	Sets all characters in a string to a specified value
`strspn`	Searches a string for a segment that is a subset of a second string
`strstr`	Searches a string for the first occurrence of a second string
`strtok`	Searches a string for tokens
`strupr`	Converts characters in a string to uppercase
`strxfrm`	Transforms one string into a second string

Borland C++ Memory and String Manipulation Functions Reference Guide

The remainder of this chapter provides detailed information for using each of the string and memory manipulation functions listed in table 11.1.

memccpy

DOS | UNIX | ANSI C | C++

Syntax

```
void *memccpy(void *dest, const void *src, int
                 c,size_t n);
```

`void *dest;`	*Destination*
`const void *src;`	*Block to copy*
`int c;`	*First character copied*
`size_t n;`	*Number of bytes copied*

Function The `memccpy` function copies a block containing the number of bytes in the `n` argument.

File(s) to Include

```
#include <mem.h>
```

or

```
#include <string.h>
```

Description The `memccpy` function copies a block of memory. The block to copy is defined in the `src` argument. The block is copied to the location pointed to by the `dest` argument. Copying from the source block stops when one of two things happens: either the character specified in the `c` argument is copied, or the number of bytes specified in the `n` argument is copied.

Value(s) Returned The pointer to the byte in the destination block following the `c` character is returned when `c` is copied. Null is returned if unsuccessful.

Related Function(s)

memcpy : copies a block with a specified length
memmove : copies a block with a specified length

Example

In the following example, memccpy copies the string in source to the string in destination. The copying stops when the g in string is copied.

```
#include <stdio.h>
#include <string.h>

int main (void)
{
char *source = "Copy this string!";
char destination [25];
char *result;

clrscr();
  result = memccpy (destination, source, 'g',
  strlen(source));
printf ("Destination string: %s\n",destination);
printf ("Resulting pointer : %s\n",result);

return 0;
}
```

memchr

DOS | UNIX | ANSI C | C++

Syntax

```
void *memchr(const void *s, int c, size_t n);
```

`const void *s;`	*Block to search*
`int c;`	*Character searched for*
`size_t n;`	*Number of bytes to search*

Function

The memchr function searches a specified number of bytes in a block for a specified character.

File(s) to Include

#include <mem.h>
or
#include <string.h>

Description The `memchr` function searches the block specified in the `s` argument for the character specified in the `c` argument. The search is limited to the number of bytes specified in the `n` argument.

Value(s) Returned The pointer to the first character matching the `c` argument is returned when successful. Null is returned if no match is found.

Related Function(s) `memcpy` : copies a block with a specified length

Example In the following example, `memchr` finds the `g` in the `source` string.

```
#include <stdio.h>
#include <string.h>

int main (void)
{
char *source = "Search this string!";
char *result;

clrscr();
result = memchr (source, 'g', strlen(source));
  printf ("Position of 'g' :
  %d\n",result-source);

return 0;
}
```

memcmp

DOS | UNIX | ANSI C | C++

Syntax

```
int memcmp(const void *s1, const void *s
           size_t n);
```

`const void *s1;`	*First block*
`const void *s2;`	*Second block*
`size_t n;`	*Number of bytes to compare*

Function The `memcmp` function compares a specified number of bytes from two blocks.

File(s) to Include

```
#include <mem.h>
```

or

```
#include <string.h>
```

Description The `memcmp` function compares the blocks specified in the `s1` and `s2` arguments. Only the number of bytes defined in the `n` argument is compared. The bytes are compared as types `unsigned char`.

Value(s) Returned One of the following is returned:

A value less than zero when `s1` is less than `s2`
Zero when `s1` is the same as `s2`
A value greater than zero when `s1` is greater than `s2`

Related Function(s) `memicmp` : compares two character arrays

Example In the following example, `memcmp` compares the strings in `string1` and `string2`.

```
#include <stdio.h>
#include <string.h>

int main (void)
{
char *string1 = "abcdefg";
char *string2 = "abcdefghij";
int result;

clrscr();
  result = memcmp (string1, string2,
  strlen(string2));
if (result < 0)
printf ("string1 is less than string2");
if (result == 0)
printf ("string1 is the same as string2");
if (result > 0)
printf ("string1 is greater than string2");

return 0;
}
```

memcpy

DOS | UNIX | ANSI C | C++

Syntax

```
void *memcpy(void *dest, const void *scr,
             size_t n);
```

`void *dest;`	*Destination block*
`const void *scr;`	*Block to copy*
`size_t n;`	*Number of bytes to copy*

Function The `memcpy` function copies a specified number of bytes from one block to another.

File(s) to Include `#include <mem.h>` or `#include <string.h>`

Description The `memcpy` function copies the block defined by the `src` argument to the block defined by the `dest` argument. The `n` argument defines the number of bytes to copy.

Value(s) Returned The pointer to the destination block is returned.

Related Function(s)

`memccpy` : copies a block with a specified length
`memmove` : copies a block with a specified length

Example In the following example, `memcpy` copies the `source` string to the `dest` string.

```
#include <stdio.h>
#include <string.h>

int main (void)
{
char *source = "123456789";
char *dest = "          ";
clrscr();
memcpy (dest, source, strlen(source));
printf ("Destination string : %s\n",dest);
return 0;
}
```

memicmp

DOS | UNIX | ANSI C | C++

Syntax

```
int memicmp(const void *s1, const void *s2,
            size_t n);
```

`const void *s1;`	*First block*
`const void *s2;`	*Second block*
`size_t n;`	*Number of bytes to compare*

Function The `memicmp` function compares two character arrays. It is not case sensitive.

File(s) to Include `#include <mem.h>`
or
`#include <string.h>`

Description The `memicmp` function compares the block defined in the `s1` argument with the block defined in the `s2` argument. The comparison is limited to the number of characters defined in the `n` argument. With the `memicmp` function, the character case (upper or lower) is ignored.

Value(s) Returned One of the following is returned:

A value less than zero when `s1` is less than `s2`
Zero when `s1` is the same as `s2`
A value greater than zero when `s1` is greater than `s2`

Related Function(s) `memcmp` : compares two blocks

Example In the following example, `memicmp` compares the strings in `string1` and `string2`.

```
#include <stdio.h>
#include <string.h>

int main (void)
{
char *string1 = "abcdefg";
char *string2 = "ABCDEFG";
int result;
```

continues

```
clrscr();
result = memicmp (string1, string2,
  strlen(string2));
if (result < 0)
printf ("string1 is less than string2");
if (result == 0)
printf ("string1 is the same as string2");
if (result > 0)
printf ("string1 is greater than string2");

return 0;
}
```

memmove

DOS | UNIX | ANSI C | C++

Syntax

```
void *memmove(void *dest, const void *src,
              size_t n);
```

`void *dest;`	*Destination*
`const void *src;`	*Block to copy*
`size_t n;`	*Number of bytes to copy*

Function The `memmove` function copies a block.

File(s) to Include `#include <mem.h>`
or
`#include <string.h>`

Description The `memmove` function copies the block specified in the `src` argument to the location returned in the `dest` argument. The `n` argument identifies the number of bytes to copy. The contents are copied correctly even if the source and destination blocks overlap.

Value(s) Returned The location of the destination block is returned in the `dest` argument.

Related Function(s)

`memccpy` : copies a block
`memcpy` : copies a block
`movmem` : copies a block

Example In the following example, `memmove` copies the `source` string to the `dest` string.

```
#include <stdio.h>
#include <string.h>

int main (void)
{
char *source = "Copy this block";
char *dest = "Copy over this!";

clrscr();
memmove (dest, source, strlen(source));
printf ("Destination string : %s\n",dest);

return 0;
}
```

memset

DOS | UNIX | ANSI C | C++

Syntax

```
void *memset(void *s, int c, size_t n);
```

`void *s;`	*Array*
`int c;`	*Character to insert*
`size_t n;`	*Number of bytes to set*

Function The `memset` function sets a predetermined number of bytes in an array to a specified character.

File(s) to Include `#include <mem.h>`
or
`#include <string.h>`

Description The `memset` function sets a number of bytes in the `s` array to the character specified in the `c` argument. The `n` argument specifies the number of characters to set.

Value(s) Returned The `s` array is returned.

Related Function(s)
`memcpy` : copies a block
`setmem` : sets a block to the specified value

Example In the following example, `memset` places a hyphen (-) over the first five `x`'s in the string.

```
#include <stdio.h>
#include <string.h>

int main (void)
{
char *string = "xxxxx Copy over x's";

clrscr();
memset (string, '-', 5);
printf ("Resulting string : %s\n",string);
return 0;
}
```

movedata

DOS | UNIX | ANSI C | C++

Syntax

```
void movedata(unsigned srcseg, unsigned srcoff,
              unsigned dstseg, unsigned dstoff,
              size_t n);
```

`unsigned srcseg;`	*Source segment*
`unsigned srcoff;`	*Source offset*
`unsigned dstseg;`	*Destination segment*
`unsigned dstoff;`	*Destination offset*
`size_t n;`	*Number of bytes to move*

Function The `movedata` function moves the block at the source address to the destination address.

File(s) to Include `#include <mem.h>`
or
`#include <string.h>`

Description The `movedata` function moves the block at the address specified in the `srcseg` and `srcoff` arguments to the address specified in the `dstseg` and `dstoff` arguments. The `n` argument identifies the number of bytes to move.

Value(s) Returned There is no return value.

Related Function(s) `movmem` : moves a block

Example The following example copies the block at 0x0000, 0x0000 to the `address` buffer.

```
#include <stdio.h>
#include <string.h>
#include <dos.h>

char buffer [25];

int main (void)
{
void far *address;
unsigned seg, off;

clrscr();
address = (void far *)buffer;
seg = FP_SEG(address);
off = FP_OFF(address);
movedata (0x0000, 0x0000, seg, off, 25);
printf ("Buffer : %s\n", buffer);

return 0;
}
```

movmem

Syntax

```
void movmem(void *src, void *dest, unsigned
            length);
```

`void *src;`	*Block to move*
`void *dest;`	*Destination*
`unsigned length;`	*Number of bytes to move*

Function The `movmem` function moves a block from one location to another.

File(s) to Include `#include <mem.h>`

Description The `movmem` function moves a block from the location specified in the `src` argument to the location specified in the `dest` argument. The block is moved correctly even if the blocks overlap.

Value(s) Returned There is no return value.

Related Function(s) `movedata` : copies a block

Example The following example moves the `source` string into the `destination` string.

```
#include <stdio.h>
#include <string.h>

int main (void)
{
char *source = "Move this block";
char *destination = "xxxxxxxxxxxxxxx";

clrscr();
movmem (source, destination, strlen(source));
printf ("Destination string : %s\n",destination);

return 0;
}
```

setmem

DOS | UNIX | ANSI C | C++

Syntax

```
void setmem(void *dest, unsigned length, char
            value);
```

`void *dest;`	*Destination*
`unsigned length;`	*Number of bytes*
`char value;`	*Value to assign*

Function The `setmem` function sets a predefined number of bytes in a block to the specified value.

File(s) to Include `#include <mem.h>`

Description The `setmem` function sets a number of bytes in the block pointed to by the `dest` argument to the value in the `value` argument. The number of bytes to set is defined in the `length` argument.

Value(s) Returned There is no return value.

Related Function(s)
`memset` : sets bytes in a block to a specified value
`strset` : set all characters in a string to a value

Example In the following example, `setmem` sets all the x's in the string to hyphens (-).

```
#include <stdio.h>
#include <string.h>

int main (void)
{
char *string = "xxxxxxxxxxxxxxxxxxx";

clrscr();
setmem (string, 20, '-');
printf ("Resulting string : %s\n",string);
return 0;
}
```

stpcpy

Syntax `char *stpcpy(char *dest, const char *src);`

`char *dest;`	*Destination string*
`const char *src;`	*Source string*

Function The `stpcpy` function copies a string.

File(s) to Include

```
#include <string.h>
```

Description The `stpcpy` function copies the string pointed to by the `src` argument to the string pointed to by the `dest` argument. The `stpcpy` function stops when the terminating null character is encountered.

Value(s) Returned The value of `dest + strlen(src)` is returned.

Related Function(s) `strcpy` : copies a string

Example The following example copies `string1` to `string2` and displays `string2`.

```
#include <stdio.h>
#include <string.h>

int main (void)
{
char *string1 = "xxxxxxxxxxxxxxxxxxxx";
char *string2 = "00000000000000000000";

clrscr();
stpcpy (string2, string1);
printf ("Destination string : %s\n",string2);

return 0;
}
```

---

strcat

DOS | UNIX | ANSI C | C++

Syntax

```
char *strcat(char *dest, const char *src);

char *dest;            Destination string
const char *src;       Source string
```

Function The `strcat` function adds one string to another.

File(s) to Include `#include <string.h>`

Description The `strcat` function adds the string specified in the `src` argument to the end of the string specified in the `dest` argument.

Value(s) Returned The pointer to the resulting string is returned.

Related Function(s) `stpcpy` : copies a string

Example The following example adds `string1` and `string2` to `string3`.

```
#include <stdio.h>
#include <string.h>

int main (void)
{
char *string1 = "xxxxxxxxxx";
char *string2 = "0000000000";
char string3[30] = "";

clrscr();
strcat (string3, string1);
strcat (string3, string2);
printf ("Final string : %s\n",string3);

return 0;
}
```

strchr

DOS | UNIX | ANSI C | C++

Syntax `char *strchr(const char *s, int c);`

`const char *s;`	*String to scan*
`int c;`	*Search character*

Function The `strchr` function searches a string for a given character.

File(s) to Include

```
#include <string.h>
```

Description The `strchr` function searches the string specified in the `s` argument for the character specified in the `c` argument. The search ends on the first occurrence of a matching character. The NULL terminator for the string is searched by the `strchr` function.

Value(s) Returned The pointer to the location of the first matching character is returned when a match is found. If no match is found, null is returned.

Related Function(s)
`strcspn` : searches a string
`strrchr` : searches a string for the last match

Example In the following example, `strchr` searches the string for `x`.

```
#include <stdio.h>
#include <string.h>

int main (void)
{
char *string = "----x----";
char *result;

clrscr();
result = strchr (string,'x');
printf ("Returned value : %d\n",result-string);

return 0;
}
```

---

strcmp

DOS | UNIX | ANSI C | C++

Syntax

```
int strcmp(const char *s1, const char *s2);
```

`const char *s1;` *First string*
`const char *s2;` *Second string*

Function The `strcmp` function compares two strings.

File(s) to Include `#include <string.h>`

Description The `strcmp` function compares the strings specified in the `s1` and `s2` arguments. The comparison begins with the first letter of the strings and continues until corresponding characters differ, or until the ends of the strings are reached.

Value(s) Returned One of the following is returned:

A value less than zero if `s1` is less than `s2`
Zero if `s1` is the same as `s2`
A value greater than zero if `s1` is greater than `s2`

Related Function(s)

`strcmpi` : compares two strings
`stricmp` : compares two strings
`strncmp` : compares one part of string with another

Example In the following example, `strcmp` compares `string1` and `string2`.

```
#include <stdio.h>
#include <string.h>

int main (void)
{
char *string1 = "----x----";
char *string2 = "----0----";
int result;

clrscr();
result = strcmp (string1, string2);
if (result < 0)
printf ("string1 < string2");
if (result == 0)
printf ("string1 = string2");
if (result > 0)
printf ("string1 > string2");

return 0;
}
```

strcmpi

DOS | UNIX | ANSI C | C++

Syntax

```
int strcmpi(const char *s1, const char *s2);
```

`const char *s1;` *First string*
`const char *s2;` *Second string*

Function The `strcmpi` macro compares two strings. It is not case sensitive.

File(s) to Include `#include <string.h>`

Description The `strcmpi` macro compares the strings specified in the `s1` and `s2` arguments. This macro is not case sensitive.

Value(s) Returned One of the following is returned:

A value less than zero if `s1` is less than `s2`
Zero if `s1` is the same as `s2`
A value greater than zero if `s1` is greater than `s2`

Related Function(s) `strcmp` : compares two strings

Example The following example compares `string1` and `string2` using the `strcmpi` function.

```
#include <stdio.h>
#include <string.h>

int main (void)
{
char *string1 = "----x----";
char *string2 = "----X----";
int result;

clrscr();
result = strcmpi (string1, string2);
if (result < 0)
printf ("string1 < string2");
if (result == 0)
printf ("string1 = string2");
if (result > 0)
printf ("string1 > string2");
```

```
return 0;
}
```

strcoll

DOS | UNIX | ANSI C | C++

Syntax `int strcoll(char *s1, char *s2);`

`char *s1;`	*First string*
`char *s2;`	*Second string*

Function The `strcoll` function compares two strings.

File(s) to Include `#include <string.h>`

Description The `strcoll` function compares the two strings specified in the `s1` and `s2` arguments using the collating sequence set by the `setlocale` function.

Value(s) Returned One of the following is returned:
- A value less than zero if `s1` is less than `s2`
- Zero if `s1` is the same as `s2`
- A value greater than zero if `s1` is greater than `s2`

Related Function(s)
- `strcmp` : compares two strings
- `setlocale` : sets the locale

Example In the following example, `strcoll` compares `string1` and `string2`.

```
#include <stdio.h>
#include <string.h>

int main (void)
{
char *string1 = "----x----";
char *string2 = "xxxx-xxxx";
int result;
```

continues

```
clrscr();
result = strcoll (string1, string2);
if (result < 0)
     printf ("string1 < string2");
if (result == 0)
     printf ("string1 = string2");
if (result > 0)
     printf ("string1 > string2");

return 0;
}
```

strcpy

DOS | UNIX | ANSI C | C++

Syntax `char *strcpy(char *dest, const char *src);`

`char *dest;`	*Destination string*
`const char *src;`	*String to copy*

Function The `strcpy` function copies a string.

File(s) to Include `#include <string.h>`

Description The `strcpy` function moves the string specified in the `src` argument to the location returned in the `dest` argument.

Value(s) Returned The pointer to the destination string is returned.

Related Function(s) `stpcpy` : copies a string

Example The following example copies the `source` string to the `destination` string.

```
#include <stdio.h>
#include <string.h>

int main (void)
{
```

```
char *source = "----x----";
char *destination = "xxxx-xxxx";

clrscr();
strcpy (destination, source);
printf ("Destination string : %s\n", destination);

return 0;
}
```

strcspn

DOS | UNIX | ANSI C | C++

Syntax

```
size_t strcspn(const char *s1, const char *s2);
```

`const char *s1;` *First string*
`const char *s2;` *Second string*

Function The `strcspn` function searches a string for segments that do not contain a subset of a specified set of characters.

File(s) to Include `#include <string.h>`

Description The `strcspn` function searches the string specified in the `s1` argument for the initial segment. The initial segment consists of characters that are not in the string specified in the `s2` argument.

Value(s) Returned The length of the found initial segment is returned.

Related Function(s)
`strchr` : searches a string for a specified character
`strrchr` : searches a string for a specified character

Example The following example searches `string1` for the first segment that doesn't contain a subset of `string2`.

```
#include <stdio.h>
#include <string.h>
```

continues

```
int main (void)
{
char *string1 = "aaabbbcccddd";
char *string2 = "xz";
int result;

clrscr();
result = strcspn (string1, string2);
printf ("Resulting intersection: %d\n",result);
return 0;
}
```

strdup

DOS | UNIX | ANSI C | C++

Syntax `char *strdup(const char *s);`

`const char *s;` *String to copy*

Function The `strdup` function copies a string to a new location.

File(s) to Include `#include <string.h>`

Description The `strdup` function copies the string specified by the `s` argument to the space allocated when the `strdup` function calls the `malloc` function. This space is not automatically freed.

Value(s) Returned If successful, the pointer to the new string is returned. Null is returned if the space could not be allocated.

Related Function(s) `free` : frees allocated memory

Example In the following example, `strdup` copies `string1`.

```
#include <stdio.h>
#include <string.h>

int main (void)
{
char *string1 = "ABCDEFG";
char *string2;
```

```
clrscr();
string2 = strdup (string1);
printf ("Duplicated string : %s\n", string2);

return 0;
}
```

_strerror

DOS | UNIX | ANSI C | C++

Syntax `char *_strerror(const char *s);`

`const char *s;` *String to generate*

Function The `_strerror` function generates a user-defined error message.

File(s) to Include `#include <string.h>`
or
`#include <stdio.h>`

Description The `_strerror` function generates the user-defined string specified in the `s` argument. The string should be fewer than 94 characters.

Value(s) Returned The pointer to the error string is returned when successful. The error string consists of the string pointed to by the `s` argument plus a colon, space, the most recent system error message, and a new line. When the string in the `s` argument is null, the pointer to the most recent error message is returned.

Related Function(s)
`perror` : prints a system error message
`strerror` : returns a pointer to an error message string

Example The following example generates the message `"Cannot duplicate handle"` when the `dup` function generates an error.

```
#include <stdio.h>
#include <string.h>

int main (void)
{
```

continues

```
int file_handle = 100;
char *message;

clrscr();
if (dup(file_handle) == -1)
     printf ("%s", _strerror ("Cannot duplicate
  handle"));

return 0;
}
```

strerror

Syntax `char *strerror(int errnum);`

`int errnum;` *Error number*

Function The `strerror` function returns the pointer to the error message associated with an error value.

File(s) to Include `#include <string.h>`
or
`#include <stdio.h>`

Description The `strerror` function retrieves the pointer to the error message associated with the error value specified in the `errnum` argument.

Value(s) Returned The pointer to the error message is returned.

Related Function(s)
`perror` : prints a system error message
`_strerror` : generates a user-defined error message

Example In the following example, `strerror` retrieves the error message for the error value 10.

```
#include <stdio.h>
#include <string.h>
```

```
int main (void)
{
char *message;

clrscr();
message = strerror(10);
printf ("Error: %s\n",message);

return 0;
}
```

stricmp

Syntax

```
int stricmp(const char *s1, const char *s2);

const char *s1;            First string
const char *s2;            Second string
```

Function The `stricmp` function compares two strings. It is not case sensitive.

File(s) to Include `#include <string.h>`

Description The `stricmp` function compares the strings specified in the `s1` and `s2` arguments and is not case sensitive. The unsigned comparison begins with the first character of each string and continues until corresponding characters differ or the ends of the strings are reached.

Value(s) Returned One of the following is returned:

- A value less than zero if `s1` is less than `s2`
- Zero if `s1` is the same as `s2`
- A value greater than zero if `s1` is greater than `s2`

Related Function(s)

`strcmp` : compares two strings
`strcmpi` : compares two strings and is not case sensitive

Example The following example compares `string1` and `string2` using `stricmp`.

```
#include <stdio.h>
#include <string.h>

int main (void)
{
char *string1 = "----x----";
char *string2 = "----X----";
int result;

clrscr();
result = stricmp (string1, string2);
if (result < 0)
     printf ("string1 < string2");
if (result == 0)
     printf ("string1 = string2");
if (result > 0)
     printf ("string1 > string2");

return 0;
}
```

---

strlen

DOS | UNIX | ANSI C | C++

Syntax `size_t strlen(const char *s);`

`const char *s;` *String to evaluate*

Function The `strlen` function determines the length of a string.

File(s) to Include `#include <string.h>`

Description The `strlen` function determines the length of the string specified in the `s` argument. The NULL terminator is not counted.

Value(s) Returned The number of characters in the string is returned.

Related Function(s) `strcmp` : compares two strings

Example The following example displays the length of the string.

```
#include <stdio.h>
#include <string.h>

int main (void)
{
char *string = "1234567890";

clrscr();
printf ("Length of string : %d\n",
  strlen(string));

return 0;
}
```

strlwr

DOS | UNIX | ANSI C | C++

Syntax `char *strlwr(char *s);`

`char *s;` *String to convert*

Function The `strlwr` function converts the uppercase letters in a string to lowercase.

File(s) to Include `#include <string.h>`

Description The `strlwr` function converts the uppercase letters in the string specified by the `s` argument to lowercase.

Value(s) Returned The pointer to the string specified in the `s` argument is returned.

Related Function(s) `strupr` : converts lowercase letters in a string to uppercase

Example The following example converts the uppercase letters in the string to lowercase.

```
#include <stdio.h>
#include <string.h>
```

continues

```
int main (void)
{
char *string = "ABCDEFG";

clrscr();
strlwr (string);
printf ("Converted string : %s\n", string);

return 0;
}
```

strncat

DOS | UNIX | ANSI C | C++

Syntax

```
char *strncat(char *dest, const char *src, size_t
               maxlen);
```

`char *dest;`	*Destination string*
`const char *src;`	*String to add to* `dest`
`size_t maxlen;`	*Maximum length of final* `dest` *string*

Function The `strncat` function adds the contents of one string to the end of another.

File(s) to Include `#include <string.h>`

Description The `strncat` function adds the contents of the string specified in the `src` argument to the end of the string specified in the `dest` argument. The final length of the destination string is limited to the length of the original destination string plus the value specified in the `maxlen` argument. A null character is appended to the resulting string.

Value(s) Returned The pointer to the final destination string is returned.

Related Function(s)

`strcat` : adds one string to the end of another
`strncmp` : compares parts of two strings

Example The following example adds `string` to `buffer` using `strncat`.

```
#include <stdio.h>
#include <string.h>

int main (void)
{
char buffer[10] = "";
char *string = "ABCDEFG";

clrscr();
strncat (buffer,string,7);
printf ("Resulting string : %s\n", buffer);

return 0;
}
```

strncmp

DOS | UNIX | ANSI C | C++

Syntax

```
int strncmp(const char *s1, const char *s2, size_t
            maxlen);
```

`const char *s1;`	*First string*
`const char *s2;`	*Second string*
`size_t maxlen;`	*Maximum number to compare*

Function The `strncmp` function compares a part of one string with a part of another string.

File(s) to Include `#include <string.h>`

Description The `strncmp` function compares parts of the two strings specified in the `s1` and `s2` arguments. Comparison begins with the first character and continues until corresponding characters differ or the number of characters specified in the `maxlen` arguments has been compared.

Value(s) Returned One of the following is returned:

A value less than zero if `s1` is less than `s2`
Zero if `s1` is the same as `s2`
A value greater than zero if `s1` is greater than `s2`

Related Function(s)

`strcmp` : compares two strings
`strcolt` : compares two strings

Example The following example compares `string1` and `string2` using `strncmp`.

```
#include <stdio.h>
#include <string.h>

int main (void)
{
char *string1 = "xx------";
char *string2 = "xxxx-xxxx";
int result;

clrscr();
result = strncmp (string1, string2,2);
if (result < 0)
printf ("string1 < string2");
if (result == 0)
printf ("string1 = string2");
if (result > 0)
printf ("string1 > string2");

return 0;
}
```

---

strncmpi

DOS | UNIX | ANSI C | C++

Syntax

```
int strncmpi(const char *s1, const char *s2,
             size_t n);
```

`const char *s1;`	*First string*
`const char *s2;`	*Second string*
`size_t n;`	*Maximum bytes to compare*

Function The `strncmpi` function compares a part of one string with a part of another. It is not case sensitive.

File(s) to Include `#include <string.h>`

Description The `strncmpi` function compares the first part of the string specified in the `s1` argument with the first part of the string specified in the `s2` argument. This function is not case sensitive. The signed comparison begins with the first character in the strings and continues until corresponding characters differ, or until the number of bytes specified in the `n` argument has been compared.

Value(s) Returned One of the following is returned:

A value less than zero if `s1` is less than `s2`
Zero if `s1` is the same as `s2`
A value greater than zero if `s1` is greater than `s2`

Related Function(s)
`strcmpi` : compares two strings; is not case sensitive
`stricmp` : compares two strings; is not case sensitive

Example In the following example, `strncmpi` compares the first two elements of `string1` and `string2`.

```
#include <stdio.h>
#include <string.h>

int main (void)
{
char *string1 = "xx------";
char *string2 = "XXxx-xxxx";
int result;

clrscr();
result = strncmpi (string1, string2,2);
if (result < 0)
      printf ("string1 < string2");
if (result == 0)
      printf ("string1 = string2");
if (result > 0)
      printf ("string1 > string2");

return 0;
}
```

strncpy

DOS | UNIX | ANSI C | C++

Syntax

```
char *strncpy(char *dest, const char *src, size_t
              maxlen);
```

`char *dest;`	*Destination string*
`const char *src;`	*Source string*
`size_t maxlen;`	*Maximum number to copy*

Function The `strncpy` function copies a specified number of characters from one string to another.

File(s) to Include `#include <string.h>`

Description The `strncpy` function copies the string specified in the `src` argument to the destination string specified by the `dest` argument. The number of characters copied is limited to the value specified in the `maxlen` argument. The destination string is padded or truncated as required.

Value(s) Returned The pointer to the destination string is returned.

Related Function(s) `strncat` : adds a part of one string to another

Example The following example copies the first five characters of `string2` into `string1` using `strncpy`.

```
#include <stdio.h>
#include <string.h>

int main (void)
{
char string1[5];
char *string2 = "123456789";

clrscr();
strncpy (string1, string2, 5);
string1[5] = '\0';
printf ("Resulting string : %s\n", string1);

return 0;
}
```

strnicmp

DOS UNIX ANSI C C++

Syntax

```
int strnicmp(const char *s1, const char *s2,
             size_t maxl);
```

`const char *s1;`	*First string*
`const char *s2;`	*Second string*
`size_t maxl;`	*Maximum number to compare*

Function The `strnicmp` function compares parts of two strings. It is not case sensitive.

File(s) to Include `#include <string.h>`

Description The `strnicmp` function compares the first parts of the strings specified in the `s1` and `s2` arguments. The signed comparison begins with the first characters of the strings and continues until corresponding characters don't match, the number of characters specified in the `maxl` argument has been compared, or the ends of the strings are reached.

Value(s) Returned One of the following is returned:

Less than zero if `s1` is less than `s2`
Zero if `s1` is the same as `s2`
Greater than zero if `s1` is greater than `s2`

Related Function(s) `strncmpi` : compares parts of two strings; is not case sensitive

Example The following example compares the first six characters of `string1` and `string2`.

```
#include <stdio.h>
#include <string.h>
```

continues

```
int main (void)
{
char *string1 = "ABCDEFG";
char *string2 = "abcdefg";
int result;

clrscr();
result = strnicmp (string1, string2, 6);
if (result < 0)
     printf ("string1 < string2");
if (result == 0)
     printf ("string1 = string2");
if (result > 0)
     printf ("string1 > string2");

return 0;
}
```

strnset

DOS | UNIX | ANSI C | C++

Syntax `char *strnset(char *s, int ch, size_t n);`

`char *s;`	*String to convert*
`int ch;`	*New character*
`size_t n;`	*Number of characters to set*

Function The `strnset` function sets a number of characters in a string to a specified character.

File(s) to Include `#include <string.h>`

Description The `strnset` function sets a number of characters in the string specified in the `s` argument to the character specified in the `ch` argument. The number of characters set to the new character value is defined in the `n` argument.

Value(s) Returned The pointer to the `s` argument is returned.

Related Function(s) `setmem` : sets a number of characters in a block to a predefined value

—

Example In the following example, `strnset` sets the first five characters of the string to `-`.

```
#include <stdio.h>
#include <string.h>

int main (void)
{
char *string = "xxxxxxxxxx";

clrscr();
strnset (string, '-', 5);
printf ("New string : %s\n", string);

return 0;
}
```

strpbrk

DOS | UNIX | ANSI C | C++

Syntax `char *strpbrk(const char *s1, const char *s2);`

`const char *s1;`	*First string*
`const char *s2;`	*Second string*

Function The `strpbrk` function searches one string for the first occurrence of any character from the second string.

File(s) to Include `#include <string.h>`

Description The `strpbrk` function searches the string specified in the `s1` argument for the first occurrence of any character in the string specified in the `s2` argument.

Value(s) Returned If a match is found, the pointer to the first match is returned. If no match is found, null is returned.

Related Function(s) `strrchr` : searches a string for the last occurrence of a character

Example In the following example, `strpbrk` searches `string1` for the characters in `string2`.

```
#include <stdio.h>
#include <string.h>

int main (void)
{
char *string1 = "abcdefg";
char *string2 = "cd";
char *result;

clrscr();
result = strpbrk (string1, string2);
printf ("First Occurrence : %c\n", *result);

return 0;
}
```

---

strrchr

DOS | UNIX | ANSI C | C++

Syntax `char *strrchr(const char *s, int ch);`

`const char *s;`	*String to search*
`int ch;`	*Character for search*

Function The `strrchr` function searches a string for the last occurrence of a specified character.

File(s) to Include `#include <string.h>`

Description The `strrchr` function searches the string specified in the `s` argument for the last occurrence of the character specified in the `ch` argument.

Value(s) Returned The pointer to the last occurrence is returned. If no match to the `ch` argument is found, null is returned.

Related Function(s) `strchr` : searches a string for the first occurrence of a specified character

Example The following example searches the string for the last occurrence of g.

```
#include <stdio.h>
#include <string.h>

int main (void)
{
char *string = "abcdefg";
char *result;

clrscr();
result = strrchr (string,'g');
printf ("Last Occurrence : %c\n", *result);

return 0;
}
```

strrev

DOS | UNIX | ANSI C | C++

Syntax `char *strrev(char *s);`

`char *s;` *String to reverse*

Function The `strrev` function reverses a string.

File(s) to Include `#include <string.h>`

Description The `strrev` function reverses the order of the characters in the string specified in the `s` argument.

Value(s) Returned The pointer to the resulting string is returned.

Related Function(s) `strcmp` : compares two strings

Example The following example reverses the order of the string to `Hello there`.

```
#include <stdio.h>
#include <string.h>
```

continues

```
int main (void)
{
char *string = "ereht olleH";
char *result;

clrscr();
strrev (string);
printf ("Reversed string : %s\n", string);

return 0;
}
```

strset

DOS UNIX ANSI C C++

Syntax `char *strset(char *s, int ch);`

`char *s;`	*String to convert*
`int ch;`	*Character to set*

Function The `strset` function sets all the characters in a string to the specified character.

File(s) to Include `#include <string.h>`

Description The `strset` function sets all the characters in the string specified by the `s` argument to the character value specified in the `ch` argument. Conversion stops when the NULL terminator is found.

Value(s) Returned The pointer to the string specified in the `s` argument is returned.

Related Function(s) `setmem` : sets all values in a block of memory

Example The following example sets the hyphens (-) in the string to `x`'s.

```
#include <stdio.h>
#include <string.h>
```

```
int main (void)
{
char *string = "------";

clrscr();
strset (string, 'x');
printf ("New string : %s\n", string);

return 0;
}
```

strspn

DOS | UNIX | ANSI C | C++

Syntax `size_t strspn(const char *s1, const char *s2);`

`const char *s1;`	*First string*
`const char *s2;`	*Second string*

Function The `strspn` function searches one string for a segment that is a subset of the second string.

File(s) to Include `#include <string.h>`

Description The `strspn` function searches the string specified in the `s1` argument for the first segment that contains a subset of the characters specified in the `s2` argument.

Value(s) Returned The length of the found segment is returned.

Related Function(s) `strcspn` : searches a string for the first segment not containing a subset of a second string

Example The following example finds the segment in `string1` that is a subset of `string2`.

```
#include <stdio.h>
#include <string.h>
```

continues

```
int main (void)
{
char *string1 = "123456";
char *string2 = "abc123";
int length;

clrscr();
length = strspn (string1, string2);
printf ("Length : %d\n", length);
return 0;
}
```

strstr

DOS | UNIX | ANSI C | C++

Syntax

```
char *strstr(const char *s1, const char *s2);
```

`const char *s1;` *First string*
`const char *s2;` *Second string*

Function The `strstr` function searches a string for the first occurrence of the second string.

File(s) to Include `#include <string.h>`

Description The `strstr` function searches the string in the `s1` argument for the string in the `s2` argument.

Value(s) Returned The pointer to the matching string in `s1` is returned if a match is found. If no match is found, null is returned.

Related Function(s) `strspn` : searches a string for the first segment that contains a subset of a second string

Example In the following example, `strstr` searches `string1` for `456`.

```
#include <stdio.h>
#include <string.h>

int main (void)
{
```

```
char *string1 = "123456";
char *string2 = "456";
char *result;

clrscr();
result = strstr (string1, string2);
printf ("Substring : %s\n", result);
return 0;
}
```

strtok

DOS | UNIX | ANSI C | C++

Syntax `char *strtok(char *s1, const char *s2);`

`char *s1;` *String of tokens*
`const char *s2;` *Separator string*

Function The `strtok` function searches one string for tokens. These tokens are separated by delimiters defined in the second string.

File(s) to Include `#include <string.h>`

Description The `strtok` function searches the string specified by the `s1` argument for tokens. The string specified in the `s2` argument contains the separators for the tokens. The first call to this function returns the pointer to the first character in the first token. The second call, using null as the first argument, returns the pointer to the first character of the second token, and so forth.

Value(s) Returned The pointer to the corresponding token is returned. When no more tokens exist, a null pointer is returned.

Related Function(s) `strcmp` : compares two strings

Example In the following example, `strtok` displays the first and second tokens in `string1`.

```
#include <stdio.h>
#include <string.h>

int main (void)
{
char *string1 = "a, b, c";
char *string2 = ",";
char *result;

clrscr();
result = strtok (string1, string2);
printf ("First Token : %s\n", result);
result = strtok (NULL, string2);
printf ("Second Token : %s\n",result);

return 0;
}
```

---

strupr

DOS | UNIX | ANSI C | C++

Syntax `char *strupr(char *s);`

`char *s;` *String to convert*

Function The `strupr` function converts the lowercase letters in a string to uppercase.

File(s) to Include `#include <string.h>`

Description The `strupr` function converts the lowercase letters in the string specified in the `s` argument to uppercase.

Value(s) Returned The pointer to the converted string is returned.

Related Function(s) `strlwr` : converts uppercase letters in a string to lowercase

Example The following example converts the letters in `string1` to uppercase.

```
#include <stdio.h>
#include <string.h>

int main (void)
{
char *string = "abcdefg";

clrscr();
strupr (string);
printf ("Converted string : %s\n", string);

return 0;
}
```

strxfrm

DOS | UNIX | ANSI C | C++

Syntax `size_t strxfrm(char *s1, char *s2, size_t n);`

`char *s1;`	*First string*
`char *s2;`	*Second string*
`size_t n;`	*Maximum characters to transform*

Function The `strxfrm` function transforms one string into a second string.

File(s) to Include `#include <string.h>`

Description The `strxfrm` function transforms the string specified in the `s2` argument into the string specified in the `s1` argument. The transformation is limited to the number of characters specified in the `n` argument.

Value(s) Returned The number of characters copied is returned.

Related Function(s)
`strcoll` : compares two strings
`strncpy` : copies from one string into another

Example In the following example, `strxfrm` transforms the first three characters of `string1` into the first three characters of `string2`.

```
#include <stdio.h>
#include <string.h>

int main (void)
{
char *string1 = "abcdefg";
char *string2 = "1234567";

clrscr();
strxfrm (string1, string2, 3);
printf ("Transformed : %s\n", string1);

return 0;
}
```

Mathematical Functions

This chapter introduces the Borland C++ functions that provide mathematical capabilities beyond the basic C math operators. The functions and macros listed in table 12.1 provide a range of capabilities from simple mathematics to type conversions.

Table 12.1. Mathematical functions.

Function	*Meaning*
abs	Returns the absolute value of an integer
acos	Calculates the arc cosine
arg	Determines the angle in the complex plane
asin	Calculates the arc sine
atan	Calculates the arc tangent
atan2	Calculates the arc tangent of x/y
atof	Converts a string to a floating-point
atoi	Converts a string to an integer
atol	Converts a string to a long value
bcd	Converts a value to binary coded decimal
cabs	Calculates the absolute value of a complex value
ceil	Rounds a value up
_clear87	Clears the floating-point status word
complex	Creates a complex number from two values
conj	Determines the complex conjugate
_control87	Changes the floating-point control word
cos	Calculates the cosine
cosh	Calculates the hyperbolic cosine
div	Divides two integers
ecvt	Converts a floating-point to a string
exp	Calculates the exponential e^x
fabs	Determines the absolute value of a floating-point number
fcvt	Converts a floating-point to a string
floor	Rounds a value down
fmod	Calculates x modulo y
_fpreset	Reinitializes the floating-point math package
frexp	Divides a number into a mantissa and exponent
gcvt	Converts a floating-point to a string

Function	*Meaning*
`hypot`	Determines the hypotenuse of a right triangle
`imag`	Returns the imaginary part of a complex value
`itoa`	Converts an integer to a string
`labs`	Determines the absolute value of a long value
`ldexp`	Returns the value of $x * 2^{exp}$
`ldiv`	Divides two long values
`log`	Calculates the natural logarithm
`log10`	Calculates the base 10 logarithm
`_lrotl`	Rotates a long value to the left
`_lrotr`	Rotates a long value to the right
`ltoa`	Converts a long value to a string
`matherr`	Handles math errors
`max`	Returns the largest of two values
`min`	Returns the smallest of two values
`modf`	Divides a double into its integer and fractional parts
`norm`	Returns the square of the absolute value of a complex number
`polar`	Returns a complex number with the specified magnitude and angle
`poly`	Calculates the specified polynomial
`pow`	Calculates the value of x^y
`pow10`	Calculates the value of 10^x
`rand`	Generates a random number
`random`	Generates a random number within a range
`randomize`	Initializes the random number generator
`real`	Returns the real part of a complex number
`_rotl`	Rotates an unsigned integer left
`_rotr`	Rotates an unsigned integer right
`sin`	Calculates the sine
`sinh`	Calculates the hyperbolic sine
`sqrt`	Returns the square root of a value

continues

Table 12.1. *(continued)*

Function	*Meaning*
`srand`	Sets a seed point for the random generator
`_status87`	Retrieves the floating-point status
`strtod`	Converts a string to a double
`strtol`	Converts a string to a long
`strtoul`	Converts a string to an unsigned long
`tan`	Calculates the tangent
`tanh`	Calculates the hyperbolic tangent
`ultoa`	Converts an unsigned long to a string

As you can see from table 12.1, many data type conversions are provided. In the C and C++ languages, as with most other languages, operations should be performed only on the proper data types. For example, integer values should not be passed to functions expecting floating-point values. Therefore, several functions provided are for type conversions. Keep in mind that the C and C++ languages do allow for the modification of types in a declaration, such as

```
x = (int) y + 3;
```

in which `x` is an integer value and `y` is a floating-point. Table 12.2 lists the types, size, and range of several of the data types defined in Borland C++.

Table 12.2. *Data types.*

Type	*Number of bits*	*Range*
unsigned char	8	0 to 255
char	8	–128 to 127
enum	16	–32768 to 32,767
unsigned int	16	0 to 65,535
short int	16	–32,768 to 32,767
int	16	–32,768 to 32,767
unsigned long	32	0 to 4,294,967,295
long	32	–2,147,483,648 to 2,147,483,647

Type	*Number of bits*	*Range*
float	32	$3.4x10^{-38}$ to $3.4x10^{38}$
double	64	$1.7x10^{-308}$ to $1.7x10^{308}$
long double	80	$3.4x10^{-4932}$ to $1.1x10^{4932}$

Integer Math

Integer math is generally used for counters, summations, and so forth. For most purposes, the operators provided in the C language are sufficient because most math operations on integer values return integer values. This is not the case, however, with division, which can return a non-integer value. For this reason, the `div` and `ldiv` functions are provided for integer math. These functions return the integer remainder and quotient in a structure of type `div_t` and `ldiv_t`, respectively.

The Borland C++ library also includes several functions for converting integer values and for calculating the absolute values of integers.

Floating-Point Math

Floating-point math is more complex than simple integer math. Floating-point math, however, provides greater flexibility and precision. The family of 80x86 microprocessors has a corresponding family of math co-processors, the 80x87s, which are specially designed for floating-point math operations. These co-processors are not necessary to execute floating-point math operations, but they significantly increase the speed of mathematically intensive software applications.

Borland C++, by default, compiles source code with the assumption that a math co-processor will be available on the machine. Therefore, instructions for the 80x87 are created. In addition to generating the 80x87 instructions, an emulation library is linked-in to interpret the 80x87 instructions, thus emulating the 80x87 if no math co-processor is found when the program is executed.

Compiler Options

You can control the way that the Borland C++ Compiler generates code through the use of compiler options. The command-line compiler options which pertain to 80x87 code are as follows:

Option	*Function*
–f	The default setting. With this option, the compiler will generate 80x87 code. In addition, the emulation library (EMU.LIB) will be linked into the program. During program execution, if an 80x87 coprocessor is detected, it will be used. If no coprocessor is detected, the emulation software is used to execute the 80x87 instructions.
–87	Used when the host machine is known to have an 80x87 coprocessor. With this option, FP87.LIB is linked into the code. Approximately 10K bytes are saved in the executable file using this option instead of –f.
–f–	Used when there is no floating-point code in the program. Choosing this option will save some time during the linking process.
–ff	Allows you to perform fast floating-point operations. Fast floating-point operations trade precision for execution speed. For most applications, the loss in precision has no effect on proper execution.

IEEE Floating-Point Format

Borland C++ uses the IEEE floating-point formats for its floating-point types. Borland C++ has three floating-point types. These are the float, double, and long double types. Floating-point values contain a mantissa and an exponent. The exponent represents the power of 2.

Under the IEEE format, the floating-point value is normalized. The exponent, for normalized values, has been adjusted so that the binary point in the mantissa lies to the right of the most significant nonzero digit. The IEEE format contains a sign bit, a mantissa, and an exponent representing the power of 2.

Borland C++ uses the 32-bit IEEE real format for the float type. The float type is used for single-precision floating-point values. Single-precision floating-point values require 4 bytes of storage. The IEEE format for the float type contains 1 sign bit, 7 exponent bits, and 24 mantissa bits. The double type follows the 64-bit IEEE real format and uses 1 sign bit, 11 exponent bits, and 52 mantissa bits. The long double type follows the 80-bit extended real format.

Most of the functions listed previously in table 12.1 are provided for manipulating floating-point values and the 80x87 processor.

Complex Math

A complex value contains a real and an imaginary part in the following form:

x + yi

in which x is the real part

y is the imaginary part

and i is the square root of –1.

Borland C++ handles complex values in two ways. The first is available through the standard C language using the complex structure prototyped in `math.h`. The second is available only through C++ and the complex class as defined in `complex.h`.

When you use the standard C language, a structure called `complex` is defined that holds the real and imaginary parts of the complex number.

```
struct complex
{
double x, y;    /* real and imaginary parts */
}
```

When you use the C++ language, the class `complex` has been defined in `complex.h`. In the `complex.h` header file, all the arithmetic operators, the stream operators << and >>, and the usual math functions (`sin`, `cos`, etc.) have been overloaded to work with complex numbers.

The majority of the mathematical functions listed in table 12.1 shown earlier support complex math when using C++ as well as `complex.h`.

BCD Math

The Borland C++ compiler, as well as the computer, operates with binary numbers. Because most of us think in decimal, the computer converts decimal to binary. For the most part, this causes no problems because any error in the conversion is extremely small.

There are times, however, when such errors can cause problems. For example, the round-off errors in conversions can create problems for financial recordkeeping. The binary coded decimal (`bcd`) type provides some advantages over normal floating-point types when you are concerned with precision. The `bcd` type offers 17-decimal digits precision and a range of $1x10^{-125}$ to $1x10^{125}$. In addition, banker's rounding is used. In banker's rounding, rounding is done to the nearest whole number. Ties go to the even digit (for example, 6.345 to two places precision would be 6.34 because the tie goes to the even digit 4).

Borland C++ Mathematical Functions Reference Guide

The remainder of this chapter provides detailed information for each of the functions listed previously in table 12.1.

abs

DOS | UNIX | ANSI C | C++

Syntax

Real Version:

```
int abs(int x);

int x;                          Value to process
```

Complex Version:

```
double abs(complex x);

complex x;                      Value to process
```

Function The `abs` function returns the absolute value of the specified integer value.

File(s) to Include Real Version:

```
#include <stdlib.h>
```

or

```
#include <math.h>
```

Complex Version:

```
#include <complex.h>
```

Description The `abs` function returns the absolute value of the value specified in the `x` argument. When called with the `stdlib.h` file included, `abs` is treated as a macro that is expanded to `inline` code. Use the `#undef` function to make the `abs` macro a function when including the `stdlib.h` file.

Value(s) Returned The real version returns an integer in the range of 0 to 32,767. The complex version returns a double value.

Related Function(s)
`cabs` : gets the absolute value of a complex number
`fabs` : gets the absolute value of a floating-point
`labs` : gets the absolute value of a long value

Example The following example calculates and displays the absolute value of –534.

```
#include <stdio.h>
#include <stdlib.h>

int main (void)
{
int value =   534;
int absvalue;

clrscr ();
absvalue = abs(value);
printf ("Initial value : %d\n",value);
printf ("Absolute value : %d\n",absvalue);

return 0;
}
```

---

acos

DOS	UNIX	ANSI C	C++

Syntax Real Version:

```
double acos(double x);

double x;                    Value
```

Complex Version:

```
complex acos(complex x);

complex x;                   Value
```

Function The `acos` function calculates the arc cosine of a value.

File(s) to Include

Real Version:
`#include <math.h>`

Complex Version:
`#include <complex.h>`

Description

The `acos` function calculates the arc cosine of the value specified in the `x` argument. For the real version, the `x` argument must range between –1 and 1. If the `x` argument is out of this range, NAN (not-a-number) is returned by the `acos` function and the global variable `errno` is set to EDOM, for domain error.

The arc cosine is calculated as follows for the complex version:

```
acos(z) = -i log(z + i sqrt(1-z^2))
```

Value(s) Returned

Real Version : A value in the range of 0 to pi is returned when the `x` argument ranges between –1 and 1.
Complex Version : The arc cosine of the value is returned.

Related Function(s)

`asin` : calculates the arc sine
`atan` : calculates the arc tangent
`cos` : calculates the cosine

Example

In the following example, `acos` calculates the arc cosine of .75.

```
#include <stdio.h>
#include <math.h>

int main (void)
{
double calc_value;

clrscr();
calc_value = acos (.75);
printf ("Arc cosine of .75 is %lf\n",calc_value);

getch();
return 0;
}
```

arg

DOS UNIX ANSI C C++

Syntax

```
double arg(complex x);
```

`complex x;` *Number in complex plane*

Function The `arg` function determines the angle of a number in the complex plane.

File(s) to Include `#include <complex.h>`

Description The `arg` function determines the angle, in radians, of the number in the complex plane specified in the `x` argument. The positive real axis has angle 0; the positive imaginary axis has angle pi.

The `arg` function is equivalent to

```
atan2 (imag(x),real(x))
```

Value(s) Returned The angle, in radians, of the number in the complex plane is returned.

Related Function(s)

`complex` : creates complex numbers
`norm` : returns the square of the absolute value
`polar` : returns a complex number with a given magnitude and angle

Example In the following example, `arg` determines the angle of the given complex value.

```
#include <complex.h>
#include <iostream.h>
#include <conio.h>

int main (void)
{
complex z;
double angle;

clrscr();
z = complex (1.5,4.2);
angle = arg(z);
```

continues

```
cout << "z = " << z << "\n";
cout << "angle (radians) = " << angle << "\n";

return 0;
}
```

asin

DOS	UNIX	ANSI C	C++

Syntax Real Version:

```
double asin(double x);
```

`double x;` *Input value*

Complex Version:

```
complex asin(complex x);
```

`complex x;` *Input value*

Function The `asin` function calculates the arc sine.

File(s) to Include Real Version:

```
#include <math.h>
```

Complex Version:

```
#include <complex.h>
```

Description The `asin` function calculates the arc sine of the value specified in the `x` argument. For the real version, arguments must range between –1 and 1. If the `x` argument is outside this range, the `asin` function returns NAN (not-a-number) and the global variable `errno` is set to EDOM, for domain error.

The complex version uses the following formula to calculate the arc sine:

```
asin(z) =  i * log(i*z + sqrt(1 z^2))
```

Value(s) Returned Real Version : A value in the range of –pi/2 to pi/2 is returned when the `x` argument ranges between –1 and 1.

Complex Version: The arc sine of the value is returned.

Related Function(s)

`acos` : calculates the arc cosine
`atan` : calculates the arc tangent
`sin` : calculates the sine

Example In the following example, `asin` calculates the arc sine of .75.

```
#include <stdio.h>
#include <math.h>
#include <conio.h>

int main (void)
{
double calc_value;

clrscr();
calc_value = asin (.75);
printf ("Arc sine of .75 is %lf\n",calc_value);

return 0;
}
```

atan

DOS | UNIX | ANSI C | C++

Syntax Real Version:

```
double atan(double x);
```

`double x;` *Input value*

Complex Version:

```
complex atan(complex x);
```

`complex x;` *Input value*

Function The `atan` function calculates the arc tangent of a value.

File(s) to Include Real Version:

```
#include <math.h>
```

Complex Version:

```
#include <complex.h>
```

Description The `atan` function calculates the arc tangent of the value specified in the `x` argument. For the complex version, the arc tangent is determined using the following formula:

```
atan(z) = -0.5 i log((1 + iz)/(1 - iz))
```

Value(s) Returned

Real Version : A value ranging from –pi/2 to pi/2 is returned.

Complex Version : The value, as determined using the formula shown previously, is returned.

Related Function(s)

`acos` : calculates the arc cosine of a value
`asin` : calculates the arc sine of a value
`atan2` : calculates the arc tangent of a value
`tan` : calculates the tangent of a value

Example In the following example, `atan` determines the arc tangent of .75.

```
#include <stdio.h>
#include <math.h>
#include <conio.h>

int main (void)
{
double calc_value;

clrscr();
calc_value = atan (.75);
printf ("Arc tangent of .75 is %lf\n",calc_value);

return 0;
}
```

---

atan2

DOS | UNIX | ANSI C | C++

Syntax `double atan2(double x, double y);`

`double x;` *Numerator for value*
`double y;` *Denominator for value*

Function The `atan2` function calculates the arc tangent of `x` divided by `y`.

File(s) to Include `#include <math.h>`

Description The `atan2` function calculates the arc tangent of the value resulting from the division of the value specified in the `x` argument by the value specified in the `y` argument.

Value(s) Returned A value ranging from –pi to pi is returned.

Related Function(s)
`acos` : calculates the arc cosine of a value
`asin` : calculates the arc sine of a value
`atan` : calculates the arc tangent of a value
`tan` : calculates the tangent of a value

Example In the following example, `atan2` determines the arc tangent of 3.0/4.0.

```
#include <stdio.h>
#include <math.h>
#include <conio.h>

int main (void)
{
double calc_value;

clrscr();
calc_value = atan2 (3.0,4.0);
printf ("Arc tangent of 3.0 / 4.0 is
  %lf\n",calc_value);
return 0;
}
```

atof

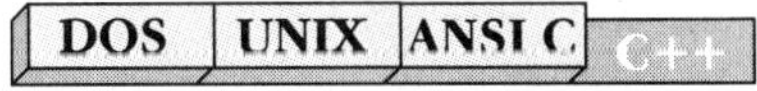

Syntax `double atof(const char *str);`

`const char *str;` *String to convert*

Function The `atof` function converts a string to a floating-point value.

File(s) to Include `#include <stdlib.h>`
or
`#include <math.h>`

Description The `atof` function converts the string pointed to by the `str` argument to a double floating-point value. The character string must be the character representation of a floating-point number and must follow the format shown as follows. Conversion ends when an unrecognized character is encountered.

[whitespace] [sign] [ddd] [.] [ddd] [e | E[sign]ddd]

in which

[whitespace] = an optional string of tabs and spaces
[sign] = the sign of the value
[ddd] = a string of digits on either or both sides of the decimal
[.] = the decimal
[e | E[sign]ddd] = the exponential notation of the value

Note: +INF and –INF, for plus and minus infinity, and +NAN and –NAN, for not-a-number, are recognized by the `atof` function.

Value(s) Returned The double floating-point value of the string is returned unless there is an overflow.

Related Function(s)
`atoi` : converts a string to an integer
`atol` : converts a string to a long value
`strtod` : converts a string to a double value

Example The following example converts the value in the `string` argument to a floating-point value.

```
#include <stdio.h>
#include <stdlib.h>

int main (void)
{
float value;
char *string = "532.5596";

clrscr();
value = atof(string);
printf ("Floating-point value = %3.4f\n",value);
```

```
printf ("String = %s\n",string);

return 0;
}
```

atoi

DOS | UNIX | ANSI C | C++

Syntax

```
int atoi(const char *str);

const char *str;          String to convert
```

Function The `atoi` function converts a string to an integer value.

File(s) to Include `#include <stdlib.h>`

Description The `atoi` function converts the string pointed to by the `str` argument to an integer value. The string must be the character representation of an integer value and must follow the format shown as follows. Conversion ends when the first unrecognized character is encountered.

[whitespace] [sign] [ddd]

in which

[whitespace] = an optional string of tabs and spaces
[sign] = an optional sign for the value
[ddd] = the string of digits

Value(s) Returned The integer value of the string is returned when `atoi` is successful. If the `atoi` function is unable to convert the string, a 0 is returned.

Related Function(s)

`atof` : converts a string to a floating-point value
`atol` : converts a string to a long value

Example The following example converts the value in the `string` argument to an integer value.

```
#include <stdlib.h>
#include <stdio.h>
```

continues

```
int main (void)
{
int value;
char *string = "8726";

clrscr();
value = atoi (string);
printf ("Integer value = %d\n",value);
printf ("String = %s\n",string);

return 0;
}
```

atol

DOS | UNIX | ANSI C | C++

Syntax `long atol(const char *str);`

`oconst char *str;` *String to convert*

Function The `atol` function converts a string to a long value.

File(s) to Include `#include <stdlib.h>`

Description The `atol` function converts the string pointed to by the `str` argument to a long value. The string must be the character representation of an integer value and must follow the format shown as follows. Conversion ends when the first unrecognized character is encountered.

[whitespace] [sign] [ddd]

in which

[whitespace] = an optional string of tabs and spaces
[sign] = the optional sign for the following digits
[ddd] = a string of digits

Value(s) Returned The value of the converted string is returned when the `atol` function is successful. If the string cannot be converted, `atol` returns a 0.

Related Function(s)

`atof` : converts a string to a floating-point value
`atoi` : converts a string to an integer value

Example The following example converts the value in the string argument to a long value.

```
#include <stdlib.h>
#include <stdio.h>

int main (void)
{
long value;
char *string = "45332754";

clrscr();
value = atol(string);
printf ("String = %s\n",string);
printf ("Value = %ld\n",value);

return 0;
}
```

bcd

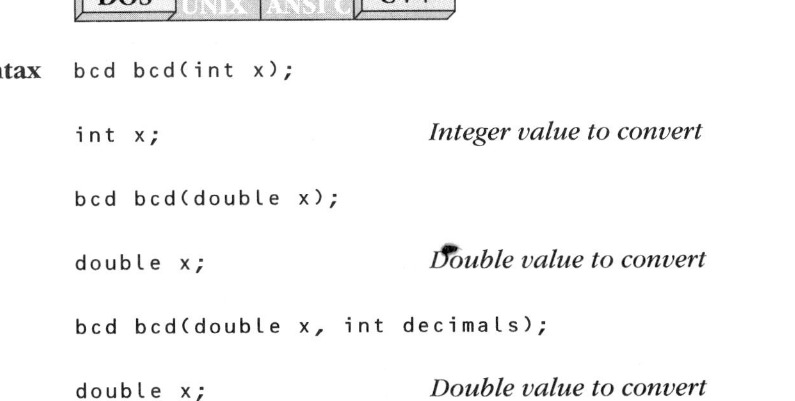

Syntax

```
bcd bcd(int x);
```

`int x;`	*Integer value to convert*

```
bcd bcd(double x);
```

`double x;`	*Double value to convert*

```
bcd bcd(double x, int decimals);
```

`double x;`	*Double value to convert*
`int decimals;`	*Number of places after decimal*

Function The `bcd` function converts a value to binary coded decimal (BCD).

File(s) to Include `#include <bcd.h>`

Description The `bcd` function converts the value specified in the `x` argument to binary coded decimal (BCD). The `decimals` argument is optional and specifies the number of digits desired after the decimal. BCD numbers range from $1x10^{-125}$ to $1x10^{125}$ and carry 17-decimal digits precision.

Value(s) Returned The converted value is returned.

Related Function(s) `real` : converts a BCD number back to float, double, or long double

Example In the following example, `bcd` converts 15.34 to binary coded decimal.

```
#include <stdio.h>
#include <bcd.h>
#include <conio.h>
#include <iostream.h>

int main (void)
{
bcd calc_value;

clrscr();
calc_value = bcd (15.34,2);
cout << "The BCD of 15.34 is " << calc_value <<
  "\n";

return 0;
}
```

cabs

DOS | UNIX | ANSI C | C++

Syntax `double cabs(struct complex z);`

`complex z;` *Input value*

Function The `cabs` macro calculates the absolute value of a complex number.

File(s) to Include `#include <math.h>`

Description The `cabs` macro calculates the absolute value of the complex number stored in the structure of type `complex`. The complex structure is as follows:

```
struct complex
{
double x, y;
};
```

This function is equivalent to the following:

```
sqrt(z.x * z.x + z.y * z.y)
```

Value(s) Returned The absolute value of `z`, a double value, is returned when successful. On overflow, `HUGE_VAL` is returned and the global variable `errno` is set to ERANGE, for result out of range.

Related Function(s)

`abs` : determines the absolute value
`fabs` : determines the absolute value of a floating point number
`labs` : determines the absolute value of a long value

Example In the following example, `cabs` determines the absolute value of the complex number in the `comp` structure.

```
#include <stdio.h>
#include <math.h>
#include <conio.h>

int main (void)
{
struct complex comp;
double calc_value;

clrscr();
comp.x = 3.2;
comp.y = 2.1;
calc_value = cabs (comp);
printf ("Absolute value of the complex number is
        %lf\n", calc_value);

return 0;
}
```

ceil

DOS | UNIX | ANSI C | C++

Syntax `double ceil(double x);`

`double x;` *Value to round*

Function The `ceil` function rounds a value up.

File(s) to Include `#include <math.h>`

Description The `ceil` function rounds the value specified in the `x` argument up to the next largest integer.

Value(s) Returned The rounded value, as a double, is returned.

Related Function(s) `floor` : rounds a value down

Example The following example rounds the value 12.34 up.

```
#include <stdio.h>
#include <conio.h>
#include <math.h>

int main (void)
{
double rounded_val;

clrscr();
rounded_val = ceil (12.34);
printf ("12.34 rounded up = %lf \n", rounded_val);

return 0;
}
```

_clear87

DOS | UNIX | ANSI C | C++

Syntax `unsigned int _clear87(void);`

Function The `_clear87` function clears the floating-point status word.

File(s) to Include `#include <float.h>`

Description The `_clear87` function clears the combination of the 80x87 status word and the conditions detected by the 80x87 exception handler. This combination is referred to as the floating-point status word.

Value(s) Returned The returned value indicates the floating-point status before calling the `_clear87` function.

Related Function(s)

`_control87` : gets or modifies the floating-point control word

`_status87` : gets the status of the 80x87

Example The following example clears the floating-point status word and prints the status before and after the call to the `_clear87` function.

```
#include <stdio.h>
#include <conio.h>
#include <float.h>

int main (void)
{
clrscr();

printf ("Status before clear = %X\n",
 _status87()); _clear87();
printf ("Status after clear = %X\n", _status87());

return 0;
}
```

complex

DOS | UNIX | ANSI C | C++

Syntax

```
complex complex(double real, double imag);
```

`double real;` *Real part*
`double imag;` *Imaginary part*

Function The `complex` function creates a complex number from two values.

File(s) to Include `#include <complex.h>`

Description The `complex` function creates a complex number from the values in the `real` and `imag` arguments. This function is the constructor for the C++ class `complex`. The `complex.h` header file overloads the `+`, `-`, `*`, `/`, `+=`, `-=`, `*=`, `/=`, `=`, `==`, and `!=` operators. Therefore, complex numbers can be used with expressions containing integers, doubles, longs, and so forth.

Value(s) Returned The complex number is returned.

Related Function(s)

`conj` : returns the complex conjugate of a complex number
`imag` : returns the imaginary part of a real number
`real` : returns the real part of an imaginary number

Example The following example displays the real and imaginary parts of the defined complex number.

```
#include <stdio.h>
#include <conio.h>
#include <iostream.h>
#include <complex.h>

int main (void)
{
complex comp_value;

clrscr();
comp_value = complex (3.1, 2.4);
cout << "Real part : " << real(comp_value) <<
  "\n";
```

```
cout << "Imag part : " << imag(comp_value) <<
  "\n";

return 0;
}
```

conj

Syntax

```
complex conj(complex x);
```

`complex x;` *Complex number*

Function The `conj` function determines the complex conjugate of a complex number.

File(s) to Include `#include <complex.h>`

Description The `conj` function calculates the complex conjugate of the complex number specified in the `x` argument. This function is equivalent to

```
complex (real(x), -imag(x))
```

Value(s) Returned The complex conjugate of the specified complex number is returned.

Related Function(s)

`complex` : creates a complex number from two values
`imag` : returns the imaginary part of a complex value
`real` : returns the real part of a complex value

Example The following example displays the complex conjugate of the specified complex number.

```
#include <stdio.h>
#include <conio.h>
#include <complex.h>
#include <iostream.h>

int main (void)
{
complex comp_num;
```

continues

```
clrscr();
comp_num = complex (4.2, 1.3);
cout << "Complex conjugate of complex 4.2, 1.3 is"
     << conj(comp_num) << "\n";

return 0;
}
```

_control87

DOS | UNIX | ANSI C | C++

Syntax

```
unsigned int _control87(unsigned int newcw,
                        unsigned int mask);
```

`unsigned int newcw;`	*New control word*
`int mask;`	*For comparison*

Function The `_control87` function retrieves or changes the floating-point control word.

File(s) to Include `#include <float.h>`

Description The `_control87` function retrieves and possibly modifies the floating-point control word. The floating-point control word, type `unsigned int`, specifies the precision, infinity, and rounding modes for floating-point values. The `newcw` and `mask` arguments evaluate and modify the floating-point control word. The `mask` argument identifies whether each bit in the control word will change. A 1 in the `mask` argument indicates that the corresponding bit in the control word will change. When a 1 bit is encountered in the `mask` argument, the corresponding bit in the control word is set to the corresponding bit in the `newcw` argument. Several examples follow.

Control Word	1010	0011	1111	0100
`mask`	0000	0100	1101	1111
`newcw`	1110	1100	1001	0011
New Control Word	1010	0111	1011	0011

Value(s) Returned The returned value represents the new control word.

Related Function(s)
`_clear87` : clears the floating-point status word
`_status87` : gets the floating-point status

Example The following example calls the `_control87` function with values 0. Therefore, the floating-point control word will not change.

```
#include <stdio.h>
#include <conio.h>
#include <float.h>

int main (void)
{
clrscr();
printf ("Status before _control87 call : %X\n",
  _status87());
_control87 (0,0);
printf ("Status after _control87 call : %x\n",
  _status87());

return 0;
}
```

cos

DOS	UNIX	ANSI C	C++

Syntax Real Version:

```
double cos(double x);

double x;                    Input value
```

Complex Version:

```
complex cos(complex x);

complex x;                   Input value
```

Function The `cos` function calculates the cosine of a value.

File(s) to Include Real Version:

```
#include <math.h>
```

Complex Version:

```
#include <complex.h>
```

Description The `cos` function calculates the cosine of the value, expressed in radians, specified in the `x` argument.

The cosine for a complex value is determined by the following formula:

```
cos(z) = (exp(i*z) + exp( i*z))/2
```

Value(s) Returned

Real Version	:	The cosine value, ranging from –1 to 1, is returned.
Complex Version	:	The calculated cosine value is returned.

Related Function(s)

`acos`	:	calculates the arc cosine of a value
`sin`	:	calculates the sine of a value
`tan`	:	calculates the tangent of a value

Example The following example calculates the cosine of .75 using the `cos` function.

```
#include <stdio.h>
#include <math.h>
#include <conio.h>

int main (void)
{
double calc_value;

clrscr();
calc_value = cos (.75);
printf ("Cosine of .75 is %lf\n",calc_value);

return 0;
}
```

---

cosh

DOS	UNIX	ANSI C	C++

Syntax Real Version:

```
double cosh(double x);

double x;
```

Input value

Complex Version:

```
complex cosh(complex x);

complex x;
```

Input value

Function The `cosh` function calculates the hyperbolic cosine of a value.

File(s) to Include Real Version:

```
#include <math.h>
```

Complex Version:

```
#include <complex.h>
```

Description The `cosh` function computes the hyperbolic cosine of the value specified in the `x` argument. The following formula is used when calculating the hyperbolic cosine of a complex number:

```
cosh(z) = (exp(z) + exp( z))/2
```

Value(s) Returned The hyperbolic cosine of the `x` argument is returned when successful. If overflow occurs, `HUGE_VAL` is returned and the global variable `errno` is set to ERANGE, for result out of range.

Related Function(s)
`acos` : calculates the arc cosine of a value
`cos` : calculates the cosine of a value

Example The following example displays the hyperbolic cosine of .75.

```
#include <stdio.h>
#include <math.h>
#include <conio.h>

int main (void)
{
double calc_value;

clrscr();
calc_value = cosh (.75);
printf ("Hyperbolic cosine of .75 is
  %lf\n",calc_value);

return 0;
}
```

div

DOS UNIX ANSI C C++

Syntax

```
div_t div(int numer, int denom);
```

`int numer;`	*Numerator*
`int denom;`	*Denominator*

Function The `div` function returns the quotient and remainder from the division of two integers.

File(s) to Include `#include <stdlib.h>`

Description The `div` function divides the numerator defined in the `numer` argument by the denominator defined in the `denom` argument, and returns the quotient and remainder in a structure of type `div_t`. The `div_t` structure is as follows:

```
typedef struct
{
int quot;            /* quotient */
int rem;             /* remainder */
} div_t;
```

Value(s) Returned The `div` function returns the remainder and quotient in a structure of type `div_t`.

Related Function(s) `ldiv` : divides two long values

Example The following example calculates and displays the quotient and remainder from the division of two integers.

```
#include <stdlib.h>
#include <stdio.h>

int main (void)
{

div_t result;

clrscr();
result = div (16,4);
printf ("16 divided by 4 :\n");
```

```
printf ("Quotient : %d\n",result.quot);
printf ("Remainder : %d\n",result.rem);

return 0;
}
```

ecvt

DOS | UNIX | ANSI C | C++

Syntax

```
char *ecvt(double value, int ndig, int *dec, int
           *sign);
```

`double value;`	*Value to convert*
`int ndig;`	*Number of digits*
`int *dec;`	*Decimal point position*
`int *sign;`	*Sign of the value*

Function The `ecvt` function converts a floating-point number to a string.

File(s) to Include `#include <stdlib.h>`

Description The `ecvt` function converts the floating-point value specified in the `value` argument to a null-terminated string. The length of the string is specified with the `ndig` argument. The `dec` argument is a pointer to the position of the decimal point relative to the beginning of the resulting string (the string has no decimal). The `sign` argument points to the value indicating the sign of the value. A zero indicates positive; a nonzero value indicates negative.

Value(s) Returned The pointer to the converted string is returned by the `ecvt` function.

Related Function(s)
`fcvt` : converts a floating-point value to a string
`gcvt` : converts a floating-point value to a string

Example The following example converts the floating-point value to a string.

```
#include <stdlib.h>
#include <stdio.h>

int main (void)
{
char *string;
double value = 12.756;
int dec, sign, ndig = 8;

clrscr();
string = ecvt (value,ndig,&dec,&sign);
printf ("Value = 12.756\n");
printf ("Significant digits = 8\n");
printf ("String = %s\n", string);
printf ("Decimal point position = %d\n", dec);
printf ("Sign = %d\n", sign);

return 0;
}
```

exp

DOS | UNIX | ANSI C | C++

Syntax Real Version:

```
double exp(double x);
```

`double x;` *Input value*

Complex Version:

```
complex exp(complex x);
```

`complex x;` *Input value*

Function The `exp` function calculates the exponential e^x.

File(s) to Include Real Version:

```
#include <math.h>
```

Complex Version;

```
#include <complex.h>
```

Description The `exp` function calculates the exponential value of e^x. For the complex version, the exponential calculation is performed with the following formula.

```
exp(x + yi) = exp(x)(cos(y) + i sin(y))
```

Value(s) Returned The calculated value is returned when successful. On overflow, `HUGE_VAL` is returned and the global variable `errno` is set to ERANGE, for result out of range. On underflow, 0.0 is returned.

Related Function(s)
`pow` : calculates x^y
`pow10` : calculates 10^x

Example The following example displays the calculated value of e^2.

```
#include <stdio.h>
#include <math.h>
#include <conio.h>

int main (void)
{
double calc_value;

clrscr();
calc_value = exp (2.0);
printf ("Calculated value is %lf\n",calc_value);

return 0;
}
```

fabs

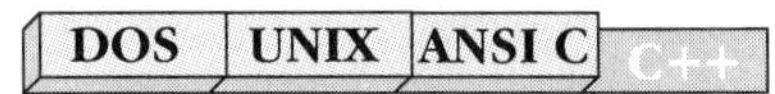

Syntax `double fabs(double x);`

`double x;` *Input value*

Function The `fabs` function determines the absolute value of a floating-point number.

File(s) to Include `#include <math.h>`

Description The `fabs` function calculates the absolute value of the value specified in the `x` argument.

Value(s) Returned The absolute value of the `x` argument is returned.

Related Function(s)
`abs` : returns the absolute value of a number
`cabs` : returns the absolute value of a complex number
`labs` : returns the absolute value of a long number

Example In the following example, `fabs` computes the absolute value of –23.345.

```
#include <stdio.h>
#include <conio.h>
#include <math.h>

int main (void)
{
double abs_value;

clrscr();
abs_value = fabs ( 23.345);
printf ("The absolute value of  23.345 is
%f\n",abs_value);

return 0;
}
```

fcvt

DOS | UNIX | ANSI C | C++

Syntax
```
char *fcvt(double value, int ndig, int *dec, int
          *sign);
```

`double value;`	*Value to convert*
`int ndig;`	*Number of digits in string*
`int *dec;`	*Position of decimal*
`int *sign;`	*Sign of value*

Function The fcvt function converts a floating-point value to a string.

File(s) to Include #include <stdlib.h>

Description The fcvt function converts the floating-point number described by the value argument to a null-terminated string with the length specified in the ndig argument. The dec argument defines the position of the decimal relative to the beginning of the string. When the dec argument is negative, the decimal is placed to the left of the returned digits. The sign argument points to the word representing the sign of the value argument. When the value argument is negative, the word pointed to by the sign argument is a nonzero value. When the value argument is positive, the word pointed to by the sign argument is 0.

Value(s) Returned The pointer to the resulting string is returned.

Related Function(s)
ecvt : converts a floating-point value to a string
gcvt : converts a floating-point value to a string

Example The following example converts the floating-point value to a string and displays both.

```
#include <stdlib.h>
#include <stdio.h>

int main (void)
{
char *string;
double value = 54.7259;
int dec, sign, ndig = 7;

clrscr();
string = fcvt(value,ndig,&dec,&sign);
printf ("Value = 54.7259\n");
printf ("Significant digits = 7\n");
printf ("String = %s\n", string);
printf ("Decimal position = %d\n",dec);
printf ("Sign = %d\n",sign);

return 0;
}
```

floor

DOS | UNIX | ANSI C | C++

Syntax

```
double floor(double x);

double x;                    Value to round
```

Function The `floor` function rounds the specified value down.

File(s) to Include `#include <math.h>`

Description The `floor` function rounds the value specified in the `x` argument down to the largest integer not greater than the `x` argument.

Value(s) Returned The rounded value is returned.

Related Function(s) `ceil` : rounds a value up

Example The following example rounds the value 31.743 down using the `floor` function.

```
#include <stdio.h>
#include <conio.h>
#include <math.h>

int main (void)
{
double floor_value;

clrscr();
floor_value = floor (31.743);
printf ("31.743 rounded down is
  %lf\n",floor_value);

return 0;
}
```

fmod

DOS UNIX ANSI C C++

Syntax

```
double fmod(double x, double y);

double x;                    Value 1
double y;                    Value 2
```

Function The `fmod` function calculates `x` modulo `y`.

File(s) to Include `#include <math.h>`

Description The `fmod` function calculates `x` modulo `y`, which is the remainder `f`, in which x=ay+f for an integer a and 0 <= f < y.

Value(s) Returned The remainder is returned except when y = 0. When y = 0, a 0 is returned.

Related Function(s) `modf` : splits a double into integer and fractional parts

Example The following example displays the calculated value of 3.0 modulo 4.0.

```
#include <stdio.h>
#include <conio.h>
#include <math.h>

int main (void)
{
double mod_value;

clrscr();
mod_value = fmod (3.0,4.0);
printf ("3.0 modulo 4.0 is %lf\n",mod_value);

return 0;
}
```

_fpreset

DOS UNIX ANSI C C++

Syntax `void _fpreset(void);`

Function The `_fpreset` function reinitializes the floating-point math package.

File(s) to Include `#include <float.h>`

Description The `_fpreset` function reinitializes the floating-point math package. It is often necessary to use this function with the `system`, `exec...`, or `spawn...` functions because in the process of opening a child process, the parent process's floating-point state may be changed.

Value(s) Returned There is no return value.

Related Function(s)

`exec...` : loads and executes a child process
`spawn...` : creates and executes a child process
`system` : issues a DOS command

Example The following example displays the status before and after the call to `_fpreset`.

```
#include <stdio.h>
#include <conio.h>
#include <float.h>

int main (void)
{
clrscr();
printf ("Status before _fpreset call : %X\n",
  _status87());
  _fpreset ();
printf ("Status after _fpreset call : %X\n",
  _status87());

return 0;
}
```

frexp

DOS | UNIX | ANSI C | C++

Syntax `double frexp(double x, int *exponent);`

`double x;`	*Input value*
`int *exponent;`	*Pointer to returned exponent value*

Function The `frexp` function divides a number into a mantissa and an exponent.

File(s) to Include `#include <math.h>`

Description The `frexp` function determines the mantissa value and integer value which, when applied to the following formula, will equal the value specified in the `x` argument. The mantissa m is returned from the function while the `exponent` argument points to the exponent `n` value.

$$m \times n^2$$

Value(s) Returned The mantissa is returned.

Related Function(s)

`exp` : calculates the exponential e^x

`ldexp` : calculates $x * 2^y$

Example In the following example, `frexp` calculates the mantissa and exponent of 4.6.

```
#include <stdio.h>
#include <conio.h>
#include <math.h>

int main (void)
{
int ex;
double man;

clrscr();
man = frexp (4.6,&ex);
printf ("Mantissa of 4.6 : %lf\n",man);
printf ("Exponent of 4.6 : %d\n",ex);

return 0;
}
```

gcvt

DOS | UNIX | ANSI C | C++

Syntax

```
char *gcvt(double value, int ndec, char *buf);
```

`double value;`	*Value to convert*
`int ndec;`	*Number of significant digits*
`char *buf;`	*Resulting string*

Function The `gcvt` function converts a floating-point value to a string.

File(s) to Include `#include <stdlib.h>`

Description The `gcvt` function converts the floating-point value defined in the `value` argument to a null-terminated ASCII string, and stores the string at the location pointed to by the `buf` argument. The resulting string contains the number of significant digits specified in the `ndec` argument and is in FORTRAN F format whenever possible. When `gcvt` is unable to use FORTRAN F format, `printf` E format is used.

Value(s) Returned The `gcvt` function returns the address of the string pointed to by the `buf` argument.

Related Function(s)

`ecvt` : converts a floating-point number to a string
`fcvt` : converts a floating-point number to a string

Example The following example converts the floating-point value to a string and displays both.

```
#include <stdlib.h>
#include <stdio.h>

int main (void)
{
char string[20];
double value = 54.7259;
int ndec = 4;

clrscr();
gcvt(value,ndec,string);
printf ("Value = 54.7259\n");
printf ("Significant digits = 4\n");
```

```
printf ("String = %s\n", string);

return 0;
}
```

hypot

DOS UNIX ANSI C C++

Syntax

```
double hypot(double x, double y);

double x;                    Side one
double y;                    Side two
```

Function The `hypot` function determines the hypotenuse of a right triangle.

File(s) to Include `#include <math.h>`

Description The `hypot` function calculates the hypotenuse of a right triangle with the length of the two perpendicular sides specified in the `x` and `y` arguments. The hypotenuse is calculated as follows:

```
z^2 = x^2 + y^2        where z >= 0
```

Value(s) Returned The hypotenuse is returned when successful. When unsuccessful, `HUGE_VAL` is returned and the global variable `errno` is set to ERANGE, for result out of range.

Related Function(s) `sqrt` : calculates the square root of a number

Example In the following example, `hypot` calculates the hypotenuse of a right triangle with perpendicular sides of length 3.0 and 4.0.

```
#include <stdio.h>
#include <conio.h>
#include <math.h>

int main (void)
{
double hyp;
```

continues

```
clrscr();
hyp = hypot (3.0,4.0);
printf ("Hypotenuse with sides 3.0, 4.0 :
  %lf\n",hyp);

return 0;
}
```

imag

Syntax `double imag(complex x);`

`complex x;` *Complex value*

Function The `imag` function returns the imaginary part of a complex number.

File(s) to Include `#include <complex.h>`

Description The `imag` function retrieves the imaginary part of the complex number specified in the `x` argument. A complex number consists of an imaginary and a real part.

Value(s) Returned The imaginary part of the complex number is returned.

Related Function(s)
`comple` : creates a complex number
`real` : returns the real part of a complex number

Example The following example displays the real and imaginary parts of the complex number.

```
#include <stdio.h>
#include <conio.h>
#include <iostream.h>
#include <complex.h>

int main (void)
{
complex c_val;
```

```
clrscr();
c_val = complex (3.0,2.3);
cout << "Real part of complex c_val is :" << real
  (c_val) << "\n";
cout << "Imag part of complex c_val is :" << imag
  (c_val) << "\n";

return 0;
}
```

itoa

DOS | UNIX | ANSI C | C++

Syntax

```
char *itoa(int value, char *string, int radix);
```

`int value;`	*Value to convert*
`char *string;`	*Resulting string*
`int radix;`	*Base used for conversion*

Function The `itoa` function converts an integer value to a string.

File(s) to Include `#include <stdlib.h>`

Description The `itoa` function converts the integer value defined in the `value` argument to a null-terminated string. The converted string is stored in the location pointed to by the `string` argument. The `radix` argument is an integer value which specifies the base (ranging from 2 to 36) used in converting the `value` argument.

Value(s) Returned The pointer to the resulting string is returned.

Related Function(s)

`ltoa` : converts a long value to a string
`ultoa` : converts an unsigned long value to a string

Example The following example converts the integer value to a string and displays both.

```
#include <stdlib.h>
#include <stdio.h>

int main (void)
{
int value = 8377;
char string[20];

clrscr();
itoa (value,string,10);
printf ("Value = 8377\n");
printf ("String = %s\n",string);
printf ("Base = 10\n");

return 0;
}
```

labs

DOS | UNIX | ANSI C | C++

Syntax `long int labs(long int x);`

`long int x;` *Value to evaluate*

Function The `labs` function determines the absolute value of a long value.

File(s) to Include `#include <stdlib.h>` or `#include <math.h>`

Description The `labs` function computes the absolute value of the long value value specified in the `x` argument.

Value(s) Returned The absolute value of `x` is returned.

Related Function(s)
`abs` : returns the absolute value of a number
`cabs` : returns the absolute value of a complex number
`fabs` : returns the absolute value of a floating-point number

Example The following example returns the absolute value of the long value.

```
#include <stdio.h>
#include <stdlib.h>

int main (void)
{
long value =  372534L;
long absvalue;

clrscr ();
absvalue = labs(value);
printf ("Initial value : %ld\n",value);
printf ("Absolute value : %ld\n",absvalue);
return 0;
}
```

ldexp

DOS | UNIX | ANSI C | C++

Syntax

```
double ldexp(double x, int exp);

double x;                  Base value
int exp;                   Exponential value
```

Function The `ldexp` function returns the calculated value of $x * 2^{exp}$.

File(s) to Include `#include <math.h>`

Description The `ldexp` function calculates the formula $x * 2^{exp}$. The `x` variable in the formula is defined in the `x` argument of the function. Similarly, the `exp` variable in the formula is defined in the `exp` argument of the function.

Value(s) Returned The calculated value is returned.

Related Function(s)

`exp` : calculates the exponential e^x

`frexp` : splits a value into a mantissa and exponent

Example The following example displays the results of the call to `ldexp`.

```
#include <stdio.h>
#include <conio.h>
#include <math.h>

int main (void)
{
double calc_val;

clrscr();
calc_val = ldexp (2.0,3.0);
printf ("2.0 * 2^3.0 = %lf\n",calc_val);

return 0;
}
```

---

ldiv

DOS UNIX ANSI C C++

Syntax `ldiv_t ldiv(long int numer, long int denom);`

`long int numer;`	*Numerator*
`long int denom;`	*Denominator*

Function The `ldiv` function returns the quotient and remainder from the division of two long values.

File(s) to Include `#include <stdlib.h>`

Description The `ldiv` function divides the numerator defined in the `numer` argument by the denominator defined in the `denom` argument. The quotient and remainder are returned in a structure of type `ldiv_t`. The `ldiv_t` structure is as follows:

```
typedef struct
{
long int quot;        /* quotient  */
long int rem;         /* remainder */
} ldiv _t;
```

Value(s) Returned The quotient and remainder are returned in a structure of type `ldiv_t`.

Related Function(s) `div` : divides two integer values

Example The following example calculates and displays the quotient and remainder from the division of two long values.

```
#include <stdlib.h>
#include <stdio.h>

int main (void)
{

ldiv_t result;

clrscr();
result = ldiv (1600L,40L);
printf ("1600 divided by 40 :\n");
printf ("Quotient : %ld\n",result.quot);
printf ("Remainder : %ld\n",result.rem);

return 0;
}
```

log

DOS	UNIX	ANSI C	C++

Syntax Real Version:

```
double log(double x);

double x;                 Input value
```

Complex Version:

```
complex log(complex x);

complex x;                Input value
```

Function The `log` function calculates the natural log of the input value.

File(s) to Include Real Version:

```
#include <math.h>
```

Complex Version:

```
#include <complex.h>
```

Description The log function calculates the natural log of the value specified in the x argument. For the complex version, the following formula is used:

```
log(z) = log(abs(z)) + i arg(z)
```

Value(s) Returned

Real Version : The calculated value is returned when successful. When the x argument is less than zero, the global variable errno is set to EDOM, for domain error. When x is 0, HUGE_VAL is returned and the global variable errno is set to ERANGE, for result out of range.

Complex Version : The calculated value is returned.

Related Function(s)

complex : creates a complex number from two values
log10 : calculates the base 10 logarithm of a value

Example The following example calculates the natural logarithm of 2.3 using log.

```
#include <stdio.h>
#include <conio.h>
#include <math.h>

int main (void)
{
double calc_val;

clrscr();
calc_val = log (2.3);
printf ("log (2.3) = %lf\n",calc_val);

return 0;
}
```

log10

DOS | UNIX | ANSI C | C++

Syntax

Real Version:

```
double log10(double x);

double x;                    Input value
```

Complex Version:

```
complex log10(complex x);

complex x;                   Input value
```

Function

The `log10` function calculates the base 10 logarithm of the input value.

File(s) to Include

Real Version:

```
#include <math.h>
```

Complex Version:

```
#include <complex.h>
```

Description

The `log10` function calculates the base 10 logarithm of the value specified in the `x` argument. The following formula is used for the complex version:

```
log10(z) = log(z) / log(10)
```

Value(s) Returned

Real Version : The calculated value is returned when successful. If the value in the `x` argument is less than zero, the global variable `errno` is set to EDOM, for domain error. If the `x` argument is 0, `HUGE_VAL` is returned.

Complex Version: The calculated value is returned.

Related Function(s)

`complex` : creates a complex number from two values
`log` : calculates the natural logarithm of a value

Example

In the following example, `log10` calculates the base 10 logarithm of 2.3.

```
#include <stdio.h>
#include <conio.h>
#include <math.h>

int main (void)
{
double calc_val;

clrscr();
calc_val = log10 (2.3);
printf ("log10 (2.3) = %lf\n",calc_val);

return 0;
}
```

_lrotl

DOS | UNIX | ANSI C | C++

Syntax

```
unsigned long _lrotl(unsigned long val, int
                      count);

unsigned long val;        Value to rotate
int count;                Number of bits to rotate
```

Function The `_lrotl` function rotates an unsigned long value to the left.

File(s) to Include `#include <stdlib.h>`

Description The `_lrotl` function rotates the unsigned long value defined in the `val` argument to the left the number of bits specified in the `count` argument.

Value(s) Returned The rotated value is returned.

Related Function(s)
`_lrotr` : rotates an unsigned long value right
`_rotl` : rotates an unsigned integer left
`_rotr` : rotates an unsigned integer right

Example The following example rotates the unsigned long value left two bits.

```
#include <stdio.h>
#include <stdlib.h>

int main (void)
{
unsigned long rot_value;
unsigned long value = 500;
int shift_bits = 2;

clrscr ();
rot_value = _lrotl (value,shift_bits);
printf ("Initial Value : %lu\n",value);
printf ("Shifted Value : %lu\n",rot_value);

return 0;
}
```

_lrotr

DOS | UNIX | ANSI C | C++

Syntax

```
unsigned long _lrotr(unsigned long val, int
                                    count);
```

`unsigned long val;` *Value to rotate*
`int count;` *Number of bits to rotate*

Function The `_lrotr` function shifts an unsigned long value to the right.

File(s) to Include `#include <stdlib.h>`

Description The `_lrotr` function shifts the unsigned long value defined in the `val` argument to the right the number of bits specified in the `count` argument.

Value(s) Returned The rotated value is returned.

Related Function(s)

`_lrotl` : rotates an unsigned long value left
`_rotl` : rotates an unsigned integer left
`_rotr` : rotates an unsigned integer right

Example The following example rotates the unsigned long value to the right two bits.

```
#include <stdio.h>
#include <stdlib.h>

int main (void)
{
unsigned long rot_value;
unsigned long value = 500;
int shift_bits = 2;

clrscr ();
rot_value = _lrotr (value,shift_bits);
printf ("Initial Value : %lu\n",value);
printf ("Shifted Value : %lu\n",rot_value);

return 0;
}
```

ltoa

DOS | UNIX | ANSI C | C++

Syntax

```
char *ltoa(long value, char *string, int radix);
```

`long value;`	*Value to convert*
`char *string;`	*Resulting string*
`int radix;`	*Base for conversion*

Function The `ltoa` function converts a long value to a string.

File(s) to Include `#include <stdlib.h>`

Description The `ltoa` function converts the long value specified in the `value` argument to a null-terminated string. The resulting string is stored at the memory location pointed to by the `string` argument. The `radix` argument (ranging from 2 to 36) specifies the base used for the conversion.

Value(s) Returned The pointer to the resulting string is returned.

Related Function(s)
`itoa` : converts an integer to a string
`ultoa` : converts an unsigned long value to a string

Example The following example converts the long value to a string and displays both.

```
#include <stdlib.h>
#include <stdio.h>

int main (void)
{
long value = 99288377L;
char string[20];

clrscr();
ltoa (value,string,10);
printf ("Value = 99288377\n");
printf ("String = %s\n",string);
printf ("Base = 10\n");

return 0;
}
```

matherr

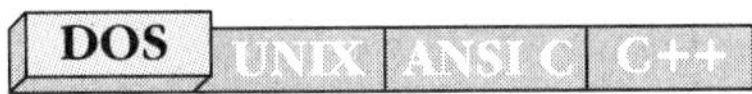

Syntax `int matherr(struct exception *e);`

`struct exception *e;` *Pointer to the* `exception` *structure*

Function The `matherr` function handles math errors and is user-modifiable.

File(s) to Include `#include <math.h>`

Description The `matherr` function traps domain and range errors generated by the math library. This function can be modified for custom error handling. If modifications are made, the new `matherr` function should return a 1 if the error is resolved and a 0 if the error cannot be resolved. The `exception` structure follows:

```
struct exception
    {
    int type;               /* type of error that
                               occurred */
    char *name;             /* pointer to name of
                               function generating
                               the error */
    double arg1, arg2;      /* arguments of the
                               function generating
                               the error */
    double retval;          /* return value of
                               matherr */
    };
```

The following constants are defined for possible math errors:

Constant	*Meaning*
DOMAIN	Argument was out of the domain of the function
SING	Argument would result in singularity
OVERFLOW	Argument would produce a value greater than MAXDOUBLE (defined in `values.h`)
UNDERFLOW	Argument would produce a value less than MINDOUBLE (defined in `values.h`)
TLOSS	Argument would produce a value with a total loss of significant digits

Value(s) Returned The default return value is 1. This occurs when the error is TLOSS or UNDERFLOW. The return value is 0 for other cases. When the return value is 0, the `errno` global variable is set to 0 and an error message is printed. When the return value is nonzero, the `errno` global variable is not set and no error message is printed.

Related Function(s) `perror` : prints a system error message

Example The following example demonstrates how the `matherr` function could be redefined to handle the `sqrt` DOMAIN problem.

```
#include <math.h>
#include <stdio.h>
```

```
#include <string.h>

int matherr (struct exception *x)
{
if (x->type == DOMAIN)
      {
      if (strcmp (x->name,"sqrt") == 0)
            {
            x->retval = sqrt( (x->arg1));
            return 1;
            }
      }
return 0;
}

int main (void)
{
double a, b;

a = -1.0;
b = sqrt(a);

printf ("Math error corrected : %lf\n",b);

return 0;
}
```

max

DOS UNIX ANSI C C++

Syntax `type) max (a,b);`

`(type) a;`	*First value*
`(type) b;`	*Second value*

Function The `max` macro returns the largest of two values.

File(s) to Include `#include <stdlib.h>`

Description The `max` macro compares the values passed in the `a` and `b` arguments and returns the largest of these values. The `a` argument, the `b` argument, and function declaration must all be the same type.

Value(s) Returned The largest number is returned.

Related Function(s) `min` : returns the smallest of two values

Example The following example returns the largest value from 13 and 11.

```
#include <stdio.h>
#include <conio.h>
#include <stdlib.h>

int main (void)
{
int biggest;
int a = 13;
int b = 11;

clrscr();
biggest =  max (a,b);
printf ("The biggest of 13 and 11 is :
  %d\n",biggest);

return 0;
}
```

---

min

DOS | UNIX | ANSI C | C++

Syntax `(type) min (a,b);`

`(type) a;`	*First value*
`(type) b;`	*Second value*

Function The `min` macro returns the smallest of two values.

File(s) to Include `#include <stdlib.h>`

Description The `min` macro compares the two values in the `a` and `b` argument and returns the smallest of the two values. The `a` argument, the `b` argument, and the function declaration must all be the same type.

Value(s) Returned The smallest value is returned.

Related Function(s) `max` : returns the largest of two values

Example The following example displays the smallest value from 13 and 11.

```
#include <stdio.h>
#include <conio.h>
#include <stdlib.h>

int main (void)
{
int smallest;
int a = 13;
int b = 11;

clrscr();
smallest =  min (a,b);
printf ("The smallest of 13 and 11 is :
  %d\n",smallest);

return 0;
}
```

modf

DOS | UNIX | ANSI C | C++

Syntax `double modf(double x, double *ipart);`

`double x;`	*Value to split*
`double *ipart;`	*Integer part*

Function The `modf` function divides a value of type `double` into its integer and fractional parts.

File(s) to Include `#include <math.h>`

Description The `modf` function divides the value specified in the `x` argument into its integer and fractional parts. The integer part is stored via the `ipart` argument whereas the fractional part is returned by the `modf` function.

Value(s) Returned The fractional part of the `x` argument is returned.

Related Function(s) `fmod` : calculates `x` modulo `y`

Example The following example displays the fractional and integer parts of 84.523.

```
#include <stdio.h>
#include <conio.h>
#include <math.h>

int main (void)
{
double frac, integer;

clrscr();
frac = modf (84.5231,&integer);
printf ("Fractional part of 84.5231 :
  %lf\n",frac);
printf ("Integer part of 84.5231 :
  %lf\n",integer);

return 0;
}
```

norm

Syntax `double norm(complex x);`

`complex x;` *Input value*

Function The `norm` function returns the square of the absolute value of the complex input value.

File(s) to Include `#include <complex.h>`

Description The `norm` function calculates and returns the square of the absolute value of the complex value specified in the `x` argument. The following formula is used for the `norm` function:

```
norm (x) returns real(x) * real(x) + imag(x) *
  imag(x)
```

Value(s) Returned The calculated value is returned. Note that this function can overflow when the real or imaginary parts of the complex value are large.

Related Function(s) `complex` : creates a complex number from two values

Example The following example displays the magnitude of the complex value using the `sqrt` and `norm` functions.

```
#include <stdio.h>
#include <conio.h>
#include <complex.h>
#include <iostream.h>

int main (void)
{
complex c_val;

clrscr();
c_val = complex (6.2,1.6);
cout << "Magnitude of c_val : " <<
  sqrt(norm(c_val)) << "\n";

return 0;
}
```

polar

DOS UNIX ANSI C C++

Syntax

```
complex polar(double mag, double angle);

double mag;                  Magnitude
double angle;                Angle
```

Function The `polar` function returns a complex number with the specified magnitude and angle.

File(s) to Include `#include <complex.h>`

Description The `polar` function returns a complex number with the magnitude specified in the `mag` argument and angle specified in the `angle` argument. The `polar` function is equivalent to the following formula:

```
complex(mag * cos(angle), mag * sin(angle))
```

Value(s) Returned The complex number is returned.

Related Function(s) `complex` : creates a complex number from two values

Example The following example displays the complex number created by `polar`.

```
#include <stdio.h>
#include <conio.h>
#include <complex.h>
#include <iostream.h>

int main (void)
{
complex c_val;

clrscr();
c_val = polar (6.2,1.6);
cout << "c_val : " << c_val << "\n";

return 0;
}
```

poly

DOS | UNIX | ANSI C | C++

Syntax

```
double poly(double x, int degree, double
            coeffs[]);
```

```
double x;              Base value
int degree;            Max degree
double coeffs[];       Coefficients of values
```

Function The poly function calculates the specified polynomial.

File(s) to Include `#include <math.h>`

Description The poly function describes a polynomial and returns the value of that polynomial. The following example explains the x, degree, and coeffs arguments.

```
double x = 3.0;
int degree = 3;
double coeffs [] = {1.0, 2.0, 3.0, 4.0};
```

With these arguments the polynomial would be

```
4.0*3^3 + 3.0*3^2 + 2.0*3 + 1.0
```

which represents

```
coeffs[3]x^3 + coeffs[2]x^2 + coeffs[1]x +
  coeffs[0]
```

Value(s) Returned The calculated value of the polynomial is returned.

Related Function(s) pow : calculates the value of x^y

Example The following example displays the result of the described polynomial.

```
#include <stdio.h>
#include <conio.h>
#include <math.h>

int main (void)
```

continues

```
{
double coeff[] = { 2.0,3.0,1.0,3.0};
double result;

clrscr();
result = poly (4.0,3,coeff);
printf ("3*4^3 + 1*4^2 + 3*4   2 = %lf\n",result);

return 0;
}
```

pow

DOS	UNIX	ANSI C	C++

Syntax Real Version:

```
double pow(double x, double y);

double x;                     Input value
double y;                     Power
```

Complex Version:

```
complex pow(complex x, complex y);
complex pow(complex x, double y);
complex pow(double x, complex y);

complex x;                    Input value
double x;                     Input value
complex y;                    Power
double y;                     Power
```

Function The `pow` function calculates the value of x^y.

File(s) to Include Real Version:

`#include <math.h>`

Complex Version:

`#include <complex.h>`

Description The `pow` function calculates the result of the value specified in the `x` argument raised to the power defined in the `y` argument. For the complex version, the following formula is used:

```
pow (base, expon) = exp(expon log (base))
```

Value(s) Returned

Real Version : The calculated value is returned when successful. If the result overflows, `HUGE_VAL` is returned and the global variable `errno` is set to ERANGE, for result out of range. If the `x` argument is less than 0, and `y` is not a whole number, the global variable `errno` is set to EDOM, for domain error. If both the `x` and `y` arguments are 0, 1 is returned.

Complex Version : The calculated value is returned when successful. If the result overflows, `HUGE_VAL` is returned and the global variable `errno` is set to ERANGE, for result out of range.

Related Function(s)

`complex` : creates a complex number from two values
`pow10` : calculates 10 raised to a value

Example The following example displays the value of 4^3.

```
#include <stdio.h>
#include <conio.h>
#include <math.h>

int main (void)
{
double result;

clrscr();
result = pow (4.0,3.0);
printf ("4.0 to the 3.0 power is %lf\n",result);

return 0;
}
```

pow10

Syntax `double pow10(int p);`

`int p;` *Power*

Function The `pow10` function raises 10 to the specified power.

File(s) to Include `#include <math.h>`

Description The `pow10` function returns the value of 10 raised to the power specified in the `p` argument.

Value(s) Returned The calculated result is returned.

Related Function(s) `pow` : calculates the value of x^y .

Example The following example displays the results of 10^4.

```
#include <stdio.h>
#include <conio.h>
#include <math.h>

int main (void)
{
double result;

clrscr();
result = pow10 (4.0);
printf ("10 to the 4.0 power is %lf\n",result);

return 0;
}
```

rand

DOS | UNIX | ANSI C | C++

Syntax `int rand(void);`

Function The `rand` function generates a random number.

File(s) to Include `#include <stdlib.h>`

Description The `rand` function generates a random number using a multiplicative congruential random number generator with period 2E32. The returned pseudorandom numbers range from 0 to RAND_MAX. RAND_MAX is defined in stdlib.h as 2E15 –1.

Value(s) Returned The generated pseudorandom number is returned.

Related Function(s)

random : generates a random number within a specified range

randomize : initializes the random number generator

Example The following example displays a random number.

```
#include <stdio.h>
#include <stdlib.h>

int main (void)
{
clrscr ();
printf ("This is a random number : %d\n",rand());

return 0;
}
```

random

DOS | UNIX | ANSI C | C++

Syntax

```
int random(int num);
```

int num; *Upper limit*

Function The random macro generates a random number within a specified range.

File(s) to Include #include <stdlib.h>

Description The random macro generates a random number between 0 and the upper limit specified in the num argument.

Value(s) Returned A random number between 0 and `num-1` is returned.

Related Function(s)
`rand` : generates a random number
`randomize` : initializes the random number generator

Example The following example generates a random number between 0 and 10.

```
#include <stdio.h>
#include <stdlib.h>
#include <time.h>

int main (void)
{
clrscr ();
randomize ();
printf ("This is a random number less than 10 :
%d\n",random(10));

return 0;
}
```

randomize

DOS | UNIX | ANSI C | C++

Syntax `void randomize(void);`

Function The `randomize` macro initializes the random number generator.

File(s) to Include
`#include <stdlib.h>`
`#include <time.h>`

Description The `randomize` macro initializes the random number generator with a random seed obtained from a call to the `time` function. Because this macro calls the `time` function, the `time.h` header file should be included in the program.

Value(s) Returned There is no return value.

Related Function(s)
`rand` : generates a random number
`random` : generates a random number within a range
`srand` : sets the seed point for the random generator

Example The following example generates a random number between 0 and 10.

```
#include <stdio.h>
#include <stdlib.h>
#include <time.h>

int main (void)
{
clrscr ();
randomize ();
printf ("This is a random number (0 10) :
  %d\n",random(10));

return 0;
}
```

real

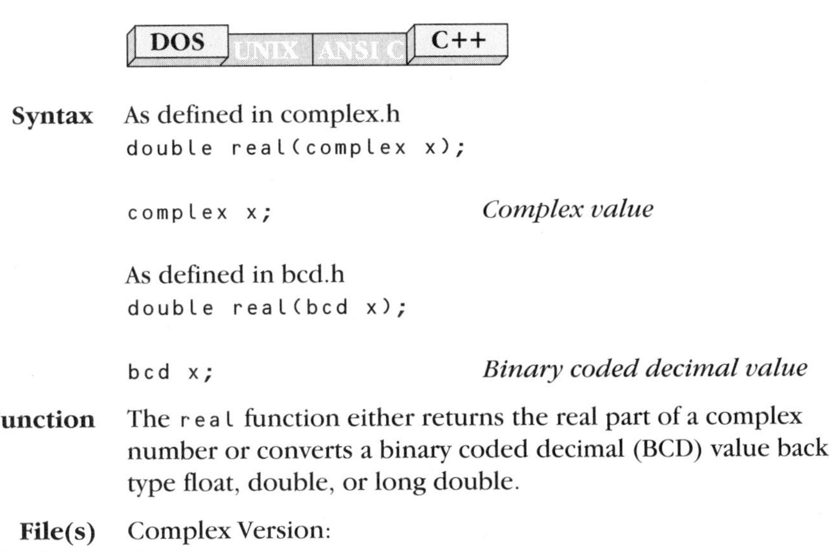

Syntax As defined in complex.h

```
double real(complex x);

complex x;
```

Complex value

As defined in bcd.h

```
double real(bcd x);

bcd x;
```

Binary coded decimal value

Function The `real` function either returns the real part of a complex number or converts a binary coded decimal (BCD) value back to type float, double, or long double.

File(s) to Include Complex Version:

```
#include <complex.h>
```

BCD:

```
#include <bcd.h>
```

Description When the x argument is complex, the real function returns the real part of the complex number specified in the x argument.

When the x argument is BCD, the real function converts the BCD value in the x argument back to its float, double, or long double type.

Value(s) Returned The appropriate value is returned.

Related Function(s)

bcd : converts to BCD
complex : creates a complex number from two values
imag : returns the imaginary part of a real number

Example The following example displays the real and imaginary parts of the complex value.

```
#include <stdio.h>
#include <conio.h>
#include <iostream.h>
#include <complex.h>

int main (void)
{
complex c_val;

clrscr();
c_val = complex (3.0,2.3);
cout << "Real part of complex c_val is :" << real
  (c_val) << "\n";
cout << "Imag part of complex c_val is :" << imag
  (c_val) << "\n";

return 0;
}
```

_rotl

DOS | UNIX | ANSI C | C++

Syntax

```
unsigned _rotl(unsigned val, int count);
```

`unsigned val;` *Value to rotate*
`int count;` *Number of bits to rotate*

Function The `_rotl` function rotates an unsigned integer value to the left.

File(s) to Include `#include <stdlib.h>`

Description The `_rotl` function rotates the unsigned integer value specified in the `val` argument to the left the number of bits specified in the `count` argument.

Value(s) Returned The rotated value is returned.

Related Function(s)
`_lrotl` : rotates an unsigned long value to the left
`_lrotr` : rotates an unsigned long value to the right
`_rotr` : rotates an unsigned integer to the right

Example The following example rotates the unsigned value left two bits.

```
#include <stdio.h>
#include <stdlib.h>

int main (void)
{
unsigned rot_value;
unsigned value = 500;
int shift_bits = 2;

clrscr ();
rot_value = _rotl (value,shift_bits);
printf ("Initial Value : %u\n",value);
printf ("Shifted Value : %u\n",rot_value);

return 0;
}
```

_rotr

DOS | UNIX | ANSI C | C++

Syntax `unsigned _rotr(unsigned val, int count);`

`unsigned val;` *Value to rotate*
`int count;` *Number of bits to rotate*

Function The `_rotr` function rotates an unsigned integer value to the right.

File(s) to Include `#include <stdlib.h>`

Description The `_rotr` function rotates the unsigned integer value specified in the `val` argument to the right the number of bits specified in the `count` argument.

Value(s) Returned The rotated value is returned.

Related Function(s)
`_lrotl` : rotates an unsigned long value to the left
`_lrotr` : rotates an unsigned long value to the right
`_rotl` : rotates an unsigned integer to the left

Example The following example rotates the unsigned value right two bits.

```
#include <stdio.h>
#include <stdlib.h>

int main (void)
{
unsigned rot_value;
unsigned value = 500;
int shift_bits = 2;

clrscr ();
rot_value = _rotr (value,shift_bits);
printf ("Initial Value : %u\n",value);
printf ("Shifted Value : %u\n",rot_value);

return 0;
}
```

sin

DOS	UNIX	ANSI C	C++

Syntax Real Version:
`double sin(double x);`

```
double x;
```
Input value

Complex Version:

```
complex sin(complex x);

complex x;
```
Input value

Function The `sin` function calculates the sine of a given value.

File(s) to Include Real Version:

```
#include <math.h>
```

Complex Version:

```
#include <complex.h>
```

Description The `sin` function computes the sine of the angle value, expressed in radians, that is specified in the `x` argument. For the complex version, the following formula is used:

```
sin(z) = (exp(i * z)    exp( i * z))/(2i)
```

Value(s) Returned The sine of the input value is returned.

Related Function(s)

`asin` : calculates the arc sine of a value
`cos` : calculates the cosine of a value
`tan` : calculates the tangent of a value

Example The following example calculates and displays the sine of .75.

```
#include <stdio.h>
#include <math.h>
#include <conio.h>

int main (void)
{
double calc_value;

clrscr();
calc_value = sin (.75);
printf ("Sine of .75 is %lf\n",calc_value);

return 0;
}
```

sinh

DOS | UNIX | ANSI C | C++

Syntax

Real Version:

```
double sinh(double x);

double x;                    Input value
```

Complex Version:

```
complex sinh(complex x);

complex x;                   Input value
```

Function

The `sinh` function calculates the hyperbolic sine of the specified value.

File(s) to Include

Real Version:

```
#include <math.h>
```

Complex Version:

```
#include <complex.h>
```

Description

The `sinh` function calculates the hyperbolic sine of the value specified in the `x` argument. The complex version uses the following formula to calculate the hyperbolic sine:

```
sinh(z) = (exp(z) - exp(-z))/2
```

Value(s) Returned

The hyperbolic sine is returned when successful. If overflow occurs, `HUGE_VAL` is returned and the global variable `errno` is set to ERANGE, for result out of range.

Related Function(s)

`cosh` : calculates the hyperbolic cosine
`tanh` : calculates the hyperbolic tangent

Example

The following example displays the hyperbolic sine of .75.

```
#include <stdio.h>
#include <math.h>
#include <conio.h>

int main (void)
{
double calc_value;
```

```
clrscr();
calc_value = sinh (.75);
printf ("Hyperbolic sine of .75 is
  %lf\n",calc_value);

return 0;
}
```

sqrt

DOS | UNIX | ANSI C | C++

Syntax Real Version:

```
double sqrt(double x);

double x;
```

Input value

Complex Version:

```
complex sqrt(complex x);

complex x;
```

Input value

Function The `sqrt` function returns the square root of a value.

File(s) to Include Real Version:

```
#include <math.h>
```

Complex Version:

```
#include <complex.h>
```

Description The `sqrt` function calculates the square root of the value specified in the `x` argument. For the real version, the value must be positive. For the complex version, the following formula is used:

```
sqrt (z) = sqrt(abs(z))(cos(arg(z)/2)+i
  sin(arg(z)/2))
```

Value(s) Returned The calculated square root is returned when successful. For the real version, when the `x` argument is negative, the global variable `errno` is set to EDOM, for domain error.

Related Function(s) `complex` : creates a complex number from two values

Example The following example calculates and displays the square root of 16.0.

```
#include <stdio.h>
#include <math.h>
#include <conio.h>

int main (void)
{
double calc_value;

clrscr();
calc_value = sqrt (16.0);
printf ("Square root of 16.0 is
  %lf\n",calc_value);

return 0;
}
```

srand

DOS | UNIX | ANSI C | C++

Syntax `void srand(unsigned seed);`

`unsigned seed;` *Seed point for random number*

Function The `srand` function initializes the random number generator.

File(s) to Include `#include <stdlib.h>`

Description The `srand` function sets the random number generator with the seed point defined in the `seed` argument. When the `seed` argument is 1, the random number generator is reinitialized.

Value(s) Returned There is no return value.

Related Function(s)

`rand` : generates a random number
`random` : generates a random number within a range
`randomize` : initializes the random number generator

Example The following example sets the random number generator seed to 34 and generates a random number.

```
#include <stdio.h>
#include <stdlib.h>

int main (void)
{
clrscr ();
srand (34);
printf ("This is a random number %d\n",rand());

return 0;
}
```

_status87

DOS UNIX ANSI C C++

Syntax `unsigned int _status87(void);`

Function The `_status87` function retrieves the floating-point status.

File(s) to Include `#include <float.h>`

Description The `_status87` function retrieves the floating-point status word. The floating-point status word is the combination of the 80x87 status word and the conditions detected by the 80x87 exception handler.

Value(s) Returned The floating-point status is returned.

Related Function(s)

`_clear87` : clears the floating-point status word
`_control87` : changes the floating-point control word

Example The following example prints the floating-point status word of the 80x87.

```
#include <stdio.h>
#include <conio.h>
#include <float.h>

int main (void)
{
clrscr();

printf ("Status before clear = %X\n",
   _status87());
_clear87();
printf ("Status after clear = %X\n", _status87());

return 0;
}
```

strtod

Syntax

```
double strtod(const char *s, char **endptr);
```

`const char *s;`	*String to convert*
`char **endptr;`	*Useful for error detection*

Function The `strtod` function converts a string to a double value.

File(s) to Include `#include <stdlib.h>`

Description The `strtod` function converts the character string pointed to by the `s` argument to a double value. The character string to be converted must follow the format:

[whitespace] [sign] [ddd] [.] [ddd] [fmt[sign]ddd]

in which

[whitespace] = optional whitespace
[sign] = the optional sign of the value
[ddd] = the optional digits
[.] = the decimal point

[ddd] = optional digits
[fmt] = optional e or E
[sign] = the optional sign of the exponent
[ddd] = optional digits

The `strtod` function recognizes +INF and –INF for plus and minus infinity. It also recognizes +NAN and –NAN for not-a-number. Conversion stops when the first character that cannot be recognized is encountered.

If `endptr` is not null, the `strtod` function sets `*endptr` at the location of the character that stopped the conversion. Therefore, `endptr` is useful for detecting errors.

Value(s) Returned The double value of the string is returned. `HUGE_VAL` is returned when overflow occurs.

Related Function(s) `atof` : converts a string to a floating-point number

Example The following example converts the string to a double value.

```
#include <stdlib.h>
#include <stdio.h>

int main (void)
{
double value;
char string[20] = "254.938";
char *endptr;

clrscr();
value = strtod (string,&endptr);
printf ("Value = %lf\n",value);
printf ("String = %s\n",string);

return 0;
}
```

strtol

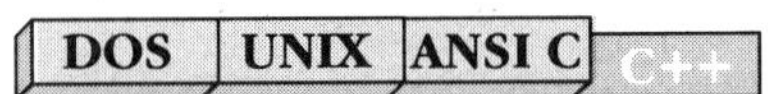

Syntax

```
long strtol(const char *s, char **endptr, int
        radix);
```

```
const char *s;          String to convert
char **endptr;          Useful for error detection
int radix;              Base for conversion
```

Function The `strtol` function converts a string to a long value.

File(s) to Include `#include <stdlib.h>`

Description The `strtol` function converts the character string pointed to by the `s` argument to a long value. The character string must be in the format:

[whitespace] [sign] [0] [x] [ddd]

in which

[whitespace] = optional whitespace
[sign] = the sign of the value
[0] = optional 0
[x] = optional x or X
[ddd] = optional digits

When the `radix` argument ranges from 2 to 36, the returned long value is expressed in the base defined by the `radix` argument. When the `radix` argument is 0, the first few characters of the `s` string determine the base of the returned long value, as follows:

First Character	*Second Character*	*String interpreted as*
0	1 to 7	Octal
0	x or X	Hexadecimal
1 to 9		Decimal

When the `radix` argument is 1, less than 0, or greater than 36, the argument is invalid.

If `endptr` is not null, the `*endptr` argument points to the character that stopped the conversion.

Value(s) Returned The value of the converted string is returned when successful. A 0 is returned when unsuccessful.

Related Function(s)

`atoi` : converts a string to an integer
`atol` : converts a string to a long value
`strtoul` : converts a string to an unsigned long value

Example The following example converts the string to a long value.

```
#include <stdlib.h>
#include <stdio.h>

int main (void)
{
long value;
char *string = "6568595";
char *endptr;

clrscr();
value = strtol (string,&endptr,10);
printf ("Value = %ld\n",value);
printf ("String = %s\n",string);
printf ("Base = 10\n");

return 0;
}
```

strtoul

DOS UNIX ANSI C C++

Syntax

```
unsigned long strtoul(const char *s, char
                        **endptr, int radix);
```

`const char *s;`	*String to convert*
`char **endptr;`	*Useful for error detection*
`int radix;`	*Base for conversion*

Function The `strtoul` function converts a string to an unsigned long value.

File(s) to Include `#include <stdlib.h>`

Description The `strtoul` function converts the character string pointed to by the `s` argument to a long value. The character string must be in the format:

[whitespace] [sign] [0] [x] [ddd]

in which

[whitespace] = optional whitespace
[sign] = the sign of the value
[0] = optional 0
[x] = optional x or X
[ddd] = optional digits

When the `radix` argument ranges from 2 to 36, the returned unsigned long value is expressed in the base defined by the `radix` argument. When the `radix` argument is 0, the first few characters of the `s` string determine the base of the returned long value, as follows:

First Character	*Second Character*	*String interpreted as*
0	1 to 7	Octal
0	x or X	Hexadecimal
1 to 9		Decimal

When the `radix` argument is 1, less than 0, or greater than 36, the argument is invalid.

If `endptr` is not null, the `*endptr` argument points to the character that stopped the conversion.

Value(s) Returned The value of the converted string is returned when successful. A 0 is returned when unsuccessful.

Related Function(s)
`atoi` : converts a string to an integer
`atol` : converts a string to a long value
`strtol` : converts a string to a long value

Example The following example converts the string to an unsigned long value.

```
#include <stdlib.h>
#include <stdio.h>
```

```
int main (void)
{
unsigned long value;
char *string = "6568595";
char *endptr;

clrscr();
value = strtoul (string,&endptr,10);
printf ("Value = %lu\n",value);
printf ("String = %s\n",string);
printf ("Base = 10\n");

return 0;
}
```

tan

DOS | UNIX | ANSI C | C++

Syntax Real Version:

```
double tan(double x);

double x;                    Input value
```

Complex Version:

```
complex tan(complex x);

complex x;                   Input value
```

Function The `tan` function calculates the tangent of a value.

File(s) to Include Real Version:

```
#include <math.h>
```

Complex Version:

```
#include <complex.h>
```

Description The `tan` function calculates the tangent of the value, defined in radians, that is specified in the `x` argument. For the complex version, the following formula is used:

```
tan(z) = sin(z) / cos(z)
```

Value(s) Returned The tangent of the x argument is returned.

Related Function(s)
atan : calculates the arc tangent of a value
cos : calculates the cosine of a value
sin : calculates the sine of a value

Example The following example calculates and displays the tangent of .75.

```
#include <stdio.h>
#include <math.h>
#include <conio.h>

int main (void)
{
double calc_value;

clrscr();
calc_value = tan (.75);
printf ("Tangent of .75 is %lf\n",calc_value);

return 0;
}
```

tanh

DOS | UNIX | ANSI C | C++

Syntax Real Version:

```
double tanh(double x);

double x;                    Input value
```

Complex Version:

```
complex tanh(complex x);

complex x;                   Input value
```

Function The tanh function calculates the hyperbolic tangent of a value.

File(s) to Include Real Version:
`#include <math.h>`

Complex Version:
```
#include <complex.h>
```

Description The `tanh` function calculates the hyperbolic tangent of the value specified in the `x` argument. For the complex version, the following formula is used:

```
tanh(z) = sinh(z) / cosh(z)
```

Value(s) Returned The hyperbolic tangent is returned.

Related Function(s)
`cosh` : calculates the hyperbolic cosine
`sinh` : calculates the hyperbolic sine

Example The following example calculates and displays the hyperbolic tangent of .75.

```
#include <stdio.h>
#include <math.h>
#include <conio.h>

int main (void)
{
double calc_value;

clrscr();
calc_value = tanh (.75);
printf ("Hyperbolic tangent of .75 is
  %lf\n",calc_value);

return 0;
}
```

ultoa

DOS | UNIX | ANSI C | C++

Syntax
```
char *ultoa(unsigned long value, char *string, int
            radix);
```

`unsigned long value;`	*Value to convert*
`char *string;`	*Converted string*
`int radix;`	*Base for conversion*

Function The `ultoa` function converts an unsigned long value to a string.

File(s) to Include `#include <stdlib.h>`

Description The `ultoa` function converts the unsigned long value defined in the `value` argument to a null-terminated string. The converted string is stored at the location pointed to by the `string` argument. The `radix` argument (ranging from 2 to 36) specifies the base for converting the `value` argument.

Value(s) Returned The converted string is returned.

Related Function(s)
`itoa` : converts an integer to a string
`ltoa` : converts a long value to a string

Example The following example converts the unsigned long value to a string.

```
#include <stdio.h>
#include <stdio.h>

int main (void)
{
unsigned long value = 62259374L;
char string [20];

clrscr();
ultoa (value,string,10);
printf ("Value = %lu\n",value);
printf ("String = %s\n",string);
printf ("Base = 10");

return 0;
```

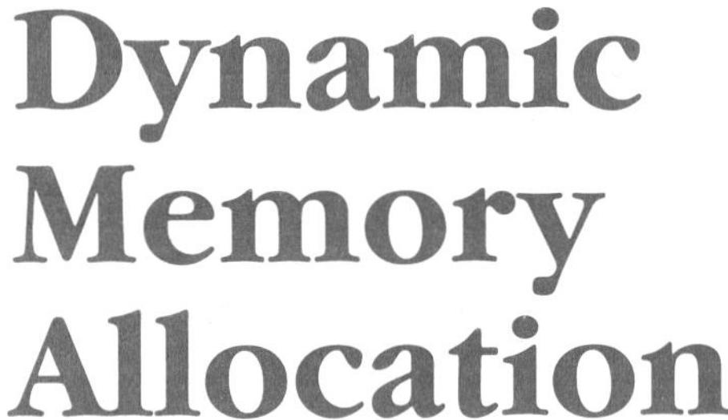

Dynamic Memory Allocation

Many applications require the capability to allocate memory during run time. Borland C++ provides a number of functions, listed in table 13.1, for dynamic memory allocation.

Table 13.1. *Dynamic memory allocation functions.*

Function	Description
`allocmem`	Allocates a DOS memory segment
`brk`	Changes data segment space allocation
`calloc`	Allocates main memory
`coreleft`	Determines amount of unused RAM
`farcalloc`	Allocates memory from the far heap
`farcoreleft`	Determines amount of unused memory in far heap
`farfree`	Frees a block from far heap
`farheapcheck`	Tests and verifies the far heap
`farheapcheckfree`	Checks free blocks of far heap for constant value
`farheapchecknode`	Tests and verifies a single node on the far heap
`farheapfillfree`	Fills free blocks of far heap with a constant value
`farheapwalk`	"Walks" through far heap node by node
`farmalloc`	Allocates memory from the far heap
`farrealloc`	Modifies allocated block in far heap
`free`	Frees an allocated block
`heapcheck`	Tests and verifies the heap
`heapcheckfree`	Checks free blocks on the heap for a constant value
`heapchecknode`	Tests and verifies a single node on the heap
`heapfillfree`	Fills free blocks on the heap with a constant value
`heapwalk`	"Walks" through the heap node by node
`malloc`	Allocates main memory
`realloc`	Reallocates main memory
`sbrk`	Modifies data segment space allocation
`setblock`	Modifies the size of an allocated block

To fully understand these functions and their use, some basic concepts must first be introduced.

Segments and Offsets

The 8086 microprocessor has 16-bit internal registers. However, it uses a 20-bit address to access up to 1,024 bytes of memory (note that this limitation applies to the 80286, 80386, and 80486 when operating in "real mode"). Because no single register on the 8086 can hold the 20-bit address, the approach of using segments and offsets (thus two 16-bit values) was implemented. The segment address is the address of the first byte of a segment. The offset is the location of an arbitrary byte with respect to the beginning of the segment. The physical address of the memory location is then determined by shifting the segment address left by four bits and adding the offset to the shifted segment address.

Typical Memory Layout

Once a program has been written, compiled, and linked, it can be executed. When a typical C program is executed, the C program is divided and stored in several components in memory (see fig. 13.1 that follows). The code segment is the location in memory where the actual instructions for your program are stored. The CS register holds the segment address of the code segment, whereas the instruction pointer (IP) maintains the offset, which determines the instruction to execute.

Fig. 13.1. Typical memory layout for a C program.

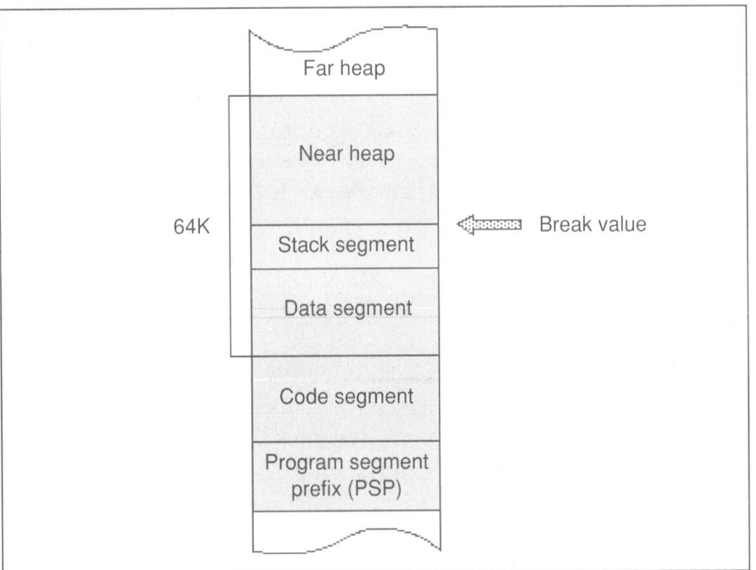

The next segment is called the data segment. The address of the data segment is maintained in the DS register. The data segment is then followed by the stack segment. The stack segment, usually 2K in size, stores local variables and passes arguments. The SP (stack pointer) register maintains the location in the stack; the SS register maintains the segment address of the stack segment. The break value marks the end of the stack segment, thus also marking the end of the space available to place the program. The break value can be altered with either the `brk` or `sbrk` functions.

The remainder of the physical memory is used according to the memory model chosen. Another segment register, not shown in the preceding figure 13.1, is used for extra segments. This segment register is called the extra segment (ES) register. The Borland C++ memory models are described in the following sections.

Tiny Memory Model

The tiny memory model represents the smallest of the memory models. This memory model should be used when minimizing the amount of memory used by the application is necessary. With this model, all four segment registers—CS, DS, SS, and ES—are set to the same address. Therefore, only 64K is available for the combination of the code, data, and stack. Only near pointers are available with the tiny memory model.

Small Memory Model

The small memory model is appropriate for most applications. The code and data segments differ with the small memory models; therefore, 64K is available for the code and 64K is available for the data and stack. Near pointers are used with the small memory model.

Medium Memory Model

The medium memory model is a good choice for larger programs that don't require much memory for storing data. With the medium memory model, far pointers are supported for the code but not for the data. The code can use up to 1 megabyte of memory, but the stack and data can use only 64K.

Compact Memory Model

The compact memory model is appropriate for applications needing little memory for code, but a lot of memory for storing data. With this model, the code is limited to 64K, whereas the data can occupy up to 1 megabyte. Far pointers are used for the data but not for the code.

Large Memory Model

The large memory model is a good choice for large applications that require a lot of memory for both code and data. In the large memory model, both the code and data use far pointers. Therefore, both the code and data can occupy up to 1 megabyte.

Huge Memory Model

The huge memory model is a good choice for large applications that require more than 64K for static data. The huge memory model uses far pointers for the data and code and avoids the 64K limit on static data.

Borland C++ Dynamic Memory Allocation Function Reference Guide

The remainder of this chapter provides detailed information for each of the Borland C++ functions used for dynamic memory allocation.

---

allocmem

Syntax `int allocmem(unsigned size, unsigned *segp);`

```
unsigned size;          Size in paragraphs
unsigned *segp;         Pointer to segment address
```

Function The `allocmem` function allocates a DOS memory segment.

File(s) to Include `#include <dos.h>`

Description The `allocmem` function allocates a block of free memory, with size defined in paragraphs (16 bytes in a paragraph) and specified in the `size` argument, using the DOS system call 0x48. The `segp` argument points to the word that is assigned to the segment address of the allocated memory block. Do not use the `allocmem` and `malloc` functions in the same program.

Value(s) Returned A –1 is returned when successful. When unsuccessful, the number of paragraphs available in the largest memory block is returned. In addition, the global variable `_doserrno` is set appropriately and the global variable `errno` is set to ENOMEM, for not enough memory.

Related Function(s) `freemem` : frees an allocated DOS memory block

Example In the following example, `allocmem` allocates a DOS memory segment.

```
#include <dos.h>
#include <alloc.h>
#include <stdio.h>

int main (void)
{
unsigned int size = 64;
unsigned int segp;

clrscr();
if (allocmem (size,&segp) == -1)
     printf ("Segment : %x\n",segp);
else
     printf ("Unable to allocate segment\n");

return 0;
}
```

brk

DOS | UNIX | ANSI C | C++

Syntax `int brk(void *addr);`

`void *addr;` *Break value*

Function The `brk` function modifies the data segment space allocation.

File(s) to Include `#include <alloc.h>`

Description The `brk` function changes the amount of space on the calling program's heap by altering the break value. The `addr` argument specifies the new break value. The break value is best defined as the address of the first location beyond the end of the data segment.

Value(s) Returned A 0 is returned when successful. When unsuccessful, a −1 is returned and the global variable `errno` is set to ENOMEM, for not enough memory.

Related Function(s)
`coreleft` : returns the amount of unused RAM
`sbrk` : changes the data segment space allocation

Example In the following example, `brk` increases the size of the space allocated to addr.

```
#include <alloc.h>
#include <stdio.h>

int main (void)
{
char *addr;

clrscr();
addr = malloc(20);
if (brk (addr+10) == 0)
      printf ("brk successfully called \n");
else
      printf ("error in call to brk\n");

return 0;
}
```

calloc

DOS | UNIX | ANSI C | C++

Syntax `void *calloc(size_t nitems, size_t size);`

`size_t nitems;` *Number of items*
`size_t size;` *Size*

Function The `calloc` function allocates main memory.

File(s) to Include `#include <stdlib.h>`
or
`#include <alloc.h>`

Description The `calloc` function dynamically allocates memory in the C memory heap. For small data models, including tiny, small, and medium models, the space between the end of the data segment and the top of the program stack is available for use. The only memory reserved is a small amount for DOS plus a small amount needed for the application.

For large data models, including the compact, large, and huge models, the space beyond the program stack to the end of physical memory is available for the heap.

The block size of the allocated memory is calculated to be the `nitems` argument multiplied by the `size` argument (`nitems` x `size`). The block of memory is cleared to 0 upon allocation. If the requested block size is greater than 64K, the `farcalloc` function must be used.

Value(s) Returned The pointer to the new block is returned. If there is not enough memory, or the `nitems` or `size` arguments are 0, null is returned.

Related Function(s)

`farcalloc` : allocates memory from the far heap
`malloc` : allocates main memory
`realloc` : reallocates main memory

Example In the following example, `calloc` allocates a block of memory.

```
#include <stdlib.h>
#include <stdio.h>

int main (void)
{
char *string = NULL;

clrscr();
string = calloc (20,sizeof(char));
if (string)
      {
      strcpy (string,"12345678912345678 9");
      printf ("Result: %s\n",string);
      }
else
      printf ("Memory not allocated\n");

free (string);
return 0;
}
```

coreleft

Syntax For tiny, small, and medium models:

```
unsigned coreleft(void);
```

For compact, large, and huge models:

```
unsigned long coreleft(void);
```

Function The `coreleft` function returns the amount of unused RAM.

File(s) to Include `#include <alloc.h>`

Description The `coreleft` function determines and returns the amount of RAM not in use. The return value differs depending on the memory model being used.

Value(s) Returned For the tiny, small, and medium models, the amount of unused memory between the top of the heap and the stack is returned.

For the compact, large, and huge models, the amount of unused memory between the highest allocated block and the end of available memory is returned.

Related Function(s) `farcoreleft` : returns the amount of unused memory in the far heap

Example In the following example, `coreleft` determines the amount of RAM not in use.

```
#include <alloc.h>
#include <stdio.h>

int main (void)
{
clrscr();

printf ("RAM not in use : %lu bytes\n", (unsigned
        long) coreleft());

return 0;
}
```

farcalloc

DOS UNIX ANSI C C++

Syntax

```
void far *farcalloc(unsigned long nunits,
                    unsigned long unitsz);
```

```
unsigned long nunits;    Number of elements
unsigned long unitsz;    Length in bytes
```

Function The `farcalloc` function allocates memory from the far heap.

File(s) to Include `#include <alloc.h>`

Description The `farcalloc` function allocates memory from the far heap. The memory is allocated for an array containing the number of elements specified in the `nunits` argument, in which each element contains the number of bytes defined in the `unitsz` argument. All available RAM and blocks larger than 64K can be allocated with the `farcalloc` function. Note that the tiny model cannot use this function.

Value(s) Returned The pointer to the allocated block is returned when successful. When unsuccessful, null is returned.

Related Function(s) `calloc` : allocates main memory

Example In the following example, `farcalloc` allocates a block of memory from the far heap.

```
#include <stdlib.h>
#include <stdio.h>
#include <alloc.h>
#include <string.h>
#include <dos.h>

int main(void)
{
char far *ptr;
char *string = "Test";

clrscr();
ptr = farcalloc(20,sizeof(char));
movedata (FP_SEG(string),FP_OFF(string),
      FP_SEG(ptr),FP_OFF(ptr),
      strlen(string));
printf ("%Fs\n",ptr);

return 0;
```

farcoreleft

DOS UNIX ANSI C C++

Syntax `unsigned long farcoreleft(void);`

Function The `farcoreleft` function determines the amount of unused memory in the far heap.

File(s) to Include `#include <alloc.h>`

Description The `farcoreleft` function determines and returns the amount of unused memory in the far heap beyond the highest allocated block. Note that the `farcoreleft` function should not be used with the tiny model.

Value(s) Returned The amount of unused memory between the highest allocated block and the end of available memory is returned.

Related Function(s) `coreleft` : returns the amount of unused RAM

Example In the following example, `farcoreleft` determines the amount of unused memory in the far heap.

```
#include <alloc.h>
#include <string.h>
#include <stdio.h>

int main (void)
{
unsigned long mem;

clrscr();
mem = farcoreleft ();
printf ("Unused memory in far heap : %lu bytes
        \n",mem);

return 0;
}
```

farfree

DOS | UNIX | ANSI C | C++

Syntax

```
void farfree(void far *block);

void far *block;
```

Block to free

Function The `farfree` function frees an allocated block from the far heap.

File(s) to Include `#include <alloc.h>`

Description The `farfree` function frees the previously allocated block of memory, pointed to by the `block` argument, from the far heap. Note that the `farfree` function cannot be used with the tiny model.

Value(s) Returned There is no return value.

Related Function(s)
`farcalloc` : allocates memory from the far heap
`farmalloc` : allocates memory from the far heap

Example In the following example, `farfree` frees the block of memory in the far heap pointed to by `ptr`.

```
#include <stdlib.h>
#include <stdio.h>
#include <alloc.h>
#include <string.h>
#include <dos.h>

int main(void)
{
char far *ptr;
char *string = "Test";

clrscr();
ptr = farmalloc(20);
movedata (FP_SEG(string),
  FP_OFF(string),FP_SEG(ptr),FP_OFF(ptr),
  strlen(string));
printf ("%Fs\n",ptr);
farfree(ptr);

return 0;
}
```

farheapcheck

DOS ~~UNIX~~ ~~ANSI C~~ ~~C++~~

Syntax `int farheapcheck(void);`

Function The `farheapcheck` function checks and tests the far heap.

File(s) to Include `#include <alloc.h>`

Description The `farheapcheck` function examines each block in the far heap. This function checks the pointers, size, and attributes of each block.

Value(s) Returned A return value of less than zero is returned when unsuccessful. A value of greater than zero is returned when successful. Some of the possible return values are as follows:

Constant	*Value*	*Meaning*
`_HEAPEMPTY`	1	There is no heap
`_HEAPOK`	2	Heap has been verified
`_HEAPCORRUPT`	–1	Heap has been corrupted

Related Function(s) `heapcheck` : checks and tests the heap

Example In the following example, `farheapcheck` checks the status of the heap.

```
#include <alloc.h>
#include <stdio.h>

int main (void)
{
char far *ptr;
int result;

clrscr();
ptr = farmalloc (20);
result = farheapcheck ();
if (result == _HEAPEMPTY)
     printf ("Heap is empty\n");
```

continues

```
if (result == _HEAPOK)
     printf ("Heap is ok\n");
if (result == _HEAPCORRUPT)
     printf ("Heap is corrupt\n");
farfree (ptr);
return 0;
}
```

farheapcheckfree

DOS | UNIX | ANSI C | C++

Syntax `int farheapcheckfree(unsigned int fillvalue);`

`unsigned int fillvalue;` *Value to check*

Function The `farheapcheckfree` function checks free blocks for a constant value.

File(s) to Include `#include <alloc.h>`

Description The `farheapcheckfree` function checks the free blocks in the far heap for the constant value specified in the `fillvalue` argument.

Value(s) Returned A value less than zero is returned when unsuccessful. A value greater than zero is returned when successful. The following constants are possible return values:

Constant	*Value*	*Meaning*
`_HEAPEMPTY`	1	There is no heap
`_HEAPOK`	2	Heap is okay
`_HEAPCORRUPT`	–1	Heap has been corrupted
`_BADVALUE`	–3	Value other than the value specified in the `fillvalue` argument was found

Related Function(s)
`farheapfillfree` : fills free blocks with a constant value
`heapcheckfree` : checks free blocks for a constant value

Example In the following example, `farheapcheckfree` checks the free blocks in the far heap for the value 1.

```
#include <alloc.h>
#include <stdio.h>

int main (void)
{
char far *ptr;
int result;

clrscr();
ptr = farmalloc (20);
farheapfillfree(1);
result = farheapcheckfree (1);
if (result == _HEAPEMPTY)
      printf ("Heap is empty\n");
if (result == _HEAPOK)
      printf ("Heap is ok\n");
if (result == _HEAPCORRUPT)
      printf ("Heap is corrupt\n");
if (result == _BADVALUE)
      printf ("Fill value not found\n");

farfree (ptr);
return 0;
}
```

farheapchecknode

Syntax `int farheapchecknode(void *node);`

`void *node;` *Node to check*

Function The `farheapchecknode` function checks and tests a single node on the far heap.

File(s) to Include `#include <alloc.h>`

Description The `farheapchecknode` function checks and tests the node on the far heap specified in the `node` argument. Note that if a node has been freed and `farheapchecknode` is called with the pointer to the freed block, the return value may be `_BADNODE` rather than the expected `_FREEENTRY`.

Value(s) Returned A value less than zero is returned when unsuccessful. A value greater than zero is returned when successful. The following constants are possible return values:

Constant	*Value*	*Meaning*
_HEAPEMPTY	1	There is no heap
_HEAPCORRUPT	–1	Heap has been corrupted
_BADNODE	–2	Node not found
_FREEENTRY	3	Node is a free block
_USEDENTRY	4	Node is a used block

Related Function(s) `heapchecknode` : checks and tests a single node on the heap

Example In the following example, `farheapchecknode` checks the node pointed to by `ptr`.

```
#include <alloc.h>
#include <stdio.h>

int main (void)
{
char far *ptr;
int result;

clrscr();
ptr = farmalloc (20);
result = farheapchecknode (ptr);
if (result == _HEAPEMPTY)
     printf ("Heap is empty\n");
if (result == _BADNODE)
     printf ("Node not found\n");
if (result == _HEAPCORRUPT)
     printf ("Heap is corrupt\n");
if (result == _FREEENTRY)
     printf ("Node is free block\n");
if (result == _USEDENTRY)
     printf ("Node is used block\n");

farfree (ptr);
return 0;
}
```

farheapfillfree

DOS UNIX ANSI C C++

Syntax

```
int farheapfillfree(unsigned int fillvalue);
```

`unsigned int fillvalue;` *Value for fill*

Function The `farheapfillfree` function fills free blocks with a constant value.

File(s) to Include

```
#include <alloc.h>
```

Description The `farheapfillfree` function fills the free blocks on the far heap with the constant value specified in the `fillvalue` argument.

Value(s) Returned A value less than zero is returned when unsuccessful. A value greater than zero is returned when successful. The following constants are possible return values for the `farheapfillfree` function:

Constant	*Value*	*Meaning*
_HEAPEMPTY	1	There is no heap
_HEAPOK	2	Heap is okay
_HEAPCORRUPT	–1	Heap has been corrupted

Related Function(s)

`farheapcheckfree` : checks free blocks for a constant value
`heapfillfree` : fills free blocks with a constant value

Example In the following example, `farheapfillfree` fills the free blocks of the far heap with the value 1.

```
#include <alloc.h>
#include <stdio.h>

int main (void)
{
char far *ptr;
int result;

clrscr();
```

continues

```
ptr = farmalloc (20);
farheapfillfree(1);
result = farheapcheckfree (1);
if (result == _HEAPEMPTY)
     printf ("Heap is empty\n");
if (result == _HEAPOK)
     printf ("Heap is ok\n");
if (result == _HEAPCORRUPT)
     printf ("Heap is corrupt\n");
if (result == _BADVALUE)
     printf ("Fill value not found\n");

farfree (ptr);
return 0;
}
```

farheapwalk

DOS | UNIX | ANSI C | C++

Syntax `int farheapwalk(struct farheapinfo *info);`

`struct farheapinfo *info;` *Heap information*

Function The `farheapwalk` function "walks," node by node, through the far heap.

File(s) to Include `#include <alloc.h>`

Description The `farheapwalk` function gets information on each node in the heap. The structure pointed to by the `info` argument is where the information on each node is located. When calling the `farheapwalk` function for the first time, the `ptr` field of the structure should be null. The structure contains the following information:

`info.ptr`	*Address of the first block*
`info.size`	*Size of the block in bytes*
`info.in_use`	*Flag to indicate if block is in use*

The `farheapwalk` function makes the assumption that the heap is correct. Therefore, `farheapcheck` should be used to verify the heap before using `farheapwalk`.

Value(s) Returned The following constants are possible return values:

Constant	*Value*	*Meaning*
`_HEAPEMPTY`	1	There is no heap
`_HEAPOK`	2	The `heapinfo` block contains valid data
`_HEAPEND`	5	End of the heap

Related Function(s)
`farheapcheck` : checks and verifies the far heap
`heapwalk` : "walks" through the heap node by node

Example In the following example, `farheapwalk` retrieves information on the nodes of the heap.

```
#include <alloc.h>
#include <stdio.h>

int main (void)
{
char far *ptr;
struct farheapinfo info;
int result;

clrscr();
ptr = farmalloc (20);
info.ptr = NULL;
result = farheapwalk (&info);
if (result == _HEAPEMPTY)
     printf ("Heap is empty\n");
if (result == _HEAPOK)
     {
     printf ("Heap is ok\n");
     printf ("In Use : %d\n",info.in_use);
     printf ("Size : %7u",info.size);
     }
if (result == _HEAPEND)
     printf ("End of heap\n");

farfree (ptr);
return 0;
}
```

farmalloc

DOS UNIX ANSI C C++

Syntax `void far *farmalloc(unsigned long nbytes);`

`unsigned long nbytes;` *Number of bytes to allocate*

Function The `farmalloc` function allocates a block of memory from the far heap.

File(s) to Include `#include <alloc.h>`

Description The `farmalloc` function allocates a block of memory, with the length specified in the `nbytes` argument, from the far heap. When you use the `farmalloc` function, all available RAM and blocks larger than 64K can be allocated. Note that the `farmalloc` function cannot be used with the tiny model.

Value(s) Returned The pointer to the allocated block is returned when successful. When unsuccessful, null is returned.

Related Function(s)
`farcalloc` : allocates memory from the far heap
`malloc` : allocates main memory

Example In the following example, `farmalloc` allocates a block of memory.

```
#include <stdlib.h>
#include <stdio.h>
#include <alloc.h>
#include <string.h>
#include <dos.h>

int main(void)
{
char far *ptr;
char *string = "Test";

clrscr();
ptr = farmalloc(20);
ptr = farrealloc(ptr,30);
movedata (FP_SEG(string),FP_OFF(string),
     FP_SEG(ptr),FP_OFF(ptr),
     strlen(string));
printf ("%Fs\n",ptr);
farfree(ptr);

return 0;
}
```

farrealloc

DOS UNIX ANSI C C++

Syntax

```
void far *farrealloc(void far *oldblock, unsigned
long nbytes);

void far *oldblock;        Pointer to block to modify
unsigned long nbytes;      New block size
```

Function The `farrealloc` function adjusts the size of an allocated block in the far heap.

File(s) to Include `#include <alloc.h>`

Description The `farrealloc` function resizes the block pointed to by the `oldblock` argument to the size specified in the `nbytes` argument. When you use the `farrealloc` function, all available RAM and blocks larger than 64K can be allocated. Note that the `farrealloc` function cannot be used with the tiny model.

Value(s) Returned The address of the reallocated block is returned when successful. Null is returned when unsuccessful.

Related Function(s)

`farmalloc` : allocates memory from the far heap
`realloc` : reallocates main memory

Example In the following example, `farrealloc` resizes the block pointed to by `ptr`.

```
#include <stdlib.h>
#include <stdio.h>
#include <alloc.h>
#include <string.h>
#include <dos.h>

int main(void)
{
char far *ptr;
char *string = "Test";

clrscr();
ptr = farmalloc(20);
ptr = farrealloc(ptr,30);
movedata (FP_SEG(string),FP_OFF(string),
      FP_SEG(ptr),FP_OFF(ptr),
      strlen(string));
printf ("%Fs\n",ptr);
farfree(ptr);
return 0;
}
```

free

DOS | UNIX | ANSI C | C++

Syntax
```
void free(void *block);

void *block;                    Block to free
```

Function The `free` function frees an allocated memory block.

File(s) to Include
```
#include <stdlib.h>
```
or
```
#include <alloc.h>
```

Description The `free` function deallocates the memory block pointed to by the `block` argument and allocated by a call to the `calloc` function, the `malloc` function, or the `realloc` function.

Value(s) Returned There is no return value.

Related Function(s) `freemem` : frees an allocated DOS memory block

Example In the following example, `free` frees the block pointed to by string.

```
#include <stdlib.h>
#include <stdio.h>

int main (void)
{
char *string = NULL;

clrscr();
string = calloc (20,sizeof(char));
if (string)
     {
     strcpy (string,"12345678912345678");
     printf ("Result: %s\n",string);
     }
else
     printf ("Memory not allocated\n");

free (string);
return 0;
}
```

heapcheck

DOS | UNIX | ANSI C | C++

Syntax `int heapcheck(void);`

Function The `heapcheck` function tests and verifies the heap.

File(s) to Include `#include <alloc.h>`

Description The `heapcheck` function tests each block in the heap. The pointers, size, and attributes of each block are checked.

Value(s) Returned A value less than zero is returned when unsuccessful. A value greater than zero is returned when successful. The following constants are possible return values:

Constant	*Value*	*Meaning*
`_HEAPEMPTY`	1	There is no heap
`_HEAPOK`	2	Heap is okay
`_HEAPCORRUPT`	–1	Heap has been corrupted

Related Function(s) `farheapcheck` : tests and verifies the far heap

Example In the following example, `heapcheck` checks the heap.

```
#include <alloc.h>
#include <stdio.h>

int main (void)
{
char *ptr;
int result;

clrscr();
ptr = malloc (20);
printf ("%s\n",ptr);
result = heapcheck ();
if (result == _HEAPEMPTY)
      printf ("No heap\n");
if (result == _HEAPOK)
```

continues

```
        printf ("Heap is ok\n");
    if (result == _HEAPCORRUPT)
        printf ("Heap is corrupt\n");

    free (ptr);
    return 0;
    }
```

heapcheckfree

Syntax `int heapcheckfree(unsigned int fillvalue);`

`unsigned int fillvalue;` *Value to check*

Function The `heapcheckfree` function checks free blocks for a constant value.

File(s) to Include `include <alloc.h>`

Description The `heapcheckfree` function checks the free blocks on the heap for the constant value specified in the `fillvalue` argument.

Value(s) Returned A value less than zero is returned when unsuccessful. A value greater than zero is returned when successful. The following constants are possible return values.

Constant	*Value*	*Meaning*
`_HEAPEMPTY`	1	There is no heap
`_HEAPOK`	2	Heap is okay
`_HEAPCORRUPT`	–1	Heap has been corrupted
`_BADVALUE`	–3	Value other than the value specified in the `fillvalue` argument was found

Related Function(s) `farheapcheckfree` : checks free blocks in the far heap for a constant value

Example In the following example, heapcheckfree checks the free blocks on the heap for the value 1.

```
#include <alloc.h>
#include <stdio.h>

int main (void)
{
char *ptr;
int result;

clrscr();
ptr = malloc (20);
heapfillfree (1);
printf ("%s\n",ptr);
result = heapcheckfree (1);
if (result == _HEAPEMPTY)
      printf ("No heap\n");
if (result == _HEAPOK)
      printf ("Heap is ok\n");
if (result == _HEAPCORRUPT)
      printf ("Heap is corrupt\n");
if (result == _BADVALUE)
      printf ("Value not found\n");

free (ptr);
return 0;
}
```

heapchecknode

Syntax `int heapchecknode(void *node);`

`void *node;` *Node to check*

Function The heapchecknode function tests and verifies a single node on the heap.

File(s) to Include `#include <alloc.h>`

Description The heapchecknode function tests and verifies the node specified in the node argument. Note that when the specified node has been freed and the heapchecknode function is called with the pointer to the freed block, the return value may be _BADNODE rather than the expected _FREEENTRY.

Value(s) Returned A value less than zero is returned when unsuccessful. A value greater than zero is returned when successful. The following constants are possible return values:

Constant	*Value*	*Meaning*
_HEAPEMPTY	1	There is no heap
_HEAPCORRUPT	–1	The heap has been corrupted
_BADNODE	–2	Node could not be found
_FREEENTRY	3	Node is a free block
_USEDENTRY	4	Flag to indicate node is used block

Related Function(s) farheapchecknode : tests and verifies a node on the far heap

Example In the following example, heapchecknode checks the node pointed to by ptr.

```
#include <alloc.h>
#include <stdio.h>

int main (void)
{
char *ptr;
int result;

clrscr();
ptr = malloc (20);
printf ("%s\n",ptr);
result = heapchecknode (ptr);
if (result == _HEAPEMPTY)
     printf ("No heap\n");
if (result == _HEAPCORRUPT)
     printf ("Heap is corrupt\n");
if (result == _BADNODE)
     printf ("Node not found\n");
if (result == _FREEENTRY)
     printf ("Node is free block\n");
if (result == _USEDENTRY)
     printf ("Node is used block\n");

free (ptr);
return 0;
}
```

heapfillfree

DOS | UNIX | ANSI C | C++

Syntax

```
int heapfillfree(unsigned int fillvalue);
```

`unsigned int fillvalue;` *Value to use as fill*

Function The `heapfillfree` function fills the free blocks on the heap with a constant value.

File(s) to Include `#include <alloc.h>`

Description The `heapfillfree` function fills the free blocks on the heap with the constant value specified in the `fillvalue` argument.

Value(s) Returned A value less than zero is returned when unsuccessful. A value greater than zero is returned when successful. The following constants are possible return values:

Constants	*Value*	*Meaning*
`_HEAPEMPTY`	1	There is no heap
`_HEAPOK`	2	Heap is okay
`_HEAPCORRUPT`	–1	Heap has been corrupted

Related Function(s) `farheapfillfree` : fills the free blocks on the far heap with a constant value

Example In the following example, `heapfillfree` fills the free blocks on the heap with the value 1.

```
#include <alloc.h>
#include <stdio.h>

int main (void)
{
char *ptr;
int result;

clrscr();
ptr = malloc (20);
heapfillfree (1);
printf ("%s\n",ptr);
```

continues

```
result = heapcheckfree (1);
if (result == _HEAPEMPTY)
     printf ("No heap\n");
if (result == _HEAPOK)
     printf ("Heap is ok\n");
if (result == _HEAPCORRUPT)
     printf ("Heap is corrupt\n");
if (result == _BADVALUE)
     printf ("Value not found\n");

free (ptr);
return 0;
}
```

heapwalk

DOS | UNIX | ANSI C | C++

Syntax

```
int heapwalk(struct heapinfo *info);
```

`struct heapinfo *info;` *Heap information*

Function The `heapwalk` function "walks" through the heap node by node.

File(s) to Include `#include <alloc.h>`

Description The `heapwalk` function gets information on each node on the heap. When using the `heapwalk` function, the `ptr` field of the `*info` structure should be set to null before the first call. The information stored in the `heapinfo` structure is as follows:

`info.ptr`	*Address of the first block*
`info.size`	*Size of the block (in bytes)*
`info.in_use`	*Flag to indicate whether block is currently in use*

The `heapwalk` function makes the assumption that the heap is correct. Therefore, `heapcheck` should be called to verify the heap prior to calling `heapwalk`.

Value(s) Returned The following constants are possible return values:

Constant	*Value*	*Meaning*
_HEAPEMPTY	1	There is no heap
_HEAPOK	2	The `heapinfo` block contains valid information
_HEAPEND	5	End of heap

Related Function(s) `farheapwalk` : "walks" through the far heap node by node

Example In the following example, `heapwalk` gets information on the nodes of the heap.

```
#include <alloc.h>
#include <stdio.h>

int main (void)
{
struct heapinfo info;
char *ptr;
int result;

clrscr();
ptr = malloc (20);
printf ("%s\n",ptr);
info.ptr = NULL;
result = heapwalk (&info);
if (result == _HEAPEMPTY)
     printf ("No heap\n");
if (result == _HEAPOK)
     {
     printf ("Heap is ok\n");
     printf ("In Use : %d\n",info.in_use);
     printf ("Size : %7u\n",info.size);
     }
if (result == _HEAPEND)
     printf ("End of heap\n");

free (ptr);
return 0;
}
```

malloc

DOS | UNIX | ANSI C | C++

Syntax `void *malloc(size_t size);`

`size_t size;` *Size of block to allocate*

Function The `malloc` function allocates main memory.

File(s) to Include `#include <stdlib.h>`
or
`#include <alloc.h>`

Description The `malloc` function allocates a block of memory with the size specified in the `size` argument. The memory is allocated from the memory heap, which is used for the dynamic allocation of variable-sized blocks.

Value(s) Returned The pointer to the allocated block of memory is returned when successful. When unsuccessful, or the `size` argument is 0, null is returned.

Related Function(s)
`calloc` : allocates main memory
`farcalloc` : allocates memory from the far heap
`farmalloc` : allocates memory from the far heap
`realloc` : reallocates main memory

Example In the following example, `malloc` allocates a block of memory.

```
#include <stdlib.h>
#include <stdio.h>

int main (void)
{
char *string = NULL;

clrscr();
string = malloc (20);
if (string)
     {
     strcpy (string,"123456789123456789");
     printf ("Result: %s\n",string);
     }
else
     printf ("Memory not allocated\n");

free (string);
return 0;
}
```

realloc

DOS | UNIX | ANSI C | C++

Syntax
```
void *realloc(void *block, size_t size);
```

`void *block;` *Memory block*
`size_t size;` *Size of block*

Function The `realloc` function reallocates main memory.

File(s) to Include
```
#include <stdlib.h>
```
or
```
#include <alloc.h>
```

Description The realloc function alters the size of the block pointed to by the `block` argument to the size defined in the `size` argument. The block pointed to by the `block` argument should have been previously allocated with the `malloc` or `calloc` functions.

Value(s) Returned The address of the reallocated block is returned when successful. If the *size* argument is 0, or the block cannot be reallocated, null is returned.

Related Function(s)
`calloc` : allocates main memory
`malloc` : allocates main memory

Example In the following example, `realloc` resizes the block of memory allocated by `malloc`.

```
#include <stdlib.h>
#include <stdio.h>

int main (void)
{
char *string = NULL;

clrscr();
string = malloc (20);
strcpy (string, "123456789123456789");
printf ("String : %s\n", string);
realloc (string, 30);
strcpy (string,
        "123456789123456789123456789");
printf ("String : %s\n", string);

free (string);
return 0;
}
```

sbrk

DOS | UNIX | ANSI C | C++

Syntax `void *sbrk(int incr);`

`int incr;` *Number of bytes to increment*

Function The `sbrk` function changes the data segment space allocation.

File(s) to Include `#include <alloc.h>`

Description The `sbrk` function changes the break value by adding the number of bytes specified in the `incr` argument. The allocated space is increased when the `incr` argument is positive, and decreased when the `incr` argument is negative.

Value(s) Returned The previous break value is returned when successful. When unsuccessful, –1 is returned and the global variable `errno` is set to ENOMEM, for not enough core.

Related Function(s) `brk` : changes data segment space allocation

Example In the following example, `sbrk` increases the break value.

```
#include <alloc.h>
#include <stdio.h>

int main (void)
{
clrscr();
sbrk (500);
printf ("%lu bytes free\n",(unsigned long)
        coreleft());

return 0;
}
```

setblock

DOS UNIX ANSI C C++

Syntax `int setblock(unsigned segx, unsigned newsize);`

`unsigned segx;`	*Segment address*
`unsigned newsize;`	*New size in paragraphs*

Function The `setblock` function changes the size of a previously allocated block.

File(s) to Include `#include <dos.h>`

Description The `setblock` function modifies the size of a memory segment identified by the segment address in the `segx` argument. The segment address in the `segx` argument is retrieved by a call to `allocmem`. The `newsize` argument defines the requested size, in paragraphs.

Value(s) Returned A –1 is returned when successful. Otherwise, the size of the largest possible block, in paragraphs, is returned and the global variable `_doserrno` is set.

Related Function(s)
`allocmem` : allocates a DOS memory segment
`freemem` : frees a previously allocated DOS memory block

Example In the following example, `setblock` changes the size of the block pointed to by `segp`.

```
#include <alloc.h>
#include <stdio.h>

int main (void)
{
unsigned int size = 32;
unsigned int segp;

clrscr();
allocmem (size,&segp);

setblock (segp,64);
printf ("Block at segment : %X\n",segp);

freemem (segp);
return 0;
}
```

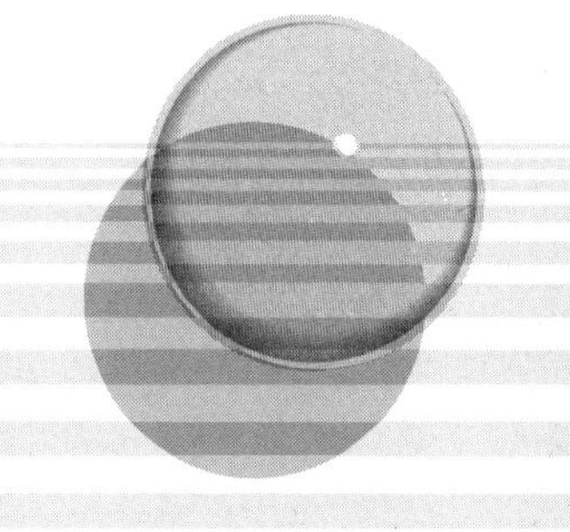

Process Control

The functions described in this chapter are used to control processes. A process can be defined as an executable program in memory and the program's associated environment. The program's environment, stored in the program segment prefix (PSP), consists of the locations of the code, the locations of the data, and the identifications of open files.

It is possible to open other processes from inside a process. In other words, you can have a program that executes another program. The program that executes the second program is called the *parent process*. The program that gets executed from another program is called the *child process*. The `execl`, `execle`, `...`, `execvpe` functions and the `spawnl`, `spawnle`, `...`, `spawnvpe` functions are used to open child processes.

Whenever a child process exists, an integer value, called the *exit code*, is returned to the parent process. An exit code of 0 is generally used to indicate a successful child process. A nonzero exit code is often used to indicate various errors.

The `raise` and `signal` functions are provided to generate and handle signals. A signal is a flag to the operating system that an error has occurred. The `raise` function is used to generate the signal. The `signal` function is used to call user-defined signal handler functions.

Table 14.1 lists the process control functions.

14

REFERENCE

Table 14.1. *Process control functions.*

Function	*Meaning*
`abort`	Abnormally terminates a program
`execl`	Loads and runs a child process; the argument pointers are passed as separate arguments
`execle`	Loads and runs a child process; the argument pointers are passed as separate arguments; the environment for the child process can be altered
`execlp`	Loads and runs a child process; the argument pointers are passed as separate arguments; this function searches the DOS PATH for the specified file
`execlpe`	Loads and runs a child process; the argument pointers are passed as separate arguments; the environment for the child process can be altered; this function searches the DOS PATH for the specified file
`execv`	Loads and runs a child process; the argument pointers are passed as an array of pointers
`execve`	Loads and runs a child process; the argument pointers are passed as an array of pointers; the environment for the child process can be altered
`execvp`	Loads and runs a child process; the argument pointers are passed as an array of pointers; this function searches the DOS PATH for the specified file
`execvpe`	Loads and runs a child process; the argument pointers are passed as an array of pointers; this function searches the DOS PATH for the specified file; the environment for the child process can be altered
`_exit`	Terminates a program
`exit`	Terminates a program
`getpid`	Gets the process identification
`raise`	Sends a software signal
`signal`	Defines signal handling actions
`spawnl`	Creates and executes a child process; the argument pointers are passed as separate arguments
`spawnle`	Creates and executes a child process; the argument pointers arc passed as separate arguments; the environment for the child process can be altered

Function	*Meaning*
`spawnlp`	Creates and executes a child process; the argument pointers are passed as separate arguments; this function searches the DOS PATH for the specified file
`spawnlpe`	Creates and executes a child process; the argument pointers are passed as separate arguments; the environment for the child process can be altered; this function searches the DOS PATH for the specified file
`spawnv`	Creates and executes a child process; the argument pointers are passed as an array of pointers
`spawnve`	Creates and executes a child process; the argument pointers are passed as an array of pointers; the environment for the child process can be altered
`spawnvp`	Creates and executes a child process; the argument pointers are passed as an array of pointers; this function searches the DOS PATH for the specified file
`spawnvpe`	Creates and executes a child process; the argument pointers are passed as an array of pointers; the environment for the child process can be altered; this function searches the DOS PATH for the specified file

Borland C++ Process Control Functions Reference Guide

The remainder of this chapter provides detailed information for using each of the functions listed in table 14.1.

abort

DOS	UNIX	ANSI C	C++

Syntax `void abort(void);`

Function The `abort` function terminates the program.

File(s) to Include `#include <stdlib.h>`
or
`#include <process.h>`

Description The `abort` function terminates the program in an abnormal way. The `abort` function writes the termination message `Abnormal program termination` on `stderr` and aborts the program by calling the `_exit` function with exit code 3.

Value(s) Returned The exit code 3 is returned to the parent process or DOS.

Related Function(s) `_exit` : terminates a program

Example The following example demonstrates the `abort` function by terminating the function before displaying the last string.

```
#include <stdio.h>
#include <stdlib.h>

int main (void)
{
clrscr ();
printf ("The program will terminate without
  displaying last line\n");
abort();
printf ("This line will not be printed\n");

return 0;
}
```

execl

DOS UNIX ANSI C C++

Syntax

```
int execl(char *path, char *arg0, *arg1, ...,
          *argn, NULL);
```

`char *path;`	*File name of the child process*
`char *arg0,...`	*Arguments for child process*
`NULL;`	*Null*

Function The `execl` function loads and runs a child process. The argument pointers are passed as separate arguments.

File(s) to Include `#include <process.h>`

Description The `execl` function loads and executes another program. The filename of the program to execute, called the child process, is specified in the `path` argument. The filename specified in the `path` argument is searched for using the standard DOS search. When the filename contains no file extension, the filename is searched for in the following way: The filename, as given, is searched for first. If not found, then the `.com` extension is added and searched for, then the `.exe` extension is added and searched for.

The `execl` function uses the `*arg..` argument pointers to form the new list of arguments. `execl` is useful when the number of arguments needed for the child process is known. Each argument is passed separately.

Value(s) Returned No value is returned when successful. However, when an error occurs, a –1 is returned and the global variable `errno` is set to one of the following:

E2BIG	Argument list too long
EACCES	Permission denied
EMFILE	Too many open files
ENOENT	Path or file name not found
ENOEXEC	Exec format error
ENOMEM	Not enough core

Related Function(s) `spawnl` : creates and executes a child process

Example In the following example, the parent process executes the child process. The child process must be compiled separately and entitled `child.exe`.

Parent Process

```
#include <conio.h>
#include <stdio.h>
#include <process.h>

void main (int argc, char *argv[])
{
clrscr();
printf ("Calling child process from
%s\n",argv[0]);
execl ("child.exe","child.exe","One","Two",NULL);
printf ("Number of parameters %d\n",argc);
perror ("exec error\n");
```

continues

```
exit (1);
}
```

Child Process

```
#include <stdio.h>
#include <stdlib.h>

void main (int argc, char **argv)
{
int x;

printf ("Running child process : \n");
for (x = 0; x < argc; x = x +1)
     printf ("%s : \n", argv[x]);
}
```

execle

DOS | UNIX | ANSI C | C++

Syntax

```
int execle(char *path, char *arg0, *arg1, ...,
           *argn, NULL, char **env);
```

`char *path;`	*Filename of child process*
`char *arg0, ...`	*Arguments for child process*
`NULL`	*Null*
`char **env;`	*New environment settings*

Function The `execle` function loads and runs a child process. The argument pointers are passed as separate arguments. The environment for the child process can be altered.

File(s) to Include `#include <process.h>`

Description The `execle` function loads and executes another program. The filename of the program to execute, called the child process, is specified in the `path` argument. The filename specified in the `path` argument is searched for using the standard DOS search. When the filename contains no file extension, the filename is searched for in the following way: The filename, as given, is searched for first. If not found, then the `.com` extension is added and searched for, then the `.exe` extension is added and searched for.

The `execle` function uses the `*arg..` argument pointers to form the new list of arguments. `execle` is useful when the number of arguments needed for the child process is known. Each argument is passed separately.

The `env` argument is an array of character pointers that can be used to specify new environment settings for the child process. Each element of the `env` argument points to a null-terminated character string in the form

```
envvar = value
```

in which `envvar` is the name of the environment variable and `value` is the new value of the environment variable. When the `env` argument is null, the child process defaults to the environment settings of the parent process.

Value(s) Returned No value is returned when successful. However, when an error occurs, a –1 is returned and the global variable `errno` is set to one of the following:

E2BIG	Argument list too long
EACCES	Permission denied
EMFILE	Too many open files
ENOENT	Path or file name not found
ENOEXEC	Exec format error
ENOMEM	Not enough core

Related Function(s) `spawnle` : creates and executes a child process

Example In the following example, the parent process executes the child process. The child process must be compiled separately and entitled `child.exe`.

Parent Process

```
#include <conio.h>
#include <stdio.h>
#include <process.h>

void main (int argc, char *argv[], char *envp[])
{
clrscr();
printf ("Calling child process from
%s\n",argv[0]);
execle
("child.exe","child.exe","One","Two",NULL,envp);
printf ("Number of parameters %d\n",argc);
```

continues

```
perror ("exec error\n");
exit (1);
}
```

Child Process

```
#include <stdio.h>
#include <stdlib.h>

void main (int argc, char **argv)
{
int x;

printf ("Running child process : \n");
for (x = 0; x < argc; x = x +1)
      printf ("%s : \n", argv[x]);
}
```

execlp

DOS ~~UNIX~~ ~~ANSI C~~ ~~C++~~

Syntax

```
int execlp(char *path, char *arg0, *arg1, ...,
            *argn, NULL);
```

`char *path;`	*Filename of child process*
`char *arg1, ...`	*Arguments for child process*
`NULL;`	*Null*

Function The `execlp` function loads and executes a child process. The argument pointers are passed as separate arguments. This function searches the DOS PATH for the specified file.

File(s) to Include `#include <process.h>`

Description The `execlp` function loads and executes another program. The filename of the program to execute, called the child process, is specified in the `path` argument. The filename specified in the `path` argument is searched for using the standard DOS search. When the filename contains no file extension, the filename is searched for in the following way: The filename, as given, is searched for first. If not found, then the `.com` extension is added and searched for, then the `.exe` extension is added and searched for.

The execlp function searches for the child process in all the directories specified by the DOS PATH variable. The execl, execle, execv, and execve functions search only the specified path or current working directory.

The execlp function uses the *arg.. argument pointers to form the new list of arguments. This function is useful when the number of arguments needed for the child process is known. Each argument is passed separately.

Value(s) Returned No value is returned when successful. However, when an error occurs, a –1 is returned and the global variable errno is set to one of the following:

E2BIG	Argument list too long
EACCES	Permission denied
EMFILE	Too many open files
ENOENT	Path or file name not found
ENOEXEC	Exec format error
ENOMEM	Not enough core

Related Function(s) spawnlp : creates and executes a child process

Example In the following example, the parent process executes the child process. The child process must be compiled separately and entitled child.exe.

Parent Process

```
#include <conio.h>
#include <stdio.h>
#include <process.h>

void main (int argc, char *argv[])
{
clrscr();
printf ("Calling child process from
%s\n",argv[0]);
execlp ("child.exe","child.exe","One","Two",NULL);
printf ("Number of parameters %d\n",argc);
perror ("exec error\n");
exit (1);
}
```

Child Process

```
#include <stdio.h>
#include <stdlib.h>
```

continues

```
void main (int argc, char **argv)
{
int x;

printf ("Running child process : \n");
for (x = 0; x < argc; x = x +1)
     printf ("%s : \n", argv[x]);
}
```

execlpe

DOS UNIX ANSI C C++

Syntax

```
int execlpe(char *path, char *arg0, *arg1, ...,
                argn, NULL, char **env);
```

`char *path;`	*Filename of child process*
`char *arg0, ...`	*Arguments for child process*
`NULL;`	*Null*
`char **env;`	*New environment variables*

Function The `execlpe` function loads and executes a child process. The argument pointers are passed as separate arguments. This function searches the DOS PATH for the specified file. The environment for the child process can be altered.

File(s) to Include `#include <process.h>`

Description The `execlpe` function loads and executes another program. The filename of the program to execute, called the child process, is specified in the `path` argument. The filename specified in the `path` argument is searched for using the standard DOS search. When the filename contains no file extension, the filename is searched for in the following way: The filename, as given, is searched for first. If not found, then the `.com` extension is added and searched for, then the `.exe` extension is added and searched for.

The `execlpe` function searches for the child process in all the directories specified by the DOS PATH variable. The `execl`, `execle`, `execv`, and `execve` functions search only the specified path or current working directory.

The `execlpe` function uses the `*arg..` argument pointers to form the new list of arguments. This function is useful when the number of arguments needed for the child process is known. Each argument is passed separately.

The `env` argument is an array of character pointers that can be used to specify new environment settings for the child process. Each element of the `env` argument points to a null-terminated character string in the form

```
envvar = value
```

in which `envvar` is the name of the environment variable and `value` is the new value of the environment variable. When the `env` argument is null, the child process defaults to the environment settings of the parent process.

Value(s) Returned No value is returned when successful. However, when an error occurs, a –1 is returned and the global variable `errno` is set to one of the following:

E2BIG	Argument list too long
EACCES	Permission denied
EMFILE	Too many open files
ENOENT	Path or file name not found
ENOEXEC	Exec format error
ENOMEM	Not enough core

Related Function(s) `spawnlpe` : creates and executes a child process

Example In the following example, the parent process executes the child process. The child process must be compiled separately and entitled `child.exe`.

Parent Process

```
#include <conio.h>
#include <stdio.h>
#include <process.h>

void main (int argc, char *argv[], char *envp[])
{
clrscr();
printf ("Calling child process from
%s\n",argv[0]);
execlpe
("child.exe","child.exe","One","Two",NULL,envp);
printf ("Number of parameters %d\n",argc);
```

continues

```
perror ("exec error\n");
exit (1);
}
```

Child Process

```
#include <stdio.h>
#include <stdlib.h>

void main (int argc, char **argv)
{
int x;

printf ("Running child process : \n");
for (x = 0; x < argc; x = x +1)
     printf ("%s : \n", argv[x]);
}
```

execv

DOS UNIX ANSI C C++

Syntax

```
int execv(char *path, char *argv[]);

char *path;                 Filename of child process
char *argv[];               Arguments for child process
```

Function The `execv` function loads and executes a child process. The argument pointers are passed as an array of pointers.

File(s) to Include `#include <process.h>`

Description The `execv` function loads and executes another program. The filename of the program to execute, called the child process, is specified in the `path` argument. The filename specified in the `path` argument is searched for using the standard DOS search. When the filename contains no file extension, the filename is searched for in the following way: The filename, as given, is searched for first. If not found, then the `.com` extension is added and searched for, then the `.exe` extension is added and searched for.

The `argv` function is an array of pointers used to pass arguments to the child process. This function is useful when the number of arguments which must be passed to the child process varies.

Value(s) Returned No value is returned when successful. However, when an error occurs, a –1 is returned and the global variable `errno` is set to one of the following:

E2BIG	Argument list too long
EACCES	Permission denied
EMFILE	Too many open files
ENOENT	Path or file name not found
ENOEXEC	Exec format error
ENOMEM	Not enough core

Related Function(s) `spawnv` : creates and executes a child process

Example In the following example, the parent process executes the child process. The child process must be compiled separately and entitled `child.exe`.

Parent Process

```
#include <conio.h>
#include <stdio.h>
#include <process.h>

void main (int argc, char *argv[])
{
clrscr();
printf ("Calling child process from
%s\n",argv[0]);
execv ("child.exe",argv);
printf ("Number of parameters %d\n",argc);
perror ("exec error\n");
exit (1);
}
```

Child Process

```
#include <stdio.h>
#include <stdlib.h>

void main (int argc, char **argv)
{
int x;

printf ("Running child process : \n");
for (x = 0; x < argc; x = x +1)
     printf ("%s : \n", argv[x]);
}
```

execve

DOS UNIX ANSI C C++

Syntax

```
int execve(char *path, char *argv[], char **env);
```

`char *path;`	*Filename of child process*
`char *argv[];`	*Arguments for the child process*
`char **env;`	*Environment variables*

Function The `execve` function loads and executes a child process. The argument pointers are passed as an array of pointers. The environment for the child process can be altered.

File(s) to Include `#include <process.h>`

Description The `execve` function loads and executes another program. The filename of the program to execute, called the child process, is specified in the `path` argument. The filename specified in the `path` argument is searched for using the standard DOS search. When the filename contains no file extension, the filename is searched for in the following way: The filename, as given, is searched for first. If not found, then the `.com` extension is added and searched for, then the `.exe` extension is added and searched for.

The `argv` argument is an array of pointers used to pass arguments to the child process. This function is useful when the number of arguments which must be passed to the child process varies.

The `env` argument is an array of character pointers which can be used to specify new environment settings for the child process. Each element of the `env` argument points to a null-terminated character string in the form

```
envvar = value
```

in which `envvar` is the name of the environment variable and `value` is the new value of the environment variable. When the `env` argument is null, the child process defaults to the environment settings of the parent process.

Value(s) Returned No value is returned when successful. However, when an error occurs, a –1 is returned and the global variable `errno` is set to one of the following:

E2BIG	Argument list too long
EACCES	Permission denied
EMFILE	Too many open files
ENOENT	Path or file name not found
ENOEXEC	Exec format error
ENOMEM	Not enough core

Related Function(s)

`spawnve` : creates and executes a child process

Example

In the following example, the parent process executes the child process. The child process must be compiled separately and entitled `child.exe`.

Parent Process

```
#include <conio.h>
#include <stdio.h>
#include <process.h>

void main (int argc, char *argv[], char *envp[])
{
clrscr();
printf ("Calling child process from
%s\n",argv[0]);
execve ("child.exe",argv,envp);
printf ("Number of parameters %d\n",argc);
perror ("exec error\n");
exit (1);
}
```

Child Process

```
#include <stdio.h>
#include <stdlib.h>

void main (int argc, char **argv)
{
int x;

printf ("Running child process : \n");
for (x = 0; x < argc; x = x +1)
     printf ("%s : \n", argv[x]);
}
```

execvp

DOS UNIX ANSI C C++

Syntax `int execvp(char *path, char *argv[]);`

```
char *path;           Filename of child process
char *argv[];         Arguments for child process
```

Function The `execvp` function loads and executes a child process. The argument pointers are passed as an array of pointers. This function searches the DOS PATH for the specified file.

File(s) to Include `#include <process.h>`

Description The `execvp` function loads and executes another program. The filename of the program to execute, called the child process, is specified in the `path` argument. The filename specified in the `path` argument is searched for using the standard DOS search. When the filename contains no file extension, the filename is searched for in the following way: The filename, as given, is searched for first. If not found, then the `.com` extension is added and searched for, then the `.exe` extension is added and searched for.

The `execvp` function searches for the child process in all the directories specified by the DOS PATH variable. The `execl`, `execle`, `execv`, and `execve` functions search only the specified path or current working directory.

The `argv` argument is an array of pointers used to pass arguments to the child process. This function is useful when the number of arguments which must be passed to the child process varies.

Value(s) Returned No value is returned when successful. However, when an error occurs, a –1 is returned and the global variable `errno` is set to one of the following:

E2BIG	Argument list too long
EACCES	Permission denied
EMFILE	Too many open files
ENOENT	Path or file name not found
ENOEXEC	Exec format error
ENOMEM	Not enough core

Related Function(s) `spawnvp` : creates and executes a child process

Example In the following example, the parent process executes the child process. The child process must be compiled separately and entitled `child.exe`.

Parent Process

```
#include <conio.h>
#include <stdio.h>
#include <process.h>

void main (int argc, char *argv[])
{
clrscr();
printf ("Calling child process from
%s\n",argv[0]);
execvp ("child.exe",argv);
printf ("Number of parameters %d\n",argc);
perror ("exec error\n");
exit (1);
}
```

Child Process

```
#include <stdio.h>
#include <stdlib.h>

void main (int argc, char **argv)
{
int x;

printf ("Running child process : \n");
for (x = 0; x < argc; x = x +1)
     printf ("%s : \n", argv[x]);
}
```

execvpe

DOS UNIX ANSI C C++

Syntax `int execvpe(char *path, char *argv[], char **env);`

`char *path;`	*Filename of child process*
`char *argv[];`	*Arguments for child process*
`char **env;`	*Environment variables*

Function The `execvpe` function loads and executes a child process. The argument pointers are passed as an array of pointers. This function searches the DOS PATH for the specified file. The environment for the child process can be altered.

File(s) to Include `#include <process.h>`

Description The `execvpe` function loads and executes another program. The filename of the program to execute, called the child process, is specified in the `path` argument. The filename specified in the `path` argument is searched for using the standard DOS search. When the filename contains no file extension, the filename is searched for in the following way: The filename, as given, is searched for first. If not found, then the `.com` extension is added and searched for, then the `.exe` extension is added and searched for.

The `execvpe` function searches for the child process in all the directories specified by the DOS PATH variable. The `execl`, `execle`, `execv`, and `execve` functions search only the specified path or current working directory.

The `argv` argument is an array of pointers used to pass arguments to the child process. This function is useful when the number of arguments that must be passed to the child process varies.

The `env` argument is an array of character pointers which can be used to specify new environment settings for the child process. Each element of the `env` argument points to a null-terminated character string in the form

```
envvar = value
```

in which `envvar` is the name of the environment variable and `value` is the new value of the environment variable. When the `env` argument is null, the child process defaults to the environment settings of the parent process.

Value(s) Returned No value is returned when successful. However, when an error occurs, a –1 is returned and the global variable `errno` is set to one of the following:

E2BIG	Argument list too long
EACCES	Permission denied
EMFILE	Too many open files
ENOENT	Path or file name not found

ENOEXEC	Exec format error
ENOMEM	Not enough core

Related Function(s) `spawnvpe` : creates and executes a child process

Example In the following example, the parent process executes the child process. The child process must be compiled separately and entitled `child.exe`.

Parent Process

```
#include <conio.h>
#include <stdio.h>
#include <process.h>

void main (int argc, char *argv[], char *envp[])
{
clrscr();
printf ("Calling child process from
%s\n",argv[0]);
execvpe ("child.exe",argv,envp);
printf ("Number of parameters %d\n",argc);
perror ("exec error\n");
exit (1);
}
```

Child Process

```
#include <stdio.h>
#include <stdlib.h>

void main (int argc, char **argv)
{
int x;

printf ("Running child process : \n");
for (x = 0; x < argc; x = x +1)
     printf ("%s : \n", argv[x]);
}
```

_exit

DOS UNIX ANSI C C++

Syntax `void _exit(int status);`

`int status;` *Exit status*

Function The `_exit` function terminates a program.

File(s) to Include `#include <stdlib.h>`
or
`#include <process.h>`

Description The `_exit` function terminates program execution. When the program is terminated, no files are closed, no output is flushed, and no `exit` functions are called. The `status` argument is used as the exit status of the process. A zero is usually used to indicate a normal exit. A nonzero value is usually used to indicate an error.

Value(s) Returned There is no return value.

Related Function(s)
`abort` : abnormally terminates a program
`exit` : terminates a program

Example In the following example, `_exit` terminates the program.

```
#include <stdio.h>
#include <stdlib.h>

int main (void)
{
clrscr ();
printf ("The program will terminate without
  displaying last line\n");
_exit(0);
printf ("This line will not be printed\n");

return 0;
}
```

---

exit

DOS	UNIX	ANSI C	C++

Syntax `void exit(int status);`

`int status;` *Exit status*

Function The `exit` function terminates the program.

File(s) to Include

```
#include <stdlib.h>
```
or
```
#include <process.h>
```

Description The `exit` function terminates a program. Unlike the `_exit` function, with `exit` all files are closed, buffered output is processed, and exit functions are called before the program is terminated. The `status` argument defines the exit status of the program. A 0 is generally used to indicate a normal exit. A nonzero value is generally used to indicate an error.

Value(s) Returned There is no return value.

Related Function(s)

`abort` : abnormally terminates a program
`_exit` : terminates a program

Example In the following example, `exit` terminates the program.

```
#include <stdio.h>
#include <stdlib.h>

int main (void)
{
clrscr ();
printf ("The program will terminate without
  displaying last line\n");
exit(0);
printf ("This line will not be printed\n");

return 0;
}
```

---

getpid

DOS | UNIX | ANSI C | C++

Syntax `unsigned getpid(void);`

Function The `getpid` function gets the process identification of a program.

File(s) to Include `#include <process.h>`

Description The `getpid` function gets the process identification number for a program. The process identification number, which uniquely identifies each ongoing process, is essential in multitasking environments.

Value(s) Returned The segment value of a program's program segment prefix (PSP) is returned.

Related Function(s) `getpsp` : gets the program's program segment prefix

Example This example retrieves and displays the program's process identification.

```
#include <stdio.h>
#include <process.h>

int main (void)
{
clrscr();
printf ("PID : %X\n", getpid());

getch();
return 0;
}
```

raise

DOS	UNIX	ANSI C	C++

Syntax `int raise(int sig);`

`int sig;` *Signal to send*

Function The `raise` function sends a software signal to the program.

File(s) to Include `#include <signal.h>`

Description The `raise` function sends the software signal specified in the `sig` argument to the program. The default action for the signal is taken when no signal handler has been installed. However, when a signal handler is installed, the signal handler will take appropriate action. Table 14.2 lists the signal types defined in the Borland C++ `signal.h` header file.

Table 14.2. Signal types.	
Signal	*Meaning*
SIGABRT	Abnormal termination
SIGFPE	Bad floating-point operation
SIGILL	Illegal instruction
SIGINT	Control break interrupt
SIGSEGV	Invalid access to storage
SIGTERM	Request for program termination

Value(s) Returned A 0 is returned when successful. A nonzero value is returned when unsuccessful.

Related Function(s)
`abort` : abnormally aborts a program
`signal` : specifies signal handling actions

Example This example raises the SIGABRT flag and abnormally aborts.

```
#include <stdio.h>
#include <signal.h>

int main (void)
{
clrscr();
printf ("Raising SIGABRT\n");
raise (SIGABRT);

return 0;
}
```

signal

DOS | UNIX | ANSI C | C++

Syntax

```
void(*signal(int sig, void (*func)
            (int sig[,int subcode])))(int);
```

`int sig;`	*Signal*
`void (*func)(int sig[,int subcode])))(int);`	*Signal handler*

Function The `signal` function defines signal handling actions.

File(s) to Include `#include <signal.h>`

Description The `signal` function defines the way in which the signal specified in the `sig` argument is handled. The signal types are listed in table 14.2. The `func` argument identifies the routine which will handle the signal. The signal handling routine can be user-defined or one of the predefined handlers listed in table 14.3.

Table 14.3. *Predefined signal handlers.*

Pointer to function	*Meaning*
SIG_DFL	Terminates the program
SIG_IGN	Ignore this type of signal
SIG_ERR	Indicates an error return from `signal`

A signal can be generated in several ways. When the signal is generated by the `raise` function or an external event, and a user-defined signal handler has been installed to handle the generated signal, the user-defined function is called with the signal type as a parameter and the action for that signal type is set to `SIG_DFL`.

When the signal type is SIGFPE, SIGSEGV, or SIGILL, the user-defined signal handler function is called with one to two extra parameters. When a signal is explicitly generated by the `raise` function, one extra parameter is used. This parameter is an integer indicating that the signal handler is being explicitly invoked. Table 14.4 lists the parameters used with each of the signal types described in this paragraph.

Table 14.4. *Extra parameter for explicitly generated signals.*

Signal	*Parameter*
SIGFPE	FPE_EXPLICITGEN
SIGSEGV	SEGV_EXPLICITGEN
SIGILL	ILL_EXPLICITGEN

Table 14.5 lists each extra parameter used to call the signal handler function when the signal type SIGFPE is generated as a result of a floating-point exception.

Table 14.5. *Parameters for floating-point exceptions.*

SIGFPE signal	*Meaning*
`FPE_INTOVFLOW`	INTO executed with OF flag set
`FPE_INTDIV0`	Integer divide by 0
`FPE_INVALID`	Invalid operation
`FPE_ZERODIVIDE`	Division by 0
`FPE_OVERFLOW`	Numeric overflow
`FPE_UNDERFLOW`	Numeric underflow
`FPE_INEXACT`	Precision
`FPE_EXPLICITGEN`	User program executed raise(SIGFPE)

When the SIGSEGV, SIGILL, or the integer-based variants of SIGFPE signals are generated as a result of processor exception, the signal handler function is called with two extra parameters. The first is the ANSI signal type. The second is an integer pointer into the stack of the interrupt handler that called the user-defined signal handler. The integer pointer points to a list of the processor registers saved when the exception occurred. These registers, in order, are BP, DI, SI, DS, ES, DX, CX, BX, AX, IP, CS, FLAGS.

SIGSEGV signals include:

`SEGV_BOUND`	Bound constraint exception
`SEGV_EXPLICITGEN`	`raise` was executed

The `SEGV_BOUND` signal is not supported by the 8088 or 8086 processors.

SIGILL signals include:

`ILL_EXECUTION`	Illegal operation attempted
`ILL_EXPLICITGEN`	`raise` was executed

The `ILL_EXECUTION` signal is not supported by the 8088, 8086, NEC V20, or NEC V30 processors.

Value(s) Returned The pointer to the previous handler routine for the specified signal type is returned when successful. When unsuccessful, `SIG_ERR` is returned and the external variable `errno` is set to EINVAL.

Related Function(s) `raise` : generates a software signal

Example This example prints lines of text until Control-C is pressed. The handler function then prints a message and terminates the program.

```
#include <stdio.h>
#include <signal.h>

void handler (void)
{
printf ("Breaking out\n");
exit (1);
}

int main (void)
{
int x;

clrscr();
signal (SIGINT,handler);
for (x=0; x<10000; x=x+1)
    printf ("Press Control-C to stop\n");

return 0;
}
```

spawnl

DOS | UNIX | ANSI C | C++

Syntax

```
int spawnl(int mode, char *path, char *arg0, arg1,
           ..., argn, NULL);
```

`int mode;`	*Mode for calling function*
`char *path;`	*Filename of child process*
`char *arg0, ...`	*Arguments for child process*
`NULL;`	*Null*

Function The `spawnl` function creates and executes a child process. The argument pointers are passed as separate arguments.

File(s) to Include `#include <process.h>`

Description The `spawnl` function creates and executes the child process defined by the `path` argument. The `mode` argument defines the way that the child and parent processes interact. The following constants can be used for the mode argument:

`P_WAIT`	Puts parent process "on hold" until child process completes its execution
`P_NOWAIT`	Continues to run the parent process while running the child process (Not available in early releases of Borland C++)
`P_OVERLAY`	Overlays child process in memory location formerly occupied by the parent process. This option is the same as the `execl`, `exec...` functions.

The filename specified in the `path` argument identifies the program to execute. The filename is searched for using the standard DOS search method. When no extension or period is specified, the exact filename is searched for. If not found, the `.com` extension is added and then searched for. If still not found, the `.exe` extension is added and then searched for.

The `arg0, ..., argn` arguments are used to define the arguments passed to the child process. Each argument is passed separately and the NULL terminator is required.

Value(s) Returned The exit status of the child process, usually a zero, is returned when successful. When unsuccessful, a –1 is returned and the global variable `errno` is set to one of the following:

E2BIG	Argument list too long
EINVAL	Invalid argument
ENOENT	Path or file name not found
ENOEXEC	Exec format error
ENOMEM	Not enough core

Related Function(s) `execl` : loads and executes a child process

Example In the following example, the parent process executes the child process. The child process must be compiled separately and entitled `child.exe`.

Parent Process

```
#include <conio.h>
#include <stdio.h>
#include <process.h>

void main (int argc, char *argv[])
{
clrscr();
printf ("Calling child process from
%s\n",argv[0]);
spawnl
(P_WAIT,"child.exe","child.exe","One","Two",NULL);
printf ("Number of parameters %d\n",argc);
perror ("exec error\n");
exit (1);
}
```

Child Process

```
#include <stdio.h>
#include <stdlib.h>

void main (int argc, char **argv)
{
int x;

printf ("Running child process : \n");
for (x = 0; x < argc; x = x +1)
     printf ("%s : \n", argv[x]);
}
```

spawnle

DOS UNIX ANSI C C++

Syntax

```
int spawnle(int mode, char *path, char *arg0,
            arg1, ..., argn, NULL, char *envp[]);
```

`int mode;`	*Mode for calling function*
`char *path;`	*Filename of child process*
`char *arg 0, ...`	*Arguments for child process*
`NULL;`	*Null*
`char *envp[];`	*New environment variables*

Function The `spawnle` function creates and executes a child process. The argument pointers are passed as separate arguments. The environment for the child process can be altered.

File(s) to Include `#include <process.h>`

Description The `spawnle` function creates and executes the child process defined by the `path` argument. The `mode` argument defines the way that the child and parent processes interact. The following constants can be used for the mode argument:

`P_WAIT`	Puts parent process "on hold" until child process completes its execution
`P_NOWAIT`	Continues to run the parent process while running the child process (Not available in early releases of Borland C++)
`P_OVERLAY`	Overlays child process in memory location formerly occupied by the parent process. This option is the same as the `execl`, `execle`, `execlp`, `exec...` functions.

The filename specified in the `path` argument identifies the program to execute. The filename is searched for using the standard DOS search method. When no extension or period is specified, the exact filename is searched for. If not found, the `.com` extension is added and then searched for. If still not found, the `.exe` extension is added and then searched for.

The `arg0, ..., argn` arguments are used to define the arguments passed to the child process. Each argument is passed separately and the NULL terminator is required.

The `envp` argument specifies the new environment settings. The `envp` argument is an array of character pointers in which each element of the array identifies a character string in the following format:

```
envvar = value
```

in which `envvar` is the environment variable name and `value` is its new associated value. If the `envp` argument is null, the child process inherits the environment settings of the parent process.

Value(s) Returned The exit status of the child process, usually a zero, is returned when successful. When unsuccessful, a –1 is returned and the global variable `errno` is set to one of the following:

E2BIG	Argument list too long
EINVAL	Invalid argument
ENOENT	Path or file name not found
ENOEXEC	Exec format error
ENOMEM	Not enough core

Related Function(s) `execle` : loads and executes a child process

Example In the following example, the parent process executes the child process. The child process must be compiled separately and entitled `child.exe`.

Parent Process

```
#include <conio.h>
#include <stdio.h>
#include <process.h>

void main (int argc, char *argv[], char *envp[])
{
clrscr();
printf ("Calling child process from
%s\n",argv[0]);
spawnle
(P_WAIT,"child.exe","child.exe","One","Two",NULL,envp);
printf ("Number of parameters %d\n",argc);
perror ("exec error\n");
exit (1);
}
```

Child Process

```
#include <stdio.h>
#include <stdlib.h>

void main (int argc, char **argv)
{
int x;

printf ("Running child process : \n");
for (x = 0; x < argc; x = x +1)
     printf ("%s : \n", argv[x]);
}
```

spawnlp

DOS UNIX ANSI C C++

Syntax

```
int spawnlp(int mode, char *path, char *arg0,
              arg1, ..., argn, NULL);
```

`int mode;`	*Mode for calling function*
`char *path;`	*Filename of child process*
`char *arg0, ...`	*Arguments for child process*
`NULL`	*Null*

Function The `spawnlp` function creates and executes a child process. The argument pointers are passed as separate arguments. This function searches the DOS PATH for the specified file.

File(s) to Include `#include <process.h>`

Description The `spawnlp` function creates and executes the child process defined by the `path` argument. The `mode` argument defines the way that the child and parent processes interact. The following constants can be used for the `mode` argument:

`P_WAIT`	Puts parent process "on hold" until child process completes its execution
`P_NOWAIT`	Continues to run the parent process while running the child process (Not available in early releases of Borland C++)
`P_OVERLAY`	Overlays child process in memory location formerly occupied by the parent process. This option is the same as the `execl`, `exec...` functions.

The filename specified in the `path` argument identifies the program to execute. The filename is searched for using the standard DOS search method. When no extension or period is specified, the exact filename is searched for. If not found, the `.com` extension is added and then searched for. If still not found, the `.exe` extension is added and then searched for.

The `spawnlp` function will search every path defined in the PATH environment variable for the specified file. The `spawnl`, `spawnle`, `spawnv`, and `spawnve` functions search only the path specified in the `path` argument or the current working directory.

The `arg0, ..., argn` arguments are used to define the arguments passed to the child process. Each argument is passed separately and the NULL terminator is required.

Value(s) Returned The exit status of the child process, usually a zero, is returned when successful. When unsuccessful, a –1 is returned and the global variable `errno` is set to one of the following:

E2BIG	Argument list too long
EINVAL	Invalid argument
ENOENT	Path or file name not found
ENOEXEC	Exec format error
ENOMEM	Not enough core

Related Function(s) `execlp` : loads and executes a child process

Example In the following example, the parent process executes the child process. The child process must be compiled separately and entitled `child.exe`.

Parent Process

```
#include <conio.h>
#include <stdio.h>
#include <process.h>

void main (int argc, char *argv[])
{
clrscr();
printf ("Calling child process from
%s\n",argv[0]);
spawnlp
(P_WAIT,"child.exe","child.exe","One","Two",NULL);
printf ("Number of parameters %d\n",argc);
perror ("exec error\n");
exit (1);
}
```

Child Process

```
#include <stdio.h>
#include <stdlib.h>

void main (int argc, char **argv)
{
int x;

printf ("Running child process : \n");
for (x = 0; x < argc; x = x +1)
     printf ("%s : \n", argv[x]);
}
```

spawnlpe

DOS UNIX ANSI C C++

Syntax

```
int spawnlpe(int mode, char *path, char *arg0,
             arg1, ..., argn, NULL, char *envp[]);
```

`int mode;`	*Mode for calling function*
`char *path;`	*Filename of child process*
`char *arg0, ...`	*Arguments for child process*
`NULL;`	*Null*
`char *envp[];`	*New environment variables*

Function The `spawnlpe` function creates and executes a child process. The argument pointers are passed as separate arguments. This function searches the DOS PATH for the specified file. The environment for the child process can be altered.

File(s) to Include `#include <process.h>`

Description The `spawnlpe` function creates and executes the child process defined by the `path` argument. The `mode` argument defines the way that the child and parent processes interact. The following constants can be used for the mode argument:

`P_WAIT`	Puts parent process "on hold" until child process completes its execution
`P_NOWAIT`	Continues to run the parent process while running the child process (Not available in early releases of Borland C++)
`P_OVERLAY`	Overlays child process in memory location formerly occupied by the parent process. This option is the same as the `execl`, `exec...` functions.

The filename specified in the `path` argument identifies the program to execute. The filename is searched for using the standard DOS search method. When no extension or period is specified, the exact filename is searched for. If not found, the `.com` extension is added and then searched for. If still not found, the `.exe` extension is added and then searched for.

The `spawnlpe` function will search every path defined in the PATH environment variable for the specified file. The `spawnl`, `spawnle`, `spawnv`, and `spawnve` functions search only the path specified in the `path` argument or the current working directory.

The `arg0, ..., argn` arguments are used to define the arguments passed to the child process. Each argument is passed separately and the NULL terminator is required.

The `envp` argument specifies the new environment settings. The `envp` argument is an array of character pointers in which each element of the array identifies a character string in the following format:

```
envvar = value
```

in which `envvar` is the environment variable name and `value` is its new associated value. If the `envp` argument is null, the child process inherits the environment settings of the parent process.

Value(s) Returned The exit status of the child process, usually a zero, is returned when successful. When unsuccessful, –1 is returned and the global variable `errno` is set to one of the following:

E2BIG	Argument list too long
EINVAL	Invalid argument
ENOENT	Path or file name not found
ENOEXEC	Exec format error
ENOMEM	Not enough core

Related Function(s) `execlpe` : loads and executes a child process

Example In the following example, the parent process executes the child process. The child process must be compiled separately and entitled `child.exe`.

Parent Process

```
#include <conio.h>
#include <stdio.h>
#include <process.h>

void main (int argc, char *argv[], char *envp[])
{
clrscr();
printf ("Calling child process from
%s\n",argv[0]);
spawnlpe (P_WAIT,"child.exe","child.exe","One",
 "Two",NULL,envp);
```

```
printf ("Number of parameters %d\n",argc);
perror ("exec error\n");
exit (1);
}
```

Child Process

```
#include <stdio.h>
#include <stdlib.h>

void main (int argc, char **argv)
{
int x;

printf ("Running child process : \n");
for (x = 0; x < argc; x = x +1)
     printf ("%s : \n", argv[x]);
}
```

spawnv

DOS UNIX ANSI C C++

Syntax `int spawnv(int mode, char *path, char *argv[]);`

`int mode;`	*Mode for calling function*
`char *path;`	*Filename of child process*
`char *argv[];`	*Arguments for child process*

Function The `spawnv` function creates and executes a child process. The argument pointers are passed as an array of pointers.

File(s) to Include `#include <process.h>`

Description The `spawnv` function creates and executes the child process defined by the `path` argument. The `mode` argument defines the way that the child and parent processes interact. The following constants can be used for the `mode` argument:

`P_WAIT`	Puts parent process "on hold" until child process completes its execution
`P_NOWAIT`	Continues to run the parent process while running the child process (Not available in early releases of Borland C++)

`P_OVERLAY`	Overlays child process in memory location formerly occupied by the parent process. This option is the same as the `execl`, `exec...` functions.

The filename specified in the `path` argument identifies the program to execute. The filename is searched for using the standard DOS search method. When no extension or period is specified, the exact filename is searched for. If not found, the `.com` extension is added and then searched for. If still not found, the `.exe` extension is added and then searched for.

The `argv` argument is an array of argument pointers which defines the arguments passed to the child process. This function is useful when the number of arguments passed to the child process varies.

Value(s) Returned The exit status of the child process, usually a zero, is returned when successful. When unsuccessful, a –1 is returned and the global variable `errno` is set to one of the following:

E2BIG	Argument list too long
EINVAL	Invalid argument
ENOENT	Path or file name not found
ENOEXEC	Exec format error
ENOMEM	Not enough core

Related Function(s) `execv` : loads and executes a child process

Example In the following example, the parent process executes the child process. The child process must be compiled separately and entitled `child.exe`.

Parent Process

```
#include <conio.h>
#include <stdio.h>
#include <process.h>

void main (int argc, char *argv[])
{
clrscr();
printf ("Calling child process from
%s\n",argv[0]);
spawnv (P_WAIT,"child.exe",argv);
printf ("Number of parameters %d\n",argc);
perror ("exec error\n");
exit (1);
}
```

Child Process

```
#include <stdio.h>
#include <stdlib.h>

void main (int argc, char **argv)
{
int x;

printf ("Running child process : \n");
for (x = 0; x < argc; x = x +1)
     printf ("%s : \n", argv[x]);
}
```

spawnve

DOS UNIX ANSI C C++

Syntax

```
int spawnve(int mode, char *path, char *argv[],
               char *envp []);
```

`int mode;`	*Mode of calling function*
`char *path;`	*Filename of child process*
`char *argv[];`	*Arguments for child process*
`char *envp[];`	*New environment variables*

Function The `spawnve` function creates and executes a child process. The argument pointers are passed as an array of pointers. The environment for the child process can be altered.

File(s) to Include `#include <process.h>`

Description The `spawnve` function creates and executes the child process defined by the `path` argument. The `mode` argument defines the way that the child and parent processes interact. The following constants can be used for the `mode` argument:

`P_WAIT`	Puts parent process "on hold" until child process completes its execution
`P_NOWAIT`	Continues to run the parent process while running the child process (Not available in early releases of Borland C++)
`P_OVERLAY`	Overlays child process in memory location formerly occupied by the parent process. This option is the same as the `execl`, `exec...` functions.

The filename specified in the `path` argument identifies the program to execute. The filename is searched for using the standard DOS search method. When no extension or period is specified, the exact filename is searched for. If not found, the `.com` extension is added and then searched for. If still not found, the `.exe` extension is added and then searched for.

The `argv` argument is an array of argument pointers which define the arguments passed to the child process. This function is useful when the number of arguments passed to the child process varies.

The `envp` argument specifies the new environment settings. The `envp` argument is an array of character pointers in which each element of the array identifies a character string in the following format:

```
envvar = value
```

in which `envvar` is the environment variable name and `value` is its new associated value. If the `envp` argument is null, the child process inherits the environment settings of the parent process.

Value(s) Returned The exit status of the child process, usually a zero, is returned when successful. When unsuccessful, a –1 is returned and the global variable `errno` is set to one of the following:

E2BIG	Argument list too long
EINVAL	Invalid argument
ENOENT	Path or file name not found
ENOEXEC	Exec format error
ENOMEM	Not enough core

Related Function(s) `execve` : loads and executes a child process

Example In the following example, the parent process executes the child process. The child process must be compiled separately and entitled `child.exe`.

Parent Process

```
#include <conio.h>
#include <stdio.h>
#include <process.h>

void main (int argc, char *argv[], char *envp[])
{
clrscr();
printf ("Calling child process from
```

```
  %s\n",argv[0]);
spawnve (P_WAIT,"child.exe",argv,envp);
printf ("Number of parameters %d\n",argc);
perror ("exec error\n");
exit (1);
}
```

Child Process

```
#include <stdio.h>
#include <stdlib.h>

void main (int argc, char **argv)
{
int x;

printf ("Running child process : \n");
for (x = 0; x < argc; x = x +1)
     printf ("%s : \n", argv[x]);
}
```

spawnvp

DOS | UNIX | ANSI C | C++

Syntax `int spawnvp(int mode, char *path, char *argv[]);`

`int mode;`	*Mode for calling function*
`char *path;`	*Filename of child process*
`char *argv[];`	*Arguments for child process*

Function The `spawnvp` function creates and executes a child process. The argument pointers are passed as an array of pointers. This function searches the DOS PATH for the specified file.

File(s) to Include `#include <process.h>`

Description The `spawnvp` function creates and executes the child process defined by the `path` argument. The `mode` argument defines the way that the child and parent processes interact. The following constants can be used for the `mode` argument:

`P_WAIT`	Puts parent process "on hold" until child process completes its execution

`P_NOWAIT`	Continues to run the parent process while running the child process (Not available in early releases of Borland C++)
`P_OVERLAY`	Overlays child process in memory location formerly occupied by the parent process. This option is the same as the `execl`, `exec...` functions.

The filename specified in the `path` argument identifies the program to execute. The filename is searched for using the standard DOS search method. When no extension or period is specified, the exact filename is searched for. If not found, the `.com` extension is added and then searched for. If still not found, the `.exe` extension is added and then searched for.

The `spawnvp` function will search every path defined in the PATH environment variable for the specified file. The `spawnl`, `spawnle`, `spawnv`, and `spawnve` functions search only the path specified in the `path` argument or the current working directory.

The `argv` argument is an array of argument pointers which defines the arguments passed to the child process. This function is useful when the number of arguments passed to the child process varies.

Value(s) Returned The exit status of the child process, usually a zero, is returned when successful. When unsuccessful, a –1 is returned and the global variable `errno` is set to one of the following:

E2BIG	Argument list too long
EINVAL	Invalid argument
ENOENT	Path or file name not found
ENOEXEC	Exec format error
ENOMEM	Not enough core

Related Function(s) `execvp` : loads and executes a child process

Example In the following example, the parent process executes the child process. The child process must be compiled separately and entitled `child.exe`.

Parent Process

```
#include <conio.h>
#include <stdio.h>
#include <process.h>
```

```
void main (int argc, char *argv[])
{
clrscr();
printf ("Calling child process from
%s\n",argv[0]);
spawnvp (P_WAIT,"child.exe",argv);
printf ("Number of parameters %d\n",argc);
perror ("exec error\n");
exit (1);
}
```

Child Process

```
#include <stdio.h>
#include <stdlib.h>

void main (int argc, char **argv)
{
int x;

printf ("Running child process : \n");
for (x = 0; x < argc; x = x +1)
     printf ("%s : \n", argv[x]);
}
```

spawnvpe

DOS UNIX ANSI C C++

Syntax

```
int spawnvpe(int modem, char *path, char *argv[],
                  char *envp[]);
```

`int mode;`	*Mode for calling process*
`char *path;`	*Filename of child process*
`char *argv[];`	*Arguments for child process*
`char *envp[];`	*New environment variables*

Function The `spawnvpe` function creates and executes a child process. The argument pointers are passed as an array of pointers. This function searches the DOS PATH for the specified file. The environment for the child process can be altered.

File(s) to Include `#include <process.h>`

Description The `spawnvpe` function creates and executes the child process defined by the `path` argument. The `mode` argument defines the way that the child and parent processes interact. The following constants can be used for the `mode` argument:

`P_WAIT`	Puts parent process "on hold" until child process completes its execution
`P_NOWAIT`	Continues to run the parent process while running the child process (Not available in early releases of Borland C++)
`P_OVERLAY`	Overlays child process in memory location formerly occupied by the parent process. This option is the same as the `execl`, `exec...` functions.

The filename specified in the `path` argument identifies the program to execute. The filename is searched for using the standard DOS search method. When no extension or period is specified, the exact filename is searched for. If not found, the `.com` extension is added and then searched for. If still not found, the `.exe` extension is added and then searched for.

The `spawnvpe` function will search every path defined in the PATH environment variable for the specified file. The `spawnl`, `spawnle`, `spawnv`, and `spawnve` functions search only the path specified in the `path` argument or the current working directory.

The `argv` argument is an array of argument pointers which defines the arguments passed to the child process. This function is useful when the number of arguments passed to the child process varies.

The `envp` argument specifies the new environment settings. The `envp` argument is an array of character pointers in which each element of the array identifies a character string in the following format:

```
envvar = value
```

in which `envvar` is the environment variable name and `value` is its new associated value. If the `envp` argument is null, the child process inherits the environment settings of the parent process.

Value(s) Returned The exit status of the child process, usually a zero, is returned when successful. When unsuccessful, a –1 is returned and the global variable `errno` is set to one of the following:

E2BIG	Argument list too long
EINVAL	Invalid argument
ENOENT	Path or file name not found
ENOEXEC	Exec format error
ENOMEM	Not enough core

Related Function(s)

`execvpe` : loads and executes a child process

Example

In the following example, the parent process executes the child process. The child process must be compiled separately and entitled `child.exe`.

Parent Process

```
#include <conio.h>
#include <stdio.h>
#include <process.h>

void main (int argc, char *argv[], char *envp[])
{
clrscr();
printf ("Calling child process from
  %s\n",argv[0]);
spawnvpe (P_WAIT,"child.exe",argv,envp);
printf ("Number of parameters %d\n",argc);
perror ("exec error\n");
exit (1);
}
```

Child Process

```
#include <stdio.h>
#include <stdlib.h>

void main (int argc, char **argv)
{
int x;

printf ("Running child process : \n");
for (x = 0; x < argc; x = x +1)
     printf ("%s : \n", argv[x]);
}
```

Text Windows and Display

The Borland C++ library contains several functions for the display and manipulation of text through the use of text windows and text attributes. The functions listed in table 15.1 provide capabilites to create text windows, control text inside text windows, and modify text attributes.

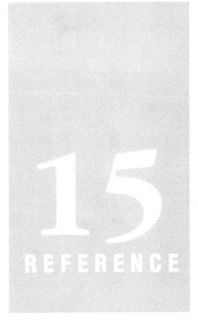

Table 15.1. Text window and display functions.

Functions	*Meaning*
clreol	Clears to the end of the line
clrscr	Clears the screen
delline	Deletes a line of text
gettext	Stores a block of text
gettextinfo	Gets information on the text mode
gotoxy	Moves the text cursor
highvideo	Sets high intensity characters
insline	Inserts a line at the cursor
lowvideo	Sets low intensity characters
movetext	Moves a block of text
normvideo	Sets normal intensity characters
puttext	Places a stored block of text
_setcursortype	Specifies the cursor type
textattr	Sets the text attributes
textbackground	Sets the text background color
textcolor	Sets the text foreground color
textmode	Sets the text mode
wherex	Gets the x location of the text cursor
wherey	Gets the y location of the text cursor
window	Defines the boundaries of the text window

Text Mode

The IBM series of personal computers and their compatibles operate, by default, in text mode. In text mode, the screen is divided into a series of character cells arranged in rows and columns. Each character cell consists of a series of pixels used to create the shape of the character to be displayed inside the cell. Figure 15.1 illustrates the text screen. The number of character cells available on the screen depends on the video hardware. Most graphics adapters and monitors support the basic black-and-white, 25-row by 80-column text modes. However, some adapters, such as the Color Graphics Adapter (CGA), Enhanced Graphics Adapter (EGA), and the Video Graphics Array (VGA), support color 25-row by 80-column text modes. In addition, the EGA supports a color 43-by-80 text mode and the VGA supports a color 50-by-80 text mode. The text modes supported by Borland C++ are described later in the chapter under `textmode` function. The text mode initialized on boot-up depends on the video hardware configuration. The functions described in this chapter are used to display text in text modes.

Fig. 15.1. The screen in text mode.

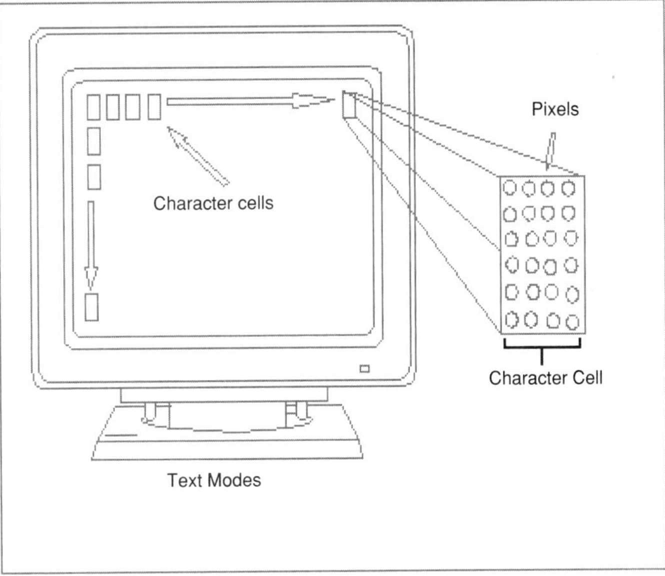

Borland C++ Text Window and Display Functions Reference Guide

The remainder of this chapter provides detailed information on each of the functions listed in table 15.1.

clreol

DOS | UNIX | ANSI C | C++

Syntax `void clreol(void);`

Function The `clreol` function clears the text line from the cursor position to the end of the line.

File(s) to Include `#include <conio.h>`

Description The `clreol` function clears all characters in the text line from the current position of the text cursor to the end of the line. Only text within the current text window will be cleared and the cursor position is not changed.

Value(s) Returned There is no return value.

Related Function(s)

`clrscr` : clears the current text window
`delline` : deletes a line of text

Example In the following example, `clreol` clears all but the first letter of the printed line when a key is pressed.

```
#include <conio.h>
#include <stdio.h>

int main (void)
{
clrscr();
printf ("Press any key to clear from 2,1 to end of
 line");
gotoxy (2,1);
getch();
clreol();

return 0;
}
```

clrscr

DOS UNIX ANSI C C++

Syntax `void clrscr(void);`

Function The `clrscr` function clears the current text window.

File(s) to Include `#include <conio.h>`

Description The `clrscr` function clears the current text window. The cursor is then placed in the upper left corner of the text window, which is text cursor position 1,1.

Value(s Returned There is no return value.

Related Function(s)
`clreol` : clears text from the cursor to end of line
`delline` : deletes a line of text

Example In the following example, `clrscr` clears the text window.

```
#include <conio.h>
#include <stdio.h>

int main (void)
{
int x;

clrscr();
for (x=1; x < 22; x = x + 1)
     {
   gotoxy(3,x);
   printf ("Press any key to clear the
   screen");
   }
getch();
clrscr();

return 0;
}
```

delline

DOS | UNIX | ANSI C | C++

Syntax `void delline(void);`

Function The `delline` function deletes a line of text from the current text window.

File(s) to Include `#include <conio.h>`

Description The `delline` function deletes the line of text containing the text cursor from the current text window.

Value(s) Returned There is no return value.

Related Function(s)
`clreol` : clears text from the cursor to end of line
`clrscr` : clears the current text window
`insline` : inserts a blank line in the text window

Example In the following example, `delline` deletes the first line of the displayed text. Note that all other lines of text move up one line when the first line is deleted.

```
#include <conio.h>
#include <stdio.h>

int main (void)
{
int x;

clrscr();
for (x=1; x < 22; x = x + 1)
     {
   gotoxy(3,x);
   printf ("Press any key to delete the first
   line");
   }
gotoxy (3,1);
getch();
delline();

return 0;
}
```

gettext

DOS | UNIX | ANSI C | C++

Syntax

```
int gettext(int left, int top, int right, int
            bottom, void *destin);
```

```
int left, top;           Upper left corner of text area
int right, bottom;       Lower right corner of text area
void *destin;            Pointer to memory buffer
```

Function The `gettext` function copies a section of text from the screen to memory.

File(s) to Include `#include <conio.h>`

Description The `gettext` function copies a rectangular section of text from the screen to the memory location pointed to by the `destin` argument. The rectangular section of the screen to copy is described by the `left`, `top`, `right`, and `bottom` arguments. The `left` and `top` arguments define the column and row coordinates of the upper left-hand corner of the rectangular region. The `right` and `bottom` arguments define the column and row coordinates of the lower right-hand corner of the rectangular region.

Each character position of the rectangular region requires two bytes of memory. The first byte is for the character; the second byte is for the character cell's attribute. The following formula can be used to determine the size requirements of the memory buffer:

```
number of bytes = height in rows x width in
  columns x 2
```

Value(s) Returned A 1 is returned if the rectangular section of text is successfully saved. A 0 is returned if the attempt to save is unsuccessful.

Related Function(s)

`movetext` : copies text from one part of the screen to another
`puttext` : places text from memory onto the screen

Example In the following example, `gettext` saves a portion of the screen.

```
#include <conio.h>
#include <stdio.h>

char textbuffer [4096];

int main (void)
{
int x;

clrscr();
for (x=1; x < 22; x = x + 1)
   {
   gotoxy(3,x);
   printf ("Save this part of the screen");
   }
gettext (3,1,32,22,textbuffer);

gotoxy (3,24);
printf ("Press any key to clear and restore screen");
getch();
clrscr();
puttext (3,1,32,22,textbuffer);

return 0;
}
```

gettextinfo

DOS | UNIX | ANSI C | C++

Syntax `void gettextinfo(struct text_info *r);`

`struct text_info *r;` *Text information*

Function The `gettextinfo` function retrieves the current text mode information.

File(s) to Include `#include <conio.h>`

Description The `gettextinfo` function retrieves information on the current text mode. This information is then placed in the `text_info` structure pointed to by the `r` argument. The `text_info` structure is as follows:

```
struct text_info
    {
```

```
unsigned char winleft;      /*left window coordinate*/
unsigned char wintop;       /*top window coordinate*/
unsigned char winright;     /*right window coordinate*/
unsigned char winbottom;    /*bottom window coordinate*/
unsigned char attribute;    /*text attribute*/
unsigned char normattr;     /*normal attribute*/
unsigned char currmode;     /*BW40,BW80,C40,C80,or
                              C4350*/
unsigned char screenheight; /*bottom minus top*/
unsigned char screenwidth;  /*right minus left*/
unsigned char curx;         /*x coordinate in window*/
unsigned char cury;         /*y coordinate in window*/
};
```

Value(s) Returned There is no return value.

Related Function(s) `window` : defines the current text window

Example The following example retrieves and displays the current text information.

```
#include <conio.h>
#include <stdio.h>

int main (void)
{
struct text_info tex;

clrscr();
gettextinfo (&tex);
printf ("Left window : %2d\n",tex.winleft);
printf ("Top window : %2d\n",tex.wintop);
printf ("Right window : %2d\n",tex.winright);
printf ("Bottom window : %2d\n",tex.winbottom);
printf ("Attribute : %2d\n",tex.attribute);
printf ("Normal attribute : %2d\n",tex.normattr);
printf ("Current mode : %2d\n",tex.currmode);
printf ("Screen height : %2d\n",tex.screenheight);
printf ("Screen width : %2d\n",tex.screenwidth);
printf ("Current x : %2d\n",tex.curx);
printf ("Current y : %2d\n",tex.cury);

return 0;
}
```

gotoxy

DOS | UNIX | ANSI C | C++

Syntax

```
void gotoxy(int x, int y);

int x, y;
```

Position to move cursor

Function The `gotoxy` function moves the text cursor to the specified point.

File(s) to Include `#include <conio.h>`

Description The `gotoxy` function positions the text cursor at the column and row coordinates specified in the `x` and `y` arguments. The x coordinate specifies the column (horizontal) position; the y coordinate specifies the row (vertical) position.

Value(s) Returned There is no return value.

Related Function(s)

`wherex` : retrieves the x position of the text cursor
`wherey` : retrieves the y position of the text cursor

Example In the following example, `gotoxy` moves the cursor diagonally across the screen while printing a line of text.

```
#include <conio.h>
#include <stdio.h>

int main (void)
{
int x,y;

clrscr();
y = 1;
for (x=1; x<25; x=x+1)
   {
   gotoxy (y,x);
   printf ("Testing gotoxy function");
   y=y+1;
   }

return 0;
}
```

highvideo

DOS | UNIX | ANSI C | C++

Syntax `void highvideo(void);`

Function The `highvideo` function selects high-intensity characters.

File(s) to Include `#include <conio.h>`

Description The `highvideo` function sets the high-intensity bit of the current foreground color, resulting in the display of high-intensity characters. Only the characters displayed after the `highvideo` function is called will be displayed as high intensity. Characters displayed before the call to `highvideo` are not affected.

Value(s) Returned There is no return value.

Related Function(s) `lowvideo` : selects low-intensity characters

Example The following example displays text using the low, normal, and high text intensities.

```
#include <conio.h>
#include <stdio.h>

int main (void)
{
clrscr();
lowvideo();
cprintf ("Low intensity characters\r\n");
normvideo();
cprintf ("Normal intensity characters\r\n");
highvideo();
cprintf ("High intensity characters\r\n");

return 0;
}
```

insline

DOS UNIX ANSI C C++

Syntax `void insline(void);`

Function The `insline` function inserts a blank line in the current text window.

File(s) to Include `#include <conio.h>`

Description The `insline` function inserts a blank line at the current cursor position. The current text color is used and only the current text window is affected.

Value(s) Returned There is no return value.

Related Function(s) `delline` : deletes a line from the current text window

Example In the following example, `insline` inserts a line in the middle of the text when a key is pressed.

```
#include <conio.h>
#include <stdio.h>

int main (void)
{
int x;

clrscr();
for (x=1; x<21; x=x+1)
   {
   gotoxy (1,x);
   printf ("Press a key to insert line on row
   10\n");
   }
gotoxy (1,10);
getch();
insline();
return 0;
}
```

lowvideo

DOS UNIX ANSI C C++

Syntax `void lowvideo(void);`

Function The `lowvideo` function selects low-intensity characters.

File(s) to Include `#include <conio.h>`

Description The `lowvideo` function clears the high-intensity bit of the currently selected foreground color, resulting in low-intensity characters. Only characters displayed after the call to the `lowvideo` function are affected. Those characters displayed before the call to the `lowvideo` function are not affected.

Value(s) Returned There is no return value.

Related Function(s) `highvideo` : selects high-intensity characters

Example The following example displays low, normal, and high-intensity characters.

```
#include <conio.h>
#include <stdio.h>

int main (void)
{
clrscr();
lowvideo();
cprintf ("Low intensity characters\r\n");
normvideo();
cprintf ("Normal intensity characters\r\n");
highvideo();
cprintf ("High intensity characters\r\n");

return 0;
}
```

movetext

DOS UNIX ANSI C C++

Syntax

```
int movetext(int left, int top, int right, int bottom,
             int destleft, int desttop);
```

`int left, top;`	*Upper left corner of block to move*
`int right, bottom;`	*Lower right corner of block to move*
`int destleft, desttop;`	*Upper left corner of destination*

Function The `movetext` function moves a rectangular block of text from one location to another.

File(s) to Include `#include <conio.h>`

Description The `movetext` function moves the rectangular block of text defined by the `left`, `top`, `right`, and `bottom` arguments to the location specified by the `destleft`, and `desttop` arguments. The `left` and `top` arguments define the upper left corner of the block to move. The `right` and `bottom` arguments define the lower right corner of the block to move. The `destleft` and `desttop` arguments define the upper left corner of the destination block.

Value(s) Returned A 0 is returned when the `movetext` function is unsuccessful. A nonzero value is returned when `movetext` is successful.

Related Function(s) `gettext` : stores a block of text to memory

Example In the following example, `movetext` moves the block of text from the top of the screen to the bottom.

```
#include <conio.h>
#include <stdio.h>

int main (void)
{
clrscr();
printf ("Move this block\n");
printf ("of text to \n");
printf ("the bottom of \n");
printf ("the screen\n");
```

```
gotoxy (1,21);
printf ("Press any key\n");
printf ("to move block\n");
getch();
movetext (1,1,20,5,1,20);

return 0;
}
```

normvideo

DOS UNIX ANSI C C++

Syntax `void normvideo(void);`

Function The `normvideo` function selects normal-intensity characters.

File(s) to Include `#include <conio.h>`

Description The `normvideo` function resets the foreground and background text attributes to their default normal-intensity settings, resulting in normal-intensity characters. Only characters displayed after the `normvideo` function is called are affected. Characters displayed before the `normvideo` function call are not affected.

Value(s) Returned There is no return value.

Related Function(s)
`lowvideo` : selects low-intensity characters
`highvideo` : selects high-intensity characters

Example The following example displays low, normal, and high-intensity characters.

```
#include <conio.h>
#include <stdio.h>

int main (void)
{
clrscr();
lowvideo();
cprintf ("Low intensity characters\r\n");
normvideo();
cprintf ("Normal intensity characters\r\n");
```

continues

```
highvideo();
cprintf ("High intensity characters\r\n");

return 0;
}
```

puttext

DOS UNIX ANSI C C++

Syntax

```
int puttext(int left, int top, int right, int bottom,
            void *source);
```

`int left, top;`	*Upper left corner of display area*
`int right, bottom;`	*Lower right corner of display area*
`void *source;`	*Text to display*

Function The `puttext` function moves text from memory to the display screen.

File(s) to Include `#include <conio.h>`

Description The `puttext` function places a block of text stored in memory to the display screen. The text in memory is pointed to by the `*source` argument. The rectangular display area in which the text will be placed is defined by the `left`, `top`, `right`, and `bottom` arguments. The `left` and `top` arguments define the column and row coordinates of the upper left corner of the display area. The `right` and `bottom` arguments define the column and row coordinates of the lower right corner of the display area.

Value(s) Returned A nonzero value is returned when the `puttext` function is successful. A 0 is returned when `puttext` is unsuccessful.

Related Function(s)

`gettext` : stores a block of text in memory
`movetext` : moves a block of text around the screen

Example In the following example, `puttext` places the text stored with the `gettext` function onto the screen.

```
#include <conio.h>
#include <stdio.h>
```

```
char textbuffer [4096];

int main (void)
{
int x;

clrscr();
for (x=1; x < 22; x = x + 1)
    {
    gotoxy(3,x);
    printf ("Save this part of the screen");
    }
gettext (3,1,32,22,textbuffer);

gotoxy (3,24);
printf ("Press any key to clear and restore screen");
getch();
clrscr();
puttext (3,1,32,22,textbuffer);

return 0;
}
```

_setcursortype

DOS UNIX ANSI C C++

Syntax `void _setcursortype(int cur_t);`

`int cur_t;` *Cursor type*

Function The `_setcursortype` function sets the appearance of the text cursor.

File(s) to Include `#include <conio.h>`

Description The `_setcursortype` function sets the appearance of the text cursor to one of the following:

`_NOCURSOR`	Turns cursor off
`_SOLIDCURSOR`	Solid cursor
`_NORMALCURSOR`	Normal underscore cursor

Value(s) Returned There is no return value.

Related Function(s)

`wherex` : gets x location of text cursor
`wherey` : gets y location of text cursor

Example The following example displays the normal, solid, and no-cursor options of the `_setcursortype` function.

```
#include <conio.h>
#include <stdio.h>

int main (void)
{
clrscr();
printf ("Normal Cursor");
_setcursortype(_NORMALCURSOR);
getch();
printf ("\nSolid Cursor");
_setcursortype(_SOLIDCURSOR);
getch();
printf ("\nNo Cursor");
_setcursortype(_NOCURSOR);
getch();
_setcursortype(_NORMALCURSOR);

return 0;
}
```

---

textattr

DOS | UNIX | ANSI C | C++

Syntax

```
void textattr(int newattr);

int newattr;
```

Attributes

Function The `textattr` function sets the text attributes.

File(s) to Include `#include <conio.h>`

Description The `textattr` function sets the foreground and background text attributes. Only characters displayed after the call to the `textattr` function will reflect the new attributes.

The `newattr` argument is an 8-bit parameter used to define the new attributes. The 8-bits are defined in the following format:

Bbbb ffff

in which

B	=	the blink enable bit (0 for no-blink, 1 for blinking)
bbb	=	the 3-bit background color (0 to 7)
ffff	=	the 4-bit foreground color (0 to 15)

Value(s) Returned There is no return value.

Related Function(s)

`textbackground` : sets the text background color
`textcolor` : sets the text foreground color

Example The following example sets the text attributes to display blinking characters with a red foreground and a blue background.

```
#include <conio.h>
#include <stdio.h>

int main (void)
{
clrscr();

   /* set to blinking, blue background, */
   /* red foreground                    */

textattr (10110100);
cprintf ("Text using the new attributes\r\n");

return 0;
}
```

textbackground

DOS UNIX ANSI C C++

Syntax `void textbackground(int newcolor);`

`int newcolor;` *New background color*

Function The `textbackground` function sets the text background color.

File(s) to Include `#include <conio.h>`

Description The `textbackground` function sets the text background color to the color specified in the `newcolor` argument. The `newcolor` argument must be an integer value ranging from 0 to 7. Only characters displayed after the call to the `textbackground` function will reflect the new background color. Table 15.2 lists the background constants and values used with the `textbackground` function.

Table 15.2. Background constants used with the `textbackground` ***function.***

Constant	*Value*
BLACK	0
BLUE	1
GREEN	2
CYAN	3
RED	4
MAGENTA	5
BROWN	6
LIGHTGRAY	7

Value(s) Returned There is no return value.

Related Function(s)

`textattr` : sets the text foreground and background colors

`textcolor` : sets the text foreground color

Example The following example displays text using the blue background.

```
#include <conio.h>
#include <stdio.h>

int main (void)
{
clrscr();

   /* set to blue background */

textbackground (1);
```

```
cprintf ("Text using the new background
color\r\n");

return 0;
}
```

textcolor

Syntax `void textcolor(int newcolor);`

`int newcolor;` *Foreground color*

Function The `textcolor` function sets the foreground character color in text modes.

File(s) to Include `#include <conio.h>`

Description The `textcolor` function selects the new foreground character color specified in the `newcolor` argument. The `newcolor` argument is selected from the constants and values shown in table 15.3. Only characters displayed after the call to the `textcolor` function will reflect the new foreground color.

***Table 15.3.** Foreground colors for use with the* `textcolor` *function.*

Constant	*Value*
BLACK	0
BLUE	1
GREEN	2
CYAN	3
RED	4
MAGENTA	5
BROWN	6
LIGHTGRAY	7
DARKGRAY	8

continues

Table 15.3. (continued)

Constant	*Value*
LIGHTBLUE	9
LIGHTGREEN	10
LIGHTCYAN	11
LIGHTRED	12
LIGHTMAGENTA	13
YELLOW	14
WHITE	15
BLINK	128

Note: BLINK is defined so that any of the colors (0 to 15) can be made to blink by adding 128, or the BLINK constant.

Value(s) Returned There is no return value.

Related Function(s)

`textattr` : sets the foreground and background text colors

`textbackground` : sets the text background color

Example The following example displays text using the blue foreground.

```
#include <conio.h>
#include <stdio.h>

int main (void)
{
clrscr();

   /* set to blue text color */

textcolor (1);
cprintf ("Text using the new text color\r\n");

return 0;
}
```

textmode

Syntax `void textmode(int newmode);`

`int newmode;` *Text mode to initiate*

Function The `textmode` function places the system in the selected text mode.

File(s) to Include `#include <conio.h>`

Description The `textmode` function places the system in the text mode defined in the `newmode` argument. Table 15.4 lists the constants and values for the text modes. When the new mode is set, the text window is reset to the entire screen and the text attributes are reset to their normal values. The `textmode` function should not be used to return to text mode from a graphics mode. Use the `restorecrt` mode to initiate a temporary text mode.

Table 15.4. *Text modes for the* `textmode` *function.*

Constant	*Value*	*Meaning*
LASTMODE	–1	Restore previous text mode
BW40	0	40-column black and white
C40	1	40-column color
BW80	2	80-column black and white
C80	3	0-column color
MONO	7	80-column monochrome
C4350	64	43-line EGA or 50-line VGA

Value(s) Returned There is no return value.

Related Function(s) `restorecrtmode` : initiates a text mode from graphics mode

Example The following example sets the text mode to black-and-white 40-column mode. The mode is reset to color 80-column mode before exiting.

```
#include <conio.h>
#include <stdio.h>

int main (void)
{
clrscr();

textmode (BW40);
cprintf ("Text in BW40 mode\r\n");
getch();
textmode(C80);

return 0;
}
```

wherex

DOS | UNIX | ANSI C | C++

Syntax `int wherex(void);`

Function The `wherex` function retrieves the horizontal (x) text cursor position.

File(s) to Include `#include <conio.h>`

Description The `wherex` function gets the horizontal, or x, position of the text cursor relative to the current text window.

Value(s) Returned The horizontal column (x) position of the text cursor, ranging from 1 to 80, is returned.

Related Function(s) `wherey` : retrieves the vertical position of the text cursor

Example The following example displays the `x` and `y` values of the cursor position.

```
#include <conio.h>
#include <stdio.h>
```

```
int main (void)
{
clrscr();
printf ("Print some text to update the\n");
printf ("the position of the cursor\n");
printf ("X position : %d\n",wherex());
printf ("Y position : %d\n",wherey());

return 0;
}
```

wherey

DOS UNIX ANSI C C++

Syntax `int wherey(void);`

Function The `wherey` function retrieves the vertical (y) position of the text cursor.

File(s) to Include `#include <conio.h>`

Description The `wherey` function retrieves the vertical (y) position of the text cursor relative to the current text window.

Value(s) Returned The window-relative vertical position of the text cursor, ranging from 1 to 25, 1 to 43, or 1 to 50, is returned.

Related Function(s) `wherex` : retrieves the horizontal position of the text cursor

Example The following example displays the x and y position of the text cursor.

```
#include <conio.h>
#include <stdio.h>

int main (void)
{
clrscr();
printf ("Print some text to update the\n");
printf ("the position of the cursor\n");
printf ("X position : %d\n",wherex());
printf ("Y position : %d\n",wherey());
```

continues

```
return 0;
}
```

window

DOS | UNIX | ANSI C | C++

Syntax

```
void window(int left, int top, int right, int
            bottom);

int left, top;         Upper left corner of text window
int right, bottom;     Lower right corner of text window
```

Function The `window` function defines the text window.

File(s) to Include `#include <conio.h>`

Description The `window` function defines the current text window. The `left` and `top` arguments define the column and row coordinates of the upper left corner of the text window. The `right` and `bottom` arguments define the column and row coordinates of the lower right corner of the text window. The minimum size of the text window is one column by one row.

Value(s) Returned There is no return value.

Related Function(s) `gettextinfo` : retrieves information on the current text window

Example The following example defines a small text window and displays a text string inside that small text window.

```
#include <conio.h>
#include <stdio.h>

int main (void)
{
clrscr();
window (5,5,15,15);
gotoxy (1,1);
cprintf ("Test the dimensions of the text
  window");

return 0;
}
```

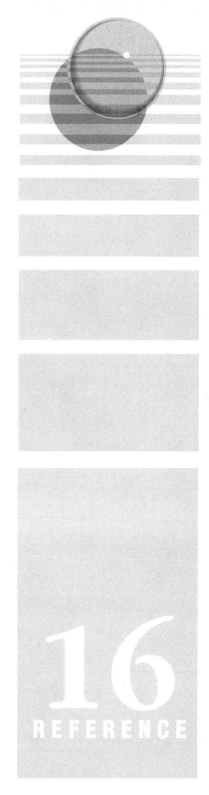

Standard Functions

This chapter introduces the functions provided in the standard library. The standard library functions, listed in table 16.1, provide routines for data conversions, memory allocation, and other miscellaneous functions.

The functions listed in table 16.1 are prototyped in the `stdlib.h` header file. Although many of these functions are ANSI C compatible, not all are. The strength of the standard functions is that most of these functions are portable between C compilers. For example, the Microsoft C compiler's `stdlib.h` header file includes almost exactly the same functions provided in Borland C's `stdlib.h`. Therefore, programs which use the standard functions are likely to be more portable.

Table 16.1. Standard library functions.

Function	*Meaning*
`abort`	Terminates the program abnormally
`abs`	Returns the absolute value of an integer
`atexit`	Registers exit functions
`atof`	Converts a string to a floating-point
`atoi`	Converts a string to an integer
`atol`	Converts a string to a long value
`bsearch`	Performs a binary search
`calloc`	Allocates main memory
`div`	Divides two integer values
`ecvt`	Converts a floating-point to a string
`_exit`	Terminates a program
`exit`	Terminates a program
`fcvt`	Converts a floating-point to a string
`free`	Frees memory
`gcvt`	Converts a floating-point to a string
`getenv`	Gets a string from the environment
`itoa`	Converts an integer to a string
`labs`	Derives absolute value of a long
`ldiv`	Divides two long values
`lfind`	Performs a linear search
`_lrotl`	Rotates an unsigned long to the left
`_lrotr`	Rotates an unsigned long to the right
`lsearch`	Performs a linear search
`ltoa`	Converts a long value to a string
`malloc`	Allocates memory
`putenv`	Puts a string into the environment
`qsort`	Performs a quick sort of an array
`realloc`	Reallocates main memory

Function	*Meaning*
`_rotl`	Rotates an unsigned integer to the left
`_rotr`	Rotates an unsigned integer to the right
`srand`	Initializes the random number generator
`strtod`	Converts a string to a double
`strtol`	Converts a string to a long
`strtoul`	Converts a string to an unsigned long
`swab`	Copies a string while switching bytes
`system`	Invokes the DOS command.com file
`ultoa`	Converts an unsigned long to a string

Borland C++ Standard Library Reference Guide

The remainder of this chapter provides detailed information on the use of each of the standard library functions.

abort

DOS | UNIX | ANSI C | C++

Syntax `void abort(void);`

Function The `abort` function terminates the program.

File(s) to Include `#include <stdlib.h>`
or
`#include <process.h>`

Description The `abort` function terminates the program in an abnormal way. The `abort` function writes the termination message `Abnormal program termination` on `stderr` and aborts the program by calling the `_exit` function with exit code 3.

Value(s) Returned The exit code 3 is returned to the parent process or DOS.

Related Function(s) `_exit` : terminates a program

Example The following example demonstrates the `abort` function by terminating the function before the last string is displayed.

```
#include <stdio.h>
#include <stdlib.h>

int main (void)
{
clrscr ();
printf ("The program will terminate without
  displaying last line\n");
abort();
printf ("This line will not be printed\n");

return 0;
}
```

abs

DOS	UNIX	ANSI C	C++

Syntax Real Version:

```
int abs(int x);|

int x;                    Value to process
```

Complex Version:

```
double abs(complex x);

complex x;                Value to process
```

Function The `abs` function returns the absolute value of the specified integer value.

File(s) to Include Real Version:

`#include <stdlib.h>`

or

`#include <math.h>`

Complex Version:

`#include <complex.h>`

Description The abs function returns the absolute value of the value specified in the x argument. When called with the stdlib.h file included, abs is treated as a macro that is expanded to inline code. Use #undef to make the abs macro a function when including the stdlib.h file.

Value(s) Returned The real version returns an integer in the range of 0 to 32,767. The complex version returns a double value.

Related Function(s)
cabs : gets the absolute value of a complex number
fabs : gets the absolute value of a floating-point
labs : gets the absolute value of a long value

Example The following example calculates and displays the absolute value of –534.

```
#include <stdio.h>
#include <stdlib.h>

int main (void)
{
int value = -534;
int absvalue;

clrscr ();
absvalue = abs(value);
printf ("Initial value : %d\n",value);
printf ("Absolute value : %d\n",absvalue);

return 0;
}
```

atexit

Syntax `int atexit(atexit_t func);`

`atexit_t func;` *Exit function*

Function The atexit function registers a function to execute upon exit.

File(s) to Include `#include <stdlib.h>`

Description The atexit function registers the function pointed to by the func argument as the exit function. When the program terminates normally, the exit function is called before returning to the operating system. The atexit function can be called up to 32 times to register up to 32 exit functions. The exit functions are called on an LIFO (last in, first out) basis.

Value(s) Returned A zero is returned when the specified function is successfully registered. A nonzero value is returned when unsuccessful.

Related Function(s)

abort : terminates the program
_exit : terminates the program
exit : terminates the program

Example In the following example, atexit registers the exit_one and exit_two exit functions. These are automatically called before program termination.

```
#include <stdio.h>
#include <stdlib.h>

void exit_one (void)
{
printf ("exit_one is executed\n");
}

void exit_two (void)
{
printf ("exit_two is executed\n");
}

int main (void)
{
clrscr ();
atexit(exit_one);
atexit(exit_two);
printf ("Exiting main function\n");

return 0;
}
```

atof

DOS | UNIX | ANSI C | C++

Syntax

```
double atof(const char *str);

const char *str;          String to convert
```

Function The `atof` function converts a string to a floating-point value.

File(s) to Include

```
#include <stdlib.h>
```
or
```
#include <math.h>
```

Description The `atof` function converts the string pointed to by the `str` argument to a double floating-point value. The character string must be the character representation of a floating-point number and use the following format. Conversion ends when an unrecognized character is encountered.

[whitespace] [sign] [ddd] [.] [ddd] [e|E[sign]ddd]

in which

[whitespace] = an optional string of tabs and spaces
[sign] = the sign of the value
[ddd] = a string of digits on either or both sides of the decimal
[.] = the decimal
[e|E[sign]ddd] = the exponential notation of the value

Note: +INF and –INF, for plus and minus infinity, and +NAN and –NAN, for not-a-number, are recognized by the `atof` function.

Value(s) Returned The double floating-point value of the string is returned unless there is an overflow.

Related Function(s)

`atoi` : converts a string to an integer value
`atol` : converts a string to a long value
`strtod` : converts a string to a double value

Example The following example converts the value in the `string` argument to a floating-point value.

```
#include <stdio.h>
#include <stdlib.h>
```

continues

```
int main (void)
{
float value;
char *string = "532.5596";

clrscr();
value = atof(string);
printf ("Floating-point value = %3.4f\n",value);
printf ("String = %s\n",string);

return 0;
}
```

atoi

DOS | UNIX | ANSI C | C++

Syntax `int atoi(const char *str);`

`const char *str;` *String to convert*

Function The `atoi` function converts a string to an integer value.

File(s) to Include `#include <stdlib.h>`

Description The `atoi` function converts the string pointed to by the `str` argument to an integer value. The string must be the character representation of an integer value and follow the format shown as follows. Conversion ends when the first unrecognized character is encountered.

[whitespace] [sign] [ddd]

in which

[whitespace] = an optional string of tabs and spaces
[sign] = an optional sign for the value
[ddd] = the string of digits

Value(s) Returned The integer value of the string is returned when `atoi` is successful. If the `atoi` function is unable to convert the string, a 0 is returned.

Related Function(s)
`atof` : converts a string to a floating-point value
`atol` : converts a string to a long value

Example The following example converts the value in the `string` argument to an integer value.

```
#include <stdlib.h>
#include <stdio.h>

int main (void)
{
int value;
char *string = "8726";

clrscr();
value = atoi (string);
printf ("Integer value = %d\n",value);
printf ("String = %s\n",string);

return 0;
}
```

atol

DOS | UNIX | ANSI C | C++

Syntax `long atol(const char *str);`

`const char *str;` *String to convert*

Function The `atol` function converts a string to a long value.

File(s) to Include `#include <stdlib.h>`

Description The `atol` function converts the string pointed to by the `str` argument to a long value. The string must be the character representation of an integer value and use the following format. Conversion ends when the first unrecognized character is encountered.

[whitespace] [sign] [ddd]

in which

[whitespace] = an optional string of tabs and spaces
[sign] = the optional sign for the following digits
[ddd] = a string of digits

Value(s) Returned The value of the converted string is returned when the `atol` function is successful. If the string cannot be converted, the `atol` function returns a 0.

Related Function(s)
`atof` : converts a string to a floating-point value
`atoi` : converts a string to an integer value

Example The following example converts the value in the `string` argument to a long value.

```
#include <stdlib.h>
#include <stdio.h>

int main (void)
{
long value;
char *string = "45332754";

clrscr();
value = atol(string);
printf ("String = %s\n",string);
printf ("Value = %ld\n",value);

return 0;
}
```

bsearch

DOS | UNIX | ANSI C | C++

Syntax

```
void *bsearch(const void *key, const void *base,
              size_t nelem, size_t  width,
              int(*fcmp)(const void *, const
              void *));
```

`const void *key;`	*Search key*
`const void *base;`	*Array to search*
`size_t nelem;`	*Number of elements*
`size_t width;`	*Width of elements*
`int(*fcmp)(const void *, const void *);`	*Comparison routine*

Function The `bsearch` function performs the binary search of an array.

File(s) to Include `#include <stdlib.h>`

Description The `bsearch` function searches an array with the number of elements specified in the `nelem` argument. The `key` argument identifies the search key. The address of the first element that matches the search key is returned. If no match is found, a 0 is returned. The `width` argument defines the number of bytes in each array element. The function defined by the `fcmp` argument is called for the comparison of two values.

Value(s) Returned The address of the first entry that matches the search key is returned when a match is found. If no match is found, a 0 is returned.

Related Function(s) `lsearch` : performs a linear search

Example The following example searches `testarray` for the value 20. A message is displayed indicating whether 20 is found.

```
#include <stdlib.h>
#include <stdio.h>

int testarray[] = {25, 38, 20, 26, 16};

int compare (const int *p1, const int *p2)
{
return (*p1 - *p2);
}

int main (void)
{
int *tempptr;
int key = 20;

clrscr();
printf ("Searching testarray for 20\n");
     tempptr = bsearch (&key,testarray,5,2,
     (int(*)(const void *, const void *))compare);
if (tempptr == 0)
     printf ("20 was not found in testarray\n");
else
     printf ("20 was found in testarray\n");

return 0;
}
```

calloc

DOS | UNIX | ANSI C | C++

Syntax

```
void *calloc(size_t nitems, size_t size);

size_t nitems;          Number of items
size_t size;            Size
```

Function The `calloc` function allocates main memory.

File(s) to Include

```
#include <stdlib.h>
```

or

```
#include <alloc.h>
```

Description The `calloc` function dynamically allocates memory in the C memory heap. For small data models, including the tiny, small, and medium models, the space between the end of the data segment and the top of the program stack is available for use. The only part of this memory reserved is a small amount for DOS plus a small amount needed for the application.

For large data models, including the compact, large, and huge models, the space beyond the program stack to the end of physical memory is available for the heap.

The block size of the allocated memory is calculated to be the `nitems` argument multiplied by the `size` argument (`nitem x size`).

The block of memory is cleared to 0 upon allocation. If the requested block size is greater than 64K, the `farcalloc` function must be used.

Value(s) Returned The pointer to the new block is returned. If there is not enough memory, or if the `nitems` or `size` arguments are 0, null is returned.

Related Function(s)

`farcalloc` : allocates memory from the far heap
`malloc` : allocates main memory
`realloc` : reallocates main memory

Example The following example uses `calloc` to allocate a block of memory.

```
#include <stdlib.h>
#include <stdio.h>
```

```
int main (void)
{
char *string = NULL;

clrscr();
string = calloc (20,sizeof(char));
if (string)
     {
     strcpy (string,"123456789123456789");
     printf ("Result: %s\n",string);
     }
else
     printf ("Memory not allocated\n");

free (string);
return 0;
}
```

div

DOS UNIX ANSI C C++

Syntax `div_t div(int numer, int denom);`

`int numer;`	*Numerator*
`int denom;`	*Denominator*

Function The `div` function returns the quotient and remainder from the division of two integers.

File(s) to Include `#include <stdlib.h>`

Description The `div` function divides the numerator defined in the `numer` argument by the denominator defined in the `denom` argument and returns the quotient and remainder in a structure of type `div_t`. The `div_t` structure is shown as follows:

```
typedef struct
     {
     int quot;    /* quotient */
     int rem;     /* remainder */
     } div_t;
```

Value(s) Returned The `div` function returns the remainder and quotient in a structure of type `div_t`.

Related Function(s) `ldiv` : divides two long values

Example The following example calculates and displays the quotient and remainder from the division of two integers.

```
#include <stdlib.h>
#include <stdio.h>

int main (void)
{

div_t result;

clrscr();
result = div (16,4);
printf ("16 divided by 4 :\n");
printf ("Quotient : %d\n",result.quot);
printf ("Remainder : %d\n",result.rem);

return 0;
}
```

ecvt

DOS | UNIX | ANSI C | C++

Syntax

```
char *ecvt(double value, int ndig, int *dec, int
           *sign);
```

`double value;`	*Value to convert*
`int ndig;`	*Number of digits*
`int *dec;`	*Decimal point position*
`int *sign;`	*Sign of the value*

Function The `ecvt` function converts a floating-point number to a string.

File(s) to Include `#include <stdlib.h>`

Description The `ecvt` function converts the floating-point value specified in the `value` argument to a null-terminated string. The length of the string is specified with the `ndig` argument. The `dec` argument is a pointer to the position of the decimal point relative to the beginning of the resulting string (there is no decimal in the string). The `sign` argument points to the value indicating the sign of the value. A zero indicates positive; a nonzero value indicates negative.

Value(s) Returned The pointer to the converted string is returned by the `ecvt` function.

Related Function(s)
`fcvt` : converts a floating-point value to a string
`gcvt` : converts a floating-point value to a string

Example The following example converts the floating-point value to a string.

```
#include <stdlib.h>
#include <stdio.h>

int main (void)
{
char *string;
double value = 12.756;
int dec, sign, ndig = 8;

clrscr();
string = ecvt (value,ndig,&dec,&sign);
printf ("Value = 12.756\n");
printf ("Significant digits = 8\n");
printf ("String = %s\n", string);
printf ("Decimal point position = %d\n", dec);
printf ("Sign = %d\n", sign);

return 0;
}
```

_exit

DOS | UNIX | ANSI C | C++

Syntax `void _exit(int status);`

`int status;` *Exit status*

Function The `_exit` function terminates a program.

File(s) to Include `#include <stdlib.h>`
or
`#include <process.h>`

Description The `_exit` function terminates program execution. When the program is terminated, no files are closed, no output is flushed, and no `exit` functions are called. The `status` argument is used as the exit status of the process. A zero is usually used to indicate a normal exit whereas a nonzero value is usually used to indicate an error.

Value(s) Returned There is no return value.

Related Function(s)
`abort` : terminates a program
`exit` : terminates a program

Example In the following example, `_exit` terminates the program.

```
#include <stdio.h>
#include <stdlib.h>

int main (void)
{
clrscr ();
printf ("The program will terminate without
        displaying last line\n");
_exit(0);
printf ("This line will not be printed\n");

return 0;
}
```

exit

DOS | UNIX | ANSI C | C++

Syntax
```
void exit(int status);

int status;
```
Exit status

Function The `exit` function terminates a program.

File(s) to Include
`#include <stdlib.h>`
or
`#include <process.h>`

Description The `exit` function terminates a program. Unlike the `_exit` function, all files are closed, buffered output is processed, and `exit` functions are called before the program is terminated. The `status` argument defines the exit status of the program. A 0 is generally used to indicate a normal exit. A nonzero value is generally used to indicate an error.

Value(s) Returned There is no return value.

Related Function(s)
`abort` : terminates a program
`_exit` : terminates a program

Example In the following example, `exit` terminates the program.

```
#include <stdio.h>
#include <stdlib.h>

int main (void)
{
clrscr ();
printf ("The program will terminate without
displaying last
line\n");
exit(0);
printf ("This line will not be printed\n");

return 0;
}
```

fcvt

DOS | UNIX | ANSI C | C++

Syntax

```
char *fcvt(double value, int ndig, int *dec, int
            *sign);
```

`double value;`	*Value to convert*
`int ndig;`	*Number of digits in string*
`int *dec;`	*Position of decimal*
`int *sign;`	*Sign of value*

Function The `fcvt` function converts a floating-point value to a string.

File(s) to Include `#include <stdlib.h>`

Description The `fcvt` function converts the floating-point number described by the `value` argument to a null-terminated string with the length specified in the `ndig` argument. The `dec` argument defines the position of the decimal relative to the beginning of the string. When the `dec` argument is negative, the decimal is placed to the left of the returned digits. The `sign` argument points to the word representing the sign of the `value` argument. When the `value` argument is negative, the word pointed to by the `sign` argument is a nonzero value. When the `value` argument is positive, the word pointed to by the `sign` argument is 0.

Value(s) Returned The pointer to the resulting string is returned.

Related Function(s)
`ecvt` : converts the floating-point value to a string
`gcvt` : converts the floating-point value to a string

Example The following example converts the floating-point value to a string and displays both.

```
#include <stdlib.h>
#include <stdio.h>

int main (void)
{
char *string;
double value = 54.7259;
int dec, sign, ndig = 7;

clrscr();
string = fcvt(value,ndig,&dec,&sign);
printf ("Value = 54.7259\n");
printf ("Significant digits = 7\n");
printf ("String = %s\n", string);
printf ("Decimal position = %d\n",dec);
printf ("Sign = %d\n",sign);

return 0;
}
```

free

DOS | UNIX | ANSI C | C++

Syntax
```
void free(void *block);
```

`void *block;` *Block to free*

Function The `free` function frees an allocated memory block.

File(s) to Include
`#include <stdlib.h>`
or
`#include <alloc.h>`

Description The `free` function deallocates the memory block pointed to by the `block` argument and allocated by a call to the `calloc` function, the `malloc` function, or the `realloc` function.

Value(s) Returned There is no return value.

Related Function(s) `freemem` : frees an allocated DOS memory block

Example In the following example, the `free` function frees memory allocated by the `calloc` function.

```
#include <stdlib.h>
#include <stdio.h>

int main (void)
{
char *string = NULL;

clrscr();
string = calloc (20,sizeof(char));
if (string)
     {
     strcpy (string,"12345678912345678 9");
     printf ("Result: %s\n",string);
     }
else
     printf ("Memory not allocated\n");

free (string);
return 0;
}
```

gcvt

DOS UNIX ANSI C C++

Syntax

```
char *gcvt(double value, int ndec, char *buf);
```

`double value;`	*Value to convert*
`int ndec;`	*Number of significant digits*
`char *buf;`	*Resulting string*

Function The `gcvt` function converts a floating-point value to a string.

File(s) to Include `#include <stdlib.h>`

Description The `gcvt` function converts the floating-point value defined in the `value` argument to a null-terminated ASCII string, and stores the string at the location pointed to by the `buf` argument. The resulting string contains the number of significant digits specified in the `ndec` argument and is in FORTRAN F format whenever possiblc. When `gcvt` is unable to use FORTRAN F format, printf E format is used.

Value(s) Returned The `gcvt` function returns the address of the string pointed to by the `buf` argument.

Related Function(s)

`ecvt` : converts a floating-point number to a string
`fcvt` : converts a floating-point number to a string

Example The following example converts the floating-point value to a string and displays both.

```
#include <stdlib.h>
#include <stdio.h>

int main (void)
{
char string[20];
double value = 54.7259;
int ndec = 4;

clrscr();
gcvt(value,ndec,string);
printf ("Value = 54.7259\n");
printf ("Significant digits = 4\n");
printf ("String = %s\n", string);
```

```
return 0;
}
```

getenv

DOS | UNIX | ANSI C | C++

Syntax

```
char *getenv(const char *name);

const char *name;          Variable name
```

Function The `getenv` function retrieves a string from the environment.

File(s) to Include `#include <stdlib.h>`

Description The `getenv` function gets the value of the variable specified in the `name` argument. The `name` argument can contain upper- and lowercase letters but cannot include the = sign. An empty string is returned if the environment variable specified in the `name` argument does not exist.

Value(s) Returned If the specified variable is found, a string value is returned. If the specified variable is not found, an empty string is returned.

Related Function(s) `putenv` : adds a string to the environment

Example The following example retrieves the COMSPEC environment variable and displays it.

```
#include <stdio.h>
#include <stdlib.h>

int main (void)
{
char *string;

string = getenv ("COMSPEC");
clrscr ();
printf ("COMSPEC = %s\n",string);

return 0;
}
```

itoa

DOS | UNIX | ANSI C | C++

Syntax

```
char *itoa(int value, char *string, int radix);

int value;              Value to convert
char *string;           Resulting string
int radix;              Base used for conversion
```

Function The `itoa` function converts an integer value to a string.

File(s) to Include `#include <stdlib.h>`

Description The `itoa` function converts the integer value defined in the `value` argument to a null-terminated string. The converted string is stored in the location pointed to by the `string` argument. The `radix` argument is an integer value which specifies the base (ranging between 2 and 36) used in converting thc `value` argument.

Value(s) Returned The pointer to the resulting string is returned.

Related Function(s)
`ltoa` : converts a long value to a string
`ultoa` : converts an unsigned long value to a string

Example The following example converts the integer value to a string and displays both.

```
#include <stdlib.h>
#include <stdio.h>

int main (void)
{
int value = 8377;
char string[20];

clrscr();
itoa (value,string,10);
printf ("Value = 8377\n");
printf ("String = %s\n",string);
printf ("Base = 10\n");

return 0;
}
```

labs

DOS | UNIX | ANSI C | C++

Syntax

```
long int labs(long int x);

long int x;                    Value to evaluate
```

Function The `labs` function determines the absolute value of a long value.

File(s) to Include

```
#include <stdlib.h>
```
or
```
#include <math.h>
```

Description The `labs` function computes the absolute value of the long value specified in the `x` argument.

Value(s) Returned The absolute value of `x` is returned.

Related Function(s)

- `abs` : returns the absolute value of number
- `cabs` : returns the absolute value of a complex number
- `fabs` : returns the absolute value of a floating-point number

Example The following example returns the absolute value of the long value.

```
#include <stdio.h>
#include <stdlib.h>

int main (void)
{
long value = -372534L;
long absvalue;

clrscr ();
absvalue = labs(value);
printf ("Initial value : %ld\n",value);
printf ("Absolute value : %ld\n",absvalue);
return 0;
}
```

ldiv

DOS UNIX ANSI C C++

Syntax

```
ldiv_t ldiv(long int numer, long int denom);
```

`long int numer;`	*Numerator*
`long int denom;`	*Denominator*

Function The `ldiv` function returns the quotient and remainder from the division of two long values.

File(s) to Include `#include <stdlib.h>`

Description The `ldiv` function divides the numerator defined in the `numer` argument by the denominator defined in the `denom` argument. The quotient and remainder are returned in a structure of type `ldiv_t`. The `ldiv_t` structure is as follows:

```
typedef struct
    {
    long int quot;        /* quotient */
    long int rem;         /* remainder */
    } ldiv_t;
```

Value(s) Returned The quotient and remainder are returned in a structure of type `ldiv_t`.

Related Function(s) `div` : divides two integer values

Example The following example calculates and displays the quotient and remainder from the division of two long values.

```
#include <stdlib.h>
#include <stdio.h>

int main (void)
{

ldiv_t result;

clrscr();
result = ldiv (1600L,40L);
printf ("1600 divided by 40 :\n");
printf ("Quotient : %ld\n",result.quot);
printf ("Remainder : %ld\n",result.rem);

return 0;
}
```

lfind

DOS UNIX ANSI C C++

Syntax

```
void *lfind(const void *key, const void *base,
            size_t *num, size_t width, int(*fcmp)
            (const void *, const void *));
```

`const void *key;`	*Search key*
`const void *base;`	*Array to search*
`size_t *num;`	*Number of elements*
`size_t width;`	*Width of elements*
`int (*fcmp)(const void *, const void *);`	*Comparison routine*

Function The `lfind` function performs a linear search.

File(s) to Include `#include <stdlib.h>`

Description The `lfind` function performs a linear search through an array of sequential elements for the value specified in the `key` argument. The array contains the number of elements defined in the `num` argument and begins at the memory location pointed to by the `base` argument. The `width` argument defines the width, in bytes, of each element of the array. The function defined by the `fcmp` argument is called by the `lfind` function to perform comparisons.

Value(s) Returned The address of the first matching array element is returned. Null is returned when no match is found.

Related Function(s)
`bsearch` : performs a binary search
`lsearch` : performs a linear search

Example The following example searches `testarray` for the value 20.

```
#include <stdlib.h>
#include <stdio.h>

int compare (int *a, int *b)
{
return (*a - *b);
}
```

continues

```
int main (void)
{
int *tempptr;
int key = 20;
int testarray[5] = {25,38,20,26,16};
int num = 5;

clrscr();
printf ("Searching testarray for 20\n");
tempptr = lfind (&key,testarray,(size_t *)&num,2,
          (int(*)(const  void *, const void
          *))compare);
if (tempptr == 0)
     printf ("20 was not found in testarray\n");
else
     printf ("20 was found in testarray\n");

return 0;
}
```

_lrotl

DOS | UNIX | ANSI C | C++

Syntax

```
unsigned long _lrotl(unsigned long val, int
                                   count);

unsigned long val;          Value to rotate
int count;                  Number of bits to rotate
```

Function The `_lrotl` function rotates an unsigned long value to the left.

File(s) to Include `#include <stdlib.h>`

Description The `_lrotl` function rotates the unsigned long value defined in the `val` argument left the number of bits specified in the `count` argument.

Returned Value(s) The rotated value is returned.

Related Function(s)

_lrotr : rotates an unsigned long value right
_rotl : rotates an unsigned integer left
_rotr : rotates an unsigned integer right

Example The following example rotates the unsigned long value to the left two bits.

```
#include <stdio.h>
#include <stdlib.h>

int main (void)
{
unsigned long rot_value;
unsigned long value = 500;
int shift_bits = 2;

clrscr ();
rot_value = _lrotl (value,shift_bits);
printf ("Initial Value : %lu\n",value);
printf ("Shifted Value : %lu\n",rot_value);

return 0;
}
```

_lrotr

DOS | UNIX | ANSI C | C++

Syntax

```
unsigned long _lrotr(unsigned long val, int
                                     count);
```

`unsigned long val;`	*Value to rotate*
`int count;`	*Number of bits to rotate*

Function The _lrotr function shifts an unsigned long value to the right.

File(s) to Include `#include <stdlib.h>`

Description The _lrotr function shifts the unsigned long value defined in the val argument to the right the number of bits specified in the count argument.

Value(s) Returned The rotated value is returned.

Related Function(s)

`_lrotl` : rotates an unsigned long value left
`_rotl` : rotates an unsigned integer left
`_rotr` : rotates an unsigned integer right

Example The following example rotates the unsigned long value to the right two bits.

```
#include <stdio.h>
#include <stdlib.h>

int main (void)
{
unsigned long rot_value;
unsigned long value = 500;
int shift_bits = 2;

clrscr ();
rot_value = _lrotr (value,shift_bits);
printf ("Initial Value : %lu\n",value);
printf ("Shifted Value : %lu\n",rot_value);

return 0;
}
```

lsearch

DOS | UNIX | ANSI C | C++

Syntax

```
void *lsearch(const void *key, void *base, size_t
              *num, size_t width, int (*fcmp)
              (const void *,const void *));
```

`const void *key;`	*Search key*
`void *base;`	*Array to search*
`size_t *num;`	*Number of elements*
`size_t width;`	*Width of elements*
`int (*fcmp)(const void *, const void *);`	*Comparison routine*

Function The `lsearch` function performs a linear search.

File(s) to Include `#include <stdlib.h>`

Description The `lsearch` function performs a linear search through an array for the value specified in the `key` argument. The array begins at the location pointed to by the `base` argument and contains the number of elements specified in the `num` argument. Each element in the array contains the number of bytes specified in the `width` argument. The function defined by the `fcmp` argument is called by the `lsearch` function to compare values. When the search is exhausted and no match is found, the value specified in the `key` argument is appended to the array.

Value(s) Returned The address of the first matching element is returned.

Related Function(s)
`bsearch` : performs a binary search
`lfind` : performs a linear search

Example The following example searches `testarray` for `Tom`.

```
#include <stdlib.h>
#include <stdio.h>

int compare (char **a, char **b)
{
return (strcmp(*a,*b));
}

int main (void)
{
char *key = "Tom";
char *testarray[5] = {"Peter", "Paul", "Mike",
  "Tom", "Jim"};
int num = 5;

clrscr();
printf ("Searching testarray for Tom\n");
lsearch (key,testarray,(size_t *)&num,sizeof
  (char *),(int(*)(const void *,
  const void *))compare);

return 0;
}
```

ltoa

DOS UNIX ANSI C C++

Syntax

```
char *ltoa(long value, char *string, int radix);
```

`long value;`	*Value to convert*
`char *string;`	*Resulting string*
`int radix;`	*Base for conversion*

Function The `ltoa` function converts a long value to a string.

File(s) to Include `#include <stdlib.h>`

Description The `ltoa` function converts the long value specified in the `value` argument to a null-terminated string. The resulting string is stored at the memory location pointed to by the `string` argument. The `radix` argument (ranging from 2 to 36) specifies the base used for the conversion.

Value(s) Returned The pointer to the resulting string is returned.

Related Function(s)
`itoa` : converts an integer to a string
`ultoa` : converts an unsigned long integer to a string

Example The following example converts the long value to a string and displays both.

```
#include <stdlib.h>
#include <stdio.h>

int main (void)
{
long value = 99288377L;
char string[20];

clrscr();
ltoa (value,string,10);
printf ("Value = 99288377\n");
printf ("String = %s\n",string);
printf ("Base = 10\n");

return 0;
}
```

malloc

DOS | UNIX | ANSI C | C++

Syntax `void *malloc(size_t size);`

`size_t size;` *Size of block to allocate*

Function The `malloc` function allocates main memory.

File(s) to Include `#include <stdlib.h>`
or
`#include <alloc.h>`

Description The `malloc` function allocates a block of memory with the size specified in the `size` argument. The memory is allocated from the memory heap, which is used for the dynamic allocation of variable-sized blocks.

Value(s) Returned The pointer to the allocated block of memory is returned when successful. When unsuccessful, or the `size` argument is 0, null is returned.

Related Function(s)

`calloc` : allocates main memory
`farcalloc` : allocates memory from the far heap
`farmalloc` : allocates memory from the far heap
`realloc` : reallocates main memory

Example In the following example, `malloc` allocates a block of memory.

```
#include <stdlib.h>
#include <stdio.h>

int main (void)
{
char *string = NULL;

clrscr();
string = malloc (20);
if (string)
     {
     strcpy (string,"12345678912345678 9");
     printf ("Result: %s\n",string);
     }
else
     printf ("Memory not allocated\n");
```

continues

```
free (string);
return 0;
}
```

putenv

DOS | UNIX | ANSI C | C++

Syntax

```
int putenv(const char *name);

const char *name;          String to add
```

Function The `putenv` function places a string in the current environment.

File(s) to Include `#include <stdlib.h>`

Description The `putenv` function adds the string defined in the `name` argument to the environment of the current process. In addition, `putenv` can either modify or delete existing environment strings.

Value(s) Returned A 0 is returned when successful. A –1 is returned when unsuccessful.

Related Function(s) `getenv` : retrieves an environment string

Example The following example retrieves the COMSPEC environment string and places it back into the environment without modifying it. However, the string could have easily been modified before being placed back into the environment.

```
#include <stdio.h>
#include <stdlib.h>

int main (void)
{
char *string;

string = getenv ("COMSPEC");
clrscr ();
printf ("COMSPEC = %s\n",string);

putenv (string);
string = getenv ("COMSPEC");
```

```
printf ("COMSPEC = %s\n", string);
printf ("String not modified\n");

return 0;
}
```

qsort

DOS | UNIX | ANSI C | C++

Syntax

```
void qsort(void *base, size_t nelem, size_t width,
           int (*fcmp)(const void *, const void
           *));
```

`void *base;`	*Points to array*
`size_t nelem;`	*Number of elements*
`size_t width;`	*Width of elements*
`int (*fcmp)(const void *, const void *);`	*For comparison*

Function The `qsort` function uses the quicksort algorithm for sorting.

File(s) to Include `#include <stdlib.h>`

Description The `qsort` function sorts the array pointed to by the base argument using the "median of three" variant of the quicksort algorithm. The array contains the number of elements specified in the `nelem` argument, with each element having the number of bytes specified in the `width` argument. The function defined by the `fcmp` argument is called for element comparison.

Value(s) Returned There is no return value.

Related Function(s)
`bsearch` : performs a binary search
`lsearch` : performs a linear search

Example The `qsort` function is used in this example to sort the array.

```
#include <stdio.h>
#include <stdlib.h>
#include <string.h>

int sort (const void *a, const void *b)
```

continues

```
{
return (strcmp (a,b));
}

int main (void)
{
char array[7][2] = {"d","a","f","g","b","e","c"};
int c;

clrscr ();

qsort ((void *)array, 7, sizeof(array[0]),sort);
for (c = 0; c < 7; c=c+1)
     printf ("%s\n",array[c]);

return 0;
}
```

rand

DOS | UNIX | ANSI C | C++

Syntax `int rand(void);`

Function The `rand` function generates a random number.

File(s) to Include `#include <stdlib.h>`

Description The `rand` function generates a random number using a multiplicative congruential random number generator with period 2e32. The returned pseudorandom numbers range from 0 to `RAND_MAX`. `RAND_MAX` is defined in `stdlib.h` as 2E15 – 1.

Value(s) Returned The generated pseudorandom number is returned.

Related Function(s)

`random` : generates a random number within a specified range

`randomize` : initializes the random number generator

Example The following example displays a random number.

```
#include <stdio.h>
#include <stdlib.h>

int main (void)
```

```
{
clrscr ();
printf ("This is a random number : %d\n",rand());

return 0;
}
```

realloc

DOS | UNIX | ANSI C | C++

Syntax

```
void *realloc(void *block, size_t size);

void *block;                Memory block
size_t size;                Size of block
```

Function The `realloc` function reallocates main memory.

File(s) to Include `#include <stdlib.h>`
or
`#include <alloc.h>`

Description The `realloc` function alters the size of the block pointed to by the `block` argument to the size defined in the `size` argument. The block pointed to by the `block` argument should have been previously allocated with the `malloc` or `calloc` functions.

Value(s) Returned The address of the reallocated block is returned when successful. If the `size` argument is 0, or the block cannot be reallocated, null is returned.

Related Function(s)
`calloc` : allocates main memory
`malloc` : allocates main memory

Example In the following example, `realloc` resizes the block of memory allocated by `malloc`.

```
#include <stdlib.h>
#include <stdio.h>

int main (void)
{
char *string = NULL;

clrscr();
string = malloc (20);
```

continues

```
strcpy (string,"123456789123456789");
printf ("String : %s\n",string);
realloc (string,30);
strcpy (string,"123456789123456789123456789");
printf ("String : %s\n",string);

free (string);
return 0;
}
```

_rotl

DOS UNIX ANSI C C++

Syntax `unsigned _rotl(unsigned val, int count);`

`unsigned val;`	*Value to rotate*
`int count;`	*Number of bits to rotate*

Function The `_rotl` function rotates an unsigned integer value to the left.

File(s) to Include `#include <stdlib.h>`

Description The `_rotl` function rotates the unsigned integer value specified in the `val` argument to the left the number of bits specified in the `count` argument.

Value(s) Returned The rotated value is returned.

Related Function(s)
`_lrotl` : rotates an unsigned long value to the left
`_lrotr` : rotates an unsigned long value to the right
`_rotr` : rotates an unsigned integer to the right

Example The following example rotates the unsigned value to the left two bits.

```
#include <stdio.h>
#include <stdlib.h>

int main (void)
{
unsigned rot_value;
unsigned value = 500;
int shift_bits = 2;
```

```
clrscr ();
rot_value = _rotl (value,shift_bits);
printf ("Initial Value : %u\n",value);
printf ("Shifted Value : %u\n",rot_value);

return 0;
}
```

_rotr

DOS | UNIX | ANSI C | C++

Syntax `unsigned _rotr(unsigned val, int count);`

`unsigned val;`	*Value to rotate*
`int count;`	*Number of bits to rotate*

Function The `_rotr` function rotates an unsigned integer value to the right.

File(s) to Include `#include <stdlib.h>`

Description The `_rotr` function rotates the unsigned integer value specified in the `val` argument to the right the number of bits specified in the `count` argument.

Value(s) Returned The rotated value is returned.

Related Function(s)
`_lrotl` : rotates an unsigned long value to the left
`_lrotr` : rotates an unsigned long value to the right
`_rotl` : rotates an unsigned integer to the left

Example The following example rotates the unsigned value to the right two bits.

```
#include <stdio.h>
#include <stdlib.h>

int main (void)
{
unsigned rot_value;
unsigned value = 500;
int shift_bits = 2;
```

continues

```
clrscr ();
rot_value = _rotr (value,shift_bits);
printf ("Initial Value : %u\n",value);
printf ("Shifted Value : %u\n",rot_value);

return 0;
}
```

---

srand

DOS | UNIX | ANSI C | C++

Syntax

```
void srand(unsigned seed);
```

`unsigned seed;` *Seed point for random number*

Function The `srand` function initializes the random number generator.

File(s) to Include `#include <stdlib.h>`

Description The `srand` function sets the random number generator with the seed point defined in the `seed` argument. When the `seed` argument is 1, the random number generator is reinitialized.

Value(s) Returned There is no return value.

Related Function(s)

`rand` : generates a random number
`random` : generates a random number within a range
`randomize` : initializes the random number generator

Example The following example sets the random number generator seed to 34 and generates a random number.

```
#include <stdio.h>
#include <stdlib.h>

int main (void)
{
clrscr ();
srand (34);
printf ("This is a random number %d\n",rand());

return 0;
}
```

strtod

DOS | UNIX | ANSI C | C++

Syntax

```
double strtod(const char *s, char **endptr);
```

`const char *s;` *String to convert*
`char **endptr;` *Useful for error detection*

Function The `strtod` function converts a string to a double value.

File(s) to Include

```
#include <stdlib.h>
```

Description The `strtod` function converts the character string pointed to by the `s` argument to a double value. The character string to be converted must follow the format:

[whitespace] [sign] [ddd] [.] [ddd] [fmt[sign]ddd]

in which

[whitespace] = optional whitespace
[sign] = the optional sign of the value
[ddd] = optional digits
[.] = the decimal points
[ddd] = optional digits
[fmt] = optional e or E
[sign] = optional sign of exponent
[ddd] = optional digits

The `strtod` function recognizes +INF and –INF for plus and minus infinity. It also recognizes +NAN and –NAN for not-a-number. Conversion stops when the first character that cannot be recognized is encountered.

If `endptr` is not null, the `strtod` function sets `*endptr` to the location of the character that stopped the conversion. Therefore, `endptr` is useful for detecting errors.

Value(s) Returned The double value of the string is returned. HUGE_VAL is returned when overflow occurs.

Related Function(s) `atof` : converts a string to a floating-point number

Example The following example converts the string to a double value.

```
#include <stdlib.h>
#include <stdio.h>

int main (void)
{
double value;
char string[20] = "254.938";
char *endptr;

clrscr();
value = strtod (string,&endptr);
printf ("Value = %lf\n",value);
printf ("String = %s\n",string);

return 0;
}
```

strtol

DOS | UNIX | ANSI C | C++

Syntax

```
long strtol(const char *s, char **endptr, int
            radix);
```

`const char *s;`	*String to convert*
`char **endptr;`	*Useful for error detection*
`int radix;`	*Base for conversion*

Function The `strtol` function converts a string to a long value.

File(s) to Include `#include <stdlib.h>`

Description The `strtol` function converts the character string pointed to by the `s` argument to a long integer value. The character string must be in the following format:

[whitespace] [sign] [0] [x] [ddd]

in which

[whitespace] = optional whitespace
[sign] = the sign of the value
[0] = optional 0
[x] = optional x or X
[ddd] = optional digits

When the `radix` argument ranges from 2 to 36, the returned long value is expressed in the base defined by the `radix` argument. When the `radix` argument is 0, the first few characters of the `s` string determine the base of the returned long value, as follows:

First Character	*Second Character*	*String interpreted as*
0	1 to 7	Octal
0	x or X	Hexadecimal
1 to 9		Decimal

When the `radix` argument is 1, less than 0, or greater than 36, the argument is invalid.

If `endptr` is not null, the `*endptr` argument points to the character that stopped the conversion.

Value(s) Returned The value of the converted string is returned when conversion is successful. A 0 is returned when conversion is unsuccessful.

Related Function(s)
`atoi` : converts a string to an integer
`atol` : converts a string to a long value
`strtoul` : converts a string to an unsigned long value

Example The following example converts the string to a long value.

```
#include <stdlib.h>
#include <stdio.h>

int main (void)
{
long value;
char *string = "6568595";
char *endptr;

clrscr();
value = strtol (string,&endptr,10);
printf ("Value = %ld\n",value);
printf ("String = %s\n",string);
printf ("Base = 10\n");

return 0;
}
```

strtoul

DOS UNIX ANSI C C++

Syntax

```
unsigned long strtoul(const char *s, char
                      **endptr, int radix);

const char *s;          String to convert
char **endptr;          Useful for error detection
int radix;              Base for conversion
```

Function The `strtoul` function converts a string to an unsigned long value.

File(s) to Include `#include <stdlib.h>`

Description The `strtoul` function converts the character string pointed to by the `s` argument to an unsigned long value. The character string must be in the format:

[whitespace] [sign] [0] [x] [ddd]

in which

[whitespace] = optional whitespace
[sign] = the sign of the value
[0] = optional 0
[x] = optional x or X
[ddd] = optional digits

When the `radix` argument ranges from 2 to 36, the returned unsigned long value is expressed in the base defined by the `radix` argument. When the `radix` argument is 0, the first few characters of the `s` string determine the base of the returned unsigned long value, as follows:

First Character	*Second Character*	*String interpreted as*
0	1 to 7	Octal
0	x or X	Hexadecimal
1 to 9		Decimal

When the `radix` argument is 1, less than 0, or greater than 36, the argument is invalid.

If `endptr` is not null, the `*endptr` argument points to the character that stopped the conversion.

Value(s) Returned The value of the converted string is returned when conversion is successful. A 0 is returned when conversion is unsuccessful.

Related Function(s)
`atoi` : converts a string to an integer
`atol` : converts a string to a long integer
`strtol` : converts a string to a long integer

Example The following example converts the string to an unsigned long value.

```
#include <stdlib.h>
#include <stdio.h>

int main (void)
{
unsigned long value;
char *string = "6568595";
char *endptr;

clrscr();
value = strtoul (string,&endptr,10);
printf ("Value = %lu\n",value);
printf ("String = %s\n",string);
printf ("Base = 10\n");

return 0;
}
```

swab

DOS | UNIX | ANSI C | C++

Syntax `void swab(char *from, char *to, int nbytes);`

`char *from;`	*String to copy from*
`char *to;`	*String to copy to*
`int nbytes;`	*Number of bytes*

Function The `swab` function moves a string while swapping bytes.

File(s) to Include `#include <stdlib.h>`

Description The `swab` function moves the string pointed to by the `from` argument to the string pointed to by the `to` argument. As the string is moved, adjacent even and odd bytes are swapped. The `nbytes` argument defines the number of bytes, which should be even.

Value(s) Returned There is no return value.

Related Function(s) `strcpy` : copies one string to another

Example The following example copies `init` to `final` while swapping bytes. The `final` string is 12345678.

```
#include <stdio.h>
#include <stdlib.h>

char init[8] = "21436587";
char final[8] = "00000000";

int main (void)
{
clrscr ();
swab (init,final,8);
printf(final);
return 0;
}
```

---

system

DOS | UNIX | ANSI C | C++

Syntax `int system(const char *command);`

`const char *command;` *DOS command*

Function The `system` function issues a DOS command.

File(s) to Include `#include <stdlib.h>`
or
`#include <process.h>`

Description The `system` function executes the DOS command, or file, specified in the `command` argument by invoking the DOS COMMAND.COM file. The string specified in the `command` argument must refer to a file or command accessible through the current directory or the PATH string.

Value(s) Returned A 0 is returned when `system` is successful. A –1 is returned when unsuccessful.

Related Function(s) See Chapter 13 for other DOS interface functions.

Example The following example generates the DOS call to `dir`.

```
#include <stdio.h>
#include <stdlib.h>

int main (void)
{
clrscr ();
printf("Current directory is :\n");
system("dir");

return 0;
}
```

ultoa

DOS | UNIX | ANSI C | C++

Syntax

```
char *ultoa(unsigned long value, char *string, int
            radix);
```

`unsigned long value;`	*Value to convert*
`char *string;`	*Converted string*
`int radix;`	*Base for conversion*

Function The `ultoa` function converts an unsigned long value to a string.

File(s) to Include `#include <stdlib.h>`

Description The `ultoa` function converts the unsigned long value defined in the `value` argument to a null-terminated string. The converted string is stored at the location pointed to by the `string` argument. The `radix` argument (ranging from 2 to 36) specifies the base for converting the `value` argument.

Value(s) Returned The converted string is returned.

Related Function(s)

`itoa` : converts an integer to a string

`ltoa` : converts a long value to a string

Example The following example converts the unsigned long value to a string.

```
#include <stdio.h>
#include <stdio.h>

int main (void)
{
unsigned long value = 62259374L;
char string [20];

clrscr();
ultoa (value,string,10);
printf ("Value = %lu\n",value);
printf ("String = %s\n",string);
printf ("Base = 10");

return 0;
}
```

Time and Date

The 80x86 series of computers uses a system clock which operates several million times per second. The system clock is primarily used to control the microprocessor but is also used to calculate the time and date. This chapter introduces the Borland C++ functions used to manipulate the time and date.

The UNIX time format expresses time in the number of seconds since 00:00:00 hours Greenwich Mean Time (GMT) on January 1, 1970. This format is easy to store and update and can easily be converted to the DOS local time and date when the time zone, the time difference between local and GMT, and the setting of daylight savings time are known. These parameters—the time zone, time difference, and daylight savings time—are stored and set with the TZ environment variable.

The Borland C++ functions listed in table 17.1 are provided to retrieve, convert, and display time and date information.

Table 17.1. Time and date functions.

Function	*Meaning*
`asctime`	Converts date and time to an ASCII string
`clock`	Determines the program execution time
`ctime`	Converts date and time to a string
`difftime`	Determines the time difference between two time events
`dostounix`	Converts from DOS to UNIX format
`ftime`	Stores the current time in a `timeb` structure
`getdate`	Gets the system date
`gettime`	Gets the system time
`gmtime`	Converts date and time to GMT
`localtime`	Converts the date and time to a structure
`mktime`	Converts the time to calendar format
`setdate`	Sets the system date
`settime`	Sets the system time
`stime`	Sets the system date and time
`strftime`	Formats the time
`time`	Gets the current time
`tzset`	Sets the TZ environment variable
`unixtodos`	Converts from UNIX to DOS format

Borland C++ Time and Date Reference Guide

The remainder of this chapter provides detailed information on the use of each of the time and date functions.

asctime

DOS | UNIX | ANSI C | C++

Syntax `char *asctime(const struct tm *tblock);`

`const struct tm *tblock;` *Time structure to convert*

Function The `asctime` function converts the date and time to ASCII.

File(s) to Include `#include <time.h>`

Description The `asctime` function converts the time and date stored in the structure pointed to by `tblock` to an ASCII string. The resulting ASCII string contains 26 characters in the format shown as follows:

```
Mon Aug 15 03:10:15 1987\n\0
```

Value(s) Returned The pointer to the character string containing the date and time is returned.

Related Function(s)

`ctime` : converts the date and time to a string
`gmtime` : converts the data and time to Greenwich mean time

Example In the following example, `asctime` converts the date and time set in the `timestr` structure to an ASCII string.

```
#include <time.h>
#include <stdio.h>

int main (void)
{
struct tm timestr;
char timestring[80];

clrscr();
timestr.tm_sec = 50;
timestr.tm_min = 25;
timestr.tm_hour = 12;
timestr.tm_mday = 12;
timestr.tm_mon = 8;
timestr.tm_year = 89;
timestr.tm_wday = 3;
```

continues

```
timestr.tm_yday = 243;
timestr.tm_isdst = 0;

strcpy (timestring,asctime(&timestr));
printf ("String : %s\n",timestring);

return 0;
}
```

clock

Syntax `clock_t clock(void);`

Function The `clock` function determines the processor time passed since the beginning of program execution.

File(s) to Include `#include <time.h>`

Description The `clock` function determines the number of seconds elapsed since the start of the program. To determine the number of seconds elapsed, the return value of the `clock` function should be divided by the value of the macro `CLK_TCK`.

Value(s) Returned The elapsed processor time since the beginning of program execution is returned by the clock function. A –1 is returned when the processor time cannot be retrieved.

Related Function(s) `time` : retrieves the current time

Example The following example prints the clock time at the beginning and end of the `for` loop.

```
#include <time.h>
#include <stdio.h>

int main (void)
{
clock_t begin, end;
int x;
```

```
clrscr();
printf ("Start : %f\n",clock()/CLK_TCK);
for (x = 1; x < 11; x = x+1)
     printf ("Counting %d\n",x);
printf ("End : %f\n",clock()/CLK_TCK);
return 0;
}
```

ctime

DOS | UNIX | ANSI C | C++

Syntax `char *ctime(const time_t *time);`

`const time_t *time;` *Pointer to time value*

Function The `ctime` function converts the date and time to a string.

File(s) to Include `#include <time.h>`

Description The `ctime` function converts the time value, pointed to by the `time` argument, into a string. The resulting string contains 26 characters in the form of the following example:

`Mon Aug 15 05:37:15 1987\n\0`

Value(s) Returned The pointer to the character string containing the date and time is returned by the `ctime` function.

Related Function(s)

`asctime` : converts the date and time to an ASCII string

`gmtime` : converts the date and time to Greenwich mean time

Example In the following example, `ctime` displays a date and time string from the current time.

```
#include <time.h>
#include <stdio.h>

int main (void)
{
time_t currtime;
char *timestring;
```

continues

```
clrscr();
currtime = time(NULL);
timestring = ctime (&currtime);
printf ("Time and date : %s\n",timestring);

return 0;
}
```

difftime

DOS | UNIX | ANSI C | C++

Syntax `double difftime(time_t time2, time_t time1);`

`time_t time2;`	*Time value 2*
`time_t time1;`	*Time value 1*

Function The `difftime` function calculates the difference between two times.

File(s) to Include `#include <time.h>`

Description The `difftime` function determines the time difference, in seconds, between two time values.

Value(s) Returned The double value representing the time difference is returned by the `difftime` function.

Related Function(s)

`clock` : determines the processor time since program execution

`time` : returns the current time

Example In the following example, `difftime` calculates the time difference between the beginning and end of the `for` loop.

```
#include <time.h>
#include <stdio.h>
#include <dos.h>

int main (void)
{
time_t begin, end;
int x;
```

```
clrscr();
printf ("Start : %f\n",clock()/CLK_TCK);
begin = time(NULL);
for (x = 1; x < 11; x = x+1)
      {
      delay (500);
      printf ("Counting %d\n",x);
      }
printf ("End : %f\n",clock()/CLK_TCK);
end = time (NULL);
printf ("The time difference, in seconds, is :
%f\n",
      difftime(end, begin));

return 0;
}
```

dostounix

DOS UNIX ANSI C C++

Syntax `long dostounix(struct date *d, struct dostime *t);`

`struct date *d;`	*Pointer to* `date` *structure*
`struct dostime *t;`	*Pointer to* `dostime` *structure*

Function The `dostounix` function converts the date and time from DOS to UNIX time format.

File(s) to Include `#include <dos.h>`

Description The `dostounix` function converts the date and time to UNIX time format. The `getdate` and `gettime` functions retrieve the date and time, respectively. The `d` argument points to the `date` structure. The `t` argument points to the `dostime` structure, which contains DOS date and time information.

Value(s) Returned The `dostounix` function returns the number of seconds since 00:00:00 on January 1, 1970 (GMT), in UNIX date and time parameters.

Related Function(s)

unixtodos : converts the date and time from UNIX to DOS format

Example

In the following example, dostounix converts the date and time retrieved by the getdate and gettime functions to UNIX format.

```
#include <time.h>
#include <stdio.h>
#include <dos.h>

int main (void)
{
time_t untime;
struct time dos_time;
struct date dos_date;
struct tm *currtime;

clrscr();
getdate(&dos_date);
gettime(&dos_time);
untime = dostounix(&dos_date, &dos_time);
currtime = localtime(&untime);
printf ("Current : %s\n",asctime(currtime));

return 0;
}
```

ftime

DOS | UNIX | ANSI C | C++

Syntax

```
void ftime(struct timeb *buf);

struct timeb *buf;
```

Pointer to the timeb *structure*

Function

The ftime function retrieves the current time and stores it in the timeb structure.

File(s) to Include

```
#include <sys\timeb.h>
```

Description The `ftime` function retrieves the current time and fills the `timeb` structure pointed to by the `buf` argument. The `timeb` function is as follows:

```
struct timeb
     {
     long time;          /* seconds since 00:00:00
                            January 1, 1970,
                            Greenwich mean time
                            (GMT) */
     short millitm;      /* number of milliseconds */
     short timezone;     /* difference in minutes
                            between GMT and local
                            time */
     short dstflag;      /* determines if daylight
                            savings time is in
                            effect */

     };
```

Value(s) Returned There is no return value.

Related Function(s)

`localtime` : converts the date and time to a structure
`time` : retrieves the current time

Example In the following example, `ftime` retrieves the current time and places it in the `time` structure.

```
#include <time.h>
#include <stdio.h>
#include <sys\timeb.h>

int main (void)
{
struct timeb time;

clrscr();
ftime (&time);
printf ("Daylight Savings ? (1) for yes, (0) for no :
      %d\n",time.dstflag);
printf ("Difference between local and GMT :
      %d\n",time.timezone);
printf ("Milliseconds : %d\n",time.millitm);
printf ("Seconds since 1/1/1970 GMT : %ld\n",time.time);

return 0;
}
```

getdate

DOS | UNIX | ANSI C | C++

Syntax

```
void getdate(struct date *datep);

struct date *datep;        Pointer to the date structure
```

Function The `getdate` function retrieves the system date.

File(s) to Include

```
#include <dos.h>
```

Description The `getdate` function retrieves the current system date. The retrieved date is then placed in the `date` structure pointed to by the `datep` argument. The date structure follows.

```
struct date
     {
     int da_year;        /* year */
     int da_day;         /* day of the month */
     char da_mon;        /* month, 1 for Jan, ...,
                            12 for Dec */
     };
```

Value(s) Returned There is no return value.

Related Function(s) `setdate` : sets the system date

Example In the following example, `getdate` retrieves the current system date.

```
#include <dos.h>
#include <stdio.h>

int main (void)
{
struct date currdate;

clrscr();
getdate (&currdate);
printf ("Year  : %d\n",currdate.da_year);
printf ("Day   : %d\n",currdate.da_day);
printf ("Month : %d\n",currdate.da_mon);

return 0;
}
```

gettime

DOS | UNIX | ANSI C | C++

Syntax `void gettime(struct time *timep);`

`struct time *timep;` *Pointer to the* `time` *argument*

Function The `gettime` function retrieves the system time.

File(s) to Include `#include <dos.h>`

Description The `gettime` function retrieves the current system time. The retrieved time is then placed in the `time` structure pointed to by the `timep` argument. The `time` structure follows:

```
struct time
      {
      unsigned char ti_min;       /* minutes */
      unsigned char ti_hour;      /* hours */
      unsigned char ti_hund;      /* hundredths of a
                                     second */
      unsigned char ti_sec;       /* seconds */
      };
```

Value(s) Returned There is no return value.

Related Function(s)
`settime` : sets the system time
`time` : gets the current time

Example In the following example, `gettime` retrieves the current system time.

```
#include <dos.h>
#include <stdio.h>

int main (void)
{
struct time currtime;

clrscr();
gettime (&currtime);
printf ("Hour              :
      %2d\n",currtime.ti_hour);
printf ("Minute            :
```

continues

```
%2d\n",currtime.ti_min);continues
printf ("Second          : %2d\n",currtime.ti_sec);
printf ("1/100th second : %2d\n",currtime.ti_hund);

return 0;
}
```

gmtime

DOS UNIX ANSI C C++

Syntax `struct tm *gmtime(const time_t *timer);`

`const time_t *timer;` *Pointer to the* `time_t` *structure*

Function The `gmtime` function converts the date and time to Greenwich mean time.

File(s) to Include `#include <time.h>`

Description The `gmtime` function converts the return value of the `time` function into Greenwich mean time. The converted time is stored in a structure of type `tm`, as follows:

```
struct tm
     {
     int tm_sec;          /* seconds */
     int tm_min;          /* minutes */
     int tm_hour;         /* hours */
     int tm_mday;         /* day of the month - 1 to
                             31 */
     int tm_mon;          /* month - 0 for Jan, 1 for
                             Feb */
     int tm_year;         /* year minus 1900, 89 for
                             1989 */
     int tm_wday;         /* weekday - 0 for
                             Sunday */
     int tm_yday;         /* day of the year - 0 to
                             365 */
     int tm_isdst;        /* nonzero if daylight
                             savings is
                             in effect */
     };
```

Value(s) Returned The pointer to the structure containing the Greenwich mean time is returned.

Related Function(s) `time` : gets the current time

Example In the following example, `gmtime` converts the local time to Greenwich mean time.

```
#include <dos.h>
#include <stdio.h>
#include <time.h>

int main (void)
{
time_t loctime;
struct tm *currtime, *gmttime;

clrscr();
loctime = time(NULL);
currtime = localtime (&loctime);
gmttime = gmtime(&loctime);
printf ("Local time : %s\n",asctime(currtime));
printf ("GMT is : %s\n",asctime(gmttime));

return 0;
}
```

localtime

DOS | UNIX | ANSI C | C++

Syntax `struct tm *localtime(const time_t *timer);`

`const time_t *timer;` *Pointer to the `time_t` structure*

Function The `localtime` function converts the date and time to a structure of type `tm`.

File(s) to Include `#include <time.h>`

Description The `localtime` function converts the date and time value, as returned by the `time` function, into a structure of type `tm` while correcting for the time zone and possible daylight savings time. The `tm` structure is as follows:

```
struct tm
     {
     int tm_sec;          /* seconds */
     int tm_min;          /* minutes */
     int tm_hour;         /* hours */
     int tm_mday;         /* day of the month - 1 to
                             31 */
     int tm_mon;          /* month - 0 for Jan, 1 for
                             Feb */
     int tm_year;         /* year minus 1900, 89 for
                             1989 */
     int tm_wday;         /* weekday - 0 for
                             Sunday */
     int tm_yday;         /* day of the year - 0 to
                             365 */
     int tm_isdst;        /* nonzero if daylight
                             savings is in effect */
     };
```

Value(s) Returned The pointer to the structure which contains the converted time is returned.

Related Function(s)
`asctime` : converts the time and date to ASCII
`ctime` : converts the time and date to a string
`gmtime` : converts the time and date to Greenwich mean time
`time` : gets the current time

Example In the following example, `localtime` adjusts the local time for time zones and daylight savings time.

```
#include <dos.h>
#include <stdio.h>
#include <time.h>

int main (void)
{
time_t loctime;
struct tm *currtime;

clrscr();
loctime = time(NULL);
currtime = localtime (&loctime);
printf ("Local time : %s\n",asctime(currtime));

return 0;
}
```

mktime

Syntax `time_t mktime(struct tm *t);`

`struct tm *t;` *Pointer to the `tm` structure*

Function The `mktime` function converts the time to a calendar format.

File(s) to Include `#include <time.h>`

Description The `mktime` function converts the time value stored in the structure pointed to by the `t` argument into a calendar time format. The calendar time format is the same format as that used by the `time` function, but the fields of the structure are not limited to the ranges defined in the `tm` structure. The `tm_wday` and `tm_yday` values are computed by the `mktime` function.

Value(s) Returned The pointer to the structure containing the converted calendar time is returned.

Related Function(s)

`localtime` : converts the date and time to a structure
`time` : gets the current time

Example In the following example, `mktime` converts the specified time and date to calendar format.

```
#include <dos.h>
#include <stdio.h>
#include <time.h>

int main (void)
{
struct tm tim;

clrscr();
tim.tm_year = 90;
tim.tm_mon = 9;
tim.tm_mday = 15;
tim.tm_hour = 8;
tim.tm_min = 45;
tim.tm_sec = 32;
tim.tm_isdst = 0;
mktime (&tim);
```

continues

```
printf ("Year : %d\n",tim.tm_year);
printf ("Month : %d\n",tim.tm_mon);
printf ("Day of month : %d\n",tim.tm_mday);
printf ("Hour : %d\n",tim.tm_hour);
printf ("Minute : %d\n",tim.tm_min);
printf ("Day of week : %d\n",tim.tm_wday);
printf ("Day of year : %d\n",tim.tm_yday);

return 0;
}
```

setdate

DOS | UNIX | ANSI C | C++

Syntax `void setdate(struct date *datep);`

`struct date *datep;` *Pointer to the* `date` *structure*

Function The `setdate` function sets the DOS date.

File(s) to Include `#include <dos.h>`

Description The `setdate` function sets the system date to the date specified in the `date` structure as pointed to by the `datep` argument. The date structure is as follows:

```
struct date
     {
     int da_year;        /* year */
     char da_day;        /* day of the month */
     char da_mon;        /* month - 1 for Jan, etc */
     };
```

Value(s) Returned There is no return value.

Related Function(s)
`getdate` : gets the system date
`gettime` : gets the system time
`settime` : sets the system time

Example The following example retrieves the current system date with the `getdate` function, sets a new system date with the `setdate` function, then restores the original system date.

```
#include <dos.h>
#include <stdio.h>

int main (void)
{
struct date olddate, newdate;

clrscr();
getdate (&olddate);
system ("date");
newdate.da_year = 1995;
newdate.da_day = 5;
newdate.da_mon = 3;
setdate (&newdate);
system ("date");
printf ("Reset to original date\n");
setdate (&olddate);
system ("date");

return 0;
}
```

---

settime

DOS | UNIX | ANSI C | C++

Syntax `void settime(struct time *timep);`

`struct time *timep;` *Pointer to the* `time` *structure*

Function The `settime` function sets the system time.

File(s) to Include `#include <dos.h>`

Description The `settime` function sets the system time to the time values in the `time` structure pointed to by the `timep` argument. The `time` structure is as follows:

```
struct time
      {
      unsigned char ti_min;       /* minutes */
      unsigned char ti_hour;      /* hours */
      unsigned char ti_hund;      /* hundredths of a
                                     second */
      unsigned char ti_sec;       /* seconds */
      };
```

Value(s) Returned There is no return value.

Related Function(s)
`getdate` : gets the current date
`gettime` : gets the current time
`setdate` : sets the DOS date

Example The following example retrieves the system time with the `gettime` function, sets a new time with the `settime` function, then restores the original system time.

```
#include <dos.h>
#include <stdio.h>

int main (void)
{
struct time oldtime, newtime;

clrscr();
gettime (&oldtime);
system ("time");
newtime.ti_min = 35;
newtime.ti_hour = 5;
newtime.ti_sec = 43;
newtime.ti_hund = 65;
settime (&newtime);
system ("time");
printf ("Reset to original time\n");
settime (&oldtime);
system ("time");

return 0;
}
```

stime

Syntax `int stime(time_t *tp);`

`time_t *tp;` *Pointer to the `timeb` structure*

Function The stime function sets the system date and time.

File(s) to Include `#include <time.h>`

Description The stime function sets the system time and date. The tp argument points to the time as measured in seconds from 00:00:00 Greenwich mean time, January 1, 1970.

Value(s) Returned The stime function returns 0.

Related Function(s)
ftime : stores the current time in a timeb structure
time : gets the current time

Example In the following example, stime sets the system time and date.

```
#include <time.h>
#include <stdio.h>

int main (void)
{
time_t timehold;

clrscr();
timehold = time(NULL);
stime (&timehold);
printf ("Number of seconds since 1/1/70 is
      %ld",timehold);

return 0;
}
```

strftime

DOS UNIX ANSI C C++

Syntax

```
size_t_cdecl strftime(char *s, size_t maxsize,
                      const char *fmt, const
                      struct tm *t);
```

char *s;	*String*
size_t maxsize;	*Maximum number of characters*

```
const char *fmt;          Format specifications
const struct tm *t;       Time to format
```

Function The `strftime` function formats a time value for output.

File(s) to Include `#include <time.h>`

Description The `strftime` function formats the time value of the `t` argument. The time value is formatted according to the specifications listed in the `fmt` argument string. The formatted time is placed in the string defined by the `s` argument. The string is limited to the size defined in the `maxsize` argument. Table 17.2 lists the format options for the resulting string.

Table 17.2. The `strftime` ***function format options.***

Format specifier	*Substituted value*
%%	Character %
%a	Abbreviated day of the week
%A	Full weekday name
%b	Abbreviate month name
%B	Full month name
%c	Date and time
%d	Two-digit day of the month (01 to 31)
%H	Two-digit hour (00 to 23)
%I	Two-digit hour (01 to 12)
%j	Three-digit day of year (001 to 366)
%m	Two-digit month as a decimal number
%M	Two-digit minute (00 to 59)
%p	AM or PM
%S	Two-digit second (00 to 59)
%U	Two-digit week number (00 to 52)
%w	Weekday (0 to 6; Sunday is 0)
%W	Two-digit week (00 to 52)
%x	Date

Format specifier	*Substituted value*
%X	Time
%y	Two-digit year without century (00 to 99)
%Y	Year with century
%	ZTime zone name

Value(s) Returned The number of characters placed in the formatted string is returned. If the number of characters required to create the string is greater than the specified `maxsize` argument, 0 is returned.

Related Function(s) `time` : gets the current time

Example The following example displays formatted time and date output using `strftime`.

```
#include <time.h>
#include <stdio.h>

int main (void)
{
time_t timesec;
struct tm *currtime;
char buffer[80];

clrscr();
timesec = time(NULL);
currtime = localtime (&timesec);
strftime(buffer,80,"%A %B %d 19%y :
%I:%M",currtime);
printf ("Current time : %s\n",buffer);

return 0;
}
```

time

Syntax `time_t time(time_t *timer);`

`time_t *timer;` *Pointer to the retrieved time*

Function The `time` function retrieves the current time.

File(s) to Include `#include <time.h>`

Description The `time` function retrieves the current time, in seconds, since 00:00:00 GMT January 1, 1970. This time value is then stored in the location pointed to by the `timer` argument. If `timer` is a null pointer, the value is not stored.

Value(s) Returned The time function returns the number of seconds elapsed since 00:00:00 GMT on January 1, 1970.

Related Function(s)
- `asctime` : converts the date and time to ASCII
- `ctime` : converts the date and time to a string
- `gmtime` : converts the date and time to Greenwich mean time

Example In the following example, `time` retrieves the current time.

```
#include <time.h>
#include <stdio.h>

int main (void)
{
time_t timesec;

clrscr();
timesec = time(NULL);
printf ("Seconds since 1/1/1970 : %ld\n",timesec);

return 0;
}
```

---

tzset

DOS | UNIX | ANSI C | C++

Syntax `void tzset(void);`

Function The `tzset` function sets the `daylight`, `timezone`, and `tzname` global variables.

File(s) to Include `#include <time.h>`

Description The `tzset` function sets the `daylight`, `timezone`, and `tzname` global variables according to the environment variable TZ. These global variables are used by the `ftime` and `localtime` functions to correct Greenwich mean time to the local time zone.

The TZ environment string has the following format:

```
TZ = zzz[+\-]d[d][lll]
```

The `zzz` field of the string represents the name of the current time zone. PST, for example, would stand for the Pacific Standard Time.

The `[+\-]d[d]` field represents the local time zone's deviation from Greenwich mean time. For example, 5 is for Eastern Standard time. Positive numbers are used to adjust westward; negative numbers are used to adjust eastward. The global variable `timezone` is calculated from this number, in which the `timezone` variable represents the number of seconds difference between Greenwich mean time and the local time zone.

The `lll` field represents the local time zone's daylight savings time. When this field is present, the global variable `daylight` is set to a nonzero value. If not present, the global variable `daylight` is set to zero.

The default value of the TZ environment string is TZ = EST5EDT.

Value(s) Returned There is no return value.

Related Function(s) `time` : gets the current time

Example In the following example, `tzset` sets the TZ variables to PST8PDT.

```
#include <time.h>
#include <stdio.h>

int main (void)
{
time_t timesec;

clrscr();
putenv("TZ=PST8PDT");
tzset();
```

continues

```
timesec = time(NULL);
printf ("Time : %s\n",
asctime(localtime(&timesec)));

return 0;
}
```

unixtodos

DOS UNIX ANSI C C++

Syntax

```
void unixtodos(long time, struct date *d, struct
                    time *t);
```

`long time;`	*UNIX format time*
`struct date *d;`	*Pointer to `date` structure*
`struct time *t;`	*Pointer to `time` structure*

Function The `unixtodos` function converts the UNIX time and date format to DOS time and date format.

File(s) to Include `#include <dos.h>`

Description The `unixtodos` function converts the UNIX date and time format specified in the `time` argument to DOS format. The date and time structures, pointed to by the `d` and `t` arguments, respectively, are filled with the converted time and date information.

Value(s) Returned There is no return value.

Related Function(s) `dostounix` : converts DOS time and date format to UNIX

Example The following example converts DOS to UNIX format, then UNIX to DOS.

```
#include <dos.h>
#include <stdio.h>

int main (void)
```

```
{
long untime;
struct date d;
struct time t;

clrscr();
getdate (&d);
gettime (&t);
untime = dostounix (&d,&t);
unixtodos (untime,&d,&t);
printf ("%ld unix format is %d %d %d DOS
format\n",untime,
         d.da_mon, d.da_day, d.da_year);

return 0;
}
```

Miscellaneous Functions

This chapter introduces miscellaneous functions that do not fit easily into previous chapters. The functions introduced in this chapter perform a variety of tasks which include performing sound effects, providing for nonlocal `goto`s, retrieving and setting locale information, and providing diagnostic capabilities. Table 18.1 lists the functions described in this chapter.

Table 18.1. Miscellaneous functions.

Function	*Meaning*
`assert`	Tests for a condition and aborts if necessary
`delay`	Delays program execution
`localeconv`	Gets information on the current locale
`longjmp`	Has the effect of a nonlocal `goto`
`matherr`	User-modifiable function for handling math errors
`nosound`	Turns the PC speaker off
`perror`	Displays a system error message
`setjmp`	Prepares the system for a nonlocal `goto`
`setlocale`	Selects a locale
`sound`	Emits a sound at the specified frequency

Borland C++ Miscellaneous Functions Reference Guide

The remainder of this chapter provides detailed information on the use of each of the functions listed in table 18.1.

assert

DOS | UNIX | ANSI C | C++

Syntax

```
void assert(int test);

int test;                    Test for abort
```

Function The `assert` function tests the specified condition and aborts if necessary.

File(s) to Include

```
#include <assert.h>
```

Description The assert function tests the condition specified in the test argument. If the test evaluates to zero, the assert macro prints an error message using stderr, and aborts the program using the abort function. The error message displayed is as follows:

```
Assertion failed: test, file filename, line
  linenum
```

in which the filename and linenum fields are the file name of the source and the line number where the assert macro appears.

Note: Placing #define NDEBUG before #include <assert.h> in the source code effectively comments out the assert statement.

Value(s) Returned There is no return value.

Related Function(s) abort : terminates a program

Example The following example aborts if the directory c:\tc\junk isn't found. Because the directory is not found (unless you have created such a directory) a –1 is returned by the chdir function. The assert function aborts on 0; therefore, a 1 must be added to the return value of the chdir function to abort when the directory is not found.

```
#include <assert.h>
#include <stdio.h>
#include <stdlib.h>

int main (void)
{
clrscr();
assert (chdir("c:\tc\junk") + 1);

      /* since c:\tc\junk isn't found,  1 is
         returned by chdir */
      /* adding 1 makes 0 causing assert to abort
         the program  */

printf ("This line is never reached");
return 0;
}
```

delay

DOS | UNIX | ANSI C | C++

Syntax

```
void delay(unsigned milliseconds);
```

`unsigned milliseconds;` *Number of milliseconds to delay*

Function The `delay` function delays execution for a specified number of milliseconds.

File(s) to Include `#include <dos.h>`

Description The `delay` function delays program execution for the number of milliseconds specified in the `milliseconds` argument.

Value(s) Returned There is no return value.

Related Function(s) `sleep` : suspends program execution for a specified number of seconds

Example In the following example, the `delay` function delays the program. The first line is displayed, followed by the second line in 10 seconds.

```
#include <dos.h>
#include <stdio.h>

int main (void)
{
clrscr();
printf ("The next line will appear in 10
seconds\n");
delay (10000);
printf ("Done\n");

return 0;
}
```

localeconv

DOS UNIX ANSI C C++

Syntax `struct lconv *localeconv(void);`

Function The `localeconv` function returns the pointer to the current locale structure.

File(s) to Include `#include <locale.h>`

Description The `localeconv` function sets up country-specific monetary and numeric formats. Borland C++ currently supports only locale C.

Value(s) Returned The pointer to the current locale structure is returned.

Related Function(s) `setlocale` : sets a locale

Example The following example retrieves the information on the current locale. The international currency symbol and fraction digits are then displayed.

```
#include <locale.h>
#include <stdio.h>

int main (void)
{
struct lconv ll;
struct lconv *current = &ll;

current = localeconv();
clrscr();
printf ("International currency symbol :
         %s\n",current->int_curr_symbol);
printf ("International fraction digits :
         %s\n",current->int_frac_digits);

return 0;
}
```

longjmp

DOS | UNIX | ANSI C | C++

Syntax
```
void longjmp(jmp_buf jmpb, int retval);
```

```
jmp_buf jmpb;              Task state
int retval;                Return value
```

Function The `longjmp` function has the effect of a nonlocal `goto`.

File(s) to Include `#include <setjmp.h>`

Description Using the `jmpb` argument, the `longjmp` function restores the task state saved with the last call to the `setjmp` function. The task state consists of all segment registers, register variables, the stack pointer, the frame base pointer, and the flags. `longjump` returns in such a way that `setjmp` appears to have returned the value `retval`.

The `setjmp` function must be called before calling the `longjmp` function. In addition, the routine that calls `setjmp` must be active when `longjmp` is called. If 0 is used as the `retval` argument for the `longjmp` function, a 1 is substituted for the 0.

Value(s) Returned There is no return value.

Related Function(s) `setjmp` : prepares for a nonlocal `goto`

Example The following example demonstrates the use of the `setjmp` and `longjmp` functions.

```
#include <stdio.h>
#include <setjmp.h>

jmp_buf jump;

void test_function (void);

int main (void)
{
int holder;
```

```
holder = setjmp (jump);
if (holder != 0)
{
     printf ("longjmp initiated with %d\n",
          holder);
      exit (holder);
}
printf ("Calling subroutine\n");
test_function();

return 0;
}

void test_function (void)
{
      longjmp (jump,1);
}
```

matherr

DOS UNIX ANSI C C++

Syntax

```
int matherr(struct exception *e);
```

`struct exception *e;` *Pointer to the* `exception` *structure*

Function The `matherr` function handles math errors and is user-modifiable.

File(s) to Include

```
#include <math.h>
```

Description The `matherr` function traps domain and range errors generated by the math library. This function can be modified for custom error handling. If modifications are made, the new `matherr` function should return a 1 if the error is resolved and a 0 if the error cannot be resolved. The exception structure follows:

```
struct exception
{
int type;    /* type of error that occurred */
char *name; /* pointer to name of function
               generating the error */
```

continues

```
    double arg1,arg2;    /* arguments of the
                            function generating
                            the error */
    double retval;       /* return value of
                            matherr */
    };
```

The following constants are defined for possible math errors.

Constant	*Meaning*
DOMAIN	Argument was out of the domain of the function
SING	Argument would result in singularity
OVERFLOW	Argument would produce a value greater than MAXDOUBLE (defined in values.h)
UNDERFLOW	Argument would produce a value less than MINDOUBLE (defined in values.h)
TLOSS	Argument would produce a value with a total loss of significant digits

Value(s) Returned

The default return value is 1. This occurs when the error is TLOSS or UNDERFLOW. The return value is 0 for other cases. When the return value is 0, the `errno` global variable is set to 0 and an error message is printed. When the return value is nonzero, the `errno` global variable is not set and no error message is printed.

Related Function(s)

`perror` : prints a system error message

Example

The following example demonstrates how the `matherr` function could be redefined to handle the `sqrt` DOMAIN problem.

```
#include <math.h>
#include <stdio.h>
#include <string.h>

int matherr (struct exception *x)
{
if (x->type == DOMAIN)
     {
     if (strcmp (x->name,"sqrt") == 0)
          {
          x->retval = sqrt(-(x->arg1));
```

```
                return 1;
                }
        }
return 0;
}

int main (void)
{
double a, b;

a = -1.0;
b = sqrt(a);

printf ("Math error corrected : %lf\n",b);

return 0;
}
```

nosound

DOS UNIX ANSI C C++

Syntax `void nosound(void);`

Function The `nosound` function turns the PC speaker off.

File(s) to Include `#include <dos.h>`

Description The `nosound` function turns the PC speaker off once it has been turned on by the `sound` function.

Value(s) Returned There is no return value.

Related Function(s) `sound` : turns the PC speaker on

Example The following example emits a 250-hertz sound for 2 seconds. The `nosound` function stops the sound.

```
#include <dos.h>
#include <stdio.h>

int main (void)
{
```

continues

```
sound (250);
delay (2000);
nosound();
return 0;
}
```

perror

DOS | UNIX | ANSI C | C++

Syntax `void perror(const char *s);`

`const char *s;` *String to print*

Function The `perror` function displays a system error message.

File(s) to Include `#include <stdio.h>`

Description The `perror` function prints the system error message for the last unsuccessful library function to the `stderr` stream. The `perror` function prints the `s` argument first, then a colon, then the message corresponding to the current value of the `errno` global variable, then a newline. The `s` argument is usually the file name of the program.

Value(s) Returned There is no return value.

Related Function(s)
`clearerr` : clears the error indication
`strerror` : returns a pointer to an error message string

Example The following example creates and displays an error message when the `junk.jnk` file (a dummy file name) can't be found.

```
#include <stdio.h>

int main (void)
{
FILE *ret;

ret = fopen ("junk.jnk","r");
if (!ret)
    perror ("Can't open file");

return 0;
}
```

setjmp

DOS | UNIX | ANSI C | C++

Syntax `int setjmp(jmp_buf jmpb);`

`jmp_buf jmpb;` *Task state*

Function The `setjmp` function prepares the system for a nonlocal `goto`.

File(s) to Include `#include <setjmp.h>`

Description The `setjmp` function reads the task state and stores it in the `jumpb` argument in preparation for a nonlocal `goto`. A task state contains all segment registers, register variables, the stack pointer, the frame base pointer, and all flags. The `longjmp` function restores the captured task state.

The `setjmp` function must be called before calling the `longjmp` function. In addition, the function which calls `setjmp` must be active.

Value(s) Returned A 0 is returned when the `setjmp` function is initially called. If the return is from the `longjmp` function, a nonzero value is returned.

Related Function(s) `longjmp` : performs a nonlocal goto

Example The following example demonstrates the use of the `setjmp` and `longjmp` functions.

```
#include <stdio.h>

int main (void)
{
FILE *ret;

ret = fopen ("junk.jnk","r");
if (!ret)
     perror ("Can't open file");

return 0;
}
```

setlocale

DOS UNIX ANSI C C++

Syntax

```
char *setlocale(int category, char *locale);

int category;            Category
char *locale;            Locale string
```

Function The `setlocale` function selects a locale.

File(s) to Include `#include <locale.h>`

Description The `setlocale` function and Borland C++ currently support only the C locale. Therefore, this function has no effect. The possible values for the category argument are as follows:

```
LC_ALL
LC_COLLATE
LC_CTYPE
LC_MONETARY
LC_NUMERIC
LC_TIME
```

Value(s) Returned The string which indicates the locale in effect before the call to `setlocale` is returned when `setlocale` is successful. Otherwise, a null pointer is returned.

Related Function(s) `localeconv` : returns a pointer to the current locale structure

Example The following example sets the locale to the C locale.

Note: the C locale is currently the only locale supported.

```
#include <locale.h>
#include <stdio.h>

int main (void)
{
char *old;

clrscr();
old = setlocale (LC_ALL,"C");
printf ("Old locale : %s\n",old);

return 0;
}
```

sound

DOS UNIX ANSI C C++

Syntax `void sound(unsigned frequency);`

`unsigned frequency;` *Frequency to emit*

Function The `sound` function turns the PC speaker on and emits a sound at the specified frequency.

File(s) to Include `#include <dos.h>`

Description The `sound` function turns the PC speaker on at the frequency specified in the `frequency` argument. The `frequency` argument is specified in hertz, or cycles per second.

Value(s) Returned There is no return value.

Related Function(s) `nosound` : turns the PC speaker off

Example The following example uses `sound` to emit a 250-hertz sound.

```
#include <dos.h>
#include <stdio.h>

int main (void)
{
sound (250);
delay (2000);
nosound();
return 0;
```

Part III

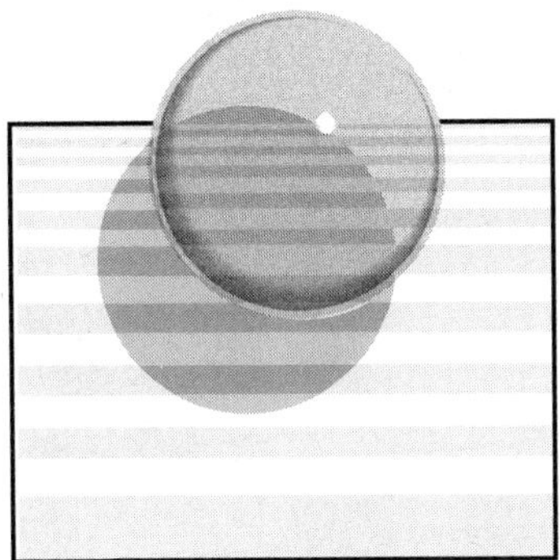

Borland C++ Programming Tools

Whitewater Resource Toolkit

The Whitewater Resource Toolkit is a powerful set of tools for building and modifying resources used in Microsoft Windows applications. With this toolkit, you can create and manage the user interface of any target Windows application. The Resource Toolkit operates inside the Windows environment and provides a variety of editors for the creation and modification of resources such as keyboard accelerators, bitmaps, cursors, icons, dialog boxes, menus, and strings.

Because the Resource Toolkit operates under Windows, you must have Windows Version 3.0, or a newer version, up and running on your system. Additional system requirements include 1MB of RAM, a graphics display and adapter, a pointing device, and at least 700K of available disk space. The Resource Toolkit can be started from the DOS prompt, the Windows Program Manager, the Windows File Manager, or the Windows MS-DOS executive.

Resources

Windows applications consist of a number of graphical elements ranging from dialog boxes to cursors. Under Windows, each element is stored as a resource that can be loaded into the application. Resources are separated from the source code, thus offering several advantages in application development. One advantage is that by separating the resource, a resource definition can be used for several applications. This eliminates development time for subsequent applications. Another advantage is that a resource can be modified without affecting the source code. This permits parallel development of resources and source code while shortening software modification phases.

It is very important to understand that resources do not define interface functionality. Resources are merely the visual representation of program elements. Table 19.1 lists the resources that can be edited by the Resource Toolkit.

***Table 19.1**. Resources edited by the Resource Toolkit.*

Resource	*Meaning*
Accelerators	Keys or key sequences used as an alternative to menu selection
Bitmaps	Series of data that represent an element, or picture, on the screen
Cursors	Screen markers used to indicate position
Dialog Boxes	Input screens that offer the user options for the application
Icons	Screen elements that can be selected to control the application
Menus	Lists of program options
Strings	The text displayed in the menus, dialog boxes, and so forth

The Resource Toolkit can edit, create, copy, view, save, and delete a variety of file types. Table 19.2 lists the various file types and provides information on how each of these file types can be manipulated by the Resource Toolkit.

***Table 19.2**. File types manipulated by the Resource Toolkit.*

Type	*Manipulation*	*Description*
.BMP (Bitmap resource file)	edit	Contains single bitmap resource in bitmap format. Files can be generated by the Toolkit and included in .RC files.

Type	*Manipulation*	*Description*
.CUR (Cursor resource file)	edit	Contains single cursor resource in bitmap format. Files can be generated by the Toolkit and included in .RC files.
.DAT (Raw data sources)	copy, rename, delete	Contains raw data resources used by the application. Files can be copied, renamed, or deleted.
.DLG (dialog box resource script file)	generated by Resource Toolkit but must be compiled by Microsoft's Resource Compiler	Contains dialog box resources in text format. Files can be generated by the Resource Toolkit or created with a text editor.
.EXE (Executable file)	edit	Contains all the application's resources and compiled program code. Resources of .EXE file can be modified and saved without recompiling source code.
.FON (Font file)	copy, rename, delete	Contains fonts used by application to delete display text. Files can be copied, renamed, or deleted.
.H (Header file)	edit	Contains symbolic names assigned to numbers that identify the action resulting from a menu selection.
.ICO (Icon resource)	edit	Contains single icon resource in bitmap format. ICO resources can be generated by Toolkit and included in .RC files.
.RC (Resource script file)	generated by Resource Toolkit but must be compiled by Microsoft's Resource Compiler	Contains resources in binary format. Resources are identified by name or number, and attributes, styles, etc. are described. Files can be generated by Toolkit or created with a text editor.

continues

Table 19.2. (continued)

Type	Manipulation	Description
.RES (Compiled Microsoft Resource Compiler File)	edit	Contains resources in binary format. Files can be edited and saved while using the Toolkit.

The Resource Manager

The Resource Manager is the main window of the Resource Toolkit. From this window, you can enter any of the resource editors, access existing resources, and create or close new files. As shown in figure 19.1 that follows, the resource manager has three sets of options: editor buttons, resource browsers, and the include button.

Fig. 19.1. The Resource Manager.

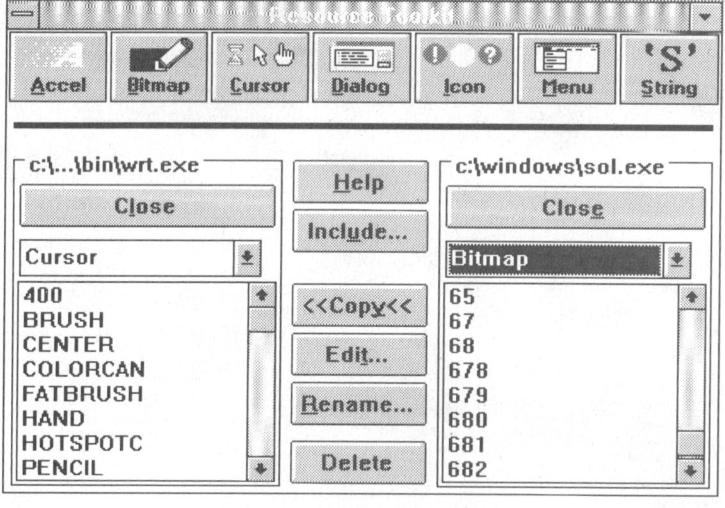

The editor buttons are used to start the resource editors. To enter one of the editors, just click on the appropriate editor button. When the editor is open, new resources can be created or existing resources can be edited.

The two resource browsers provide the capability to open files. The two browsers can be used to open two files simultaneously. It is therefore easy to copy resources from one file to another.

The include button allows you to select the resource types to display. When the include button is "clicked," a dialog box opens, listing the resource types that can be edited or copied.

The features of the Resource Manager are easy to use and operation is intuitive. The remainder of this chapter provides information on the editors included in the Resource Manager. Table 19.3 lists the keys used to move around inside the various editors. Ctrl-Enter is used to add another row to the editor tables.

***Table 19.3**. Keys for moving around the editor tables.*

Key	*Meaning*
Up Arrow	Moves up one row
Down Arrow	Moves down one row
Tab	Moves to the right one column
Shift-Tab	Moves to the left one column
Right Arrow	Moves cursor to the right one space in the current field
Left Arrow	Moves cursor to the left one space in the current field
Home	Moves the cursor to the first position of the current field
End	Moves the cursor to the last position of the current field

The Accelerator Editor

The Accelerator Editor creates and edits accelerator resources. Accelerators are *hot keys* or *key sequences* used as alternatives to selecting menu options with the mouse. The Accelerator Editor is shown in figure 19.2.

The Accelerator Editor stores accelerator resources in an accelerator table that normally contains seven columns, or eight when a header file is open. This accelerator table defines the use and function of the specified accelerators. The eight columns of the accelerator table are defined as follows.

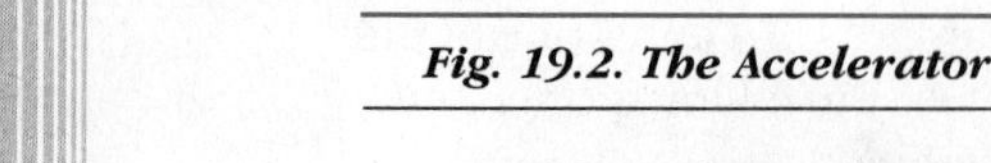

Fig. 19.2. The Accelerator Editor.

Accelerator: C:\BORLANDC\BIN\WRT.EXE WRT

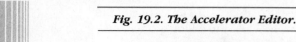

File Edit Header Help

Type	Key	Code	Shift	Ctrl	Alt	Value	Invert
Virtkey	HOME	36	No	No	No	309	Yes
Virtkey	END	35	No	No	No	308	Yes
Virtkey	F3	114	No	No	No	114	Yes
Virtkey	DELETE	46	No	No	No	304	Yes
Virtkey	F1	112	No	No	No	699	Yes
Ascii	^O	15				999	Yes
Ascii	^L	12				641	Yes
Virtkey	BACK	8	No	No	Yes	300	Yes
Virtkey	ESCAPE	27	No	No	No	27	Yes

The Type Column

The Type column defines the accelerator as a virtual key or ASCII code. To define the accelerator according to a virtual key definition, move to the Type column and press the spacebar to the desired type, or press the V key. To define the accelerator according to an ASCII code, move to the Type column and press the spacebar to the desired type, or press the A key.

The Key Column

The Key column defines the actual key or key sequence that represents the accelerator. To define the accelerator, first move to the Key column, then press the desired key or key sequence. For example, if you want Ctrl-G to be an accelerator, move to the Key column and press Ctrl-G. The ASCII or virtual key representation (whichever is selected in the Type column) will appear in the Key column.

The Code Column

The Code column displays the keyboard scan code—the key ID number for the keyboard—for the accelerator key or key sequence defined in the Key column. The Code column is filled automatically when the Key column is filled. The displayed keyboard scan code varies depending on the ASCII or virtual key selection made in the Type column.

The Shift Column

The Shift column is filled only when the Type column is set to virtual key. The Shift column, which is filled automatically, indicates whether the Shift key must be pressed to activate the specified accelerator. The fields in this column can be modified by moving to the column, then the appropriate field, and pressing the spacebar to cycle between the yes and no options, or by pressing the Y (yes) or N (no) keys.

The Ctrl Column

The Ctrl column is filled only when the Type Column is set to virtual key. The Ctrl column, which is filled automatically, indicates whether the Ctrl key must be pressed to activate the specified accelerator. The fields in this column can be modified by moving to the column, then the appropriate field, and pressing the spacebar to cycle between the yes and no options, or by pressing the Y (yes) or N (no) keys.

The Value Column

The Value column displays the integer ID number for the accelerator specified in the Key Column. This ID number loads the accelerator into the application's source code.

The Invert Column

The Invert column specifies whether the main menu item associated with the specified accelerator should be highlighted when the accelerator is pressed.

The Symbol Column

The Symbol column displays the symbol that has a matching ID number in the header file for the current accelerator. This symbol can be used to load the accelerator into the application.

Table 19.3, shown earlier, lists the keys used to move around inside the editors. Ctrl-Enter is used to add another row to the accelerator table.

The Bitmap Editor

The Bitmap Editor is a graphics tool for creating and editing bitmap resources (see fig. 19.3). Bitmap resources describe a picture and can be either two-color or sixteen-color images. The maximum size for each bitmap is 200-by-200 pixels. The defaults for each bitmap are 72-by-72 pixels using 16 colors.

The Bitmap Editor provides a number of drawing tools similar to those in paintbrush programs. These tools are described in the *Drawing Tools* section later in this chapter.

Fig. 19.3. The Bitmap Editor.

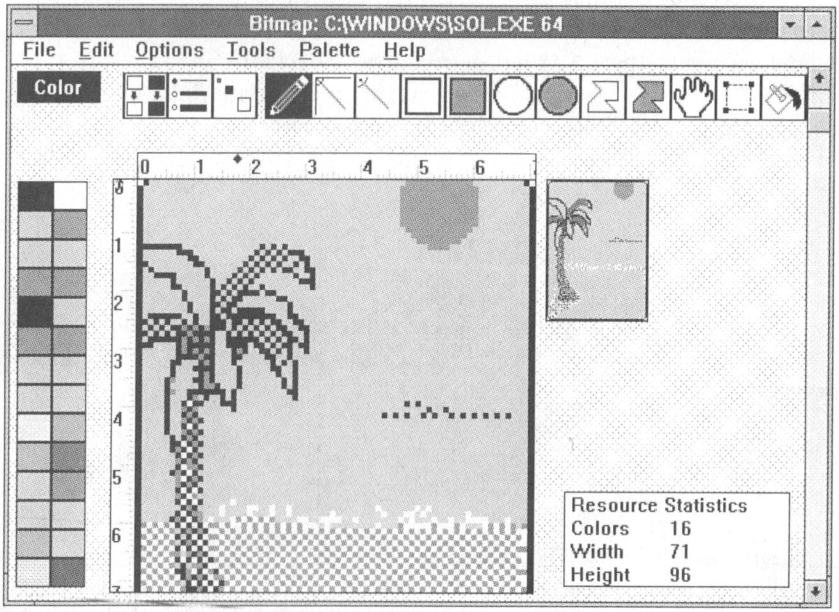

The Cursor Editor

The Cursor Editor is a graphics tool for creating and editing cursor resources (see fig. 19.4). Cursor resources are bitmaps that represent the current location of the mouse. Different cursor bitmaps can be used to represent different cursor modes.

When creating a cursor, the dimensions and number of colors to use in the cursor bitmap must be defined in the WRT.DAT file. The WRT.DAT file stores resolution information in records for various device drivers. Each record in the file contains fields that describe a particular device. The fields are described as follows:

Field	*Description*
Name:	Contains the name which describes the device; maximum length of 10 characters
Number of colors:	Contains the number of colors available for the bitmap
Cursor width:	Contains the width, in pixels, of a cursor
Cursor height:	Contains the height, in pixels, of a cursor
Icon width:	Contains the width, in pixels, of an icon
Icon height:	Contains the height, in pixels, of an icon

The Cursor Editor provides a number of drawing tools similar to those in paintbrush programs. These tools are described in the *Drawing Tools* section later in this chapter.

The Icon Editor

The Icon Editor is a graphics tool for creating and editing icon resources (see fig. 19.5). Icons are bitmaps that represent applications or actions within an application.

When creating an icon, the dimensions and number of colors to use in the cursor bitmap must be defined in the WRT.DAT file. The WRT.DAT file stores resolution information in records for various device drivers. Each record in the file contains fields that describe a particular device. The fields are described as follows:

Field	*Description*
Name:	Contains the name which describes the device; maximum length of 10 characters
Number of colors:	Contains the number of colors available for the bitmap
Cursor width:	Contains the width, in pixels, of a cursor

continues

Field	*Description*
Cursor height:	Contains the height, in pixels, of a cursor
Icon width:	Contains the width, in pixels, of an icon
Icon height:	Contains the height, in pixels, of an icon

Fig. 19.4. The Cursor Editor.

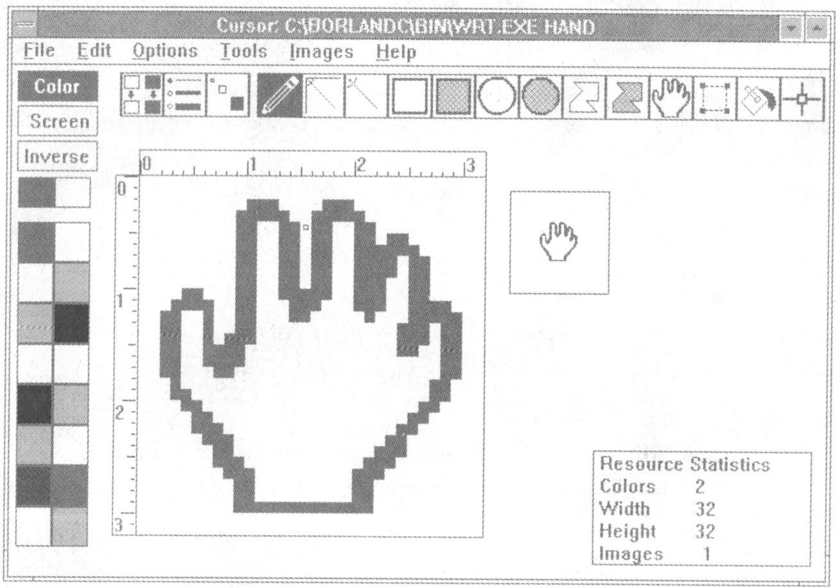

The Icon Editor provides a number of drawing tools similar to those in paintbrush programs. These tools are described in the *Drawing Tools* section that follows.

Drawing Tools

The Bitmap, Cursor, and Icon Editors contain a series of drawing tools used to create and edit bitmaps. Information for using these tools is provided in this section.

Each of the three editors used to create and edit bitmaps contains six basic parts, as follows:

- The Color Palette
- The Tools Palette
- The Editing Area
- The Rulers
- The View Window
- The Resource Statistics

A brief description of each part follows.

Fig. 19.5. The Icon Editor.

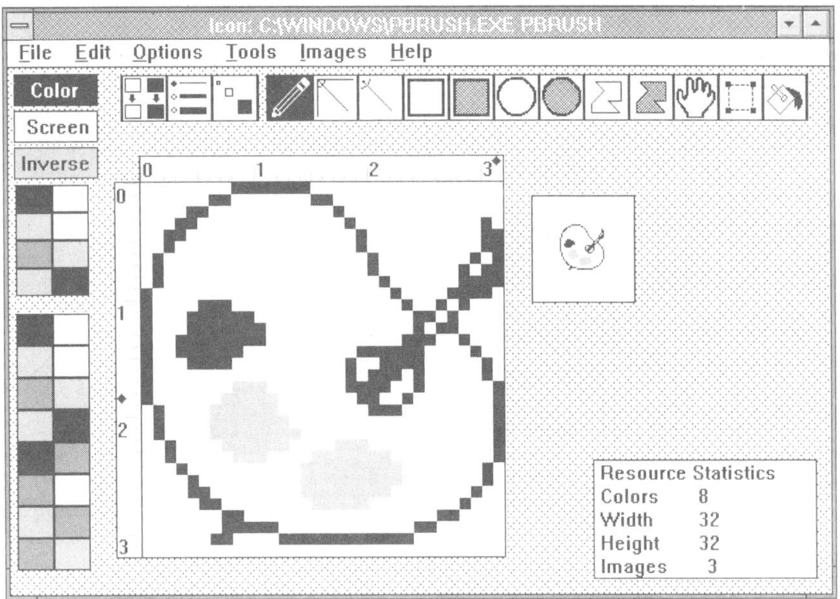

The Color Palette

The Color Palette appears on the left-hand side of the screen. It displays all the available colors for creating the bitmap and the current drawing color. The color palette varies among the editors (see table 19.4).

For the Bitmap Editor, 28 colors are available for use. When a 16-color bitmap is specified, the first 16 colors are solid, true colors. The remainder of the colors are shades of some of the first 16 colors. When a 2-color bitmap is specified, black, white, and 26 shades of gray are available. The colors in the Bitmap Editor color palette can be changed by first selecting the color, then selecting Edit Color. The red, blue, and green fields of each color can then be modified.

For the Cursor Editor, only black and white are available. However, 16 screen and inverse colors are available for use on the lower palette.

For the Icon Editor, the number of colors in the palette depends on the device specified in the WRT.DAT file. In addition, the colors available in the lower palette depend on the color mode and device in use.

When using the Cursor or Icon Editors, three color modes are available. These are the Color, Screen, and Inverse Modes. The color mode is selected by "clicking" the appropriate button.

Table 19.4. *Color modes for the Cursor and Icon Editors.*

Mode	*Meaning*
Color Mode	Indicates that the colors used in the bitmap will maintain their true colors no matter what background is specified.
Screen Mode	Specifies the screen's background color. Using this mode makes all images drawn subsequent to the selection take on the color of the background.
Inverse Mode	Specifies the inverse color of the screen color. All images drawn after the selection of this mode will be drawn in the inverse of the screen color.

Tools Palette

The Tools Palette is displayed across the top of the screen. These tools are similar to those in many graphics and paint packages and are used to create and edit bitmaps for the Bitmap, Cursor, and Icon Editors.

To use the drawing tools, select a color from the color palette, then choose the desired tool. Table 19.5 provides a description of each tool and its drawing methods.

Table 19.5. Tools in the Tools Palette.

Tool	*Function*
Toggle	Draws with the inverse of a color when using the Pencil Tool. When Toggle is off (the default), drawing is accomplished with the color selected from color palette. When on, drawing is accomplished with the inverse of the color of the pixel at the current position of the cursor.
Line Width	Selects the line width, in pixels. Three line thicknesses are provided: 1 (the default), 3, and 5 pixels. All lines drawn by the editors use this line width.
Magnifying	Selects the scale of the editing area. Three options are provided: actual size, 4 times actual size (the default), and 8 times actual size.
Pencil	Creates free-hand lines. The pencil is moved by the mouse and drawing occurs the entire time the mouse button is pressed.
Line	Draws a straight line between any two points at any angle.
Constrained Line	Draws a straight line that is a multiple of 45 degrees (0, 45, 90, 135, 180, 225, 270, 315, 360 degrees).
Rectangle	Draws an unfilled rectangle.
Filled Rectangle	Draws a rectangle filled with the current color.
Ellipse	Draws an unfilled ellipse.
Filled Ellipse	Draws an ellipse filled with the current color.
Polygon	Draws an unfilled polygon. Each side of the polygon is defined by clicking at the starting point and dragging to the next point. The polygon is automatically closed by the Polygon Tool.
Filled Polygon	Draws a polygon filled with the current color. Each side of the polygon is defined by clicking at the starting point and dragging to the next point. The polygon is automatically closed by the Filled Polygon Tool.
Selecting	Selects an existing object in the editing area. By selecting an object, it can be copied onto the Clipboard. From the Clipboard, the object can be modified with the operations available in the Edit menu.
Pouring	Fills an area with the current color, first evaluating the color value of the pixel at the current cursor position, then converting that pixel to the current color and moving in all directions, changing each pixel that matches the pixel value evaluated at the starting cursor position. The Pouring Tool stops filling the area when, in all directions, a pixel value is found other than that of the evaluated pixel.
Hot Spot	Used with the Cursor Editor to define a cursor hot spot. A hot spot is one point on the screen which identifies where a cursor operation will occur.

The Editing Area

The Editing Area is the area of the screen where the bitmaps are actually created and/or modified. This area can be actual size, four times actual size, or eight times actual size.

The Rulers

The Rulers are used to provide precise information on the location of the cursor relative to the Editing Area.

The View Window

The View Window shows the bitmap being created and/or modified as it would appear in the application. For the Bitmap Editor, the bitmap is shown in actual size. For the Cursor and Icon Editors, the View Window is larger than actual size.

The Resource Statistics

The Resource Statistics appear in the bottom right corner of the editor. The statistics displayed include the number of colors available for creating and/or modifying the bitmap, the pixel height of the bitmap, and the pixel width of the bitmap.

The Dialog Box Editor

The Dialog Box Editor is used to create and edit dialog box resources. Dialog boxes are resources which contain controls for the window application's user interface. The dialog box editor is shown in figure 19.6.

The Dialog Box Editor is similar to a paint program and has two palettes, the Tools Palette and the Alignment Palette.

Fig. 19.6. The Dialog Box Editor.

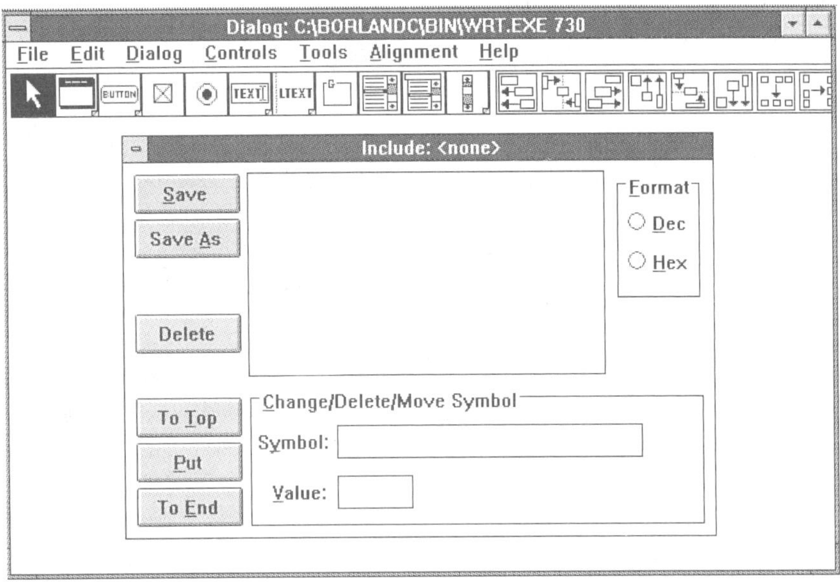

The Tools Palette

The Tools Palette provides a list of tools used to create the dialog box and its controls. Table 19.6 describes the tools available in the Tools Palette. The Tools menu can also be used to select the appropriate tool.

***Table 19.6.** The Tools Palette of the Dialog Box Editor.*

Tool	*Function*
Pointer	Activated automatically when a tool is selected. The pointer is then displayed, allowing you to draw with a selected tool, choose a dialog box, or modify existing controls.
Dialog Box	Creates either a standard or a captioned dialog box. A standard dialog box has no title bar and can't be moved within an application. A captioned dialog box has a title bar and can be moved within an application.
Control	Create push buttons, check boxes, radio buttons, edit fields, static text, group boxes, list boxes, combo boxes, scroll bars, and icons. Control Tools are described in table 19.7 that follows.

Table 19.7. *Control Tools in Tools Palette of Dialog Box Editor.*

Tool	*Purpose*
Button	Creates standard push buttons. A standard push button must be selected before it can be activated and is the tool selected by default.
Default Button	Creates default push button, which is automatically selected when a dialog box is open. Only one default push button should be defined for each dialog box.
Check Box	Develops options which can be checked on or off.
Radio Button	Creates a series of options. Only one option can be selected at any time. A set of radio buttons must be defined as a logical group.
Edit Controls	Used for text entry. Single line edit, multiple line edit, multiple line edit with vertical scrolling, and multiple line edit with vertical and horizontal scrolling styles are provided.
Text	Displays static text. Three formatting options are provided: left-justified formatting, right-justified formatting, and centered text.
Group Box	Groups push buttons, check boxes, or radio buttons. Group box surrounds buttons with a titled border, but buttons must be defined as a logical group using the Set Group option under the Dialog menu for the user to move between options with the cursor keys.
List Box	Creates a list box, a list of text items. List boxes are often used to show a file list and scroll bars are provided to permit the vertical scrolling of the list. List boxes can be customized.
Combo Box	Creates a combo box, which combines features of edit and list box. Single combo box, drop-down combo box, and drop-down list combo box styles are provided. Simple combo box displays both edit area and list box. Drop-down combo box displays combo box first. List box is opened whenever the down arrow on the right is selected. Drop-down list combo box behaves like the drop-down combo box. Difference is that the drop-down combo box provides flexible entry of text. The drop-down list combo box limits text entry to items in the list box.
Standard Scroll Bar	Creates a scroll bar with standard width.
Scroll Bar	Creates a scroll bar with a specified width.
Icon	Creates a box where an icon can be placed. The box is automatically sized by Windows.
Custom Control	Creates a box for placing a customized control. A custom control must have a dynamic-link library that fully defines the control's procedures and functionality.

The Alignment Palette

The Alignment Palette positions and adjusts the size of controls. The Alignment Tools in the Alignment Palette provide the power to make your controls perfectly spaced and aligned. The procedure for using each of the Alignment Tools is the same. First, one control is selected. The selection is designated as the standard for sizing or alignment. Other controls can then be selected while pressing the Shift key. The selected controls will be aligned or sized according to the standard control and the Alignment Tool chosen.

Table 19.8 describes the Alignment Tools. The Alignment Menu can also be used to select the Alignment Tools.

Table 19.8. *The Alignment Tools in the Alignment Palette.*

Tool	*Purpose*
Align Left	Aligns all the selected controls with the standard control's left border. Vertical positioning is not changed.
Align Right	Aligns all the selected controls with the standard control's right border. Vertical positioning in not changed.
Align Top	Aligns all the selected controls with the standard control's top border. Horizontal positioning is not changed.
Align Bottom	Aligns all the selected controls with the standard control's bottom border. Horizontal positioning is not changed.
Center on Horizontal	Aligns the centers of the selected controls with the standard control's horizontal axis. Horizontal positioning is not changed.
Center on Vertical	Aligns the centers of the selected controls with the standard control's vertical axis. Vertical positioning is not changed.
Spread Horizontally	Evenly spaces selected controls horizontally through dialog box's width. Standard control has no special significance with this tool.
Spread Vertically	Evenly spaces selected controls vertically through dialog box. Standard control has no special significance with this tool.
Make Same Size	Makes all the selected controls the same size as the standard control. Positioning is not changed.

The Menu Editor

The Menu Editor creates and edits menu resources. Its several features include a menu table, movement buttons, style and attribute fields, and a test window. The Menu Editor is shown in figure 19.7.

Fig. 19.7. The Menu Editor.

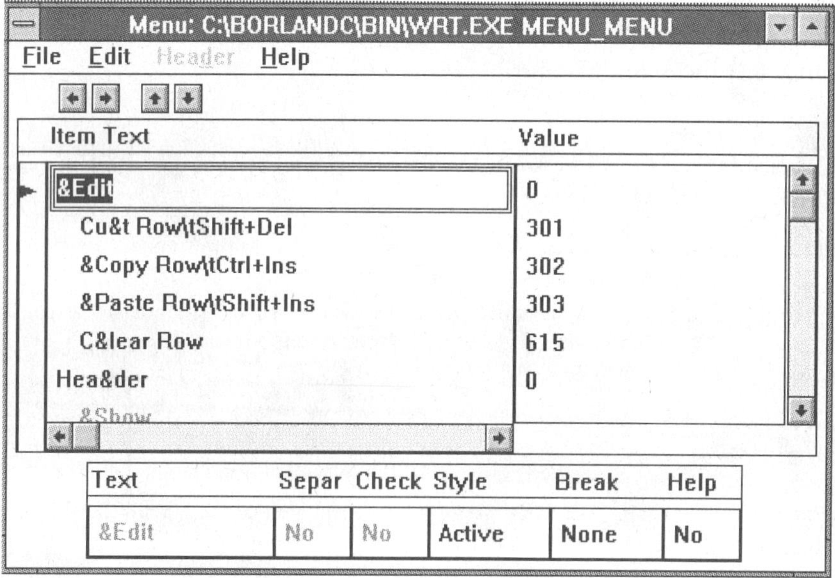

The Menu Table

The menu table, which contains an Item Text field and a Value field, appears when the Menu Editor is opened. The Item Text field is used for entering and editing text for the menu items. The Value field is used to enter or edit a value for the current item. An additional field, which shows the symbolic name for each menu item, is shown when a header file is open. Table 19.3, shown earlier, lists the keys used to move around the menu table.

The Item Text Field

The Item Text field lists the text that will actually appear on the menu. This field can contain any alphanumeric character and has a maximum length of 255 characters. The ampersand (&) character defines an activation key. For example, the Text field `&Remove` would define the character R as the activation key for the Remove menu item. Although the Item Text field will appear as `&Remove`, the actual menu item will appear as `Remove` on the menu with the R being underscored. A tab mark can also be inserted into the Item Text field by using \t. The tab mark is useful for lining up menu options.

The Value Field

The Value field contains the ID number for the menu item. The ID number is the unique integer value between 0 and 65,535 that is returned when the menu item is selected. This value is useful when developing the source code that describes the action resulting from a menu selection.

The Symbol Field

The Symbol field appears only when a header file is open. The symbol whose ID number in the header file matches the value for the current menu item is shown in this field. The symbol can be used rather than the ID in the Value field in the application's source code.

The Movement Buttons

Four movement buttons are provided above the menu table for moving through the information on a menu item. The Left and Right movement buttons are used to move through a menu item's hierarchy. The Up and Down movement buttons are used to change the position of the menu relative to other menu items.

The Up and Down Movement Buttons

The Up and Down movement buttons move an item up or down the menu hierarchy. Windows applications use a hierarchy of menus to represent levels. Each menu item in a top-level menu can offer other menu options which in turn offer more options. At each level, the items of the pop-up menus are indented to represent the hierarchic level of the menu. To move the hierarchic level of a particular menu

item, the Up and Down Movement Buttons are provided. The Left movement button moves the item up one level. The Right Movement Button moves the item down one level. All menus assigned to the moved item are also moved.

The Left and Right Movement Buttons

The Left and Right movement buttons change the position of menu items. The Up movement button moves the menu item up on the menu. The Down movement button moves the menu item down on the menu. A menu item can be moved only up or down from its current level in the menu hierarchy. The Up and Down Movement Buttons are used to change the menu item's hierarchy.

The Style and Attributes Fields

Style and Attribute fields are provided below the menu table. These fields define menu styles and attributes. Features include the ability to add separator lines, use checkmarks, define text styles, align columns, and assign help attributes.

Separator Lines

Separator lines—lines that divide menu items—can be easily added to menus by inserting a blank line (press Ctrl-Enter) into the menu table and typing YES in the Separator field. For each blank line, a separator line can be inserted.

Checkmarks

Checkmarks can be placed on menu items to indicate that they are turned on. Many menu items are merely switches to turn features on or off. For this type of menu item, checkmarks are good indicators of the menu item's status. To indicate that a checkmark should be used for the menu item, type YES in the menu item's check field.

Text Style

The Text Style of the menu item is set by the Style field. The three options for the Style field are Active, Inactive, and Gray. The text is displayed normally when the Active style is specified. The Active style also indicates that the menu item is active. The Inactive style indicates that the menu item is initially inactive. Text is displayed normally with the Inactive style. The Gray style indicates that the menu item does not return a value when selected. Text is displayed as gray text, indicating that the menu item cannot be selected.

Menu Item Alignment

Two types of breaks can be defined for menu item alignment. These breaks are the bar and column breaks. To define the breaks, type NONE, COLUMN, or BAR in the Break field. None is used to indicate that no break is defined. Column indicates that the menu item will begin a new column. All text subsequent to the setting of the column break is aligned with the new column. The Bar break is the same as the Column break except that a vertical bar is inserted between the columns.

The Help Attribute

The Help attribute can be set for top-level menu items and for only one item in a menu. The Help attribute is set by typing YES in the Help field of the menu item.

The Test Window

A test window is provided above the menu table and is used to test the menu as it is developed. The menus displayed in the Test Window behave exactly as they will in the application. Each time the Text Window is used, the menu reflects all current changes to the menu.

The String Editor

The String Editor is provided to create and edit string resources. String resources are used by the application to display text such as error messages or captions. The String Editor is shown in figure 19.8.

The String Editor defines strings with a String Table containing two or three columns. The first column holds the integer value of the string ID. The second column contains the string as it will be displayed on the screen. The third column appears when a header file is open and shows the symbolic name for the string ID. Table 19.3, shown earlier, lists the keys used to move around inside the String Table.

The Header Editor

The Header Editor is provided to allow you to create and edit symbolic constants, also called symbols. Symbols are defined to be global constants which are set to equal the ID numbers for various resources. By defining a symbol for an ID number, symbols can be substituted for ID numbers when developing source code. The Header Editor is shown in figure 19.9.

Fig. 19.8. The String Editor.

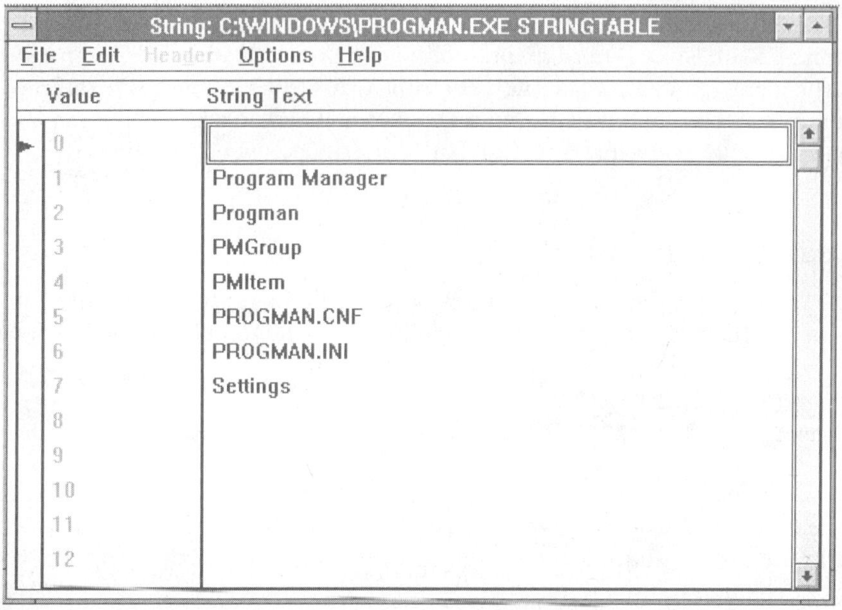

Fig. 19.9. The Header Editor.

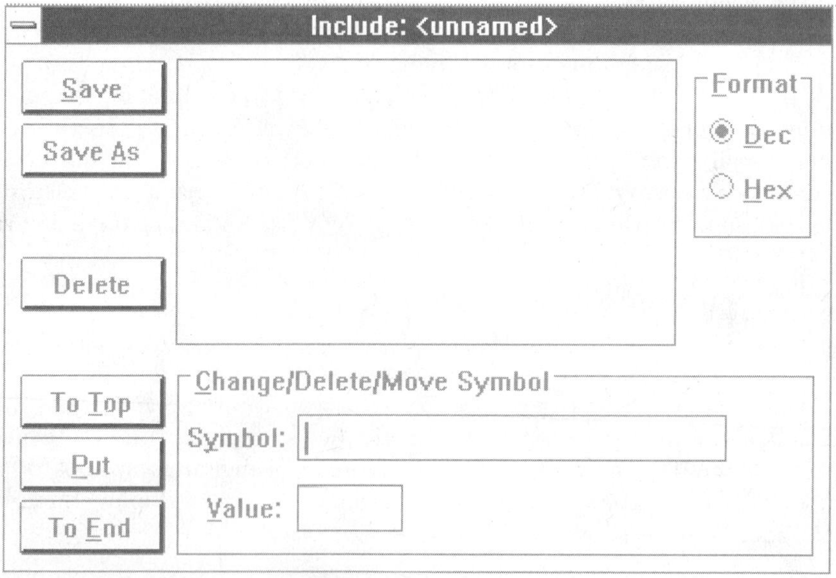

Turbo Assembler

Assembly language is extremely powerful and provides full control over the microprocessor. A low-level language, each line of assembly language code is fundamental in its operation. Assembly language source code is generally quite lengthy. This, on the surface, may be a negative factor to many. However, assembly language programs, when developed correctly, run more efficiently and produce more compact executable code than high-level language code.

As with every other language, there are tradeoffs with assembly language. When using assembly language for software development, ease of development is traded for overall operating efficiency. With high-level languages, operation efficiency is traded for ease of development.

Although some software programs are generated entirely in assembly language, this is rare. Most software programs are generated in a high-level language with assembly language subroutines or macros. By using assembly language for the time-critical, repetitive operations, overall operation speed can be optimized without giving up the ease of development provided by the high-level language.

Turbo Assembler provides a multi-pass command-line assembler for the 80x86 and 80x87 processor families, and produces object code from the source file. This object code can then be turned into executable code using TLINK.EXE.

The procedure for developing executable assembly language programs with Turbo Assembler is as follows:

1. Create the source code using a text editor which produces an ASCII file.
2. Assemble the program using Turbo Assembler. Turbo Assembler is invoked by typing TASM at the command line.
3. If errors occur, edit the source code with the text editor and repeat step 2. Proceed to step 4 if no errors occurred.
4. Link the object code produced in the previous steps using TLINK.EXE.
5. If errors occur, modify the source code using the text editor and start over from step 2. If no errors occurred, continue with step 6.
6. Run the executable file produced in step 4. If it operates correctly, you are done. If it operates incorrectly, modify the source code with the text editor and start over from step 2.

Turbo Assembler provides you with some control over the assembly process in the form of command-line options. Command-line options can be used when invoking Turbo Assembler to control the way the assembler will behave. Table 20.1 provides a list of the command-line options.

Table 20.1. *Command-line options.*

Option	*Meaning*
/a	Specifies alphabetical segment-ordering
/b	Included for compatibility. Performs no action and has no effect on assembly
/c	Enables cross-referencing in listing file
/d	Defines a symbol
/e	Generates floating-point emulator instructions
/h or /?	Displays a help screen
/i	Sets an Include file path
/j	Defines an assembler startup directive
/kh	Sets the maximum number of symbols allowed

Option	*Meaning*
/l	Generates a listing file
/la	Shows high-level interface code in listing file
/m	Sets the maximum number of assembly passes
/ml	Treats symbols as case-sensitive
/mu	Converts symbols to uppercase
/mv#	Sets the maximum length of symbols
/mx	Makes public and external symbols case-sensitive
/n	Suppresses symbol table in listing file
/o	Generates overlay code
/op	Generates overlay code for the Phar Lap Linker
/p	Checks for impure code in protected mode
/q	Suppresses .OBJ records not needed for linking
/r	Generates real floating-point instructions
/s	Specifies sequential segment-ordering
/t	Suppresses messages on successful assembly
/v	Included for compatibility. Performs no action and has no effect on assembly
/w	Controls the generation of warning messages
/x	Includes false conditionals in listing file
/z	Displays source lines along with error messages
/zd	Enables line-number information in object files
/zi	Enables debug information in object file

The source code of an assembly language program is primarily made up of directive and instruction mnemonics with the following format:

<label> <instruction/directive> <operands> <;comment>

in which

<label> = an optional symbolic name

<instruction/directive> = the mnemonic for an instruction or directive

<operands> = a combination of constants, memory references, register references, or text strings required for the instruction or directive

<;comment> = an optional comment.

The remainder of this chapter provides a listing and brief description of the 80x86 processor instructions, 80x87 co-processor instructions, directives, operators, and predefined symbols used by Turbo Assembler. This chapter is not meant to provide full reference materials for each instruction, directive, operator, and symbol. The intent is to provide tables to be used by programmers who are familiar with assembly language to quickly review the resources available under Turbo Assembler.

Processor Instructions

Table 20.2 provides a listing of processor instructions used by the 80x86 processors. The Turbo Assembler Quick Reference Guide, included with Borland C++, provides full reference information for each instruction.

Table 20.2. *Processor instructions.*

Instruction	*Meaning*
AAA	ASCII adjust after addition
AAD	ASCII adjust before division
AAM	ASCII adjust AX after multiply
AAS	ASCII adjust AL after subtraction
ADC	Add with carry
ADD	Add
AND	Logical AND
ARPL	Adjust RPL field of selector
BOUND	Check array index against bounds
BSF	Bit scan forward
BSR	Bit scan reverse
BSWAP	Byte swap
BT	Bit test

Instruction	Meaning
BTC	Bit test and complement
BTR	Bit test and reset
BTS	Bit test and set
CALL	Call procedure
CBW	Convert byte to word
CDQ	Convert doubleword to quadword
CLC	Clear carry flag
CLD	Clear direction flag
CLI	Clear interrupt flag
CLTS	Clear task switched flag
CMC	Complement carry flag
CMP	Compare two operands
CMPS	Compare string operands
CMPSB	Compare bytes
CMPSW	Compare words
CMPSD	Compare doublewords
CMPXCHG	Compare and exchange
CWD	Convert word to doubleword; uses DX:AX as the destination
CWDE	Convert word to doubleword; uses EAX as the destination
DAA	Decimal adjust AL after addition
DAS	Decimal adjust AL after subtraction
DEC	Decrement by one
DIV	Unsigned divide
ENTER	Make stack frame for procedure parameters
HLT	Halt
IDIV	Signed divide
IMUL	Signed multiply
IN	Input from port
INC	Increment by one

continues

Table 20.2. (continued)

Instruction	*Meaning*
INS	Input from port to string
INSB	Input byte from port
INSW	Input word from port
INSD	Input doubleword from port
INT	Call to interrupt procedure;
INTO	Call to interrupt procedure; interrupt number is 4
INVD	Invalidate cache
INVLPG	Invalidate TLB entry
IRET	Interrupt return
IRETD	Interrupt return
JA	Jump if above
JAE	Jump if above or equal
JB	Jump if below
JBE	Jump if below or equal
JC	Jump on carry
JCXZ	Jump if CX=0
JE	Jump if equal
JECXZ	Jump if ECX = 0
JG	Jump if greater than
JGE	Jump if greater than or equal
JL	Jump if less than
JLE	Jump if less than or equal
JMP	Jump
JNA	Jump if not above
JNAE	Jump if not above or equal
JNB	Jump if not below
JNBE	Jump if not below or equal
JNC	Jump on no carry

Instruction	*Meaning*
JNE	Jump if not equal
JNG	Jump if not greater than
JNGE	Jump if not greater than or equal
JNL	Jump if not less than
JNLE	Jump if not less than or equal
JNO	Jump on no overflow
JNP	Jump on no parity
JNS	Jump on not sign
JNZ	Jump on not zero
JO	Jump on overflow
JP	Jump on parity
JPE	Jump on parity even
JPO	Jump on parity odd
JS	Jump on sign
JZ	Jump on zero
LAHF	Load flags into AH register
LAR	Load access rights byte
LEA	Load effective address offset
LEAVE	High-level procedure exit
LGDT/LIDT	Load global/interrupt descriptor table register
LGS, LSS, LFS, LDS, LES	Load full pointer
LLDT	Load local descriptor table register
LMSW	Load machine status word
LOCK	Assert LOCK# signal prefix
LODS	Load string operand
LODSB	Load byte
LODSW	Load word
LODSD	Load doubleword

continues

Table 20.2. (continued)

Instruction	*Meaning*
LOOP	Loop control with CX counter
LOOP cond	Loop control with CX/ECX counter
LSL	Load segment limit
LTR	Load task register
MOV	Move to/from special registers
MOVS	Move data from string to string
MOVSB	Move byte
MOVSW	Move word
MOVSD	Move doubleword
MOVSX	Move with sign-extend
MOVZX	Move with zero-extend
MUL	Unsigned multiplication of AL or AX
NEG	Two's complement negation
NOP	No operation
NOT	One's complement negation
OR	Logical inclusive OR
OUT	Output to port
OUTS	Output string to port
OUTSB	Output byte
OUTSW	Output word
OUTSD	Output doubleword
POP	Pop a word from the stack
POPA	Pop all general registers; pops the eight 16-bit general registers
POPAD	Pop all general registers; pops the eight 32-bit general registers
POPF	Pop from stack into FLAGS
POPFD	Pop from stack into EFLAGS register
PUSH	Push operand onto the stack
PUSHA	Push all general registers; 16-bit general registers

Instruction	*Meaning*
PUSHAD	Push all general registers; 32-bit general registers
PUSHF	Push flags register onto the stack; decrement stack pointer by 2
PUSHFD	Push flags register onto the stack; decrement stack pointer by 4
RCL	Rotate left
RCR	Rotate right
ROL	Rotate left
ROR	Rotate right
REP	Repeat following string operation
REPE	Repeat while equal
REPZ	Repeat while zero
REPNE	Repeat while not equal
REPNZ	Repeat while not zero
RET	Return from procedure
SAHF	Store AH into flags
SAL	Arithmetic shift left
SAR	Arithmetic shift right
SHL	Shift left
SHR	Shift right
SBB	Integer subtraction with borrow
SCAS	Compare string data
SCASB	Scan string for byte
SCASW	Scan string for word
SCASD	Scan string for doubleword
SETA	Set byte if above or equal
SETB	Set byte if below
SETBE	Set byte if below or equal
SETC	Set byte on carry
SETE	Set byte if equal
SETG	Set byte if greater than

continues

Table 20.2. (continued)

Instruction	*Meaning*
SETGE	Set byte if greater than or equal
SETL	Set byte if less than
SETLE	Set byte if less than or equal
SETNA	Set byte if not above
SETNAE	Set byte if not above or equal
SETNB	Set byte if not below
SETNBE	Set byte if not below or equal
SETNC	Set byte on no carry
SETNE	Set byte if not equal
SETNG	Set byte if not greater than
SETNGE	Set byte if not greater than or equal
SETNL	Set byte if not less than
SETNO	Set byte on no overflow
SETNP	Set byte on no parity
SETNS	Set byte on not sign
SETNZ	Set byte if not zero
SETO	Set byte on overflow
SETP	Set byte on parity
SETPE	Set byte on parity even
SETPO	Set byte on parity odd
SETS	Set byte on sign
SETZ	Set byte if zero
SGDT	Store global/interrupt descriptor table; store GDTR
SIDT	Store global/interrupt descriptor table; store IDTR
SHLD	Double precision shift left
SHRD	Double precision shift right
SLDT	Store local descriptor table register
SMSW	Store machine status word

Instruction	Meaning
STC	Set carry flag
STD	Set direction flag
STI	Set interrupt enable flag
STOS	Store string data
STOSB	Store in byte
STOSW	Store in word
STOSD	Store in doubleword
STR	Store task register
SUB	Integer subtraction
TEST	Logical compare
VERR	Verify a segment for reading
VERW	Verify a segment for writing
WAIT	Wait until BUSY# pin is inactive
WBINVD	Write-back and invalidate cache
XADD	Exchange and add
XCHG	Exchange memory/register with register
XLAT	Table look-up translation
XLATB	Table look-up translation; no operand form
XOR	Logical exclusive OR

Co-processor Instructions

Table 20.3 provides a listing of processor instructions used by the 80x87 numeric co-processors. The Turbo Assembler Quick Reference Guide, included with Borland C++, provides full reference information for each of these instructions.

Table 20.3. Co-processor instructions.

Instruction	*Meaning*
F2XM1	Compute 2^x-1
FABS	Absolute value
FADD	Add real
FADDP	Add real and pop
FBLD	Packed decimal (BCD) load
FBSTP	Packed decimal (BCD) store and pop
FCHS	Change sign
FCLEX	Clear exceptions
FNCLEX	Clear exceptions; no operand
FCOM	Compare real
FCOMP	Compare real and pop
FCOMPP	Compare real and pop twice
FCOS	Cosine of ST(0)
FDECSTP	Decrement stack pointer
FDISI	Disables interrupts
FNDISI	Disables interrupts; no operand
FDIV	Divide real
FDIVP	Divide real and pop
FDIVR	Divide real reversed
FDIVRP	Divide real reversed and pop
FENI	Enable interrupts; no operands
FNENI	Enable interrupts
FFREE	Free register
FIADD	Integer add
FICOM	Integer compare
FICOMP	Integer compare and pop
FIDIV	Integer divide
FIDIVR	Integer divide reversed

Instruction	*Meaning*
FILD	Integer load
FIMUL	Integer multiply
FINCSTP	Increment stack pointer
FINIT	Initialize processor
FNINIT	Initialize processor; no operand
FIST	Integer store
FISTP	Integer store and pop
FISUB	Integer subtract
FISUBR	Integer subtract reversed
FLD	Load real
FLDCW	Load control word
FLDENV	Load environment
FLDLG2	Load $\log_{10}2$
FLDLN2	Load $\log_{e}2$
FLDL2E	Load $\log_{2}e$
FLDL2T	Load $\log_{2}10$
FLDPI	Load P (pi)
FLDZ	Load +0.0
FLD1	Load +1.0
FMUL	Multiply real
FMULP	Multiply real and pop
FNOP	No operation
FPATAN	Partial arctangent
FPREM	Partial remainder
FPREM1	Partial remainder; 387 and i486 only
FPTAN	Partial tangent
FRNDINT	Round to integer
FRSTOR	Restore saved state
FSAVE/FNSAVE	Save state

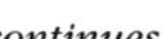
continues

Table 20.3. (continued)

Instruction	*Meaning*
FSCALE	Scale
FSETPM	Set protected mode
FSIN	Sine of ST(0)
FSINCOS	Sine and cosine of ST(0)
FSQRT	Square root
FST	Store real
FSTCW/FNSTCW	Store control word
FSTENV/FNSTENV	Store environment
FSTP	Store real and pop
FSTSW/FNSTSW	Store status word
FSTSW AX/FNSTSW AX	Store status word to AX
FSUB	Subtract real
FSUBP	Subtract real and pop
FSUBR	Subtract real reversed
FSUBRP	Subtract real reversed and pop
FTST	Test stack top against +0.0
FUCOM/FUCOMP/FUCOMPP	Unordered compare
FWAIT	Wait
FXAM	Examine stack top
FXCH	Exchange registers
FXTRACT	Extract exponent and significant
FYL2X	$Y * \log_2 X$
FYL2XP1	$Y * \log_2(X+1)$
F2XM1	2^X-1

Directives

Table 20.4 provides a listing of the directives used by Turbo Assembler. The Turbo Assembler Quick Reference Guide provides full reference information for each of these directives.

Table 20.4. *Directives.*

Directive	*Meaning*
.186	Enables assembly of 80186 processor instructions
.286	Enables assembly of non-privileged 80286 processor instructions and 80287 co-processor instructions
.286C	Enables assembly of non-privileged 80286 processor instructions and 80287 co-processor instructions
.286P	Enables assembly of all 80286 processor instructions and 80287 co-processor instructions
.287	Enables assembly of 80287 numeric co-processor instructions
.386	Enables assembly of non-privileged 80386 processor instructions and 80387 co-processor instructions
.386C	Enables assembly of non-privileged 80386 processor instructions and 80387 co-processor instructions
.386P	Enables assembly of all 80386 processor instructions and 80387 co-processor instructions
.387	Enables assembly of 80387 co-processor instructions
.486	Enables assembly of non-privileged instructions for the 80486 processor
.486C	Enables assembly of non-privileged instructions for the 80486 processor
.486P	Enables assembly of protected mode instructions for the 80486 processor
.8086	Enables assembly of 8086 processor instructions only (the default processor instruction mode)
.8087	Enables assembly of 8087 co-processor instructions only (the default co-processor instruction mode)
:	Defines a near code label
=	Defines a numeric equate

continues

Table 20.4. (continued)

Directive	*Meaning*
ALIGN	Rounds up the location counter to a power-of-two address boundary
.ALPHA	Sets alphanumeric segment-ordering
ARG	Sets up arguments on the stack for procedures
ASSUME	Specifies the segment register used to calculate the effective addresses for all labels and variables defined under a given segment or group
%BI	Sets the width of the object code field
CATSTR	Concatenates several strings into one string
.CODE	Defines the start of a code segment; MASM only
CODESEG	Defines the start of a code segment; Ideal or MASM
COMM	Defines a communal variable
COMMENT	Starts a multiline comment
%COND	Show all statements in conditional blocks in the listing
CONST	Defines the start of the constant data segment
.CREF	Reverses the effects of any %XCREF or .XCREF directives
%CREF	Allows cross-reference information to be accumulated for all symbols encountered from this point forward in the source file
%CREFALL	Causes all subsequent symbols in the source file to appear in the cross-reference listing
%CREFREF	Disables listing of unreferenced symbols in cross-reference
%CREFUREF	Lists only the unreferenced symbols in cross-reference
%CTLS	Causes listing control directives to be placed in the listing file
.DATA	Defines the start of the initialized data segment; MASM
DATASEG	Defines the start of the initialized data segment; Ideal
.DATA?	Defines the start of the uninitialized data segment
DB	Allocates and initializes a byte of storage
DD	Allocates and initialzes 4 bytes of storage
%DEPTH	Sets the size of the depth field in the listing file
DF	Allocates and initializes 6 bytes of storage

Directive	*Meaning*
DISPLAY	Outputs a quoted string to the screen
DOSSEG	Enables DOS segment-ordering at link time
DP	Allocates and initializes 6 bytes of storage
DQ	Allocates and initializes 8 bytes of storage
DT	Allocates and initializes 10 bytes of storage
DW	Allocates and initializes 2 bytes of storage
ELSE	Starts an alternative conditional assembly block
ELSEIF	Starts a nested conditional assembly block
EMUL	Causes all subsequent co-processor instructions to be generated as emulated instructions
END	Marks the end of a source file
ENDIF	Marks the end of a conditional IF-xxx assembly block
ENDM	Marks the end of a repeat block or a macro definition
ENDP	Marks the end of a procedure
ENDS	Marks the end of the current segment, structure, or union
EQU	Defines a string, alias, or numeric equate
.ERR	Forces an error on that line in the source file; MASM only
ERR	Forces an error on that line in the source file; MASM or Ideal
.ERR1	Forces an error to occur on pass 1 of assembly
.ERR2	Forces an error to occur on pass 2 of assembly
.ERRB	Forces an error to occur if an argument is blank
.ERRDEF	Forces an error to occur if the symbol is defined
.ERRDIF	Forces an error to occur if arguments differ (this is case sensitive)
.ERRDIFI	Forces an error to occur if arguments differ (this is not case sensitive)
.ERRE	Forces an error to occur if the expression is false
.ERRIDN	Forces an error to occur if the arguments are the same (this is case sensitive)
.ERRIDNI	Forces an error to occur if the arguments are the same (this is not case sensitive)
ERRIF	Forces an error to occur if the expression is true

continues

Table 20.4. (continued)

Directive	*Meaning*
ERRIF1	Forces an error to occur on pass 1 of assembly
ERRIF2	Forces an error to occur on pass 2 of assembly
ERRIFB	Forces an error if the argument is blank
ERRIFDEF	Forces an error if the symbol is defined
ERRIFDIF	Forces an error if the arguments are different (this is case sensitive)
ERRIFDIFI	Forces an error if the arguments are different (this is not case sensitive)
ERRIFE	Forces an error if the expression is false
ERRIFIDN	Forces an error if the arguments are identical (this is case sensitive)
ERRIFIDNI	Forces an error if the arguments are identical (this is not case sensitive)
ERRIFNB	Forces an error if the argument is not blank
ERRIFNDEF	Forces an error if the symbol is not defined
.ERRNB	Forces an error if the argument is not blank
.ERRNDEF	Forces an error if the symbol is not defined
.ERRNZ	Forces an error to occur if the expression is true
EVEN	Rounds up the location counter to the next even address
EVENDATA	Rounds up the location counter to the next even address in a data segment
EXITM	Terminates macro or block-repeat expansion
EXTRN	Indicates that a symbol is defined in another module
.FARDATA	Defines the start of a far initialized data segment; MASM
FARDATA	Defines the start of a far initialized data segment; MASM or ideal
.FARDATA?	Defines the start of a far uninitialized data segment
GLOBAL	Defines a global symbol
GROUP	Associates a group name with one or more segments
IDEAL	Enters the Ideal assembly mode
IF	Initiates a conditional block that causes the assembly of certain statements when the corresponding expression is true

Directive	*Meaning*
IF1	Initiates a conditional block that causes the assembly of certain statements when the assembly pass is pass one
IF2	Initiates a conditional block that causes the assembly of certain statements when the assembly pass is pass two
IFB	Initiates a conditional block that causes the assembly of certain statements when the corresponding argument is blank
IFDEF	Initiates a conditional block that causes the assembly of certain statements when the corresponding symbol is defined
IFDIF	Initiates a conditional block that causes the assembly of certain statements when the corresponding arguments differ (this is case sensitive)
IFDIFI	Initiates a conditional block that causes the assembly of certain statements when the corresponding arguments differ (this is not case sensitive)
IFE	Initiates a conditional block that causes the assembly of certain statements when the corresponding expression is false
IFIDN	Initiates a conditional block that causes the assembly of certain statements when the corresponding arguments are identical (this is case sensitive)
IFIDNI	Initiates a conditional block that causes the assembly of certain statements when the corresponding arguments are identical (this is not case sensitive)
IFNB	Initiates a conditional block that causes the assembly of certain statements when the corresponding argument is not blank
IFNDEF	Initiates a conditional block that causes the assembly of certain statements when the corresponding symbol is not defined
%INCL	Enables the listing of include files
INCLUDE	Includes source code from another file
INCLUDELIB	Causes the linker to include a specified library at link time
INSTR	Finds the position of the first occurrence of one string in a second string
IRP	Repeats a block of statements with string substitution
IRPC	Repeats a block of statements with character substitution
JUMPS	Causes Turbo Assembler to look at the address of a conditional jump instruction

continues

Table 20.4. (continued)

Directive	*Meaning*
LABEL	Defines a symbol to be of a specified type
.LALL	Enables the listing of macro expansions
.LFCOND	Shows all statements in conditional blocks in the listing
%LINUM	Sets the width of the line-number field in the listing file
%LIST	Shows source lines in the listing; MASM or Ideal
.LIST	Shows source lines in the listing; MASM only
LOCAL	Defines local variables for macros and procedures
LOCALS	Enables local symbols
MACRO	Defines a macro
%MACS	Enables listing of macro expansions
MASM	Enters MASM assembly mode
MASM51	Enables assembly of some of MASM 5.1 enhancements
MODEL	Sets the memory model for simplified segmentation directives; MASM or Ideal
.MODEL	Sets the memory model for simplified segmentation directives; MASM only
MULTERRS	Allows multiple errors to be reported on a single source line
NAME	Sets the object file's module name
%NEWPAGE	Starts a new page in the listing file
%NOCONDS	Disables the placement of statements in conditional blocks in the listing file
%NOCREF	Disables cross-reference listing information accumulation
%NOCTLS	Disables placement of listing-control directives
NOEMUL	Causes all subsequent numeric co-processor instructions to be generated as real instructions
%NOINCL	Disables listing of source lines from INCLUDE files
NOJUMPS	Disables stretching of conditional jumps enabled with JUMPS
%NOLIST	Disables output to the listing file
NOLOCALS	Disables local symbols enabled with LOCALS

Directive	*Meaning*
%NOMACS	Lists only macro expansions that generate code
NOMASM51	Disables MASM 5.1 enhancements enabled with MASM51
NOMULTERRS	Allows only one error to be reported on a source line
NOSMART	Disables code optimizations
%NOSYMS	Disables placement of the symbol table in the listing file %NOTRUNC Prevents truncation of fields whose contents are longer than the corresponding fields' widths
NOWARN	Disables specified or all warning messages
ORG	Sets the location counter in the current segment to the specified address
%OUT	Displays text on the screen
P186	Enables assembly of 80186 instructions
P286	Enables assembly of 80286 and 80287 instructions
P286N	Enables assembly of non-privileged 80286 instructions and 80287 instructions
P286P	Enables assembly of all 80286 instructions and 80287 instructions
P287	Enables assembly of 80287 co-processor instructions
P386	Enables assembly of all 80386 processor instructions and 80387 co-processor instructions
P386N	Enables assembly of non-privileged 80386 instructions and 80387 co-processor instructions
P386P	Enables assembly of all 80386 instructions and 80387 co-processor instructions
P387	Enables assembly of 80387 co-processor instructions
P486	Enables assembly of all 80486 processor instructions
P486N	Enables assembly of non-privileged 80486 processor instructions
P8086	Enables assembly of 8086 processor instructions (this is the default mode)
P8087	Enables assembly of 8087 co-processor instructions (this is the default mode)

continues

Table 20.4. (continued)

Directive	*Meaning*
%PAGESIZE	Sets the listing page height and width and starts a new page
%PCNT	Sets the segment:offset field width in the listing file
PNO87	Prevents the assembling of co-processor instructions
%POPLCTL	Resets the listing controls to the settings prior to when the %PUSHLCTL directive was issued
PROC	Defines the start of a procedure
PUBLIC	Declares a symbol accessible from other modules
PUBLICDLL	Declares symbols accessible as dynamic link entry points from other modules
PURGE	Removes a macro definition
%PUSHLCTL	Saves the current listing controls
QUIRKS	Allows the assembly of source files which use one of the true MASM bugs
RADIX	Sets the default radix for integer constants; MASM only
RADIX	Sets the default radix for integer constants; MASM or Ideal
RECORD	Defines a record name that contains bit fields
REPT	Repeats a block of statements
RETCODE	Generates a near or far return
RETF	Generates a far return from a procedure
RETN	Generates a near return from a procedure
.SALL	Suppresses the listing of all statements in macro expansions
SEGMENT	Defines the segment name with full attribute control
.SEQ	Sets sequential segment-ordering
.SFCOND	Prevents FALSE statements in conditional blocks from appearing in the listing file
SIZESTR	Assigns a number of characters
SMART	Enables all code optimizations
.STACK	Defines the start of the stack segment; MASM
STACK	Defines the start of the stack segment; MASM or ideal

Directive	*Meaning*
STRUC	Defines a structure
SUBSTR	Defines a new string
SUBTTL	Sets the subtitle in the listing file; MASM
%SUBTTL	Sets the subtitle in the listing file; MASM or Ideal
%SYMS	Enables symbol table placement in the listing file
%TABSIZE	Sets the number of columns between tabs in the listing file
%TEXT	Sets the width of the source field in the listing file
.TFCOND	Toggles conditional block-listing mode
TITLE	Sets the title in the listing file; MASM
%TITLE	Sets the title in the listing file; MASM or Ideal
%TRUNC	Truncates the listing fields that are too long
UDATASEG	Defines the start of an uninitialized data segment
UFARDATA	Defines the start of an uninitialized far data segment
UNION	Defines a union
USES	Indicates which registers or single-token data items should be pushed at the beginning of the procedure or popped at the end
WARN	Enables some or all warning messages
.XALL	Causes only the macro expansions that generate code or data to be listed
.XCREF	Disables cross-reference listing information accumulation
.XLIST	Disables subsequent output to the listing file

Operators

Table 20.5 lists the operators provided by Turbo Assembler. The Turbo Assembler Quick Reference Guide provides full reference information for each of these operators.

Table 20.5. Operators.

Operator	*Meaning*
()	Marks an expression for priority evaluation
*	Multiplies two integer expressions
+ (binary)	Adds two expressions
+ (unary)	Indicates that an expression is positive
– (binary)	Subtracts one expression from another
– (unary)	Changes the sign of an expression
.	Selects a structure member
/	Divides two integer expressions
:	Generates segment or group override
?	Initializes with indeterminate data
[ ]	MASM mode: Specifies addition or register indirect memory operands Ideal mode: Specifies a memory reference
AND	Performs bit-by-bit logical AND
BYTE/BYTE PTR	Forces an address expression to be byte size
CODEPTR	Returns the default procedure address size
DATAPTR	Forces address expressions to model-dependent size
DUP	Repeats a data allocation operation
DWORD/DWORD PTR	Forces an address expression to be doubleword size
EQ	Returns TRUE if two expressions are equal
FAR/FAR PTR	Forces an address expression to be a far code pointer
FWORD/FWORD PTR	Forces an address expression to be 32-bit far pointer size
GE	Returns TRUE if one expression is greater than or equal to another
GT	Returns TRUE if one expression is greater than another
HIGH	Returns the high part, 8 bits or type size, of an expression

Operator	*Meaning*
LARGE	Sets an expression's offset size to 32 bits
LE	Returns TRUE if one expression is less than or equal to another
LENGTH	Returns the number of data elements allocated
LOW	Returns the low part, 8 bits or type size, of an expression
LT	Returns TRUE is one expression is less than another
MASK	Returns a bit mask for a record field or an entire record
MOD	Returns the remainder from the division of two expressions
NE	Returns TRUE if the expressions are not equal
NEAR/NEAR PTR	Forces an address expression to be a near code pointer
NOT	Performs a bit-by-bit complement of an expression
OFFSET	Returns the offset of an expression
OR	Performs a bit-by-bit logical OR of two expressions
PROC/PROC PTR	Forces an address expression to be a near or far code pointer
PTR	Forces an address expression to have type size
PWORD/PWORD PTR	Forces an address expression to be 32-bit far pointer size
QWORD/QWORDPTR	Forces an address expression to be quadword size
SEG	Retrieves the segment address of an expression
SHL	Shifts the value of an expression to the left
SHORT	Forces an expression to be a short code pointer
SHR	Shifts the value of an expression to the right
SIZE	Returns the size of a data item
SMALL	Sets an expression's offset size to 16 bits
SYMTYPE	Returns the byte that describes an expression

continues

Table 20.5. (continued)

Operator	*Meaning*
TBYTE/TBYTE PTR	Forces an address expression to be 10-byte size
THIS	Creates an operand whose address is the current segment and location counter
.TYPE	Returns the byte that describes the mode and scope of an expression
TYPE	Applies the type of an existing variable or structure member to another variable or structure member
UNKNOWN	Removes type information from an address expression
WIDTH	Returns the width, in bits, of a field in a record or of an entire field
WORD/WORD PTR	Forces an address expression to be word size
XOR	Performs a bit-by-bit logical XOR of two expressions

Predefined Symbols

Table 20.6 lists the predefined symbols for Turbo Assembler. The Turbo Assembler Quick Reference Guide provides full reference information for each of these symbols.

Table 20.6. Predefined symbols.

Symbol	*Meaning*
$	Represents the current location counter within the current segment
@code	Alias equate for .CODE segment name
@CodeSize	Numeric equate that indicates code memory model (0 = near, 1 = far)
@CPU	Numeric equate that returns information about current processor directive

Symbol	*Meaning*
@curseg	Alias equate for current segment
@data	Alias equate for near data group name
@DataSize	Numeric equate which indicates the date memory model (0 = near, 1 = far, 2 = huge)
??date	String equate for today's date
@fardata	Alias equate for initialized far data segment name
@fardata?	Alias equate for uninitialized far data segment name
@FileName	Alias equate for the current assembly file name
??filename	String equate for the current assembly file name
@Model	Numeric equate representing the model currently in effect
@Startup	Label that marks the beginning of the startup code
??time	String equate for the current time
??version	Numeric equate for the current Turbo Assembler version number
@WordSize	Numeric equate which indicates 16 or 32 bit segments (2 = 16 bit, 4 = 32 bit)

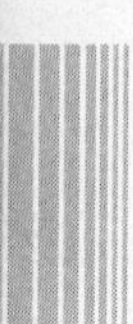

Introduction to the Turbo Debugger

Turbo Debugger is a source-level debugger that provides the capability to detect, find, and fix errors in your programs. Turbo Debugger can be used to analyze Turbo C, Turbo Pascal, Turbo Assembler, Microsoft C, or MASM programs. In addition, new features have been added which allow you to debug Microsoft Windows applications.

Turbo Debugger helps you to analyze your program through its tracing, back tracing, stepping, viewing, inspecting, changing, and watching features. These terms are defined as follows:

Tracing	The ability to execute the program one line at a time.
Back Tracing	The ability to execute the program one line at a time beginning at the bottom and going to the top.
Stepping	The ability to execute the program one line at a time while skipping procedure or function calls.

Viewing — The ability to view the state of the program relative to variables, values, breakpoints, the stack, a log, a data file, a source file, CPU code, memory, registers, co-processor information, object and class hierarchies, execution history, or program output.

Inspecting — The ability to view the contents of data structures.

Changing — The ability to change the value of a global or local variable.

Watching — The ability to isolate variables and view their values as the program executes.

This chapter provides reference information for using Turbo Debugger. It is not a guide to debugging programs with Turbo Debugger. The information in this chapter includes descriptive information on the components of the Turbo Debugger environment, including command-line options (see table 21.2), menus, and hot keys. This information can be used to quickly identify and find the features of the debugger environment.

Table 21.1. *Command-line options.*

Option	*Meaning*
-c	Loads the specified configuration file
-do	Runs Turbo Debugger on a secondary display
-dp	Uses screen flipping to show the debugger on one page and the program on another
-ds	Uses screen swapping, the default option
-h or -?	Displays a list of Turbo Debugger command-line options and syntax
-i	Enables process ID switching
-k	Enables keystroke recording
-l	Forces Turbo Assembler to open in assembler mode with the CPU window open
-m	Sets the size of the working heap to the specified number of kilobytes
-p	Enables mouse support
-r	Enables debugging of a remote system using the serial link
-rp	Sets the remote link port to the specified port
-rs	Sets the remote link speed to the specified baud rate
-sc	Ignores case when entering symbol names
-sd	Sets one or more source directories

Option	*Meaning*
-sm	Sets the symbol table reserved memory size
-vg	Saves a complete graphics image on the program screen
-vn	Disables 43/50 line display
-vp	Enables the EGA/VGA palette save
-w	Indicates remote debugging program is WREMOTE
-y	Sets the overlay pool size in main memory
-ye	Sets the overlay pool size in EMS memory

The ≡ Menu

The ≡ Menu, often called the System Menu, provides environment options (see Fig. 21.1). These options are Repaint Desktop, Restore Standard, and About. Table 21.2 describes these options.

Table 21.2. *Environment options of the ≡ Menu.*

Option	*Purpose*
Repaint Desktop	Recreates the screen; useful when a portion of the screen has been corrupted by pop-up menus, memory-resident programs, and so forth
Restore Layout	Resets the environment to the standard window layout
About	Displays information about Turbo Debugger

The File Menu

The File Menu primarily provides file and DOS access (see Fig. 21.2). The options for the File Menu are Open, Change Dir, Get Info, DOS Shell, Resident, Symbol Load, Table Relocate, DLL Symbol load, and Quit. These options are described in table 21.3.

Fig. 21.1. The System Menu.

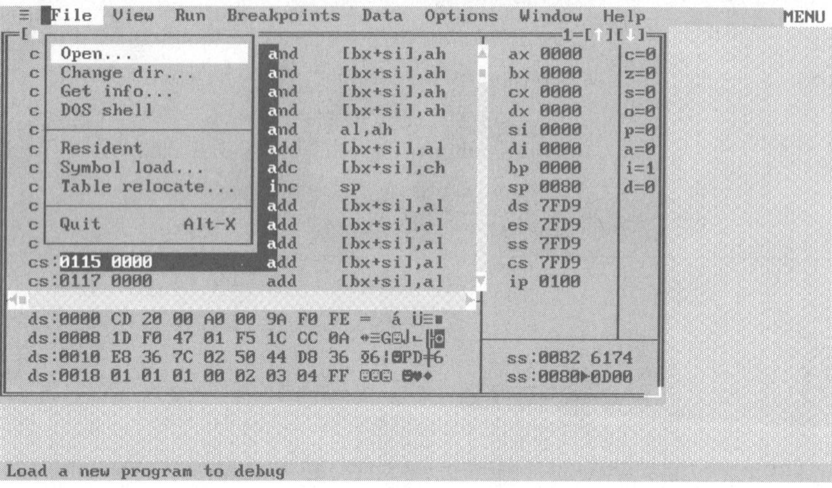

Table 21.3. Options of the File Menu.

Option	*Purpose*
Open	Allows you to select a program to load into the environment for debugging
Change Dir	Provides the ability to change the current working directory
Get Info	Displays program information
DOS Shell	Allows you to get to the DOS prompt
Resident	Forces Turbo Debugger to terminate and stay resident
Symbol Local	Loads a symbol table independent of the executable file
Table Relocate	Allows you to set the base segment of the symbol table
Quit	Quits Turbo Debugger and returns you to DOS

View Menu

The View Menu offers several options which allow you to view various aspects of your program (see Fig. 21.3). The options for the View Menu are Breakpoints, Stack, Log, Watches, Variables, Module, File, CPU, Dump, Registers, Numeric Processor, Execution History, Hierarchy, Windows Messages, and Another. Thesc options are described in table 21.4.

Fig. 21.2. The File Menu.

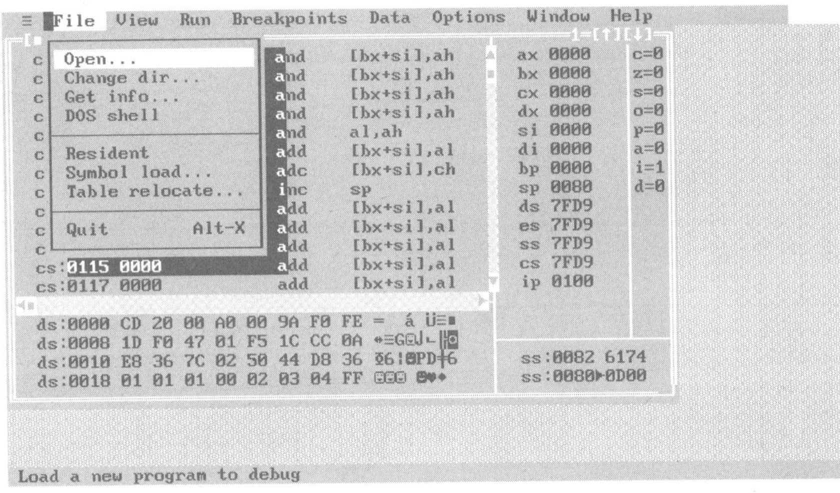

Table 21.4. Options of the View Menu.	
Option	*Purpose*
Breakpoints	Displays the breakpoints in your program
Stack	Allows you to view the function-calling stack
Log	Displays a log of events and data
Watches	Displays watched variables
Variables	Allows you to view global and local variables
Module	Displays the program source module
File	Displays the disk file as ASCII or hex
CPU	Allows you to view CPU instructions, data, and the stack
Dump	Displays a raw data dump
Registers	Displays CPU registers and flags
Numeric Processor	Allows you to view co-processor or emulator information
Execution History	Displays the assembler code saved for backtracking or keystroke playback
Hierarchy	Displays the object or class type list and a hierarchy tree
Windows Messages	Displays a list of Windows messages for your program

continues

Table 21.4 (continued)	
Option	*Purpose*
Another	Allows you to make another window with the following options:
Module	Makes another Module window
Dump	Makes another Dump window
File	Makes another File window

Fig. 21.3. The View Menu.

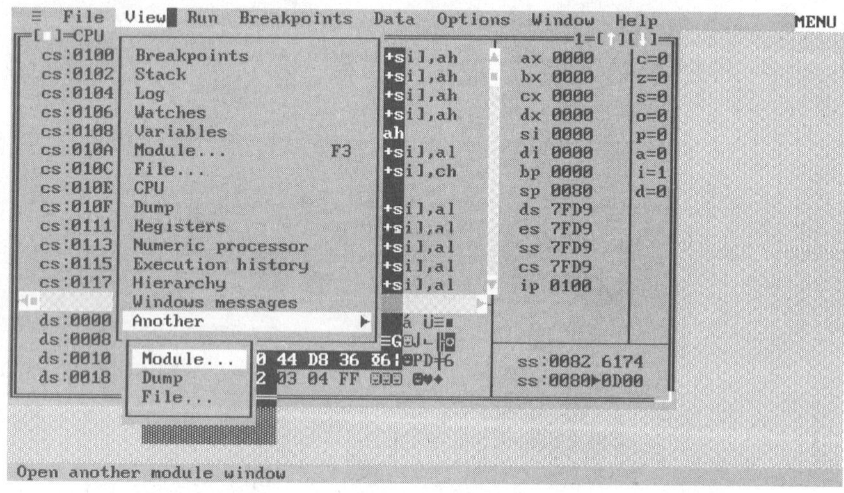

The Run Menu

The Run Menu provides options for executing specific portions of the target program (see Fig. 21.4). The options for the Run Menu are Run, Go to Cursor, Trace Into, Step Over, Execute to, Until Return, Animate, Back Trace, Instruction Trace, Arguments, and Program Reset. These options are described in table 21.5.

Table 21.5. Options of the Run Menu.	
Option	*Purpose*
Run	Executes your program until a breakpoint is reached, execution is interrupted, or the program ends
Go to Cursor	Executes the program from the beginning up to the point where the cursor is located in the current Module window or CPU Code pane
Trace Into	Executes one line of source code or one instruction
Step Over	Executes one line of source code or one instruction but skips over all procedure or function calls
Execute To	Executes the program from the beginning to the address specified by the user
Until Return	Continues the execution of the program until the current function has finished and control is returned to the calling function
Animate	Executes each line of code while updating screen information with each execution
Back Trace	Similar to the Trace Into option except that Back Trace moves through the code backwards
Instruction Trace	Executes one machine instruction
Arguments	Allows you to define any command-line arguments needed for your program
Program Reset	Reloads your program

Breakpoints Menu

The Breakpoints Menu controls the breakpoints in the program (see Fig. 21.5). The options under the Breakpoints Menu are Toggle, At, Changed Memory Global, Expression True Global, and Delete All. These options are described in table 21.6.

Table 21.6. Options of the Breakpoints Menu.	
Option	*Purpose*
Toggle	Toggles the breakpoint (if off, then on; if on, then off) at the cursor
At	Sets a breakpoint at the address you specify

continues

Table 21.6 (continued)

Option	*Purpose*
Changed Memory Global	Allows you to set a global breakpoint on a memory area
Expression True Global	Sets a global breakpoint on an expression
Hardware Breakpoint	Allows you to set a general purpose hardware breakpoint
Delete All	Allows you to remove all the breakpoints in the program

Fig. 21.4. The Run Menu.

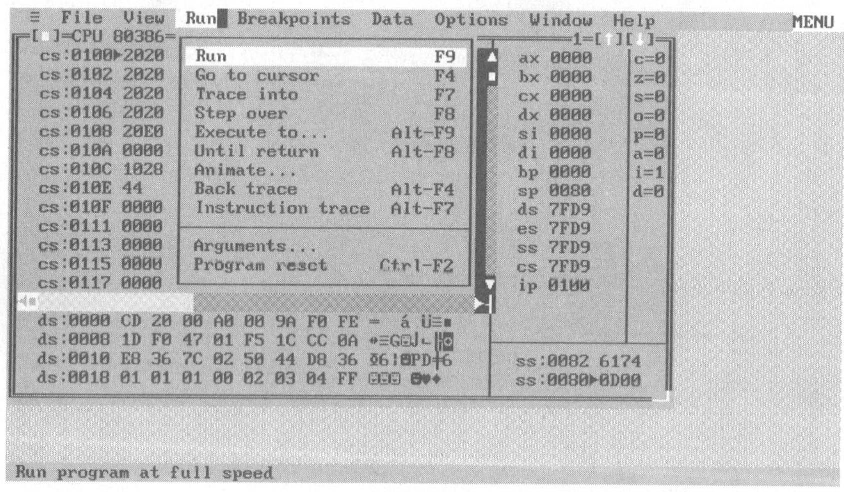

Data Menu

The Data Menu offers options which allow you to examine and modify program data (see Fig. 21.6). The options under the Data Menu are Inspect, Evaluate/Modify, Add Watch, and Function Return. Table 21.7 describes these options.

Fig. 21.5. The Breakpoints Menu.

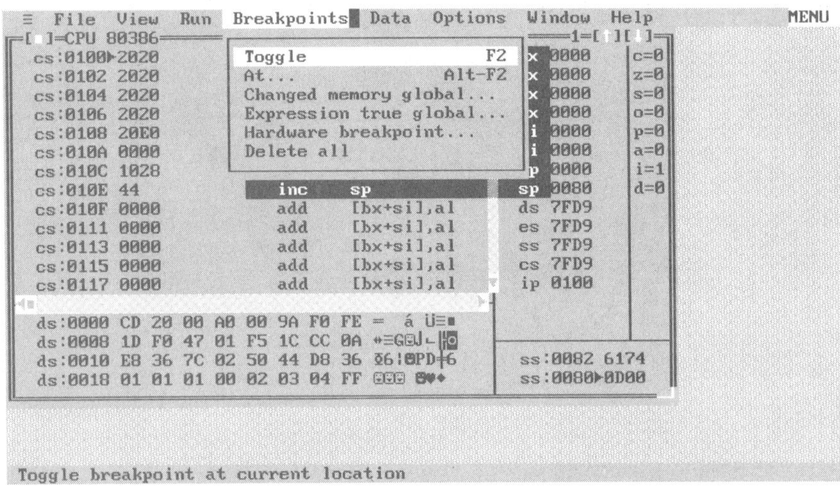

Table 21.7. Options of the Data Menu.	
Option	*Purpose*
Inspect	Displays the contents of the program variable or expression that you define
Evaluate/Modify	Evaluates an expression
Add Watch	Allows you to add a variable to the Watch window
Function Return	Allows you to examine the value returned from a function

Options Menu

The Options Menu provides several options which affect the overall appearance and operation of the Turbo Debugger environment (see Fig. 21.7). The options under the Options Menu are Language, Macros, Display, Path for Source, Save Options, and Restore Options. Table 21.8 describes these options.

Fig. 21.6. The Data Menu.

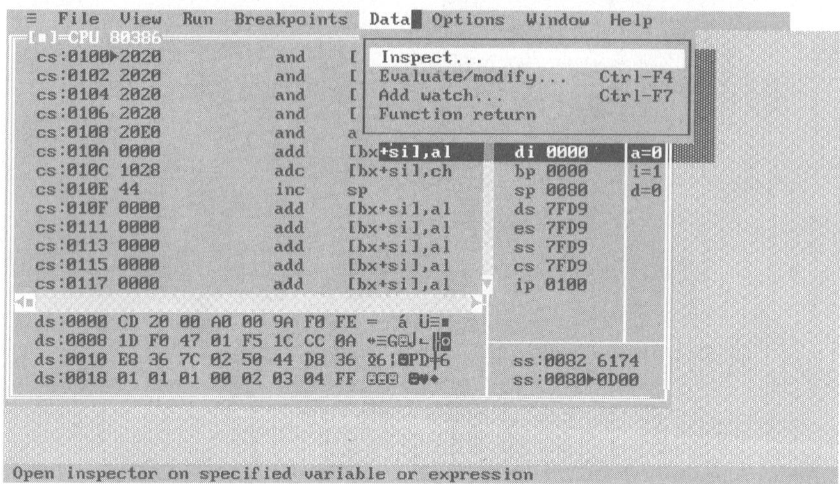

Table 21.8. Options of the Options Menu.

Option	*Purpose*
Language	Defines the expression language from the source module
Macros	Provides macro control with the following options:
Create	Initiates macro keystroke recording
Stop Recording	Ends macro keystroke recording
Remove	Allows you to remove a macro
Delete All	Removes all keystroke macros
Display Options	Allows you to customize the screen display. Custom features include display swapping, integer format, screen lines, and tab size
Path for Source	Specifies the path for the source files
Save Options	Allows you to save any changes to the configuration
Restore Options	Resets the environment to the values in the configuration file on your disk

Fig. 21.7. The Options Menu.

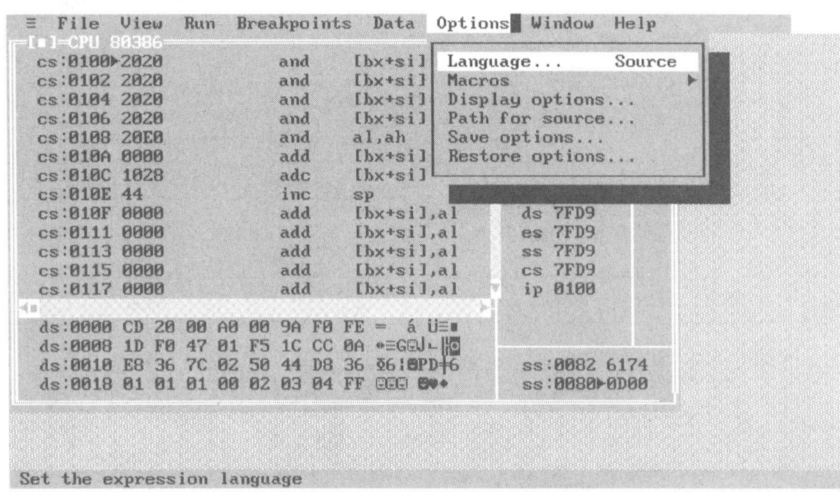

Windows Menu

The Windows Menu provides options for window management (see Fig. 21.8). The options for the Windows Menu are Zoom, Next, Next Pane, Size/Move, Iconize/Restore, Close, Undo Close, Dump Pane to Log, User Screen, Open Window List, and Window Pick. These options are described in table 21.9.

***Table 21.9.** Options of the Windows Menu.*

Option	*Purpose*
Zoom	Makes the active window the full size of the screen
Next	Makes the next window the active window
Next Pane	Takes you to the next pane in a window
Size/Move	Moves or resizes a window
Iconize/Reduce	Reduces the current window to an icon, or turns an icon into a window
Close	Closes the active window
Undo Close	Reverses the effects of the last Close option
Dump Pane to Log	Writes the contents of the current pane to the Log window

continues

Table 21.9 *(continued)*

Option	*Purpose*
User Screen	Displays the output of the program
Open Window List	Displays a list of open windows
Window Pick	Allows you to display a menu of open menus when more than 9 are open onscreen

Fig. 21.8. The Windows Menu.

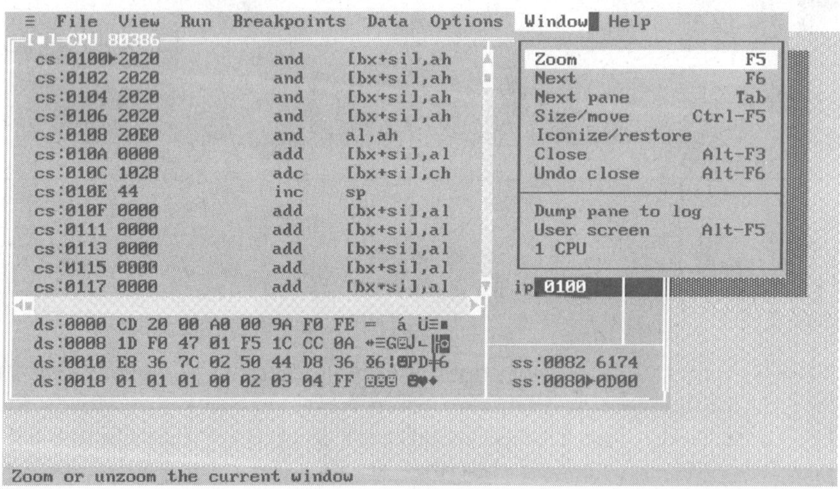

Help Menu

The Help Menu provides options which allow you to access on-line help information (see Fig. 21.9). The options under the Help Menu include Index, Previous Topic, and Help on Help. Table 21.10 describes these options.

Table 21.10. Options of the Help Menu.

Option	*Purpose*
Index	Displays the index for the on-line help features
Previous Topic	Allows you to recall the last help screen
Help on Help	The Help on Help option is used to provide helpful information on the use of the on-line help

Fig. 21.9. The Help Menu.

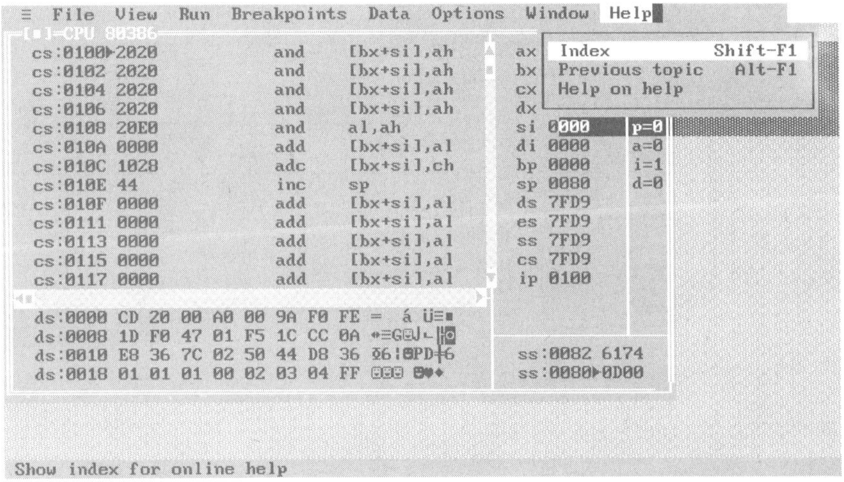

```
≡ File View Run Breakpoints Data Options Window Help
[■]=CPU 80386
cs:0100►2020      and   [bx+si],ah    ax  Index            Shift-F1
cs:0102 2020      and   [bx+si],ah    bx  Previous topic   Alt-F1
cs:0104 2020      and   [bx+si],ah    cx  Help on help
cs:0106 2020      and   [bx+si],ah    dx
cs:0108 20E0      and   al,ah         si 0000   p=0
cs:010A 0000      add   [bx+si],al    di 0000   a=0
cs:010C 1028      adc   [bx+si],ch    bp 0000   i=1
cs:010E 44        inc   sp            sp 0080   d=0
cs:010F 0000      add   [bx+si],al    ds 7FD9
cs:0111 0000      add   [bx+si],al    es 7FD9
cs:0113 0000      add   [bx+si],al    ss 7FD9
cs:0115 0000      add   [bx+si],al    cs 7FD9
cs:0117 0000      add   [bx+si],al    ip 0100

ds:0000 CD 20 00 A0 00 9A F0 FE
ds:0008 1D F0 47 01 F5 1C CC 0A
ds:0010 E8 36 7C 02 50 44 D8 36      ss:0082 6174
ds:0018 01 01 01 00 02 03 04 FF      ss:0080►0D00

Show index for online help
```

Turbo Debugger is easy to use and provides an excellent debugging environment. The Turbo Debugger environment is menu-driven. Several hot keys are provided to minimize mouse-clicks and maximize efficiency. Tables 21.11 through 21.20 list the hot keys for each of the menus in the Turbo Debugger environment.

Table 21.11. *The function keys.*

Function Key	*Menu Option*
F1	Brings up Help
F2	Breakpoints | Toggle
F3	View | Module
F4	Run | Go to Cursor
F5	Window | Zoom
F6	Window | Next Window
F7	Run | Trace Into
F8	Run | Step Over
F9	Run | Run

Table 21.12. *Hot keys to get to the menus.*

Hot Keys	*Menu Selected*
Alt-Space	≡ Menu
Alt-B	Breakpoint Menu
Alt-D	Data Menu
Alt-F	File Menu
Alt-H	Help Menu
Alt-O	Options Menu
Alt-R	Run Menu
Alt-V	View Menu
Alt-W	Window Menu

Table 21.13. *Hot keys for the File Menu.*

Hot Keys	*Menu Option*
Alt-X	File | Quit

Table 21.14. *Hot keys for the View Menu.*	
Hot Keys	*Menu Option*
F3	View | Module

Table 21.15. *Hot keys for the Run Menu.*	
Hot Keys	*Menu Option*
F9	Run | Run
F4	Run | Go to cursor
F7	Run | Trace into
F8	Run | Step Over
Alt-F9	Run | Execute to
Alt-F8	Run | Until Return
Alt-F4	Run | Back Trace
Alt-F7	Run | Instruction Trace
Ctrl-F2	Run | Program Reset

Table 21.16. *Hot keys for the Breakpoints Menu.*	
Hot Keys	*Menu Option*
F2	Breakpoints | Toggle
Alt-F2	Breakpoints | At

Table 21.17. *Hot keys for the Data Menu.*	
Hot Keys	*Menu Option*
Ctrl-F4	Data | Evaluate/Modify
Ctrl-F7	Data | Add Watch

Table 21.18. *Hot keys for the Options Menu.*

Hot Keys	*Menu Option*
Alt=	Options | Macros | Create
Alt-	Options | Macros | Stop Recording

Table 21.19. *Hot keys for the Windows Menu.*

Hot Keys	*Menu Option*
F5	Window | Zoom
F6	Window | Next
Tab	Window | Next Pane
Ctrl-F5	Window | Size/Move
Alt-F3	Window | Close
Alt-F6	Window | Undo Close
Alt-F5	Window | User Screen

Table 21.20. *Hot keys for the Help Menu.*

Hot Keys	*Menu Option*
Shift-F1	Help | Index
Alt-F1	Help | Previous Topic
F1-F1	Help | Help on Help

Introduction to Turbo Profiler

Turbo Profiler is a performance analyzer software tool. With this tool you can analyze and measure a program's performance by monitoring processor time, disk access, keyboard input, printer output, and interrupt activity. By carefully studying these activities and their statistical reports, you can optimize your program.

This chapter provides reference information for using Turbo Profiler. It is not intended to be a full-blown guide to profiling your programs. Rather, this chapter provides descriptive information on the components of Turbo Profiler including command-line options (see Table 22.1), menus, and hot keys. The information in this chapter can be used to quickly identify and find the many features of Turbo Profiler. You can enter the Turbo Profiler environment by typing TPROF at the DOS prompt.

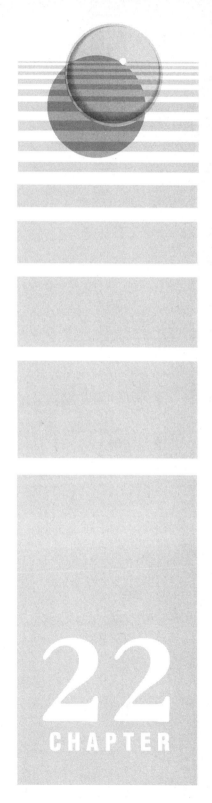

Table 22.1. *Command-line options for Turbo Profiler.*

Option	*Meaning*
-c	Reads the specified configuration file
-do	Runs Turbo Profiler on a secondary display
-dp	Displays Turbo Profiler on one page while displaying the output of the profiled program on another page
-ds	Keeps Turbo Profiler on one screen and the program under analysis on another screen
-h, -?	Brings up the help screen
-i	Enables process ID switching
-m	Sets the size of the working heap to the specified number of kilobytes
-p	Enables mouse support
-r	Enables profiling on a remote system using the serial link
-rp	Sets the remote link port to the specified port
-rs	Sets the baud rate for the remote link
-sc	Ignores the case of symbol names
-sd	Defines one or more paths for source files
-vg	Saves a complete graphics image on the program screen
-vn	Disables the 43/50 line display
-vp	Enables the saving of the EGA/VGA palette
-y	Sets the size of the overlay area to the specified number of kilobytes
-ye	Sets the size of the EMS overlay area to the specified number of 16K pages

The ≡ Menu

The ≡ Menu, often called the System Menu, has three options (see Fig. 22.1). These options, described in table 22.2, are Repaint Desktop, Restore Standard, and About.

Table 22.2. Options of the ≡ Menu.

Option	*Purpose*
Repaint Desktop	Redraws the screen; useful when a part of the screen has been corrupted by memory-resident programs and so forth
Restore Standard	Sets the screen to the configuration specified in the configuration file; in other words, the screen is restored to its startup state
About	Provides version and copyright information about Turbo Profiler

Fig. 22.1. The ≡ , or System, Menu.

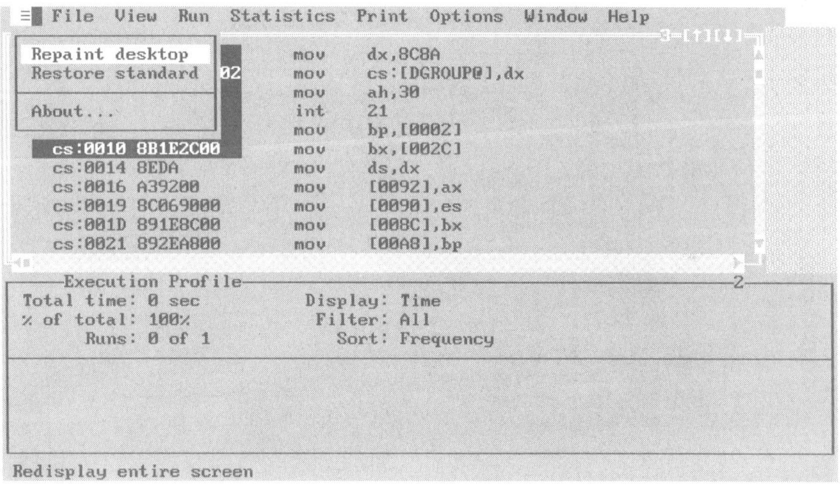

The File Menu

The File Menu basically provides the file and DOS interface (see Fig. 22.2). The options under the File Menu are Open, Change Dir, Get Info, DOS Shell, and Quit. Table 22.3 describes these options.

Table 22.3. Options of the File Menu.	
Option	*Purpose*
Open	Allows you to open a file by either specifying the filename at the prompt or selecting a file from a list of files
Change Dir	Specifies a new current working directory
Get Info	Provides information on the program being analyzed and about the system's current memory configuration
DOS Shell	The DOS Shell option takes you to the DOS prompt; typing EXIT takes you back to Turbo Profiler
Quit	The Quit option removes Turbo Profiler from memory and takes you to the DOS prompt

Fig. 22.2. The File Menu.

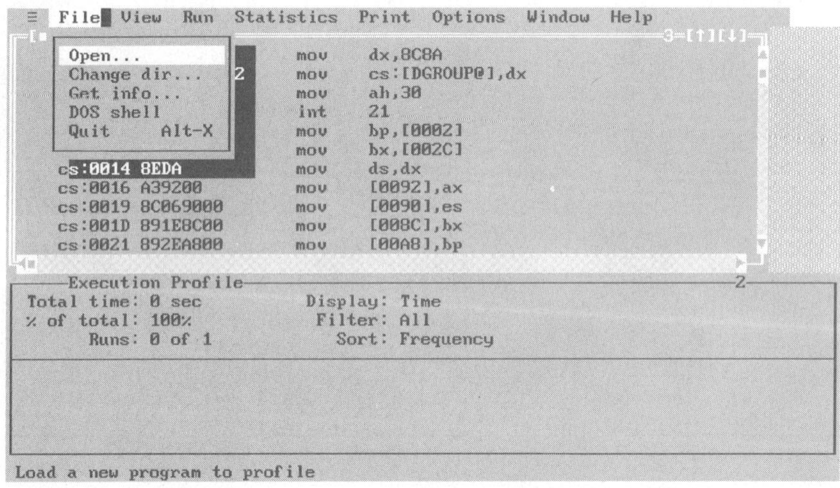

The View Menu

The View Menu allows you to view various performance information about the program being analyzed (see Fig. 22.3). The options for the View Menu are Module, Execution Profile, Callers, Overlays, Interrupts, Files, Areas, Routines, Disassembly, and Text File. These options are described in table 22.4.

Table 22.4. Options of the View Menu.

Option	*Purpose*
Module	Allows you to list the source code for the program being analyzed
Execution Profile	The Execution Profile option is used to open the Execution Profile window which displays the program's profile statistics
Callers	Opens the Callers window, which displays the call paths for each marked routine in the program
Overlays	Opens the Overlays window, which provides information about overlay activity for Turbo Pascal, Turbo C, and Turbo Assembler programs
Interrupts	Allows you to open the Interrupts window, which lists video, disk, keyboard, DOS, and mouse interrupt events
Files	Displays file activity information resulting from your program
Areas	Opens the Areas window, which lists information about the marked profile areas of the program
Routines	Provides a list of routines which can be used as area markers
Disassembly	Allows you to open the Disassembly window, which displays the current area in the Module window as disassembled source code
Text File	Provides the capability to view or modify ASCII text files

Fig. 22.3. The View Menu.

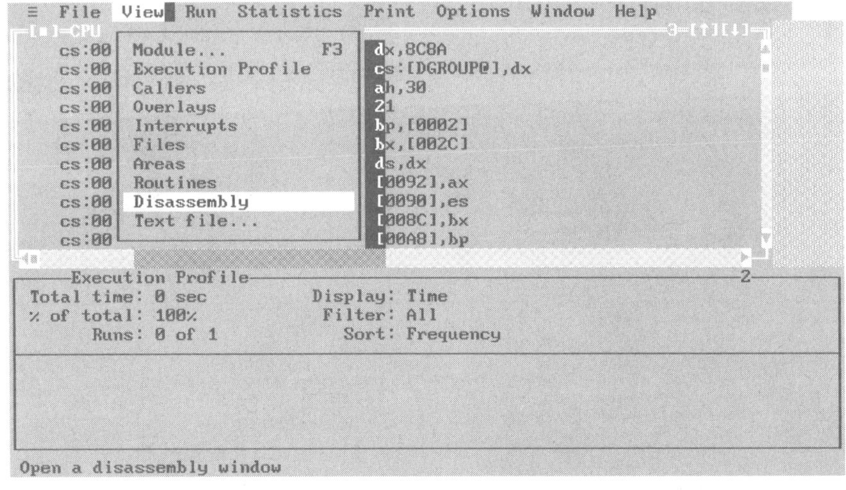

The Run Menu

The Run Menu allows you to run your program (see Fig. 22.4). The three options for the Run Menu, described in table 22.5, are Run, Program Reset, and Arguments.

Table 22.5. *Options of the Run Menu.*

Option	*Purpose*
Run	Executes the program and collects statistics on the program's performance
Program Reset	Allows you to reload your program from the disk and start the program again
Arguments	Defines command-line arguments for the program being analyzed

Fig. 22.4. The Run Menu.

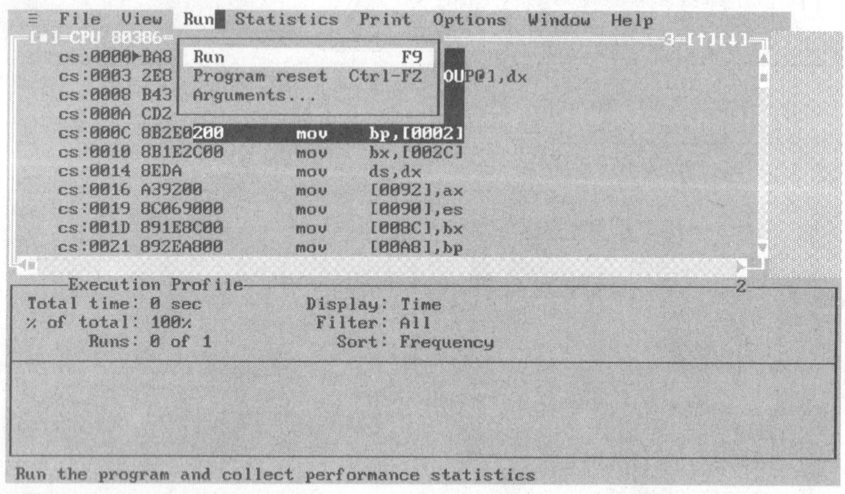

The Statistics Menu

The Statistics Menu specifies what statistics will be collected and how they will be collected (see Fig. 22.5). The options under the Statistics Menu are Callers, Files, Interrupts, Overlays, Profiling Options, Accumulation, Delete All, Save, and Restore. These options are described in table 22.6.

Table 22.6. *Options of the Statistics Menu.*

Option	*Purpose*
Callers	Allows the profiler to get statistics on those routines which call other routines
Files	Collects statistics about the files which are opened and about all read and write operations
Interrupts	Provides the capability to collect statistics on the interrupts generated by your program
Overlays	Used to turn on or turn off statistics collection for the program overlays
Profiling Options	Allows you to specify the profile mode, the number of times your program will run, the maximum number of areas, and the clock speed
Accumulation	Toggles automatic data collection
Delete All	Removes all of the statistics collected during the current profiling session
Save	Saves all the collected statistics and all area information
Restore	Restores all the saved options, settings, and statistical information from a previously saved profiling session

The Print Menu

The Print Menu allows you to print the contents of an open profiler window (see Fig. 22.6). The options for the Print Menu are Statistics, Module, or Options. These options are described in table 22.7.

Fig. 22.5. The Statistics Menu.

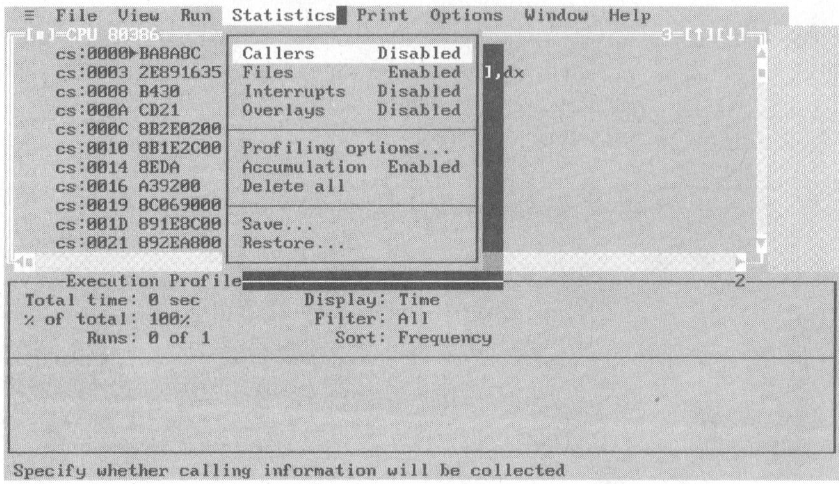

Table 22.7. Options of the Print Menu.

Option	Purpose
Statistics	Prints all the open profiler windows, except the Module window, to a printer or file
Module	Allows you to print the specified program module to a printer or file
Options	Sets print options including the number of characters per line and the number of lines per page while specifying whether graphics or ASCII characters should be printed and whether output should be sent to a file or to the printer

The Options Menu

The Options Menu lets you define macros and customize the operation and appearance of Turbo Profiler (see Fig. 22.7). The options for the Options Menu are Macros, Display Options, Path for Source, Save Options, and Restore Options. Table 22.8 describes these options, including those of the Macros option, which are Create, Stop Recording, Remove, and Delete All.

Fig. 22.6. The Print Menu.

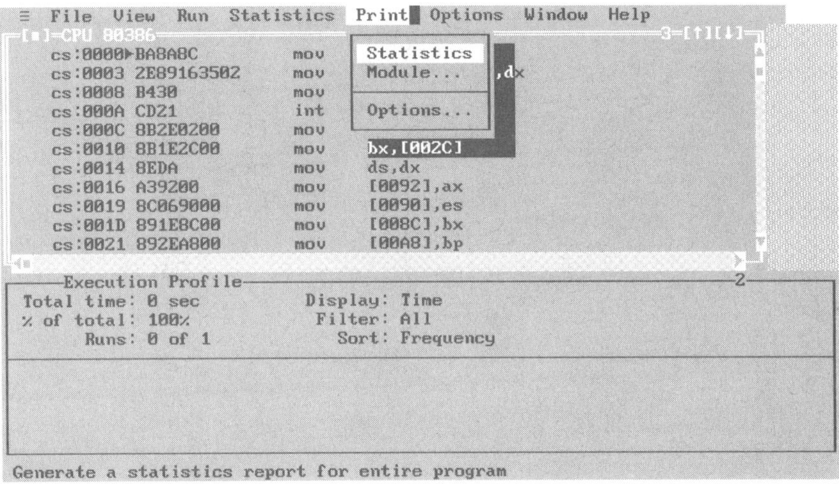

***Table 22.8.** Options of the Options Menu.*

Option	*Purpose*
Macros	Allows you to define and delete macros using the following options:
Create	Initializes a macro and begins keystroke recording
Stop Record	Stops the recording of keystrokes
Remove	Removes a macro
Delete All	Deletes all macros and resets the key definitions
Display Options	Provides selections for the display mode; under this option, you can specify whether display swapping should be used, the number of lines on the screen, the tab size, and the width of the names display
Path for Source	Allows you to specify one or more directories where source code can be found
Save Options	Stores the current profiler options to a configuration file
Restore Options	Sets up the environment according to the specified configuration file

Fig. 22.7. The Options Menu.

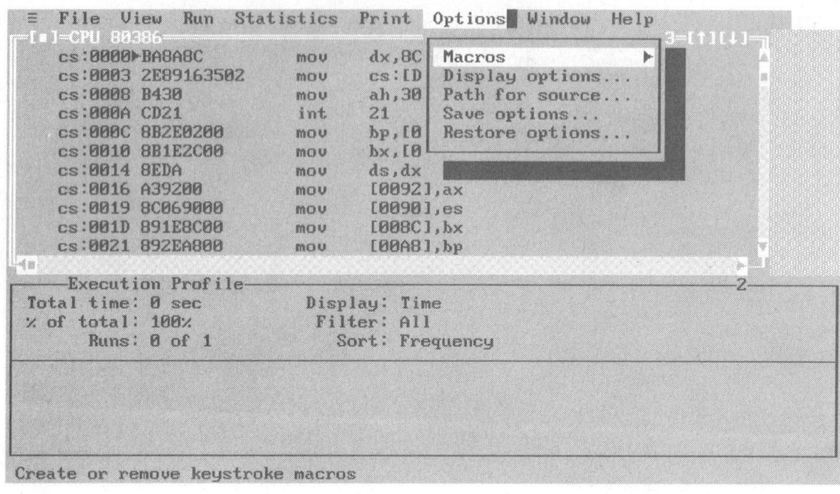

The Window Menu

The Window Menu provides options for windows management (see Fig 22.8). The Window Menu options are Zoom, Next, Next Pane, Size/Move, Iconize/Restore, Close, Undo Close, and User Screen. These options are described in table 22.9.

Table 22.9. *Options of the Window Menu.*

Option	*Purpose*
Zoom	Makes the active window the size of the screen
Next	Makes the next window active
Next Pane	Moves the cursor to the next pane in the current window
Size/Move	Changes the location or size of the active window
Iconize/Restore	Reduces the active window to an icon, or makes the active icon a window
Close	Closes the active window
Undo Close	Reverses the last close
User Screen	Allows you to view the full-screen output from your program

Fig. 22.8. The Window Menu.

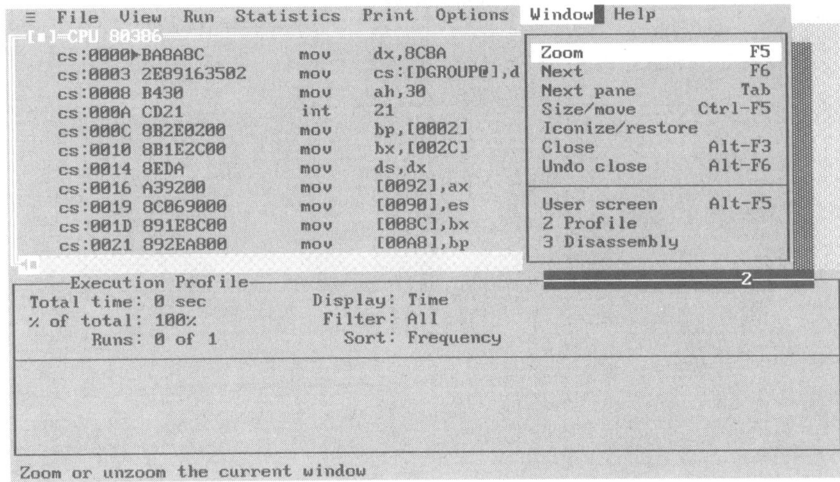

The Help Menu

The Help Menu provides access to the on-line help information (see Fig. 22.9). The options under the Help Menu are Index, Previous Topic, and Help on Help. These options are described in table 22.10.

***Table 22.10.** Options of the Help Menu.*

Option	*Purpose*
Index	Lists an index to the help information
Previous Topic	Brings up the last help screen you viewed
Help on Help	Provides helpful information on how to use on-line help

Fig. 22.9. The Help Menu.

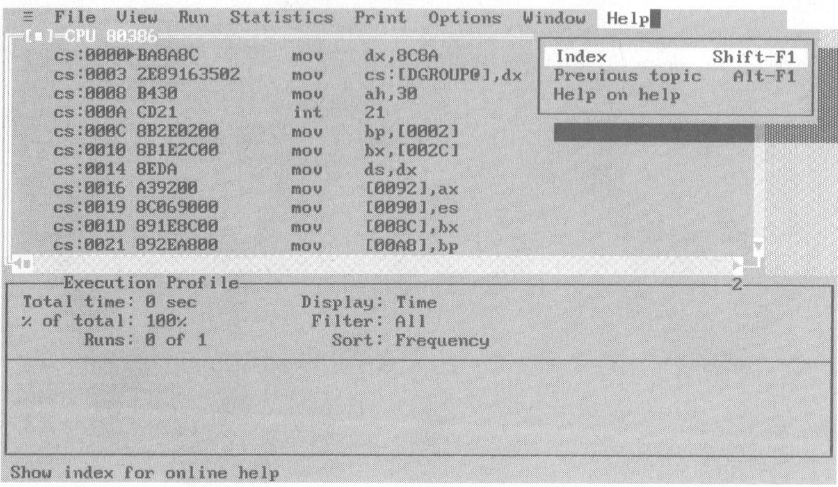

Turbo Profiler is very easy to use and provides vital information for optimizing your programs. The Turbo Profiler is menu-driven and provides several hot keys to minimize mouse clicks and maximize efficiency. Tables 22.11 through 22.17 list the hot keys for each of the menus in the Turbo Profiler environment.

Table 22.11. *Function keys.*

Function Key	*Menu Option*
F1	Brings up help
F3	View | Module
F5	Window | Zoom
F6	Window | Next
F9	Run | Run

Table 22.12. *Hot keys for the File Menu.*

Hot Keys	*Menu Option*
Alt-X	File | Quit

Table 22.13. Hot keys for the View Menu.

Hot Keys	*Menu Option*
F3	View | Module

Table 22.14. Hot keys for the Run Menu.

Hot Keys	*Menu Option*
F9	Run | Run
Crtl-F2	Run | Program Reset

Table 22.15. Hot keys for the Options Menu.

Hot Keys	*Menu Option*
Alt =	Options | Macros | Create
Alt -	Options | Macros | Stop Recording

Table 22.16. Hot keys for the Window Menu.

Hot Keys	*Menu Option*
F5	Window | Zoom
F6	Window | Next
Tab	Window | Next Pane
Ctrl-F5	Window | Size/Move
Alt-F3	Window | Close
Alt-F6	Window | Undo Close
Alt-F5	Window | User Screen

Table 22.17. Hot keys for the Help Menu.

Hot Keys	*Menu Option*
Shift-F1	Help | Index
Alt-F1	Help | Previous Topic
F1-F1	Help on Help

Bibliography

Borland C++ Programmer's Guide to Graphics,
SAMS, 1991.

DOS Programmer's Reference, **2nd Ed.,**
Que Corporation, 1989.

Quick Reference Guide,
Turbo Assembler, Borland International, Inc., 1990.

Programmer's Guide,
Borland C++, Borland International, Inc., 1990.

User's Guide,
Borland C++, Borland International, Inc., 1990.

Whitewater Resource Toolkit User's Guide,
Borland C++, Borland International, Inc., 1990.

Reference Guide,
Borland C++, Borland International, Inc., 1990.

User's Guide,
Turbo Debugger, Borland International, Inc., 1990.

User's Guide,
Turbo Profiler, Borland International, Inc., 1990.

Index

Symbols

A

B

C

D

E

G

H

I

N

O

P

Q-R

S

T

U

V

W

Free Catalog!

Mail us this registration form today, and we'll send you a free catalog featuring Que's complete line of best-selling books.

Name of Book ______________________

Name ______________________

Title ______________________

Phone ( ) ______________________

Company ______________________

Address ______________________

City ______________________

State ____________ ZIP ____________

Please check the appropriate answers:

1. Where did you buy your Que book?
   - ☐ Bookstore (name: ____________)
   - ☐ Computer store (name: ________)
   - ☐ Catalog (name: ____________)
   - ☐ Direct from Que
   - ☐ Other: ____________

2. How many computer books do you buy a year?
   - ☐ 1 or less
   - ☐ 2-5
   - ☐ 6-10
   - ☐ More than 10

3. How many Que books do you own?
   - ☐ 1
   - ☐ 2-5
   - ☐ 6-10
   - ☐ More than 10

4. How long have you been using this software?
   - ☐ Less than 6 months
   - ☐ 6 months to 1 year
   - ☐ 1-3 years
   - ☐ More than 3 years

5. What influenced your purchase of this Que book?
   - ☐ Personal recommendation
   - ☐ Advertisement
   - ☐ In-store display
   - ☐ Price
   - ☐ Que catalog
   - ☐ Que mailing
   - ☐ Que's reputation
   - ☐ Other: ____________

6. How would you rate the overall content of the book?
   - ☐ Very good
   - ☐ Good
   - ☐ Satisfactory
   - ☐ Poor

7. What do you like *best* about this Que book?

   ____

   ____

8. What do you like *least* about this Que book?

   ____

   ____

9. Did you buy this book with your personal funds?
   - ☐ Yes ☐ No

10. Please feel free to list any other comments you may have about this Que book.

    ____

    ____

    ____

QUE

Order Your Que Books Today!

Name ______________________

Title ______________________

Company ______________________

City ______________________

State ____________ ZIP ____________

Phone No. ( ) ______________________

Method of Payment:

Check ☐ (Please enclose in envelope.)

Charge My: VISA ☐ MasterCard ☐

American Express ☐

Charge # ______________________

Expiration Date ______________________

Order No.	Title	Qty.	Price	Total

You can **FAX** your order to **1-317-573-2583.** Or call **1-800-428-5331, ext. ORDR** to order direct.
Please add $2.50 per title for shipping and handling.

Subtotal	
Shipping & Handling	
Total	

QUE

NO POSTAGE
NECESSARY
IF MAILED
IN THE
UNITED STATES

BUSINESS REPLY MAIL
First Class Permit No. 9918 Indianapolis, IN

Postage will be paid by addressee

11711 N. College
Carmel, IN 46032

NO POSTAGE
NECESSARY
IF MAILED
IN THE
UNITED STATES

BUSINESS REPLY MAIL
First Class Permit No. 9918 Indianapolis, IN

Postage will be paid by addressee

11711 N. College
Carmel, IN 46032